ON
EXHIBIT

The Art Lover's
TRAVEL GUIDE
to American Museums

*"The finest guide
to American museums"*

—The New England
Review of Books

By Patti Sowalsky and Judith Swirsky

Published by ON EXHIBIT Fine Art Publications, P. O. Box 59734, Potomac,
MD 20859.

Distributed worldwide by D. A. P./Distributed Art Publishers.
Tel (212) 473-5119 Fax: (212) 673-2887
636 Broadway, 12th Floor, New York, NY 10012.

Printed in the U.S.A.

ISBN: 0-9633650-2-9

Dedication

To Jerry and Leo, our husbands
and best friends.

ACKNOWLEDGEMENTS

No Man — or in this case two women — is an island. Even in the somewhat solitary process of writing a book, the help, counsel, and encouragement of others is essential. We owe a debt of thanks first to our children John and Susan Sowalsky and Marjorie and Larry Zelner who have solved numerous technical problems for us with their expertise. The assistance given to us by Julie Strauss, Alice Mansfield, Susie Liberman and Suzanne McDermott is also deeply appreciated. A special note of thanks is extended to Ron Feldman of Ronald Feldman Fine Arts who recognized that a good resource to fine art museums was long overdue, and who helped us to make *On Exhibit* a reality. We are deeply grateful as well for the aid and support of our corporate sponsor, Irvin Feld and Kenneth Feld Productions, Inc. as well as to the many exhibition services that have supplied us with invaluable information.

Finally, we want to thank the thousands of art lovers and hundreds of participating museums who have enthusiastically supported our effort.

TABLE OF CONTENTS

ON EXHIBIT

INTRODUCTION

At last! Now you can know, before you go, with *On Exhibit*, the ultimate annual guide to fine art museums in America. Those of us who travel on business or pleasure, and love to explore interesting art museums, will never again miss a little gem or important exhibition for lack of information. Like you, we are among the millions of art lovers who enjoy visiting museums wherever we go. All too often finding reliable information, especially about little known hidden treasures, is difficult, if not totally impossible. Even high-quality exhibitions in major cities are often overlooked simply because newspaper and magazine reviews appear just as the show is about to close or, frequently, contain no information regarding the admission or ticket requirements that might be necessary for attendance.

On Exhibit solves all of these problems. It is a complete reference guide to museums, art centers and fine art institutions throughout America. We know that you will be surprised and delighted with this quick, yet comprehensive overview of the country's artistic riches.

IMPORTANT INFORMATION

In the museum world, nothing is written in stone. **All** hours, fees, days closed, and **especially** exhibitions, including those **not** marked as tentative, are subject to change at any time. The information in *On Exhibit* is as accurate as possible at the time of publication. However, we strongly suggest that you call to confirm any exhibition you wish to see. We particularly request that you note the exclamation point "!". This is used as an important symbol in the book to remind you to call or check for information or any other verification.

Please note that exhibitions at most college and university museums are only scheduled during the academic year. In addition, some museums that have no exhibition listings simply did not have the information available at press time. Please call ahead to any museum for an update.

Not all museums responded to our request for information, and they, therefore, have abbreviated listings.

Every effort has been made to check the accuracy of all museum information, as well as exhibition schedules. If you find any inaccuracies, please accept our apologies — but do let us know. Finally, if we have inadvertently omitted your favorite museum, a letter to us would be most appreciated, so we can include it in the 1996 edition.

HOW TO USE THIS GUIDE

On Exhibit has been designed to be reader-friendly.

All museums are listed in a logical alphabetical progression of state and then city within each state.

Most permanent collection and museum facility information is expressed in easily recognized standard abbreviations. These are explained both in the front of the book — and, for your convenience, on the back of the enclosed bookmark.

Group tour reservations must be arranged well in advance. When calling be sure to check on group size requirements and fee information.

As a reminder, it is recommended that students and seniors always present proper I.D.'s in order to qualify for museum fee discounts wherever they are offered.

EXPLANATION OF CODES

The coding system we have developed for this guide is made up **primarily** of standardized, easy to recognize abbreviations. All codes are listed under their appropriate categories.

MAIN CATEGORIES

AM	American	IND	Indian
AF	African	IMPR	Impressionist
AN/GRK	Ancient Greek	JAP	Japanese
AN/R	Ancient Roman	LAT/AM	Latin American
AS	Asian	MEX	Mexican
BRIT	British	MED	Medieval
BYZ	Byzantine	NAT/AM	Native American
CH	Chinese	OC	Oceanic
CONT	Contemporary	OM	Old Masters
DU	Dutch	OR	Oriental
EGT	Egyptian	P/COL	Pre-Columbian
EU	European	P/RAPH	Pre-Raphaelite
FL	Flemish	REG	Regional
FR	French	REN	Renaissance
GER	German	RUSS	Russian
IT	Italian	SP	Spanish

MEDIUM

CER	Ceramics	PHOT	Photography
DEC/ART	Decorative Arts	POST	Posters
DRGS	Drawings	PTGS	Paintings
GR	Graphics	SCULP	Sculpture
PER/RMS	Period Rooms	W/COL	Water Colors

ON EXHIBIT

SUBJECT MATTER

AB	Abstract	FIG	Figurative
ANT	Antiquities	FOLK	Folk Art
ARCH	Architectural	LDSCP	Landscape
CART	Cartoon	PRIM	Primitive
EXP	Expressionist	ST/LF	Still Life
ETH	Ethnic		

REGIONS

E	East	S	South
MID/E	Middle East	W	West
N	North		

PERM/COLL   Permanent Collection

The punctuation marks used for the permanent collection codes denote the following:

The colon : is used after a major category to indicate sub-listings with that category. For example, "AM: ptgs, sculp" indicates that the museum has a collection of American paintings and sculpture.

The semi-colon ; indicates that one major category is ending and another major category listing is beginning. For example, "AM: ptgs; SP: sculp; DU; AF" indicates that the museum has collections that include American paintings, Spanish sculpture, and works of Dutch and African origin.

A number added to any of the above denotes century, i.e., EU: ptgs 19, 20 = European Painting of the 19th and 20th Centuries.

MUSEUM SERVICES

Y	Yes
!	symbol for Call to Confirm or for Further Information
HDC/ACC	Handicapped Accessibility
REST/FAC	Restaurant Facilities
ADM	Admission
SUGG/CONT	Suggested Contribution — Pay What You Wish, But You Must Pay Something
VOL/CONT	Voluntary Contribution — Free Admission, Contribution Requested.
F	Free
F/DAY	Free Day
SR CIT	Senior Citizen, with I.D. (Age may vary)
GT	Group Tours
DT	Drop in Tours
MUS/SH	Museum Shop
H/B	Historic Building
S/G	Sculpture Garden
TBA	To Be Announced
TENT!	Tentatively Scheduled
ATR!	Advance Tickets Required - Call
CAT	Catalog
WT	Exhibition Will Travel - see index of travelling exhibitions
WT*	Only or Last US venue for this exhibition

HOLIDAYS

ACAD!	Academic Holidays — Call For Information
LEG/HOL!	Legal Holidays — Call For Information
THGV	Thanksgiving
MEM/DAY	Memorial Day
LAB/DAY	Labor Day

M	Monday	T	Thursday
TU	Tuesday	F	Friday
W	Wednesday	SA	Saturday
	S	Sunday	

ALABAMA

BIRMINGHAM

Birmingham Museum of Art
2000 8th Ave. North, **Birmingham, AL 35203**
TEL: 205-254-2566
HRS: 10-5 Tu-Sa; Noon-5 S   DAY CLOSED: M   HOL: 1/1; THGV, 12/25
VOL/CONT: Y   ADM: F   HDC/ACC: Y   PARKING: Y; Adjacent to the museum   MUS/SH: Y
REST/FAC: Y; Restaurant   GR/T: Y   GR/PH: Call ahead to reserve   S/G: Y
PERM/COLL: AM: ptgs; EU: ptgs; OR; AF; P/COL; DEC/ART; PHOT

Following two years of renovation and expansion planned by architect Edward Larabee Barnes, the Birmingham Museum of Art, with 15,000 works in its permanent collection is the largest municipal museum in the Southeast. **NOT TO BE MISSED:** New multi-level outdoor Sculpture Garden featuring a waterfall designed by sculptor Elyn Zimmerman and two mosaic lined pools designed by artist Valerie Jaudon; Newly acquired Mitt Collection of 18th C French paintings & decorative arts.

ON EXHIBIT/95:

9/20/94 - 5/8/95   HONOR THY FATHER AND MOTHER: A MULTI-MEDIA INSTALLATION BY LORENZO PACE — Sound, video, and computer modules enhance the effects of this 9-section vignette by Pace, an Alabama-born artist whose assembled objects evoke chapters in his ancestral African past and in the African presence in today's South.

12/14/94 - 3/12/95   IN OPEN AIR: OUTDOOR PHOTOGRAPHY FROM THE COLLECTION OF THE BIRMINGHAM MUSEUM OF ART — Landscape photographs by William Haney Jackson, Linda Connor, Ansel Adams, Eliot Porter, and William Christenberry will be featured in this exhibit.

3/4 - 4/30/95   CLEARLY ART: PILCHUCK'S GLASS LEGACY — The 80 objects on exhibit by 66 artists trained by noted glass artist Dale Chihuly, in the famous Pacific Northwest Pilchuck Glass Factory, will trace the 23 year history of this school and assess its impact on the studio glass movement in the U.S.   CAT   WT

7/22 - 9/17/95   BOTTICELLI TO TIEPOLO: THREE CENTURIES OF ITALIAN PAINTINGS FROM BOB JONES UNIVERSITY — Forty great master paintings that trace the development of Italian painting from the High Renaissance through the Baroque and Rococo periods will include works by Tintoretto, Reni, Guercino and others.   CAT   WT

10/7 - 12/31/95   ECHIZEN: EIGHT HUNDRED YEARS OF JAPANESE STONEWARE — The history of one of the traditional and great kiln sites in Japan will be traced in the 75 objects in this exhibition on loan from every major private and public collection in Japan.

DAPHNE

American Sport Art Museum and Archives
Affiliate Institution: U. S. Sports Academy
One Academy Dr., **Daphne, AL 36526**
TEL: 205-626-3303
HRS: 10-2 M-F   DAY CLOSED: Sa, S   HOL: LEG/HOL, ACAD!
ADM: F   HDC/ACC: Y   PARKING: Y; Free   MUS/SH: Y   GR/T: Y
GR/PH: 205-626-3303   DT: Y   TIME: 10-2 M-F
PERM/COLL: AM: ptgs, sculp, gr all on the single theme of American sports heros

The largest collection of sports art in America may be found at this museum which also features works highlighting an annual sport artist of the year. **NOT TO BE MISSED:** "The Pathfinder," a large sculpture of a hammer-thrower by John Robinson where the weight of the ball of the hammer is equal to the rest of the entire weight of the body of the figure.

ON EXHIBIT/95:
A rotating schedule of bi-monthly exhibitions is featured. Call for specifics.

1

ALABAMA

DOTHAN

Wiregrass Museum of Art
126 N. College St., **Dothan, AL 36302**
TEL: 205-794-3871
HRS: 10-5 Tu-Sa; 1-5 S   DAY CLOSED: M   HOL: LEG/HOL!
ADM: F
HDC/ACC: Y   PARKING: Y; Ample and free   GR/T: Y   GR/PH: call 205-794-3871
H/B: Y; Located in former 1912 electric plant
PERM/COLL: REG

Featured on the main floor galleries of this newly established art institution are a variety of works that reflect the ever changing world of art with emphasis on solo exhibits showcasing important emerging artists of the South. The museum is located in the southeast corner of Alabama approximately 100 miles from Montgomery. **NOT TO BE MISSED:** ARTventures, a "hands on" gallery for children, schools, & families

ON EXHIBIT/95:

1/7 - 2/12/95	BIENNIAL INVITATIONAL
2/18 - 3/19/95	ART OF WEST AFRICA
3/25 - 4/23/95	YAM '95
4/29 - 4/30/95	ESKIMO ART
5/6 - 6/4/95	BOTANICAL ART
1/10 - 8/27/95	ROLAND HOCKETT
7/29 - 8/27/95	CHRIS HARTSFIELD
8/28 - 9/29/95	MUSEUM CLOSED TO PREPARE FOR GRAND OPENING: PHASE TWO
9/30/95	GRAND OPENING - PHASE TWO: DECORATIVE ARTS (Main Gallery) & PERMANENT COLLECTION (Blumberg Gallery)

FAYETTE

Fayette Art Museum
530 Temple Ave. N., **Fayette, AL 35555**
TEL: 205-932-8727
HRS: 9-Noon & 1-4 M-F   DAY CLOSED: Sa, S   HOL: LEG/HOL!
ADM: F   HDC/ACC: Y   PARKING: Y; Ample parking with spaces for the handicapped
GR/T: Y   GR/PH: call 205-932-8727   DT: Y   TIME: daily during museum hours   H/B: Y
PERM/COLL: AM: ptgs 20; FOLK

Housed in a 1930s former school house, this collection consists mainly of folk works as well as a 1,500 piece collection of art that spans the career of Lois Wilson (1905-1980). **NOT TO BE MISSED:** The largest collection of folk art in the Southeast.

ON EXHIBIT/95:
Rotating exhibitions drawn from the 2,000 piece permanent collection.

ALABAMA

GADSDEN

Gadsden Museum of Fine Arts
2829 W. Meighan Blvd., **Gadsden, AL 35904**
TEL: 205-546-7365
HRS: 10-4 M-W & F; 10am-8pm T; 1-5 S   DAY CLOSED: Sa.   HOL: LEG/HOL!
VOL/CONT: Y   ADM: F
HDC/ACC: Y   PARKING: Y; Free and ample   GR/T: Y   GR/PH: call 205-546-7365
PERM/COLL: EU: Impr/ptgs; CONT; DEC/ART

As of Janurary, 1995 the Gasden Museum of Arts will be located in the renovated historic Duncan Department Store whose antique atmosphere will be retained in combination with a new state-of-the-art museum facility.

HUNTSVILLE

Huntsville Museum of Art
700 Monroe St., S.W., **Huntsville, AL 35899**
TEL: 205-535-4350
HRS: 10-5 Tu-F; 9-5 Sa; 1-5 S   DAY CLOSED: M   HOL: 1/1, THGV, 12/25
ADM: F   HDC/ACC: Y; Totally accessible with wheelchairs available   PARKING: Y; Limited free parking in the civic center building in which the museum is located; metered parking in garage across the street.
GR/T: Y   GR/PH: call 205-535-4350   DT: Y   TIME: 3:00 2 times per month on S!
PERM/COLL: AM: ptgs, drgs, phot, sculp, folk, dec/art, reg 18-20; EU: works on paper; OR; AF

Focusing on American paintings and graphics from the 18th through the 20th century as well as on works by regional artists, the Huntsville Museum promotes the recognition and preservation of artistic heritage in its own and other southeastern states. Located across from Bif Spring Park in downtown Huntsville, the museum serves as the leading visual arts center in north Alabama. **NOT TO BE MISSED:** Large Tiffany style stained glass window.

ON EXHIBIT/95:

10/23/94 - 1/8/95	JAMES ROSENQUIST: TIME DUST, THE COMPLETE GRAPHIC WORKS: 1962-1992 — 115 works accompanied by related studies and collages will be presented in this first time retrospective of the distinguished career of American printmaker, Rosenquist. WT
1/15 - 3/5/95	ENCOUNTERS: ROBERT COX — Recent work by Cox, an outstanding regional artist will be featured in a recurring series of solo exhibitions.
1/29 - 3/26/95	MADE IN ALABAMA: A STATE LEGACY — Alabama-made decorative arts from the 18th through the early 20th century will be featured.
4/16 - 6/11/95	INTERNATIONAL LATHE-TURNED OBJECTS: CHALLENGE V — Contemporary lathe-turned objects from around the world. CAT WT
4/16 - 6/11/95	BREAKING THE MOLD: NEW DIRECTIONS IN GLASS — Works by nationally emerging contemporary artists.
5/14 - 7/16/95	AMERICAN PORTRAIT MINIATURES FROM THE COLLECTION OF LINDA AND RAYMOND WHITE — Miniature portrait paintings rendered in watercolor on ivory (late 18th - early 20th centuries) will be on loan from this major regional private collection.

3

ALABAMA

Huntsville Museum of Art - continued

7/2 - 9/3/95	ALABAMA IMPACT — Works by important regional and nationally acclaimed contemporary Alabama artists.
7/30 - 9/24/95	ENCOUNTERS: CLIFTON PEARSON — As above, recent work by outstanding regional artist Pearson will be featured in a recurring series of solo exhibitions.
ONGOING	VIEWS OF THE COLLECTION — Recent acquisitions, 19th & 20th century American and non-Western art, and other notable objects from the permanent collection will be on view.

MOBILE

The Fine Arts Museum of the South at Mobile
4850 Museum Dr., Langan Park, **Mobile, AL 36608**
TEL: 205-343-2667
HRS: 10-5 Tu-S   DAY CLOSED: M   HOL: LEG/HOL! CITY/HOL!
ADM: F   HDC/ACC: Y; Ramps, elevators, restrooms   PARKING: Y; Free parking on site of main museum
MUS/SH: Y   GR/T: Y   GR/PH: call 205-343-2667   S/G: Y
PERM/COLL: AM: 19; AF; OR; EU; DEC/ART; CONT/CRAFTS

Beautifully situated on a lake in the middle of Langan Park, this museum offers the visitor an overview of 2,000 years of culture represented by more than 4,000 pieces in its permanent collection. **PLEASE NOTE:** There is a downtown gallery of this museum (FAMOS downtown) located at 300 Dauphin St. (205-694-0533), OPEN 8:30-4:30 M-F. This space is handicapped accessible and offers metered and lot parking. **NOT TO BE MISSED:** Boehm porcelain bird collection; 20th-century decorative arts collection.

ON EXHIBIT/95:

11/18/94 - 1/1/95	GASTON LACHAISE: SCULPTURE AND DRAWING — Ample and exaggerated female forms, the trademark of this modern American sculptor, will be seen in this 45-piece overview of his work. Twenty of his drawings will also accompany the exhibition. CAT WT
1/13 - 2/26/95	STYLES, STRANDS, AND SEQUENCES: AMERICAN REALIST PAINTING AND DRAWING FROM THE PHILIP DESIND COLLECTION — 47 works dating from 1932-1990 attest to the keen eye of this revered octagenarian American art collector and gallery owner. CAT
1/14 - 2/12/95	MEDICINE'S GREAT JOURNEY: ONE HUNDRED YEARS OF HEALING — Photo perspectives
3/11 - 5/7/95	ALABAMA IMPACT: CONTEMPORARY ARTISTS WITH ALABAMA TIES CAT
5/14 - 6/26/95	MOBILE ART ASSOCIATION SPRING/SUMMER JURIED EXHIBITION
5/19 - 7/9/95	TALES AND TRADITIONS: STORYTELLING IN TWENTIETH CENTURY AMERICAN CRAFT — Nearly 70 works by 70 artists working in a variety of media that includes weaving, furniture, ceramics, and jewelry will exhibit their unique representations of portraits and scenes relating to historical events and political issues. CAT WT
7/14 - 8/6/95	PRINTS FROM THE PERMANENT COLLECTION
8/18 - 10/15/95	MADE IN ALABAMA 1819-1930: A STATE LEGACY — 200 objects from private collections, many of which have never been on public view, will include ceramics, furniture, metals, paintings, photographs, and textiles. CAT

4

The Fine Arts Museum of the South at Mobile - continued

10/20 - 12/3/95	LOUISE LYONS HEUSTIS (1865-1951) — A retrospective exhibition of the work of this Mobile-born painter. CAT
10/20 - 12/3/95	GENERATIONS IN BLACK AND WHITE: PHOTOGRAPHS BY CARL VAN VECHTEN — 43 vintage photographic portraits (1932-1962) of notable African-Americans. CAT WT
12/10/95 - 1/21/96	MOBILE ART ASSOCIATION ANNUAL JURIED EXHIBITION
12/8/94 - 1/28/95	ALONE IN A CROWD: PRINTS BY AFRICAN-AMERICAN ARTISTS OF THE 1930's AND 1940'S FROM THE COLLECTION OF REBA AND DAVE WILLIAMS — The works of 41 African-American printmakers working in a wide variety of styles and techniques during the Depression decades (many under the auspices of the WPA) will be on view in this 106 piece exhibition. CAT WT

EXHIBITIONS AT FAMOS DOWNTOWN:

1 - 2/95	REFLECTIONS OF THE EIGHTEENTH CENTURY FROM MOBILE COLLECTIONS
11/10 - 12/29/95	THE WATERCOLOR AND GRAPHIC ARTS SOCIETY OF MOBILE'S ANNUAL JURIED EXHIBITION

MONTGOMERY

Montgomery Museum of Fine Arts

One Museum Dr., P.O. Box 230819, **Montgomery, AL 36117**
TEL: 205-244-5700
HRS: 10-5 Tu-Sa; till 9 T; Noon-5 S   DAY CLOSED: M   HOL: LEG/HOL!
ADM: F
HDC/ACC: Y; Fully accessible   PARKING: Y; Ample and free   MUS/SH: Y   REST/FAC: Y; 11-2 Tu-Sa
GR/T: Y   GR/PH: call 205-244-5700 tour coord.
PERM/COLL: AM: ptgs, gr, drgs 18-20; EU: ptgs, gr, sculp, dec/art 19; CONT/REG; BLOUNT COLLECTION OF AM ART

Situated like a jewel in its lake-studded parklike setting, the Montgomery Museum features among its treasures the Blount collection that documents the evolution of American art from the 18th century to the present. **NOT TO BE MISSED:** "A Peaceable Kingdom With Quakers Bearing Banners" by Edward Hicks; "Interactive Gallery" for children

ON EXHIBIT/95:

1/28 - 3/5/95	MONTGOMERY ART GUILD 31ST MUSEUM EXHIBITION
2/4 - 3/5/95	LIVELY TIMES AND EXCITING EVENTS: THE DRAWINGS OF BILL TAYLOR
3/19 - 5/28/95	FACE OF THE GODS: ART AND ALTARS OF AFRICA AND THE AFRICAN AMERICAS — Artistic and ritualistic traditions carried from Africa to America during the last 2 centuries will be seen in the 20 altars (some still in use) and 120 works of art presented in this exhibition. CAT WT
6/22 - 9/10/95	THE FIGURE IN AMERICAN SCULPTURE: A QUESTION OF MODERNITY
9/26 - 11/26/95	BILTMORE
12/3/95 - 1/28/96	MADE IN ALABAMA

5

ALABAMA

UNIVERSITY

University of Alabama Moody Gallery of Art
Garland Hall, **University, AL 35487**
TEL: 205-348-5967
HRS: 8:30-4:30 M-F; 2-5 S; Summer, 10-4 M-F   DAY CLOSED: Sa   HOL: ACAD!
ADM: F   HDC/ACC: Y; Gallery on one floor, no stairs
PARKING: Y   GR/T: Y   GR/PH: call 205-348-5967
DT: Y   TIME: staff member always on duty for tours
PERM/COLL: PTGS, DRGS, GR, SCULP

The permanent collection of this institution consists mainly of works on paper which are on display one time a year during the summer months.

ALASKA

ANCHORAGE

Anchorage Museum of History and Art
121 W. Seventh Ave., **Anchorage, AK 99501**
TEL: 907-343-4326
HRS: 9-6 M-S mid May-mid Sept; 10-6 Tu-Sa, 1-5 S rest of the year   HOL: LEG/HOL!
ADM: Y   ADULT: $4.00   CHILDREN: F (under 18)   STUDENTS: $4.00   SR CIT: $3.50
HDC/ACC: Y   MUS/SH: Y   REST/FAC: Y; Cafe   GR/T: Y   GR/PH: call 907-343-6187
DT: Y   TIME: 12 & 2 daily for art collection
PERM/COLL: ETH

For 25 years the Anchorage Museum of History & Art has been dedicated to the collection, preservation, and exhibition of Alaskan ethnology, history, and art.

ON EXHIBIT/95:

1/8 - 2/26/95	WILLIAM KEITH: CALIFORNIA'S POET PAINTER — 135 landscape paintings that span the career (late 1860's -1911) of one of the leading turn-of-the-century artists will be on exhibit. CAT WT
1/4 - 1/9/95	ALASKA POSITIVE — A biennial juried photographic exhibition.
2/5 - 3/12/95	EARTH, FIRE AND FIBRE — A major biennial juried craft exhibition.
2/5 - 3/12/95	MIKE SIRL — Featured in his first museum exhibition will be Sirl's metal sculptures of common every-day objects which he often arranges in an installation setting that implies metaphorical narrative.
3/12 - 4/16/95	LAURENCE AHVAKANA — Sculptural works in marble and in such non-traditional materials as neon, steel and plastic that reflect the traditional stories and art of Ahvakana's Inuit culture will be featured in this exhibition.
3/19 - 4/30/95	THE ARTIST'S HAND (BANK OF AMERICA COLLECTION) — On exhibit will be 56 works dating from 1965-1990 by such noted artists as David Hockney, Jonathan Borofsky, David Salle and Robert Longo that show the remarkable range of contemporary drawing.
4/11 - 9/24/95	DALE CHIHULY: INSTALLATIONS 1964-1995 — Major works by Chihuly, America's foremost glass artist will be seen in the largest contemporary exhibition ever mounted at this museum. WT
10/1 - 11/5/95	RAREFIED LIGHT — Annual juried photographic exhibition.
10/8 - 11/19/95	BOTH ART AND LIFE: GEMINI G.E.L. AT 25 — Since its founding 25 years ago, many distinguished artists have produced work in this influential printmaking workshop. For this exhibition selections from the print suites of such artists as John Baldessari, Jonathan Borofsky, Mark de Suvero, Richard Diebenkorn, Ellsworth Kelly and Roy Lichtenstein who have worked at Gemini will be on view accompanied by educational text panels describing various printmaking techniques and photographs of the artists at work. CAT WT
11/19 - 12/31/95	BRIAN BOLDON: SOLO EXHIBITION — In this installation by contemporary ceramic artist Boldon, clay models of animals placed in a series of animated positions that resemble a circus ring will allow the viewer to experience a carnival-like atmosphere.

7

ALASKA

Anchorage Museum of History and Art - continued

11/26/95 - 1/31/96   ROZZE REDMOND — Painted in the tradition of the New York School, several of Redmond's large abstract images will be seen in this exhibition.

11/26/94 - 1/31/96   5TH INTERNATIONAL SHOEBOX SCULPTURE — On exhibit will be 80 pieces of sculpture from around the world all of which are no larger than the size of a regular shoe box.   WT

KETCHIKAN

Totem Heritage Center
601 Deermount, **Ketchikan, AK 99901**
TEL: 907-225-5900
HRS: 8-5 Daily (mid May-Sep); 1-5 Tu-F (mid Oct-May - no adm fee)
F/DAY: S pm   ADM: Y   ADULT: $2.00
HDC/ACC: Y
PERM/COLL: CONT: N/W Coast Indian art; Totem poles

FLAGSTAFF

Northern Arizona University Art Museum and Galleries
Box 6021, **Flagstaff, AZ 86011-6021**
TEL: 602-523-3471
HRS: 9-5 M-F; 1-4 S   DAY CLOSED: Sa   HOL: LEG & ACAD HOL!
VOL/CONT: Y   ADM: F   HDC/ACC: Y   PARKING: Y; Free   MUS/SH: Y
PERM/COLL: GR; PTGS; SCULP

The collection at this university museum is comprised mainly of works from the southwestern region of the United States and from Mexico.

ON EXHIBIT/95:   Exhibitions include displays of the permanent collection and other bodies of work both contemporary and historic in nature.

MESA

Mesa Southwest Museum
53 N. Macdonald, **Mesa, AZ 85201**
TEL: 602-644-2571
HRS: 10-5 Tu-Sa; 1-5 S   DAY CLOSED: M   HOL: LEG/HOL!
ADM: Y   ADULT: $4.00   CHILDREN: $2.00 (3-12)   STUDENTS: $3.50   SR CIT: $3.50
HDC/ACC: Y   PARKING: Y; Street parking in front of the museum & covered parking directly behind the museum on the first level of the parking garage. Handicapped spaces located in front of the museum.   MUS/SH: Y
GR/T: Y   GR/PH: call 602-644-3553 or 3071
PERM/COLL: ETH; P/COL; CER

Changing exhibitions of ancient to contemporary works based on Southwestern themes are featured in this multi-faceted museum. **NOT TO BE MISSED:** "Finding The Way," by Howard Post; "Superstition Sunrise," full-color wall mural by Jim Gucwa; "Hohokam Life," by Ka Graves, a series of watercolor interpretations of Hohokam Indian life (300 B.C.-1450 A.D.)

ON EXHIBIT/95:
1 - 3/95	COMMUNITY ARTS EXHIBITIONS
3 - 5/95	INTO THE CANYON — A photographic exhibition of the geology, paleontology and archaeology of the Grand Canyon.
3 - 5/95	THE ART OF KARL DOWHIE — Contemporary Southwestern landscapes.
6 - 9/95	XICANINDIO ARTES RETROSPECTIVE — A 20 year art organization overview as seen in contemporary artworks by Latin American and Native American artists.

PHOENIX
The Heard Museum
22 E. Monte Vista Rd., **Phoenix, AZ 85004**
TEL: 602-252-8840
HRS: 9:30-5 M-Sa; Noon-5 S; Till 9 pm W   HOL: LEG/HOL!
F/DAY: 5-9 W   ADM: Y   ADULT: $5.00   CHILDREN: F (under 4) !   STUDENTS: $4.00   SR CIT: $4.00
HDC/ACC: Y; Barrier free   PARKING: Y; Free   MUS/SH: Y   GR/T: Y   GR/PH: 602-252-8840 (Activities coord.)
DT: Y   TIME: Many times daily!
PERM/COLL: NAT/AM; ETH; AF; OR; OC; SO/AM

ARIZONA

The Heard Museum - continued

The collection of the decorative and fine arts of the Heard Museum, which spans the history of Native American Art from the pre-historic to the contemporary, is considered the most comprehensive collection of its kind in the entire country. Named after the Heards who founded the museum based on their great interest in the culture of the native people of Arizona, the museum is housed in part of the original Heard home called Casa Blanca. **NOT TO BE MISSED:** Experience the cultures of 3 Native American tribes with hands-on family oriented "Old Ways, New Ways"

ON EXHIBIT/95:

9/24/94 - 10/1/95	NATIVE AMERICAN FINE ARTS INVITATIONAL — Installation art, cutting-edge sculpture, and paintings will highlight what's current in Native American fine art.
11/11/94 - 10/95	WATCHFUL EYES: NATIVE AMERICAN WOMEN ARTISTS — Works by 70 contemporary 20th-century Native American women artists.
11/94 - 7/95	READ MULLAN TEXTILES/REHOUSING — Award-winning Navajo textiles created during the 1950's to 70's when regional styles of weaving gained great national acclaim and recognition will be on exhibit.
1/21/95 - 9/96	FOLLOWING THE SUN AND THE MOON: HOPI KACHINA DOLLS — From the permanent collection, this display will feature an array of Kachina dolls from the early 1900's to present day examples.
3/4 - 3/5/95	37th ANNUAL GUILD INDIAN FAIR & MARKET
4/7 - 4/15/95	7TH ANNUAL GUILD NATIVE AMERICAN STUDENT ARTS & CRAFTS SHOW — An exhibit and sale of works by Native American students from throughout the U.S.
THROUGH 6/95	RAIN — The significance of rain in Native American culture is explored through a presentation of art and artifacts.
9/95 - 8/96	INVENTING THE SOUTHWEST: THE FRED HARVEY COLLECTION — Baskets, pottery, jewelry, painting and other art from this noted collection will be on view.
10/28/95 - 1/14/96	DAY OF THE DEAD EXHIBIT: MUERTOS DE GUSTO — This exhibition of "Muertos de Gusto" which translates to "Thrilled to Death," defines the Mexican tradition of the celebration of death which is at once both humorous and sad and serves as a reminder that life is brief and should be enjoyed to the fullest. Coinciding with this exhibition is the Dia de Muertos Festival, 10/95, held on the grounds of the Museum.

ON PERMANENT DISPLAY

NATIVE PEOPLES OF THE SOUTHWEST: THE PERMANENT COLLECTION OF THE HEARD MUSEUM — A magnificent display of superb Native American artifacts including pottery, baskets, jewelry, weaving and kachina dolls.

OLD WAYS, NEW WAYS — A state-of-the-art interactive exhibit that features enjoyable hands-on art activities for the entire family.

PHOENIX

Phoenix Art Museum
1625 N. Central Ave., **Phoenix, AZ 85004-1685**
TEL: 602-257-1222
HRS: 10-5 Tu, T-Sa; 10-9 W, Noon-5 S   DAY CLOSED: M   HOL: 1/1, 7/4, THGV, 12/25
F/DAY: W   ADM: Y   ADULT: $4.00   CHILDREN: F (under 6)   STUDENTS: $1.50   SR CIT: $3.00
HDC/ACC: Y   PARKING: Y; Ample parking around the museum   MUS/SH: Y
GR/T: Y   GR/PH: call 602-257-1880   DT: Y   TIME: 2:00 daily & 6:00 on W
PERM/COLL: AM: Western, cont; AS; EU: 18-19

Phoenix Art Museum - continued

The Phoenix, one of the largest art museums in the Southwest, has a broad range of fine and decorative art dating from the Renaissance to today. A special treat for families is the hands-on "Attack Gallery" and the Thorne Miniature Rooms of historic interiors. The museum will remain open and fully operational during a major 2 year 20 million dollar expansion and renovation program scheduled for completion in 1996. **NOT TO BE MISSED:** "Attack Gallery" for children and their families; Thorne Miniature Rooms of historic interiors.

ON EXHIBIT/95:

12/21/94 - 2/19/95	PICTURING HISTORY: AMERICAN PAINTING 1770-1930 — For the first time in the U.S., an exhibition of paintings will highlight pivotal events in American history. Over 70 works ranging from depictions of Columbus' voyage, the first Thanksgiving, the American Revolution & Civil War, and other significant historical events will be seen in this unique overview of American history. CAT WT
10/1/94 - 1/29/95	ANCIENT CHINA-MODERN CLAY: INFLUENCES ON FIVE CERAMIC ARTISTS — 30 objects by 5 contemporary potters whose works reinterpret many of the classical aspects of traditional Chinese ceramics.
2/16 - 4/15/95	CHINESE SNUFF BOTTLES
3/11 - 5/11/95	FRANK LLOYD WRIGHT AND JAPANESE ART — An exhibition of never before seen Japanese textiles, furniture, prints, screens, fans, and scrolls from Wright's Archives will show how important the influence of Japanese esthetics was upon his own artistic processes.
7/8 - 10/1/95	CIEN ANOS De CREATIVIDAD: LATIN AMERICAN WOMEN ARTISTS — In the first large-scale exhibition of its kind, works by 35 20th century Latin American women artists emphasize the importance of their artistic contributions. WT
10/21 - 11/19/95	THE 30TH ANNUAL COWBOY ARTISTS OF AMERICA EXHIBITION AND SALE
12/2/95 - 2/25/96	THE TASTE OF TWO EARLS: PAINTINGS FROM ITALY AT BURGHLEY HOUSE — 60 Old Master paintings will be on loan from the grandest Elizabethan house in England. CAT WT

PHOENIX

Plotkin Judiaca Museum of Greater Phoenix
3310 N. 10th Ave., **Phoenix, AZ 85013**
TEL: 602-264-4428
HRS: 10-3 Tu-T; Noon-3 S; Open after Fri. Evening Services; DAY CLOSED: M, F, Sa
HOL: LEG/HOL!; JEWISH HOL!
VOL/CONT: Y ADM: F HDC/ACC: Y; Restrooms; Museum on ground floor (no steps)
PARKING: Y; Free behind building MUS/SH: Y GR/T: Y GR/PH: call 602-264-4428
PERM/COLL: JEWISH ART

Considered to be one of the most important centers of Jewish art and culture in the Southwest, the Plotkin Museum holdings span 5,000 years of Jewish history and heritage. PLEASE NOTE: It is advised to call ahead for summer hours! **NOT TO BE MISSED:** Recreated composite neighborhood synagogue of Tunis housed in the Bush Gallery.

ON EXHIBIT/95:

10/94 - through 6/95	DIAMONDS IN THE DESERT: 75TH ANNIVERSARY OF TEMPLE BETH ISRAEL — A 4 gallery exhibition on the 75 year history (1920-1995) of the Temple Beth Israel congregation that will include photographs, artifacts and other relative items.

11

ARIZONA

PRESCOTT

Prescott's Phippen Museum of Western Art
4701 Hwy 89 N, **Prescott, AZ 86301**
TEL: 602-778-1385
HRS: 1-4 daily (Jan & Feb); 10-4 M & W-Sa, 1-4 S (Mar-Dec)   DAY CLOSED: Tu   HOL: 1/1, THGV, 12/25
ADM: Y   ADULT: $2.00   CHILDREN: F (under 6)   STUDENTS: $1.00   SR CIT: $1.50
HDC/ACC: Y   PARKING: Y; Free and ample   MUS/SH: Y
PERM/COLL: PTGS, SCULP

Paintings and sculpture of western America including contemporary Native American and Anglo artists' works are featured. **NOT TO BE MISSED:** 3 foot high bronze of Father Keno by George Phippen; spectacular view and historic wagons in front of the museum

ON EXHIBIT/95:

1/7 - 3/7/95	ARIZONA HISTORY THROUGH ART: EARLY RANCHING
3/10 - 4/18/95	CONTEMPORARY SOUTHWEST PAINTERS
4/21 - 6/12/95	NICOLAI FECHIN — Major works from the Taylor Museum Collection, Colorado Springs, Co. WT
6/13 - 7/13/95	TBA
7/14 - 9/19/95	THE GINGER RENNER COLLECTION OF CHARLES RUSSELL PAINTINGS AND BRONZES
9/22 - 11/14/95	FIVE LADY PAINTERS OF EARLY PRESCOTT — Kate Cory, Ada Rigden, Mable Laurence, Lillian Wilhelm Smith, and Clara Dooner Pillips
11/17 - 12/31/95	9TH ANNUAL ARIZONA HOLIDAYS FINE ART AND CRAFT SHOW

SCOTTSDALE

Fleisher Museum
17207 N. Perimeter Dr., **Scottsdale, AZ 85255**
TEL: 602-585-3108
HRS: 10-4 Daily   HOL: LEG/HOL!
ADM: F
HDC/ACC: Y; Entrance & elevators   PARKING: Y; Free and ample   MUS/SH: Y
GR/T: Y   GR/PH: 602-585-3108
H/B: Y; All materials used in building indiginous to State of Arizona   S/G: Y
PERM/COLL: AM/IMPR; ptgs, sculp (California School)

Located in the 261 acre Perimeter Center, the Fleisher Museum was, until recently, the first and only museum to feature California Impressionist works. More than 80 highly recognized artists of this genre are represented in the permanent collection. **NOT TO BE MISSED:** "Mount Alice at Sunset" by Franz A. Bischoff, best known as the "King of the Rose Painters."

ON EXHIBIT/95:

2/3 - 5/17/95	ARTHUR G. RIDER: AMERICAN IMPRESSIONIST — 70 paintings and 7 pencil sketches by Rider (1886-1979) considered the ultimate practitioner of Impressionist color theory will be on view accompanied by archival photographs. WT

ARIZONA

SCOTTSDALE

Scottsdale Center for the Arts
7383 Scottsdale Mall, **Scottsdale, AZ 85251**
TEL: 602-994-2787
HRS: 10-5 M-W; 10-8 T-Sa; Noon-5 S   HOL: LEG/HOL!
VOL/CONT: Y   ADM: F
HDC/ACC: Y   PARKING: Y; Free and ample parking   MUS/SH: Y
GR/T: Y   GR/PH: call 602-994-2315 Joyce Erickson   DT: Y   TIME: 1:30 S
PERM/COLL: CONT; REG

Four exhibition spaces and a beautiful outdoor sculpture garden are but a part of this community oriented multi-disciplinary cultural center. **NOT TO BE MISSED:** "The Dance" a bronze sculpture (1936) by Jacques Lipchitz; "Ambient Landscape" by Janet Taylor; "Time/Light Fusion" sculpture (1990) by Dale Eldred

ON EXHIBIT/95:

10/21/94 - 2/5/95
A MUSEUM IN THE MAKING: THE JANSSEN COLLECTION OF FINE ART — Some of the finest examples of the CoBrA (an acronym for Copenhagen, Brussels and Denmark) art movement as well as outstanding contemporary works by American artists will be selected for viewing from this noteworthy collection.

11/4/94 - 1/1/95
NEO-DADA: REDEFINING ART, 1958-62 — In this traveling exhibition, works by Duchamp and Schwitters, grand masters of the artform will be joined by those created as a direct result of their influence. Works by 31 well-known artists in the field including Jasper Johns, Claes Oldenburg, Yoko Ono, John Cage, Andy Warhol and others will be featured.   WT

12/24/94 - 2/5/95
RICHARD LAUGHARN: CROSSING DESERTS — Photographer Richard Laugharn compares and contrasts the cultures of the arid Sonoran and Saharan Deserts concentrating both on similar architectural traditions and the differences of each culture's relationship to the land.

1/13 - 3/12/95
PAINTER AND PATRON: THE SANTA FE COLLECTION — Less than 50 years after its inception in 1869, the Santa Fe Railroad began collecting American works by artists tied to the history and development of the Southwest. Some of the finest examples of work by Thomas Moran, Joseph Sharp, Irving Couse, Oscar E. Burninghaus, and others from the collection will be featured in this exhibition.

1/13 - 3/12/95
WOMEN OF THE WEST: SELECTIONS FROM THE SANTA FE COLLECTION — Works by women whose artistic achievements helped to shape the perceptions of the Southwest will be selected for viewing from the Santa Fe Collection.

2/17 - 4/16/95
ROBERT COLESCOTT: THE ONE-TWO PUNCH — Richly painted cartoonish caricatures that appear in Colescott's emotionally charged depictions of history parody familiar images of George Washington, Shirley Temple, van Gogh, and Cezanne by often presenting them in blackface in an attempt to debunk society's cultural and historical myths.

3/11 - 4/14/95
THE PRESENCE OF ABSENCE: MEL ROMAN AND JAMES MONTFORD — A collaborative multi-media installation by two artists, one white and the other black, that both illuminates the achievements of African-American filmmakers and artists and comments on society's neglect and abuse of them.

3/24 - 5/21/95
THE STUDIO MUSEUM IN HARLEM: TWENTY FIVE YEARS OF AFRICAN-AMERICAN ART — In celebration of the Studio Museum's 25th anniversary, this traveling exhibition will highlight paintings, sculpture, and works on paper created between 1968-1993 by noted African-American artists.   WT

ARIZONA

Scottsdale Center for the Arts - continued

3/24 - 5/21/95   NANCY O'CONNOR: I COULDN'T HEAR NOBODY PRAY — Black cowboy life in South Texas is documented in O'Connor's manipulated photographs presented along with sound, projected images, writings, and some personal belongings of the cowboys themselves.

6/2 - 8/20/95   LARRY SULTAN: PICTURES FROM HOME — Family photographs accompanied by the vocal commentary of his mother and father explore the often complicated emotional issues about the nature of photography, family relationships, and memory.   WT

6/2 - 8/20/95   IN THE LAST HOUR: SANDY SKOGLAND PHOTOGRAPHS AND SCULPTURES — Life-size interiors filled with a bizarre array of objects created by the artist over the past 13 years will be seen along with an installation of her most recent large-scale environment called "The Cocktail Party."

5/7 - 8/27/95   MUSEUM IN THE MAKING: SELECTIONS FROM THE JANSSEN COLLECTION OF FINE ART — An exhibition of additional works from the collection as described above.

5/19 - 8/13/95   SEAN O'DONNELL: PASTEOGRAPHY — Three dimensional collages made from images taken from newspapers and magazines are blended together in a virtually seamless manner by the use of an air brush. Mounted in found frames, the artist enhances the compositions by incorporating light and movement which is activated by pressing a button at the bottom of the frame.

TEMPE

University Art Museum

Affiliate Institution: Arizona State University
Nelson Fine Arts Center & Mathews Center, **Tempe, AZ 85287-2911**
TEL: 602-965-ARTS
HRS: 10-9 Tu, 10-5 W-Sa, 1-5 S (Nelson Ctr.); 10-5 Tu-Sa (Matthews Ctr.)   DAY CLOSED: M   HOL: LEG/HOL!
VOL/CONT: Y   ADM: F   HDC/ACC: Y   PARKING: Y; Metered parking in front of museum & visitors lot behind museum on corner of 10th St. & Myrtle   MUS/SH: Y   GR/T: Y   GR/PH: call 602-965-5254   H/B: Y; Award winning new building by Antoine Predock.
PERM/COLL: AM: ptgs, gr; EU: gr 15-20; AM: crafts 19-20; LAT/AM: ptgs, sculp; CONT; AF; FOLK

For 40 years the ASU Art Museum, founded to broaden the awareness of American visual arts in Arizona, has been a vital resource within the valley's art community. The ASU Art Museum consists of both the Nelson Center and the Matthews Center. **NOT TO BE MISSED:** ASU Zoo (Whimsical works of animal art in all media)

ON EXHIBIT/95:

10/7/94 - 1/8/95   PETER GREENAWAY'S DRAWINGS AND FILMS — Artworks by this British filmmaker inspired by certain aspects and elements of the films he created.

11/18/94 - 1/29/95   DREAMING WITH OPEN EYES — A 30 year retrospective of the sculpture of Fritz Scholder.

12/9/94 - 2/5/95   REDEFINING THE LATHE-TURNED OBJECT III — Traditional vessels as well as innovative sculpture and furniture, all created on the lathe will be featured in this international juried exhibition and mini-conference.

1/29 - 4/15/95   ART UNDER DURESS: EL SALVADOR 1980 - PRESENT — Works of art and video documentary document the effects of the recent 12 year long war waged in El Salvador.

ONGOING AT THE NELSON CENTER:

   MEXICAN ART FROM THE LATIN AMERICAN COLLECTION — Superb paintings by such past masters as Rivera, Siqueiros and Tamayo, joined by those of contemporary artists are displayed with examples of vice-regal religious statuary and baroque-inspired Mexican retablos.

14

ARIZONA

TUCSON

Center for Creative Photography
Affiliate Institution: University of Arizona
Tucson, AZ 85721
TEL: 602-621-7968
HRS: 11-5 M-F; Noon-5 S   DAY CLOSED: Sa   HOL: LEG/HOL!
ADM: F   HDC/ACC: Y; Ramp & electronic door
PARKING: Y; Metered public parking in garage on NE corner of Speedway & Park   MUS/SH: Y
GR/T: Y   GR/PH: call 602-621-7968 education dept
PERM/COLL: PHOT 19-20

The singular focus of this collection is on the photographic image, its history, and its documentation. **NOT TO BE MISSED:** Works by Ansel Adams, Richard Avedon, Imogen Cunningham, Laura Gilpin, Marion Palfi, & Edward Weston

ON EXHIBIT/95:

11/13/94 - 1/22/95	LOLA ALVEREZ BRAVO: IN HER OWN LIGHT
11/13/94 - 1/22/95	SELECTIONS FROM THE PERMANENT COLLECTION: THE PERSONAL DOCUMENTARY
1/29 - 3/26/95	ART MUSEUM
4/2 - 5/28/95	WITHIN THIS GARDEN: PHOTOGRAPHS BY RUTH THORNE-THOMSEN
4/2 - 5/28/95	PATTERNS OF CONNECTION: LEAH KING-SMITH
6/4 - 9/10/95	ARTHUR TRESS: THE WURLITZER TRILOGY

Tucson Museum of Art
140 N. Main Ave., **Tucson, AZ 85701**
TEL: 602-624-2333
HRS: 10-4 M-Sa; Noon-4 S; closed M June, July, & Aug.   HOL: LEG/HOL!
F/DAY: Tu   ADM: Y   ADULT: $2.00   CHILDREN: F (under 12)   STUDENTS: $1.00   SR CIT: $1.00
HDC/ACC: Y; No stairs; has ramp & elevator   PARKING: Y; Free lot on north side of building; lot on east side of building free with validation of ticket; commercial underground parking garage under city hall across street.
MUS/SH: Y   REST/FAC: Y; Janos Restaurant in neighboring J. Corbett House
GR/T: Y   GR/PH: call 602-624-2333
DT: Y   TIME: Daily during museum hours   H/B: Y; Located on the site of the original Presidio   S/G: Yes
PERM/COLL: P/COL; AM: Western; CONT/SW; SP: colonial; MEX

Past meets present in this 70-year-old museum and historic home complex set in the Plaza of the Pioneers. The contemporary museum building itself is a wonderful contrast to five of Tucson's most prominent historic homes that are all situated in an inviting parklike setting. PLEASE NOTE: Historic Fish House on Maine Ave. will open in the fall of 1995 as a museum of Western American Art and will feature special exhibitions of Western Art. **NOT TO BE MISSED:** Pre-Columbian collection

ON EXHIBIT/95:

11/4/94 - 1/1/95	NEW MEXICAN TIN WORK

15

ARIZONA

Tucson Museum of Art - continued

11/11/94 - 1/1/95	DIRECTIONS: WILL SAUNDERS
11/20/94 - 3/31/95	EL NACIMIENTO — For the 19th year, 200 hand painted miniature terra cotta Mexican nativity figures will be displayed in intricately arranged tableaus.
12/16/94 - 2/12/95	THIRTY YEARS IN THE ARENA: LOUISE SERPA PHOTOGRAPHS
1/13 - 3/12/95	CAMPBELL SOUP TUREEN EXHIBIT — 500 years of Western decorative arts will be seen in this unique display of European and American soup tureens. WT
2/24 - 3/26/95	AMERICAN WOMEN ARTISTS AND THE WEST SHOW AND SALE
3/24 - 5/14/95	L. B. CURTIS
3/24 - 5/21/95	GRONK: A LIVING SURVEY — Paintings, notebook sketches, and other memorabilia will be included in a 20-year overview of this Los Angeles Chicano artist. WT
4/7 - 6/4 95	PICTURING THE FRONTIER: THE URUGUAYAN SCENES OF JUAN MANUEL BLANES — 40 masterful works that depict the social and political environment of 19th century life on the plains in Uruguay and Argentina. WT
6/16 - 8/6/95	ARIZONA BIENNIAL
8/18 - 10/8/95	AMAZON RITUAL FEATHER WORK — Ritual life of 64 Amazonian tribes as expressed in aesthetic featherwork will be highlighted in this exhibition.
7/21 - 9/17/95	INTERMOUNTAIN WEAVERS GUILD ANNUAL JURIED SHOW
10/7 - 12/3/95	SELECTIONS FROM THE ELI BROAD FOUNDATION Contemporary artworks on loan from the extensive holdings of this major Los Angeles collection will be featured in this exhibit.
10/20 - 12/10/95	CONTEMPORARY SOUTHWEST IMAGES X: THE STONEWALL FOUNDATION SERIES (Artist on exhibit TBA)
11/19/95 - 3/26/96	TWENTIETH ANNIVERSARY OF EL NACIMIENTO (See above listing)

TUCSON

University of Arizona Museum of Art
Olive and Speedway, Tucson, AZ 85721
TEL: 602-621-7567
HRS: 9-5 M-F, Noon-4 S (Sep-mid May); 10-3:30 M-F, Noon-4 S (mid May thru Aug)   DAY CLOSED: Sa
HOL: LEG/HOL!; ACAD!
ADM: F   HDC/ACC: Y; Automatic doors, elevators
PARKING: Y; $1.00 per hour in garage on the NE corner of Park Ave. & Speedway Blvd. (Free on Sundays)
MUS/SH: Y   GR/T: Y   GR/PH: call 602-621-7567
DT: Y   TIME: 12:15 first & last W Month (Sept-Apr)
PERM/COLL: IT: Kress Collection 14-19; CONT/AM: ptgs, sculp; CONT/EU: ptgs, sculp; OR: gr; CONT: gr; AM: ptgs, gr

One of the most complete university collections of Renaissance and later European and American works can be enjoyed when visiting the Tucson based University of Arizona Museum of Art. **NOT TO BE MISSED:** 61 plaster models & sketches by Jacques Lipchitz; 26 panel retablo of Ciudad Rodrigo by Gallego (late 15th C)

16

University of Arizona Museum of Art - continued

ON EXHIBIT/95:

1/5 - 2/26/95
MARK ROTHKO: THE SPIRIT OF MYTH — 24 expressionist landscape, still life, figure studies and portrait paintings by Rothko from the 30's and 40's will document the critical period in the evolution of the artist's style that was a forerunner of his later abstract atmospheric color field works.

1/19 - 3/5/95
DREAMWEAVERS — Paintings of fantasy art and children's book illustrations by 7 highly regarded artists working in this field.

2/26 - 3/23/95
ARIZONA ON PAPER — Works by 8 Arizona artists that recently toured the Slovak Republic.

4/2 - 4/23/95
MASTER OF FINE ARTS THESIS EXHIBITION

ARKANSAS

FORT SMITH

Fort Smith Art Center
423 N. 6th St., **Fort Smith, AR 72901**
TEL: 501-784-2787
HRS: 9:30-4:30 Tu-Sa ; 2-4 S; closed 1st Sa of the month from noon on   DAY CLOSED: M   HOL: 7/4; 12/25 - 1/1
VOL/CONT: Y   ADM: F
HDC/ACC: Y; To lower floor   PARKING: Y; Free   MUS/SH: Y   GR/T: Y   GR/PH: call 501-782-6371
H/B: Y; Pilot House for Belle Grove Historic District
PERM/COLL: CONT/AM: ptgs, gr, sculp, dec/arts

Located mid-state on the western border of Oklahoma, the Fort Smith Art Center, housed in the Pilot House for Belle Grove Historic District, features an impressive collection of porcelain Boehm birds that are on display year round. **NOT TO BE MISSED:** Large Boehm Porcelain Collection

ON EXHIBIT/95:   Rotating monthly exhibitions

LITTLE ROCK

The Arkansas Arts Center
MacArthur Park, **Little Rock, AR 72203**
TEL: 501-372-4000
HRS: 10-5 M-Sa; Noon-5 S, Hol.   HOL: 12/25
VOL/CONT: Y   ADM: F   HDC/ACC: Y; Galleries, restaurant, museum shop accessible by elevator or ramp
PARKING: Y; Free   MUS/SH: Y
REST/FAC: Y; Restaurant 11:30-1:30 M-F   GR/T: Y   GR/PH: 501-372-4000
H/B: Y; Housed in a 1840 Greek Revival building   S/G: Y
PERM/COLL: AM: drgs 19-20; EU: drgs; AM: all media; EU: all media; OR; CONT/CRAFTS

Housed in an 1840 Greek Revival building, the art center features American and European drawings along with a variety of contemporary crafts.

ON EXHIBIT/95:
11/18/94 - 1/8/95	MAD HATTER TEA PARTY
	WORKS FROM THE PERMANENT COLLECTION
11/20/94 - 1/8/95	TOYS DESIGNED BY ARTISTS
1/6 - 2/19/95	LET US MARCH ON! SELECTED CIVIL RIGHTS PHOTOGRAPHS OF ERNEST C. WITHERS
1/13 - 2/19/95	AFRICAN-AMERICAN WORKS FROM THE PERMANENT COLLECTION
1/13 - 2/19/95	ODD NERDRUM: THE DRAWINGS — 25 charcoal drawings by this contemporary Norwegian-born artist will be featured in the first American exhibition of his work. CAT WT
1/15 - 2/26/95	QUILT INTERNATIONAL
1/20 - 3/5/95	PAUL ROTTEREDAM: A DRAWING RETROSPECTIVE

The Arkansas Arts Center - continued

2/24 - 4/2/95	POST 1950 ABSTRACT WORKS FROM THE PERMANENT COLLECTION
3/5 - 4/15/95	ORIENTAL CARPETS FROM THE HUNTINGTON MUSEUM, W. VA. (TENT!)
3/10 - 6/4/95	FRENCH OIL SKETCHES AND THE ACADEMIC TRADITION — 125 paintings ranging from the Baroque, Rococo, Neoclassic, Romantic, and Realistic periods which recorded the initial spontaneous thoughts of the artists represented in this exhibition will be seen in the first traveling exhibition of its kind.　　　　CAT　WT
3/10 - 4/9/95	MID-SOUTHERN WATERCOLORISTS SILVER ANNIVERSARY EXHIBITION
4/7 - 5/14/95	THE BARRETT HAMILTON YOUNG ARKANSAS ARTISTS COMPETITION AND EXHIBITION
4/14 - 6/95	CUBISM AND ITS LEGACY: WORKS FROM THE PERMANENT COLLECTION
5/19 - 6/25/95	PRINTS, DRAWINGS & PHOTOGRAPHS
6/9 - 7/30/95	AL ALLEN: RETROSPECTIVE
6/11 - 7/9/95	PERMANENT COLLECTION (Decorative Arts Museum)
9/95 - 11/26/95	DRIVEN TO CREATE: THE ANTHONY PETULLA COLLECTION OF SELF-TAUGHT AND OUTSIDER ART　　　　WT
9/8 - 11/5/95	ALONE IN A CROWD: PRINTS BY AFRICAN AMERICAN ARTISTS OF THE 1930'S AND 40'S FROM THE COLLECTION OF REBA AND DAVE WILLIAMS — The works of 41 African-American printmakers working in a wide variety of styles and techniques during the Depression decades (many under the auspices of the WPA) will be on view in this 106 piece exhibition.　　　　CAT　WT
9/22 - 11/26/95	HANS BURKHARDT: DRAWINGS
11/13/95 - 1/31/96	ADOLPH GOTTLIEB PICTOGRAPHS — An exhibition that allows the viewer to understand how Gottlieb, a founding member of the Abstract Expressionist group, combined and integrated a diverse range of elements (from classical, African, modern, Native American and Tlingit) into his own distinctive grid-like creations.　CAT　WT

PINE BLUFF

The Arts & Science Center for Southeast Arkansas
701 Main St., **Pine Bluff, AR 71601**
TEL: 501-536-3375
HRS: 8-5 M-F, 10-4 Sa, 1-4 S　HOL: LEG/HOL!
ADM: F
HDC/ACC: Y　PARKING: Y; Free　GR/T: Y　GR/PH: call 501-536-3375　DT: Y
PERM/COLL: EU: ptgs 19; AM: ptgs, gr 20; OM: drgs; CONT/EU: dgrs

A new building opened in Sept. '94, houses a nearly 1,000 piece collection of fine art that includes one of the country's most outstanding permanent collections of African-American artworks. The museum also contains a noted collection of American drawings (1900 to the present) which are always on view. **NOT TO BE MISSED:** Collection of African-American art by Tanner, Lawrence, Bearden and others; Art Deco & Art Nouveau bronzes

ARKANSAS

The Arts & Science Center for Southeast Arkansas - continued

ON EXHIBIT/95:

9/24/94 - 1/31/95	SELECTIONS FROM THE PERMANENT COLLECTION
12/19/94 - 2/15/95	ART FROM WITHIN
1/1 - 1/28/95	SMALL WORKS ON PAPER
1/23 - 3/3/95	AFRICAN-AMERICAN ARTISTS
3/3 - 3/26/95	SET DECORATORS ART
3/10 - 4/19/95	SELECTIONS FROM THE PERMANENT COLLECTION
4/1 - 4/30/95	KIMONOS
4/24 - 6/9/95	STERLING COLLECTION OF BOTANICAL PAINTINGS
5/8 - 8/18/95	IRENE ROSENZWEIG BIENNIAL EXHIBITION

BAKERSFIELD

Bakersfield Museum of Art

1930 R St., **Bakersfield, CA 93301**
TEL: 805-323-7219
HRS: 10-4 M-Sa   DAY CLOSED: M   HOL: LEG/HOL!& AUG
VOL/CONT: Y   ADM: Y   ADULT: $2.00   CHILDREN: F (under 12)   STUDENTS: $1.00   SR CIT: $1.00
HDC/ACC: Y; Entrance, restrooms   PARKING: Y; Free and ample parking   MUS/SH: Y
GR/T: Y   GR/PH: call 805-323-7219
PERM/COLL: PTGS; SCULP; GR; REG

Works by California regional artists are the main focus of this museum and its collection. Box lunches available 3 days in advance to tour groups may be enjoyed among the sculptures and flowers of the museum's gardens. **NOT TO BE MISSED:** The Artist Guild Show in the lobby where works by local professional artists are individually highlighted on a monthly basis.

ON EXHIBIT/95:

12/15/94 - 1/15/95	THROUGH THE LOOKING GLASS AND DRAWING OF LIFE: ELIZABETH LAYTON — A paired exhibition that reflects the views of an elderly and witty woman artist.
1/20 - 2/26/95	ADDITIONS TO THE B. M. A. COLLECTION — Works never before shown in the gallery will be on exhibit.
3/24 - 5/5/95	MAYNARD DIXON: PORTRAITS OF NATIVE AMERICANS — 42 portrait drawings dating from 1900-1933 that reflected native Californian Dixon's compassion and fascination with Native-American people will be seen in this exhibition. WT
5/13 - 6/17/95	VISUAL ARTS FESTIVAL — 7th annual juried art exhibit of Kern County artists.
6/23 - 7/30/95	ARCHITECTURE OF ARTHUR DYSON — Drawings, plans and three-dimensional models by this award winning architect will be on view.
9 - 11/95	CALIFORNIA IMPRESSIONISTS FROM THE IRVINE MUSEUM

BERKELEY

Judah L. Magnes Memorial Museum

Russell St., **Berkeley, CA 94705**
TEL: 510-549-6950
HRS: 10-4 S-T   DAY CLOSED: F, Sa   HOL: Jewish & FEDERAL/HOL!
SUGG/CONT: Y   ADULT: $3.00
HDC/ACC: Y; Most galleries   PARKING: Y; Plentiful street parking   MUS/SH: Y   GR/T: Y!
H/B: Y; 1908 Berkeley landmark building (Burke Mansion)   S/G: Y
PERM/COLL: FINE ARTS; JEWISH CEREMONIAL ART, RARE BOOKS & MANUSCRIPTS; ARCHIVES OF WESTERN U.S. JEWS

Founded in 1962, the Judah L. Magnes Memorial Museum is the third largest Jewish museum in the Western Hemisphere and the first Jewish museum to be accredited by the American Association of Museums. Literally thousands of prints and drawings by nearly every Jewish artist past and present are represented in the permanent collection. **NOT TO BE MISSED:** "The Jewish Wedding" by Trankowsky; Menorahs 14-20th C.; Room of Remembrance.

CALIFORNIA

Judah L. Magnes Memorial Museum - continued

ON EXHIBIT/95:

10/16/94 - 2/12/95   BREAKING THE MOLD: THE INNOVATIVE LEGACY OF HAROLD PARIS — Installation, video, handmade-paper works, and sculpture are included in the exhibition of this visionary artist.

2/26 - 6/31/95   A MAJOR EXHIBITION ON JUDAH L. MAGNES IN HONOR OF THE 75TH ANNIVERSARY OF HEBREW UNIVERSITY IN JERUSALEM

6/11 - 9/15/95   RECENT ACQUISITIONS

10/95 - 1/96   JEWS OF INDIA

BERKELEY

University Art Museum and Pacific Film Archive
Affiliate Institution: University of California
2625 Durant Ave., **Berkeley, CA 94720**
TEL: 510-642-1207
HRS: 11-5 W-S; 11-9 T   DAY CLOSED: M, Tu   HOL: LEG/HOL!
F/DAY: T pm   ADM: Y   ADULT: $6.00   CHILDREN: F (under 12)   STUDENTS: $4.00   SR CIT: $4.00
HDC/ACC: Y; Fully accessible; ramps to all galleries and entrances   PARKING: Y; Several commercial lots in the area; also Student Union Garage, & other. For further information call Parking Services at 510-642-4283.
MUS/SH: Y   REST/FAC: Y; Cafe 11-7:30 W-Sa; 11-4 S, M & Tu
GR/T: Y   GR/PH: call 510-642-8344 education dept.   DT: Y   TIME: 12:15 T   (Curator's Choice)   S/G: Y
PERM/COLL: AM: all media 20; VISUAL ART

Since its founding in the 1960's with a bequest of 45 Hans Hoffman paintings from the artist himself, the UAM, with collections spanning the full range of the history of art, has become one of the largest and most important university art museums in the country. The museum building, a work of art in itself, is arranged with overlapping galleries to allow for the viewing of works from multiple vantage points. **NOT TO BE MISSED:** Contemporary collection including masterpieces by Calder, Cornell, Frankenthaler, Still, Rothko, and others

ON EXHIBIT/95:

9/28/94 - 2/19/95   FACE OF THE GODS: ART AND ALTARS OF THE AFRICAN-AMERICAS — Artistic and ritualistic traditions carried from Africa to America during the last 2 centuries will be seen in the 20 altars (some still in use) and 120 works of art presented in this exhibition.   CAT   WT

12/14/94 - 5/28/95   AMERICAN FOLK ART FROM THE CARNOCHAN COLLECTIONS — Paintings, drawings, sculpture and a wonderful collection of weathervanes dating from the late 18th and 19th centuries will be presented for exhibition from one of the most important collections of American folk art in California.

12/17/94 - 2/26/95   INSIDE THE LARGE SMALL HOUSE: THE RESIDENTIAL DESIGN LEGACY OF WILLIAM W. WURSTER (Theater Gallery) — An exhibition of the designs of this important and influential mid-twentieth century architect.

University Art Museum and Pacific Film Archive - continued

1/11 - 4/9/95	IN A DIFFERENT LIGHT — An in-depth examination of the works of both gay and straight artists and how their various yet often mutually invigorating creations have evolved out of 20th century American cultural styles and icons.
3/15 - 6/18/95	URBAN REVISIONS: CURRENT PROJECTS FOR THE PUBLIC REALM — The relationship between architecture and urban design is explored in this exhibit of innovative urban planning and design through the projects developed by 18 young and mid-career American architects and teams of architects. WT
4/15 - 7/2/95	JUMPING LINES: TAPA PAINTINGS FROM UIAKU, PAPUA-NEW GUINEA — In association with the Greenpeace organization and in an effort to prevent the ecological threat of massive logging in the Uiaku area, the indigenous artists are attempting to develop a market with tapa (bark cloth) paintings in order to foster an economic alternative to selling their logging rights. In this exhibition 40 examples of their tapa paintings will be featured.
4/19 - 7/2/95	SUSAN FRECON: WATERCOLORS — An exhibition of Frecon's beautifully colored abstract paintings.
6/14 - 9/24/95	GOYA/CHAGOYA — Artist/curator Enrique Chagoya comments on Goya's influence.
8/23 - 11/19/95	THE NEW CHILD: THE ORIGINS OF MODERN CHILDHOOD IN ENGLISH ART 1730-1830 — Changing ideas of childhood as seen through the works of Reynolds, Gainsborough and others.
12/6/95 - 2/11/96	EARLY 20TH CENTURY CALIFORNIA ARTISTS

CLAREMONT

Montgomery Gallery

Affiliate Institution: Pomona College
Montgomery Gallery- 330 College Ave., **Claremont, CA 91711**
TEL: 714-621-8283
HRS: 1-5 W-S (During exhibitions)   DAY CLOSED: M, Tu   HOL: ACAD! & LEG/HOL!
ADM: F   HDC/ACC: Y; Both galleries are wheelchair accessible   PARKING: Y; Free and ample street parking
MUS/SH: Y   GR/T: Y   GR/PH: call 714-621-8283   H/B: Y; Listed NRHP
PERM/COLL: AM: ptgs 19-20; AM: cer 20; AM: gr, drgs; EU: gr, drgs; JAP: gr; NAT/AM; KRESS PANELS: 15-16

The Montgomery Gallery of Pomona College and the Lang Gallery of Scripps College are united under the title of the Galleries of the Claremont Colleges. Included in their permanent collections are woodblock prints by the Japanese master, Hiroshige, and watercolors by American artist Millard Sheets. Please note that many objects in the permanent collection, though not on permanent exhibition, may be seen by prior arrangement.

ON EXHIBIT/95:

9/94 - 5/95	"FOCUS" EXHIBITIONS — Small short-term exhibitions of works from the permanent collection.
1/22 - 3/26/95	(IN)FORMING THE VISUAL: (RE)PRESENTING WOMEN OF AFRICAN DESCENT — Through a variety of media that incorporate devalued stereotypes and denigrating caricatures, this exhibition of works by a number of contemporary Black women artists addresses the ways in which Black women have been and continue to be represented in American culture.

CALIFORNIA

DAVIS

Richard L. Nelson Gallery & The Fine Arts Collection, UC Davis
Affiliate Institution: Univ. of California
Davis, CA 95616
TEL: 916-752-8500
HRS: Noon-5 M-F; 2-5 S   DAY CLOSED: Sa   HOL: LEG/HOL! ACAD/HOL
VOL/CONT: Y   ADM: F   HDC/ACC: Y; Completely accessible
PARKING: Y; On campus on lots 1, 2, 5, 6 (Handicapped), & 10; $2.00 parking fee charged weekdays
MUS/SH: Y   GR/T: Y   GR/PH: Call 916-752-8500
PERM/COLL: DRGS, GR, PTGS 19; CONT; OR; EU; AM; CER

The gallery, which has a 2,500 piece permanent collection aquired primarily through gifts donated to the institution since the 1960's presents an ongoing series of changing exhibitions. **NOT TO BE MISSED:** "Bookhead" and other sculptures by Robert Arneson; Deborah Butterfield's "Untitled" (horse).

DOWNEY

Downey Museum of Art
10419 Rives Ave., **Downey, CA 90241**
TEL: 310-861-0419
HRS: Noon-5 W-S   DAY CLOSED: M, Tu   HOL: LEG/HOL!
VOL/CONT: Y   ADM: F
HDC/ACC: Y   PARKING: Y; Ample free off-street parkingLIB: GR/T: Y   GR/PH: call 310-861-0419
PERM/COLL: REG: ptgs, sculp, gr, phot 20; CONT

With over 400 modern works and contemporary works by Southern California artists, the Downey Museum has been the primary source of art in this area for the past 35 years.

ON EXHIBIT/95:   Approximately 6 exhibitions are presented annually.

FRESNO

Fresno Art Museum
2233 N. First St., **Fresno, CA 93703**
TEL: 209-485-4810
HRS: 10-5 Tu-F; Noon-5 Sa, S   DAY CLOSED: M   HOL: LEG/HOL!
F/DAY: Tu   ADM: Y   ADULT: $2.00   CHILDREN: F (under 16)   STUDENTS: $1.00   SR CIT: $1.00
HDC/ACC: Y   PARKING: Y; Free   MUS/SH: Y   REST/FAC: Y!; T ONLY 11:30-2:00
GR/T: Y   GR/PH: call 209-485-4810   S/G: Y
PERM/COLL: P/COL; MEX; CONT/REG; AM: gr, sculp

In addition to a wide variety of changing exhibitions, pre-Columbian Mexican ceramic sculpture, French Post-impressionist graphics, and American sculptures from the permanent collection are always on view. **NOT TO BE MISSED:** Hans Sumpf Gallery of Mexican Art containing pre-Columbian ceramics through Diego Rivera masterprieces.

24

Fresno Art Museum - continued

ON EXHIBIT/95:

10/4/94 - 4/4/95	DAVID ALFARO SIQUEIROS: LITHOGRAPHS GIFTED BY JAMES AND BARBARA JOHNSON AND BY KATHLEEN LUSTGARTEN — Lithographs by one of Mexico's most renowned artists reveal his revolutionary devotion to his people and to the beauty of the land.
10/4/94 - 4/4/95	MANUEL JIMENEZ: WOODCARVER FROM THE VALLEY OF OAXACA — On exhibit will be aniline dyed wooden sculptures by Jimenez, an artist who lives a simple rural life but whose works reveal the dynamic influences of his Mexican culture and his love for the beauty of his rural surroundings.
10/28/94 - 1/8/95	JEANNETTE MAXFIELD LEWIS: A CENTENNIAL CELEBRATION — Paintings and etchings by this California artist will be seen in a retrospective of her renderings of the human condition, architecture and landscape.
11/18/94 - 2/26/95	GRAND ILLUSIONS — Photographs by George Hurrell of the luminaries of Hollywood's "Golden Age" of the 1920's, 30's, and 40's will be on exhibit.
11/15/94 - 1/8/95	JOY JOHNSON: COLOR OF LIGHT — In celebration of the feminine spirit, Johnson will create a temple installation that will fill the entire lobby of the museum.
11/11/94 - 1/8/95	HENRI MATISSE: JAZZ — Lithographs from Matisse's famous Jazz series.
12/7/94 - 3/5/95	THE NABIS: PRINTS FROM THE DEAN COLLECTION — The Nabis, a group of artists formed in Paris in the 1890's, created works influenced by the Japanese print that will be seen in this exhibition along with examples of their subjective representations of nature.
1/13 - 3/5/95	ROBERT CREMEAN: WORKS ON PAPER — New acquisitions from George and LaVona Blair.
1/17 - 5/28/95	JOHN BATTENBERG: MOUNTAIN CAT SERIES — Battenberg's life size bronze sculptures of the California cougar in a variety of dynamic poses will transform the Museum's lobby to a mountain top in the wilds of the Sierra.
1/13 - 3/5/95	HARDY HANSON: UNNATURAL HISTORIES — An exhibition of meticulous assemblages by Santa Cruz artist, Hanson, that explores the subconscious.
3/3 - 4/2/95	MANUEL MARTINEZ: ARTIST-INTERPRETER — Martinez's pencil drawings and paintings that render images of the homeless will be on view.
3/7 - 4/30/95	HOWARD SCHATZ: HOMELESS PORTRAITS OF AMERICANS IN HARD TIMES — 75 black and white photographs accompanied by audio interviews of the homeless will be seen in this exhibition of the work of San Francisco resident, Schatz, who is also the author of the book "Reds."
3/12 - 5/28/95	THE ART OF ERIC CARLE: CHILDREN'S BOOK ILLUSTRATIONS — Drawings, sketches and paintings by this much loved children's author and illustrator.
3/14 - 4/19/95	ON THE LEVEL: WALKING THE STREETS WITH MIKE McGARVIN: PHOTOS OF HOMELESS AMERICANS — Photographs of Fresno street people taken by McGarvin over a period of 10 years.
3/14 - 6/18/95	A DAY IN THE COUNTRY: PRINTS FROM THE DEAN COLLECTION — Leisure times in the lives of Parisians between the Franco Prussian War and World War I are depicted in this exhibition.
4/4 - 4/30/95	HANS TEGABO: ARTIST-INTERPRETER — Contemporary ceramic (clay) sculpture.
4/4 - 4/30/95	JIM ENTZ: ARTIST INTERPRETER — An installation of sculpture created on-site by Entz from the bark of the Cork Oak tree adjacent to the Museum's cafe will be accompanied by his jewel-like three dimensional paintings.

CALIFORNIA

Fresno Art Museum - continued

4/11 - 8/13/95	ALFREDO ZALCE: ETCHINGS FROM THE BLAIR COLLECTION — The social struggle of the Mexican people is reflected in these etchings of ordinary people involved in everyday tasks, created by the artist from 1945 through 1967.
4/11 - 8/13/95	GEORGE LOPEZ: WOOD ARTISAN OF CARDOVA, NEW MEXICO: WOOD-CARVINGS FROM THE PETESCH COLLECTION — Following in the footsteps of the religious santos carvers of Spain, Lopez, with his unadorned direct carvings, was considered a national treasure during the last years of his life.
4/25 - 8/13/95	THE JANET HUGHES PERUVIAN PRE-COLUMBIAN COLLECTION — This extensive collection of Pre-Columbian Peruvian ceramics, wooden objects, textiles and gold artifacts on view in this exhibition is a recent gift to the museum.
5/9 - 9/5/95	AMAZON ART: RITUALS — 250 objects that include drawings on the rituals of life and death in the Amazon from the collection of Adam Mekler will be joined in this exhibition by spectacular feathered ornaments, musical instruments, shrunken heads, and a number of full body costumes. Music and video presentations will provide additional enrichment to the museum visitor's sense of the rich cultures of the people of the South American forests.
6/6 - 8/13/95	KIM ABELES ENCYCLOPEDIA PERSONA: A FIFTEEN YEAR SURVEY — Political awareness and questions relevant to contemporary life are addressed by Los Angeles artist Abeles in the 82 objects, assemblages, sculptures and installations exhibited in this 15-year retrospective of her work.
6/27 - 8/13/95	FOLIOS FROM THE DEAN COLLECTION — A display of limited edition books and folios of prints published especially for collectors in late 19th century Paris.

ON EXHIBIT AT THE FRESNO AIRPORT SATELLITE GALLERY:

11/94 - 2/95	FOLK ART DOLLS FROM AROUND THE WORLD: ERMA GROSSE COLLECTION
3/95 - 5/95	NANCY YOUDELMAN: ASSEMBLAGE
6/95 - 8/95	AMAZON ART FROM THE MEKLER COLLECTION

FRESNO

Fresno Metropolitan Museum
1555 Van Ness Ave., **Fresno, CA 93721**
TEL: 209-441-1444
HRS: 11-5 daily   HOL: LEG/HOL!
F/DAY: 1st W   ADM: Y   ADULT: $4.00   CHILDREN: $3.00 (4-12)   STUDENTS: $3.00   SR CIT: $3.00
HDC/ACC: Y   PARKING: Y; Ample parking in free lot adjacent to the museum   MUS/SH: Y
GR/T: Y   GR/PH: call 209-441-1444   H/B: Y
PERM/COLL: AM: st/lf 17-20; EU; st/lf 17-20; EU; ptgs 16-19; PHOT (Ansel Adams)

Located in the historic "Fresno Bee" building, the Fresno Metropolitan Museum is the largest cultural center in the central San Joaquin Valley. **NOT TO BE MISSED:** Oscar & Maria Salzar collection of American & European still-life paintings 17th to early 20th centuries.

ON EXHIBIT/95:

1/21 - 4/15/95	CHANGING FACES OF OUR LAND — 80 photographs by Joe Munroe that serve as a slice of Americana, capture the changes in farming and rural life during the quarter century after World War II through images of people, their animals, machinery, and the land.

26

CALIFORNIA

Fresno Metropolitan Museum - continued

1/27 - 4/30/95	REVOLUTION AT THE SPEED OF LIGHT — Although this is essentially a major science exhibit, it does feature the art related aspects of a laser light show, interactive laser displays and holograms.
4/22 - 10/8/95	FOLK ART OF PERU
5/15 - 9/3/95	RAINFORESTS OF THE WORLD
6/10 - 7/30/95	FLIGHTS OF FANCY: PHOTOGRAPHS BY JACQUES-HENRI LARTIQUE, 1904-1922 — 84 modern prints of Lartique's early photographs of flight. BROCHURE WT
8/13 - 11/19/95	DAVID SHIPLEY ASSEMBLAGE
8/19 - 11/12/95	ITALIAN PAINTINGS FROM BURGHELY HOUSE — 60 Old Master paintings will be on loan from the grandest Elizabethan house in England. CAT WT

IRVINE

The Irvine Museum
18881 Von Karman Ave. 12th Floor, **Irvine, CA 92715**
TEL: 714-476-0294
HRS: 11-5 Tu-Sa   HOL: LEG/HOL!
ADM: F   HDC/ACC: Y   PARKING: Y; First hour free with validation   GR/T: Y   GR/PH: call 714-476-0294
PERM/COLL: California Impressionist Art 1890-1930

Opened in Jan. 1993, this new museum places its emphasis on the past by promoting the preservation and display of historical California art with particular emphasis on the School of California Impressionism (1890-1930).

ON EXHIBIT/95:

10/15/94 - 1/15/95	CARTER LIBRARY
2/23 - 6/17/95	IRVINE MUSEUM COLLECTION
9/19/95 - 1/21/96	PALM SPRINGS DESERT MUSEUM
10/95 - 1/96	ARTHUR G. RIDER: AMERICAN IMPRESSIONIST — 70 paintings, and 7 pencil sketches by Rider (1886-1976) considered the ultimate practitioner of Impressionist color theory will be on view accompanied by archival photographs. WT

The Severin Wunderman Museum
3 Mason St., **Irvine, CA 92718**
TEL: 714-472-1138
HRS: 9-4:30 M-F   DAY CLOSED: Sa, S   HOL: LEG/HOL!
SUGG/CONT: Y   ADULT: $3.00   CHILDREN: F (under 17)   STUDENTS: $2.00   SR CIT: $2.00
PARKING: Y; Marked visitor spaces adjacent to the building in which the museum is located   MUS/SH: Y
GR/T: Y   GR/PH: call 714-472-1138   DT: Y   TIME: always available
PERM/COLL: WORLD'S LARGEST COLLECTION OF WORKS BY JEAN COCTEAU

On a rotating basis the 10 year old Wunderman Museum illustrates the diversity of media used by Jean Cocteau in creating his pastels, drawings, paintings, ceramics, sculpture, theater properties, lithographs, and tapestries.

27

CALIFORNIA

The Severin Wunderman Museum - continued

ON EXHIBIT/95:

11/7/94 - 2/7/95	VASLAV NIJINSKY: ART BY AND ABOUT THE WORLD'S GREATEST DANCER — On exhibit will be costumes, works by Nijinsky, and images of this great artist who was a close friend of Cocteau in Paris during the years of the Ballet Russes.
2/14 - 5/5/95	HARLEQUINADE OF JEAN COCTEAU — Representations of Harlequin as Jean Cocteau in his many guises.
5/15 - 8/31/95	THE NEO-HUMANISTS AND THEIR CIRCLE — "A private world of emotionally charged dreams" that reflect the human condition will be seen in the personal visions of Pavel Tchelitchew, Christian Berard, Eugene Berman and others who appeared as "The Neo-Humanists," a group promoted by Cocteau in the Galerie Druet in Paris in 1926.
9/10 - 12/29/95	THE STYLE OF JEAN COCTEAU — The definition of style as the ulitmate aspect of all art will be highlighted in this exhibition of works by Cocteau, who was considered the first individual to distinguish between style and fashion.

LA JOLLA

Mingei International Museum of World Folk Art

University Towne Centre, 4405 La Jolla Village Dr., 1-7, **La Jolla, CA 92038**
TEL: 619-453-5300
HRS: 11-5 Tu-Sa, 2-5 S   DAY CLOSED: M   HOL: LEG/HOL!
ADM: Y   ADULT: $3.00   CHILDREN: $1.00   STUDENTS: $3.00   SR CIT: $3.00
HDC/ACC: Y; Outdoor elevator leads to museum that is all on one level   PARKING: Y; Parking a short distance from the museum in the University Towne Centre lots   MUS/SH: Y   GR/T: Y   GR/PH: call 619-453-5300 to reserve
PERM/COLL: FOLK: Jap, India, Af, & over 70 other countries; international doll coll.; Palestinian costumes

Dedicated to furthering the understanding of World Folk Art, the collection at Mingei International is displayed in an innovatively designed contemporary architectural space. **NOT TO BE MISSED:** A small wax doll (clothed in its original fabric and a bonnet characteristic of the Tudor period) that once belonged to a lady-in-waiting to English Queen, Mary Stuart.

ON EXHIBIT/95:

1/17 - 3/12/95	UNCOMMON BEAUTY IN COMMON OBJECTS: THE LEGACY OF AFRICAN-AMERICAN CRAFT ART
4/7 - 10/15/95	KINDRED SPIRITS: THE ELOQUENCE OF FUNCTION IN AMERICAN SHAKER AND JAPANESE ARTS OF DAILY LIFE
11/17 - FOR 5 OR 6 MONTHS	THE BEAD: SMALL, PORTABLE ART OBJECT

LAGUNA BEACH

Laguna Art Museum

307 Cliff Dr., **Laguna Beach, CA 92651**
TEL: 714-494-6531
HRS: 11-5 Tu-S   DAY CLOSED: M   HOL: 1/1, 7/4, THGV, 12/25
ADM: Y   ADULT: $4.00   CHILDREN: F (under 12)   STUDENTS: $3.00   SR CIT: $3.00
HDC/ACC: Y; Completely wheelchair accessible   PARKING: Y; Metered street parking only   MUS/SH: Y
GR/T: Y   GR/PH: By appt - call ahead to reserve   DT: Y   TIME: 2:00 Tu, W, Sa, S
PERM/COLL: AM: cont/art; PHOT; CALIF: early - mid 20

Laguna Art Museum - continued

The Laguna Art Museum, which celebrated its 75th birthday in 1993, is the oldest cultural institution in Orange County. American art with a special emphasis on California artists is the focus of the collection at the main museum, while contemporary art by California artists is on view at the South Coast Plaza Branch in Costa Mesa. **NOT TO BE MISSED:** Collection of avant-garde photographic prints.

ON EXHIBIT/95:

10/30/94 - 2/26/95	LIT FROM WITHIN: AMISH QUILTS OF LANCASTER COUNTY — Quilts to the Amish reflect their ideals of simplicity, harmony and a reverence for tradition. In this exhibition of 30 quilts created between 1880-1950, large color field areas with finely stitched designs reveal the Amish penchant for "less is more" simplicity in their lives and aesthetics of design.
3/11 - 6/18/95	CHICANO PRINTMAKING: THE ROLE OF SELF-HELP GRAPHICS — On exhibit will be 70 examples from the Laguna Art Museum's permanent collection of Chicano prints, the largest of its kind in the nation. Created by Mexican-American and Latino artists working with Self-Help Graphics in Los Angeles, the works on view reveal a highly charged and emotional content that is the result of a mixture of Chicano symbolism, American Pop culture, contemporary urban life and Catholic iconography.　　CAT
2/24 - 6/18/95	PAINTINGS FROM PARADISE: CALIFORNIA IMPRESSIONISM FROM THE COLLECTION OF THE LAGUNA ART MUSEUM — Featured will be early 20th century romanticized plein air Impressionist paintings of the southern California landscape still untouched at that time by the encroachment of freeways and housing tracts.
6/22 - 10/8/95	TWILIGHT AND REVERIE: CALIFORNIA TONALIST PAINTINGS, 1890-1930 — Inspired by the natural conditions of the fog and mist in the northern California atmosphere, artists created quiet, contemplative tonalist mood paintings of nature that will be featured in this exhibition.
7/29 - 10/8/95	EYE TATTOOED AMERICA — Tattoo art, so popular today that its acceptance has created a new "folk art" tradition, has had a long and somewhat disreputable reputation. This unusual exhibition traces the history of the tattoo from its origins in ancient Africa and Europe, to the penchant for them by certain segments of the 19th century upper classes, to the transforming acceptance of the practice of this art from the 1960's to today.
10/27/95 - 1/21/96	LLYN FOULKES: BETWEEN A ROCK AND A HARD PLACE — In this retrospective of paintings and assemblages representing Foulkes' visions of the underside of American life and mythology, the artist himself will accompany the artworks by performing his own music and reading his own poems.

LANCASTER

Lancaster Museum/Art Gallery
44801 North Sierra Hwy., **Lancaster, CA 93534**
TEL: 805-723-6250
HRS: 11-4 Tu-Sa; 1-4 S　DAY CLOSED: M
HOL: LEG/HOL! & 1-2 WEEKS BEFORE OPENING OF EACH NEW EXHIBIT!
ADM: F　HDC/ACC: Y; Wheelchair accessible　PARKING: Y; Ample and free　MUS/SH: Y
GR/T: Y　GR/PH: call 805-723-6250
PERM/COLL: REG, PHOT

About 75 miles north of Los Angeles, in the heart of America's Aerospace Valley, is the City of Lancaster Museum, a combined history and fine art facility that serves the needs of one of the fastest growing areas in southern California. The gallery offers 8 to 9 rotating exhibitons annually.

CALIFORNIA

Lancaster Museum/Art Gallery - continued

ON EXHIBIT/95:

1/28 - 3/12/95	10TH ANNUAL JURIED ART EXHIBITION
5/6 - 6/5/95	CAVE AND ROCK EXHIBITION
6/17 - 7/30/95	LANCASTER PHOTOGRAPHY ART EXHIBITION
8/12 - 9/24/95	SLAVIC ART EXHIBITION
10/7 - 11/26/95	NATIVE AMERICAN ART EXHIBITION
12/9/95 - 1/14/96	ANTELOPE VALLEY PEOPLE PLACES AND THINGS EXHIBITION

LONG BEACH

Long Beach Museum of Art

2300 E. Ocean Blvd., **Long Beach, CA 90803**
TEL: 310-439-2119
HRS: 10-5 W-S; till 8 F; Sculpture Garden open 7-6 daily   DAY CLOSED: M, Tu   HOL: LEG/HOL!
F/DAY: F 5-8pm   ADM: Y   ADULT: $2.00   CHILDREN: F (under 12)   STUDENTS: $1.00   SR CIT: $1.00
HDC/ACC: Y   PARKING: Y; Free street parking   MUS/SH: Y   REST/FAC: Y; Outdoor cafe
GR/T: Y   GR/PH: Call 310-439-2119   DT: Y   TIME: 1:00 Sa, S   H/B: Y   S/G: Y
PERM/COLL: REG 19-20; EU 19-20; CONT/SCULP; GER: 20; AM: 19-20; EU: Modernists 20; CALIF: postwar ptgs, sculp; VIDEOS

Situated on a bluff overlooking the Pacific Ocean, the Long Beach museum is housed in a 1912 California Arts & Crafts-style residence and carriage house. Its fine holdings of modern and California regional art were enhanced, in 1979, with the bequest of an important collection of 20th century German art from the estate of Milton Wichner. Included in this collection are numerous works by Jawlensky, Kandinsky, Feininger, Moholy-Nagy, and Fischinger. **NOT TO BE MISSED:** The Mexican "Days of the Dead Festival" held each fall; the Children's Cultural Festival held each spring (please call for specifics for both events); one of the largest collection of artists' videos in the country.

ON EXHIBIT/95:

3/5 - 5/21/95	MUSIC BOX — For this exhibit 17 artists will create new objects with musical melodies.

University Art Museum

Affiliate Institution: California State University, Long Beach
1250 Bellflower Blvd., **Long Beach, CA 90840**
TEL: 310-985-5761
HRS: Noon-8 Tu-T; Noon-5 F-S   DAY CLOSED: M   HOL: ACAD/HOL! LEG/HOL!
SUGG/CONT: Y   ADULT: $1.00   CHILDREN: $.50   STUDENTS: $F   SR CIT: $0.50
HDC/ACC: Y; Ample access to gallery located on 5th floor of library
PARKING: Y; Parking permits may be purchased for Lot A just beyond the Visitor Information Kiosk; advance reservations may be made for Lot 12   MUS/SH: Y   GR/T: Y   GR/PH: 310-985-5761 education dept.   S/G: Y
PERM/COLL: CONT: drgs, gr; SCULP

Walking maps are available for finding and detailing the permanent site-specific Monumental Sculpture Collection owned by this outstanding university art museum and located throughout its 322 acre campus. **NOT TO BE MISSED:** Extensive collection of contemporary works on paper.

30

LOS ANGELES

California Afro-American Museum
600 State Drive, Exposition Park, **Los Angeles, CA 90037**
TEL: 213-744-7432
HRS: 10-5 Tu-S   DAY CLOSED: M   HOL: 1/1 THGV, 12/25
ADM: F
HDC/ACC: Y; Restrooms, parking, ramps
PARKING: Y; Limited ($3.00 fee) next to museum   MUS/SH: Y
GR/T: Y   GR/PH: call 213-744-7432
PERM/COLL: BENJAMIN BANNISTER: drgs; TURENNE des PRES: ptgs; GAFTON TAYLOR BROWN: gr; AF: masks; AF/AM: cont   NOTE: The permanent collection is not on permanent display!

The primary goal of this museum is the collection and preservation of art and artifacts documemting the Afro-American experience in America. Exhibitions and programs focus on contributions made to the arts and various other facets of life including a vital forum for playwrights and filmmakers. The building itself features a 13,000 square foot sculpture court through which visitors pass into a spacious building topped by a ceiling of tinted bronze glass.

Fisher Gallery, University of South California
Affiliate Institution: University of Southern California
823 Exposition Blvd., **Los Angeles, CA 90089**
TEL: 213-740-4561
HRS: Noon-5 Tu-F, 11-3 Sa (closed during summer)   DAY CLOSED: M   HOL: LEG/HOL! SUMMER
ADM: F
HDC/ACC: Y   PARKING: Y; Visitor parking on campus through Gate 1
PERM/COLL: EU: ptgs, gr, drgs; AM: ptgs, gr, drgs; PTGS 15-20 (ARMAND HAMMER COLL; ELIZABETH HOLMES FISHER COLL.)

Old master paintings from the Dutch and Flemish schools as well as significant holdings of 19th century British and French art are two of the strengths of the Fisher Gallery. Please note that the collection is available to museums, scholars, students, and the public by appointment.

ON EXHIBIT/95:

5/9/94 - 4/1/95	IN SEARCH OF...USC'S BAROQUE MASTERS FROM THE ARMAND HAMMER COLLECTION — Major works by Baroque masters Rubens, van Dyck, van Ostade, Jacob Ruisdale and others from this outstanding collection will be featured in this exhibition of 12 Dutch and Flemish paintings. CAT
11/16/94 - 1/22/95	TAKE 2...AT FISHER GALLERY AND CALIFORNIA AFRO-AMERICAN MUSEUM — In the 2nd city-wide biennial LAX (The Los Angeles Exhibition) works by 13 Los Angeles artists created during the past 2 years will be on view. CAT
2/22 - 4/22/95	THE ART OF EXAGGERATION: PIRANESI'S PERSPECTIVES ON ROME — Exaggerated scale, chiaroscuro, illusionism and fantasy will be seen in the works of Italian architectural draughtsman, Piranesi (1720-78) with a display of 24 bound volumes featuring his views of Rome. CAT

CALIFORNIA

LOS ANGELES

Gene Autry Western Heritage Museum
4700 Western Heritage Way, **Los Angeles, CA 90027-1462**
TEL: 213-667-2000
HRS: 10-5 Tu-S   DAY CLOSED: M   HOL: THGV, 12/25
ADM: Y   ADULT: $7.00   CHILDREN: $3.00 (2-12)   STUDENTS: $5.00   SR CIT: $5.00
HDC/ACC: Y   PARKING: Y; Free parking adjacent to the museum   MUS/SH: Y
REST/FAC: Y; Golden Spur Cafe for breakfast & lunch   GR/T: Y   GR/PH: call 213-667-2000
PERM/COLL: FINE & FOLK ART

Fine art is but one aspect of this mulit-dimensional museum that acts as a showcase for the preservation and understanding of both the real and mythical historical legacy of the American West. **NOT TO BE MISSED:** Los Angeles Times Children's Discovery Gallery; Spirit of Imagination

ON EXHIBIT/95:

12/10/94 - 2/12/95	CRAFTING DEVOTIONS: TRADITION IN CONTEMPORARY NEW MEXICO SANTOS
2/25 - 5/7/95	THUNDERING HOOVES: FIVE CENTURIES OF HORSE POWER IN THE AMERICAN WEST
5/20 - 10/1/95	WALT DISNEY'S WILD WEST
5/20 - 10/95	PATCHWORK SOUVENIRS: QUILTS FROM THE 1933 CHICAGO WORLD'S FAIR — A special adjunct to the 1933 Chicago World's Fair was a quilt making contest sponsored by Sears, Roebuck & Co. Over 25,000 hand-made quilts were entered containing subjects and themes that today serve as historical records of the past. Never studied as a group before, the quilts in this exhibition will be accompanied by archival photos and other souveniers from the fair. BROCHURE WT
10/14/95 - 1/96	WOMEN ARTISTS OF THE WEST WT

Grunwald Center for the Graphic Arts
Affiliate Institution: UCLA
405 N. Hilgard Ave., **Los Angeles, CA 90024-1620**
TEL: 310-825-3783
HRS: 11-5 W-F; 11-7 Tu; 1-5 Sa-S; (STUDY ROOM 9-5 M-F BY/APPT ONLY)   DAY CLOSED: M
ADM: F
HDC/ACC: Y; To upper & lower level galleries   PARKING: Y; $5.00 parking fee on premises   MUS/SH: Y
GR/T: Y!   DT: Y!   S/G: Y
PERM/COLL: OM: gr, drgs; GR, DRGS, PHOT 19-20

One of the finest and most comprehensive university collections of graphic arts in the country, the Grunwald, which is part of the UCLA museum system, has works ranging from Old Master prints and drawings to contemporary artworks by modern masters. **NOT TO BE MISSED:** Frank Lloyd Wright Japanese print collection; 850 landscape graphics & drawing collection.

LOS ANGELES

Laband Art Gallery

Affiliate Institution: Loyola Marymount University
Loyola Blvd. at W. 80th St., **Los Angeles, CA 90045**
TEL: 310-338-2880
HRS: 11-5 W-F; Noon-4 Sa (Sep-May)   DAY CLOSED: M, S   HOL: JUN - AUG.; THGV; EASTER WEEKEND
ADM: F
HDC/ACC: Y
PERM/COLL: FL: om; IT: om; DRGS; GR

The Laband Art Gallery usually features exhibitions based on multicultural projects relating to Latin and Native American subjects, current social and political issues, and Jewish & Christian spiritual traditions.
ON EXHIBIT/95:

1/18 - 2/25/95	JEROME WITKIN: THE HEROIC PAINTER IN A DIMINISHED AGE (TENT!) — 25 monumental realist paintings that reflect the tragedies of 20th century modern life will be on view in the first major southern California showing of New York artist Witkin's work. CAT
4/26 - 6/3/95	LOS ANGELES PRINTMAKING SOCIETY 13TH NATIONAL EXHIBITION — A biennial exhibition that features the most recent developments in printmaking in both the U.S. and Mexico. CAT
8/23 - 10/7/95	THOUGHT WORKS @ L.A. — Conceptual exhibit of LMU's five teaching artists.
10/28 - 12/9/95	THE WOMEN'S MOVEMENT AND CERAMIC ART — 4 themes at 4 southern California galleries in addition to the Laband Gallery will be presented for this exhibition.

LOS ANGELES

Los Angeles County Museum of Art

5905 Wilshire Blvd., **Los Angeles, CA 90036**
TEL: 213-857-6000
HRS: 10-5 W & T; 10-9 F (except for Japanese Art Pavilion); 11-6 Sa, S   DAY CLOSED: M, Tu
HOL: 1/1, THGV, 12/25
F/DAY: 2nd W   ADM: Y   ADULT: $6.00   CHILDREN: $1.00 (6-17)   STUDENTS: $4.00   SR CIT: $4.00
HDC/ACC: Y; Fully accessible with wheelchairs available   PARKING: Y; Paid parking available in lot directly across the street from the entrance to the museum.   MUS/SH: Y   REST/FAC: Y; 2 Cafes
GR/T: Y   GR/PH: call 213-857-6108   DT: Y   TIME: Frequent & varied (call for information)!
PERM/COLL: AN/EGT: sculp, ant; AN/GRK: sculp, ant; AN/R: sculp, ant; CH: ptgs, sculp, cer; JAP: ptgs, sculp, cer; AM/ART; EU/ART; DEC/ART

The diversity and excellence of the collections of the Los Angeles Museum offer the visitor to this institution centuries of art to enjoy from ancient Roman or pre-Columbian art to modern paintings, sculpture, and photography. PLEASE NOTE: The Pavillion for Japanese Art is the only gallery NOT open on Friday evening. All other galleries WITH THE EXCEPTION of the Pre-Columbian, Chinese & Korean galleries are open on an alternating gallery schedule. **NOT TO BE MISSED:** Micro-mosaic collection; George de La Tour's "Magdelene with the Smoking Flame", 1636-1638; "Under the Trees" by Cezanne (recently acquired)

33

CALIFORNIA

Los Angeles County Museum of Art - continued

ON EXHIBIT/95:

9/8/94 - 2/5/95   ACROSS THE SEAS: TEXTILES AND THE MEETING OF CULTURES — From the permanent collection, 50 outstanding examples of textile art created by craftsmen from Peru, Europe, Africa, Japan, China, India and the Middle East will demonstrate the diversity of their many cultures as reflected in their costumes, textiles and dress.

10/9/94 - 1/8/95   PAINTING THE MAYA UNIVERSE: ROYAL CERAMICS OF THE CLASSICAL PERIOD — Drawn from public and private collections throughout North and Central America, the 98 vessels and related Late Classic Mayan objects on view (A.D. 550-900) reflect the complexity of the Mayan civilization through the technical & aesthetic accomplishments of their ceramic artists.   CAT   WT

10/23/94 - 1/8/95   R. B. KITAJ: A RETROSPECTIVE — In this 100 work retrospective of Kitaj, a Cleveland-born artist who moved to England in 1957 and helped to launch the British Pop-Art movement, paintings, drawings and pastels from every phase of his distinguished 35 year career will be on view.   CAT   WT

11/6/94 - 1/22/95   THE PEACEFUL LIBERATORS: JAIN ART FROM INDIA — A major exhibition of 150 historically significant artworks relating to one of the oldest and most important religions of India.   WT

11/17/94 - 2/12/95   ANNIE LEIBOVITZ: PHOTOGRAPHS 1970-1990 — For this venue, new works will be added to the traveling exhibition of photographic portraits by Leibovitz.

12/22/94 - 3/12/95   ITALIAN PANEL PAINTING OF THE EARLY RENAISSANCE — From the permanent collection, 18 14th to 16th-century panel paintings both sacred and secular in nature will be on exhibit accompanied by information prepared by the museum's staff that shows various stages of restoration and conservation of these panels.

2/16 - 4/30/95   THE PRINTS OF ROY LICHTENSTEIN — 100 of Lichtenstein's lithographs, etchings, screenprints, woodcuts, and works that combine several processes will be shown with related sculptures made concurrently with the prints. Included will be rare prints from the 50's, contemporary images of the 60's, and present examples of his work.   CAT   WT

2/26 - 4/30/95   THE FIGURE IN AMERICAN SCULPTURE: A QUESTION OF MODERNITY

3/12 - 5/7/95   COMMON FORMS, HIGH ART: THREE CENTURIES OF AMERICAN FURNITURE

3/12 - 5/14/95   AMERICAN PAINTERS OF MODERN LIFE: IMPRESSIONISM AND REALISM — Prints and drawings

4/6 - 7/16/95   SOMETHING OLD, SOMETHING NEW: EUROPEAN AND AMERICAN WEDDING DRESSES, 1830-1990

4/13 - 7/30/95   SIGMAR POLKE

5/3 - 7/30/95   JAPANESE FOLK TEXTILES

6/8 - 9/10/95   EMIL NOLDE: THE PAINTER'S PRINTS

6/15 - 9/3/95   ANNETTE MESSAGER

6/25 - 9/10/95   CÉZANNE AND PISSARO: AN IMPRESSIONISTIC COLLABORATION

PLEASE NOTE: Because some of the above exhibitions were quite tentative at press time, it is suggested that you call ahead to confirm.

LOS ANGELES

Los Angeles Municipal Art Gallery

Affiliate Institution: Barnsdall Art Park
4804 Hollywood Blvd., **Los Angeles, CA 90027**
TEL: 213-485-4581
HRS: 12:30-5 Tu-S   DAY CLOSED: M   HOL: 1/1, 12/25
ADM: Y   ADULT: $1.00   CHILDREN: F (under 12)   STUDENTS: $1.00   SR CIT: $1.00
HDC/ACC: Y; including handicapped parking   PARKING: Y; Ample free parking in the Park
DT: Y   TIME: house only $3.00 (adult) Tu-S Noon, 1, 2, 3   H/B: Y; 1921 Frank Lloyd Wright Hollyhock House
PERM/COLL: CONT: S/Ca art

The Los Angeles Municipal Art Gallery of the Barnsdall Art Park is but one of several separate but related arts facilities. Included in this group is the Frank Lloyd Wright Hollyhock House, (open Tu-S Noon-3), and the Junior Arts Center Gallery, (open 12:30-5 Tu-S). **NOT TO BE MISSED:** Frank Lloyd Wright Hollyhock House & drawings

ON EXHIBIT/95:

1/31 - 4/2/95	SOCIAL ENGAGEMENTS
4/18 - 6/18/95	CYCLES: JUDY DATER
7/5 - 8/27/95	1995 LOS ANGELES JURIED EXHIBITION
REST OF THE YEAR:	TBA

The Los Angeles Art Association

825 N. La Cienega Blvd., **Los Angeles, CA 90069**
TEL: 310-652-8272
HRS: Noon-5 Tu-Sa   DAY CLOSED: M, S   HOL: LEG/HOL!
VOL/CONT: Y   ADM: F
HDC/ACC: Y; But very limited   PARKING: Y; Free in rear of building

For 67 years the gallery of the Los Angeles Art Association has been exhibiting and promoting some of the most important California artists on the art scene today. Solo exhibitions are presented in the newly designed Helen Wurdemann Gallery.

The Museum of African American Art

4005 Crenshaw Blvd., 3rd Floor, **Los Angeles, CA 90008**
TEL: 213-294-7071
HRS: 11-6 W-Sa; Noon-5 S   DAY CLOSED: M-T   HOL: 1/1, EASTER, THGV, 12/25
ADM: F
HDC/ACC: Y; Elevator to third floor gallery location   PARKING: Y; Free   MUS/SH: Y
PERM/COLL: AF: sculp, ptgs, gr, cer; CONT/AM; sculp, ptgs, gr; HARLEM REN ART

Located on the third floor of the Robinsons May Department Store.

CALIFORNIA

LOS ANGELES

The Museum of Contemporary Art, Los Angeles

250 S. Grand Ave., California Plaza, **Los Angeles, CA 90012**
TEL: 213-626-6222
HRS: 11-5 Tu, W, F, Sa, S; 11-8 T   DAY CLOSED: M   HOL: 1/1, THGV, 12/25
F/DAY: 5-8 T   ADM: Y   ADULT: $6.00   CHILDREN: F (under 12)   STUDENTS: $4.00   SR CIT: $4.00
HDC/ACC: Y; Fully accessible, wheelchairs available   PARKING: Y; For weekends - California Plaza Parking
Garage (enter from lower Grand Ave) parking fee charged. For weekdays - The Music Center Garage $6.00 for 4
hours ($14.00 deposit required upon entry with $8.00 returned with ticket validated at museum.   MUS/SH: Y
REST/FAC: Y; Cafe 8:30-4 Tu-F; 11-4:30 Sa, S   GR/T: Y   GR/PH: call 213-621-1751   education dept.
DT: Y   TIME: 1:00 & 2:00 T-S, call 213-621-1751   H/B: Y; First American building commission by Arata Isozaki
PERM/COLL: CONT: all media

The Museum of Contemporary Art (MOCA) is the only institution in Los Angeles devoted exclusively
to art created from 1940 to the present by modern-day artists of international reputation. The museum
is located in two unique spaces: MOCA at California Plaza, the first building designed by Arata
Isozaki; and MOCA at the Temporary Contemporary, a former warehouse renovated by Frank Ghery.
PLEASE NOTE: The Temporary Contemporary will reopen in May 1995 after the surrounding
redevelopment project is finished. Shuttle bus service between the two spaces will resume with the
reopening of the building.

ON EXHIBIT/95:
MOCA EXHIBITIONS AT CALIFORNIA PLAZA:

12/18/94 - 3/12/95	GARY HILL — Since the early 1970's Seattle-born artist Hill has created videotapes and installations that chart new technological and aesthetic territory. This survey concentrates on the sculptural and environmental aspects of his work. CAT WT
1/22 - 3/26/95	FOCUS SERIES: SHERRIE LEVINE — In this installation entitled "Newborn," Levine, who borrows directly from major artists of the 20th century, recreates in translucent white glass Constantine Brancusi's marble sculpture "Newborn" which she places on top of a black baby grand piano.
1/22 - 3/26/95	FOCUS SERIES: PIERO MANZONI: DRAWINGS — At the time of his death at the age of 30 in 1963, Manzoni was one of Italy's most important contemporary artists. In this first exhibition of his work in California, a series of his "Line" drawings (single lines drawn in ink on strips of paper rolled up and placed in sealed, cylindrical cardboard containers) will be on view.
2/12 - 5/21/95	INSTALLATIONS: SELECTIONS FROM THE PERMANENT COLLECTION, PART TWO
2/12 - 5/21/95	CY TWOMBLY: A RETROSPECTIVE — Twombly, one of the most important American artists of the last half of this century, has pursued an imageless form of painting that combines elements of gestural abstraction, drawing, and writing in a personal manner. This exhibition of paintings, works on paper, and selected sculptures surveys his entire career and includes crucial, rarely seen works from private European collections. CAT WT
6/18 - 9/3/95	CLAES OLDENBURG: AN ANTHOLOGY — On exhibit will be 200 drawings, collages and sculptures by Oldenburg, a key figure of the Pop Art movement. CAT WT

MOCA EXHIBITIONS AT THE TEMPORARY CONTEMPORARY:

8 - 9/95	ACTION OCCUPATION — In celebration of the re-opening of MOCA at the Temporary Contemporary, movement artist/choreographer Elizabeth Streb and her "Ringside" company will perform one newly commissioned and 6 existing works.

36

The Museum of Contemporary Art, Los Angeles - continued

10/8/95 - 1/7/96   1965-1975: RECONSIDERING THE OBJECT OF ART — The broad range of practices associated with conceptual art that challenged and redefined traditional forms of art-making during the 10 year span between '65 -'75 will be highlighted in this major international exhibition.

LOS ANGELES

UCLA at the Armand Hammer Museum of Art and Cultural Center

10899 Wilshire Blvd., **Los Angeles, CA 90024**
TEL: 310-443-7000
HRS: 11-7 Tu-Sa, 11-6 S   DAY CLOSED: M   HOL: 1/1, THGV, 12/25; OTHERS!
ADM: Y   ADULT: $4.50   CHILDREN: F (under 17)   STUDENTS: $3.00   SR CIT: $3.00
HDC/ACC: Y; Ramps and elevator   PARKING: Y; Underground visitor parking available for a nominal fee
MUS/SH: Y   GR/T: Y   GR/PH: call 310-443-7041   DT: T   TIME: 1:00 Tu, T & S!
PERM/COLL: EU: 15-19

With the largest collection of works by Daumier in the country (more than 10,000) and an 18 page Codex by Leonardo da Vinci illustrated with 360 original drawings that document his theories of hydraulics and engineering, the Armand Hammer Museum is considered a major U.S. artistic cultural resource. The museum, opened in 1991, is now part of UCLA. It houses the collections of the Wight Art Gallery and the Grunwald Center for the Graphic Arts (one of the finest university collections of graphic arts in the country with 35,000 works dating from the Renaissance to the present). **NOT TO BE MISSED:** Five centuries of Masterworks: over 100 works by Rubens, Rembrandt, van Gogh, Cassatt, Goya, Monet, and others.

ON EXHIBIT/95:

11/1/94 - 1/1/95   THE FRENCH RENAISSANCE IN PRINTS FROM THE BIBLIOTHEQUE NATIONALE de FRANCE, PARIS — In the first comprehensive survey of the origins of Renaissance printmaking in France, works by over 50 artists active during the 16th to the early 17th centuries that document the artistic development and production of the medium will be on exhibit.   CAT   WT

1/17 - 3/26/95   PHOTOGRAPHS FROM THE COLLECTION OF THE J. PAUL GETTY MUSEUM — A historical overview of the medium of photography will be seen in the 175 works selected for this exhibition. Included will be 19th-century examples of the discovery and invention of photography and daguerreotypes, as well as documentary, painterly and experimental works of the 20th century.

4/18 - 6/11/95   RENE MAGRITTE — 65 works, many of which come from The Menil Collection in Houston, and span the career of this noted Belgian surrealist, will be on view.

7/2 - 8/27/95   PACIFIC DREAMS: CURRENTS OF SURREALISM IN EARLY CALIFORNIA ART — Subjective currents in California art that bring to light exceptional yet relatively unexplored works created during the years spanning the Depression to the Cold War will be presented in this exhibition.   CAT

9/26/95 - 1/3/96   JUDY CHICAGO'S "THE DINNER PARTY": A RETROSPECTIVE — Early works by Chicago will be shown with related examples by contemporary feminist artists of the 80's providing a reevaluation of her controversial "Dinner Party" and its impact on feminist art & theory from the 1960's through the mid-1990's.   CAT

CALIFORNIA

LOS ANGELES

Watts Towers Arts Center
1727 E. 107th St., **Los Angeles, CA 90002**
TEL: 213-569-8181
HRS: 9-4 Tu-S (Watts Tower Art Center); Watts Tower open Sa, S! $1.00 adults   DAY CLOSED: M
HOL: LEG/HOL!
ADM: F
HDC/ACC: Y   PARKING: Y; Visitors parking lot outside of Arts center
GR/T: Y   GR/PH: Call ahead for weekday Tower tours
PERM/COLL: AF; CONT; WATTS TOWER

Fantastic lacy towers spiking into the air are the result of a 33 year effort by the late Italian immigrant sculptor Simon Rodia. His imaginitive use of the "found object" resulted in the creation of one of the most unusual artistic structures in the world.

MALIBU

Frederick R. Weisman Museum of Art
Affiliate Institution: Pepperdine Center for the Arts, Pepperdine University
24255 Pacific Coast Highway, **Malibu, CA 90263**
TEL: 310-456-4851
HRS: 11-5 Tu-S   DAY CLOSED: M   HOL: LEG/HOL!
ADM: F
HDC/ACC: Y; Completely accessible with ramps and elevators   PARKING: Y; Free
GR/T: Y   GR/PH: call 310-456-4851   DT: Y   TIME: call for specifics!
PERM/COLL: PTGS, SCULP, GR, DRGS, PHOT 20

Opened in 1992, this museum's permanent collection and exhibitions focus primarily on 19th & 20th-century art. **NOT TO BE MISSED:** Selections from the Frederick R. Weisman Art Foundation.

ON EXHIBIT/95:

1/7 - 3/4/95	FIRST ARTIST OF THE WEST: PAINTINGS AND WATERCOLORS BY GEORGE CATLIN FROM THE GILCREASE MUSEUM — 35 outstanding oil paintings and 25 rare watercolors by Catlin, the first artist to devote his entire career to the depiction of images of the West created during his many sojourns there, will be seen in this exhibition. Considered among the most enduring images in American culture, these works reflect his romanticized and idealized notions of Indian life. CAT WT
3/14 - 4/9/95	PERMANENT COLLECTION AND LONG TERM LOANS FROM THE FREDERICK R. WEISMAN ART FOUNDATION — On view in the upper gallery.
4/29 - 7/16/95	PERMANENT COLLECTION AND LONG TERM LOANS FROM THE FREDERICK R. WEISMAN ART FOUNDATION — On view in the upper gallery.
7/29 - 9/24/95	HEAD, HEART AND HAND: ELBERT HUBBARD AND THE ROYCROFTERS — In celebration of the 100th anniversary of the Western New York craft colony founded by Elbert Hubbard, this major exhibition (the first of its kind devoted to all aspects of Roycroft production and aesthetics) will feature more than 200 examples of such finely crafted items as furniture, metalwork, ceramics, and leather goods in addition to period photographs of the community at work and play. CAT WT

MALIBU

The J. Paul Getty Museum
17985 Pacific Coast Highway, **Malibu, CA 90265**
TEL: 310-458-2003
HRS: 10-5 Tu-S (BY RESERVATION ONLY)   DAY CLOSED: M   HOL: 7/4, 1/1, THGV, 12/25
ADM: F
HDC/ACC: Y; Parking, ramps, elevators, some wheelchairs, & other amemities
PARKING: Y; Advance parking reservations are a must! Call 310-458-2003, 9-5 daily for information & reservations
MUS/SH: Y   REST/FAC: Y; 9:30-4:30 (Lunch 11-2:30)
H/B: Y; Museum building based on 1st century Roman villa
PERM/COLL: AN/GRK; AN/R; EU: ptgs, drgs, sculp; DEC/ART; AM: phot 20; EU: phot 20; Illuminated Manuscripts

The outstanding collections of the Getty Museum are housed in the recreation of the Villa dei Papiri, an ancient Roman country house. Modern casts of ancient sculpture and illusionistic wall paintings decorate the gardens. **NOT TO BE MISSED:** "Irises" by Vincent van Gogh, 1889; Pontormo's "Portrait of Cosimo I de Medici", c. 1537; "Bullfight Suerte de Varas" by Goya, 1824 (recently acquired).

ON EXHIBIT/95:

THROUGH 3/95 — THE GETTY KOUROS — An exhibition that examines both sides of the ongoing controversy involving the authenticity of the Getty Kouros.

7/26/94 - 2/12/95 — THE MAKING OF A MEDIEVAL BOOK — This largely hands-on exhibition demonstrates the entire process of how medieval manuscript books were made from the preparation of the parchment, to the writing and illumination, to the final binding.

10/13/94 - 1/15/95 — A PASSION FOR ANTIQUITIES: ANCIENT ART FROM THE COLLECTION OF BARBARA AND LAWRENCE FLEICHMAN — For the first time ever, 200 works from this magnificent collection will be on public view. Among the many remarkable sculptures, wall paintings, terracotta vases and jewelry will be treasures that include the head of a large Cycladic idol (2500 B.C.), a 4th century Macedonian grave stele, a rare southern Italian vase, and a late Hellenistic bronze vessel containing relief decoration and silver inlay.   CAT   WT

10/25/94 - 1/8/95 — THE INTERNATIONAL STYLE: COURTLY ART AROUND THE YEAR 1400 — 19 illuminated manuscripts and one panel painting highlight the flowering of European court art between 1380-1420.   WT

10/25/94 - 1/8/95 — CLASSICISM AND NEOCLASSICISM IN FRENCH DRAWING, 1600-1860 — Works by 25 artists including Lorrain, Poussin and David that show a reverence for antiquity and technical mastery in French draftsmanship from the early 17th to the early 19th century.

12/6/94 - 2/12/95 — FREDERICK SOMMER: POETRY AND LOGIC — Recently acquired by the museum, this outstanding display of works by one of America's foremost living photographers includes some of his most notable surrealist images of desert landscapes, figurative studies, portraits and abstract studies.

1/10 - 3/26/95 — MICHAELANGELO'S REST ON THE FLIGHT INTO EGYPT SEEN IN CONTEXT — One of less than a dozen works by Michaelangelo in the U.S., this recently acquired drawing will be the centerpiece of an exhibition that includes reproductions of comparative works from other collections, an explanation of the drawing's technique, and a look at the history of the drawing.

1/24 - 4/9/95 — ILLUMINATED SECULAR MANUSCRIPTS — Twenty western European 13th to 15th-century works of such secular sources as epic romances, historical chronicles and books of law will be on exhibit.

CALIFORNIA

The J. Paul Getty Museum - continued

2/21 - 6/18/95	HIDDEN WITNESS: JACKIE NAPOLEAN WILSON COLLECTION
2/21 - 6/18/95	CARRIE MAE WEEMS REACTS TO HIDDEN WITNESS
3/28 - 6/11/95	DRAPERY AND COSTUME IN EUROPEAN DRAWINGS OF THE 15TH - 18TH CENTURIES
6/13 - 8/27/95	FLEMISH DRAWINGS, 1500-1660

MONTEREY

Monterey Peninsula Museum of Art

559 Pacific St., **Monterey, CA 93940**
TEL: 408-372-7591
HRS: 10-4 Tu-Sa; 1-4 S   DAY CLOSED: M   HOL: LEG/HOL!
SUGG/CONT: Y   ADULT: $3.00   CHILDREN: F (under 12)   STUDENTS: $1.50
HDC/ACC: Y; Entrance ramp to ground floor; elevator; restrooms
PARKING: Y; Street parking and paid lots nearby to main museum   MUS/SH: Y
GR/T: Y   GR/PH: Call Barbara Call to reserve   DT: Y   TIME: 2:00 S; 1:00 Sa & S for La Mirada   H/B: Y
PERM/COLL: REG/ART; AS; PACIFIC RIM; FOLK; ETH; GR; PHOT

With a focus on its ever growing collection of California regional art, The Monterey Peninsula Museum is planning a modern addition to its original building, La Mirada, the adobe portion of which dates back to the late 1700's when California was still under Mexican rule. PLEASE NOTE: The combined entry fee for La Mirada (an extension of the museum located at 720 Via Mirada) and the museum is $5.00 adult, $4.00 student (with I.D.), children free under 12, and free entry to all on the 1st Sunday of the month. **NOT TO BE MISSED:** Painting and etching collection of works by Armin Hansen

MORGANA

Hearst Art Gallery

Affiliate Institution: St. Mary's College
Box 5110, **Morgana, CA 94575**
TEL: 510-631-4379
HRS: 11-4:30 W-S   DAY CLOSED: M, Tu   HOL: LEG/HOL!
VOL/CONT: Y   ADM: F
HDC/ACC: Y   PARKING: Y; Free   MUS/SH: Y   GR/T: Y   GR/PH: call 510-631-4379
PERM/COLL: AM: Calif. ldscp ptgs 19-20; IT: Med/sculp; EU: gr; AN/CER; CHRISTIAN RELIGIOUS ART 15-20

Contra Costa County, not far from the Bay Area of San Francisco, is home to the Hearst Art Gallery, built with the aid of the William Randolph Hearst Foundation. Located on the grounds of St. Mary's College, one of its most outstanding collections consists of Christian religious art representing many traditions, cultures and centuries. **NOT TO BE MISSED:** Paintings by William Keith (1838 - 1911), noted California landscape painter

40

Hearst Art Gallery - continued

ON EXHIBIT/95:

1/11 - 2/26/95   SAINT MARY'S COLLEGE ART FACULTY — A once in four year presentation of faculty artworks.

3/18 - 4/30/95   ICONS AND EASTER EGGS OF IMPERIAL RUSSIA — Fifty 15th-19th century icons, many embellished with jewels and precious metals, will be accompanied in this exhibition by Easter eggs from a noted private collection.   CAT

6/10 - 7/30/95   WILLIAM KEITH: THE COLLECTION COMES HOME — 50 outstanding landscapes that have been on a national tour for over 2 years return home to the Hearst Art Gallery to join newly acquired and restored works, all by William Keith, known as California's Poet Painter.   BOOK

9 - 12/95   TBA

NEWPORT BEACH

Newport Harbor Art Museum

850 San Clemente Dr., **Newport Beach, CA 92660**
TEL: 714-759-1122
HRS: 10-5 Tu-S   DAY CLOSED: M   HOL: 1/1, THGV, 12/25
F/DAY: Tu   ADM: Y   ADULT: $4.00   CHILDREN: F (under 12)   STUDENTS: $2.00   SR CIT: $2.00
HDC/ACC: Y; Ramps; museum on one level   PARKING: Y; Free off-street parking   MUS/SH: Y
REST/FAC: Y; 11:30-2:20 M-F   GR/T: Y   GR/PH: call 714-759-1122
DT: Y   TIME: 12:15 & 1:15 Tu-F; 2:00 Sa, S   S/G: Y
PERM/COLL: REG: Post War Ca. art (PLEASE NOTE: The permanent collection is not usually on display).

With an emphasis on contemporary and modern art, the Newport Harbor Art Museum, founded in 1962, also features post World War II California art. The museum is dedicated to the promotion of pace-setting trends in contemporary and cutting-edge works of art.

ON EXHIBIT/95:

1/13 - 3/19/95   JOCHEN GERZ — In his first U.S. show, recent photo-text installations of images drawn from the natural environment will be highlighted in an overview of two decades of work by this internationally acclaimed German conceptual photographer.   CAT   WT

OAKLAND

The Oakland Museum

1000 Oak St, **Oakland, CA 94607**
TEL: 510-238-3401
HRS: 10-5 W-Sa; Noon-7 S   DAY CLOSED: M, Tu   HOL: 1/1, 7/4, THGV, 12/25
ADM: F
HDC/ACC: Y; Wheelchair accessible including phones and restrooms
PARKING: Y: Entrance on Oak & 12th St. small fee charged   MUS/SH: Y   REST/FAC: Y
GR/T: Y   GR/PH: 510-273-3514   DT: Y   TIME: 2:00 weekdays; by request on weekends   S/G: Y
PERM/COLL: REG/ART; PTGS; SCULP; GR; DEC/ART

CALIFORNIA

The Oakland Museum - continued

The art gallery of the multi-purpose Oakland Museum, also known as "The Museum of California," features works by important regional artists that document the visual history and heritage of the state. Of special note is the Kevin Roche - John Dinkaloo designed building itself, a prime example of progressive museum architecture complete with terraced gardens. PLEASE NOTE: One-person exhibitions are mounted 3 times a year at the Oakland Museum Sculpture Court at City Center, 1111 Broadway, Oakland (open 7-7 M-F, 8-4 Sa, 10-4 S; Free admission) **NOT TO BE MISSED:** California art

ON EXHIBIT/95:

7/27/94 - 1/8/95	AN IMPROMPTU EXHIBITION OF OUTDOOR SCULPTURE — In conjunction with the International Sculpture Conference in San Francisco in Aug. the museum will install 24 outdoor sculptures in a variety of media on the museum's terraces, along walkways outside 3rd floor galleries and on the roof garden.
9/24/94 - 1/8/95	25 YEARS OF COLLECTION CALIFORNIA — On the occasion of the Museum's 25th anniversary, 4 artists will create a series of imaginative installations by combining objects acquired during the museum's first quarter century.
11/5/94 - 5/7/95	CHOICES: RECENT ACQUISITIONS — On exhibit will be a selection of paintings, watercolors, drawings, sculpture and photographs acquired by the museum over the past 2 years.
1/28 - 4/30/95	PHOTOGRAPHS FROM THE PERMANENT COLLECTION (working title) — 40 photographs selected for viewing from the more than 5,000 works in the permanent collection will feature both classic images by Cunningham, Adams and Weston as well as contemporary examples of the medium.
1/28 - 5/14/95	TWILIGHT AND REVERIE: CALIFORNIA TONALIST PAINTINGS — 60 paintings by 12 California Tonalist artists working between 1890 and 1920 will demonstrate the concern they had with capturing quiet, contemplative scenes of nature at both dawn and dusk by employing the use of blurred imagery and mysterious lighting effects. CAT
2/25 - 6/11/95	PACIFIC DREAMS: CURRENTS OF SURREALISM AND FANTASY IN CALIFORNIA ART, 1934-1957 — 90 works by 35 artists will be featured in the first major museum exhibition to examine the development of myth, magic and fantasy in California art from the Depression to the Cold War. WT
6/10 - 10/29/95	DOROTHEA LANGE: ARCHIVE OF AN ARTIST — In commemoration of the centennial of her birth, 100 images will be selected for viewing from the more than 40,000 of Lange's prints and negatives in the permanent collection of the museum. From little-known images and many that have never been seen before, to such classic icons as her "Migrant Mother," all will celebrate her entire distinguished photographic career.
7/1 - 9/24/95	GUY ROSE: AMERICAN IMPRESSIONIST — Nearly 65 works will be featured in the first major museum exhibition of the works of Guy Rose (1867-1925), one of California's most highly acclaimed landscape and figurative Impressionist painters active during the first 2 decades of the 20th century. CAT
7/22 - 11/12/95	THE ART OF PETER VOULKOS — In the first major exhibition of the work of Bay Area ceramic artist Peter Voulkos, an acknowledged leader of the national and international ceramics revolution that began in California in the 1950's, examples from every period of his creative oeuvre will be on display. CAT
9/16/95 - 1/28/96	SILVER AND GOLD: CALIFORNIA CASED IMAGES — 50 "cased" images by the best-known daguerreotypists will highlight the California Gold Rush era (1849-1860) through images of the Gold Rush country and mining activity to street scenes of San Francisco. Included will be portraits showing the ethnic diversity of miners and other Californians living during these times.

The Oakland Museum - continued

10/21/95 - 1/7/96	LIA COOK: MATERIAL ALLUSIONS — In this exhibition, the focus on the meaning of cloth and what it suggests about our contemporary human experience will be seen in the 25 pieces on view created by Cook during the past 15 years. CAT
11/25/95 - 2/24/96	FINDING FORM — Installations created by using found, recycled, fabricated and sometimes odd materials such as wax, grocery lists, keys and the like will be seen in the works of the 5 sculptors featured in this exhibition.

OXNARD

Carnegie Art Museum
424 S. C St., **Oxnard, CA 93030**
TEL: 805-385-8157
HRS: 10-5 T, 11-6 F, 10-5 Sa, 1-5 S (Museum closed between exhibits)   DAY CLOSED: M
HOL: MEM/DAY, LAB/DAY, THGV, 12/25
VOL/CONT: Y   ADM: F   HDC/ACC: Y   PARKING: Y; Free parking in the lot next to the museum
MUS/SH: Y   GR/T: Y   GR/PH: call 805-385-9157   H/B: Y
PERM/COLL: CONT/REG; EASTWOOD COLL.

Originally built in 1906 in the neo-classic style, the Carnegie, located on the coast just south of Ventura, served as a library until 1980. Listed NRHP **NOT TO BE MISSED:** Collection of art focusing on California painters from the 1920's to the present.

ON EXHIBIT/95:

12/3/94 - 1/15/95	MASTERS IN OUR MIDST SERIES: FROM THE EDGE/POSTCARDS BY KIM LOUCKS KAISER
12/3/94 - 2/26/95	THE PAINTINGS OF WILLIAM ROPER
	KENTE: THE CLOTH OF GHANA
1/21 - 2/26/95	MASTERS IN OUR MIDST SERIES: ORIENTAL WATERCOLOR BY VENTURA COUNTY ARTISTS
3/10 - 6/4/95	CALIFORNIA WATERCOLOR OF THE 1930'S & 40'S
6/17 - 9/3/95	DEPRESSION SILVER: ART DECO ALUMINUM
9/16 - 11/19/95	CONTEMPORARY LATINO PAINTERS FROM THE SANCHEZ COLLECTION
ONGOING:	8-10 works from the Museum's permanent collection of 20th century California art

PALM SPRINGS

Palm Springs Desert Museum, Inc.
101 Museum Drive, **Palm Springs, CA 92262**
TEL: 619-325-7186
HRS: Open Sep 17/94 - Apr 30/95: 10-4 Tu-T & Sa-S; 1-8 F   DAY CLOSED: M   HOL: LEG/HOL! & SUMMER
F/DAY: 1st F   ADM: Y   ADULT: $5.00   CHILDREN: F (under 6))   STUDENTS: $2.00   SR CIT: $4.00
HDC/ACC: Y; South entrance handicapped ramp   PARKING: Y; Free parking in the north Museum lot, the south lot (which has a handicap entrance); daily pay parking (free of charge in the evening) in the Desert Fashion Plaza shopping center lot across the street from the museum.   MUS/SH: Y
REST/FAC: Y; Gallery Cafe open 11-3 daily & 1-8 F   GR/T: Y   GR/PH: call 619-325-7186
DT: Y   TIME: 2 Tu-S (Nov-May)   H/B: Y; Architectural landmark   S/G: Y
PERM/COLL: CONT/REG

CALIFORNIA

Palm Springs Desert Museum, Inc. - continued

Contemporary American art with special emphasis on the art of California and other western states is the main focus of the 4,000 piece collection of the Palm Springs Desert Museum. The museum is housed in a splendid modern structure made of materials that blend harmoniously with the surrounding landscape. PLEASE NOTE: The museum will close for the summer this year on 4/30/95 in order to allow for expansion and construction. **NOT TO BE MISSED:** Leo S. Singer Miniature Room Collection; Miniature of Thomas Jefferson Reception Room at the State Department.

ON EXHIBIT/95:

9/17/94 - 1/8/95	ALLAN HOUSER: A LIFE IN ART — Sculptural works that are both abstract and repersentational by Houser, a recently deceased leading figure in contemporary American Indian art. WT
12/16/94 - 2/19/95	JOHN BUCK: SCULPTURE AND WOODBLOCK PRINTS — Woodblock prints and 10 sculptures will be featured in the first comprehensive survey of contemporary Montana artist Buck's work.
1/24 - 4/30/95	MASTERS OF THE TAOS TRADITION: THE GERALD PETERS COLLECTION — From the collection of collector and gallery owner Gerald Peters, an exhibition of paintings by many now famous artists who founded New Mexico's renowned Taos Society of Artists in the first half of the 20th century.
3/1 - 4/30/95	AGNES PELTON: POET OF NATURE — A retrospective exhibition of 50 paintings by Pelton (1881-1961), a pioneer American modernist and former resident of the Palm Springs area. CAT WT
3/7 - 4/2/95	ARTISTS COUNCIL ANNUAL EXHIBITION — A juried exhibition of 50 paintings and sculptures by local and national artists.
4/4 - 4/30/95	DESERT WILDFLOWERS — 25 photographs that show the color and diversity of springtime wildflowers in the Coachella Valley.

PALO ALTO

Palo Alto Cultural Center
1313 Newell Rd., **Palo Alto, CA 94303**
TEL: 415-329-2366
HRS: 10-5 Tu-Sa; till 10 T; 1-5 S   HOL: 1/1, 7/4, 12/25
ADM: F   HDC/ACC: Y; No steps in building   PARKING: Y; Free and adjacent to the center   MUS/SH: Y
GR/T: Y   GR/PH: call 415-329-2366   DT: Y   TIME: call for information
PERM/COLL: CONT/ART; HIST/ART

Located in a building that served as the town hall from the 1950's to 1971, this active community art center mounts special exhibitions on a regular rotating basis.

ON EXHIBIT/95:

11/20/94 - 2/5/95	THE GOLD SHOW — Contemporary exploration of the media of gold through examples of Ororone photography, contemporary fiber, painting and sculptural jewelry.
11/20/94 - 2/5/95	CLAUDIA BERNARDI — Presented will be "Frescoes on Paper," creations by the artist on paper from Brazilian woodcuts.
11/20/94 - 2/5/95	CRIES FROM THE INVISIBLE: AN INSTALLATION BY ENRIQUE CHAGOYA & CLAUDIA BERNARDI — A site-specific installation inspired by the Argentine Forensic Anthropology Team's work in Argentina, El Salvador and Ethiopia.

44

Palo Alto Cultural Center - continued

2/23 - 4/30/95	WINDOWS TO THE MIND: SELECTED BOOKS FROM STANFORD SPECIAL COLLECTIONS — Chosen from the largest special collection of its kind on the West Coast will be the Nuremberg Chronicle, a 15th century Book of Hours, and artist-illustrated books published by Vollard.
2/23 - 5/28/95	THE PAINTED POEM — Presented will be picture poems and contemporary paintings that employ the use of text.
6/22 - 8/13/95	CHRISTOPHER BROWN: WORKS ON PAPER — This first Bay Area exhibition of Brown's work will include etchings, woodcuts, lithographs and pastels. CAT
6/22 - 8/13/95	PASTEL AS PAINTING — Contemporary artists of drawings who enter the realm of painting will be featured in this exhibition.
8/27 - 9/24/95	RADIUS 1995 — A juried exhibition of works by artists living in cities adjacent to the Palo Alto Cultural Center.
8/27 - 9/24/95	FRAME OF REFERENCE — An invitational exhibition and sale where each participating artist is given a 6 x 9" wooden frame with which to create a piece.
10/15/95 - 1/96	CONCEPT IN FORM: ARTISTS' SKETCHBOOKS AND MAQUETTES

PASADENA

Norton Simon Museum
411 W. Colorado Blvd., **Pasadena, CA 91105**
TEL: 818-449-6840
HRS: Noon-6 T-S   DAY CLOSED: M-W   HOL: 1/1, THGV, 12/25
ADM: Y   ADULT: $4.00   CHILDREN: F(under 12)   STUDENTS: $2.00   SR CIT: $2.00
HDC/ACC: Y; Wheelchair access & availability   PARKING: Y; Ample parking available at the museum
MUS/SH: Y   GR/T: Y   GR/PH: call Nancy Gubin 818-449-6840   S/G: Y
PERM/COLL: EU: ptgs 15-20; sculp 19-20; IND: sculp; OR: sculp; EU/ART 20; AM/ART 20

Thirty galleries with 1,000 works from the permanent collection that are always on display plus a beautiful sculpture garden make the internationally known Norton Simon Museum home to one of the most remarkable and renowned collections of art in the world. The seven centuries of European art on view from the collection contain remarkable examples of work by Old Master, Impressionist, and important modern 20th century artists. **NOT TO BE MISSED:** IMP & POST/IMP Collection including a unique set of original master bronzes by Degas.

ON EXHIBIT/95:

THROUGH 1/15/95	EYE-TO-EYE WITH REMBRANDT: ETCHED PORTRAITS AND SELF-PORTRAITS — An examination of Rembrandt's technical and stylistic innovations.
9/15/94 - 3/12/95	PHOTOGRAPHY — 50 important photographs from the permanent collection by such masters as Ansel Adams, Edward Weston and Imogen Cunningham will be featured.
11/17/94 - 9/10/95	THE SPIRIT OF MODERNISM: GALKA SCHEYER IN THE NEW WORLD — A major painting and print exhibition of over 200 works that celebrates Scheyer's life and shows much of her important collection. Included will be works by renowned Blue Four artists Kandinsky, Klee, Feininger and Jawlensky. Also on exhibit will be major works by Picasso, Kokoshka, Archipenko, Nolde, Schwitters and others.

CALIFORNIA

Norton Simon Museum - continued

1/19 - 7/9/95	LANDSCAPE PRINTS & DRAWINGS — Landscapes by Claude, Rembrandt, Goya and others.
3/16 - 9/17/95	JAPANESE PRINTS — Woodblock prints of landscapes from the permanent collection.
5/19/94 - 3/95	STILL LIFE — All of the still life masterpieces from the collection will be on view.
7/13/95 - 1/7/96	BOTANICAL STUDIES
9/14/95 - 5/19/96	BRAVO — Photographs by Manuel Alvarez Bravo.
9/14/95 - 5/19/96	LATIN AMERICAN PRINTS — Prints in the permanent collection by Rufino Tamayo, Diego Rivera, and other early 20th century Latin American artists will be on exhibit.
9/21/95 - 3/24/96	SMALL DEVOTIONAL OBJECTS — Small sculptures used in worship will be on display.

PASADENA

Pacific Asia Museum

46 N. Los Robles Ave., **Pasadena, CA 91101**
TEL: 818-449-2742
HRS: 10-5 W-S   DAY CLOSED: M, Tu   HOL: 1/1, MEM/DAY, 7/4, THGV, 12/25, 12/31
F/DAY: 3rd Sa   ADM: Y   ADULT: $3.00   CHILDREN: F (under 12)   STUDENTS: $1.50   SR CIT: $1.50
HDC/ACC: Y; Limited - no second level access   PARKING: Y; Free parking at the Pasadena Mall southwest of the museum; $3.00 fee at lot north of museum   MUS/SH: Y   GR/T: Y   GR/PH: call 818-449-2742
DT: Y   TIME: 2pm S   H/B: Y; California State Historical Landmark   S/G: Y
PERM/COLL: AS: cer, sculp; CH: cer, sculp; OR/FOLK; OR/ETH; OR/PHOT

The Pacific Asia Museum is the only one in Southern California devoted exclusively to the arts of Asia. The collection, housed in a gorgeous 1924 structure built in the Chinese Imperial Palace style, features a lovely authentic Chinese courtyard garden added in 1979. Listed NRHP. **NOT TO BE MISSED:** Chinese courtyard garden

ON EXHIBIT/95:

8/3/94 - 5/21/95	THE EVOLVING DREAMTIME: CONTEMPORARY ART BY INDIGENOUS AUSTRALIANS - SELECTIONS FROM THE KELTON FOUNDATION COLLECTION — The evolution of this art movement in a historical context will be highlighted with selections from the largest and most comprehensive collection of its kind outside of Australia. Works by both male and female artists from all of the major Aboriginal settlements will be included. WT
12/10/94 - 1/22/95	3 PERSON EXHIBITION (NEON SCULPTURE)
2/8 - 8/27/95	A GATHERING PLACE: ARTMAKING BY ASIAN-PACIFIC WOMEN IN TRADITIONAL AND CONTEMPORARY DIRECTIONS — A comparison of traditionally inspired works by Asian/Pacific Island master artists from local communities with those of contemporary artists using post-modernist artistic techniques.
6/7 - 9/3/95	CHINA'S RENAISSANCE IN BRONZE: THE ROBERT H. CLAGUE COLLECTION OF LATER CHINESE BRONZES (1100-1900) — Based on vessels from China's Great Bronze Age which began around 1600 B.C., these examples echo the shapes and motifs of their ancient counterparts but are infused with new patterns, functions and even new meanings.
9/13/95 - 5/18/96	HANGING SCROLLS BY TS'UI TXU-FAN (CUI ZIFAN) — Hanging scrolls in ink and in color by Chinese artist Cui Zifan, born 1915.
11/95 - 3/96	IMPORTANT ASIAN ARTIFACTS FROM SOUTHERN CALIFORNIA COLLECTIONS AND RARELY SEEN OBJECTS FROM THE PERMANENT COLLECTION

PENN VALLEY

Museum of Ancient & Modern Art

11392 Pleasant Valley Rd., **Penn Valley, CA 95946**
TEL: 916-432-3080
HRS: 10-5 DAILY   HOL: 1/1, EASTER, 7/4, LAB/DAY, THGV, 12/25
ADM: F   HDC/ACC: Y   PARKING: Y; Free and plentiful   MUS/SH: Y   GR/T: Y   GR/PH: call 916- 432-3080
DT: Y   TIME: upon request if available
PERM/COLL: AN/GRK; AN/R; ETRUSCAN; GR; CONT; DU; FR; GER; CONT/AM; DEC/ART; PHOT

Although the permanent collection has been assembled over a short 20-year period, the scope and extent of its holdings is truly mind-boggling. In addition to the outstanding collection of ancient Western Asiatic artworks, the museum features a group of historical art books containing woodcuts, etchings and engravings printed as early as 1529, a wonderful assemblage of African masks and sculptures from over 20 different tribes, and a superb group of Rembrandt etchings and other European masterpieces. The museum is located approximately 50 miles northeast of Sacramento. **NOT TO BE MISSED:** One of the largest collections of 18th Dynasty Egypt in the U.S.; Theodora Van Runkel Collection of Ancient Gold; Hall of Miniatures; the TIME MACHINE.

ON EXHIBIT/95:

10/94 - 6/95	THE TIME MACHINE: INSTALLATION
1/95 - 3/95	ROMAN COLISEUM: AN ARCHITECTURAL EXTRAVAGANZA
3/95 - 6/95	A THOUSAND WALLS: ANCIENT TEMPLES
6/95 - 9/95	EGYPTIAN PYRAMIDS: A STAIRWAY TO HEAVEN
9/95 - 12/95	VANISHING POINT

RIVERSIDE

California Museum of Photography

Affiliate Institution: Univ. of California
3824 Main St., **Riverside, CA 92521**
TEL: 909-784-FOTO
HRS: 11-5 M, W-Sa; Noon-5 S; till 8:30 pm W (Apr-Nov)   DAY CLOSED: Tu   HOL: LEG/HOL!
F/DAY: W   ADM: W   ADULT: $2.00   CHILDREN: F (under 12)   STUDENTS: $1.00   SR CIT: $1.00
HDC/ACC: Y   PARKING: Y; Street parking and several commercial lots and garages nearby.   MUS/SH: Y
GR/T: Y   GR/PH: call 714-787-4787   DT: Y   TIME: 2:00 Sa
PERM/COLL: PHOT 19-20; CAMERA COLLECTION

Converted from a 1930's Kress dimestore into an award winning contemporary space, this is one of the finest photographic museums in the country. In addition to a vast number of photographic prints the museum features a 6,000 piece collection of photographic apparatus. **NOT TO BE MISSED:** "Images and Apparatus," a "please touch" Interactive Gallery; Watkins Screen, a huge antique 1880's English oak screen that holds 26 enormous albumen prints by Watkins of the American West; 6,000 piece collection of Ansel Adams photographs.

CALIFORNIA

California Museum of Photography - continued

ON EXHIBIT/95:

11/12/94 - 2/12/95	HOW FAR HAVE WE COME? PAST AND PRESENT MEDIA IMAGES OF AFRICAN-AMERICANS — On view will be a set of 20 stereographs (3-D photographs that were a popular form of entertainmemt at the turn-of-the-century) that depict the historic "Coon Series," believed at the time to be true documents of African-American life.
12/3/94 - 2/19/95	THE ETERNAL RETURN: VISIONS OF CHILDHOOD — Multi-media works by 5 mid-career and emerging artists explore the nature of their childhood memories and the thin line that exists between bliss, dread, and the realm of the imagination.
3/4 - 4/30/95	GARDEN OF EARTHLY DELIGHTS: PHOTOGRAPHS OF EDWARD WESTON AND ROBERT MAPPLETHORP — 45 photographs by each artist dealing with the figure, the portrait and the still life will allow the viewer to compare and contrast the styles of these two men, both of whom challenged the artistic conventions of their day. WT

RIVERSIDE

Riverside Art Museum
3425 Seventh St., **Riverside, CA 92501**
TEL: 909-684-7111
HRS: 10-4 M-Sa   DAY CLOSED: S   HOL: Last 2 Weeks Aug; LEG/HOL!
ADM: F   HDC/ACC: Y   PARKING: Y; Limited free parking at museum; metered street parking   MUS/SH: Y
REST/FAC: Y; Open weekdays   GR/T: Y   GR/PH: call 714-684-7111   DT: Y   TIME: daily upon request
H/B: Y; 1929 building designed by Julia Morgan, architect of Hearst Castle
PERM/COLL: PTGS, SCULP, GR

Julia Morgan, the architect of the Hearst Castle also designed this handsome and completely updated museum building in 1929. Listed on the NRHP, the museum is located in the Los Angeles/Palm Springs area. Aside from its professionally curated exhibitions, the museum displays the work of area students during the month of May.

SACRAMENTO

Crocker Art Museum
216 O St., **Sacramento, CA 95814**
TEL: 916-264-5423
HRS: 10-5 W-S; till 9 T   DAY CLOSED: M, Tu   HOL: LEG/HOL!
ADM: Y   ADULT: $4.50   CHILDREN: $2.00 (7-17)
HDC/ACC: Y   PARKING: Y; On-site paid parking   MUS/SH: Y   GR/T: Y   GR/PH: call 916-449-5527
DT: Y   TIME: !   H/B: Y; Over 100 years old
PERM/COLL: PTGS: REN-20; OM/DRGS 15-20; CONT; OR; SCULP

This inviting Victorian gingerbread mansion, the oldest public art museum in the West, was built in the 1870's by Judge E. B. Crocker. It is filled with his collection of more than 700 European and American paintings displayed throughout the ballroom and other areas of the original building. Contemporary works by northern California artists are on view in the light-filled, modern wing whose innovative facade is a re-creation of the Crocker home. **NOT TO BE MISSED:** Early California painting collection.

48

Crocker Art Museum - continued

ON EXHIBIT/95:

11/11/94 - 1/15/95	MORLEY BAER'S CALIFORNIA — 20 of the photographic images taken by Baer between 1947-1993 reflect his fascination and reverence for the California landscape. What makes his work unusual is the variety of ways in which he has creatively approached the same themes over the past 5 decades of his career offering various and complex compositions and viewpoints to oft-photographed subjects.
12/2/94 - 1/8/95	BUILDING A COLLECTION: A DECADE OF GIFTS — 10 years of acquisitions to the permanent collection of the Crocker Museum which include international ceramics, Persian & Indian miniature paintings, contemporary & 19th century northern California art and European art will be featured in this exhibition.
1/20 - 3/5/95	IMAGE AND MEMORY: LATIN AMERICAN PHOTOGRAPHY, 1880-1992 — On view will be an overview of Latin American photography from early examples which were influenced by European technology and aesthetics to contemporary present day works. BOOK WT
3/10 - 5/7/95	TBA/CONTEMPORARY ART
3/16 - 6/4/95	TAGGER ART IE: — Graffiti art
3/24 - 5/14/95	NOH MASKS BY ADAM ZILLINGER AND THE ARIAKE NOMEN CIRCLE OF JAPAN — 55 masks created for the Noh theater by native Californian, Zollinger, the only American artist to create masks for the Noh theater, will be presented with others by Japanese teachers and colleagues from the Ariake Nomen Circle of mask makers in Fukuoka, Japan.
5/12 - 7/95	18TH CENTURY FRENCH DRAWINGS
6/1 - 7/23/95	CROCKER ART MUSEUM INVITATIONAL EXHIBITION
8/13 - 10/8/95	TBA
10/26 - 12/31/95	WESTERN ARTISTS COLLECTING AFRICAN ART — The influence of African art on Western artists will be seen in the 41 African objects on display owned by 26 contemporary artists who live and work in New York.

SAN DIEGO

Museum of Contemporary Art, San Diego
1001 Kettner Blvd., San Diego, CA 92101
TEL: 617-454-3541
HRS: 10-5 Tu & T-S-S; 10-9 W   DAY CLOSED: M   HOL: 1/1, 2nd week Aug., THGV, 12/25
F/DAY: 10-9 W   ADM: Y   ADULT: $3.00   CHILDREN: F (under 13)   STUDENTS: $1.00   SR CIT: $1.00
HDC/ACC: Y   PARKING: Y; 2 hour free street parking at La Jolla; validated $2.00 2 hour parking at America Plaza garage for downtown location during the week plus some metered street parking and pay lots nearby.   MUS/SH: Y
GR/T: Y   GR/PH: call 619-454-3541, ex 180   DT: Y   TIME: 2pm Sa, S & 6:30 T (downtown branch)   S/G: Y
PERM/COLL: CONT: ptgs, sculp, drgs, gr, phot

Perched on a bluff overlooking the Pacific Ocean, this 50 year old museum features major examples of contemporary art (since the 1950's) by highly regarded national and international artists as well as works by emerging new talents. There is also a downtown branch at America Plaza that will be open during the renovation of the main museum at La Jolla which is scheduled for closure for approximately 18 months beginning in 1/94. Both branches will operate as one museum with 2 permanent locations when the main museum reopens in early 1996.

CALIFORNIA

SAN DIEGO

Museum of Photographic Arts
1649 El Prado, Balboa Park, **San Diego, CA 92101**
TEL: 619-239-5262
HRS: 10-5 Daily   DAY CLOSED: M   HOL: LEG/HOL!
F/DAY: 2nd Tu   ADM: Y   ADULT: $3.00   CHILDREN: F (under 12)
HDC/ACC: Y   PARKING: Y; Available free throughout Balboa Park   MUS/SH: Y
GR/T: Y   GR/PH: CALL 619-239-5262   DT: Y   TIME: 1:00 Sa, S
PERM/COLL: PHOT

Now in its 12th year, the Museum of Photographic Arts, situated in the heart of beautiful Balboa Park, is housed in an original 1915 structure built for the Panama-California Exposition. Devoted exclusively to the care and collection of photographic works of art, the museum is in the process of an expansion project that will more than triple its present space.

ON EXHIBIT/95:

11/2/94 - 1/8/95	FOR THE LOVE OF FORM: PHOTOGRAPHY OF HARRY CALLHAN — 100 photographs will be on view in a survey of Callhan's work from landscape studies of the early 1940's to images taken over the last decade.
1/11 - 3/19/95	INFORMED BY FILM — In celebration of the 100th anniversary of film, this exhibition will present the work of photographers who have furthered the interaction between still and moving pictures.
3/22 - 5/21/95	A SHADOW BORN OF EARTH: NEW PHOTOGRAPHY IN MEXICO — Works by 16 young Mexican artists that explore the techniques of photomontage, photographic manipulation, large-scale Polaroid photography and photography constructed tableau will be featured in this exhibition. CAT WT
5/24 - 6/18/95	RECENT ACQUISITIONS FROM THE PERMANENT COLLECTION
6/21 - 9/10/95	PHOTOGRAPHY AND BEYOND: THE FRENCH VANGUARD — From established masters to emerging talents, works by French avant-garde photographers will be featured in this exhibition that is a joint venture between The Israel Museum and The Boca Raton Museum of Art. CAT WT
9/12 - 11/5/95	POINTS OF ENTRY: WORLDS LOST/A NATION FOUND (working subtitle) — The reality of the American Dream as experienced by immigrants will be the subject of this three-part photographic exhibition. 125 images from daguerrotypes to contemporary work will cover four specific geographic "points of entry" used by immigrants coming into the U.S. PLEASE NOTE: There will be one catalog published that will include all 3 portions of this exhibition. CAT WT
9/12 - 11/15/95	POINTS OF ENTRY: TRACING CULTURES (working subtitle) — Works by living immigrant artists who, in experiencing cultural dislocation, are striving to retain their cultural identity and language rather than become part of the American "melting pot." CAT WT

SAN DIEGO
San Diego Museum of Art
1450 El Prado, Balboa Park, **San Diego, CA 92101**
TEL: 619-232-7931
HRS: 10-4:30 Tu-S   DAY CLOSED: M   HOL: 1/1, THGV, 12/25
ADM: Y   ADULT: $6.00   CHILDREN: $2.00 (6-17)   SR CIT: $5.00
HDC/ACC: Y   PARKING: Y; Parking is available in Balboa Park and in the lot in front of the museum.
MUS/SH: Y   REST/FAC: Y; Sculpture Garden Cafe 11:30-1:30 Tu-S (To reserve: 232-7931 ex250)
GR/T: Y   GR/PH: call 619-232-7931   DT: Y   TIME: 10, 11, 1, & 2 Tu-T & Sa; 1 & 2 F, S
H/B: Y; Built in 1926, the facade is similar to one at Univ. of Salamanca   S/G: Y
PERM/COLL: IT/REN; SP/BAROQUE; DU; AM: 20 EU; ptgs, sculp 19; AS; AN/EGT; P/COL

Whether strolling through the treasures in the sculpture garden or viewing the masterpieces inside the Spanish Colonial style museum building, a visit to this institution, in San Diego's beautiful Balboa Park, is a richly rewarding and worthwhile experience. Family oriented self-led discovery guides of the collection are available in both English and Spanish. **NOT TO BE MISSED:** Frederick R. Weisman Gallery of Calif. art; Thomas Eakin's "Elizabeth With a Dog;" Works by Toulouse-Lautrec.

ON EXHIBIT/95:

12/10/94 - 1/15/95	PASSIONATE VISIONS OF THE AMERICAN SOUTH: SELF TAUGHT ARTISTS FROM 1940 TO THE PRESENT — 270 works from 110 private and public collections (and 23 states) will be featured in an overview of painting and sculpture by Southern self-taught artists selected solely on the basis of artistic merit.
3/18 - 5/28/95	ROTHKO: THE SPIRIT OF MYTH - EARLY PAINTINGS FROM THE 1930'S AND 1940'S — 24 figurative and transitional works will be on view.
4/26 - 4/29/95	ART ALIVE — An annual event that features floral interpretations of the museum's permanent collection.
6/4 - 7/31/95	DISCOVERING ELLIS RULEY— 62 works by this self-taught African-American artist reveal his instinctive genius for composition and color as expressed in the medium of ordinary housepaint on posterboard.
7/29 - 9/24/95	GAUGUIN AND THE SCHOOL OF PONT-AVEN — Featured will be paintings, works on paper, and polychrome wood sculptures by Gauguin and other of his famous 19th century art school contemporaries. CAT WT

Timken Museum of Art
1500 El Prado, Balboa Park, **San Diego, CA 92101**
TEL: 619-239-5548
HRS: 10-4:30 Tu-Sa; 1:30-4:30 S   DAY CLOSED: M   HOL: LEG/HOL!; MONTH OF SEPT
VOL/CONT: Y   ADM: F   HDC/ACC: Y   GR/T: Y   GR/PH: call 619-239-5548   DT: Y   TIME: 10-12 Tu-T
PERM/COLL: EU: om/ptgs 13-19; AM: ptgs 19; RUSS/IC 15-19; GOBELIN TAPESTRIES

Superb examples of European and American paintings and Russian Icons are but a few of the highlights of the Timkin Museum of Art located in beautiful Balboa Park, site of the former 1915-16 Panama California Exposition. Treasures displayed within the six galleries and the rotunda of this museum make it a "must see." **NOT TO BE MISSED:** "Portrait of a Man" by Frans Hals; "The Magnolia Flower" by Martin Johnson Heade.

ON EXHIBIT/95:

12/1/94 - 1/15/95	"DEATH OF THE VIRGIN" BY PETER CHRISTUS — A conservation show on this Flemish masterpiece.
10/95	THE PAINTINGS OF STEPHEN HANNOCK — Presented in celebration of the 30th anniversary of the Timkin Museum of Art.

CALIFORNIA

SAN FRANCISCO

Asian Art Museum of San Francisco
Affiliate Institution: The Avery Brundage Collection
Golden Gate Park, **San Francisco, CA 94118**
TEL: 415-668-8922
HRS: 10-5 W-S; 10am-8:45pm 1st W each month   DAY CLOSED: M, Tu   HOL: 1/1, THGV, 12/25
F/DAY: !   ADM: Y   ADULT: $5.00   CHILDREN: F (under 12)   STUDENTS: $2.00   SR CIT: $3.00
HDC/ACC: Y; Elevator, restrooms, wheelchairs available
PARKING: Y; Free parking in lot east of the museum building and at both ends of the Music Concourse
GR/T: Y   GR/PH: call 415-668-8922
DT: Y   TIME: frequent daily tours!
PERM/COLL: OR: arts; MID/E: arts; BRUNDAGE COLLECTION (80 % OF THE HOLDINGS OF THE MUSEUM)

With a 12,000 piece collection that covers 40 countries and 6,000 years, the Asian Museum is the largest of its kind outside of Asia. **NOT TO BE MISSED:** Earliest dated Chinese buddha (338 A.D.).

ON EXHIBIT/95:

11/30/94 - 1/29/95	LATTER DAYS OF THE LAW: IMAGES OF CHINESE BUDDHISM, 850-1850 — On exhibit are 83 richly painted, woven, embroidered and printed objects that defy the notion that the religious persecutions of the Tang dynasty in 845 led to a decline of the law in China. They did, in fact, result in a productive period of change and restructuring as reflected in the works on view.
12/8/94 - 2/5/95	SNUFF BOTTLES FROM THE COLLECTIONS OF HUMPHREY HUI AND CHRISTOHPER SIN — 238 snuff bottles, each one a unique and remarkable miniature work of art, will be featured in this exhibition.
2/28 - 4/30/95	POJAGI: KOREAN WRAPPING CLOTHS OF THE CHOSON DYNASTY — According to Korean beliefs, good fortune (pok) is enclosed or captured in Pojagi, beautiful wrapping cloths that were utilized for wrapping, covering, storing and carrying. Many of these wonderful textiles will be on view in this exhibition.
8 - 10/95	MONGOL RENAISSANCE: BUDDHIST MONKS OF THE HIGH STEPPE — An examination of Tibetan-style Buddhism with its concept of reincarnation that resulted from an attempt in the 16th-century to reunite nomadic tribes that came together under the rule of Genghis Kahn 3 centuries earlier.

Cartoon Art Museum
665 Third St., Fourth Floor, **San Francisco, CA 94107**
TEL: 415-546-9481
HRS: 11-5 W-F; 10-5 Sa; 1-5 S   DAY CLOSED: Tu   HOL: 1/1, 7/4, THGV, 12/25
ADM: Y   ADULT: $3.00   CHILDREN: $1.00 (under 12)   STUDENTS: $2.00   SR CIT: $2.00
HDC/ACC: Y; Sidewalk ramps & elevator; museum all one level   PARKING: Y; Street parking; lot one block south at Third & King.   MUS/SH: Y   GR/T: Y   GR/PH: call 415-546-3922   DT: Y   TIME: upon request if available
PERM/COLL: CARTOON ART; GRAPHIC ANIMATION

Original cartoon art, newspaper strips, political cartoons, and animation cells are but a few of the many facets to be explored in this most unique museum.

CALIFORNIA

SAN FRANCISCO

Coit Tower
1 Telegraph Hill, **San Francisco, CA**
TEL: 415-274-0203
HRS: 9-4:30 daily (winter); 10-5:30 daily (summer)
ADM: F   PARKING: Y; very limited timed parking
PERM/COLL: murals

Though not a museum, art lovers should not miss the newly restored Depression-era murals that completely cover the interior of this famous San Francisco landmark. 25 social realist artists working under the auspices of the WPA participated in creating these frescoes that depict rural and urban life in California during the 1930's. Additional murals on the second floor may be seen only at 11:15 on Saturday mornings. The murals, considered one of the city's most important artistic treasures, and the spectacular view of San Francisco from this facility are a "must see" when visiting this city.

The Fine Arts Museums of San Francisco
Affiliate Institution: M. H. DeYoung Mem. Mus. & Calif. Palace of Legion of Honor
Calif. Palace of the Legion of Honor
Lincoln Park, **San Francisco, CA 94121**
TEL: 415-750-3600
HRS: 10-8:45 W; 10-5 T-S   DAY CLOSED: M, Tu
HOL: Most holidays that fall on M & Tu, when the museum is regularly closed
F/DAY: Y!   ADM: Y   ADULT: $5.00   CHILDREN: F (under 12)   STUDENTS: $2.00   SR CIT: $3.00
HDC/ACC: Y   PARKING: Y; Free parking in the park   MUS/SH: Y   REST/FAC: 2 Cafes open 10am-4pm
GR/T: Y   GR/PH: 425-750-3638   H/B: Y; Calif. Palace of Legion of Honor modeled on Hotel de Salm in Paris
PERM/COLL: DeYoung: PTGS, DRGS, GR, SCULP; AM: dec/art; BRIT: dec/art; AN/EGT; AN/R; AN/GRK; AF; OC. California Palace of Legion of Honor: EU: 13-20; REN; IMPR: drgs, gr

The DeYoung Museum: Situated in the heart of Golden Gate Park, the DeYoung features a premier collection of American art. The California Palace of the Legion of Honor: One of the most dramatic museum buildings in the country, the Palace of the Legion of Honor houses one of the world's finest collections of Rodin sculpture. It will, however, be closed until 11/95 for renovation. **NOT TO BE MISSED:** Rodin's "Thinker" (Legion of Honor); Textile collection (DeYoung).

ON EXHIBIT/95:
M. H. DEYOUNG:

7/20/94 - 1/1/95	IMPRESSIONS OF AN ERA: PARIS 1870-1914 — Charming portrayals of everyday society will be seen in this exhibition of Impressionist and Post-Impressionist paintings, drawings, prints, sculpture, posters, photographs and costumes.
9/28/94 - 3/95	DRESSED FOR DANCE — Dance costumes from the Museum's collection that reveal the development of the "tutu" will be seen in this exhibit which also features a classic costume worn by the legendary Russian dancer Anna Pavlova as well as works on paper related to the subject of ballet.
10/19/94 - 1/1/95	ERLE LORAN: ARTIST, COLLECTOR, AND SCHOLAR — On exhibit will be paintings and writings by Loran who, at the age of 89 is still a prominent and active figure in Bay Area art circles. Loren, who has been active artistically since 1936, is best known for his modernist watercolors of Bay Area life and landscapes, many of which will be on view.

CALIFORNIA

The Fine Arts Museums of San Francisco - continued

12/17/94 - 3/5/95	A GIFT TO AMERICA: MASTERPIECES OF EUROPEAN PAINTING FROM THE SAMUEL H. KRESS COLLECTION — 60 Italian, Dutch, French, Flemish, and Spanish masterpiece paintings from the 16th through 18th centuries will emphasize the remarkable scope and depth of one of the most distinguished art collections ever assembled by a private individual. Four prominent museums, all recipients of major works from the Kress Collection, will loan their paintings (which have been apart for more than 30 years) in order to reunite them for this splendid exhibition. CAT
2/22 - 4/30/95	RAYMOND SAUNDERS: BLACK PAINTINGS — In this exhibition for well-known Bay Area artist, Saunders, large collaged compositions reflecting popular culture, biographical themes, and African-American art & life are juxtaposed on expansive black backgrounds. Working on this theme since 1975, this is the first time that a show of 12 to 14 of his creations will be on view at the DeYoung.
3/25 - 5/29/95	MONET: LATE PAINTINGS OF GIVERNY FROM THE MUSÉE MARMOTTAN — 22 of Monet's famous garden scenes created between 1903-1926, some never seen before in the U.S., will be on view in this second and last American venue for this exclusive exhibition. Of particular note will be several very large canvases from this remarkable collection. WT
6/24 - 9/10/95	FACING EDEN: 100 YEARS OF LANDSCAPE ART IN THE BAY AREA — In celebration of the M. H. de Young Memorial Museum's centennial, this multi-media exhibition will pay homage to the regional sensitivity of the very landscape that helped to foster the Museum's existence in Golden Gate Park. CAT
7/15 - 11/26/95	DWIGHT STRONG COLLECTION OF AFRICAN ART — 40 African masks and figures that focus on the little-known artistic tradition of Western Equatorial Africa will be featured in this exhibition.
9/95 - 11/95	PERGAMON: THE TELEPHOS FRIEZE RESTORED — An exhibition of important Hellenistic Greek sculpture featuring the conserved and restored Telephos Frieze which originally covered the interior walls of the Great Altar at Pergamon. WT

SAN FRANCISCO

The Friends of Photography, Ansel Adams Center
250 Fourth St., San Francisco, CA 94103
TEL: 415-495-7000
HRS: 11-5 Tu-S; 11-8 1st T of the month   DAY CLOSED: M   HOL: LEG/HOL!
ADM: Y   ADULT: $4.00   CHILDREN: $2.00 (12-17)   STUDENTS: $3.00   SR CIT: $2.00
HDC/ACC: Y; Restrooms, ramp (front of bldg), wheelchair lift (side of bldg)
PARKING: Y; Several commercial parking facilities located nearby   MUS/SH: Y
GR/T: Y   GR/PH: call 415-495-7000 (eductation dept)   DT: Y   TIME: 1:15 Sa
PERM/COLL: PHOT; COLLECTION OF 125 VINTAGE PRINTS BY ANSEL ADAMS AVAILABLE FOR STUDY ONLY

Founded in 1967 by a group of noted photographers including Ansel Adams, Brett Weston, and Beaumont Newhall, the non-profit Friends of Photography is dedicated to expanding public awareness of photography and to exploring the creative development of the media.

ON EXHIBIT/95:

8/31/94 - 1/8/95	PERCEPTION: ART & INVENTION — Photographic perception from pre-photographic images to stop-action photography will be reviewed in this exhibition which explores the history, technology, fine art and social impact of photography within both its historical and contemporary context.

54

The Friends of Photography, Ansel Adams Center - continued

12/7/94 - 1/8/95	CHRISTINE TAMBLYN — SHE LOVES IT, SHE LOVES IT NOT: WOMEN AND TECHNOLOGY — Issues of women's use of technology will be examined in this interactive CDROM disc created by Tamblyn in collaboration with Marjorie Franklin & Paul Tomkins.
1/18 - 3/12/95	TALKING PICTURES: PEOPLE SPEAK ABOUT THE PHOTOGRAPHS THAT SPEAK TO THEM — Comments by 70 famous and non-famous people on photographs they have selected that have changed their lives. BOOK
1/19 - 3/12/95	THE FRIENDS OF PHOTOGRAPHY ANNUAL AWARD WINNERS
3/22 - 5/7/95	INSCRUTABLE OBJECTS: IMAGE AND ICON IN RECENT PHOTOGRAPHY — A survey of recent work by photographic artists who use iconic and mysterious subject matter and whose works reflect their concern with the elusive identity of objects.
7/19 - 9/3/95	NAGASAKI JOURNEY: THE PHOTOGRAPHS OF YOSUKE YAMAHATA — 95 photographs by this late Japanese photographer will be presented in commemoration of the 50th anniversary of the bombing of Hiroshima and Nagasaki. CAT WT
9/13 - 11/5/95	POINTS OF ENTRY: TRACING CULTURES — Three interrelated exhibitions, each developed by an outstanding American photographic museum, will concentrate on recent photography and photo-related installations that deal with the theme of issues of origin, acculturation, displacement and loss within the context of contemporary American life. PLEASE NOTE: There will be one catalog that will include all 3 portions of this exhibition. CAT WT
11/15/95 - 1/7/96	POINTS OF ENTRY (EXHIBIT 2) — As above, from the Center for Creative Photography in Tucson, Az., this portion of the exhibition will focus primarily on the works of European artists of the mid-20th century, many of whom escaped from Nazi persecution. CAT WT

SAN FRANCISCO

The Mexican Museum

Affiliate Institution: Fort Mason Bldg. D.
Laguna & Marina Blvd., **San Francisco, CA 94123**
TEL: 415-441-1445
HRS: Noon-5 W-S; Noon-8 first W of month only   DAY CLOSED: M, Tu   HOL: LEG/HOL!
ADM: Y   ADULT: $3.00   CHILDREN: F (under 10)   STUDENTS: $2.00   SR CIT: $2.00
HDC/ACC: Y; Ramp at front of building   PARKING: Y; Plentiful and free   MUS/SH: Y
GR/T: Y   GR/PH: call 415-202-9704   H/B: Y; Fort Mason itself is a former military site in Golden Gate Rec. Area
PERM/COLL: MEX; MEX/AM; FOLK; ETH

With more than 9,000 objects in its collection, the Mexican Museum, founded in 1975, is the first institution of its kind devoted exclusively to the art and culture of Mexico and its people. **NOT TO BE MISSED:** "Family Sunday," a hands-on workshop for children offered the second Sunday of each month (call 415-202-9704 to reserve).

ON EXHIBIT/95:

12/14/94 - 3/12/95	THE ART OF THE SANTERA — An examination of the 20th-century phenomenon of women as santeras (saint-makers) in what was once a male dominated field. The exhibit will focus on 20 santeras and examine the differences in their works from those made by men.

CALIFORNIA

The Mexican Museum - continued

3/29 - 6/18/95   XICANO PROGENY: INVESTIGATIVE AGENTS, EXECUTIVE COUNCIL, AND OTHER REPRESENTATIVES FROM THE SOVEREIGN STATE OF AZTLAN — Installation pieces that use "techno" mediums to deal with the theme of "Chicanismo".
         CAT

6/28 - 11/27/95   SACRED GIFTS: PRECOLUMBIAN ART AND CREATIVITY — On exhibit will be examples of terracotta, stone, shells, featherwork and pure metal objects from the historic cultures of Mesoamerica and South America that serve to define the pre-columbian peoples' belief in the interrelationship between nature and art.   CAT   WT

12/6/95 - 3/10/96   FROM THE WEST: CHICANO NARRATIVE PHOTOGRAPHERS — Constructions of "The West" by Chicano photographers that reveal the effects of cultural notions of America, Mexico, and Mexican-Americans.   CAT   WT

SAN FRANCISCO

Museo Italoamericano
Ft. Mason Center, Bldg. C, **San Francisco, CA 94123**
TEL: 415-673-2200
HRS: Noon-5 W-S; open till 8pm 1st W of the month   DAY CLOSED: M, Tu   HOL: LEG/HOL!
F/DAY: 1st W   ADM: Y   ADULT: $2.00   CHILDREN: F   STUDENTS: $1.00   SR CIT: $1.00
HDC/ACC: Y   PARKING: Y; Ample free parking   MUS/SH: Y   GR/T: Y   GR/PH: call 415-673-2200
PERM/COLL: IT & IT/AM: ptgs, sculp, phot 20

This unique museum, featuring the art of many contemporary Italian and Italian-American artists was established in 1978 to promote public awareness and appreciation of Italian art and culture. Included in the collection are such modern masters as Francesco Clemente. Sandro Chia, and Luigi Lucioni, to name but a few. **NOT TO BE MISSED:** "Tavola della Memoria", a cast bronze sculpture from 1961 by Arnaldo Pomodoro; Mark Di Suvero's steel sculpture "Wittgenstein's Ladder", 1977.

San Francisco Art Institute Galleries
800 Chestnut St, **San Francisco, CA 94113**
TEL: 415-771-7020
HRS: 10-5 Tu-Sa; Till 8 T; Noon-5 S   DAY CLOSED: S, M   HOL: LEG/HOL!
ADM: F   HDC/ACC: Y   PARKING: Y; Street parking only

Founded in 1871, the Art Institute is the oldest cultural institution on the West Coast and one of San Francisco's designated historical landmarks. The main building is a handsome Spanish colonial style building designed in 1926 by architect Arthur Brown. Featured in the Walter/Bean Gallery are exhibitions by artists from the Bay Area and across the nation. **NOT TO BE MISSED:** Mural by Diego Rivera.

ON EXHIBIT/95:

1/30 - 2/4/95   ANNUAL AUCTION PREVIEW — Works in all media by more than 100 artists.

2/16 - 3/19/95   JOYCE J. SCOTT: IMAGES CONCEALED — An installation by Baltimore-based African-American artist, Scott.

3/30 - 4/30/95   1995 ADELINE KENT AWARD EXHIBITION — For the 35th time, a display of work by a talented and promising California artist chosen for this award.

6/1 - 7/2/95   KOSEN OHTSUBO — An installation by this Tokyo-based artist will be on view.

11/13/95 - 1/13/96   114TH ANNUAL EXHIBITION

SAN FRANCISCO

San Francisco Craft & Folk Art Museum
Landmark Building A, Fort Mason, **San Francisco, CA 94123-1382**
TEL: 415-775-0990
HRS: 11-5 Tu-F & S; 10-5 Sa; open till 8pm 1st W of the month   DAY CLOSED: M   HOL: 1/1, THGV, 12/25
F/DAY: 1st W   ADM: Y   ADULT: $1.00   CHILDREN: $0.50 (12-17)   SR CIT: $0.50
HDC/ACC: Y; Limited to first floor only   PARKING: Y; Ample and free   MUS/SH: Y
REST/FAC: Y; Right next door to famous Zen vegetarian restaurant, Greens
H/B: Y; Building served as disembarkation center during WW II & Viet Nam
PERM/COLL: No permanent collection

6 to 10 witty and elegant exhibitions of American and international contemporary craft and folk art are presented annually in this museum, part of a fascinating, cultural waterfront center in San Francisco.

ON EXHIBIT/95:

1/7 - 3/12/95	CONTEMPORARY ART OF BOTSWANA
	EDITH HEATH (pottery)
3/18 - 5/28/95	THREE GUATEMALAN FOLK ART PAINTERS — This exhibition will include actual samples of the costumes shown in the paintings.
3/18 - 5/28/95	WHAT BACCUS DRINKS FROM — An invitational exhibition of wine goblets by contemporary artists working in mixed media.
6/3 - 8/6/95	FOLK ART AND LABOR
	OTTO AND VIVIKA HEINO: MASTER POTTERS
8/12 - 10/22/95	ART OF THE PHILIPPINES
10/28 - 12/31/95	EARTH, WOOD AND AIR — Works by contemporary artists Margaret Ford, Ronna Neuenschwander, Bob Brady and Terry Terell
10/28 - 12/31/95	PENITENTI FIGURES OF NEW MEXICO

San Francisco Museum of Modern Art
151 Third St., **San Francisco, CA 94103**
TEL: 415-357-4000
HRS: 11-6 Tu-S, till 9 T   DAY CLOSED: M   HOL: 1/1, 7/4, THGV, 12/25
ADM: Y   ADULT: $7.00   CHILDREN: F (under 13)   STUDENTS: $3.50   SR CIT: $3.50
HDC/ACC: Y; Totally wheelchair accessible   PARKING: Y; Pay garages at Fifth & Mission, the Moscone Center Garage (255 Third St.), and the Hearst Garage at 45 Third St.   MUS/SH: Y
REST/FAC: Y; Cafe that opens onto breathtaking 5-story museum atrium   GR/T: Y   GR/PH: call 415-357-4191
DT: Y   TIME: daily (call 415-357-4096) or inquire in lobby
PERM/COLL: AM: ab/exp ptgs; GER: exp; MEX; REG; PHOT; FAUVIST: ptgs; S.F. BAY AREA ART; VIDEO ARTS

A trip to San Francisco, if only to visit the new (opening Jan. 18, 1995) home of this 60-year-old museum, would be worthwhile for any art lover. Housed in a light filled architecturally brilliant and innovative building designed by Mario Botta, the museum features the most comprehensive collection of 20th century art on the West Coast. It is interesting to note that not only is this structure the largest new American art museum to be built in this decade, it is also the second largest single facility in the U.S. devoted to modern art.

57

CALIFORNIA

San Francisco Museum of Modern Art - continued

PLEASE NOTE THE FOLLOWING: 1. Admission is half price from 5-9 on Thursday evenings; 2. Spotlight tours are conducted every Thursday and live jazz in the galleries is provided on the 3rd Thursday of each month; 3. Special group tours called "Modern Art Adventures" can be arranged (415-357-4191) for visits to Bay Area private collections, artists' studios, and a variety of museums and galleries in the area. **NOT TO BE MISSED:** "Woman in a Hat" by Matisse, one of 30 superb early 20th c. works from the recently donated Elise Hass Collection.

ON EXHIBIT/95:

1/18 - 4/30/95	PUBLIC INFORMATION: DESIRE, DISASTER, DOCUMENT (working title) — In this exhibition, works by 3 generations of artists will document the influence photography has had on the development of contemporary art over the past 30 years. The continuum between photography, painting, sculpture, film, video and slide installations will be highlighted with appropriate works presented from each discipline. CAT
1/18 - 4/2/95	WILLIAM KLEIN'S NEW YORK — In the first comprehensive presentation of his work, 150 of Klein's photographs will reveal his bold and direct approach to his subject matter often utilized as a statement against conventional technique.
1/18 - 6/25/95	MARIO BOTTA: THE DESIGN OF THE SAN FRANCISCO MUSEUM OF MODERN ART (working title) — 60 works that include drawings, sketches and models demonstrate Swiss architect Botta's plans for the artistic evolution and development of the new building he designed for the S. F. MOMA.
1/18 - ONGOING	FROM MATISSE TO DIEBENKORN: WORKS FROM THE PERMANENT COLLECTION — Many of the very best works from the museum's permanent collection will be shown in the vastly expanded gallery space of the new museum building. Included in this exhibition will be prime examples of European & American Modernism, Surrealism, Abstract Expressionism, and California Art. In addition to highlighting individual artists such as Matisse, Klee, Still and Guston, the exhibition will also feature a room-sized light installation by James Turrell.
1/18 - 6/18/95	INTO A NEW MUSEUM: RECENT GIFTS/RECENT ACQUISITIONS OF CONTEMPORARY ART, PART 1 — In honor of the new building and the 60th anniversary of the museum this exhibition will feature important works acquired as gifts or recent acquisitions. Part II of this exhibition will be presented beginning in the summer of '95 in the 4th floor galleries.
1/18 - 6/25/95	PAUL KLEE: HIGHLIGHTS OF THE DJERASSI COLLECTION (working title) — Focusing on paintings, watercolors and some drawings, this exhibition will present over 20 works on extended loan to the museum from the Carl Djerassi Collection.
6/1 - 8/27/95	JAPANESE ART AFTER 1945: SCREAM AGAINST THE SKY (TENT! dates) — In the largest survey of postwar Japanese art ever mounted, 200 works by 70 artists will be on view. WT
REST OF 1995	PERMANENT COLLECTION EXHIBITS

SAN JOSE

Rosicrucian Egyptian Museum and Art Gallery
Rosicrucian Park, **San Jose, CA 95191**
TEL: 408-947-3636
HRS: 9-5 Daily   HOL: 1/1, THGV, 12/25
ADM: Y   ADULT: $6.00   CHILDREN: $3.50 (7-15)   STUDENTS: $4.00   SR CIT: $4.00
PARKING: Y; Free lot at corner of Naglee and Chapman plus street parking   MUS/SH: Y
GR/T: Y   GR/PH: 408-287-2807   DT: Y   TIME: rock tomb only periodically during day
PERM/COLL: ANT: ptgs, sculp, gr; CONT: emerging Bay Area artists

Without question the largest Egyptian collection in the West, the Rosicrucian is a treasure house full of thousands of objects and artifacts from ancient Egypt. Even the building itself is styled after Egyptian temples and, once inside, the visitor can experience the rare opportunity of actually walking through a reproduction of the rock tombs cut into the cliffs at Beni Hasan 4,000 years ago. **NOT TO BE MISSED:** A tour through the rock tomb, a reproduction of the ones cut into the cliffs at Beni Hasan 4,000 years ago; Egyptian gilded ibis statue in Gallery B.

San Jose Museum of Art
110 S. Market St., **San Jose, CA 95113**
TEL: 408-294-2787
HRS: 10-5 Tu-Sa; 10am-8pm T;   DAY CLOSED: M   HOL: LEG/HOL!
F/DAY: 1st T   ADM: Y   ADULT: $5.00   CHILDREN: $3.00 (6-17)   STUDENTS: $3.00   SR CIT: $3.00
HDC/ACC: Y; Building and restrooms are wheelchair accessible
PARKING: Y; Paid public parking is available in several locations within 3 blocks of the museum.   MUS/SH: Y
REST/FAC: Y; "The Artful Cup" open during museum hours   GR/T: Y   GR/PH: call 408-294-2787
DT: Y   TIME: most afternoons!; T pm; 12:30 & 2:30 weekends   H/B: Y; 1892 Richardsonian Romanesque   S/G: Y
PERM/COLL: AM: 19-20; NAT/AM; CONT

Contemporary art is the main focus of this vital and rapidly expanding museum. Originally housed in a landmark building that once served as post office/library, the museum added 45,000 square feet of exhibition space in 1991 to accommodate the needs of the cultural renaissance now underway in San Jose. In 1994, the Whitney Museum of American Art in New York agreed to send the San Jose Museum of Art four large exhibitions drawn from the Whitney's permanent collection. Each exhibition will be installed for a period of 18 months. **NOT TO BE MISSED:** Children's Discovery Museum

ON EXHIBIT/95:

4/94 - 10/29/95   AMERICAN ART 1900-1940: A HISTORY RECONSIDERED. SELECTIONS FROM THE WHITNEY MUSEUM OF AMERICAN ART — More than 100 choice works by 70 notable artists including Edward Hopper, Georgia O'Keeffe, Thomas Hart Benton, and others will be on loan from the permanent collection of the Whitney Museum in New York City. This exhibition which offers an overview of the development of American art between the turn of the century and World War II, is the first of 4 planned exhibitions that are the result of a unique collaboration between the San Jose & the Whitney Museums. ATR (call 408-998-BASS). PLEASE NOTE: Some same-day tickets will also be available at the door.

2/4 - 4/23/95   ANDY GOLDSWORTHY — A series of installations by this British sculptor based on the theory of the physical properties of the natural world will be accompanied by photographs of his work process. Particular emphasis will be on works inspired by the natural resources of California.

CALIFORNIA

San Jose Museum of Art - continued

5/13 - 7/30/95	CHRISTOPHER BROWN — Recent paintings based on the Civil War and other works employing the use of historical subjects will be included in this exhibition of nearly 30 works by Chris Brown, a well-known Bay Area artist. **WT**
8/5 - 9/17 95	RECENT ACQUISITIONS TO THE PERMANENT COLLECTION
10/95 - 1/96	DALE CHILULY: INSTALLATIONS, 1964-1994 — A 30 year survey of marvelous and fantastic glass creations by this modern master of the medium. **WT**

SAN MARINO

Huntington Library, Art Collections and Botanical Gardens
1151 Oxford Rd., **San Marino, CA 91108**
TEL: 818-405-2141
HRS: 1-4:30 Tu-F; 10:30-4:30 Sa, S   DAY CLOSED: M   HOL: LEG/HOL!
SUGG/CONT: Y   ADULT: $7.50   CHILDREN: F (under 12)   STUDENTS: $4.00   SR CIT: $6.00
HDC/ACC: Y   PARKING: Y; On grounds behind Pavillion   MUS/SH: Y
REST/FAC: Y; 1-4 Tu-F; 11:30-4:00 Sa, S; ENG.TEA 1-3:45 Tu-F; Noon-3:34 Sa, S
GR/T: Y   GR/PH: call 818-405-2140   DT: Y   TIME: introductory slide show given during day
H/B: Y; 1910 estate of railroad magnate, Henry E. Huntington   S/G: Y
PERM/COLL: BRIT: ptgs, drgs, sculp, cer 18-19; EU: ptgs, drgs, sculp, cer 18; FR: ptgs, dec/art, sculp 18; REN: ptgs; AM: ptgs, sculp, dec/art 18-20

The multi-faceted Huntington Library, Art Collection & Botanical Gardens makes a special stop at this complex a must. Known for containing the most comprehensive collections of British 18th & 19th century art outside of London, the museum also houses an outstanding American collection and a library that is one of the greatest research libraries in the world. **NOT TO BE MISSED:** "Blue Boy" by Gainsborough; "Pinkie" by Lawrence; Gutenberg Bible; 12 acre desert garden; Japanese garden.

ON EXHIBIT/95:

9/27/94 - 1/15/95	WILLIAM BLAKE'S ILLUMINATED PRINTS — The largest selection of English poet and artist William Blake's illuminated books ever shown in the U.S. will kick off the year-long celebration of the Huntington's 75th anniversary. In addittion to an interactive video that allows visitors to access all of Blake's prints, drawings, and paintings in the Huntington's collection, the exhibit will feature the only known copy of his first illuminated book.
12/13/94 - 2/26/95	STRIKING IMPRESSIONS: CHILDE HASSAM AS PRINTMAKER — 50 etchings, lithographs and printed books by Hassam, who started his career as a graphic artist and illustrator will allow the viewer to assess how his exploration of the impact of light at different times of the day was central to the development of the American Impressionist aesthetic.
2/95 - 5/95	BRITISH MEZZOTINTS
3/95 - 5/95	TIFFANY EXHIBITION
6/95 - 8/95	"THE HUNTINGTON COLLECTS"
FALL 95	HOGARTH
12/95	CHILDE HASSAM

60

CALIFORNIA

SAN SIMEON

Hearst San Simeon State Historical Monument
750 Hearst Castle Rd., **San Simeon, CA 93452-9741**
TEL: 805-927-2020
HRS: 8:20-3:20 (tours only; to reserve call toll free 1-800-444-4445)   HOL: 1/1, THGV, 12/25
ADM: Y   ADULT: $14.00   CHILDREN: $8.00 (6-12)   HDC/ACC: Y; Limited   PARKING: Y; Free and plentiful
for cars, buses, & RV'S   MUS/SH: Y   GR/T: Y   GR/PH: evening also 805-927-2020   H/B: Y
PERM/COLL: IT/REN: sculp, ptgs; MED: sculp, ptgs; DU; FL; SP; AN/GRK: sculp; AN/R: sculp; AN/EGT: sculp

One of the prize attractions in the state of California is San Simeon, the enormous (165 rooms) and elaborate former home of William Randolph Hearst. The sculptures and paintings displayed throughout the mansion are a mixture of religious and secular art and antiquities attesting to the keen eye Mr. Hearst had for collecting. PLEASE NOTE: a 10% discount for groups of 12 or more has recently been implemented. Evening tours are available for a fee of $25 adults and $13 for children ages 6-12. **NOT TO BE MISSED:** Paintings and sculptures by Gerome, Canova, & Thorvaldson; a collection of 155 Greek vases.

SANTA ANA

The Bowers Museum of Cultural Art
2002 N. Main St., **Santa Ana, CA 92706**
TEL: 714-567-3600
HRS: 10-4 Tu-S; till 9pm T   DAY CLOSED: M   HOL: 1/1, 12/25
ADM: Y   ADULT: $4.50   CHILDREN: $1.50 (5-12)   STUDENTS: $3.00   SR CIT: $3.00
HDC/ACC: Y; Wheelchair accessible   PARKING: Y; Free parking lot on the S.W. corner of Main & 20th.
MUS/SH: Y   REST/FAC: Y; 11:30-3 Tu & W; 11:30-3 & 4:30-8 T & F; 11:30-4:30 Sa; 10-4:30 S
GR/T: Y   GR/PH: call 714-567-3680   DT: Y   TIME: 1 & 2 daily
PERM/COLL: PACIFIC RIM 19-20; P/COL: cer; AM; dec/art 19-20; AF; N/AM: eth; S/AM: eth

Dedicated to the display & interpretation of the fine art of the indigenous peoples of the Americas, the Pacific Rim, & Africa, the Bowers, with its multi-faceted collection, is the largest museum in Orange County. The museum, housed in a recently restored Spanish mission-style building (1932), has also added a number of large exhibit halls for changing exhibits. **NOT TO BE MISSED:** "Seated Priest" from Oaxaca, Mexico (Classic Period); "Seated Shaman" from Colima, Mexico (200 BC-200 AD).

ON EXHIBIT/95:
1/22 - 4/2/95	BETWEEN EMPIRES: THE ARTISTIC LEGACY OF PREHISPANIC PANAMA — From private and public collections, the largest exhibition ever assembled of Prehistoric Panama's little known but powerful artistic traditions will be seen in unique abstract and representational paintings on ceramic forms.
1/22 - 4/2/95	RIVER OF GOLD: PRE-COLUMBIAN TREASURES FROM SITIO CONTE — Splendid Pre-Columbian goldworks (circa 700-1100 A.D.) excavated during a University of Pennsylvania expedition to Panama in 1940, will be featured along with an abundance of information about the culture that produced them. CAT WT
4/30 - 9/17/95	CALIFORNIA NATIVE ART —A display of 150 California Indian art objects from Eureka to San Diego will include examples of basketry, sand paintings, feathered costumes, headdresses, stone carvings, jewelry, and music.
7/2 - 9/24/95	CHINESE SNUFF BOTTLES FROM THE PAMELA R. LESSING FRIEDMAN COLLECTION — Snuff bottles in a vast array of materials, designs and symbolism will be selected for viewing from one of the foremost collections in the country. CAT
10/29/95 - 2/2/96	SWORD OF HEAVEN — Japanese Samuri swords and scabbards magnificently hand-crafted before the advent of the gun will be featured in this exhibition designed to also explain the origins, art and philosophy behind their manufacture.

61

CALIFORNIA

SANTA BARBARA

Santa Barbara Museum of Art
1130 State St., **Santa Barbara, CA 93101-2746**
TEL: 805-963-4364
HRS: 11-5 Tu-W & F-Sa; 11-9 T; Noon-5 S   DAY CLOSED: M   HOL: 1/1, THGV, 12/25
F/DAY: T&1stS   ADM: Y   ADULT: $4.00   CHILDREN: F (under 6)   STUDENTS: $2.50   SR CIT: $3.00
HDC/ACC: Y; Outside ramp; elevator to all levels   PARKING: Y; 2 city parking lots each one block away from the
museum MUS/SH: Y   GR/T: Y   GR/PH: call 805-963-4364 ext. 334   DT: Y   TIME: 1:00 Tu-S; Noon W & Sa
PERM/COLL: AN/GRK; AN/R; AN/EGP; AS; EU: ptgs 19; CONT; PHOT

With 15,000 works of art, a considerable number for a community of its size, the Santa Barbara
Musum offers a variety of collections that range from antiquities of past centuries to the contemporary
creations of today. **NOT TO BE MISSED:** Fine collection of representative works of American Art

ON EXHIBIT/95:

10/22/94 - 3/12/95	THE ART WE LIVE WITH: AMERICAN DECORATIVE ARTS — 18th century folk objects and furniture will be joined by such heirlooms as a tea service, hooked rugs, dolls and paintings that serve to recreate the everyday life of the times.
11/5/94 - 3/12/95	SACRED GIFTS: PRE-COLUMBIAN ART & CREATIVITY — 120 extraordinary objects made of clay, stone, gold, wood, shell and plant fibers, all materials that the Pre-Columbian peoples considered sacred will be presented in this exhibit. Highlighted will be several items on public view for the first time including a rare Mixtec scull inlaid with turquoise mosaic and gold-copper alloy, a miniature clay figurine of a Maya warrior (A.D. 550-800), a bronze mask with shell-inlaid eyes, and a large ceramic vessel containing a vulture and trophy head from ancient Costa Rica. CAT WT
1/19/94 - 2/19/95	DALE CHIHULY: INSTALLATIONS 1964-1992 — Among the many free form glass sculptures by this internationally renowned modern-day glass artist will be large-scale installation works that serve to illustrate how Chihuly pushes the limits of the medium in which he works.
12/3/94 - 1/29/95	MASTERING THE MEDIUM, PART I — In this exhibition the viewer will be able to compare and contrast 80 works, many of which have never been shown before, that serve as an overview of 400 years of the etching medium. Works by such artists as Rembrandt and Goya, to Whistler, Picasso and John Cage will all be represented in this exhibit. BROCHURE
2/18 - 5/14/95	OLD MASTER DRAWINGS — On view will be 60 European works from the permanent collection that range chronologically from a 16th century work by Flemish artist Dirk Vellaert to Christo's proposal of 1980 for his Pont Neuf Project in Paris.
3/11 - 5/21/95	LATIN AMERICAN ART: PHOTOGRAPHS — Drawn from the permanent collection and from the Marjorie & Leonard Vernon Collection will be prime images by Latin American master photographers including works by Manuel Alvarez Bravo, Luis Gonzlaez Palma, Sebattiao Salgado and others.
4/8/95	REINSTALLATION OF THE AMERICAN COLLECTION — This reinstallation will allow for the showcasing of the most important examples of American art in the permanent collection of the Museum.
6/10 - 8/13/95	FROM THE OCEAN OF PAINTING: INDIA'S POPULAR PAINTING TRADITION — In the first major exhibition of its kind in the U.S., 100 folk, tribal and popular paintings of India, ranging in date from 1589 to today will be on loan from American and European private and public collections. CAT WT

Santa Barbara Museum of Art - continued

5/20 - 8/27/95	PAINTED PRAYERS: THE RITUAL ART OF INDIAN WOMEN – PHOTOGRAPHS BY STEPHEN HUYLER — 35 photographs by Huyler that document the tradition passed down from mothers to daughters in India of painting the surfaces of their homes in order to encourage good luck and ward off danger and evil will be featured in this exhibition.
9/2 - 11/5/95	ANNE BRIGHAM: POET, PAGAN, PHOTOGRAPHER — 60 photographs that survey the past 20 years of pictorialist Brigham's work will be featured in this solo exhibition. CAT WT
10/21/95	MASTERING THE MEDIUM, PART II: REINSTALLATION OF THE ASIAN COL-LECTION — Prints and etchings from the Museum's important permanent collection.
10/21/95	REINSTALLATION OF THE ASIAN COLLECTION — On view will be artworks from the Museum's impressive 2,500 piece collection of Asian art which spans a period of 2,000 years and includes the cultures of China, India, Japan, Korea, Tibet and Southeast Asia. Religious sculptures, Chinese ceramics, paintings, Japanese woodblock prints, textiles and decorative arts will be featured.

SANTA BARBARA

University Art Museum, Santa Barbara

Affiliate Institution: University of California
Santa Barbara, CA 93106
TEL: 805-893-2951
HRS: 10-4 Tu-Sa; 1-5 S & HOL   DAY CLOSED: M   HOL: 1/1, 7/4, EASTER, THGV, 12/25
ADM: F   HDC/ACC: Y; wheelchair accessible   MUS/SH: Y   GR/T: Y   GR/PH: call 805-893-2951
DT: Y   TIME: 2:00 Sa & 12:15 alternate Tu
PERM/COLL: IT: ptgs; GER: ptgs; FL: ptgs; DU: ptgs; P/COL; ARCH/DRGS; GR; OM: ptgs; AF; ARCH; DRGS

Outstanding among the many thousands of treasures in the permanent collection is one of the world's finest groups of early Renaissance medals and plaquettes. **NOT TO BE MISSED:** 15th through 17th century paintings from the Sedgwick Collection; Architectural drawing collection; Morgenroth Collection of Renaissance medals and plaquettes.

ON EXHIBIT/95:

1/11 - 2/26/95	RENEE STOUT: DEAR ROBERT, I'LL SEE YOU AT THE CROSSROADS — With a focus on the history and mystery of Mississippi blues musician Robert Johnson (1911-1938), African-American artist Stout creates an installation that explores the intersection of African roots and new world culture.
1/11 - 2/26/95	REPRESENTING AMERICA: THE TREVEY COLLECTION OF REALIST PRINTS — Important printworks by 3 generations of major Amaerican artists will be on loan from this collection.
1/11 - 2/26/95	GLENN LIGON: THE NARRATIVES — A suite of etchings newly acquired by the museum reinterprets many published slave narratives of the 19th century for the contemporary audience.
3/15 - 4/23/95	CERAMIC GESTURES: NEW WORK BY MAGDALENE ODUNDO — Extraordinary fired and burnished hand-crafted contemporary clay vessels by Kenyan-born artist Odundo, that reflect elements of her African heritage and the influence of Native American pottery will be seen in this exhibition.
3/15 - 4/23/95	SOPHIE CALLE — Concepts of personal identity will be explored in this retrospective exhibition of French conceptual artist Calle.
SPRING/95	STUDENT EXHIBITIONS

CALIFORNIA

SANTA CLARA

DeSaisset Museum
Affiliate Institution: Santa Clara University
Santa Clara, CA 95053
TEL: 408-554-4528
HRS: 11-4 Tu-S   DAY CLOSED: M   HOL: LEG/HOL!
ADM: F   HDC/ACC: Y; Wheelchair lift (no access ramp or elevator)
PARKING: Y; Free in front of museum with free parking permit at front gate   GR/T: Y   GR/PH: call 408-554-4528
H/B: Y; Adjacent to Mission Santa Clara
PERM/COLL: AM: ptgs, sculp, gr EU; ptgs, sculp, gr 16-20 AS; dec/art; AF; CONT: gr, phot, IT/REN: gr

Serving Santa Clara University and the surrounding community, the de Saisset, since its inception in 1955, has become an important Bay Area cultural resource. **NOT TO BE MISSED:** The largest public collection of works by early 20th century artist, Henrietta Shore

ON EXHIBIT/95:

THROUGH 1996	FROM CLASSICAL GREECE TO THE EARLY TWENTIETH CENTURY: SELECTIONS FROM THE STANFORD UNIVERSITY MUSEUM OF ART AND THE DeSAISSET MUSEUM — A survey of 2500 years of Western art history.
1/14 - 3/10/95	CHESTER ARNOLD: PAINTINGS (working title)
4/6 - 4/9/95	ART AND FLOWERS
5/6 - 8/15/95	FROM THE COLLECTION OF HELEN HOYNSTON: WORKS FROM THE PERMANENT COLLECTION (working title)
5/6 - 8/15/95	HENRIETTA SHORE: WORKS FROM THE PERMANENT COLLECTION (working title)
THROUGH 1995	CALIFORNIA HISTORY COLLECTION — Historical and ethnographic artifacts from pre-contact Native America to the founding of Mission Santa Clara by the Franciscans in 1777.
THROUGH 3/95	SELECTIONS FROM THE PERMANENT COLLECTION

Triton Museum of Art
1505 Warburton Ave., **Santa Clara, CA 95050**
TEL: 408-247-3754
HRS: 10-5 W-F; Till 9pm Tu; Noon-5 Sa-S   DAY CLOSED: HOL: LEG/HOL!
VOL/CONT: Y   ADM: F
HDC/ACC: Y; Fully Accessible   PARKING: Y; Free parking adjacent to the museum   MUS/SH: Y
GR/T: Y   GR/PH: call 408-247-3754   S/G: Y
PERM/COLL: AM: 19-20; REG; NAT/AM; CONT/GR

Located in a seven acre park adjacent to the City of Santa Clara, the Triton has grown by leaps and bounds to keep up with the cultural needs of its rapidly expanding "Silicon Valley" community. The museum is housed in a visually stunning building that opened its doors to the public in 1987. **NOT TO BE MISSED:** Paintings by American Impressionist Theodore Wores; "Native Americans: Yesterday & Today" (on permanent display)

ON EXHIBIT/95:

1/95 - 2/95	LA BELLE EPOQUE: THE ELIZABETH DEAN COLLECTION — Works by Henri de Toulouse-Lautrec and his contemporaries including Bonnard, Manet, Mucha, Tissot and others will be on exhibit.

64

CALIFORNIA

Triton Museum of Art - continued

1/95 - 2/95	PAINTINGS & DRAWINGS BY ALBERT SMITH
3/95 - 4/95	2ND BIENNIAL DRAWING AND PRINTMAKING COMPETITION AND EXHIBITION
3/4 - 4/95	SELECTIONS FROM THE PERMANENT COLLECTION
4/95 - 5/95	NEW WORKS BY CALIFORNIA ARTISTS: LUCY GAYLORD
5/95 - 6/95	LOS TRES: DIEGO RIVERA, JOSE CLEMENTE OROZCO, & DAVID ALFARO SIQUEIROS
7/95 - 8/95	GEORGIA O'KEEFFE

SANTA CRUZ

The Art Museum of Santa Cruz County
702 Front St., **Santa Cruz, CA 95060**
TEL: 408-429-1964
HRS: 11-4 Tu-S; Till 8 T   DAY CLOSED: M   HOL: LEG/HOL!
F/DAY: 1st T mo   ADM: Y   ADULT: $2.50   CHILDREN: F (under 12)   STUDENTS: $2.00   SR CIT: $2.00
HDC/ACC: Y   PARKING: No on site parking. Some garages nearby.   MUS/SH: Y
REST/FAC: Y; indoor courtyard/cafe   GR/T: Y   GR/PH: call 408-429-1964   DT: Y   TIME: Noon
PERM/COLL: CONT

The Art Museum of Santa Cruz County, located at the McPherson Center for Art and History, presents exhibitions from the permanent collection which emphasizes contemporary works, changing exhibitions of internationally renowned artists, and group exhibitions that demonstrate various art techniques, mediums, crafts and historic periods.

ON EXHIBIT/95:

12/17/94 - 2/13/95	MYTH AND MAGIC — A presentation of the works of 15 artists from the Tamayo Institute in Oxaca, Mexico.
2/25 - 4/16/95	EVERY PICTURE TELLS A STORY — Children's author/illustrator, Steven Kellog
2/11 - 3/26/95	THE BEAUTIFUL OBJECT — Jewelry of Lynda Watson Abbott
4/15 - 5/29/95	DRESSING THE TEXT — Books from small presses
5/95	MARGARET RINKOVSKY — Debut exhibition
7/95	PLEIN AIR — Early California painters from the Irvine Collection
10/95	JAZZ — Kuumbwa 20 year Anniversary Exhibition
10/95	WARHOL: ENDANGERED SPECIES — Warhol prints

65

CALIFORNIA

SANTA MONICA

Santa Monica Museum of Art
2437 Main St., **Santa Monica, CA 90405**
TEL: 310-399-0433
HRS: 11-6 W, T, S; 11-10 F, Sa   DAY CLOSED: M, Tu   HOL: 1/1, 7/4, THGV, 12/25
SUGG/CONT: Y   ADULT: $4.00   CHILDREN: $1.00 (under 12)   STUDENTS: $2.00   SR CIT: $2.00
HDC/ACC: Y; Wheelchair accessible   PARKING: Y; Validated parking at Edgemar or across the street at the Santa Monica City Lot #11; on-site parking for the disabled   MUS/SH: Y   GR/T: Y   GR/PH: call 310-399-0433
H/B: Y; Located in former Ice House
PERM/COLL: NO PERMANENT COLLECTION

Located in the former 1908 Imperial Ice Company building, this museum with its 25 foot ceilings provides ideal space for large scale works of art. Devoted to the display of art by living artists, it is the only contemporary art museum in the area.

ON EXHIBIT/95:

11/18/94 - 1/15/95	DONALD KRIEGER: BLACK MARIA — An multi-media installation that explores the implications and consequences of Thomas Edison's invention of the phonograph and the first motion picture studio known as the Black Maria.
11/18/94 - 1/15/95	THE LAYERED LOOK: TOWARDS AN AESTHETIC OF ACCUMULATION AMONG SIX LOS ANGELES ARTISTS — The Layered Look is an exhibition that is a hybrid assemblage and installation created by 6 artists who use objects or materials to create a greater affect.
1/26 - 3/19/95	MARGARET NIELSEN: A 25 YEAR RETROSPECTIVE — In the first comprehensive retrospective exhibition to be mounted for this little understood Los Angeles-based artist, examples from 4 distinct periods in her career that chart both her personal and appropriated iconography will be presented. CAT
1/26 - 5/25/95	1995 ARTIST PROJECTS SERIES — 3 commissioned site-specific works by Los Angeles area artists.
DATES TBA	PARALLEL DIALOGUE/ PARALLEL TENSIONS — Works by artists from Mexico, Ireland and the U.S. will address the ever-shifting notion of national identity.

SANTA ROSA

Sonoma County Museum
425 Seventh Ave., **Santa Rosa, CA 95401**
TEL: 707-579-1500
HRS: 11-4 W-S   DAY CLOSED: M, Tu   HOL: LEG/HOL!
ADM: Y   ADULT: $2.00   CHILDREN: F (UNDER 12)   STUDENTS: $1.00   SR CIT: $1.00
HDC/ACC: Y; Wheelchair accessible   PARKING: Y; Free parking in Museum's east lot or in adjacent parking garage.   MUS/SH: Y   GR/T: Y   GR/PH: call 707-579-1500   H/B: Y; 1910 Federal Post Office
PERM/COLL: AM: ptgs 19 ; REG

The museum is housed in a 1909 Post Office & Federal Building that was restored and moved to its present downtown location. It is one of the few examples of Classical Federal Architecture in Sonoma County. **NOT TO BE MISSED:** Collection of works by 19th century California landscape painters

ON EXHIBIT/95:

11/18/94 - 2/12/95	CHINESE HOLIDAY EXHIBIT

66

Sonoma County Museum - continued

12/16/94 - 2/12/95	WINEMAKERS - DEBO
2/24 - 5/7/95	100 YEARS OF CARTOONS
5/19 - 8/13/95	WORLD WAR II HOMEFRONT — A mixed-media exhibition
5/21 - 7/23/95	NO LAUGHING MATTER
8/18/95	ARTISTRY IN WOOD
	ArTRAILS PREVIEW

STANFORD

Stanford University Museum and Art Gallery
Lomita Dr. & Museum Way, **Stanford, CA 94305**
TEL: 415-723-4177
HRS: 10-5 Tu-F; 1-5 Sa, S   DAY CLOSED: M   HOL: 1/1, 7/4, THGV, 12/25
VOL/CONT: Y   ADM: F
HDC/ACC: Y; Limited to Rodin Sculpture Collection only   PARKING: Y; Metered parking at the Museum
MUS/SH: Y   DT: Y   TIME: 2:00 W, Sa, S (Rodin); 12:15 T!
PERM/COLL: PHOT; PTGS; SCULP (RODIN COLLECTION); DEC/ART; GR; DRGS; OR; CONT/EU

Due to severe earthquake damage the museum will be closed indefinitely. However the Art Gallery is open with a regular schedule of exhibitions. **NOT TO BE MISSED:** Rodin sculpture collection

ON EXHIBIT/95:

1/10 - 3/21/95	SPIRIT OF THE EARTH: MASKS BY DAVID NEEL — The 20 dramatic, colorful and thought-provoking masks on view by Neel, a 3rd generation Kwagiutl carver, comment on such contemporary issues as overpopulation, racism and other social concerns.
1/10 - 4/30/95	NATHAN OLIVEIRA: "THE WINGS" — Recent large paintings accompanied by earlier sketches on the theme of birds in flight will be seen in the works of Oliveira, a Stanford University Art Professor Emeritus.
1/17 - 3/21/95	HISTORY OF THE ARTIST FROM THE 16TH THROUGH THE 19TH CENTURY: PRINTS AND ILLUSTRATED BOOKS FROM THE STANFORD MUSEUM AND UNIVERSITY LIBRARIES — Images of and by artists in this exhibition will include portraits (of Carracci, Titian, David and Gericault), scenes of student artists studying models, painters in their studios, views of exhibitions, and caricatures, to name but a few.
3/28 - 4/30/95	A SCHOLAR COLLECTS: SELECTIONS FROM THE DWIGHT MILLER COLLECTION — Professor Miller's connoisseurship and elevated sense of taste will be seen in European and Californian works selected from his personal collection for this exhibition as a celebration of his 31 year association with Stanford University.
7/1 - 9/3/95	PHOTOGRAPHS FROM THE ALINDER COLLECTION — A survey of the history of photography from prints by 19th century pioneers of the medium to 20th century masters will be selected for viewing from the collection the Alinder Family which has been donating works to the museum annually for the past 15 years.
9/26 - 12/15/95	"OUR ART, OUR VOICES: NATIVE AMERICAN PERSPECTIVES" — In celebration of the 25th anniversary of the founding of the American Indian program at Stanford University, an exhibition of 90 works from the permanent collection (many that have never been seen before) will include examples of northern California basketry, Haida argillites, Northwest Coast carved wooden objects, Southwestern pottery & beadwork, and quillwork from several Plains groups.

CALIFORNIA

STOCKTON

The Haggin Museum
1201 N. Pershing Ave., **Stockton, CA 95203**
TEL: 209-462-1566
HRS: 1:30-5 Tu-S   DAY CLOSED: M   HOL: 1/1, THGV, 12/25
SUGG/CONT: Y   HDC/ACC: Y; Call in advance to arrange for use of elevator, ground level entry
PARKING: Y; Free street parking where available   MUS/SH: Y   GR/T: Y   GR/PH: call 209-462-1566
DT: Y   TIME: 1:45 Sa
PERM/COLL: AM: ptgs 19; FR: ptgs 19; AM: dec/art; EU: dec/art

Wonderful examples of 19th century French and American paintings from the Barbizon, French Salon, Rocky Mountain, and Hudson River Schools are displayed in a setting accented by a charming array of decorative art objects. **NOT TO BE MISSED:** "Lake in Yosemite Valley" by Bierstadt; "Gathering for the Hunt" by Rosa Bonheur

ON EXHIBIT/95:
MID 11/94 - EARLY 1/95

> MAINTAINING CULTURAL DIVERSITY IN A CHANGING WORLD — Images of minority groups struggling to maintain their unique identities within larger populations will be seen in an exhibition of photographs by Maty Altier.

MID 11/94 - 1/29/95   THE ART OF STOCKTON'S HMONG COMMUNITY — Textile art by Hmong women.

7/1 - 10/15/95   ART IN A JUGULAR VEIN: THE ART OF MAD MAGAZINE

7/8 - 9/10/95   INSIDE A LARGE SMALL HOUSE: THE RESIDENTIAL DESIGN LEGACY OF WILLIAM WURSTER (TENT! Dates)

10/1/95 - 1/28/96   THE BRUCE KAMMERLING COLLECTION OF ANTIQUITIES (TENT! Dates)

12/10/95 - 1/21/96   DR. HOWARD HAMMOND: SILVERSMITH

VENTURA

Ventura County Museum of History & Art
100 E. Main St., **Ventura, CA 93001**
TEL: 805-653-0323
HRS: 10-5 Tu-S   DAY CLOSED: M   HOL: 1/1, THGV, 12/25
F/DAY: 2nd Tu   ADM: Y   ADULT: $2.00 CHILDREN: F (under 12)   STUDENTS: $2.00   SR CIT: $2.00
HDC/ACC: Y   PARKING: Y; No charge at adjacent city lot   MUS/SH: Y   GR/T: Y   GR/PH: call 805-653-0323
DT: Y   TIME: 1:30 S; "ask me" docents often on duty
PERM/COLL: PHOT; CONT/REG; REG

Art is but a single aspect of this museum that also features historical exhibitions relating to the history of the region. **NOT TO BE MISSED:** 3-D portraits of figures throughout history by George Stuart. Mr. Stuart has created nearly 200 figures which are rotated for viewing every 4 months. He occasionally lectures on his works (call for information!).

Ventura County Museum of History & Art - continued

ON EXHIBIT/95:

1/14 - 3/5/95	13TH ANNUAL ASSEMBLY OF THE ARTS — A juried exhibition open to artists living in Ventura County.
3/25 - 5/7/95	THE JAPANESE IN VENTURA COUNTY — The history and cultural traditions of this ethnic group in Ventura County from 1900 to the present will be examined in this exhibition.
5/20 - 7/16/95	OTTO & VIVIKA HEINO, CERAMIC ARTISTS — On view will be works by these well-known Ojai artists.
7/30 - 9/22/95	THE HISTORY OF RANCHING ON SANTA ROSA ISLAND
10/6 - 12/31/95	HENRY CHAPMAN FORD: VIEWS OF THE MISSION & SELECTED PAINTINGS — On exhibit will be etchings and paintings by this early California artist including his famous portfolio of views of the Missions.

COLORADO

ASPEN

The Aspen Art Museum
590 N. Mill St., **Aspen, CO 81611**
TEL: 303-925-8050
HRS: 10-6 Tu-Sa; Noon-6 S (summer); Noon-6 Tu-S & till 8pm T (other)   DAY CLOSED: M
HOL: 1/1, THGV, 12/25, OTHER!
F/DAY: T pm   ADM: Y   ADULT: $3.00   CHILDREN: F (under 12)   STUDENTS: $2.00   SR CIT: $2.00
HDC/ACC: Y   PARKING: Y   MUS/SH: Y   GR/T: Y   GR/PH: call 303-925-8050
H/B: Y; The museum is housed in a former hydroelectric plant (c.1855)   S/G: Y
PERM/COLL: SCULP

Located in an area noted for its natural beauty and access to numerous recreational activities, this museum, with its emphasis on art, offers the visitor a chance to explore the cultural side of life in the community. A free reception is offered every Thursday evening from 6-8 pm for refreshments and gallery tours.

ON EXHIBIT/95:

11/17/94 - 1/29/95	FOCUS ON COLORADO: THE FRONT RANGE —Sculpture and paintings by 3 contemporary artists from the Front Range will be on exhibit.
12/8/94 - 4/9/95	JAMES TURRELL — On view will be an installation of intangible light projections that will transform the lower gallery.
2/9 - 4/9/95	PRE-COLUMBIAN TEXTILES
6/95	WILLIAM WEGMAN: PHOTOGRAPHS
	MICHAEL DAVID: FIGURATIVE ENCAUSTIC PAINTINGS

BOULDER

Leanin' Tree Museum of Western Art
6055 Longbow Dr., **Boulder, CO 80301**
TEL: 1-800-777-8716
HRS: 8-4:30 M-F; 10-4 Sa   DAY CLOSED: S   HOL: LEG/HOL!
VOL/CONT: Y   ADM: F   HDC/ACC: Y; Elevator   PARKING: Y; Free   MUS/SH: Y
PERM/COLL: WESTERN: sculp, ptgs, reg; CONT/REG

This unusual museum, just 40 minutes from downtown Denver, is housed in the corporate offices of Leanin'Tree, producers of Western greeting cards. Over 200 original oil paintings and 80 bronze sculptures by members of the Cowboy Artists of America are displayed within its walls. **NOT TO BE MISSED:** One of the largest privately owned collections of Western art in the U.S.

University of Colorado Art Galleries
Affiliate Institution: University of Colorado/Boulder
Campus Box 318, **Boulder, CO 80309**
TEL: 303-492-8300
HRS: 8-5 M-F, 8-8 Tu, Noon-4 Sa; Summer: 8-4:30 M-F   DAY CLOSED: S
HOL: 1/1, 7/4, CHRISTMAS VACATION
VOL/CONT: Y   ADM: F
HDC/ACC: Y   PARKING: Y; Paid parking in Euclid Auto Park directly south of the building
PERM/COLL: PTGS 19-20; GR 19-20; PHOT 20; DRGS 15-20; SCULP 15-20

70

University of Colorado Art Galleries - continued

ON EXHIBIT/95:

1/14 - 3/4/95   COREEN SIMPSON — A one woman photography show by this NewYork-based artist.

1/14 - 3/4/95   IMAGES OF PENANCE, IMAGES OF MERCY: SANTOS AND THE CEREMONIES OF THE AMERICAN SOUTHWEST — On exhibit will be a major collection of santos (religious folk art) featuring images and sculptures from 1860-1910.

COLORADO SPRINGS

Colorado Springs Fine Arts Center

30 W. Dale St., **Colorado Springs, CO 80903**
TEL: 719-593-3567
HRS: 9-5 Tu-F; 10-5 Sa; 1-5 S   DAY CLOSED: M   HOL: LEG/HOL!
F/DAY: Sa 10-12; 5-7 Tu   ADM: Y   ADULT: $3.00   CHILDREN: $1.00 (6-12)
STUDENTS: $1.50   SR CIT: $1.50
HDC/ACC: Y   PARKING: Y; In rear of museum   MUS/SH: Y   REST/FAC: Y; 11:30-3:00 Tu-F (summer only)
GR/T: Y   GR/PH: call 719-475-2444   S/G: Y
PERM/COLL: AM: ptgs, sculp, gr 19-20; REG; NAT/AM: sculp; CONT: sculp

Located in an innovative 1930's building that incorporates Art Deco styling with a Southwestern Indian motif, this multi-faceted museum is a major center for cultural activities in the Pikes Peak region. **NOT TO BE MISSED:** Collection of Charles Russell sculpture and memorabilia; hands-on tactile gallery called "Eyes of the Mind."

ON EXHIBIT/95:

10/1/94 - 1/8/95   THE INFORMING SPIRIT: ART OF THE AMERICAN SOUTHWEST AND WEST COAST CANADA, 1925-1945

12/3/94 - 1/15/95   ART AND THE ANIMAL

1/14 - 2/26/95   TAYLOR MUSEUM BIENNIAL: A JURIED EXHIBITION OF FINE CRAFT

3/4 - 4/23/95   WATERMEDIA VI: PIKES PEAK WATERCOLOR SOCIETY INVITATIONAL

5/6 - 8/95   DE COLORES: MEXICAN FOLK ART FROM THE TAYLOR MUSEUM COLLECTION

6/3 - 8/95   COVERING THE WEST: THE BEST OF SOUTHWEST ART MAGAZINE

SPRING 1995   SUBVERSIVE THREADS: TEXTILES AS TEXT IN GUATAMALA

PERMANENT   THE TALPA CHAPEL

ONGOING: SACRED LAND: INDIAN AND HISPANIC CULTURES OF THE SOUTHWEST

         ART OF THE AMERICAN WEST: CHARLES M. RUSSELL GALLERIES

         EYES OF THE MIND: TACTILE GALLERY

THRU SPRING 1995   NATIVE AMERICAN COLLECTION OPEN STORAGE — Open storage exhibition of Native/American art from the permanent collection

COLORADO

COLORADO SPRINGS

Gallery of Contemporary Art
Affiliate Institution: University of Colorado Springs
Austin Bluffs Pkwy., **Colorado Springs, CO 80933**
TEL: 719-593-3567
HRS: 10-4 M-F, 1-4 Sa   DAY CLOSED: S   HOL: LEG/HOL!
ADM: Y   ADULT: $1.00   CHILDREN: F (under 12)   STUDENTS: $0.50   SR CIT: $0.50
HDC/ACC: Y; Wheelchair accessible   PARKING: Y; Metered pay parking available
GR/T: Y   GR/PH: call 719-593-3567
PERM/COLL: None

This non-collecting university art gallery, one of the most outstanding contemporary art centers in the nation, concentrates on cutting edge exhibitions of contemporary art with approximately 6 exhibitions throughout the year. It is the only gallery in the Colorado Springs (Pikes Peak) region to feature contemporary art.

ON EXHIBIT/95:

12/1/94 - 1/6/95	ART & THE LAW: NINETEENTH ANNUAL EXHIBITION — An annual invitational of contemporary artists who interpret the relationship between law and society.
1/13 - 2/10/95	THE DILEMMA OF CHILDBIRTH: CONTEMPORARY ISSUES — In addition to interpretive dance, performance art, and lectures, contemporary issues concerned with women and childbirth will be addressed in sculpture, computer imagery, photography and video images.
2/24 - 3/31/95	UCCS BIENNIAL ART FACULTY
8 - 10/95	MONGOL RENAISSANCE: BUDDHIST MONKS OF THE HIGH STEPPE — This exhibition presents a unique view of Mongolian Buddhist life.

DENVER

The Denver Art Museum
14th Ave. & Bannock, **Denver, CO 80204**
TEL: 303-640-2295
HRS: 10-5 Tu-Sa; Noon-5 S   DAY CLOSED: M   HOL: LEG/HOL!
F/DAY: Sa   ADM: Y   ADULT: $3.00   CHILDREN: F (under 5)   STUDENTS: $1.50   SR CIT: $1.50
HDC/ACC: Y; Ramp at main entrance   PARKING: Y; Public pay lot located south of the museum on 13th St.; 2 hour metered street parking in front of the museum   MUS/SH: Y   REST/FAC: Y; Lunch served 11-2
GR/T: Y   GR/PH: call 303- 640-2007   DT: Y   TIME: Noon-12:30 F; (optional express lunch available)
H/B: Y; Designed by Gio Ponti in 1893   S/G: Y
PERM/COLL: AM: ptgs, sculp, dec/art 19; IT/REN: ptgs; FR; ptgs 19-20; OR; P/COL; SP; AM: cont; NAT/AM

With over 40,000 works featuring 19th century American art, a fine Asian and Native American collection, and works from the early 20th century Taos group, the Denver Art Museum houses the largest and most comprehensive art collection between Kansas City and Los Angeles. **NOT TO BE MISSED:** The outside structure of the building itself, entirely covered with one million grey Corning glass tiles.

ON EXHIBIT/95:

10/15/94 - 9/3/95	ADORNMENT FOR ETERNITY: STATUS AND RANK IN CHINESE ORNMENTS — From the Mengdiexuan Collection, 124 gold, silver, bronze and jade Chinese items of personal adornment dating from the 6th century B.C. through the 18th century A.D. will be on display. CAT

COLORADO

The Denver Art Museum - continued

10/29/94 - 1/29/95	CHISLED WITH A BRUSH: ITALIAN SCULPTURE 1850-1925 — 32 small-scale sculptures from the Gilgore Collection will be featured in this exhibition of late 19th & early 20th century Italian works. **CAT**
12/3/94 - 2/5/95	AMERICAN IMPRESSIONISM AND REALISM: THE PAINTING OF MODERN LIFE, 1885-1915 — 75 works that thematically concern the city, country and home created by artists of two distinct but related art movements will feature such artists as Mary Cassatt, John Singer Sargent, William Merrit Chase, Childe Hassam, and "Ashcan School" members Robert Henri, John Sloan and others. **CAT WT**
7/15 - 9/9/95	JACOB LAWRENCE: THE MIGRATION SERIES — The shifting population of African-Americans from the rural South to the urban North just before and after World War II may be seen in Lawrence's chronologically arranged narrative series of 60 panels. It is the first time these panels have been exhibited together in over 20 years. **CAT WT**
7/8 - 10/1/95	CIEN ANOS De CREATIVIDAD: LATIN AMERICAN WOMEN ARTISTS — In the first large-scale exhibition of its kind, works by 35 20th-century Latin American women artists emphasize the importance of their artistic contributions. **WT**

DENVER

Museo De Las Americas
861 Santa Fe Drive, **Denver, CO 80204**
TEL: 303-571-4401
HRS: 10-5 Tu-Sa, S!   DAY CLOSED: M   HOL: 1/1, 7/4, THGV, 12/25
ADM: Y   ADULT: $2.50   CHILDREN: F (under 12)   STUDENTS: $1.00   SR CIT: $1.00
HDC/ACC: Y   PARKING: Y; 2 hour non-metered street parking   MUS/SH: Y
GR/T: Y   GR/PH: Call to arrange for certain exhibitions
H/B: Y; Housed in a former J.C. Penny store built in 1924
PERM/COLL: HISPANIC COLONIAL ART; CONT LAT/AM

The Museo de las Americas, opened 7/94, is the first Latino museum in the Rocky Mountain region dedicated to showcasing the art, history, and culture of the people of the Americas from ancient times to the present.

ON EXHIBIT/95:

10 - 12/95	CIEN ANOS De CREATIVIDAD: LATIN AMERICAN WOMEN ARTISTS — In the first large-scale exhibition of its kind, works by 20th century Latin American women artists will emphasize the importance of their artistic contributions. **WT**

Museum of Western Art
1727 Tremont Pl., **Denver, CO 80202**
TEL: 303-296-1880
HRS: 10-4:30 Tu-Sa and by appointment!   DAY CLOSED: S, M   HOL: 1/1, THGV, 12/25
ADM: Y   ADULT: $3.00   CHILDREN: F (under 7)   STUDENTS: $2.00   SR CIT: $2.00
HDC/ACC: Y; Wheelchairs available   PARKING: Y; Commercial parking lots adjacent to museum building
MUS/SH: Y   GR/T: Y   GR/PH: call 303-296-1880   DT: Y   TIME: upon request during summer   H/B: Y
PERM/COLL: AM: Regional Western ptgs & sculp

COLORADO

Museum of Western Art - continued

The history of the building that houses one of the most important collections of Classic Western Art in the world is almost as fascinating as the collection itself. Located in the historic "Navarre" building, this 1880 Victorian structure, originally used as a boarding school, later became infamous as a bordello and gambling hall. Today images of the West from landscape to action to Native American themes are housed within the award-winning renovated galleries of this outstanding gem of a museum. **NOT TO BE MISSED:** "Cows Scull on Red" by Georgia O'Keeffe

ON EXHIBIT/95:
ONGOING   WORKS ON PAPER FROM THE PERMANENT COLLECTION

DENVER

The Turner Museum
773 Downing, **Denver, CO 80218**
TEL: 303-832-0924
HRS: 2-5 M-F; Noon-3 S; also open daily by appt.!   HOL: !
ADM: Y   ADULT: $7.50   STUDENTS: $5.00   SR CIT: $5.00
HDC/ACC: Y   PARKING: Y; Over 40 spaces plus on street parking across from the musuem building.
MUS/SH: Y   REST/FAC: Y!   GR/T: Y! GR/PH: group rates available:303-832-0924   DT: Y
H/B: Y; Former Governor's House   S/G: Y
PERM/COLL: J. M. W. TURNER COLLECTION (including rare original prints); THOMAS MORAN PTGS

The Turner Museum, one of Denver's best kept secrets, intimately acquaints you with every aspect of the works of English artist J. M. W. Turner. Elegant meals arranged by appointment allow one to dine among the more than 2,000 works of art. PLEASE NOTE: It is advisable to call ahead before visiting as the museum is actively looking to move to a larger facility and may do so at any time. **NOT TO BE MISSED:** "Genius Unfolding," two series of proofs

ON EXHIBIT/95:
10/94 - 3/96	ALLEGORIES OF TURNER
THROUGH 6/1/95	TURNER'S SEA
THROUGH 6/1/95	TURNER'S ANGELS — Illustrations to the poems of John Milton
ONGOING	TURNER'S COSMIC OPTIMISM

ENGLEWOOD

The Museum of Outdoor Arts
7600 E. Orchard Rd. #160 N., **Englewood, CO 80111**
TEL: 303-741-3609
HRS: Open daily during daylight hours year-round   HOL: LEG/HOL!
ADM: Y   ADULT: $3.00   CHILDREN: $1.00   STUDENTS: $1.00   SR CIT: $1.00   HDC/ACC: Y
PERM/COLL: SCULP

Fifty five major pieces of sculpture ranging from contemporary Colorado artists to those with international reputations are placed throughout the 400 acre Greenwood Plaza business park, located just south of Denver, creating a "museum without walls." A color brochure with a map is provided to lead visitors through the collection.

PUEBLO

Sangre Decristo Arts & Conference Center & Children's Center
210 N. Santa Fe Ave., **Pueblo, CO 81003**
TEL: 719-543-0130
HRS: 11-4 M-Sa   DAY CLOSED: S   HOL: LEG/HOL!
ADM: F
HDC/ACC: Y; Fully accessible   PARKING: Y; 2 free lots   MUS/SH: Y   GR/T: Y   GR/PH: call; 719-543-0130
PERM/COLL: AM: Regional Western 19-20; REG: ldscp, cont

A broad range of Western Art is represented in the collection covering works from the 19th and early 20th century through contemporary Southwest and modern regionalist pieces. **NOT TO BE MISSED:** Francis King collection of Western Art; Art of the "Taos Ten."

ON EXHIBIT/95:
WHITE GALLERY EXIBITIONS

1/14 - 3/11/95	A SELECTION OF CONTEMPORARY PAINTINGS FROM PAKISTAN — Diverse artworks by 50 contemporary artists that run the gamut from realism to nonobjective, and from traditional miniatures to abstract expressionism will be seen in the first exhibition of its kind to be shown in the U.S.
3/25 - 5/20/95	WHIIRLIGIGS AND WEATHERVANES: CONTEMPORARY SCULPTURE — 38 creative, fanciful and humorous sculptures by 23 artists that are updated versions of their traditional folk art counterparts will be on exhibit.
6/3 - 9/9/95	LUIS JIMENEZ: MAN ON FIRE — On view will be colorful large-scale cast fiberglass sculptures by this renowned New Mexican artist depicting the life of the Hispanic people who live on "la frontera," the border along the Rio Grande River that divides Texas and Mexico. WT
9/23 - 11/18/95	LAURA GILPIN: PHOTOGRAPHS OF THE SOUTHWEST - THE ORMAN COLLECTION OF PUEBLO, COLORADO — 44 silverprints by Gilpin, a 20th century photographic master committed to working toward a greater understanding of the poeple, customs and land of the Southwest will be featured in this exhibit along with Southwest native artifacts from the Orman Collection.
12/1 - 12/30/95	FESTIVAL OF THE TREES — A variety of imaginative tree decorations created by local artists working with school children.

HOAG GALLERY EXHIBITIONS

1/14 - 3/11/95	TBA
4/15 - 5/27/95	BARRY DOLAN — Unusual stained glass works by Dolan that include sculpture, handmade wood and glass furniture will be on exhibit.
6/9 - 8/19/95	EPPIE ARCHULETA — Loomworks by this award-winning San Luis Valley weaver will be on exhibit.
9/2 - 10/28/95	PAUL PLETKA — One of each of the 27 lithographs created by this "neo-surrealist" Colorado artist will be on view.
11/11/95 - 1/6/96	BILL ZINANTI AND DON MITCHELL — Freely played flat forms and bright colors will be seen in the whimsical sculptures of Don Mitchell and the drawings of Bill Zinanti.

REGIONAL GALLERY EXHIBITIONS

1/21 - 3/18/95	TRADITIONAL ARTS OF PAKISTAN — From the collection of Pueblo residents and Pakistan natives Dr. & Mrs. Nalik Hasan, will be a stunning array of objects from traditional Pakistan culture including rugs, furniture and even Mrs. Hasan's own wedding dress.
4/1 - 5/27/95	DAVE McKEAN — Featured will be McKean's large canvases filled with explosions of color.

COLORADO

Sangre Decristo Arts & Conference Center & Children's Center - continued

6/9 - 8/19/95	JERRY DE LA CRUZ — Large-scale surrealist paintings, collage work and alabaster sculpture will be on view in the multimedia exhibit of the work of this local artist.
6/9 - 8/12/95	TONY ORTEGA AND GEORGE RIVERA - A MIGRANT CHILD'S DREAM: FARMWORKER ADVENTURES OF CHOLO, VATO AND PANO — Monoprints by Ortega and text by Rivera from their recently published children's story about a young boy and his dog will be featured in this exhibit.
5/95	FIDEL ROBERTO NIETO — Beginning in May, Nieto will paint large colorful murals that may be viewed on-site as he works. Please call ahead for particulars.
9/2 - 10/28/95	DAVID CARICATO — Intricately made gourd figures, hand carved wooden sculptures and colorful paintings will be seen in this mulitmedia exhibition of works by Pueblo artist Caricato.
11/1/95 - 1/6/96	JOANNE BATTISTE — An exhibition of magical, playful and enchanting paintings.

KING GALLERY EXHIBITIONS

2/24 - 5/6/95	EAST MEETS WEST: THE LURE OF THE FRONTIER — The significant visual impact of the land west of the Mississippi will be seen in the works on view by a variety of artists including examples by each of the Taos Ten.
5/20 - 7/29/95	A CELEBRATION OF SEASONS: HIGHLIGHTS FROM THE FRANCIS KING COLLECTION — Featured will be works that pay tribute to the changing of seasons in the Southwest.
8/12 - 11/4/95	OF THE EARTH AND SKY: NATIVE AMERICANS OF THE SOUTHWEST — An outstanding array of paintings, etchings and bronze sculptures that capture the majesty of the Southwest will be on view from the Center's collection and from local private collections.
11/18/95 - 2/10/96	WESTERN AMERICA: LANDSCAPES AND INDIANS (TENT!) — From the collection of Mr. & Mrs. Norman "Buzz" Rieger, will be a spectacular display of western American art.

TRINIDAD

A. R. Mitchell Memorial Museum of Western Art

150 E. Main St., P.O. Box 95, **Trinidad, CO 81082**
TEL: 719-846-4224
HRS: 10-4 M-Sa (early Apr-through Sep); Oct-Mar by appt.   DAY CLOSED: S   HOL: 7/4
VOL/CONT: Y   ADM: F
HDC/ACC: Y; Main floor and restrooms   PARKING: Y; Street parking on Main St.; parking in back of building
MUS/SH: Y   REST/FAC: Y; Lunch (by appt.) every Fri. June-Sept.   GR/T: Y   GR/PH: call 719-846-4224
DT: Y   TIME: often available upon request   H/B: Y
PERM/COLL: AM: ptgs; HISP: folk; AM: Western

Housed in a charming turn of the century building that features its original tin ceiling and wood floors, the Mitchell contains a unique collection of early Hispanic religious folk art and artifacts from the old West both of which are displayed in a replica of an early Penitente Morada. The museum is located in southeast Colorado just above the New Mexico border. **NOT TO BE MISSED:** 250 works by Western artist/illustrator Arthur Roy Mitchell

BRIDGEPORT

The Discovery Museum
4450 Park Ave., **Bridgeport, CT 16604**
TEL: 203-372-3521
HRS: 10-5 Tu-Sa; Noon-5 S   DAY CLOSED: M   HOL: LEG/HOL!
ADM: Y   ADULT: $6.00   CHILDREN: $4.00   STUDENTS: $4.00   SR CIT: $4.00
HDC/ACC: Y; Totally accessible   PARKING: Y; Ample on-site parking   MUS/SH: Y   REST/FAC: Y; Cafeteria
GR/T: Y   GR/PH: call 203-372-3521 to reserve
PERM/COLL: AM: ptgs, sculp, phot, furniture 18-20; IT/REN & BAROQUE: ptgs (Kress Coll)

14 unique hands-on exhibitions that deal with color, line and perspective, the Bridgeport Brass Collection, and a 300 piece permanent collection of 18th - 20th century American art are but 3 of the special features of The Discovery Museum. **NOT TO BE MISSED:** The Hoppin Collection of 19th century mourning pictures, samplers and silhouettes; Mid 1950's paintings & murals from the Bridgeport Brass Collection that document the history of the company and of the area.

ON EXHIBIT/95:

10/2/94 - 1/8/95	BETWEEN EAST AND WEST: CONTEMPORARY CHINESE ARTISTS
1/95 - 3/95	WOMEN PRINTMAKERS
4/95 - 5/95	ROOTS AND REALITY - AFRICAN-AMERICAN ARTISTS
6/26 - 8/14/95	35TH ANNUAL BARNUM FESTIVAL JURIED ART EXHIBITION
8/22 - 9/18/95	CONNECTICUT CONTEMPORARY: BARNUM AWARD WINNERS
10/2/95 - 1/96	AWARD WINNERS FROM THE CONNECTICUT COMMISSION ON THE ARTS

Housatonic Museum of Art
510 Barnum Ave., **Bridgeport, CT 06608**
TEL: 203-579-6727
HRS: 10-4 M-Tu; 1-8 W, T; F (By Appointment only)   DAY CLOSED: Sa, S   HOL: LEG/HOL! ACAD!
ADM: F   HDC/ACC: Y
PARKING: Y; Free parking in student lot across the street; call ahead to arrange for handicapped parking behind the building
PERM/COLL: AM 19-20; EU: 19-20; AF; CONT: Lat/Am; CONT: reg; ASIAN; CONT: Hispanic

With a strong emphasis on contemporary and ethnographic art, the rapidly expanding Housatonic Museum displays works from the permanent collection throughout the buildings of the college with which it is associated, and in a gallery built especially for the display of temporary exhibitions.

ON EXHIBIT/95:

3 - 4/95	AMERICAN PAINTINGS
6 - 7/95	LANDSCAPE PAINTINGS/DRAWINGS FROM THE COLLECTION
8/95	CLOSED
9 - 10/95	AFRICAN ETHNOGRAPHY FROM THE PERMANENT COLLECTION

CONNECTICUT

BROOKLYN

New England Center for Contemporary Art, Inc.
Route 169, **Brooklyn, CT 06234**
TEL: 203-774-8899
HRS: 10-5 Tu-F; 1-5 Sa, S   DAY CLOSED: Tu   HOL: 1/1, THGV, 12/25
ADM: F   HDC/ACC: Y   PARKING: Y; Free and ample   MUS/SH: Y   S/G: Y
PERM/COLL: AM: cont/ptgs; CONT/SCULP; OR: cont/art

In addition to its sculpture garden, great emphasis is placed on the display of the contemporary arts of China in this art center which is located on the mid-east border of the state near Rhode Island. **NOT TO BE MISSED:** Collection of contemporary Chinese art; Collection of artifacts from Papea, New Guinea

FARMINGTON

Hill-Stead Museum
35 Mountain Rd., **Farmington, CT 06032**
TEL: 206-677-4787
HRS: 11-3-Tu-S (NOV 1-APR 30); 10- 4:30 Tu-S (MAY 1-OCT 31)   DAY CLOSED: M   HOL: 1/1, 12/25
ADM: Y   ADULT: $6.00   CHILDREN: $3.00 (6-12)   STUDENTS: $5.00   SR CIT: $5.00
HDC/ACC: Y; First floor only; advance notice required   PARKING: Y   MUS/SH: Y
GR/T: Y!   GR/PH: 203-677-4787   DT: Y TIME: hour-long tours on the hour & half hour
H/B: Y; National Historical Landmark
PERM/COLL: FR: Impr/ptgs; GR:19; OR: cer; DEC/ART

Hill-Stead, located in a suburb of Hartford, is a Colonial Revival home that was originally a "gentleman's farm" built by Alfred Atmore Pope at the turn of the century to house his still intact collection of early French Impressionist paintings. **NOT TO BE MISSED:** Period furnishings; French Impressionist paintings

GREENWICH

The Bruce Museum
Museum Drive, **Greenwich, CT 06830**
TEL: 203-869-0376
HRS: 10-5 Tu-Sa; 2-5 S   DAY CLOSED: M   HOL: LEG/HOL! MONDAYS EXCEPT SCHOOL VACATIONS
F/DAY: Tu   ADM: Y   ADULT: $2.50   CHILDREN: F (under 5)   STUDENTS: $2.00   SR CIT: $2.00
HDC/ACC: Y   PARKING: Y; On-site parking available   MUS/SH: Y
H/B: Y;   original 1909 Victorian manor is part of the museum
PERM/COLL: AM: ptgs, gr, sculp 19; AM: cer, banks; NAT/AM; P/COL; CH: robes

In addition to wonderful 19th century American works of art, the recently restored and renovated Bruce Museum also features a unique collection of mechanical and still banks, North American and pre-Columbian artifacts, and an outstanding department of natural history. Housed partially in its original 1909 Victorian manor, the museum is just a short stroll from the fine shops and restaurants in the charming center of historic Greenwich.

CONNECTICUT

The Bruce Museum - continued

ON EXHIBIT/95:

12/11/94 - 1/29/95	JOSIAH WEDGEWOOD: EXPERIMENTAL POTTER — Examples of Jasperware, red-figure Greco-Etruscan vases, a copy of the Portland vase and other objects will be featured in this display of Wedgewood ceramics. WT

1/22 - 4/23/95   AN EXHIBIT OF THE DRAWINGS OF MAJOR ARTISTS OF THE 1980'S

5/7 - 6/25/95   MULTIPLE EXPOSURE: THE GROUP PORTRAIT IN PHOTOGRAPHY   WT

7/2 - 8/29/95   THE ABSTRACT URGE   WT

9/10 - 12/31/95   THE MOBILE, THE STABILE, THE ANIM

GREENWICH

Historical Society of the Town of Greenwich, Inc.
39 Strickland Rd., **Greenwich, CT 06807**
TEL: 203-869-6899
HRS: Noon-4 Tu-F; 1-4 S   DAY CLOSED: M, Sa   HOL: 1/1, THGV, 12/25
ADM: Y   ADULT: $4.00   CHILDREN: F (under 12)   STUDENTS: $3.00   SR CIT: $3.00
HDC/ACC: Y; but quite limited!   PARKING: Y   GR/T: Y   GR/PH: call 203-869-6899
H/B: Y; Located in 18th century Bush-Holley House
PERM/COLL: DEC/ART 18-19; AM: Impr/ptgs

American Impressionist paintings and sculpture groups by John Rogers are the important fine art offerings of the Historical Society, housed in the 1732 Bush-Holley House. It was in this house, location of the first Impressionist art colony, that many of the artists in the collection resided while painting throughout the surrounding countryside. **NOT TO BE MISSED:** Childe Hassam etchings of the Bush-Holley House and site; over 50 John Rogers sculpture groups

ON EXHIBIT/95:   Changing exhibitions of local history may be seen in addition to the permanent collection of paintings and sculptures.

HARTFORD

Wadsworth Atheneum
600 Main St., **Hartford, CT 06103-2990**
TEL: 203-278-2670
HRS: 11-5 Tu-S, Till 8 pm 1st T of the month   DAY CLOSED: M   HOL: 1/1, THGV, 7/4, 12/25
F/DAY: T; Sa before noon ADM: Y ADULT: $5.00 CHILDREN: F (under 13) STUDENTS: $4.00 SR CIT: $4.00
HDC/ACC: Y; Wheelchair access through Avery entrance on Atheneum Square
PARKING: Y: Limited metered street parking; some commercial lots nearby   MUS/SH: Y
REST/FAC: Y; 11:30-2:30 Tu-F, 12-3:00 Sa, Noon-3 S (brunch); tea till 3:30 S
GR/T: Y   GR/PH: call 203-278-2670 ex 323   DT: Y   TIME: 1:00 T; 2:00 Sa, S (Sep-Jun); Noon Sa, S (Jun-Aug)
H/B: Y   S/G: Y
PERM/COLL: AM: ptgs, sculp, drgs, dec/art; FR: Impr/ptgs; SP; IT; DU: 17; REN; CER; EU: OM 16-17; EU: dec/art

79

CONNECTICUT

Wadsworth Atheneum - continued

Founded in 1842, the Wadsworth Atheneum is the oldest museum in continuous operation in the country. It has recently been promised works from the estate of artist Sol Lewitt to add to its prime and broad ranging collections. In 1994 two important oil paintings by Picasso; namely, "The Women of Algiers" and "The Artist" were given as gifts to the Atheneum making its collection of works by Picasso one of the fullest in New England museums. **NOT TO BE MISSED:** Caravaggio's "Ecstasy of St. Francis;" Wallace Nutting collection of pilgrim furniture; Colonial period rooms; African-American art (Fleet Gallery).

ON EXHIBIT/95:

10/2/94 - 2/26/95	CHENEY TEXTILES: A CENTURY OF SILK — An exhibition of fine silks manufactured from 1838-1955 by the Cheney brothers at their mills in Manchester, Conn.
10/9 - 1/22/95	FROM THESE ROOTS: IMAGES OF AFRICAN-AMERICAN FAMILY LIFE — More than 40 photographs, pastels, oil paintings and etchings from the Amistad Foundation Collection that reveal aspects of African-American family life will be on exhibit.
1/22 - 4/2/95	THE PAINTINGS OF SYLVIA PLIMACK MANGOLD — Mangold's paintings of her contemporary interpretations of landscapes from the mid 60's to the present will be featured .
1/22 - 4/2/95	MATRIX: 20TH ANNIVERSARY CELEBRATION — On display will be examples of art by contemporary artists whose works have been on view over the past 20 years in the museum's MATRIX Gallery of Contemporary Art.
1/29 - 3/26/95	JEAN-MICHEL BASQUIAT: THE BLUE RIBBON PAINTINGS — Paintings by Basquiat that comment on urban street culture and societal concerns. CAT WT
4/2 - 8/20/95	ART DECO STYLE — An illustration of the evolving of the Art Deco style from the early curvilinear to the later rectilinear style will be seen in this exhibition of clothing, furniture and artwork.
5/7 - 7/8/95	THE GENIUS OF FERDINAND HOLDER — Portraits, landscapes and symbolist works by Holder (1853-1918), a noted artist of his day, who was a friend of Corot & Courbet. WT
10/7 - 12/3/95	SHAKER FURNITURE: THE ART OF CRAFTSMANSHIP — 19th-century objects and furniture of simplicity, order and fine craftsmanship from the first and most influential Shaker community in New Lebanon, New York will be seen in the first major exhibition of its kind in America. WT

MIDDLETOWN

Davison Art Center

Affiliate Institution: Wesleyan University
301 High St., **Middletown, CT 06457**
TEL: 203-347-9411
HRS: Noon-4 Tu-F; 2-5 Sa, S (Sep-mid June); Noon-4 Tu-F (mid June-mid July)   DAY CLOSED: M
HOL: ACAD! LEG/HOL !   VOL/CONT: Y   ADM: F
PARKING: Y; On street parking   GR/T: Y   GR/PH: call 203-347-9411, x 2401   H/B: Y; Historic 1830'S Alsop House
PERM/COLL: GR 15-20; PHOT 19-20; DRGS

Historic Alsop House (1830), on the grounds of Wesleyan University, is home to a fine permanent collection of prints, photographs and drawings.

Davison Art Center - continued

ON EXHIBIT/95:

1/18 - 3/10/95   REMBRANDT'S PRINTS — From the Davison Art Center's permanent collection, approximately 50 experimental etchings (1634-1661) will be included in a comprehensive survey of Rembrandt's works based on the themes of biblical subjects, portraits, genre and landscapes.

1/18 - 3/10/95   JOSEPH REED: TRAVEL SKETCHBOOKS 1974-1994 — Works in pencil, watercolor and acrylic based on 20 years of travel throughout the U.S., Europe, and India by Reed, an artist and professor of English at Wesleyan.

3/28 - 6/4/95   BLOCK/PLATE/STONE: WHAT A PRINT IS — From the Davison Art Center Collection, a comprehensive survey of printmaking from 1500 to the present will address many of the questions about the techniques and history of the medium.

NEW BRITAIN

The New Britain Museum of American Art
56 Lexington St., **New Britain, CT 06052**
TEL: 203-229-0257
HRS: 1-5 Tu-S   DAY CLOSED: M   HOL: 1/1, EASTER, 7/4, THGV, 12/25
ADM: F
HDC/ACC: Y; Entrance, elevators, restrooms   PARKING: Y; Free on street parking   MUS/SH: Y
GR/T: Y   GR/PH: call 203-229-0257
PERM/COLL: AM: ptgs, sculp, gr 18-20

The New Britain Museum, only minutes from downtown Hartford, and housed in a turn of the century mansion, is one of only five museums in the country devoted exclusively to American art. The collection covers 250 years of artistic accomplishment including the nation's first public collection of illustrative art. A recent bequest by Olga Knoepke has added 26 works by Edward Hopper, George Tooker and other early 20th century Realist artworks to the collection. PLEASE NOTE: Tours for the visually impaired are available with advance notice. **NOT TO BE MISSED:** Thomas Hart Benton murals; Childe Hassam painting collection

ON EXHIBIT/95:

1/21 - 3/5/95   GARY ERBE RETROSPECTIVE   WT

1/22 - 4/22/95   WORLD WAR II ILLUSTRATION — Works from the museum's permanent collection of illustration.

3/17 - 5/7/95   IMAGES OF LABOR AND THE WORKPLACE — Paintings and works on paper from the permanent collection.

6/11 - 7/2/95   CONNECTICUT WOMEN ARTISTS — A juried contemporary exhibition.

7/29 - mid 9/95   MEMBERS SHOW

mid 10 - 12/95   I KNOW WHAT I LIKE (TENT! dates) — Works from the permanent collection selected for viewing by community members from New Britain and surrounding areas.

CONNECTICUT

NEW CANAAN

Silvermine Guild Art Center
1037 Silvermine Rd., **New Canaan, CT 06840**
TEL: 203-966-5617
HRS: 11-5 W-Sa; Noon-5 S   DAY CLOSED: M   HOL: 1/1, 7/4, 12/25, & HOL. falling on Mondays
ADM: F   HDC/ACC: Y; Ground level entries to galleries   PARKING: Y; Ample and free   MUS/SH: Y
GR/T: Y   GR/PH: call 203-966-5617
H/B: Y; The Silvermine Guild was established in 1922 in a barn setting   S/G: Y
PERM/COLL: NO PERMANENT COLLECTION

Housed in an 1890 barn and established as one of the first art colonies in the country, the vital Silvermine Guild exhibits works by well known and emerging artists. Nearly 30 exhibitions are presented yearly in the original New Canaan galleries and in the Metro Gallery extension in Stamford.

ON EXHIBIT/95:
1/7 - 2/5/95	NEW MEMBERS/FACULTY
2/11 - 3/12/95	BETTE SHAPIRO ONE-PERSON SHOW
	ROBERT LOEBELL ONE-PERSON SHOW
3/18 - 4/23/95	CRAFT AMERICA '95
5/12 - 6/9/95	46TH ANNUAL ART OF THE NORTHEAST USA
6/17 - 7/16/95	GORDON NICUMIS AND JAMES JACKSON BURT
	GUILD GROUP SHOW
7/22 - 8/20/95	5TH ANNUAL SCHOOL OF ART STUDENT SHOW
8/16 - 10/1/95	M. SCOTT PITNER ONE-PERSON SHOW
	VIRGINIA MURRAY ONE-PERSON SHOW
	JAN HURDOCK & SARA AUGENBRAUN TWO-PERSON SHOW
10/7 - 11/5/95	UNITED NATIONS SHOW
11/19 - 12/24/95	1995 HOLIDAY SHOW AND SALE OF ART AND CRAFT

NEW HAVEN

Yale Center for British Art
Affiliate Institution: Yale University
1080 Chapel St, **New Haven, CT 06520**
TEL: 203-432-2800
HRS: 10-5 Tu-Sa; Noon-5 S   DAY CLOSED: M   HOL: LEG/HOL!
ADM: F   HDC/ACC: Y; Entire building is fully accessible
PARKING: Y; Parking lot behind the Center and garage directly across York St.   MUS/SH: Y
GR/T: Y   GR/PH: call 203-432-2858   DT: Y   TIME: Introductory & Architectural tours on Sa
H/B: Y; Last building designed by noted American architect, Louis Kahn
PERM/COLL: BRIT: ptgs, drgs, gr 16-20

A remarkable range of art is contained in this center whose focus both in its permanent collection and special exhibits is British art of the past and present. The collection is housed in the last building designed by the late great American architect, Louis Kahn. **NOT TO BE MISSED:** "Golden Age" British paintings by Turner, Constable, Hogarth, Gainsborough, Reynolds.

82

Yale Center for British Art - continued

ON EXHIBIT/95:

11/16/94 - 1/22/95   WENCESLAUS HOLLAR: A BOHEMIAN ARTIST IN ENGLAND — 210 prints and 40 watercolors & drawings by England's first great etcher (1607-1677) will be seen in the U.S. for the first time. Works by artists who influenced him, such as Rembrandt, and those who were influenced by him, such as Francis Place, will accompany those of Hollar's in this exhibition.   WT

11/19/94 - 1/29/95   FANCY PIECES: GENRE MEZZOTINTS BY ROBERT ROBINSON AND HIS CONTEMPORARIES — From the permanent collection, a 60 work overview of the mezzotints of decorative painter and stage designer, Robinson (1674-1706), that defines English Baroque taste will be seen in his so-called fancy pieces whose subject matter ranges from architectural caprices to rustic landscapes and still lifes.

2/4 - 4/9/95   BARBARA HEPWORTH — In the first major retrospective since before her death in 1975, 75 carvings & bronzes and 30 drawings will cover the scope of the remarkable career of this noted British sculptor.

NEW HAVEN

Yale University Art Gallery

Affiliate Institution: Yale University
1111 Chapel St., **New Haven, CT 06520**
TEL: 203-432-0600
HRS: 10-5 Tu-Sa; 2-5 S   DAY CLOSED: M   HOL: 1/1, 7/4, THGV, 12/25 ;MONTH OF AUGUST
ADM: F   HDC/ACC: Y; entrance at 201 York St., wheelchairs available, barrier free
PARKING: Y; Metered street parking plus parking garage on York St.   MUS/SH: Y
GR/T: Y   GR/PH: call 203-432-0620 education dept.   DT: Y   TIME: Noon W & other!   S/G: Y
PERM/COLL: AM: ptgs, sculp, dec/art; EU: ptgs, sculp; FR: Impr, Post/Impr; OM: drgs, gr; CONT: drgs, gr; IT/REN: ptgs; P/COL; AF: sculp; CH; AN/GRK; AN/EGT

Founded in 1832 with an original bequest of 100 works from the John Trumbull Collection, the Yale University Gallery has the distinction of being the oldest museum in North America. Today over 100,000 works from virtually every major period of art history are in the outstanding collection of this highly regarded university museum. **NOT TO BE MISSED:** "Night Cafe" by van Gogh

ON EXHIBIT/95:

9/16/94 - 1/8/95   CHARLES DEMUTH POSTER PORTRAITS: 1923-29 — Images of Marsden Hartley, Georgia O'Keefe, Arthur Dove, John Marin and others, all close avant-garde American artist associates of Demuth, will be seen together for the first time in this exhibition of his portraits of them.   CAT

9/17/94 - 1/8/95   ART AND DESIGN OF THE 1920'S: SELECTIONS FROM THE PERMANENT COLLECTION — Paintings and sculptures by Leger, Archipenko, Joseph Stella and others accompanied by furniture and decorative objects by Frank Lloyd Wright, Paul Frankl and Rene Lalique will be on exhibit as a complement to the exhibit listed above.

1/20 - 3/26/95   THE RE(EN)VISIONED EMBLEM — Contemporary post-modern emblems (allegorical designs that combine text with images to represent abstract ideas or cultural commonplaces) will be created in a variety of media by invited artists and will be juxtaposed in this exhibit with 16th & 17th century antecedents.

CONNECTICUT

Yale University Art Gallery - continued

2/10 - 4/16/95   PAINTING THE MAYA UNIVERSE: ROYAL CERAMICS OF THE CLASSIC PERIOD —100 splendid examples that reveal the thematic richness and technical brilliance of the Classic Mayan civilization (A.D. 550-850).

2 - 7/95   CONTEMPORARY PAINTINGS GIVEN TO THE YALE ART GALLERY BY THURSTON TWIGG-SMITH

4/4 - 7/11/95   PRODIGAL SON NARRATIVES 1480-1980 — Themes of human virtue and vice through the centuries will be seen in this exhibition that examines the evolution of prodigal son imagery.

4/28 - 7/9/95   RONI HORN: INNER GEOGRAPHY — 13 watercolors and graphite drawings inspired by the dramatic landscape of Iceland, a country she has visited frequently over the past 2 decades will be accompanied in this exhibit by books recording her sense of place.

10/14 - 12/31/95   MEL BOCHNER: THOUGHT MADE VISIBLE, 1966-1973 — In this major retrospective of the early work of Bochner, a seminal figure of Post-Minimalist and Conceptual art, 12 wall and floor installations in which he fuses the operation of the intellect with that of feeling will explain his artistic philosophy of "doing" rather than making his art.
CAT

NEW LONDON

Lyman Allyn Art Museum

625 Williams St., **New London, CT 06320**
TEL: 203-443-2545
HRS: 1-5 Tu-F & S, till 9pm W, 11-5 Sa; (JUN-LAB/DAY: 10-5 Tu-Sa, till 9 W, 1-5 S)   DAY CLOSED: M
HOL: LEG/HOL!
ADM: Y   ADULT: $3.00   CHILDREN: F (under 12)   STUDENTS: $2.00   SR CIT: $2.00
HDC/ACC: Y; Wheelchair accessible except for auditorium   PARKING: Y; Free parking on the premises
MUS/SH: Y   GR/T: Y   GR/PH: call 203-443-2545   DT: Y   TIME: Free highlight tours 2:00 W & S
PERM/COLL: AM: ptgs, drgs; EU: ptgs, drgs; AM: dec/art 17-20; EU: dec/art 16-20; OR; AF; ANT

The Deshon Allyn House, a 19th century whaling merchants home located on the grounds of the fine arts museum and furnished with period pieces of furniture and decorative arts, is open by appointment to those who visit the Lyman Allyn Art Museum. **NOT TO BE MISSED:** 19th century Deshon Allyn House open by appointment only

ON EXHIBIT/95:

9/13/94 - 1/8/95   PERMANENT COLLECTION: 20TH CENTURY ART

10/9/94 - 1/2/95   SIMEON BRAGUIN CREATES

11/25/94 - 1/22/95   ALL THINGS GREAT AND SMALL: DOLLHOUSES & MINIATURES

3/19 - 5/7/95   LIVING LEGENDS — Ethnic folk art by living Connecticut artists

4/2 - 5/14/95   LORETTA KRUPINSKI: BLUE WATER JOURNAL — Book illustrations

5/15 - 5/26/95   TABLES FOR TWO — An exhibition of whimsical artistic table top expressions designed by community members.

6/2 - 7/30/95   THE LIEBERTS: FATHER AND DAUGHTER

6/18 - 9/3/95   INVESTING IN THE DREAM: CONNECTICUT'S COMMITTMENT TO IMAGINATION — Connecticut Commission on the Arts Award Winners

OUTDOORS ON THE MUSEUM GROUNDS:
    SCULPTURE BY SOL LEWITT, CAROL KREEGER DAVIDSON, NIKI KETCHMAN, DAVID SMALLEY, GAVRIEL WARREN, JIM VISCONTI AND ROBERT TAPLIN

CONNECTICUT

NORWICH

The Slater Memorial Museum
Affiliate Institution: The Norwich Free Academy
108 Crescent St., **Norwich, CT 06360**
TEL: 203-887-2506
HRS: 9-4 M-F; 1-4 Sa, S (Sep-Jun); 1-4 Tu-S (Jul-Aug)   HOL: LEG/HOL! STATE/HOL!
ADM: F   PARKING: Y; Free alongside museum. However parking is not permitted between 1:30-2:30 during the week to allow for school buses to operate.   MUS/SH: Y   GR/T: Y   GR/PH: call 203-887-2506
H/B: Y; 1888 Romanesque building designed by architect Stephen Earle
PERM/COLL: AM: ptgs, sculp, gr; DEC/ART; OR; AF; POLY; AN/GRK; NAT/AM

Opened in 1886, the original three story Romanesque structure has expanded from its original core collection of antique sculpture castings to include a broad range of 17th through 20th century American art. This museum has the distinction of being one of only two fine arts museums in the U.S. to be located on the campus of a secondary school. **NOT TO BE MISSED:** Classical casts of Greek, Roman and Renaissance sculpture.

ON EXHIBIT/95:
12/4/94 - 1/19/95	THE AMERICAN INDIAN EXHIBIT
12/4/94 - 1/19/95	AMERICAN STEAM ENGINES BY ROBERT HAUSCHILD
12/4/94 - 1/19/95	JUNE OWEN: SOLO SHOW
1/29 - 3/9/95	AARON ROSENSTREICH RETROSPECTIVE
1/29 - 3/9/95	GRAPHICS
6/18 - 8/24/95	COLLECTOR'S GALLERY: WORKS OF ART FOR SALE

OLD LYME

Florence Griswold Museum
96 Lyme St., **Old Lyme, CT 06371**
TEL: 203-434-5542
HRS: 10-5 Tu-Sa; 1-5 S (Summer); 1-5 W-S (Winter)   DAY CLOSED: M   HOL: LEG/HOL!
ADM: Y   ADULT: $3.00   CHILDREN: F (under 12)   STUDENTS: $3.00   SR CIT: $2.00
HDC/ACC: Y   PARKING: Y; Ample and free   MUS/SH: Y   GR/T: Y   GR/PH: call 203-434-5542
DT: Y   TIME: daily upon request   H/B: Y
PERM/COLL: AM: Impr/ptgs; DEC/ART

The beauty of the Old Lyme Connecticut countryside in the early part of the 20th century attracted dozens of artists to the area. Many of the now famous American Impressionists worked here during the summer and lived in the Florence Griswold boarding house, which is now a museum that stands as a tribute to the art and artists of that era. **NOT TO BE MISSED:** The Chadwick Workplace: newly opened and restored as early 20th century artists' studio workplace of American Impressionist, William Chadwick. Free with admission. Call ahead for hours and dates open.

ON EXHIBIT/95:
Temporary exhibitions usually from the permanent collection.

EACH DECEMBER	CELEBRATION OF HOLIDAY TREES — A month long display of trees throughout the house. Every year a new theme is chosen and each tree is decorated accordingly.

CONNECTICUT

RIDGEFIELD

The Aldrich Museum of Contemporary Art
258 Main St., **Ridgefield, CT 06877**
TEL: 203-438-4519
HRS: 1-5 W-S   DAY CLOSED: M, Tu   HOL: LEG/HOL!
ADM: Y   ADULT: $3.00   CHILDREN: F (under 12)   STUDENTS: $2.00   SR CIT: $2.00
HDC/ACC: Y   PARKING: Y; Free   MUS/SH: Y
GR/T: Y   GR/PH: call 203-438-4519
DT: Y   TIME: 3:00 S   H/B: Y   S/G: Y
PERM/COLL: CONT: ptgs, sculp

The 30 year old Aldrich Museum of Contemporary art offers the visitor a unique blend of modern art housed within the walls of a building dating back to 1783. One of the first museums in the country dedicated solely to contemporary art, the Aldrich enjoys its reputation of being a champion of new talent. **NOT TO BE MISSED:** Outdoor Sculpture Garden.

ON EXHIBIT/95:	Changing quarterly exhibitions of contemporary art featuring works from the permanent collection, collectors works, regional artists, and installations of technological artistic trends.
10/2/94 - 1/8/95	PROMISING SUSPECTS
1/22 - 5/7/95	PISTILS & STAMENS
3/4 - 4/16/95	CONNECTICUT COMMISSION
5/21 - 9/17/95	EYE TO I

STAMFORD

Whitney Museum of American Art at Champion
Atlantic St. & Tresser Blvd., **Stamford, CT 06921**
TEL: 203-358-7630
HRS: 11-5 Tu-Sa   DAY CLOSED: S, M   HOL: 1/1, 7/4, THGV, 12/25
ADM: F
HDC/ACC: Y: No stairs; large elevator from parking garage
PARKING: Y: Free on-site parking   MUS/SH: Y
GR/T: Y   GR/PH: call 203-358-7652   DT: Y   TIME: 12:30 Tu, T, Sa

This Whitney Museum branch, governed by its parent organization on Madison Avenue in N.Y.C., has no permanent collection but features special exhibitions of American Art primarily of the 20th century. Many of the works are drawn from the Whitney's permanent collection of over 10,000 works of art.

ON EXHIBIT/95:
Call for current exhibition and special events information.

STORRS

The William Benton Museum of Art, Connecticut State Art Museum
Affiliate Institution: University of Connecticut
245 Glenbrook Rd. U-140, **Storrs, CT 06269-2140**
TEL: 203-486-4520
HRS: 10-4:30 Tu-F; 1-4:30 Sa, S   HOL: LEG/HOL!
ADM: F
HDC/ACC: Y; Entrance at rear of building; museum is fully accessible   PARKING: Y; Weekdays obtain visitor's pass as sentry booth & proceed to metered parking. Weekends or evenings park in metered or unmetered spaces in any campus lot. Handicapped spaces in visitor's lot behind the Museum.   MUS/SH: Y
GR/T: Y   GR/PH: Call 203-486-1705 Education office
PERM/COLL: EU: 16-20; AM: 17-20; KATHE KOLLWITZ: gr; REGINALD MARSH: gr

Installed in "The Beanery," the former 1920's Gothic style dining hall of the university, the Benton has, in the relatively few years it's been open, grown to include a major 3,000 piece collection of American art. **NOT TO BE MISSED:** "Helene de Septeuil" by Mary Cassatt.

ON EXHIBIT/95:

1/25 - 3/17/95	CONNECTICUT COMMISSION ON THE ARTS AWARD WINNERS 1980-1994
3/28 - 6/11/95	DAVID BAKALAR POTOGRAPHIC COLLECTION Please Note: this exhibition will be closed 4/14 - 4/17 & 5/27 - 5/29.
SUMMER	IVAN G. OLINSKI (Date TBA)
10/31 - 12/22/95	SHAPING AN AMERICAN LANDSCAPE: THE ARTS AND ARCHITECTURE OF CHARLES A. PLATT

DELAWARE

WILMINGTON

Delaware Art Museum
2301 Kentmere Pkwy., **Wilmington, DE 19806**
TEL: 302-571-9590
HRS: 10-5 Tu-Sa; Noon-5 S   DAY CLOSED: M   HOL: 1/1, THGV, 12/25
F/DAY: 10-1 Sa   ADM: Y   ADULT: $5.00   CHILDREN: F (under 6)   STUDENTS: $2.50   SR CIT: $3.00
HDC/ACC: Y; Fully accessible   PARKING: Y; Free lot behind museum   MUS/SH: Y
GR/T: Y   GR/PH: call 302-571-9590
PERM/COLL: AM: ptgs 19-20; BRIT: P/Raph; GR; SCULP; PHOT

Begun as a repository for the works of noted Brandywine Valley painter/illustrator Howard Pyle, the Delaware Art Museum has grown to include other collections of note especially in the areas of Pre-Raphaelite painting and contemporary art. **NOT TO BE MISSED:** "Summertime" by Edward Hopper; "Milking Time" by Winslow Homer

ON EXHIBIT/95:

11/18/94 - 2/19/95	HOWARD PYLE AND NORMAN ROCKWELL: LASTING LEGACIES — This major exhibition of 95 paintings, drawings and watercolors will trace the development of two of America's premier illustrators and provide the opportunity to compare and contrast their individual styles. Over 300 actual Saturday Evening Post covers of Rockwell's images will be included at this venue. WT
THROUGH 3/5/95	INSPIRATION AND EXPLORATION: AMERICAN ARTISTS AND THE LURE OF THE SOUTHWEST — From the permanent collection a selection of paintings and works on paper by John Sloan, Robert Henri, Marsden Hartley and others who were inspired by the beauty and majesty of the West.
3/3 - 4/30/95	SIMPLY MADE IN AMERICA — Simple everyday and found objects that are used by artists to create their works thereby giving throwaway items new meaning and use.
5/19 - 5/21/95	ART IN BLOOM — Floral designs that compliment paintings of flowers from the museum's permanent collection.
5/12 - 7/9/95	BEVERLY BUCHANAN: SHACK WORKS — Drawings, paintings and sculptures by Buchanan that comment on the sense of survival of oppressed Americans by paying tribute to their imagination and improvisational abilities.
8/11 - 10/15/95	VISIONS OF LOVE AND LIFE: ENGLISH PRE-RAPHAELITE ART — 103 paintings, drawings, sculptures and examples of stained glass by many of the best of the Pre-Raphaelite artists will be featured in the only Northeast venue for this exhibition. WT

Art Museum of the Americas

201 18th St., N.W., **Washington, DC 20006**
TEL: 202-458-6016
HRS: 10-5 Tu-Sa   DAY CLOSED: S, M   HOL: LEG/HOL!
VOL/CONT: Y   ADM: F   PARKING: Y; Metered street parking   GR/T: Y   GR/PH: call 202-458-6301
PERM/COLL: 20th C LATIN AMERICAN ART

Established in 1976, and housed in a Spanish colonial style building completed in 1912, this museum contains the most comprehensive collection of 20th century Latin American art in the country. **NOT TO BE MISSED:** The loggia behind the museum opening onto the Aztec Gardens.

ON EXHIBIT/95:   Exhibitions are displayed on a rotating basis.

Arthur M. Sackler Gallery

1050 Independence Ave., SW, **Washington, DC 20560**
TEL: 202-357-3200
HRS: 10-5:30 Daily   HOL: 12/25
ADM: F   HDC/ACC: Y; All levels accessible by elevator
PARKING: Y; Free 3 hour parking on Jefferson Dr; some metered street parking   MUS/SH: Y
GR/T: Y   GR/PH: call 202-357-4880 ex 245   DT: Y   TIME: 2:30 M-F; 1:30 Sa, S; other call 357-3200
PERM/COLL: CH: jade sculp; JAP: cont/cer; PERSIAN: ptgs; NEAR/E: an/silver

Opened in 1987 under the auspices of the Smithsonian Institution, the Sackler Gallery, named for its benefactor, houses magnificent objects of Asian art. **NOT TO BE MISSED:** Japanese lacquer wedding planquin; Chinese jade hound.

ON EXHIBIT/95:

8/14/94 - 5/30/95	LANDSCAPE AS CULTURE: PHOTOGRAPHS BY LOIS CONNOR — Taken with a 100 year old banquet camera, approximately 80 large-format platinum prints of the architecture and landscape of China and other Asian countries will document how people shape their environment.
11/20/94 - 7/9/95	A BASKETMAKER IN RURAL JAPAN — 103 intricate and varied woven baskets designed for use in rural life during the 64 year career of Japenese bamboo craftsman Hiroshima Kazuo (born 1915) will be on loan from the Smithsonian's National Museum of Natural History. BOOK
12/24/94 - 9/24/95	PAINTINGS FROM SHIRAZ (working title) — 8 bound manuscripts and 20 individual paintings created from the 14th - 16th centuries in the Persian city of Shiraz will be featured in this exhibition.
9/24/95 - 11/10/96	RAIDERS AND TRADERS ON CHINA'S NORTHERN FRONTIER — Gilded, tinned and bronze tools, belts & fittings for horses, and gold and silver items from China's northern region will demonstrate the resulting artistic influence of contact and inter-relationships between China's urban dwellers and their nomadic neighbors. CAT

CONTINUING INDEFINITELY:

LUXURY ARTS OF THE SILK ROUTE EMPIRES

METALWORK AND CERAMICS FROM ANCIENT IRAN

SCULPTURE OF SOUTH AND SOUTHEAST ASIA

THE ARTS OF CHINA

MONSTERS, MYTHS AND MINERALS

DISTRICT OF COLUMBIA

The Corcoran Gallery of Art
17th St. & New York Ave., NW, **Washington, DC 20006**
TEL: 202-638-3211
HRS: 10-5 M & W-S; Till 9pm T   DAY CLOSED: Tu   HOL: 1/1, 12/25
SUGG/CONT: Y   ADULT: $3.00   CHILDREN: F (under 12)   STUDENTS: $1.00   SR CIT: $1.00
HDC/ACC: Y   PARKING: Y; Limited metered parking on street; commercial parking lots nearby
MUS/SH: Y   REST/FAC: Y; Cafe 11:30-4:40 daily & till 8 T; Jazz Brunch 11-2 S (202-638-1590)
GR/T: Y   GR/PH: 202-786-2374   DT: Y   TIME: 12:30 daily & 7:30 pm T
PERM/COLL: AM & EU: ptgs, sculp, works on paper 18-20

The beautiful Beaux Art building designed to house the collection of its founder, William Corcoran, contains works that span the entire history of American art from the earliest limners to the cutting edge works of today's contemporary artists. In addition to being the oldest art museum in Washington, the Corcoran has the distinction of being one of the three oldest art museums in the country. **NOT TO BE MISSED:** "Mt. Corcoran" by Bierstadt; "Niagara" by Church; Restored 18th century French room Salon Dore.

ON EXHIBIT/95:

9/24/94 - 1/8/95	LOUISE BOURGEOIS: THE LOCUS OF MEMORY: WORKS 1982-1993 — 27 large-scale sculptures and 31 works on paper will be featured in the first comprehensive exhibition of Bourgeois' work in over a decade. CAT WT
10/5/94 - 1/2/95	FROM THE COLLECTION: DANIEL GARBER — 15 to 19 of Garber's prints and drawings from the permanent collection will be on display along with a recent bequest to the museum of his oil painting entitled "Afternoon, Ellicot City," the only Washington metropolitan scene ever to be painted by the artist.
11/1/94 - 1/23/95	FROM THE COLLECTION: INSIDE/OUTSIDE, PERSONAL EXPRESSIONS IN PHOTOGRAPHY
11/17/94 - 1/16/95	VACLAV HAVEL: A WORD ABOUT WORDS — In this unusual exhibition the words used by Havel in accepting the International Peace Prize of the German Booksellers Association in 1989 are combined with collages by Jiri Kolar derived from text settings of the Guttenburg Bible.
12/3/94 - 2/6/95	LARRY SULTAN: PICTURES FROM HOME — The promise and failure of the post-World War II American dream is explored by Sultan who uses past & present photographs of his own family as seen in the snapshots, home movie stills, and other photographic images in this exhibition. CAT WT
12/10/94 - 2/13/95	FAMILY LIVES: PHOTOGRAPHY BY TINA BARNEY, NIC NICOSIA, AND CATHERINE WAGNER — Psychological and emotional relationships between people and their surroundings are explored by these 3 artists in narrative works that are equal parts autobiographical, fact and theatrical fiction. BROCHURE
1/14 - 2/20/95	FROM THE COLLECTION: COUNTDOWN TO ETERNITY, PHOTOGRAPHS OF DR. MARTIN LUTHER KING, JR. IN THE 1960'S BY BEN FERNANDEZ
1/25 - 5/1/95	FROM THE COLLECTION: ALPHONSE LEGROS AND PRINTMAKING
mid-2 - mid 4/95	FROM THE COLLECTION: COLOR AND ABSTRACTION: WASHINGTON, D.C. (1955-1975)
2/25 - 4/10/95	RECENT ACQUISITIONS

The Corcoran Gallery of Art - continued

3/4 - 5/7/95
PASSIONATE VISIONS OF THE AMERICAN SOUTH: SELF-TAUGHT ARTISTS FROM 1940 TO THE PRESENT — In this first-time exhibition and overview of painting and sculpture by Southern self-taught artists selected solely on the basis of merit will feature 220 works by 80 artists. CAT WT

3/11 - 5/15/95
PEDRO MEYER: TRUTHS & FICTIONS, A JOURNEY FROM DOCUMENTARY TO DIGITAL PHOTOGRAPHY — The transition of the photographic medium from its photochemical origins to electronic imaging created with computer technologies, the ink jet printer and interactive CD-ROM discs will be featured in this exhibition. A CD-ROM electronic catalog will be produced in conjunction with the exhibition.

5/3 - 7/31/95
FROM THE COLLECTION...STARS AND DEWS AND DREAMS OF NIGHT, DRAWINGS, PAINTINGS AND PRINTS BY ARTHUR B. DAVIES

5/3 - 8/7/95
FROM THE COLLECTION: PHOTOGRAPHS

5/6 - 7/9/95
ALFRED STEIGLITZ'S CAMERA NOTES — Published quarterly for 6 years (1897-1903) by the Camera Club of New York, "Camera Notes" was edited by Steiglitz, a founding member of the club. In this exhibition 88 photogravures and 3 silver prints that appeared in this journal will be on view. CAT WT

5/20 - 9/10/95
THE PERVASIVENESS OF MEMORY, SCULPTURE BY MARGEAUZ, ANN MESSNER, ELIZABETH NEWMAN AND LUCY PULS — Contemporary artists who use found objects to create sculptural works whose symbolic images serve as icons for the self.

7/14 - 9/4/95
AMERICAN POLITICIANS — 150 19th & 20th century images will be presented in the first survey of history that demonstrates the way in which photographers and politicians have used each other to convey both the hope and cynicism of American politics. Featured will be major themes of campaigning, meeting the press and leisure time. BOOK

8/2 - 10/30/95
FROM THE COLLECTION...MAURICE PRENDERGAST, AMERICAN PAINTER AND PRINTMAKER

9/2 - 12/29/95
DISCOVERING ELLIS RULEY — Folk artworks by Ruley, a self-taught African artist whose works were inspired by animals in the woods, and were created by using ordinary house paint on posterboard.

9/16 - 11/19/95
RAISED BY WOLVES: PHOTOGRAPHS AND DOCUMENTS OF RUNAWAYS BY JIM GOLDBERG — Goldberg juxtaposes photographs, documents, text, video and other objects in an emotionally charged multimedia installation that weaves a narrative about young Americans who leave dysfunctional families and live instead on the streets of San Francisco and Hollywood.

9/30 - 12/18/95
SCULPTURE BY NICK KEMPS — Multi-media complex contemporary sculptural forms.

11 - 12/95
RICHARD BOLTON, COMMUNITY: EXCHANGE — Organized by Richard Bolton, the concept for a sharing of ideas and the ability to electronically alter images between the residents of Abidjan, Ivory Coast and Washington, D.C. will be realized through the interplay between participants in this new artistic community who will be electronically linked to one another.

11/96 - 2/96
17TH-CENTURY DUTCH ARTISTS IN THE CORCORAN COLLECTION

12/16/95 - 2/19/96
PAINTING OUTSIDE PAINTING: 44TH BIENNIAL EXHIBITION OF CONTEMPORARY AMERICAN PAINTING — In the 3rd in a series of contemporary biennials, paintings that address the issue of expanding the conventional boundaries of painting will be featured.

DISTRICT OF COLUMBIA

Dumbarton Oaks Research Library & Collection
1703 32nd St., NW, **Washington, DC 20007**
TEL: 202-342-3200
HRS: 2-5 Tu-S   DAY CLOSED: M   HOL: LEG/HOL!
VOL/CONT: Y   ADM: F
HDC/ACC: Y; Partial access to collection   PARKING: On-street parking only   MUS/SH: Y
GR/T: Y   GR/PH: call 202-337-0348
H/B: Y; 19th-century mansion is site where plans for U.N. Charter were created
PERM/COLL: BYZ; P/COL; AM: ptgs, sculp, dec/art; EU: ptgs, sculp, dec/art

This 19th century mansion, site of the international conference of 1944 where the charter for the United Nations was incorporated, is best known for its rare collection of Byzantine and Pre-Columbian art. Beautifully maintained and now owned by Harvard University, Dumbarton Oaks is also home to a magnificent French Music Room and to 16 manicured acres that contain formally planted perennial beds, fountains and a profusion of seasonal flower gardens. **NOT TO BE MISSED:** Music room; Gardens (open daily Apr - Oct, 2-6 PM, $3.00 adult, $2.00 children/seniors; 2-5 PM daily Nov-Mar, Free).

ON EXHIBIT/95:   No changing exhibitions, permanent collection only on display.

Federal Reserve Board Art Gallery
2001 C St., **Washington, DC 20551**
TEL: 202-452-3686
HRS: 11:30-2 M-F or by reservation   HOL: LEG/HOL! WEEKENDS
ADM: F
HDC/ACC: Y; Off 20th St.   PARKING: Y; Street parking only   H/B: Y; Designed in 1937 by Paul Cret
PERM/COLL: PTGS, GR, DRGS 19-20 (with emphasis on late 19th C works by Amer. expatriates); ARCH: drgs of Paul Cret PLEASE NOTE: The permanent collection may be seen by appointmemt only.

Founded in 1975, the collection consisting of both gifts and loans of American and European works of art by public minded individuals, acquaints visitors with American artistic and cultural values. **NOT TO BE MISSED:** The atrium of this beautiful building is considered one of the most magnificent public spaces in Washington, D.C.

ON EXHIBIT/95:

1/24 - 3/17/95   THE FRAME IN AMERICA — 75 examples from the High Victorian Style to the development of metal frames in the 60's will offer a historical survey of American frame styles. In addition information of the relationship of the painting to the frame and some tools and materials used in the crafting of frames will be included.

4/11 - 6/2/95   SUSAN CRILE: THE FIRE OF WAR — Paintings and drawings that relate Crile's impressions of the aftermath of the 1990-91 Persian Gulf War where she spent 10 days in the oil fields when they were still burning.

6/27 - 9/8/95   STILL-LIFES BY JOHN WHITE ALEXANDER — On exhibit will be 25 paintings and watercolors, many of which have not been on view since the death of the artist in 1915, that include rich table top images and still-lifes with figures.

10/10 - 12/1/95   FIGURATIVE ART IN ANCIENT ISRAEL — 35 ancient figurative works from the Neolithic, Chalcolithic, Bronze Age, Israelite, Roman and Crusader Periods will be on view.

92

Fondo Del Sol Visual Arts & Media Center

2112 R St., NW, **Washington, DC 20008**
TEL: 202-483-2777
HRS: 12:30-5:30 Tu-Sa   DAY CLOSED: S, M   HOL: LEG/HOL!
SUGG/CONT: Y   ADULT: $3.00   CHILDREN: F   STUDENTS: $1.00   SR CIT: $1.00
HDC/ACC: Y   MUS/SH: Y   GR/T: Y   GR/PH: multi-lingual, call 202-483 2777
PERM/COLL: PR/COL; HISP; LATI

Promoting the works of artists of color is the main thrust of this artist-run multi-ethnic museum which is located on a quiet street lined with many art galleries.

Freer Gallery of Art

Jefferson Dr. at 12th St., SW, **Washington, DC 20560**
TEL: 202-357-2700
HRS: 10-5:50 Daily   HOL: 12/25
ADM: F   HDC/ACC: Y; Entry from Independence Ave.; elevators; restrooms
PARKING: Y; Free 3 hour parking on the Mall   MUS/SH: Y   GR/T: Y   GR/PH: 202-357-4880 (tour coordinator)
DT: Y   TIME: 11:30 & 2:30 weekdays; 1:30 weekends   H/B: Y; Listed NRHP
PERM/COLL: OR: sculp, ptgs, cer; AM/ART 20; (FEATURING WORKS OF JAMES McNEILL WHISTLER; PTGS

One of the many museums in the nation's capitol that represent the results of a single collector, the Freer Gallery focuses primarily on the arts of all of Asia. After 4 1/2 years of extensive renovation the completely refurbished museum features a new underground exhibition area which connects it to its neighbor, the Arthur M. Sackler Gallery of Asian Art. **NOT TO BE MISSED:** "Harmony in Blue and Gold," The Peacock Room by James McNeill Whistler

ON EXHIBIT/95:

6/11/94 - 2/95	MASTERPIECES OF CHINESE CALLIGRAPHY — All 4 major Chinese scripts (seal, clerical, running and cursive) and 4 primary formats (hanging scroll, handscroll, album leaf and folding fan) will be seen in the 27 works on display dating from the mid-first century B.C. to the 20th century.
8/27/94 - 5/95	BEYOND PAPER: CHINESE CALLIGRAPY ON OBJECTS — Chinese calligraphy as it appears on utilitarian objects that date from the 7th to the 19th centuries will be seen in the 36 items on display.
5/14 - 12/95	WHISTLER AND JAPAN — A exhibition drawn from the Freer's permanent collection that allows the viewer to compare and contrast the influence of Japanese art on Whistler's work as seen in this group of his paintings called "the Japanese paintings" presented with actual Japanese prints, paintings and decorative items.
ONGOING:	ANCIENT EGYPTIAN GLASS — 15 rare and brilliantly colored glass vessels created during the reigns of Amenhotep III (1391-1353 B.C.) and Akhenaten (1353-1335 B.C.) will be highlighted in this exhibition.

DISTRICT OF COLUMBIA

Hillwood Museum
4155 Linnean Ave., NW, **Washington, DC 20008**
TEL: 202-686-8500
HRS: 9, 10:30, Noon, 1:30, 3:00 Tu-Sa (By reservation only)   DAY CLOSED: S, M   HOL: FEB. & LEG/HOL!
ADM: Y   ADULT: $10.00   CHILDREN: $5.00   STUDENTS: $5.00   SR CIT: $10.00
HDC/ACC: Y   PARKING: Y; Free parking on the grounds of the museum   MUS/SH: Y
REST/FAC: Y; Reservations accepted (202) 686-8893)   GR/T: Y   GR/PH: 202-686-5807   S/G: Y
PERM/COLL: RUSS: ptgs, cer , dec/art; FR: cer, dec/art, glass

The former home of Marjorie Merriweather Post, heir to the Post cereal fortune, is filled with the art and decorative treasures of Imperial Russia amassed by her when her husband was ambassador to the Soviet Union after the revolution. PLEASE NOTE: In depth special interest tours may be arranged by appointment. **NOT TO BE MISSED:** Carl Faberge's Imperial Easter Eggs and other of his works; glorious gardens surrounding the mansion

ON EXHIBIT/95:   NOTE: children under 12 are not permitted in the house. There are no changing exhibitions.

Hirshhorn Museum and Sculpture Garden
Affiliate Institution: Smithsonian Institution
Independence Ave. at Eighth St., NW, **Washington, DC 20560**
TEL: 202-357-2700
HRS: 10-5:30 Daily   HOL: 12/25
ADM: F   HDC/ACC: Y; Through glass doors near fountain on plaza
PARKING: Y; Free 3 hour parking on Jefferson Dr.; some commercial lots nearby   MUS/SH: Y
REST/FAC: Y; Plaza Cafe - summer only!   GR/T: Y   GR/PH: call 202-357-3235
DT: Y   TIME: 10:30, 12, 1:30 M-Sa; 12:30 S   S/G: Y
PERM/COLL: CONT: sculp, art; AM: early 20th; EU: early 20th; AM: realism since Eakins

Endowed by the entire collection of its founder, Joseph Hirshhorn, this museum focuses primarily on modern and contemporary art of all kinds and cultures plus newly acquired works. One of its most outstanding features is its extensive sculpture garden. **NOT TO BE MISSED:** Rodin's "Burghers of Calais;" Larry River's "History of the Russian Revolution;" gallery of works by Francis Bacon, third floor

ON EXHIBIT/95:

11/3/94 - 1/29/95	BRUCE NAUMAN — In his first major retrospective since 1970, a survey of 50 works in all media except for drawings will be on view. CAT WT
11/17/94 - 2/12/95	DIRECTIONS – GARY SIMMONS — "Erasures," 10 blackboard-like panels showing half-erased chalk drawings of cartoon characters from the past that stereotype African-Americans will be seen in the first exhibition of Simmons' work. For this venue he will also create an on-site monumental wall drawing. BROCHURE WT
3/15 - 5/25/95	DIRECTIONS – CINDY SHERMAN: FILM STILLS — 70 black and white photographs of Sherman's trademark self-images in which she appears in various costumes and disguises will be on view. These works, made between 1978-1980 have never been shown together in their entirety before. BROCHURE
6/15 - 9/10/95	SEAN SCULLY: TWENTY YEARS, 1976-1995 — 30 large-scale abstract paintings and 31 related watercolors will be seen in the first survey of Scully's work to tour both nationally and internationally. CAT WT

94

DISTRICT OF COLUMBIA

Hirshhorn Museum and Sculpture Garden - continued

7/20 - 10/22/95   DIRECTIONS -- MARTIN KIPPENBERGER — Drawings and collages by German artist, Kippenberger.

10/19/95 - 1/15/96   STEPHAN BALKENHOL — Wood-carved figurative sculptures by German artist Balkenhal will be seen in the first major North American exhibition of his work.
CAT   WT

Howard University Gallery of Art
2455 6th St., NW, **Washington, DC 20059**
TEL: 202-806-7070
HRS: 9:30-4:30 M-F; 1-4 S (may be closed some Sundays in summer!)   DAY CLOSED: Sa   HOL: LEG/HOL! ADM: F
HDC/ACC: Y   PARKING: Y; Metered parking; Free parking in the rear of the College of Fine Arts evenings and weekends   GR/T: Y   GR/PH: call 202-806-7070 (Scott Baker)
PERM/COLL: AF/AM: ptgs, sculp, gr; EU: gr; IT: ptgs, sculp (Kress Collection); AF

In addition to an encyclopedic collection of African and African-American art and artists there are 20 cases of African artifacts on permanent display in the east corridor of the College of Fine Arts. PLEASE NOTE: It is advisable to call ahead in the summer as the gallery might be closed for inventory work. **NOT TO BE MISSED:** The Robert B. Mayer Collection of African Art

ON EXHIBIT/95:
11/1/94 - 1/6/95   GIFTS FROM THE PAST: RESTORED AND RECOVERED TREASURES FROM THE HOWARD UNIVERSITY PERMANENT COLLECTION

STUDENT AND FACULTY EXHIBITIONS ARE PLANNED FROM 2/1 - 6/2/95. CALL FOR SPECIFICS.

The Kreeger Museum
2401 Foxhall Rd., **Washington, DC 20007**
TEL: 202-337-3050
HRS: Tours only at 10:30 & 1:30 Tu-Sa   DAY CLOSED: M
HOL: LEG/HOL!; call for information on some additional closures
SUGG/CONT: Y   ADULT: $5.00
HDC/ACC: Y; Limited to first floor only   PARKING: Y; Free parking for 15 cars on the grounds of the museum.
DT: Y   TIME: 10:30 & 1:30 Tu-Sa   S/G: Y
PERM/COLL: EU: ptgs, sculp 19, 20; AM: ptgs, sculp 19, 20; AF

Designed by noted American architect, Philip Johnson, as a stunning private residence for David Lloyd and Carmen Kreeger the home has now become a museum that holds the remarkable art collection of its former owners. With a main floor filled with Impressionist and post-Impressionist paintings and sculpture, and fine collections of African, contemporary, and Washington Color School art on the bottom level, this newly opened museum is a "must see" for art lovers traveling to the D.C. area. PLEASE NOTE: Only 15 people at a time are allowed on each 2 hour tour of this museum at the hours specified and only by reservation made WELL in advance of a visit.

DISTRICT OF COLUMBIA

The National Gallery of Art
4th & Constitution Ave., N.W., **Washington, DC 20565**
TEL: 202-737-4215
HRS: 10-5 M-Sa; 11-6 S   HOL: 1/1, 12/25
ADM: F   HDC/ACC: Y; Fully accessible; wheelchairs available
PARKING: Y; Limited metered street parking; free 3 hour mall parking as available.   MUS/SH: Y
REST/FAC: Y; 3 restaurants plus Espresso bar   GR/T: Y   GR/PH: call 202-842-6247   DT: Y   TIME: daily!
PERM/COLL: EU: ptgs, sculp, dec/art 12-20: OM; AM: ptgs, sculp, gr 18-20; REN: sculp; OR: cer

The two buildings that make up the National Gallery, one classical and the other ultra modern, are as extraordinary and diverse as the collection itself. Considered one of the premier museums in the world, more people pass through the portals of the National Gallery annually than almost any other museum in the country. Self-guided tour brochures of the permanent collection for families as well as walking tour brochures for adults are available for use in the museum. In addition, advance reservations may be made for tours given in a wide variety of foreign languages. **NOT TO BE MISSED:** The only Leonardo Da Vinci oil painting in an American museum collection; Opening Sept. 1995 - Micro Gallery, an interactive computer information system with 17 workstations that allow visitors to research any work of art in the entire permanant collection.

ON EXHIBIT/95:

9/18/94 - 1/22/95	MILTON AVERY: WORKS ON PAPER — 55 works including several original etching plates & carved woodblocks will be presented in this exhibition of Avery's prints, many of which have been donated by the Avery family as part of the gift to the nation on the occasion of the National Gallery's 50th anniversary. CAT WT
10/30/94 - 1/8/95	THE PRINTS OF ROY LICHTENSTEIN — 100 of Lichtenstein's lithographs, etchings, screenprints, woodcuts and works that combine several processes will be shown with related sculptures made concurrently with the prints. Included will be rare prints from the 50's, contemporary images from the 60's, and present examples of his work. CAT WT
12/18/94 - 4/16/95	ITALIAN RENAISSANCE ARCHITECTURE: BRUNELLESCHI TO MICHEL-ANGELO — Highlighting this exhibition of important architectural models and 46 related paintings, drawings, prints and medals will be the largest and most elaborate extant Renaissance architectural model, namely that of St. Peter's, built on a scale of one to thirty in the mid 1500's by Antinio da Sangallo. Two models by Michelangelo of St. Peter's (one of the dome and supporting drum and the other of the apse vault for the south hemicycle) will also be featured. BROCHURE CAT WT
12/18/94 - 4/16/95	TOULOUSE-LAUTREC: MARCELLE LENDER IN "CHILPERIC" — A focus exhibition that features Lautrec's grand masterpiece "Marcelle Lender Dancing the Bolero in Chilperic" (1895-1986). Two related paintings by Lautrec will also be shown. BROCHURE
1/29 - 4/23/95	THE GLORY OF VENICE: ART IN THE EIGHTEENTH CENTURY — 200 works of art by such great 18th century Venetian masters as Guardi, Canaletto, Piranesi, Tiepolo and others will be seen in the first international exhibition of their works. CAT WT
2/12 - 5/7/95	CLAES OLDENBURG: AN ANTHOLOGY — On exhibit will be 200 drawings, collages and sculptures by Oldenburg, a key figure of the Pop Art movement. CAT WT
2/19 - 8/6/95	IMITATION AND INVENTION: OLD MASTER PRINTS AND THEIR SOURCES — 65 well known 16th & 17th century prints will be shown with those prints that inspired them and that they in turn inspired. Works by Rembrandt, van Leyden, Durer, Mantegna and the like will explore the many facets of borrowing from early sources and innovatively adapting them in later works. BROCHURE WT

The National Gallery of Art - continued

5/14 - 9/17/95
ARISHILE GORKY: THE BREAKTHROUGH YEARS — 45 paintings and drawings from Gorky's mature years (1940-1948) will document the artist's crucial role as a link between European surrealism and American abstract expressionism. Highlighted in this exhibition will be his painting "The Liver is the Cock's Comb," a work that is rarely allowed to travel. CAT WT

5/28 - 8/20/95
JAMES McNEILL WHISTLER — 200 paintings, watercolors, pastels and prints that survey every aspect of Whistler's career will be presented in the most important exhibition of his works since his memorial exhibition in 1904-1905. CAT WT*

6/4 - 9/4/95
PIET MONDRIAN: 1872-1944 — In the first major exhibition of his work since the 70's, an assembly of works covering his entire career, on loan from collections throughout Europe and America, will allow the viewer to trace the major steps in Mondrian's artistic evolution. CAT WT

9/24/95 - 1/7/96
JOHN SINGLETON COPLEY IN ENGLAND — 30 masterful history and portrait paintings that are considered important monuments of British painting will be featured in this exhibition that includes such well known works as "Watson and the Shark" and "The Death of Major Peirson." Copley, an expatriate American, fled to England in 1774 in order to avoid the Revolutionary War and he remained there until his death 41 years later. CAT WT

10/1 - 12/31/95
OLD MASTER DRAWINGS FROM CHATSWORTH — 100 of the finest old master drawings assembled by the Dukes of Devonshire at Chatsworth will include many that have rarely or never before been exhibited in the U.S. Stunning works by a myriad of masters including Ghirlandaio, Leonardo da Vinci, Raphael, Parmiganino, Carracci, Rembrandt, Rubens, van Dyck, Brueghel, Poussin, Durer and Lorrain will be on view. CAT WT

10/1 - 12/31/95
THE TOUCH OF THE ARTIST: MASTER DRAWINGS FROM THE WOODNER FAMILY COLLECTION — More than 100 drawings that span 5 centuries of artistic achievement collected by the late Ian Woodner over the course of 35 years will be featured in this exhibition. The works on view, all selected from the superb Woodner core collection of old master and modern drawings are permanently housed at the National Gallery of Art. CAT WT*

10/15/95 - 1/28/96
WINSLOW HOMER — In the first exhibition of this magnitude in 3 decades, 230 paintings and works on paper that cover every aspect of Homer's artistic career will be on view. CAT WT

11/12/95 - 2/11/96
JOHANNES VERMEER — On loan from private and public sources worldwide, will be 19 of the 35 known works by this Dutch master, many of which will be restored for this exhibition. "Lady Writing a Letter with Her Maid," a painting recently recovered after having been stolen from the National Gallery of Ireland some years before will be included in this exhibition. CAT WT*

THROUGH 4/16/95
JASPER FRANCIS CROPSEY'S "THE SPIRIT OF WAR" AND "THE SPIRIT OF PEACE" — For the first time in more than a centruy, these two 19th century pendant works will be on view. BROCHURE WT*

National Museum of African Art
Affiliate Institution: Smithsonian Institution
950 Independence Ave., N.W., **Washington, DC 20560**
HRS: 10-5:30 Daily   HOL: 12/25
ADM: F   HDC/ACC: Y; Fully accessible elevators, restrooms, telephones, water fountains
PARKING: Y; Free 3 hour parking along the Mall   MUS/SH: Y   GR/T: Y!   GR/PH: DT: Y!
PERM/COLL: AF/ART

DISTRICT OF COLUMBIA

National Museum of African Art - continued

Opened in 1987, The National Museum of African Art has the distinction of being the only museum in the country dedicated to the collection, exhibition, conservation and study of the arts of Africa south of the Sahara.

ON EXHIBIT/95:

11/17/94 - 2/26/95   MOHAMMED OMER KAHLIL, PRINTMAKER/AMIR NOUR, SCULPTOR — Works by two Sudanese artists will be featured in this exhibition. Those by Kahlil will consist of etchings in which he explores graphic techniques, color contrasts, pattern and texture in creations inspired in one case by the music of Bob Dylan and in the other by his visit to the ancient site of Petra in Jordon. Nour's steel and bronze volumetric sculptures reflect inspiration from several sources including gourds, snakes and childhood memories of life.

11/23/94 - 3/27/95   GRACE KWAMI SCULPTURE: AN ARTIST'S BOOK BY ATTA KWAMI — In a book consisting of 48 unnumbered, folded pages that open like the legs of a spider (or annasi which in Ghanaian culture symbolizes wisdom and ingenuity) Kwami explores the artwork of his mother through his own artistic creation.

5/24 - 9/4/95   NUBIA: EGYPT'S ANCIENT RIVAL IN AFRICA — A rare view of the artistic achievements of Nubian culture from 3,100 B.C. to 400 A.D. will be seen in the hundreds of examples of metal, glass, ceramics, statuary and funerary inscriptions featured in this exhibition. Produced by these ancient yet sophisticated people, the objects on display reveal the culture of the Nubians and provide a perspective on their centuries-old volatile relationship with their rival Egyptian neighbors.   WT

PERMANENT EXHIBITIONS:

IMAGES OF POWER AND IDENTITY — 121 objects both from the permanent collection and on loan to the museum will be grouped according to major geographical & cultural regions of sub-Saharan Africa.

ROYAL BENIN ART IN THE COLLECTION OF THE NATIONAL MUSEUM OF AFRICAN ART — 21 15th to 19th century metalworks in copper alloy and brass, many made from the lost-wax process, will highlight an artistic medium often associated with the artisans of Benin (Nigeria).

THE ART OF THE PERSONAL OBJECT — Aesthetically important and interesting utilitarian objects reflect the artistic culture of various African societies.

PURPOSE AND PERFECTION: POTTERY AS A WOMAN'S ART IN CENTRAL AFRICA — Female artistry in Africa is observed in this display of pottery from the permanent collection of the museum.

National Museum of American Art
Affiliate Institution: Smithsonian Institution
8th & G Sts., N.W., **Washington, DC 20560**
TEL: 202-357-2700
HRS: 10-5:30 DAILY   HOL: 12/25
ADM: F
HDC/ACC: Y; Ramp to garage & elevator at 9th & G Sts., NW; all restrooms
PARKING: Y; Metered street parking with commercial lot nearby   MUS/SH: Y   REST/FAC: Y; 11-3:30 Daily
GR/T: Y   GR/PH: call 202-357-3111   DT: Y   TIME: Noon on weekdays; 2:00 on weekends
H/B: Y; Housed on Old Patent Office (Greek Revival architecture) mid 1800'S
PERM/COLL: AM: ptgs, sculp, gr, cont/phot, drgs, folk, Impr; AF/AM

National Museum of American Art - continued

All aspects of American art from the earliest works by limners to emerging artists of today are shown within the walls of this mid-19th century Greek Revival building. **NOT TO BE MISSED:** George Catlin's 19th C American Indian paintings; Thomas Moran's Western Landscape paintings; James Hampton's "The Throne of the Third Heaven of the Nation's Millenium General Assembly"

ON EXHIBIT/95:

9/16/94 - 1/2/95	MAN ON FIRE: LUIS JIMENEZ — Dramatic monumental fiberglass sculptures and related graphic works by Mexican-American artist Jimenez will be featured in his first major museum retrospective. BILINGUAL CAT BOOK
9/16/94 - 1/8/95	WORKS BY JESSE TREVINO: NEW YORK, VIETNAM, SAN ANTONIO — Diverse aspects of Mexican-American culture will be revealed in the paintings and drawings of Trevino, considered to be one of the finest realist contemporary artists working in the U.S. today. On view will be images relating to his military service in Vietnam, as well as protrayals of his family, friends, and urban landmarks of San Antinio's West Side.
10/28/94 - 2/2/95	FREE WITHIN OURSELVES: AFRICAN-AMERICAN ART FROM THE NATIONAL MUSEUM OF AMERICAN ART — From the 18th century to the 1980's, this exhibition of paintings and sculptures by more than 30 major artists that celebrate the achievements of African-American artists will include works by Frederick Brown, Jacob Lawrence, Lois Mailou Jones, Keith Morrison, Alma Thomas, Sam Gilliam and others. A new documentary video featuring 5 contemporary African-American artists will accompany this exhibition.
2/10 - 5/21/95	JIM NUTT RETROSPECTIVE — On exhibit will be the first major survey of the artists' work in over a decade. Nutt is commonly associated with the style of figurative art known as Chicago Imagism, a unique fusion of Surrealism, Pop Art and a personal expression that was equally informed by folk and popular art. Included will be some 120 paintings, drawings and objects from the early "Hairy Who" cartoon inspired reverse paint on plexiglass of the mid to late 60's to his black and white paintings of the 80's and his recent imaginative portraits. CAT WT
3/17 - 7/4/95	WILL BARNET: AN INTIMATE VIEW FROM THE MUSEUM'S COLLECTION — Paintings, prints, and newly acquired drawings from the collection of the museum that span 6 decades of Barnet's work will feature early social realist images of the 30's, figurative abstractions of the 40's & 50's, and portrait and figure works of the 60's and beyond.
6/2 - 8/20/95	RECENT ACQUISITIONS ON PAPER — Forty 20th century prints, drawings and watercolors acquired by the museum between 1991 & 1994 will be on view.
6/30 - 10/29/95	SECRETS OF THE DARK CHAMBER: THE ART OF THE AMERICAN DAGUERREOTYPE — 150 daguerreotype images in a thematic arrangement of portraits, landscapes, and cultural and social relationships will be seen in this exhibition that highlights the important role they played in the invention and modernization of 19th-century American photography. Nearly 3/4 of the works on display have never been published.
11/17/95 - 3/17/96	METROPOLITAN LIFE: THE ASHCAN ARTISTS AND THEIR NEW YORK, 1897-1913 — 100 works 6 members of the "Ashcan School" or "The Eight" will be featured in this exhibition that documents the many aspects of everyday life in New York at the turn of the century.

DISTRICT OF COLUMBIA

The National Museum of Women in the Arts
1250 New York Ave., N.W., **Washington, DC 20005**
TEL: 202-783-5000
HRS: 10-5 M-Sa; Noon-5 S   DAY CLOSED: M   HOL: 1/1, THGV, 12/25
VOL/CONT: Y   ADM: F   ADULT: $3.00   CHILDREN: F   STUDENTS: $2.00   SR CIT: $2.00
HDC/ACC: Y; Wheelchairs available   PARKING: Y; Paid parking lots nearby   MUS/SH: Y
REST/FAC: Y; 11-2:30 M-F   GR/T: Y   GR/PH: call 202-783-5000 education dept.
H/B: Y; 1907 Renaissance Revival building by Waddy Wood
PERM/COLL: PTGS, SCULP, GR, DRGS, 15-20; PHOT

Unique is the word for this museum established in 1981 and located in a splendidly restored 1907 Renaissance Revival building. The more than 800 works in the permanent collection are the result of the personal vision and passion of its founder, Wilhelmina Holladay, to elevate and validate the works of women artists throughout the history of art. **NOT TO BE MISSED:** Rotating collection of portrait miniatures (late 19th - early 20th c.) by Eulabee Dix; Lavinia Fontana's "Portrait of a Noblewoman"

ON EXHIBIT/95:

6/30/94 - 1/29/95	EULABEE DIX PORTRAIT MINIATURES: AN AMERICAN RENAISSANCE — 40 works by Dix, painted between 1895 and 1936 will be joined by examples by other artists in her circle, all of whom worked as miniaturists at the turn of the century in response to a resurgence of interest in the 400 year history of the art form. BROCHURE
11/94 - 2/95	MARY ELLEN MARK: 25 YEARS — More than 100 works will be seen in this first time retrospective for Marks, an internationally acclaimed photographer and photo-journalist best known for the often gritty and gripping portrayal of her subject matter. CAT
12/1/94 - 2/5/95	THE WASHINGTON PRINT CLUB: 30TH ANNUAL EXHIBITION — Highlighting printmakers from the 18th century to the present day, the exhibition focuses this year on the theme of women artists.
10/11/95 - 1/7/96	AT CENTURY'S END: NORWEGIAN ARTISTS AND THE FIGURATIVE TRADITION 1890/1990 — The link between innovative Norwegian artists of the 19th century and the recent re-emergence of the figurative tradition in works by contemporary artists will be addressed in this exhibition.

National Portrait Gallery
Affiliate Institution: Smithsonian Institution
F St. at 8th, N.W., **Washington, DC 20560**
TEL: 202-357-1447
HRS: 10-5:30 Daily   HOL: 12/25
ADM: F   HDC/ACC: Y; Through garage entrance corner 9th & G ST.
PARKING: Y; Metered street parking; some commercial lots nearby   MUS/SH: Y   REST/FAC: Y; 11-3:30
GR/T: Y   GR/PH: call 202-357-2920   DT: Y   TIME: inquire at information desk
H/B: Y; This 1836 Building served as a hospital during the Civil War   S/G: Y
PERM/COLL: AM: ptgs, sculp, drgs

Housed in an old Patent Office built in 1836, and used as a hospital during the Civil War, this museum allows the visitor to explore U.S. history as told through portraiture. **NOT TO BE MISSED:** Gilbert Stuart's portraits of George Washington & Thomas Jefferson; Self Portrait by John Singleton Copley.

DISTRICT OF COLUMBIA

National Portrait Gallery - continued

ON EXHIBIT/95:

10/14/94 - 2/20/95	POINTS OF VIEW: SINGLE SUBJECT/MULTIPLE ARTISTS — Among the 16 sitters by the more than 50 20th-century artists in this exhibition are a series of seven portraits of Igor Stravinsky painted over a 55 year period of his lifetime, 6 portraits of Paul Robeson as both an activist and an actor, and images of Man Ray as interpreted by Arnold Newman, Andy Warhol, David Hockney and Alexander Calder.

12/2/94 - 5/29/95   FEDERAL PROFILES: SAINT MÉMIN IN AMERICA, 1793 - 1814 — Portraits of Thomas Jefferson, Stephen Decatur, Merriweather Lewis and Mother Elizabeth Ann Seton by this French émigré artist, one of the most prolific portrait painters in Federal America, will be seen in this exhibition accompanied by engravings, watercolors, chalk drawings and copperplates that help to explain his working methods and techniques.
CAT

12/9/94 - 5/29/95   RECENT ACQUISITIONS

2/10 - 11/19/95   "AGITATE! AGITATE! AGITATE!:" THE LIFE OF FREDERICK DOUGLASS — In commemoration of the centennial of Douglass' death, this exhibition will present an overview of his life and legacy through photographs, paintings, prints, documents and other memorabilia.
CAT

2/24/95 - 1/1/96   FROM TRUMAN TO CLINTON — 27 original Time Magazine presidential portraits will be on view.

4/7 - 8/13/95   IN PURSUIT OF THE BUTTERFLY: PORTRAITS OF JAMES McNEILL WHISTLER — From his earliest student days to his last years spent in London, the 80 works in this exhibition, presented in conjunction with a retrospective of Whistler's work at the National Gallery, chronicle all aspects of the artist's public and private life.

6/6 - 12/3/95   RECENT ACQUISITIONS

6/16 - 8/13/95   THE PASSIONATE OBSERVER: PHOTOGRAPHS BY CARL VAN VECHTEN — In his 30 years behind the camera (1880-1964) Van Vechten, a music critic, novelist and journalist, produced a body of 15,000 images strictly for his own pleasure. As part of the international modernist movement he, through many of his portraits seen in this exhibition, acted as a bridge between the Harlem Renaissance and the other musical, artistic and literary worlds of New York.

10/6/95 - 1/28/96   CECILIA BEAUX AND THE ART OF PORTRAITURE — In the first major retrospetive for Beaux, a highly acclaimed turn-of-the-century portrait artist, 75 paintings and drawings, some never before seen publicly, will allow the viewer to assess her marvelous talent.
CAT

The Phillips Collection
1600 21st St., N.W., **Washington, DC 20009**
TEL: 202-387-2151
HRS: 10-5 Tu-Sa; Noon-7 S (open till 8:30 for "Artful Evenings" call for info)   HOL: 1/1, 7/4, 12/25, THGV
ADM: Y   ADULT: $6.50   CHILDREN: F (under 18)   STUDENTS: $3.25   SR CIT: $3.25
HDC/ACC: Y; All galleries accessible by wheelchair
PARKING: Limited metered parking on street; commercial lots nearby   MUS/SH: Y
REST/FAC: Y; Cafe 10:45-4:30 M-Sa; Noon-6:15 S   GR/T: Y   GR/PH: call 202-387-2151, ext 247
DT: Y   TIME: 2:00 W & Sa   H/B: Y   S/G: Y
PERM/COLL: AM: ptgs, sculp 19-20; EU: ptgs, sculp, 19-20

DISTRICT OF COLUMBIA

The Phillips Collection - continued

Housed in the 1897 former residence of the Duncan Phillips family, the core collection represents the successful culmination of one man's magnificent obsession with collecting the art of his time. **NOT TO BE MISSED:** Renoir's "Luncheon of the Boating Party;" Sunday afternoon concerts that are free with the price of museum admission and are held Sept. through May at 5pm; "Artful Evenings" ($5.00 pp) for socializing, art appreciation, entertainment, drinks and refreshments.

ON EXHIBIT/95:

9/24/94 - 1/2/95	THE PICTOGRAPHS OF ADOLPH GOTTLIEB — For the first time, this rare assemblage of over 60 works (1941-1952) from museum and private collections will allow the viewer to understand how Gottlieb, a founding member of the Abstract Expressionist group, combined and integrated a diverse range of pictographic elements (from classical, African, modern, Native American and Tlingit) into his own distinctive grid-like creations. ATR (May be purchased through Ticketmaster) CAT WT
11/15/94 - 3/19/95	AMERICAN MODERNIST PHOTOGRAPHY: WORKS FROM WASHINGTON COLLECTIONS — American master photoworks by Steichen, Stieglitz, Strand, Cunningham, Adams and others will be selected for viewing from private collections in the Washington area.
1/21 - 3/26/95	THE WILLIAM S. PALEY COLLECTION — From the private collection of the late founder of CBS, paintings, sculpture and drawings ranging from the 2nd half of the 19th century to the early 1970's will be on view. The visitor to the exhibition at this venue will have the opportunity to compare and contrast works of the same era amassed by both Duncan Phillips and William Paley, two important and highly individual collectors who were also contemporaries. CAT WT
3/21 - 7/16/95	SMALL PAINTINGS AND WORKS ON PAPER — Works from the permanent collection will be shown.
5/20 - 8/27/95	DOROTHEA LANGE: AMERICAN PHOTOGRAPHS — In the first retrospective of her work, 230 photographs that include Lange's images of American migrant families of the 1930's, and photos of the wartime relocation of Japanese-Americans, will be seen along with other powerful works that comment on American life from the 30's through the 50's. CAT
7/18 - 11/12/95	WORKS ON PAPER — A one room installation of works from the permanent collection.
9/23/95 - 1/7/96	ARTHUR DOVE, MARSDEN HARTLEY, JOHN MARIN, GEORGIA O'KEEFFE, AND ALFRED STIEGLITZ: IN THE AMERICAN GRAIN — The development of modernism as an independent American art form will be assessed in the 87 works by these 5 renowned American talents. In addition to the paintings, drawings, watercolors, photographs and collages selected from the permanent collection, archival material will allow the viewer to add to his understanding of this important 20th-century American art movement. WT

Renwick Gallery of the National Museum of American Art
Affiliate Institution: Smithsonian Institution
Pennsylvania Ave. at 17th St., N.W., **Washington, DC 20560**
TEL: 202-357-2247
HRS: 10-5:30 Daily   HOL: 12/25
ADM: F   HDC/ACC: Y; Ramp that leads to elevator at corner 17th & Pa. Ave.
PARKING: Limited street parking; commercial lots and garages nearby   MUS/SH: Y
GR/T: Y   GR/PH: M-T 10-1 call 202-357-3111   H/B: Y; French Second Empire style designed in 1859 by James Renwick, Jr.
PERM/COLL: CONT/AM: crafts; AM: ptgs

DISTRICT OF COLUMBIA

Renwick Gallery of the National Museum of American Art - continued

Built in 1859 and named not for its founder, William Corcoran, but rather for its architect, James Renwick, this charming French Second Empire style building is known primarily for its displays of American crafts. The museum in 1994, became the recipient of the entire KPMG Peat Marwick corporate collection of American crafts. **NOT TO BE MISSED:** Grand Salon furnished in the styles of the 1860's & 1870's.

ON EXHIBIT/95:

10/28/94 - 2/5/95   CONTEMPORARY CRAFTS AND THE SAXE COLLECTION — From whimsical figurative sculptures, to works of abstraction, to imaginative vessel forms, 124 contemporary craft objects from this impressive collection will highlight the important strides made in the field of crafts during the decade of the 80's.   BOOK   WT

11/10/94 - 2/5/95   ALLAN WEST MEETS EAST: FOUR FOLDING SCREENS — On view will be 4 large-scale brightly colored and expressionistic screens by West, an American artist living in Tokyo, that combine his interpretations of traditional Japanese landscapes with the influence of American Color Field painting.

3/31 - 6/18/95   UNCOMMON BEAUTY IN COMMON OBJECTS: THE LEGACY OF AFRICAN-AMERICAN CRAFT ART — In one of the first circulating exhibitions of its kind, diverse works of African-American crafts in fiber, jewelry, furniture, quilts, basketry, leather, glass and metal by recognized and emerging artists will be featured.

3/31 - 6/18/95   MARRIAGE IN FORM: KAY SEKIMACHI AND BOB STOCKSDALE — In the first retrospective exhibition for each of these artists who are married to each other, 36 baskets and woven wall hangings by Sekimachi and 42 turned wooden bowls by Stocksdale will be on view.   WT

Sasakawa Peace Foundation
1819 L St., N.W., **Washington, DC 20036**
TEL: 202-296-6694
HRS: 10-6 M-F; 10-4 3rd Sa of each month   HOL: LEG/HOL!
ADM: F
HDC/ACC: Y; Fully accessible

Contemporary Japanese art which contains both Eastern and Western elements is highlighted in the special exhibitions scheduled on a regular basis in this recently opened facility. Like its sister counterpart in Tokyo, this gallery provides the opportunity to showcase contemporary Japanese art and to explore how both Japanese and non-Japanese American artists have been influenced by Japanese culture.

ON EXHIBIT/95:

1/12 - 3/18/95   BEYOND EAST AND WEST: A ROB BARNARD RETROSPECTIVE, 1974-1994 — Japanese and American influences combine in this wonderful group of ceramics that push the expressive potential of pottery to its limits.

3/30 - 5/30/95   KOJI IKUTA: MEZZOTINT WORKS — Traditional Japanese themes of nature are captured through the dark European technique of scoring and tinting copper printing plates.

6/8 - 7/28/95   THE TREE, PART II — Japanese artists respond through their art to the works of American painters presented in The Tree, Part I in the summer of 1994.

9/14 - 11/30/95   TAZUKO ICHIKAWA — Wooden sculpture.

DISTRICT OF COLUMBIA

Sewall-Belmont House
144 Constitution Ave., N.W., **Washington, DC 20002**
TEL: 202-546-3989
HRS: 10-3 Tu-F; Noon-4 Sa, S   DAY CLOSED: M   HOL: 1/1, THGV, 12/25
VOL/CONT: Y   ADM: F
PARKING: Limited street parking only   GR/T: Y   GR/PH: 202-546-3989
DT: Y   TIME: 10-3 Tu-F; Noon-4 Sa, S   H/B: Y
PERM/COLL: SCULP, PTGS

Paintings and sculpture depicting heroines of the women's rights movement line the halls of the historic Sewall-Belmont House. One of the oldest houses on Capitol Hill, this unusual museum is dedicated to the theme of women's suffrage.

ON EXHIBIT/95:   No traveling exhibitions

FLORIDA

BELLEAIR

Florida Gulf Coast Art Center, Inc.
222 Ponce deLeon Blvd., **Belleair, FL 34616**
TEL: 813-584-8634
HRS: 10-4 M-F (Pilcher Gallery); 10-4 M-Sa, Noon-4 S (Shillard Smith Gallery)   HOL: LEG/HOL!
ADM: F
HDC/ACC: Y   PARKING: Y; Ample free parking   MUS/SH: Y   GR/T: Y   GR/PH: call 407-539-2181
DT: Y   TIME: call for information   S/G: Y
PERM/COLL: AM: ptgs 1940-1950'S

In operation for 50 years this art center, just south of Clearwater near Tampa, features a permanent collection of over 700 works of art (late 19th - 20th c) with a focus on American artists including Isabel Bishop, Breckenridge, Bricher, and Inness. PLEASE NOTE: The Pilcher Gallery houses works from the permanent collection while the Smith Gallery is host to traveling exhibitions.

ON EXHIBIT/95:

12/3/94 - 1/29/95	MILTON AVERY: WORKS ON PAPER — 35 works on paper by "America's Matisse" will be featured. CAT
2/11 - 4/9/95	FLORIDA REALISM: JOHN BRIGGS, CLYDE BUTCHER, HANSON MULFORD — Florida's fragile ecology and the urgency of protecting the environment is explored through painting and photography. CAT
4/22 - 6/18/95	AMERICAN-CUBAN, CUBAN-AMERICAN, THIRTY-FIVE — Presented will be works by several Cuban artists in their 30's, some of whom came to the U.S. after the Cuban Revolution 35 years ago and others who are recent arrivals, that will allow for contrast and comparison of their individaul experiences through their unique creations.
9/16 - 11/19/95	SOUTHEASTERN FINE CRAFTS BIENNIAL INVITATIONAL, I — A multi-media exhibition of exceptional work created by Southeastern artists. GALLERY BROCHURE WT
12/2/95 - 1/28/96	SOUTHEASTERN WATERCOLOR VIII — Both traditional and innovative works will be featured in this premier Southeastern juried exhibition. CAT

BOCA RATON

Boca Raton Museum of Art
801 W. Palmetto Park Rd., **Boca Raton, FL 33486**
TEL: 407-392-2500
HRS: 10-4 M-F; Noon-4 Sa, S   HOL: LEG/HOL!
SUGG/CONT: Y
HDC/ACC: Y   PARKING: Y; Free   MUS/SH: Y   GR/T: Y   GR/PH: call 407-392-2500
DT: Y   TIME: daily!   S/G: Y
PERM/COLL: PHOT; PTGS 20

With the addition to its permanent holdings in 1990 of late 19th & 20th century art from the collection of Dr. and Mrs. John Mayers, the Boca Raton Museum of Art is well worth a visit–even on a sunny day! Look for news of the new Boca Raton Museum building to be completed in a nearby location in 1996. The newly expanded facility, over 4 football fields long, will allow for display of a large portion of the permanent collection. Due to the museum's impending move to its new facility, no exhibitions have been scheduled for the remainder of the year after 4/95.

FLORIDA

Boca Raton Museum of Art - continued

ON EXHIBIT/95:

11/25/94 - 1/8/95   BERNAR VENET: NEW AND RECENT SCULPTURE AND DRAWINGS — Large-scale sculpture on the grounds with additional sculpture and drawings in the galleries by this internationally acclaimed French artist.   CAT

1/13 - 3/1/95   PHOTOGRAPHY AND BEYOND: NEW EXPRESSIONS IN FRANCE — From established masters to emerging talents, works by French avant-garde photographers will be featured in this exhibition that is a joint venture between the Israel Museum and the Boca Raton Museum of Art.   CAT   WT

3/5 - 4/16/95   MASTERPIECES OF AMERICAN MODERNISM: SELECTIONS FROM A PRIVATE COLLECTION — Featured will be major works by many of America's greatest modern masters including paintings by O'Keeffe, Demuth, Hartley, Dove, Scheeler, Marin, Davis and others.

3/5 - 4/16/95   HARVEY SADOW: A JOURNEY IN CLAY — A ceramic tableau by Florida artist, Sadow, comprised of plates and bowls forms a landscape image that is part real and part fantasy.   CAT

CORAL GABLES

Lowe Art Museum

Affiliate Institution: University of Miami
1301 Stanford Dr., **Coral Gables, FL 33146**
TEL: 305-284-3536
HRS: 10-5 Tu-Sa; Noon-5 S   DAY CLOSED: M   HOL: ACAD!
ADM: Y   ADULT: $4.00   CHILDREN: $1.00 (6-12)   STUDENTS: $2.00   SR CIT: $3.00
HDC/ACC: Y; Ramp, parking & doors accessible   PARKING: Y; On premises   MUS/SH: Y
GR/T: Y   GR/PH: By reserv. 305-284-2024   S/G: Y
PERM/COLL: REN: ptgs, sculp (Kress Collection); SP; P/COL; AF; EU: dec/art; OR: ptgs, sculp, gr, cer; AM: ptgs, gr; LAT/AM; NAT/AM

Since its establishment in 1950, the Lowe has acquired such a superb and diverse permanent collection that it is recognized as one of the major fine art resources in Florida. More than 7,000 works from a wide array of historical styles and periods including the Kress Collection of Italian Renaissance and Baroque Art, and the Cintas Collection of Spanish Old Master paintings are represented in the collection. **NOT TO BE MISSED:** Kress Collection of Italian Renaissance and Baroque art

ON EXHIBIT/95:

12/8/94 - 2/6/95   LATIN AMERICAN ART FROM MIAMI COLLECTIONS — Trends in 20th century Latin American art will be seen in the wide diversity of drawings, paintings and watercolors selected for viewing from some of Miami's most distinguished collections.

12/8 94 - 2/6/95   SOUTH AMERICAN INDIAN PAINTINGS BY GEORGE CATLIN — From the National Gallery of Art in Washington, D.C., a selection of 35 works created between 1854-1860 that depict South American Indian tribal life and serve as an important record of 19th century South American Indian culture.

2/16 - 4/2/95   IMPERIAL RUSSIAN PORCELAIN FROM THE RAYMOND F. PIPER COLLECTION — 86 opulent and extravagant porcelains from the Imperial Porcelain Factory in St. Petersburg, Russia, created between the reigns of Elizabeth I and Nicholas II, will be featured in this exhibition.   CAT   WT

Lowe Art Museum - continued

4/13 - 5/28/95	THE MICCOSUKEE: A VISUAL COMMENTARY — Text of memories, opinions, and reactions to life today will be accompanied by transcriptions of oral history in this photo documentary exhibition that explores contemporary Seminole and Miccosukee Indian society of Florida.
6/8 - 7/31/95	PABLO PICASSO'S "SUITE VOLLARD" — Named after his art dealer, Ambroise Vollard, this suite of 100 copper plate engravings completed between 1927-1937, include the themes of the sculptor's studio, Rembrandt, and the Minotaur.
9/14 - 10/29/95	WALTER O. EVANS COLLECTION OF AFRICAN-AMERICAN ART — A multi-media exhibition that traces the evolution of African-American art .
11/9 - 12/24/95	IMAGE AND MEMORY: LATIN AMERICAN PHOTOGRAPHY, 1880-1992 — Important historical, social, political and aesthetic forces in Latin American life and culture since 1880 are seen in the diversity of Latin American photography on view in this exhibition.

DAYTONA BEACH

Museum of Arts and Sciences
1040 Museum Blvd., **Daytona Beach, FL 32014**
HRS: 9-4 Tu-F; Noon-5 Sa, S   DAY CLOSED: M   HOL: LEG/HOL!
ADM: Y   ADULT: $3.00   CHILDREN: $1.00   STUDENTS: $1.00
HDC/ACC: Y   PARKING: Y; Ample free parking   MUS/SH: Y   GR/T: Y   GR/PH: call 904-255-0285
PERM/COLL: REG: ptgs, gr, phot; AF; P/COL; EU: 19; AM: 18-20; FOLK; CUBAN: ptgs 18-20; OR; AM: dec/art, ptgs, sculp 17-20

The Museum of Arts and Sciences which serves as an outstanding cultural resource in the state of Florida has recently completed a new wing designed to add thousands of square feet of new gallery space. The new entrance to the museum features a nature drive through Tuscawill Park. **NOT TO BE MISSED:** The Dow Gallery of American Art, a collection of over 200 paintings, sculptures, furniture, and decorative arts (1640-1910).

ON EXHIBIT/95:

1/14 - 4/16/95	WALTER GAUDNEK: LABYRINTHS AND NEW WORK — A 2,000 square-foot three-dimensional interactive walk-through maze-like painting by German-born artist Gaudnek will be accompanied by an exhibition of others of his paintings in a second gallery.
3/11 - 10/22/95	TROPICAL COLORS: IMAGES OF CUBA, FLORIDA AND THE BAHAMAS, 1898-1904 — On exhibit will be 100 original romantic polychrome images by William Henry Jackson, one of the most respected 19th century American photographers.
4/22 - 9/24/95	19TH CENTURY JEWELRY FROM THE LEVINE COLLECTION — 200 masterpieces of English and Continental gold, micromosaic, semi-precious and precious jewelry will be on view.
5/13 - 9/24/95	OCEAN PALETTE — Undersea photographs by Larry Bell show Florida's diverse aquatic environments.
5/20 - 9/24/95	FEATS OF CLAY: THE BARNETT BANK ALL FLORIDA INVITATIONAL On exhibit will be objects by cutting-edge Florida artists who work in clay.

FLORIDA

DAYTONA BEACH

Southeast Museum of Photography
Affiliate Institution: Daytona Beach Community College
1200 Volusia Ave., **Daytona Beach, FL 32115**
TEL: 904-254-4475
HRS: 10-3 Tu-F; 5-7 Tu; 1-4 S   DAY CLOSED: Sa, M   HOL: LEG/HOL!
ADM: F   HDC/ACC: Y   PARKING: Y; On college campus
GR/T: Y   GR/PH: call 904-254-4475
DT: Y   TIME: 20 minute "Art for Lunch" tours!
PERM/COLL: PHOT

Thousands of photographs from the earliest daguerreotypes to the latest experiments in computer assisted manipulation are housed in this modern 2 floor gallery space. Examples of nearly every photographic process in the medium's 150 year old history is represented in this collection.

ON EXHIBIT/95:

1/10 - 3/3/95	CRITICAL MASS: A COLLABORATIVE EXHIBITION BY MERIDEL RUBEN-STEIN, WOODY AND STEINA VASKULKA AND ELLEN ZWEIG — An installation of several environments that depict the events and characters relating to the history of the Manhattan Project and the creation of the first atom bomb.
1/10 - 3/3/95	BARBARA NORFLEET: AESTHETICS OF DEFENSE — In remembrance of the 25th anniversary of the bombing of Japan, this exhibition presents a chilling display of photographs of nuclear test sites.
1/10 - 3/3/95	GILLES PERESS: FAREWELL TO BOSNIA — Bridging the gap between art and journalism, this photographic exhibition documents the daily struggles of the citizens of Sarajevo and Mostar as seen by Peress during his stay there from March to September, 1993.
1/10 - 3/3/95	ROBERT O. ZELLER, JR.: CIVIL WAR PHOTOGRAPHS OF ANTIETAM — 15 original vintage stereo-graphs and large plate folio prints by Civil War photographer, Alexander Gardner.
3/14 - 6/26/95	WATER'S EDGE: PHOTOGRAPHS BY SALLY GALL — Black and white romantic images of gelatin silver-print landscapes created by the manipulation of selectively diffused lighting.
3/14 - 6/26/95	INWARD EYE: A MODERN INTERPRETATION OF ROMANTICISM — In this exhibition the works of 6 contemporary artists using a wide variety of techniques will present photographic works that deal with the common theme of neo-Romanticism through the genre of landscape.
3/14 - 6/26/95	THE PERSISTENCE OF BEAUTY, THE PERSISTENCE OF PAIN: LUIS GONZALES PALMAS — In his theatrically posed and manipulated photographic images, Palmas addresses the themes of pain and oppression experienced by Mayans and Guatamalans of mixed racial origin.
3/14 - 6/26/95	MARIA MARTINEZ CANAS: BLACK TOTEMS — Small photographic inserts within larger shapes and frames present fragmented images of cities, landscapes and nudes that reflect the artist's disconnection with her native Cuba.
7/11 - 8/15/95	PHOTOGRAPHS BY WILFRED THESIGER: A MOST CHERISHED POSSESSION — 70 photographs that span Thesiger's travels in the Middle East and Northern Africa over a 50 year period will be seen in the first North American exhibition of his work.

Southeast Museum of Photography - continued

7/11 - 8/15/95	PHOTOGRAPHY BY CINTAS FELLOWS — Sponsored by the Cintas Foundation, this exhibition of photography by Cuban-American artists is designed to highlight their artistic accomplishments and to encourage professional development of Cuban expatriate artists.
7/11 - 8/15/95	FORGOTTEN FLORIDA: FARM SECURITY ADMINISTRATION PHOTOGRAPHS OF FLORIDA — Photographic images that show how poor men, women and children worked and survived in Florida during the Great Depression.
9/7 - 12/15/95	PICTURING PARADISE: COLONIAL PHOTOGRAPHY OF SAMOA, 1875-1925 — Rare photographs on loan from collections worldwide will be assembled in the first major study of the use of photography in the construction of the West's images of paradise.
9/7 - 12/15/95	THIRD DIMENSION: CONTEMPORARY PHOTOGRAPHIC SCULPTURE — Ways in which the medium of photography can be presented in three dimensional form is explored in this exhibition.

DELAND

The Deland Museum of Art
600 N. Woodland Blvd., **DeLand, FL 32720-3447**
TEL: 904-734-4371
HRS: 10-4 Tu-Sa, 1-4 S   DAY CLOSED: M   HOL: LEG/HOL!
ADM: Y   ADULT: $2.00   CHILDREN: $1.00 (4-12)   STUDENTS: $1.00   SR CIT: $2.00
HDC/ACC: Y   PARKING: Y; Free and ample   MUS/SH: Y
GR/T: Y   GR/PH: call 904-734-4371   DT: Y   TIME: !
H/B: Y; Building is 1892 Taylor Family Mansion
PERM/COLL: AM: 19-20; CONT: reg; DEC/ART; NAT/AM

The Deland, opened in the New Cultural Arts Center in 1991, is located between Daytona Beach and Orlando. It is a fast growing, vital institution that offers a wide range of art and art-related activities to the community and its visitors. PLEASE NOTE: The permanent collection is not usually on display.

ON EXHIBIT/95:

1/13 - 3/17/95	GARY MONROE: ONE-MAN EXHIBITION — This photographic exploration of the DeLand area will address issues of multicultural socialization through documentation of African-American and Hispanic families, as well as images of the landscape, political events, community events and historic landmarks. CAT
1/13 - 3/17/95	SLAYTON UNDERHILL: ONE-MAN SHOW — 30 paintings and photographs that concern themselves with the "multiplicity of things" by senior Florida artist, Underhill.
3/31 - 5/28/95	HURRICANE ANDREW ART QUILTS — 40 quilts by 10 fiber artists whose collaborative efforts have resulted in multi-media personal statements that comment on their experiences of living through a violent life-changing storm.
6/2 - 8/27/95	EXPEDITION: EVERGLADES - RIVER OF GRASS — Curated by gallery owner, Sherry French, this 50 work multi-media exhibition addresses issues of the continuing deterioration of the flora and fauna within the Florida Everglades. CAT

FLORIDA

FT. LAUDERDALE

Museum of Art, Inc.
1 E. Las Olas Blvd., **Ft. Lauderdale, FL 33301**
HRS: 11-9 Tu; 10-5 W-Sa; Noon-5 S   DAY CLOSED: M   Galleries closed mid Aug - early Sept.   HOL: LEG/HOL!
ADM: Y   ADULT: $5.00   CHILDREN: F (under 12)   STUDENTS: $2.00   SR CIT: $4.00
HDC/ACC: Y; Parking area & ramp near front door; wheelchairs available
PARKING: Y; Metered parking ($.50 per hour) at the Municipal Parking facility on S.E. 1st Ave. bordering the
museum on the East side.   MUS/SH: Y   GR/T: Y   GR/PH: call 305-525-5500 ex 39
DT: Y   TIME: 1:00 & 6:30 Tu; 1:00 T & F   H/B: Y; Built by renowned architect Edward Larrabee Barnes   S/G: Y
PERM/COLL: AM: gr, ptgs, sculp 19-20; EU: gr, ptgs, sculp 19-20; PR/COL; AF; OC; NAT/AM

Aside from an impressive permanent collection of 20th century European and American art, this
museum is home to the William Glackens collection, the most comprehensive collection of works by
the artist and others of his contemporaries who, as a group, are best known as "The Eight" and/or the
Ashcan School. **NOT TO BE MISSED:** The William Glakens Collection

ON EXHIBIT/95:

11/4/94 - 1/22/95	ELECTRONIC SUPER HIGHWAY: NAM JUNE PAIK IN THE 90'S — Fabricated especially for The Museum of Art, Paik's monumental multi-television monitor installation that addresses the significance of the electronic media on modern culture will fill the entire first floor gallery. CAT (both written & video) WT
11/4/94 - 1/15/95	ALFRED EISENSTAEDT PHOTOGRAPHS — In celebration of Eisenstaedt, a pioneer photojournalist who has enjoyed a long and legendary career as a Life Magazine photographer, this exhibition will include his images of important historical events, portraits of famous people, and vignettes of ordinary people involved in everyday life.
12/20/94 - 5/7/95	FERNANDO BOTERO MONUMENTAL SCULPTURES AND DRAWINGS — In one of the most prestigious exhibitions the museum has ever mounted, 100 drawings and 14 large-scale sculptures by the internationally famous Columbian artist, Botero will be on exhibit.
1/20 - 8/13/95	SELECTIONS FROM THE CoBrA COLLECTION
2/10 - 4/2/95	MY PEOPLE: THE PORTRAITS OF ROBERT HENRI — In the first major exhibition of the artist's works in 10 years, portraits painted over a 30 year period by Henri, a member and mentor of a group of painters at the turn of the century known as "The Eight," will be on view.
2/10 - 4/2/95	HENRI'S DISCIPLES: WILLIAM GLAKENS AND JOHN SLOAN — Hung thematically and chronologically, 40 works by Henri, Glakens and Sloan, all close associates who painted between 1893-1928, will demonstrate how each artist though depicting the same subject matter developed distinctive and individual styles.
4/21 - 6/18/95	SOUTH FLORIDA COLLECTS — Borrowed from approximately 30 collectors will be artworks, most of which have never been seen publicly, that will include works by de Kooning, Lichtenstein, Mapplethorpe, and Noguchi.
5/18 - 8/13/95	BEDIA COLLECTION — Two vessels created by Bedia himself will be shown with his collection of sculptures and vessels from primative cultures in Africa, South America, Australia and Oceania.
5/18 - 8/13/95	SELECTIONS FROM THE PERMANENT COLLECTION
5/18 - 8/13/95	GOTZ
6/25 - 8/13/95	WORKS IN PROGRESS (INTERACTIVE)

GAINSVILLE

Samuel P. Harn Museum of Art
Affiliate Institution: Univ. of Florida
Gainsville, FL 32611
HRS: 11-5 Tu-F; 10-5 Sa; 1-5 S (last adm. is 4:45)   DAY CLOSED: M   HOL: STATE HOL!
ADM: F
HDC/ACC: Y; Wheelchair accessible   PARKING: Y; Ample and free   MUS/SH: Y
GR/T: Y   GR/PH: call 904-392-9826   DT: Y   TIME: 2:00 Sa, S
PERM/COLL: AM: ptgs, gr, sculp; EU: ptgs, gr, sculp; P/COL; AF; OC; IND: ptgs, sculp; JAP: gr ; CONT

Although opened to the public only as recently as 1990, the Harn Museum has one of the strongest collections of African art in the region and is one of Florida's three largest art museums. **NOT TO BE MISSED:** African art collection; A Distant View: Florida Paintings by Herman Herzog

ON EXHIBIT/95:

1/23/94 - 8/13/95	HUMAN AND DIVINE IN ANCIENT AMERICAN ART — 138 objects from the permanent collection depict human beings and divinities from 6 major cultural pre-Columbian regions of the Americas. BROCHURE
4/3/94 - 10/96	TRADITIONAL ART FROM THE SEPIK RIVER: IMAGES OF PAPUA NEW GUINEA — Items of ritual art that include objects both for warfare and for everyday life will be featured in this exhibition. BROCHURE
11/6/94 - 2/26/95	AMERICA'S MIRROR: PAINTING IN THE UNITED STATES 1859-1950 FROM THE COLLECTION OF THE GEORGIA MUSEUM OF ART, UNIVERSITY OF GEORGIA, ATHENS — 55 paintings that document the growth of American history and art history through an overview of such themes as genre, still life, landscape and the like will include outstanding examples by members of "The 8" (A.K.A. the Ashcan School).
1/15 - 3/12/95	LIFE LINES: AMERCIAN MASTER DRAWINGS FROM THE MUNSON-WILLIAMS PROCTOR INSTITUTE — 56 drawings by 56 of America's foremost master artistsCAT
1 - 2/92	TURNING AROUND THE CENTRE: SHIRAZEH HOUSHIARY — Four lead & gold leaf contemporary sculptures based on the square and four graphite & acrylic drawings on paper mounted on aluminum are featured in this rotunda exhibition. CAT
3/12 - 6/5/95	30TH ANNIVERSARY DEPARTMENT OF ART, COLLEGE OF FINE ARTS FACULTY EXHIBITION BROCHURE
3/19 - 5/14/95	ARNOLD MESCHES: A RETROSPECTIVE — Various themes in contemporary society will be addressed in this exhibition of 40 large-scale paintings by New York artist, Mesches. CAT WT
3/26 - 5/21/95	REMBRANDT ETCHINGS: SELECTIONS FROM THE CARNEGIE MUSEUM OF ART — 51 portrait, narrative, genre, figurative, landscape and religious themes by Rembrandt will be seen in this exhibition of his etchings. BOOKLET WT
8/27 - 10/22/95	IMAGES OF PENANCE, IMAGES OF MERCY: SOUTHWESTERN SANTOS IN THE LATE 19TH CENTURY — An exhibition of religious folk art from northern New Mexico and southern Colorado. CAT
9/3 - 12/3/95	CONTEMPORARY JAPANESE CERAMICS FROM THE POLK MUSEUM OF ART — Contemporary ceramics by artists from the Shinto, Bizen and Hagi districts of Japan whose works reflect their reverence for the spiritual and aesthetic traditions of their historic artisan forefathers.
9/3 - 12/3/95	20TH CENTURY AMERICAN CERAMICS FROM THE EVERSON MUSEUM — 40 traditional and innovative works from one of the major museum collections in the U.S. will be featured.

FLORIDA

Samuel P. Harn Museum of Art - continued

10/15 - 11/27/95	TREASURES OF THE CORNELL FINE ARTS MUSEUM — 50 American paintings, prints and drawings accompanied by glass works by Louis Comfort Tiffany will be selected for viewing from one of the most comprehensive fine arts collections in the state of Florida. CAT
12/17/95 - ONGIONG	SPIRIT EYES, HUMAN HANDS: WEST AFRICAN ART FROM THE HARN MUSEUM COLLECTION — A re-installation of 90 objects from the permanent collection that have been on an extended exhibition tour. CAT

HOLLYWOOD

Hollywood Art Museum
2015 Hollywood Blvd., **Hollywood, FL 33020**
TEL: 305-927-6455
HRS: 1-4- M-F (Sep-June)   DAY CLOSED: Sa, S
ADM: F
PERM/COLL: AF; CONT: sculp, ptgs

The Hollywood Museum, which had the distinction of presenting the first solo exhibition of the works of sculptor Duane Hansen, will be closed indefinitely for renovation and expansion. Plans are to rename this facility the Hollywood Museum of Arts and Science.

JACKSONVILLE

Cummer Gallery of Art
829 Riverside Ave., **Jacksonville, FL 32204**
TEL: 904-356-6857
HRS: 10-9:30 Tu, 10-4 W-F, Noon-5 Sa, 2-5 S   DAY CLOSED: M   HOL: 1/1, EASTER, 7/4, THGV, 12/25
ADM: Y   ADULT: $3.00   CHILDREN: $1.00; F under 5   SR CIT: $2.00
HDC/ACC: Y; Ramps, restrooms, etc.   PARKING: Y; Opposite museum at 829 Tiverside Ave.   MUS/SH: Y
GR/T: Y   GR/PH: call 904-356-6857   DT: Y   TIME: 10-3 Tu-F(by appt); 3:00 S (w/o appt)
H/B: Y; Garden founded in 1901   S/G: Y
PERM/COLL: AM: ptgs; EU: ptgs; OR; sculp; CER; DEC/ART; AN/GRK; AN/R; P/COL; IT/REN

Named for its founders and located on the picturesque site of the original family home, visitors can travel through 4,000 years of art history along the chronologically arranged galleries of the Cummer Museum. Though the building itself is relatively new, the original formal gardens remain for all to enjoy. **NOT TO BE MISSED:** One of the earliest and rarest collections of Early Meissen Porcelain in the world

ON EXHIBIT/95:

11/18/94 - 1/27/95	OLD MASTERS OF THE 15TH AND 16TH CENTURY — Prints
1/27 - 4/14/95	EXHIBITION OF PRINTS TBA
1/24 - 3/5/95	ART OF THE EYE
2/10 - 3/19/95	TOWARDS MODERNISM: THE COLLECTION OF MR. AND MRS. JAMES BEAL

112

Cummer Gallery of Art - continued

4/14 - 6/23/95	JACKSONVILLE WATERCOLOR SOCIETY ANNUAL EXHIBITION (TENT!)
5/12 - 7/9/95	LOUIS SULLIVAN
6/23 - 8/25/95	EXHIBITION OF PRINTS TBA
7/7 - 9/3/95	ART IN CHINA: POST 1989
8/25 - 11/17/95	COLLECTION OF MR. AND MRS. GUNTER (TENT!)
9/15 - 12/17/95	THE HERSON COLLECTION (TENT!) OR
	SOUTHERN ARTS FEDERATION ANNUAL (TENT!)
10/27 - 12/30/95	MEISSEN
11/17/95 - 1/26/96	EXHIBITION OF PRINTS TBA

JACKSONVILLE

Jacksonville Art Museum
4160 Boulevard Center Dr., **Jacksonville, FL 32207**
HRS: 10-4 Tu, W,F ; 10-10 T; 1-5 Sa, S   DAY CLOSED: M   HOL: LEG/HOL!
ADM: F
HDC/ACC: Y   PARKING: Y; Free and ample   MUS/SH: Y   GR/T: Y   GR/PH: call 904-398-8336
DT: Y   TIME: upon request if available   S/G: Y
PERM/COLL: CONT; P/COL

The finest art from classic to contemporary is offered in the Jacksonville Museum, the oldest museum in the city. **NOT TO BE MISSED:** Collection of Pre-Columbian art on permanent display

ON EXHIBIT/95:

1/18/94 - 1/8/95	HOLIDAY TABLES: ARTFUL INSPIRATIONS — Now in the 6th year of what has become an annual tradition, 40 artists, architects and designers will create vignettes of fantasy table settings deriving their inspiration from an original work of art within the museum.
11/18/94 - 1/8/95	CLYDE BUTCHER: PHOTOGRAPHS - THE MAJESTY OF THE FLORIDA LANDSCAPE — Dramatic photographs of some of the still pristine environments that exist in the middle of the state of Florida.
1/19 - 2/26/95	SALLY MANN: STILL TIME — Photographs
3/16 - 4/30/95	AFRICAN-AMERICAN WORKS ON PAPER: THE COCHRAN COLLECTION — 75 works by an abundance of renowned African-American artists will be on exhibit.
3/16 - 6/3/95	SELECTED JACKSONVILLE ARTISTS
6/15 - 7/30/95	JACKSONVILLE COALITION OF VISUAL ARTS JURIED EXHIBITION
6/15 - 7/30/95	PERMANENT COLLECTION
	PRE-COLUMBIAN CERAMICS
6/15 - 10/15/95	FLORIDA FILM PIONEER: RICHARD NORMAN — On view will be posters and memorabilia in addition to films produced by Norman in the early 1920's especially for African-American audiences.

FLORIDA

LAKELAND

Polk Museum of Art
800 E. Palmetto, **Lakeland, FL 33801**
TEL: 813-688-7743
HRS: 10-4 Tu-Sa; Noon-4 S   DAY CLOSED: M   HOL: LEG/HOL!
VOL/CONT: Y   ADM: F
HDC/ACC: Y; Fully accessible by wheelchair; "Hands-On" for visually impaired
PARKING: Y; Free lot in front of museum   MUS/SH: Y   GR/T: Y   GR/PH: call 813-688-7743   S/G: Y
PERM/COLL: P/COL; REG; AS: cer, gr; EU: cer, glass, silver 15-19: AM: 20; REG

Located in central Florida about 40 miles east of Tampa, the 37,000 square foot Polk Museum of Art facility offers a complete visual and educational experience to visitors and residents alike. The Pre-Columbian Gallery with its self-activated slide presentation and its hands-on display for the visually handicapped is but one of the innovative aspects of this vital community museum and cultural center. **NOT TO BE MISSED:** "El Encuentro" by Gilberto Ruiz; Jaguar Effigy Vessel from the Nicoya Region of Costa Rica (middle polychrome period, circa A.D. 800-1200)

ON EXHIBIT/95:

9/94 - 7/30/95	CONTEMPORARY WORKS BY FLORIDA ARTISTS FROM THE PMA COLLECTION
1/6 - 2/26/95	ORIENTAL SCROLLS FROM THE PMA COLLECTION
1/14 - 3/12/95	MODERN MASTERS: THE COLLECTION OF THE SARA LEE CORPORATION — Paintings and sculptures selected for viewing from this distinguished collection will include examples of works by Braque, Chagall, Degas, Dufy, Gauguin, Giacometti, Leger, Matisse, Picasso, Renoir, Pissaro, Rouault, Sisley, Soutine and Toulouse-Lautrec. CAT
3/3 - 4/30/95	EUROPEAN CERAMICS FROM THE PMA COLLECTION
4/1 - 7/30/95	FIFTH ALL-FLORIDA BIENNIAL
6/3 - 7/30/95	SPIRIT EYES, HUMAN HANDS: AFRICAN ART FROM THE SAMUEL P. HARN MUSEUM OF ART — The 85 African artifacts on view were all created to manipulate spiritual powers and allow for interaction between the spiritual world and the human world. CAT WT
9 - 11/95	THE INVISIBLE FORCE — In this exhibition of works by ten artists from different parts of the world who chose to work in Florida, issues including cross-cultural practices, trans-migration and nomadism will be addressed. CAT

MAITLAND

Maitland Art Center
231 W. Packwood Ave., **Maitland, FL 32751-5596**
TEL: 407-539-2181
HRS: 10-4:30 M-F; Noon-4:30 Sa, S   HOL: LEG/HOL!
VOL/CONT: Y   ADM: F
HDC/ACC: Y; All public areas and facilities remodeled to be accessible
PARKING: Y; Across the street from the Art Center with additional parking just west of the Center
MUS/SH: Y   GR/T: Y   GR/PH: call 407-539-2181   DT: Y   TIME: upon request if available
H/B: Y; State of Florida Historic Site
PERM/COLL: REG: past & present

Maitland Art Center - continued

The stucco buildings of the Maitland Center are so highly decorated with murals, bas reliefs, and carvings done in the Aztec-Mayan motif, that they are a must-see work of art in themselves. Listed NRHP) NOT TO BE MISSED: Works of Jules Andre Smith, (1890-1959), artist and founder of the art center

ON EXHIBIT/95:

12/10/94 - 1/22/95	THE BALLET: PHOTOGRAPHS BY MAX WALDMAN — The Nutcracker ballet is the unifying theme of this exhibition which features photographs taken of three world class ballet companies.
1/28 - 3/12/95	DALE KENNINGTON: TIME AND PLACE — 24 photo-realist works by Ms. Kennington will be on view.
3/18 - 4/30/95	ROBERT RIVERS, GRAPHICS — Figurative etchings and drawings with mixed media.
5/6 - 6/18/95	THE ART OF MICRONESIA — 14 story boards and a variety of Micronesian artifacts from a private collection will be featured.
7/15 - 9/3/95	FLORIDA DREAMS — Some of the more venerable attractions that visitors see when exploring Florida will be featured in text panels by Jerome Stern and 75 photographs by Gary Monroe.
9/9 - 10/15/95	ART THREE BY...THE 1995 JURIED EXHIBITION
10/26 - 10/31/95	"THE ARTIST'S TABLE" — Several highly regarded interior and floral designers from Florida will create vignets based on subjects chosen from works of well-known artists.
11/10 - 12/10/95	THE ART OF INDIA — Watercolors and photographs of the art and architecture of the Rajput Maha Rawals.
12/16/95 - 1/21/96	ANGELS, HEAVENLY AND EARTHBOUND — Artistic creations based on the theme of angels by eleven 1995 M.F.A. graduates of the Philadelphia Academy of Fine Arts.

MELBOURNE

Brevard Art Center and Museum Inc.

1463 Highland Ave., **Melbourne, FL 32935**
TEL: 407-242-0737
HRS: 10-5 Tu-Sa; 1-5 S   DAY CLOSED: M   HOL: LEG/HOL!
ADM: Y   ADULT: $3.00   CHILDREN: $2.00   HDC/ACC: Y; Ramps, restrooms, wheelchairs available
PARKING: Y; Free and ample in lot on Pineapple Ave. in front of the museum   MUS/SH: Y
GR/T: Y   GR/PH: Call 407-242-0737   DT: Y   TIME: 2-4 Tu-F; 12:30-2:30 Sa; 1-5 S
PERM/COLL: OR; REG: works on paper

Serving as an active community cultural center, the Brevard, located on the east coast in the middle of the state, is housed in one of Melbourne's historic districts. The art center features exhibitions of its rapidly growing permanent collection, major traveling exhibitions, and works by important nationally and regionally recognized artists. **NOT TO BE MISSED:** Works by American women artists including Louise Nevelson, Isabel Bishop, and Janet Fish

ON EXHIBIT/95:

12/7/94 - 1/7/95	FLORIDA COUNTRY CHRISTMAS — Miniature villages, quilts and traditional furniture will be featured in the 5th annual Christmas extravaganza.
1/14 - 3/12/95	THE ART OF HOLOGRAPHY — More than 40 original holograms by nationally known artists will be on exhibit.

FLORIDA

Brevard Art Center and Museum Inc. - continued

4/7 - 5/22/95   ANSEL ADAMS — On view from the collection of the Mitsubushi Corporation will be more than 70 of Ansel Adams' world famous photographic images.

MIAMI

Center for the Fine Arts

101 W. Flagler St., **Miami, FL 33130**
TEL: 305-375-1700
HRS: 10-5 Tu-Sa; till 9 T; Noon-5 S   DAY CLOSED: M   HOL: 1/1, THGV, 12/25
ADM: Y   ADULT: $5.00   CHILDREN: $2.00 (6-12)   STUDENTS: $2.50   SR CIT: $2.50
HDC/ACC: Y; Elevator on N.W. 1st St.   PARKING: Y; Discounted rates with validated ticket and Metro-Dade Center Garage, 50 NW 2nd Ave. & City of Miami Govt. Center Garage, 270 NW 2nd Ave.   MUS/SH: Y
GR/T: Y   GR/PH: Call 305-375-1724   H/B: Y; Designed by Philip Johnson 1983   S/G: Y
PERM/COLL: NONE; SPECIAL EXHIBITIONS ONLY

Although this is a non-collecting institution, the Center for the Fine Arts receives and initiates many important traveling exhibitions each year. Their stunning facility was designed and built in 1983 by noted American architect Philip Johnson.

ON EXHIBIT/95:

11/13/94 - 1/8/95   ABSTRACTION: A TRADITION OF COLLECTING IN MIAMI — 70 works on loan from private collections in Miami trace the development of abstract painting from the 1940's to the 90's through examples by such modern masters as de Kooning, Hans Hoffman, Lee Krasner, Brice Marsden, Elsworth Kelly, Frank Stella and others.

1/17 - 3/12/95   LIFE IN A BOUNDLESS LAND: THE GAUCHO SCENES OF JUAN MANUEL BLANES — Historical and cultural parallels between 19th century North and South American art will be seen in this exhibition that contrasts the works of Blanes with North American counterparts such as Bierstadt, Bingham and Eakins.   WT

1/2 - 4/30/95   NEW WORK: ROBERTO JUAREZ — A large scale work-in-progress inspired by the recent death of several of his freinds will allow the viewer to observe Juarez as he layers his canvas with such items as peat moss, rice paper, charcoal drawings, oil or acrylic paints, and urethane.

1/28 - 4/16/95   GUILLERMO KUITCA: BURNING BEDS — A major retrospective of 34 paintings, 80 drawings and installation of 60 painted mattresses by Argentine painter Kuitca that deal with such life themes as the vulnerability of childhood, the conflicted feelings of adolescence, the invincible power of manhood, and the torment of isolation. Also included in this highly introspective exhibit will be his recent conceptual paintings of maps.

3/25 - 5/14/95   JOSEPH BEUYS: DRAWINGS, OBJECTS, PRINTS — In this retrospective of the work of German artist, Beuys, items created between the 1940's and 1986 will include works on paper of gestural human anatomy, drawings in a series, and other objects that express the artist's fascination with natural science.

5/6 - 7/30/95   ANDRES SERRANO: 1983-1994 — In the first major retrospective of the work of Hispanic photographer, Serrano, 60 mostly large format images that focus on the themes of Nomads, the Ku Klux Klan, and The Morgue (Cause of Death) series will be on view.
    WT

9/9 - 11/5/95   CARIBBEAN VISIONS: CONTEMPORARY PAINTING AND SCULPTURE — Cross-cultural dynamics will be seen in the variety of works presented in this exhibition by Spanish, French, English and Dutch speaking Caribbean artists.

10/7 - 12/24/95   NEW WORK: BARBARA NEIJNA — A large-scale minimalist sculptural installation will be created by Neijna for the New Work Gallery.

116

MIAMI

Miami-Dade Community College Kendall Campus Art Gallery
11011 Southwest 104th St., **Miami, FL 33176-3393**
TEL: 305-237-2322
HRS: 8-4 M & T; Noon-7:30 Tu-W (Jun-early Aug); 8-4 M, T, F; Noon-7:30 Tu, W (Other)   DAY CLOSED: Sa, S
HOL: 12/25, LEG/HOL!
ADM: F   HDC/ACC: Y   PARKING: Y; Free parking anywhere in student lots except for areas prohibited as marked
REST/FAC: Y; Restaurant   DT: Y
PERM/COLL: CONT: ptgs, gr, sculp, phot; GR: 15-19

With nearly 600 works in its collection, the South Campus Art Gallery is home to original prints by renowned artists of the past including Whistler, Tissot, Ensor, Corot, Goya, and those of a more contemporary ilk including Hockney, Dine, Lichtenstein, Warhol and others. **NOT TO BE MISSED:** "The Four Angels Holding The Wings," woodcut by Albrecht Durer, 1511.

The Art Museum at Florida International University
University Park, PC 110, **Miami, FL 33199**
TEL: 305-348-2890
HRS: 10-9 M; 10-5 Tu-F; Noon-4 Sa   DAY CLOSED: S   HOL: ACAD! LEG/HOL!
ADM: F   HDC/ACC: Y   PARKING: Y; Metered parking available in the PC parking area across from the Museum
GR/T: Y   GR/PH: Call 305-348-2890   S/G: Y
PERM/COLL: GR: 20; P/COL; CONT/HISPANIC (CINTAS FOUNDATION COLL); ARTPARK AT FIU

Major collections acquired recently by this fast growing institution include the Coral Gables' Metropolitan Museum and Art Center's holdings of African, Oriental, Pre-Columbian, & 18-20th century American & Latin American Art and long-term loan of the Cintas Fellowship Foundation Collection of contemporary Hispanic art. **NOT TO BE MISSED:** "Museum Without Walls" Art Park, brochure with self-guided tour provided

ON EXHIBIT/95:

1/13 - 2/18/95	AMERICAN ART TODAY: NIGHT PAINTINGS — Contemporary artists interpret the traditional theme of the Nocturne.
3/3 - 4/5/95	SHEILA NATASHA SIMROD FRIEDMAN — A retropective of the work of poetess and designer, Friedman.
10/13 - 12/17/95	DICTATED BY LIFE: MARSDEN HARTLEY'S GERMAN PAINTINGS AND ROBERT INDIANA'S HARTLEY ELEGIES WT

MIAMI BEACH

Bass Museum of Art
2121 Park Ave., **Miami Beach, FL 33139**
TEL: 305-673-7530
HRS: 10-5 Tu-Sa; 1-5 S; 1-9 2nd & 4th W of the month   DAY CLOSED: M   HOL: LEG/HOL!
F/DAY: Tu   ADM: Y   ADULT: $5.00   CHILDREN: $2 (6-12) $3 to17   STUDENTS: $4.00   SR CIT: $4.00
HDC/ACC: Y   PARKING: Y; On-site metered parking and street metered parking   MUS/SH: Y
GR/T: Y   GR/PH: 305-673-7530   S/G: Y
PERM/COLL: PTGS, SCULP, GR 19-20; REN: ptgs, sculp; MED; sculp, ptgs; PHOT

FLORIDA

Bass Museum of Art - continued

Just one block from the beach in Miami in the middle of a 9 acre park is one of the great cultural treasures of Florida. Located in a stunning 1930 Art Deco building the museum is home to more than 6 centuries of artworks including a superb 500 piece collection of European art donated by the Bass family for whom the museum is named. **NOT TO BE MISSED:** "Samson Fighting the Lion," woodcut by Albrecht Dürer

ON EXHIBIT/95:

12/6/94 - 2/26/95	TOMIE OHTAKE: NEW PAINTINGS 1989-1994 — In celebration of the 80th birthday of this Japanese-born Brazilian artist, 20 of his paintings that concern themselves with such visual issues as the power of vibrations emanating from the picture plane, are created in a style that is totally different from that of traditional Brazilian art. CAT WT
12/15/94 - 1/29/95	ALL THAT GLITTERS: ART DECO JEWELRY — An exhibition that focuses on how the Purist, Bauhaus, and other artistic movements of the 20's, 30's, and 40's impacted on the jewelry designs of those decades.
3/17 - 5/28/95	LEGACY OF A RUSSIAN EMPRESS: OLD MASTER PAINTINGS FROM THE PALACE OF PAVLOVSK — A selection of 16th to 18th-century Western European masterworks from the Palace of Pavlovsk in St. Petersburg, Russia collected by members of the Imperial family and the Empress Maria in particular will be featured in this exhibition.
6/14 - 8/13/95	ALONE IN A CROWD: PRINTS BY AFRICAN-AMERICAN ARTISTS OF THE 1930'S AND 1940'S FROM THE COLLECTION OF REBA AND DAVE WILLIAMS — The creations of 45 African-American printmakers working in a wide variety of styles and techniques during the Depression decades (many under the auspices of the WPA) will be on view in this 125 piece exhibition. CAT WT
7 - 8/95	DESIGN DIASPORA: BLACK ARCHITECTS AND INTERNATIONAL ARCHI-TECTURE (Exact dates TBA) — In the first traveling exhibition of its kind, the works of 50 prominent contemporary black architects from 11 countries will be on view. Included in this exhibition of over 70 built designs are nearly 200 photographs, drawings, plans and design models.

NAPLES

Philharmonic Center for the Arts
5833 Pelican Bay Blvd., **Naples, FL 33963**
TEL: 813-597-1111
HRS: OCT-JUN: 10-4 M-Sa, Noon-5 S   HOL: LEG/HOL!
ADM: F   HDC/ACC: Y   PARKING: Y; Free   MUS/SH: Y   GR/T: Y
DT: Y   TIME: 11am M-Sa (OCT, MAY, JUN); 11 am Tu, T & Sa (other!)   S/G: Y

Four art galleries, two sculpture gardens, and spacious lobbies where sculpture is displayed are located within the confines of the beautiful Philharmonic Center. Museum quality temporary exhibitions are presented from September through May of each year.

ON EXHIBIT/95:

12/8/94 - 1/8/95	AMERICA: THE PHOTOGRAPHS OF HIROJI KUBOTA — Large-scale color photographs of every corner and aspect of American life taken by this Japanese artist who used more than 3,000 rolls of film for this project over the course of a 3 year period of travel. WT

FLORIDA

Philharmonic Center for the Arts - continued

1/17 - 2/25/95	FROM DEEP ROOTS TO NEW GROUND: THE GULLAH LANDSCAPES OF JONATHAN GREEN — Paintings and bold-shaped compositions that interpret the artist's childhood memories during the 50's and 60's of the Gullah culture of the Atlantic Sea Islands will be seen in expressive story-telling vignettes.
1/17 - 2/25/95	ENGAGED CULTURES: TEN CONTEMPORARY LATINO ARTISTS/A DIFFERENT AMERICA — Paintings, sculptures and mixed-media artworks by 10 contemporary artists of Latino descent.
3/6 - 4/8/95	PAINTINGS BY ROBERT VICKERY — Paintings in egg-tempera by one of the foremost American realist artists working today.
3/6 - 4/8/95	A TIBETAN EXPERIENCE — Lushly detailed sculptures and paintings on fabric of Buddhist gods and goddesses from a private collection in Italy will be on view.
4/18 - 5/21/95	MAJOR LEAGUE/MINOR LEAGUE: AMERICA'S BASEBALL STADIUMS BY JIM DOW — Photographer Dow's brilliantly colored large-scale images of baseball stadiums run the gamut from small town ball fields to state-of-the-art contemporary stadiums.
4/18 - 5/21/95	HISTORY/MYSTERY: PHOTOGRAPHY BY JERRY N. UELSMANN, 1957-1993 — 100 of Uelsmann's photographs taken between 1957-1993 will be featured in this major retrospective of his work. WT
10/3 - 11/5/95	INTERNATIONAL LATHE-TURNED OBJECTS: CHALLENGE V — Contemporary lathe-turned objects from around the world. WT

NORTH MIAMI

COCA/Center of Contemporary Art
12340 Northeast 8th Ave., **North Miami, FL 33161**
TEL: 305-893-6211
HRS: 10-4 M-F, 1-4 Sa   DAY CLOSED: S   HOL: 1/1, THGV, 12/25
ADM: F   HDC/ACC: Y   PARKING: Y; Free parking in front and on the sides of the building.
GR/T: Y   GR/PH: call in advance to reserve
PERM/COLL: CONT

In operation since 1981, this small but vital center for the contemporary arts will open a new state-of-the-art building in Dec. 1995, that will provide an exciting and innovative facility for exhibitions, lectures, films and performances.

ON EXHIBIT/95:

12/15/94 - 1/28/95	NEW PAINTING — New painters in South Florida and New York will be on view.
2/9 - 3/28/95	ART + ARCHITECTURE = MIAMI — Unique collaborations between artist and architects in Miami and Miami Beach have transformed existing and created exciting new buildings throughout the area. In this exhibition photographs, drawings, maquettes and scale models of many of the most unusual projects will be featured.
4/6 - 5/27/95	ARTISTS COLLECT (working title) — Artworks that artists collect and how that artwork stimulates the making of their own creations is the subject of this exhibition.
6/15 - 8/12/95	TERESITA FERNANDEZ — A large scale installation by this Miami artist.
9/14 - ?	CHARLES GWATHMEY: ARCHITECTURE — The work of the architectural firm of Gwathmey-Siegel Architects who designed the new COCA museum facility will be seen in an exhibition of photographs, drawings, maquettes and video installations.

119

FLORIDA

OCALA

Appleton Museum of Art
4333 E. Silver Springs Blvd., **Ocala, FL 32670**
TEL: 904-236-5050
HRS: 10-4:30 Tu-Sa; 1-5 S   DAY CLOSED: M   HOL: 1/1
ADM: Y   ADULT: $3.00   CHILDREN: F (under 18)   STUDENTS: $2.00
HDC/ACC: Y; Elevators, wheelchairs, and reserved parking available
PARKING: Y; Free   MUS/SH: Y
REST/FAC: Y; Courtside Cafe   GR/T: Y   GR/PH: call 904-236-5050   DT: Y   TIME: 1:15 Tu-F
PERM/COLL: EU; PR/COL; AF; OR; DEC/ART

The Appleton Museum in central Florida, home to one of the finest art collections in the Southeast, is currently planning to open another wing in the fall of 1995 to display even more of its ever expanding collection. Situated among acres of tall pines and magnolias, the dramatic building sets the stage for the many treasures that await the visitor within its walls. **NOT TO BE MISSED:** Rodin's "Thinker," Bouguereau's "The Young Shepherdess" and "The Knitter;" 8th-century Chinese Tang Horse.

ON EXHIBIT/95:
   9/6 - 11/12/95   THE HOUND OF HEAVEN: A PICTORIAL SEQUENCE, R.H. GAMMELL

                              PLEASE NOTE: No other special exhibitions for 1995 are currently scheduled due to the museum's impending construction project.

ORLANDO

Orlando Museum of Art
2416 North Mills Ave., **Orlando, FL 32803**
TEL: 407-896-4231
HRS: 9-5 Tu-Sa; Noon-5 S   DAY CLOSED: M   HOL: LEG/HOL!
ADM: Y   ADULT: $4.00   CHILDREN: $2.00 (4-11)   STUDENTS: $4.00   SR CIT: $4.00
HDC/ACC: Y
PARKING: Y; Free on-site parking for 200 cars in the front of the museum; overflow lot approximately 1/8 mile away.
MUS/SH: Y   GR/T: Y   GR/PH: Call 407-896-4231 ex 260
DT: Y   TIME: 1:00 W & 2:00 S
PERM/COLL: P/COL; AM; 19-20; AM: gr 20; AF

In existence since 1924, the Orlando Museum recently completed Phase One of its expansion program. The museum has been designated by the state of Florida as a "Major Cultural Institution." **NOT TO BE MISSED:** Permanent collection of Pre-Columbian artifacts (1200 BC to 1500 AD) complete with "hands-on" exhibit

ON EXHIBIT/95:
   10/22/94 - 1/8/95   MY PEOPLE: THE PORTRAITS OF ROBERT HENRI — Wonderful portraits by Henri, leader of "The Eight" or "The Ashcan School" created between 1900-1930 will be seen in this exhibit that includes images of Irish & Spanish peasants, gypsies, New York immigrants and Southwestern and American Indian subjects. PLEASE NOTE: This exhibit will be closed 11/7 - 11/24 for the annual Festival of Trees.   CAT   WT

Orlando Museum of Art - continued

12/1/94 - 2/19/95	JANE HAMMOND ARTIST AS MAGICIAN — In this exhibition contemporary artist Hammond utilizes a prefixed set of 276 images which she recombines for each new painting thus suggesting new and mysterious associations among the images on view.
1/15 - 2/19/95	1995 BIENNIAL JURIED EXHIBITION — Works by local and regional artists.
3/19 - 5/28/95	19TH CENTURY AMERICAN PAINTINGS FROM THE MASCO COLLECTION — 45 works from one of the finest collections of 19th & early 20th-century American art will be on exhibit.
4/1 - 6/4/95	AMERICAN ART POTTERY FROM THE COLLECTION OF THE CHARLES HOSMER MORSE MUSEUM OF AMERICAN ART — 125 of the finest objects from the 700 piece collection of the Morse Museum's collection of American art pottery will be selected for viewing in the first large-scale exhibition of this collection.
5/14 - 7/2/95	WHITE MOUNTAIN PAINTERS — 45 oil paintings and 5 watercolors (1834-1926) by artists inspired by the beauty of the New Hampshire landscape will be seen in this exhibition. BROCHURE WT
ONGOING:	
	SELECTIONS FROM THE PAUL AND RUTH TISHMAN COLLECTION OF AFRICAN ART LOANED BY THE WALT DISNEY WORLD COMPANY — One of the finest collections of its kind in size and quality.
	PRE-COLUMBIAN ART GALLERY — 150 Pre-Columbian artifacts (1200 BC to 1500 AD).
	GLIMMERS OF A FORGOTTEN REALM: MAYA ARCHAEOLOGY FROM CARACOL, BELIZE — Recent discoveries from one of the most important classic Maya cities.
	ART ENCOUNTER — A hands-on art exhibition for young children sponsored by the Walt Disney Company.
	PEGGY CROSBY STUDENT GALLERY — "Young at Art" student work.

PALM BEACH

Hibel Museum of Art
150 Royal Poinciana Plaza, **Palm Beach, FL 33480**
TEL: 407-833-6870
HRS: 10-5 Tu-Sa; 1-5 S   DAY CLOSED: M   HOL: 1/1, 7/4, THGV, 12/25
ADM: F
HDC/ACC: Y; Through rear door; all works displayed on ground floor
PARKING: Y; Free parking in the rear of the museum and the Royal Poinciana Plaza in front of the museum
MUS/SH: Y   GR/T: Y   GR/PH: call 407-833-6870   DT: Y   TIME: Upon request if available
PERM/COLL: EDNA HIBEL: all media

The Hibel is the world's only publicly owned non profit museum dedicated to the art of a single living American woman.

FLORIDA

PALM BEACH

The Society of the Four Arts
Four Arts Plaza, **Palm Beach, FL 33480**
TEL: 407-655-7226
HRS: 10-5 M-Sa; 2-5 S (Dec 4 - Apr 17)   HOL: Museum closed May-Oct
SUGG/CONT: Y   ADULT: $3.00
HDC/ACC: Y   PARKING: Y; Ample free parking   GR/T: Y   GR/PH: Call 407-655-7226   S/G: Y
PERM/COLL: SCULP

Rain or shine, this museum provides welcome relief from the elements for all vacationing art fanciers with monthly exhibitions of paintings or decorative arts. **NOT TO BE MISSED:** Philip Hulitar Sculpture Garden

ON EXHIBIT/95:

1/7 - 2/5/95	FRENCH OIL SKETCHES OF THE 17TH, 18TH AND 19TH CENTURIES — 125 paintings ranging from the Baroque, Rococo, Neoclassic, Romantic and Realistic periods which recorded the first spontaneous thoughts of the artists represented in this exhibition will be seen in the first traveling exhibition of its kind. CAT WT
2/11 - 3/12/95	NOSTALGIC JOURNEYS: AMERICAN ILLUSTRATION FROM THE COLLECTION OF THE DELAWARE ART MUSEUM — Paintings and drawings from the "Golden Age of American Illustration" will provide the viewer with a delightful nostalgic journey that appeals to both young and old. Images created for classic stories by artists such as Howard Pyle and N. C. Wyeth will be shown with those of Arthur Dove, John Sloan, William Glackens and George Luks, members of the realist circle known as "The Eight" or "The Ashcan School." WT
3/18 - 4/16/95	AUGUSTUS VINCENT TACK: LANDSCAPE OF THE SPIRIT — A major comprehensive retrospective that traces the career of this American painter (1870-1949) from the impressionist style of his early years to his later spiritual abstractions. CAT WT

PENSACOLA

Pensacola Museum of Art
407 S. Jefferson St., **Pensacola, FL 32501**
TEL: 904-432-6247
HRS: 10-5 Tu-F; 10-4 Sa; 1-4 S   DAY CLOSED: M   HOL: LEG/HOL!
VOL/CONT: Y   ADM: F   HDC/ACC: Y
PARKING: Y; Free vacant lot across street; also 2 hour metered and non-metered street parking nearby.
MUS/SH: Y   GR/T: Y   GR/PH: 904-432-6247 reservation required
DT: Y   TIME: ! check for availability   H/B: Y
PERM/COLL: CONT/AM: ptgs, gr, works on paper

Now renovated and occupied by the Pensacola Museum of Art, this building was in active use as the city jail from 1906 - 1954.

ON EXHIBIT/95:

12/6/94 - 1/20/95	MARTIN JOHNSON HEADE: THE FLORAL AND BIRD STUDIES FROM THE ST. AUGUSTINE HISTORICAL SOCIETY — Studies that were later used in his completed works and that demonstrate the creative process of this brilliant artist are the focus of this exhibition. CAT WT

122

Pensacola Museum of Art - continued

12/6/94 - 2/5/95	ECHOES: THE TRADITION CONTINUES - AN EXHIBITION OF FOLK ART BY RECIPIENTS OF THE FLORIDA FOLK HERITAGE AWARDS
1/6 - 2/19/95	HISTORY/MYSTERY: PHOTOGRAPHS BY JERRY N. UELSMANN, 1957-1993 — 100 of Uelsmann's photographs taken between 1957-1993 will be featured in this major retrospective of his work. WT
2/1 - 4/1/95	NAIVE AMERICAN PAINTINGS FROM THE NATIONAL GALLERY OF ART — 33 19th century paintings featuring portraits, historical events, landscapes, still lifes and genre scenes by unknown and well established artists will be on view. WT
4/8 - 5/31/95	HERMAN LEONARD: JAZZ PHOTOGRAPHS
4/15 - 5/28/95	MASTER SILVER BY PAUL STORR, HIS CONTEMPORARIES AND FOLLOWERS — A dazzling display of English Regency neoclassic silver by one of the most highly regarded names in the English history of this craft will be seen in this exhibition. WT
6/6 - 7/6/95	SELECTIONS FROM THE PERMANENT COLLECTION
6/9 - 8/18/95	THROUGH THE LOOKING GLASS: DRAWINGS BY ELIZABETH LAYTON — An exhibition of 31 largely psychological self-portraits by this self-taught artist employing the technique of "blind" drawing (where the artist does not look down at the paper while working). CAT WT
7/14 - 8/11/95	THE MEMBERS SHOW
8/22 - 10/10/95	THE SPIRIT OF WEST AFRICAN TEXTILES FROM THE COLLECTION OF RODA AND GILBERT GRAHAM
8/26 - 9/24/95	ORIGINS OF ABSTRACT EXPRESSIONISM: THE LINE AS SYMBOL — 20 works from the permanent collection that explore the use of line as expression, symbol and form in the creation of a work of art.
10/1 - 11/15/95	WOOD AND WOOD CARVING FROM THE INDEX OF AMERICAN DESIGN — Naturalistic watercolor renderings that depict 19th century American objects made of wood will be on loan from the National Gallery of Art. WT
10/17 - 12/11/95	TREASURES: THE METROPOLITAN COLLECTION OF THE ART MUSEUM AT FLORIDA INTERNATIONAL UNIVERSITY
11/22/95 - 1/17/96	GEORGE RODRIGUE: THE BLUE DOG

SARASOTA

John and Mable Ringling Museum of Art
5401 Bay Shore Rd., **Sarasota, FL 34243**
TEL: 813-355-5101
HRS: 10-5:30 Daily HOL: 1/1, THGV, 12/25
F/DAY: Sa ADM: Y ADULT: $8.50 CHILDREN: F (12 & under) SR CIT: $7.50
HDC/ACC: Y ; All art & circus galleries; first floor only of mansion PARKING: Y; Free MUS/SH: Y
REST/FAC: Y; 11-4 DAILY GR/T: Y GR/PH: call 813-355-5101
DT: Y TIME: call 813-351-1660 (recorded message)
H/B: Y ; Ca'D'Zan was the winter mansion of John & Mable Ringling S/G: Y
PERM/COLL: AM: ptgs, scupl; EU: ptgs, sculp 15-20; DRGS; GR; DEC/ART; CIRCUS MEMORABILIA

Sharing the grounds of the museum is Ca'd'Zan, the winter mansion of circus impresario John Ringling and his wife Mable. Their personal collection of fine art in the museum features one of the country's premier collections of European, Old Master, and 17th century Italian Baroque paintings. **NOT TO BE MISSED:** The Rubens Gallery - a splendid group of paintings by Peter Paul Rubens.

FLORIDA

John and Mable Ringling Museum of Art - continued

ON EXHIBIT/95:

10/13/94 - 1/1/95	A GOLDEN HARVEST: PAINTINGS BY ADAM PYNACKER RECENT ACQUISITIONS
2/4 - 5/14/95	STRIKE A POSE: PORTRAITURE FROM THE JOHN AND MABLE RINGLING MUSEUM OF ART — Superb examples of 500 years of European & American portraiture from Renaissance times to the present. CAT
6/15 - 8/13/95	THE GREAT COLLECTORS: FLORIDA'S RICHEST TREASURES
9/8 - 11/19/95	PHOTOGRAPHS BY SEBASTIAO SALGADO
12/4/95 - 1/31/96	KINGS, QUEENS, AND SOUP TUREENS

ST. PETERSBURG

Florida International Museum
100 Second St. North, **St. Petersburg, FL 33701**
TEL: 813-824-6734
HRS: 9am - 8pm daily
ADM: Y   ADULT: $12.00   CHILDREN: $5.00 (5-16)   SR CIT: $10.75
HDC/ACC: Y; Fully accessible with wheelcharis available free of charge
PARKING: Y; On-site garage parking with entry at 218 Second Ave. North   MUS/SH: Y
REST/FAC: Y; On-site food service   GR/T: Y   GR/PH: Call for reservations and information

What could be more fitting - or more fabulous - than to inaugurate the opening of this new museum in the U.S. city of St. Petersburg, Fl., with Russian treasures from the Moscow Kremlin Museums that represent over 300 years of collecting by the Czars and Czarinas of Russia's former Imperial Family! Created to host grand-scale traveling exhibitions from some of the world's most prestigious museums, Florida International Museum promises to be an exciting addition to the American art scene.

ON EXHIBIT/95:

1/11 - 5/11/95	TREASURES OF THE CZARS — A magnificent collection of 250 items produced by the greatest craftsmen of the Czarist period of Russia will be featured in a rare display of treasure, most of which has never before been permitted to leave the confines of the Kremlin Museums. In addition to a dazzling display of golden chalices, richly jeweled icons, gospel covers, crucifixes, coronation uniforms, royal clothing, jewelry, and splendid church vestments, several objects of special note will be the sable-trimmed crown used in the coronation of Peter the Great, the Tricentennial "Easter Egg" by Fabergé, and the Throne of Paul I (c. 1591). PLEASE NOTE: Advance tickets for a specific day AND time of entry for this exhibition are a MUST! Call 1-800-777-9882 to charge with Visa or MasterCard. You may order by mail by sending check or money order to Florida International Museum, 100 Second St. North, St. Petersburg, Fl. 33701 (be sure to add $1.00 extra for postage and handling). Tickets are also available at the **Museum Box Office**. Only 15 people at a time are permitted on a tour which lasts 1½ to 2 hours. Special rates are available for groups of 20 or more.

ST. PETERSBURG

Museum of Fine Arts-St. Petersburg Florida
255 Beach Dr., N.E., **St. Petersburg, FL 33701**
TEL: 813-896-2667
HRS: 10-5 Tu-Sa; 1-5 S; 3rd T each month open till 9PM   DAY CLOSED: M   HOL: 12/25, 1/1
SUGG/CONT: Y   F/DAY: S   ADULT: $5.00   CHILDREN: F (under 6)   STUDENTS: $2.00   SR CIT: $3.00
HDC/ACC: Y
PARKING: Y; Visitors parking lot. Parking also available on Beach Dr. & Bayshore Dr.
GR/T: Y   GR/PH: Call 813-894-4638 (tour coord.)   DT: Y   TIME: 10, 11, 1 & 2 Tu-F   S/G: Y
PERM/COLL: AM: ptgs, sculp, drgs, gr; EU: ptgs, sculp, drgs, gr; P/COL; DEC/ART

With the recent addition of 10 new galleries, the Museum of Fine Arts, considered one of the finest museums in the southeast, is truly an elegant showcase for its many treasures that run the gamut from Dutch and Old Master paintings to the largest collection of photography in the state. PLEASE NOTE: Spanish language tours are available by advance appointment. **NOT TO BE MISSED:** Gallery of Steuben crystal

ON EXHIBIT/95:

12/4/94 - 1/15/95	MASTER SILVER BY PAUL STORR, HIS CONTEMPORARIES AND FOLLOWERS — Works by Paul Storr, a master English silversmith working in the English Regency style, will be accompanied by other examples of the craft by his contemporaries and followers. CAT WT
1/12 - 6/11/95	THREE CENTURIES OF RUSSIAN PAINTING FROM THE STATE TRETYAKOV GALLERY, MOSCOW — Rare religious icons from the 17th century accompanied by 51 18th & 19th century paintings that survey all the movements in Russian art during the Romanov reign (1613-1917) will be on view in conjunction with the innaugural exhibition entitled "Treasures of the Czars" at the Florida International Museum.
1/12 - 6/11/95	RUSSIAN TREASURES FROM A LA VIELLE RUSSIE — Russian decorative art treasures from this renowned New York gallery will be on view.
7/2 - 8/6/95	BARBARA MORGAN: PHOTOGRAPHS, DRAWINGS, PRINTS AND WATER-COLORS — Powerful and emotionally charged photographic images of the dance will be presented with Morgan's works of people and nature which are combined with light abstraction and are created through her innovative ability to develop upon traditional methods of photomontage and light drawings. CAT
9/24 - 11/19/95	SPOTLIGHT 95: AMERICAN CRAFTS COUNCIL SOUTHEAST JURIED SHOW — 50 outstanding craft items in a variety of media by 46 Florida artists will be on display in the premier craft showcase in Florida. CAT
12/3/95 - 1/31/96	MINISALON: CZECHOSLOVAKIA'S DISSIDENT ARTISTIC VOICE — First organized in 1984 by dissident Czechoslovakian artist Joska Skalnich, this collection of 244 works were never allowed by the then repressive government to be shown. In fact, Skalnich who was jailed for arranging this exhibition has, since then, been appointed as Cultural Advisor under President Vaclav Havel. The exhibition itself, which has been declared a national treasure, will be placed on permanent exhibition after this tour in the Czech National Museum. CAT WT

FLORIDA

ST. PETERSBURG

Salvador Dali Museum
100 Third St. S., **St. Petersburg, FL 33701**
TEL: 813-896-2667
HRS: 9:30-5:30 Tu-Sa; Noon-5:30 S & M   HOL: LEG/HOL!
ADM: Y   ADULT: $5.00   CHILDREN: F (9 & under)   STUDENTS: $3.50   SR CIT: $4.00
HDC/ACC: Y   PARKING: Y   MUS/SH: Y   GR/T: Y   GR/PH: Call 813-896-2667
DT: Y   TIME: call 813-823-3767
PERM/COLL: SALVADOR DALI: ptgs, sculp, drgs, gr

Unquestionably the largest and most comprehensive collection of Dali's works in the world, the museum holdings amassed by Dali's friends A. Reynolds and Eleanor Morse include 93 original oils, 100 watercolors and drawings, 1,300 graphics, sculpture, and objects d'art that span his entire career.

ON EXHIBIT/95:

9/25/94 - 1/29/95	MEMORIES OF SURREALISM — Suites of reproductive images of 3 of Dali's original works will include 12 colored photo-lithographs of "Memories of Surrealism," four colored lithographs of "Visions Surrealiste," and 6 drypoint engravings of "Dalinian Fantasia."
2/3 - 2/12/95	SURREALIST STUDENT ART EXHIBIT
2/18 - 8/27/95	GALUCHKA: DALI'S RUSSIAN MUSE: GALA AND DALI IN PHOTOGRAPHS BY ROBERT DESCHARNES — 90 photographs of Dali's Russian wife, Gala, (or Galuchka as he fondly called her) that document her life (1884-1982) by Robert Descharnes, photographer, friend and personal secretary of the artist.

TALLAHASSEE

Florida State University Fine Arts Gallery and Museum
Fine Arts Bldg., **Tallahassee, FL 32306**
TEL: 904-644-6836
HRS: 10-4 M-F; 1-4 Sa (closed weekends during summer)   HOL: ACAD! AUG
ADM: F   HDC/ACC: Y
PARKING: Y; Metered parking in front of the building with weekend parking available in the lot next to the museum
GR/T: Y   GR/PH: call 904-644-6836   DT: Y   TIME: upon request if available
PERM/COLL: EU; OR; CONT; PHOT; GR; P/COL: Peruvian artifacts; JAP: gr

With 7 gallery spaces, this is the largest art museum within 2 hours driving distance of Tallahassee.
NOT TO BE MISSED: Works by Judy Chicago

ON EXHIBIT/95:

2/17 - 4/2/95	ANSEL ADAMS PHOTOGRAPHS: COLLECTION OF THE MITSUBISHI ESTATE
2/17 - 4/2/95	THE POLITICS OF WOMEN'S TEXTILES
2/24 - 4/2/95	SELECTIONS: JUDY CHICAGO'S BIRTH PROJECT
5/9 - 8/5/95	ARTISTS' LEAGUE
	PERMANENT COLLECTION
9/7 - 10/9/95	COMBINED TALENTS: THE FLORIDA NATIONAL

TALLAHASSEE

Lemoyne Art Foundation, Inc.
125 N. Gadsden, **Tallahassee, FL 32301**
TEL: 904-22-8800
HRS: 10-5 Tu-Sa; 1-5 S   DAY CLOSED: M   HOL: 1/1, 7/4, 12/25 (may be closed during parts of Aug!)
ADM: F
HDC/ACC: Y   PARKING: Y; parking lot adjacent to the Helen Lind Garden and Sculptures; also, large lot across
street available weekends and evenings   MUS/SH: Y   DT: Y   TIME: daily when requested   H/B: Y   S/G: Y
PERM/COLL: CONT/ART; sculp

Located in an 1852 structure in the heart of Tallahassee's historic district, the Lemoyne is named for
the first artist known to have visited North America. Aside from offering a wide range of changing
exhibitions annually, the museum provides the visitor with a sculpture garden that serves as a setting
for beauty and quiet contemplation. **NOT TO BE MISSED:** Three recently acquired copper
sculptures by George Frederick Holschuh

ON EXHIBIT/95:

1/20 - 2/19/95	JERRY CUTLER/UNIVERSITY OF FLORIDA PAINTER: "RHETORICAL LANDSCAPES"
2/24 - 3/26/95	JOHN ROBERGE: TALLAHASSEE DEMOCRAT ARTIST "BLACK & WHITE & READ ALL OVER"
3/31 - 4/30/95	MAJORIE KINNAN RAWLINGS
6/9 - 7/9/95	ARTISTS OF SOUTH FLORIDA
7/14 - 8/5/95	SUMMER FUND RAISER: WEARABLE ART
9/8 - 10/8/95	CURTIS AND YVONNE TUCKER: DOUBLE VISIONS — African-American ceramics
10/13 - 11/5/95	THE TALLAHASSEE WATERCOLOR SOCIETY'S 10TH ANNUAL EXHIBITION & JEWELRY INVITATIONAL '95
11/13 - 12/31/95	THE 32ND ANNUAL HOLIDAY FUNDRAISER

TAMPA

Museum of African American Art
1308 N. Marion St., **Tampa, FL 33602**
TEL: 813-272-2466
HRS: 10-4:30 Tu-Sa, 1-4:30 S   DAY CLOSED: M   HOL: 1/1, EASTER, THGV, 12/25
ADM: Y   ADULT: $2.00   CHILDREN: $1.00 (K-12)   SR CIT: $1.00
HDC/ACC: Y; 1st floor gallery and restrooms; elevator to 2nd floor by spring '95   PARKING: Y; Free and ample
MUS/SH: Y   GR/T: Y   GR/PH: Call ahead to reserve
PERM/COLL: AF/AM ART: late 19-20

Paintings, drawings, sculpture, prints and traditional African art are housed in this museum which has
one of the oldest, most prestigious and comprehensive collections of African-American art in the
country. Established in 1991 with the acquisition of the Barnett-Aden Collection of African-American
Art, the collection includes works by such notable African-American artists as Edward M. Bannister,
Henry Ossawa Tanner, Jacob Lawrence, Lois Mailou Jones, William H. Johnson and others. **NOT TO
BE MISSED:** "Negro Boy" by Hale Woodruff; "Little Brown Girl" by Laura Wheeler Waring.

FLORIDA

TAMPA

Tampa Museum of Art
600 North Ashley Dr., **Tampa, FL 33602**
TEL: 813-274-8130
HRS: 10-5 Tu & T-Sa; 10-9 W; 1-5 S   DAY CLOSED: M   HOL: 12/25, 1/1, 7/4, 12/25
VOL/CONT: Y   ADM: F   F/DAY: 10-1 Sa   ADULT: $3.50   CHILDREN: $2.00 (6-18)   STUDENTS: $2.50
SR CIT: $3.00   HDC/ACC: Y; Wheelchairs available, follow signs to handicapped entrance
PARKING: Y; At the Curtis Hixon garage (for information call 813-223-8130)   MUS/SH: Y
GR/T: Y   GR/PH: call 813-223-8130   DT: Y   TIME: 1:00 W, Sa, S
PERM/COLL: PTGS: 19-20; GR: 19-20; AN/GRK; AN/R; PHOT

A new wing featuring a superb 400 piece collection of Greek and Roman antiquities dating from 3000 BC to the 3rd century A.D. is one of the highlights of this comprehensive and vital art museum. The Tampa Museum also offers an exciting array of ever changing exhibitions drawing on its permanent collection and on loaned pieces from private, corporate, and international sources. Please note the 11/94 opening of the new Florida Gallery where exhibitions that focus on the works of emerging artists will be presented. **NOT TO BE MISSED:** Joseph V. Noble Collection of Greek & Southern Italian antiquities

ON EXHIBIT/95:

11/13/94 - 1/29/95	A GOLDEN LEGACY: ANCIENT JEWELRY FROM THE BURTON Y. BERRY COLLECTION — 500 examples of ancient precious jewelry from the countries of the Eastern Mediterranean dating from the Bronze Age through the 14th century will be on exhibit from this extraordinary collection.
11/20/94 - 1/8/95	FERDE PACHECO: YBOR CITY REMEMBERED 1935-1945
11/20/94 - 1/15/95	MEXICO: A LANDSCAPE REVISITED — 60 paintings, some more than 200 years old, that capture the changing nature and perception of the Mexican landscape will include works by Rivera, Siquieros, Velasco and others.
12/18/94 - 2/5/95	CHILDREN AND WAR: IMAGES OF MY CHILDHOOD IN CROATIA — Artworks that include prose and poetry created by 6-14 year old Croatian children during the recent war in the Balkans will be featured in this exhibition.
1/15 - 2/26/95	MARRIAGE IN FORM: KAY SEKIMACHI AND BOB STOCKSDALE — A 30 year retrospective for this artistic husband and wife team, two pioneers of American Craft who work in their respective media of fiber and wood. WT
1/22 - 3/12/95	NEW YORK REALISM: PAST AND PRESENT — From works by early 20th century artists Thomas Hart Benton & Georgia O'Keeffe to present day examples by Richard Estes, this exhibition will focus on the changing nature of American Realism as seen in the 90 images on display, all dealing with the theme of New York City.
2/12 - 4/9/95	CONTEMPORARY RUSSIAN PHOTOGRAPHY — 70 contemporary photographic works will be featured as a complimentary exhibition to the "Treasures of the Czars" at the newly opened Florida International Museum in St. Petersburg, Florida.
2/19 - 4/2/95	RESHAPING THE URBAN ENVIRONMENT — Drawings accompanied by wall texts, a video and a park bench prototype will be featured in this exhibition by environmental artist Alan Sonfist who was involved in the creation of the new Curtis Hixon Park in Tampa.
3/12 - 5/7/95	GRADY KIMSEY: A SURVEY OF WORK — Figurative totem-like creations fashioned by Floridian artist Kimsey from small scale found objects resulting in highly personalized works that are fetishistic in quality will be on view.

128

FLORIDA

Tampa Museum of Art - continued

3/26 - 5/14/95	SCULPTURAL CONCERNS: CONTEMPORARY AMERICAN METALWORKING — 150 handcrafted metalworks by 53 artists offer a survey of the medium with a display of jewelry, hollowware, sculpture, furniture and maquettes.
4/16 - 6/4/95	ART OF RECYCLING — $6,000 in scholarships and awards in this juried exhibition will be given to the most outstanding participating students who use recylced materials in the creation of their artworks.
4/30 - 7/9/95	PRINTS FROM THE PERMANENT COLLECTION
5/28 - 8/21/95	NATIONAL ADDY AWARD WINNING ART
5/28 - 8/21/95	THE AMERICAN SCENE: THE DR. ROBERT B. & DOROTHY M. GRONLUND COLLECTION OF TWENTIETH-CENTRURY AMERICAN PRINTS — In this examination of a myriad of facets of American life, works by over 40 artists including George Bellows, John Marin, Isabel Bishop, Stuart Davis, Adolph Dane and others from this wonderful collection will be on exhibit.
6/11 - 8/6/95	PRINTMAKING PROCESS AND TECHNIQUES
6/25 - 8/27/95	SELF-TAUGHT, OUTSIDER ART: THE ANTHONY PETULLA COLLECTION WT
8/27 - 10/15/95	ART UNITES THE WORLD
9/10 - 11/12/95	THE LAMPS OF TIFFANY — An exhibition of 34 table lamps, 3 floor lamps, 7 chandeliers and 2 windows all created in the stained glass techniques and patterns of the renowned Louis Comfort Tiffany (1848-1933).

TAMPA

USF Contemporary Art Museum
Affiliate Institution: College of Fine Arts
4202 E. Fowler Ave., **Tampa, FL 33620**
TEL: 813-974-2849
HRS: 10-5 M-F; 1-4 Sa (closed Sa Jun, Jul & State/Hol)   DAY CLOSED: S   HOL: ACAD!
ADM: F
HDC/ACC: Y
PARKING: Y; Free parking in front of museum (parking pass available from museum security guard)
GR/T: Y   GR/PH: Call 813-974-2849   DT: Y
PERM/COLL: CONT: phot, gr

Located in a new building on the Tampa campus, the USF Contemporary Art Museum houses one of the largest selections of contemporary prints in the Southeast.

ON EXHIBIT/95:

1/6 - 2/25/95	NEW EDITIONS (TENT!) — New multiples by Jessica Diamond, Sol Lewitt and Lawrence Weiner.
1/13 - 3/4/95	ALFREDO JAAR — An installation reflecting on the plight of refugees fleeing to Florida.
3/10 - 5/6/95	MARK STOCK

FLORIDA

VERO BEACH

Center for the Arts, Inc.
3001 Riverside Park Dr., **Vero Beach, FL 32963**
TEL: 407-231-0707
HRS: 10-4:30 Daily & till 8 T (Oct-Apr); 10-4:30 Tu-Sa, 1-4:30 S, till 8 T   HOL: LEG/HOL!
SUGG/CONT: Y   ADULT: $2.00   HDC/ACC: Y; Fully accessible   PARKING: Y; Ample free parking on north side of building   MUS/SH: Y   GR/T: Y   GR/PH: call 407-231-0707 ex 25   DT: Y   S/G: Y
PERM/COLL: AM/ART 20

The Center for the Arts is the recent recipient of the entire 138 piece collection from the Alternative Museum of New York. Included in the bequest are many works on paper by contemporary New York artists and emerging Florida artists. **NOT TO BE MISSED:** "The Photographer," life-like sculpture by Duane Hanson; "Royal Tide V" by Louise Nevelson; "Watson and the Shark" by Sharron Quasius.

ON EXHIBIT/95:
MAIN GALLERY

THROUGH 1/8/95	COLLECTOR'S CHOICE
1/28 - 3/5/95	CLASSICAL OBJECTS (TENT!)
3/25 - 4/30/95	AMERICA'S MIRROR — Painting in the U.S. 1850-1950 from the Georgia Museum Collection
5/13 - 6/18/95	MELVIN EDWARDS (TENT!)
7/1 - 9/3/95	MARIA VON MATTHIESSEN: SONGS FROM THE HILLS
9/16 - 11/12/95	ALEXANDER CALDER
11/24/95 - 1/10/96	COLLECTOR'S CHOICE
THROUGH 1/8/95	BORIS MARGO
1/28 - 3/5/95	NARMAN LIEBMAN
3/12 - 4/23/95	DRAWINGS BY FLORIDA ARTISTS
5/28 - 6/25/95	STATEWIDE COMPETITION
7/2 - 7/30/95	SLAYTON UNDERHILL
8/6 - 9/10/95	TBA
9/17 - 11/12/95	FLORIDA DREAMS

WEST PALM BEACH

Norton Gallery and School of Art
1451 S. Olive Ave., **West Palm Beach, FL 33401**
TEL: 407-832-5194
HRS: 10-5 Tu-Sa; 1-5 S   DAY CLOSED: M   HOL: 1/1, MEM/DAY, 7/4, THGV, 12/25
SUGG/CONT: Y   ADULT: $5.00   CHILDREN: F (under 12)   STUDENTS: $2.00
HDC/ACC: Y   PARKING: Y; Free lot behind museum   MUS/SH: Y   REST/FAC: Y; Outdoor buffet!
GR/T: Y   GR/PH: Call 407-832-5196 (education office)   DT: Y   TIME: 2:00 daily (Oct. thru May)
PERM/COLL: AM: ptgs, sculp 19-20; FR: ptgs, sculp 19-20; OR: sculp, cer

Started in 1940 with a core collection of French Impressionist and modern masterpieces as well as fine works of American painting, the Norton holdings now include major pieces of contemporary sculpture, and a noteworthy collection of Asian art. It is no wonder that the Norton enjoys the reputation of being one of the finest small museums in the United States. **NOT TO BE MISSED:** Paul Manship's frieze across the main facade of the museum flanked by his sculptures of Diana and Actaeon

FLORIDA

Norton Gallery and School of Art - continued

ON EXHIBIT/95:

11/9/94 - 1/8/95	ARTISTS OF THE AMERICAN SCENE: A SELECTION FROM THE DR. ROBERT B. & DOROTHY M. GRONLUND COLLECTION OF TWENTIETH CENTURY AMERICAN PRINTS — 65 works by major 20th century artists will be on view from this local Florida collection. **WT**
11/19/94 - 1/8/95	THE PADDOCK FAMILY COLLECTION OF PRE-COLUMBIAN ART — 70 vessels, figures, gold, and tapestries (1200 B.C - 1600 A.D.) from Peru, Ecuador and Columbia will be selected for viewing from the Paddock family private collection.
12/10/94 - 2/5/95	MAN RAY'S MAN RAY'S — Early paintings from the Dada years, plus photographs and constructions of the 20's - 40's will be featured in this exhibition drawn from the private collection of the artist's family. Many of the items on view have never before been seen in public.
1/14 - 2/26/95	INTIMATE NATURES: ANSEL ADAMS AND THE CLOSE VIEW — An exhibition of 50 of Adams' gelatin silver photographic prints that will include some of the best of his trademark panoramic views as well as a little seen body of close-up interpretations of nature. **WT**
2/11 - 4/2/95	REORDERING REALITY: PRECISIONIST DIRECTIONS IN AMERICAN ART (1915-1941) — Georgia O'Keeffe, Charles Sheeler, Paul Strand, Charles Demuth and Stuart Davis will be featured in this exhibition of 125 American Precisionist works. Cubism, the stylistic basis for Precisionism, was the catalyst that led these artists to simplify their subjects by paring them down to basic geometric forms, a reflection on the American industrial landscape of their day. **WT**
3/4 - 4/23/95	THE GATE OF THE PRESENT — An exhibition of architecture in Lego bricks.
3 - 4/95	CINDY SHERMAN: ATUEUR (exact dates TBA) — Sherman, whose photographs of herself in the various and sundry guises that have become her trademark, will have those of her works shown which deal with the themes of voyeurism in the depiction of women throughout time.

WINTER PARK

The Charles Hosmer Morse Museum of American Art

151 East Welbourne Ave., **Winter Park, FL 32789**
TEL: 407-645-5311
HRS: 9:30-4 Tu-Sa; 1-4 S   DAY CLOSED: M   HOL: 1/1, MEM/DAY, 7/4, LAB/DAY, THGV, 12/25
ADM: Y   ADULT: $2.50   CHILDREN: $1.00   STUDENTS: $1.00
HDC/ACC: Y; call ahead to schedule visit 407-644-3686   PARKING: Y; At rear of museum   MUS/SH: Y
GR/T: Y   GR/PH: call 407-645-5311   DT: Y   TIME: available during regular hours
PERM/COLL: Tiffany Glass; AM: ptgs (early 20); AM: art pottery 19-20

More than 4,000 pieces of Tiffany glass were rescued in 1957 from the ruins of Laurelton Hall, Tiffany's Long Island home by Florida millionaire Hugh McKean and his wife. These form the basis, along with superb works by early 20th century artists including Emile Galle, Frank Lloyd Wright, Maxfield Parish, George Innis, and others, of the collection at this most unique little-known gem of a museum. PLEASE NOTE: The museum is moving in Mar., 1995 to new and larger quarters at 445 Park Ave. North, Winter Park, Fl. 33789 **NOT TO BE MISSED:** "The Dinkey Bird" by Maxfield Parrish

131

FLORIDA

WINTER PARK

The George D. And Harriet W. Cornell Fine Arts Museum
Affiliate Institution: Rollins College
Rollins College- Box 2765, **Winter Park, FL 32789**
TEL: 407-646-1500
HRS: 10-5 Tu-F; 1-5 Sa, S   DAY CLOSED: M   HOL: 1/1, 7/4, LAB/DAY, THGV, 12/25
ADM: F
HDC/ACC: Y   PARKING: Y; Free parking in the adjacent "H" Lot & in the parking lot next to the Field House
GR/T: Y   GR/PH: call 407-646-2526
PERM/COLL: EU: ptgs, Ren-20; SCULP; DEC/ART; AM: ptgs, sculp 19-20; PHOT; SP: Ren/sculp

Considered one of the most outstanding musuems in Central Florida, the Cornell, located on the campus of Rollins College, houses fine examples in many areas of art including American landscape painting, French portraiture, works of Renaissance and Baroque masters, and contemporary prints. **NOT TO BE MISSED:** Paintings from the Kress Collection; "Christ With The Symbols of The Passion," by Lavinia Fontana

ON EXHIBIT/95:

11/12/94 - 1/8/95	BOTH ART AND LIFE: GEMINI G.E.L. AT 25
1/13 - 3/5/95	THE EARLY PRINTS OF EDVARD MUNCH
3/11 - 5/7/95	THE BLOOMSBURY CIRCLE: ENGLISH PAINTINGS FROM THE KENNETH CURRY COLLECTION
3/11 - 5/7/95	REVERBERATIONS: DIPTYCHS & TRIPTYCHS FROM THE SOUTHEAST MUSEUM OF PHOTOGRAPHY
6/3 - 9/17/95	LAND AND SEA SCAPES FROM THE PERMANENT COLLECTION
9/23 - 11/5/95	DORIS LEEPER: A RETROSPECTIVE

ALBANY

Albany Museum of Art
311 Meadowlark Dr., **Albany, GA 31707**
TEL: 912-439-8400
HRS: 10-5 Tu-Sa, till 7pm W   DAY CLOSED: S, M   HOL: LEG/HOL!
SUGG/CONT: Y   F/DAY: Tu & Sa   ADULT: $3.00   CHILDREN: F (under 12)   STUDENTS: $1.00
SR CIT: $2.00
HDC/ACC: Y   PARKING: Y; Ample free parking   MUS/SH: Y   GR/T: Y   GR/PH: call 912-439-8400   DT: Y
PERM/COLL: AM: all media 19- 20; EU: all media 19-20; AF: 19-20; AM: dec/art 18-20; EU: dec/art 18-20; REG;
AM: cont

With one of the largest collections of traditional African art in the South, the Albany Museum, started in 1964, is also home to an important collection of contemporary American art. **NOT TO BE MISSED:** A 1,500 piece collection of African art that includes works from 18 different cultures.

ON EXHIBIT/95:

1/8 - 2/26/95	ECHOES OF OUR PAST: PALMER HAYDEN — In the 40 paintings by African-American artist Hayden, on loan from the Museum of African Art, vivid and vital images of many of the unheroic experiences of the Black man in America will be seen. CAT WT
1/10 - 5/1/95	JONI MABE
3/5 - 5/8/95	MAUDE GATEWOOD
6/15 - 8/30/95	PAUL CHOJNOWSKI: ALTERNATE VISIONS
9/16/95 - 1/1/96	AMERICAN CRAFT: BREAKING BARRIERS

ATHENS

Georgia Museum of Art
Affiliate Institution: The University of Georgia
Jackson St., North Campus, **Athens, GA 30602**
TEL: 706-542-3255
HRS: 9-5 M-Sa; 1-5 S   HOL: LEG/HOL!
ADM: F   HDC/ACC: Y; Rear of building via Jackson St.
PARKING: Y; The museum is within walking distance of downtown parking. On weekends, parking is available on Jackson St.   MUS/SH: Y   GR/T: Y   GR/PH: call 706-542-3255   H/B: Y
PERM/COLL: AM: sculp, gr; EU: gr; JAP: gr; IT/REN: ptgs (Kress Collection); AM: ptgs 19-20

The Georgia Museum of Art, located on the campus of the University of Georgia in Athens has grown from its modest beginnings in 1945 with the 100 piece collection donated by Alfred Holbrook to more than 5,000 works now included in its permanent holdings. **NOT TO BE MISSED:** American paintings from the permanent collection on view continually in the South gallery.

ON EXHIBIT/95:

11/19/94 - 1/15/95	INK, PAPER, METAL AND WOOD; HOW TO RECOGNIZE AND UNDERSTAND CONTEMPORARY ARTISTS' PRINTS — 80 prints, drawn mainly from Crown Point Press in San Francisco, will include works by such contemporary artistic luminaries as Chuck Close, Richard Diebenkorn, Wayne Thiebaud, Helen Frankenthaler and others. CAT

GEORGIA

Georgia Museum of Art - continued

1/21 - 3/19/95	SPIRIT EYES, HUMAN HANDS: AFRICAN ART FROM THE SAMUEL P. HARN MUSEUM OF ART — 90 works grouped according to spiritual themes will be on loan from the Harn, a museum that houses one of the best collections of African art in the Southeast.
1/28 - 3/19/95	THE HUDSON RIVER SCHOOL IN GEORGIA COLLECTIONS — Created between 1830-1880, 25 Hudson River School paintings, watercolors and drawings from public and private collections will be on exhibit.
1/28 - 3/19/95	A GEORGIA SAMPLER — A display of paintings, sculpture, photography, metalwork and video created by 12 artists living and working in Georgia will showcase the remarkable scope of the arts in the state.
4/1 - 5/14/95	HOUSE AND HOME: SPIRITS OF THE SOUTH — 80 photographs, 14 sculptures and 12 large drawings by Max Belcher, Beverly Buchanan and William Christenberry address the rapidly disappearing tradition of Southern vernacular architecture and design. CAT
4/1 - 5/14/95	OTHER ROOTS: PAINTED PHOTOGRAPHS BY JYNN MARSHALL LINNEMEIER — Black and white photographs by Linnemeier that she paints to resemble Middle Eastern miniatures will be on view.
5/27 - 6/25/95	TREASURES OF BRENAU
7/8 - 8/6/95	JOSEF KLINE SCULPTURES — On exibit will be 40 works of figurative sculpture and drawings by this German-born immigrant to America (1902-1992) who lived and worked in Atlanta and who was placed in an internment camp during the Second World War as a suspected spy for Germany.
7/8 - 9/10/95	NOSTALGIC JOURNEY: AMERICAN ILLUSTRATIONS FROM THE COLLECTION OF THE DELAWARE ART MUSEUM — Paintings and drawings from the "Golden Age of American Illustration" will provide the viewer with a delightful nostalgic journey that appeals to both young and old. Images created for classic stories by artists such as Howard Pyle and N. C. Weyth will be shown with those of Arthur Dove, John Sloan, William Glakens and George Luks, members of the realist circle known as "The Eight" or "The Ashcan School." WT
8/12 - 9/17/95	MEXICAN TEXTILES, LINE AND COLOR — Textiles and garments from over 85 cultures in Mexico accompanied by videos that demonstrate weaving and embroidery techniques will be featured in this exhibition.
9/23 - 11/19/95	HORACE BRISTOL — Among the nearly 80 photographs in this exhibition that document the career of a master 20th-century photographer will be those of Depression-era migrant workers that were the inspiration for John Steinbeck's "The Grapes of Wrath."
9/30 - 11/26/95	DANCING IN A GARDEN OF LIGHT — Glassworks by 17 notable western North Carolina glass artists will serve to document the development of the studio glass movement over the past 30 years.

ATLANTA

Hammonds House Galleries and Resource Center
503 Peoples St., **Atlanta, GA 31310**
TEL: 404-752-8730
HRS: 10-6 Tu-F; 1-5 Sa, S   DAY CLOSED: M   HOL: LEG/HOL!
ADM: Y   ADULT: $2.00   CHILDREN: $1.00   STUDENTS: $1.00   SR CIT: $1.00
HDC/ACC: Y; Barrier free   PARKING: Y; Free 32 car lot on the corner of Lucile & Peoples; some street parking also available   MUS/SH: Y   DT: Y   TIME: Upon request
H/B: Y; 1857 East Lake Victorian House restored in 1984 by Dr. Otis T. Hammonds
PERM/COLL: AF/AM: mid 19-20; HAITIAN: ptgs; AF: sculp

Hammonds House Galleries and Resource Center - continued

As the only fine art museum in the Southeast dedicated to the promotion of art by peoples of African descent, Hammonds House features changing exhibitions of nationally known African-American artists. Works by Romare Bearden, Sam Gilliam, Benny Andrews, James Van Der Zee and others are included in the 125 piece collection. **NOT TO BE MISSED:** Romare Bearden Collection of post 60's serigraphs; Collection of Premiere Contemporary Haitian Artists

ON EXHIBIT/95:

11/13/94 - 1/25/95	MOYO OKEDIJI AND TAYO ADENAIKE — A three-way confluence of traditional cultural expression, Western influence and contemporary American aesthetics will be seen in the work of these two Nigerian artists.
2/2 - 3/26/95	CHARLES WHITE — Works by White, an artist best known for his 1930's murals depicting African-American life and for his later drawings and paintings of individuals.
4/9 - 6/4/95	TERRY ADKINS — Mixed-media works that combine found objects into "tangible interpretations of sound" by Washington D.C.-born sculptor, Adkins.

ATLANTA

High Museum of Art
1280 Peachtree St., N.E., **Atlanta, GA 30309**
TEL: 404-733-4400
HRS: 10-5 Tu-T, Sa; 10am-9pm F; Noon-5 S   DAY CLOSED: M   HOL: 1/1, THGV, 12/25
F/DAY: 1-5 T   ADM: Y   ADULT: $6.00   CHILDREN: $2.00 (6-17)   STUDENTS: $4.00   SR CIT: $4.00
HDC/ACC: Y; Ramps, elevator, wheelchairs available   PARKING: Y; Limited paid parking on deck of Woodruff Art Center Building on the side of the museum; some limited street parking   MUS/SH: Y
GR/T: Y   GR/PH: call 404-898-1145   DT: Y   TIME: call before visiting for schedule
H/B: Y; Building designed by Richard Meier, 1983
PERM/COLL: AM: dec/art 18-20; EU: cer 18; AM: ptgs, sculp 19; EU: ptgs, sculp, cer, gr, REN- 20; PHOT 19-20; AM; cont (since 1970)

The beauty of the building designed in 1987 by architect Richard Meier is a perfect foil for the outstanding collection of art within the walls of the High Museum itself. The museum, part of the Robert W. Woodruff Art Center, is a must see for every art lover who visits Atlanta. **NOT TO BE MISSED:** The Virginia Carroll Crawford Collection of American Decorative Arts; The Frances and Emory Cocke Collection of English Ceramics.

ON EXHIBIT/95:

10/8/94 - 1/15/95	ART AT THE EDGE: JEM COHEN — In a 3-channel video installation, film and video artist Cohen, who traveled to Berlin, Dresden, Prague, Budapest and Krakow in 1992 & 1993, presents his interpretation of the cultural heritage of these cities which he feels are "being carted away to the trashbin."
12/13/94 - 2/12/95	THE HERTER BROTHERS: EUROPEAN FURNITURE MAKERS IN THE AMERICAN GILDED AGE — Furniture by these Stuttgart-born, European-trained craftsmen who worked in New York will be on view in the first comprehensive exhibition of its kind. The Herter Brothers were adept at blending high style, elegant design, rare woods and excellent craftsmanship for America's most famous 19th century patrons including Wm. Vanderbilt, Jay Gould and Frederick Church. CAT WT

GEORGIA

High Museum of Art - continued

1 - 2/95   ART AT THE EDGE: ANGE LECCIA — As part of an ongoing series of exhibitions by contemporary artists, Corsican/French artist, Leccia, will project her monumental video images of antique and medieval statuary from dusk to dawn against the facade of a major downtown building off-site of the museum.

1/14 - 4/9/95   VENICE AND THE ARTISTIC IMAGINATION: PRINTS BY TIEPOLO, CANALETTO AND WHISTLER FROM THE WEIL COLLECTION — 90 etchings from this superb private collection will focus on the theme of Venice as interpreted by three of the greatest printmakers in the history of art.   CAT WT

1/28 - 3/5/95   IN CELEBRATION OF BLACK HISTORY MONTH PHOTOGRAPHS BY PRENTICE H. POLK AND JAMES VANDERZEE — From the permanent collection, images by 2 pioneering African-American photographers; namely, James VanDerZee (1886-1983) and Prentice H. Polk (1889-1984) will be on exhibit.

2/1/95 - ONGOING   ABOUT MASKS: THE HIGH MUSEUM OF ART EDUCATION GALLERY — The new education gallery at the Museum will present an exhibition designed to be an enjoyable and educational experience for visitors of all ages. In adddition to replicas and touchable items, there will be masks from all cultures and for varied purposes including those used for work (such as welding and hockey masks), for festive occasions (such as Mardi Gras and Halloween), for theater productions and for ceremonial functions. Visitors will be encouraged to create their own masks in the hands-on area of the gallery.

2/28 - 5/21/95   TREASURES OF VENICE: PAINTINGS FROM THE MUSEUM OF FINE ARTS, BUDAPEST — 55 paintings (16th - 18th centuries) from one of the finest and largest collections of Venetian art outside of Venice itself, will include works by Venetian artists that demonstrate the vitality of 300 continuous years of artistic tradition.   WT

4/15 - 8/6/95   ART AT THE EDGE: SOCIAL TURF — Four contemporary artists of different ethnic backgrounds whose interpretations of everyday scenes as viewed from beneath the surface of the obvious will be seen in their works on display in this exhibition.

4/25 - 6/25/95   JACOB LAWRENCE: THE MIGRATION SERIES — 60 narrative paintings that detail the flight of African-Americans from the rural South to the urban North before and after World War I will be reunited in this exhibition.   CAT WT

6/13 - 9/10/95   SHAKER FURNITURE: THE ART OF CRAFTSMANSHIP — 19th-century objects and furniture of simplicity, order and fine craftsmanship from the first and most influential Shaker community in New Lebanon, New York will be seen in the first major exhibition of its kind in America.   WT

8/19 - 12/31/95   THE COTTON STATES AND INTERNATIONAL EXPOSITION ATLANTA 1895 — In commemoration of the centennial of the Cotton States and International Exhibition held in Atlanta in 1895, the High Museum is presenting an overview of the fair with particular focus on the fine artworks that were shown at that time. Included in this re-creation will be paintings, sculptures, drawings, prints and architectural renderings that were originally presented at the exposition as well as works by Mary Cassatt, Winslow Homer, Thomas Eakins, Theodore Robinson and James McNeill Whistler.

10/10/95 - 1/7/96   SEAN SCULLY: TWENTY YEARS, 1976-1995 — 40 large-scale abstract paintings accompanied by 40 related watercolors will be seen in the first survey of Scully's work to tour nationally and internationally.   CAT WT

136

ATLANTA

High Museum of Folk Art & Photography Galleries at Georgia-Pacific Center
30 John Wesley Dobbs Ave., **Atlanta, GA 30303**
TEL: 404-577-6940
HRS: 10-5 M-Sa   DAY CLOSED: S   HOL: LEG/HOL!
ADM: F
HDC/ACC: Y   PARKING: Y; Paid parking lot in the center itself with a bridge from the parking deck to the lobby; other paid parking lots nearby   MUS/SH: Y   DT: Y

Folk art and photography are the main focus in the 4,500 square foot exhibition space of this Atlanta facility formally called The High Museum of Art at Georgia-Pacific Center.

ON EXHIBIT/95:

10/15/94 - 1/14/95	WORKERS, AN ARCHAEOLOGY OF THE INDUSTRIAL AGE: PHOTOGRAPHS BY SEBASTIAO SALGADO — 250 powerful images by this renowned Brazilian-born photographer celebrate the nobility of the men, women and children worldwide who still labor with their hands and bodies even as the need for their labor diminishes with the approach of the 21st century. Many of the images in this exhibition have never before been seen or published. CAT WT
1/7 - 4/8/95	A PROPER LIKENESS: PLAIN STYLE PORTRAITS IN GEORGIA COLLECTIONS — 30 18th and 19th century portraits by limners, many of which have never before been on view, will be featured in this exhibit that reveals their "plain-style" caracteristics of flat compositions, repetition of patterns, bold colors, and an uncompromising emphasis on revealing a true likeness.
1/28 - 4/15/95	COMMODITY IMAGE — 80 contemporary photographic works by a variety of artists expressing individual styles and points of view investigate the surface appearance of social myths and the fantasies of beauty & wealth in present-day society. WT
4/22 - 7/8/95	EXECUTIVE MODEL: AN INSTALLATION BY RON JUDE (working title) — Large-format photographs by Atlanta artist Ron Jude inaugurate the first in a series of annual exhibitions that feature the works of young, emerging photographers from both the U.S. and abroad.
7/15 - 10/7/95	TALKING PICTURES: PEOPLE SPEAK ABOUT THE PHOTOGRAPHS THAT SPEAK TO THEM — The way in which photography impacts on our lives will be seen in the 65 images chosen by 65 famous and not-so famous people whose lives have been changed by the specific photographic images they have selected. BOOK WT

Michael C. Carlos Museum of Art and Archaeology
Affiliate Institution: Emory University
571 South Kilgo St., **Atlanta, GA 30322**
TEL: 404-727-4282
HRS: 10-5 M-T; 10-9 F; 10-5 Sa; Noon-5 S   HOL: 1/1, THGV, 12/25
SUGG/CONT: Y   ADULT: $3.00
HDC/ACC: Y   PARKING: Y; Visitor parking for a small fee at the Boisfeuillet Jones Building; free parking on campus except in restricted areas. Handicapped parking Plaza level entrance on So. Kilgo St.   MUS/SH: Y
REST/FAC: Y; Cafe   GR/T: Y   GR/PH: call 404-727-0519   H/B: Y
PERM/COLL: AN/EGT; AN/GRK; AN/ROM; P/COL; AS; AF; OC; WORKS ON PAPER 14-20

GEORGIA

Michael C. Carlos Museum of Art and Archaeology - continued

Founded on the campus of Emory Univeristy in 1919 (making it the oldest art museum in Atlanta), this distinguished institution, in 1991, changed its name to the Michael C. Carlos Museum in honor of its long time benefactor. A dramatic new 35,000 square foot building opened in the spring of 1993 is a masterful addition to the original Beaux-Arts edifice. **NOT TO BE MISSED:** Carlos Collection of Ancient Greek Art; Thibadeau Collection of pre-Columbian Art; recent acquisition of rare 4th c Volute-Krater by the Underworld painter of Apulia

ON EXHIBIT/95:

9/10/94 - 2/13/95	THE BODY BEAUTIFUL: ANCIENT EQUIDORIAN CERAMIC FIGURES IN THE COLLECTION OF THE BANCO CENTRAL DEL EQUADOR
10/15/94 - 1/2/95	ART OF NIGERIA FROM THE WILLIAM S. ARNETT COLLECTION — 100 19th & 20th century works from several regions in Africa will be on view from this distinguished collection.
1 - 4/95	DRAWN FROM LIFE: THE HUMAN PRESENCE IN 17TH - 20TH CENTURY EUROPEAN AND AMERICAN DRAWING
2/4 - 5/14/95	REFLECTIONS OF WOMEN IN THE NEW KINGDOM: EGYPTIAN ART FROM THE BRITISH MUSEUM — All of the 100 artworks in this exhibition which include sculptures, jewelry, papyri, and decorative art, will attempt to exemplify the ways in which women were perceived in ancient Egypt.
6 - 9/95	AFRICAN ART: UNITY IN DIVERSITY — Sculpture, ritual instruments, tools, masks and utilitarian objects from different African cultures reflect the influence upon them of representational art imposed by the Colonialist "other."
9/22 - 11/19/95	FRENCH OIL SKETCHES OF THE SEVENTEENTH, EIGHTEENTH, AND NINETEENTH CENTURIES — Paintings ranging from the Baroque, Rococo, Neoclassic, Romantic and Realistic periods which recorded the initial spontaneous thoughts of the artists represented in this exhibition will be seen in the first traveling exhibition of its kind. CAT WT
Thru 5/95	SACRED SPACES, FAMOUS FACES — This long term installation includes 19th century architectural models of Olympia, Delphi, and Athens, as well as plaster casts of many famous works of Greek art.
ONGOING:	A HISTORY OF WESTERN ARCHITECTURE: AN INSTALLATION ON LOAN FROM THE METROPOLITAN MUSEUM OF ART — 210 plaster casts of Western architectural elements and sculpture.
	NORTHERN DRIFT — An outdoor sculpture by Sir Anthony Caro which can be seen on-site through the Olympic Games in 1996.
	AFRICAN ART
	ASIAN ART

ATLANTA

Ogelthorpe University Museum

Affiliate Institution: Ogelthorpe University
4484 Peachtree Road, NE, **Atlanta, GA 30319**
TEL: 404-364-8555
HRS: 11-4 Tu-F; 1-4 S, other by appt!   DAY CLOSED: M & Sa   HOL: LEG/HOL!
ADM: F   HDC/ACC: Y   PARKING: Y; Free and ample
MUS/SH: Y   GR/T: Y   GR/PH: Call 404-365-8555 to reserve   DT: Y   TIME: Upon request if available
PERM/COLL: Realsitic figurative art, historical, metaphysical and international art

138

Ogelthorpe University Museum - continued

Established just over one year ago, this museum, dedicated to showing realistic art, has already instituted many "firsts" for this area including the opening of each new exhibition with a free public lecture, the creation of an artist-in-residence program and a regular series of chamber music concerts. In addition, the museum is devoted to creating and sponsoring its own series of original and innovative special exhibitions instead of relying on traveling exhibitions from other sources. **NOT TO BE MISSED:** 14th century Kamakura Buddha from Japan; "The Three Ages of Man" by Giorgione (on extended loan); 18th century engravings illustrating Shakespeare's plays

ON EXHIBIT/95:

2/5 - 3/19/95	GEORGIA O'KEEFFE
4/2 - 9/24/95	NAVAJO WEAVING

AUGUSTA

Morris Museum of Art
One 10th Street, **Augusta, GA 30901-1134**
TEL: 706-724-7501
HRS: 10-5:30 Tu-Sa; 1-5 S; till 8pm 1st F of the month   DAY CLOSED: M   HOL: 12/25, 1/1, THGV
F/DAY: S   ADM: Y   ADULT: $2.00   CHILDREN: F (under 12)   STUDENTS: $1.00   SR CIT: $1.00
HDC/ACC: Y; Elevators in main lobby direct to 2nd floor museum, ramps to bldg.
PARKING: Y; Free in marked spaces in West Lot; paid parking in city lot at adjacent hotel.   MUS/SH: Y
GR/T: Y   GR/PH: call 706-724-7501
PERM/COLL: REG: portraiture (antebellum to contemporary), still lifes, Impr, cont; AF/AM

Rich Southern architecture and decorative appointments installed in a contemporary office building present a delightful surprise to the first time visitor. Included in this setting are works of art that represent a broad-based survey of the history of painting in the south. **NOT TO BE MISSED:** The Southern Landscape Gallery

ON EXHIBIT/95:

1/11 - 2/12/95	AUGUSTA COLLECTS — Paintings on loan from private collections in the Augusta area.
3/3 - 5/7/95	LOUISIANA ART FROM THE COLLECTION OF ROGER HOUSTON OGDEN — 65 masterpieces of Southern painting acquired over a 25 year period of collecting by Ogden, a New Orleans attorney, will include examples of Antebellum portraiture, landscape art, impressionism, 20th century and contemporary artworks.
5/18 - 7/9/95	HOUSE AND HOME: SPIRITS OF THE SOUTH — Photographs, sculptures, paintings and drawings, some created specifically for this show by Beverly Buchanan, William Christenberry and Max Belcher all explore the theme of past and present life in the South as seen through images of the cabin, shack, and house, visual metaphors for the simple and humble life.
SUMMER	TBA

GEORGIA

COLUMBUS

The Columbus Museum
1251 Wynnton Rd., **Columbus, GA 31906**
TEL: 706-649-0713
HRS: 10-5 Tu-Sa; 1-5 S   DAY CLOSED: M   HOL: LEG/HOL!
SUGG/CONT: Y   HDC/ACC: Y; Fully accessible   PARKING: Y; Ample and free   MUS/SH: Y
GR/T: Y   GR/PH: call 706-649-0713
PERM/COLL: PTGS; SCULP; GR 19-20; DEC/ART; REG; FOLK

The new Mediterranean style addition to the Columbus Museum has added 30,000 feet of well lit exhibition space that provides a splendid setting for its permanent collection of works by American masters of the 19th & 20th centuries. **NOT TO BE MISSED:** "Fergus, Boy in Blue" by Robert Henri

ON EXHIBIT/95:

10/16/94 - 1/8/95	THE BEAUTY IN THE BEAST: AMERICAN ARTISTS OBSERVE THE HORSE — Aesthetic responses to the horse as a subject of art will be examined in this exhibition.
10/30/94 - 1/8/95	PENLAND OVERLOOK — A comprehensive overview of decorative arts and crafts will be seen in 106 works by 48 artisans in residence over the last several decades at North Carolina's renowned Penland School.
11/94 - 3/95	COLUMBUS AND THE LAND OF AYLLON
2/5 - 4/2/95	WILLIAM H. JOHNSON: A RETROSPECTIVE — In this retrospective of 54 paintings by Johnson, a noted 20th-century African-American artist, issues concerning African-American achievements in the arts, the contributions of an African-American individual, and African-American subjects in modern American art will be addressed. WT
4/30 - 6/25/95	MY PEOPLE: THE PORTRAITS OF ROBERT HENRI — 50 wonderful portraits by Henri, leader of "The Eight" or "The Ashcan School" created between 1900-1930 will be seen in this exhibit that includes images of Irish & Spanish peasants, gypsies, New York immigrants and Southwestern and American Indian subjects. CAT WT
6/11 - 8/20/95	OUR LAND/OURSELVES: AMERICAN INDIAN CONTEMPORARY ARTISTS — 86 works on paper by 29 contemporary Native American artists who address the issue of their bond between the land and its inhabitants by using metaphysical, allegorical, political and metaphorical sources of reference. WT
8/6 - 9/24/95	TALES AND TRADITIONS: STORYTELLING IN TWENTIETH-CENTURY AMERICAN CRAFT — Nearly 70 objects by 70 artists working in a variety of media that includes weaving, furniture, ceramics and jewelry will exhibit their unique representations of portraits and scenes relating to historical events and political issues. CAT WT
11/26/95 - 2/4/96	OF EARTH AND COTTON — Depression-era Library of Congress Farm Security Administration photographs of Southern farm laborers will be accompanied by an installation by Jackie Brookner entitled "Made of Earth" that consists of 30-50 sculptures of the feet of farm laborers. The purpose of this exhibition is to highlight the plight of past and present farm workers, their ties to the earth, and agriculture's effects on society. WT

140

GEORGIA

SAVANNAH

Telfair Academy of Arts and Sciences, Inc.
121 Barnard St., Savannah, GA 31401
TEL: 912-232-1177
HRS: 10-5 Tu-Sa; 2-5 S   DAY CLOSED: M   HOL: LEG/HOL!
F/DAY: S   ADM: Y   ADULT: $3.00   CHILDREN: $.50 (6-12)   STUDENTS: $1.00   SR CIT: $1.00
HDC/ACC: Y; Use President St. entrance   PARKING: Y; Metered street parking   MUS/SH: Y
GR/T: Y   GR/PH: call 912-232-1177   DT: Y   TIME: on occasion!
H/B: Y; 1819 Regency Mansion designed by William Jay
PERM/COLL: AM: Impr & Ashcan ptgs; AM: dec/art; Brit: dec/art; FR: dec/art

Named for its founding family and housed in a Regency mansion designed in 1818 by architect William Jay, this museum contains the largest and most important collection of the drawings and pastels of Kahlil Gilbran. The Telfair, which is the oldest public art museum in the Southeast, also has major works by many of the artists who have contributed so brilliantly to the history of American art. **NOT TO BE MISSED:** Original Duncan Phyfe furniture; casts of the Elgin Marbles

ON EXHIBIT/95:

12/6/94 - 2/12/95   CONTEMPORARY GEORGIA ARTISTS — On view will be two-dimensional works by 6-10 contemporary Georgia artists.

3/14 - 4/30/95   500 YEARS OF PRINTMAKING FROM THE TELFAIR COLLECTION — Works by Goya, Durer, Piranesi, Whistler and others will document the history of printmaking.

5/15 - 11/19/95   CLASSICAL SAVANNAH — From the Telfair's permanent collection, classically inspired regional fine and decorative arts, with an emphasis on those created between 1800-1840, will be complemented in this exhibition by important pieces on loan from private sources.   CAT

12/5/95 - 1/28/96   ALFRED STIEGLITZ'S CAMERA NOTES — Published quarterly by the Camera Club of New York, "Camera Notes," (1897-1903) was edited by Stieglitz, a founding member of the club. In this exhibition a complete set of every photogravure that ever appeared in this journal will be on view.   CAT   WT

12/5 95 - 1/28/96   THE PASSIONATE OBSERVER: PHOTOGRAPHS BY CARL VAN VECHTEN — 59 photographs taken of famous artists and writers by Van Vechten, during the time he was a music critic for the New York Times (from the 1930's through the 1960's), will include youthful images of Truman Capote, Salvador Dali, George Gershwin, Eugene O'Neill and others.   CAT

HAWAII

HONOLULU

The Contemporary Museum
2411 Makiki Heights Drive, **Honolulu, HI 96822**
TEL: 808-526-1322
HRS: 10-4 Tu-Sa; Noon-4 S   DAY CLOSED: M   HOL: LEG/HOL! F/DAY: 3rd T
ADM: Y   ADULT: $5.00   CHILDREN: F (under 12)
HDC/ACC: Y   PARKING: Y; Free but very limited parking   MUS/SH: Y   REST/FAC: Y; Cafe   S/G: Y
PERM/COLL: AM: cont; REG

Terraced gardens with stone benches overlooking exquisite vistas complement the museum structure in a perfect hillside setting. Inside are modernized galleries in which the permanent collection of art of the past 40 years is displayed. **NOT TO BE MISSED:** David Hockney's environmental installation "L'Enfant et les Sortileges" built for a Ravel opera

ON EXHIBIT/95:

1/25 - 3/26/95	DAVID NASH - VOYAGES AND VESSELS
4/5 - 6/11/95	JOHN BUCK - A SURVEY EXHIBITION
6/21 - 8/20/95	THE CONTEMPORARY MUSEUM BIENNIAL
8/30 - 11/5/95	CHRISTOPHER BROWN WT
	RECENT WORKS BY RICK MILLS
11/14/95 - 1/14/96	THE ARTIST'S HAND - DRAWINGS FROM THE BANK AMERICA CORPORATION ART COLLECTION

Honolulu Academy of Arts
900 S. Beretania St., **Honolulu, HI 96814-1495**
TEL: 808-532-8701
HRS: 10-4:30 Tu-Sa; 1-5 S   DAY CLOSED: M   HOL: LEG/HOL!
VOL/CONT: Y   ADM: F   ADULT: $4.00   CHILDREN: F (under 12)   STUDENTS: $2.00   SR CIT: $2.00
HDC/ACC: Y; Wheelchair access & parking at Ward Ave. gate (call 532-8759 to reserve)
PARKING: Y; Lot parking at the Academy Art Center for $1.00 with validation; some street parking also available
MUS/SH: Y   REST/FAC: Y; 11:30-1:00 Tu-F; Supper 6:30 S call 808-531-8865
GR/T: T   GR/PH: call 808-538-3693 ex 255   DT: Y   TIME: 11:00 Tu -Sa; 1:00 S
H/B: Y; 1927 Building Designed By Bertram G. Goodhue Assoc.   S/G: Y
PERM/COLL: OR: all media; AM: all media; EU: all media; HAWAIIANA COLLECTION

Thirty galleries and six garden courts form the basis of Hawaii's only general art museum. This internationally respected institution features extensive notable collections that span the history of art and come from nearly every corner of the world. **NOT TO BE MISSED:** James A. Michener collection of Japanese Ukiyo-e Woodblock prints; Kress Collection of Italian Rennaissance Paintings.

ON EXHIBIT/95:

THROUGH 2/12/95	RECENT PHOTOGRAPHY ACQUISITIONS
2/2 - 3/26/95	ISLAND ANCESTORS: OCEANIC ART FROM THE MASCO COLLECTION — 76 objects from New Guinea, Polynesia, Micronesia and Melanesia that date from Oceania's pre-colonial history will be featured in this exhibition. WT BOOK

142

Honolulu Academy of Arts - continued

2/2 - 3/26/95	SPIRIT STONES OF CHINA
2/16 - 4/16/95	RAYMOND HAN
2/16 - 3/31/95	JUDY DATER: CYCLES
3/16 - 6/18/95	TOMB TREASURES FROM CHINA: THE BURIED ART OF ANCIENT XI'AN — 62 3rd century B.C.to 8th century A.D archaelogical treasures from the recently excavated Xi'an tomb of the First Emperor, Qin Shihuangdi, will be highlighted by a group of 7 life-sized terracotta warrior figures. Superb examples of bronze, ceramic, jade, gold and silver works will also be on display in the first U.S. exhibition of artifacts from this ancient Chinese city. ATR EXTENDED HOURS ON ALTERNATE FRIDAYS FOR THIS EXHIBITION WT
4/13 - 5/21/95	REVELATIONS III: RECENT ACQUISITIONS, 1988-1995
4/13 - 5/21/95	VOLUNTEERS' CHOICE: 25TH ANNIVERSARY
4/20 - 6/11/95	LAURA RUBY: NANCY DREW SERIES
6/8 - 8/6/95	SELECTIONS OF 20TH CENTURY ART FROM THE ACADEMY'S COLLECTION
6/8 - 8/6/95	MORRIS GRAVES: PAINTINGS OF CHINESE RITUAL
6/15 - 7/30/95	RON HO
8/31 - 10/15/95	MASTERPIECES OF INDIAN ART IN THE CHRISTENSEN FUND COLLECTION
8/31 - 10/15/95	IMPERIAL RUSSIAN PORCELAIN FROM THE RAYMOND F. PIPER COLLECTION — Opulent and extravagant porcelains from the Imperial Porcelain Factory in St. Petersburg, Russia, created between the reigns of Elizabeth I and Nicholas II, will be featured in this exhibition. WT
8/8 - 12/31(?)/95	HAWAII AND ITS PEOPLE — Works from the permanent collection
11/16 - 12/31/95	ARTISTS OF HAWAII

IDAHO

BOISE

Boise Art Museum

670 S. Julia Davis Dr., **Boise, ID 83702**
TEL: 208-345-8330
HRS: 10-5 Tu-F; Noon-5 Sa, S (winter); 10-5 M-F, Noon-5 Sa, S & HOL (summer)
HOL: LEG/HOL!
ADM: Y   ADULT: $3.00   CHILDREN: $1.00 (grades 1-12)   STUDENTS: $2.00   SR CIT: $2.00
HDC/ACC: Y   PARKING: Y; Free and ample parking   MUS/SH: Y   GR/T: Y   GR/PH: 208-345-8330
DT: Y   TIME: 12:15 Tu, 1:00 Sa
PERM/COLL: REG; GR; OR; AM: (Janss Collection of American Realism)

Home of the famed Glenn C. Janss Collection of American Realism, the Boise Art Museum in its parkland setting is considered the finest art museum in the state of Idaho. **NOT TO BE MISSED:** "Art in the Park," held every September, is one of the largest art and crafts festivals in the region.

ON EXHIBIT/95:

12/3/94 - 1/29/95	IMPERIAL RUSSIAN PROCELAIN FROM THE RAYMOND F. PIPER COLLECTION — 86 opulent and extravagant historical porcelains from the Imperial Porcelain Factory in St. Petersburg, Russia, created between the reigns of Elizabeth I and Nicholas II, will be on view. WT
12/8/94 - 1/29/95	JAMES BARSNESS: CURRENT WORK — Works by Barsness that are an unusual combination of Renaissance-like painting combined with modern comic-book drawing all accented by some gold leaf and ballpoint pen.
2/4 - 4/2/95	BETWEEN HOME AND HEAVEN: CONTEMPORARY AMERCIAN LANDSCAPE PHOTOGRAPHY — Both traditional and non-traditional images created since the 1970's by the photographers in this exhibition include romantic views of the wilderness, panoramas, studio-fabricated "landscapes" and documentary subjects. WT
2/4 - 4/2/95	FLOW: A TRANSCONTINENTAL SOUNDWORK BY PATRICK ZENTZ — Zentz's large-scale sculptural instruments create diverse musical scores by including his interpretations of the sounds of wind, waves, traffic and even the whosh of a high-rise elevator.
4/29 - 6/18/95	AMERCIAN NAIVE PAINTING FROM THE NATIONAL GALLERY OF ART — 33 19th century paintings featuring portraits, historical events, landscapes, still lifes and genre scenes by unknown and well established artists will be on exhibit. WT
6/24 - 8/20/95	IDAHO TRIENNIAL

ILLINOIS

CARBONDALE

University Museum
Affiliate Institution: Southern Illinois University
Carbondale, IL 62901
TEL: 618-453-5388
HRS: Acad: 9-3 Tu-Sa; 1:30-4:30 S   DAY CLOSED: M   HOL: ACAD & LEG/HOL!
ADM: F   HDC/ACC: Y   PARKING: Y; Metered lot just East of the Student Center (next to the football stadium)
MUS/SH: Y   GR/T: Y   GR/PH: call 618-453-5388   DT: Y   TIME: upon request if available   S/G: Y
PERM/COLL: AM: ptgs, drgs, gr; EU: ptgs, drgs, gr, 13-20; PHOT 20; SCULP 20; CER; OC; DEC/ART

Continually rotating exhibitions feature the fine and decorative arts as well as those based on science related themes of anthropology, geology, natural history, and archaeology. **NOT TO BE MISSED:** In the sculpture garden, two works by Ernert Trova, "AV-A-7" and "AV-YELLOW LOZENGER," and a sculpture entitled "Starwalk" by Richard Hunt.

ON EXHIBIT/95:

1/17 - 3/10/95	REGIONAL KNIFE MAKERS
3/7 - 5/5/95	US/MEXICO PRINTS
3/21 - 8/10/95	ARTS, SCIENCE AND HUMANITIES - 125 YEARS OF COLLECTING
4/7 - 4/30/95	CLAY CUP: JURIED INVITATIONAL COMPETITION
6/13 - 8/5/95	ROSA LEA FASSLER: THREE GENERATIONS OF QUILT MAKERS
8/22 - 9/29/95	MICKEY PAULOS PAINTINGS
8/22 - 10/1/95	ROBERTS ELLIOTT FRANCIS: THE VELVET HAMMER (BLACKSMITH)
8/22 - 9/24/95	POLLY AND MARION MITCHELL: SCHERINSCHNIT & GERMAN, SCANDINAVIAN AND SHAKER BOXES
10/6 - 10/29/95	ALLEN MOORE PAINTINGS
11/4 - 12/15/95	JOCK McDONALD: PHOTOGRAPHER

CHAMPAIGN

Krannert Art Museum
Affiliate Institution: University of Illinois
500 E. Peabody Dr., **Champaign, IL 61820**
TEL: 217-333-1860
HRS: 10-5 Tu, T-Sa; 10am-8pm W; 2-5 S   DAY CLOSED: M   HOL: 1/1, EASTER, LAB/DAY, 12/25
VOL/CONT: Y   ADM: F   HDC/ACC: Y; Ramps, elevators   PARKING: Y; On-street metered parking
MUS/SH: Y   REST/FAC: Y; Cafe/bookstore   GR/T: Y   GR/PH: call 217-333-1860   DT: Y   TIME: !
PERM/COLL: P/COL; AM: ptgs; DEC/ART; OR; GR; PHOT; EU: ptgs; AS; AF; P/COL; ANT

Located on the campus of the University of Illinois, the Krannert is the second largest art museum in the state. Among the 8,000 works of art ranging in date from the 4th millennium BC to the present is the highly acclaimed Krannert collection of Old Master paintings. **NOT TO BE MISSED:** "Christ After the Flagellation," by Murillo; "Portrait of Cornelius Guldewagen, Mayor of Haarlem," by Frans Hals.

ON EXHIBIT/95:

11/4/94 - 1/8/95	VERNON FISHER: RETURN TO BASE

145

ILLINOIS

Krannert Art Museum - continued

11/19/94 - 1/22/95	ALFRED NOW: CONTEMPORARY AMERICAN CERAMICS
	CONTEMPORARY CERAMICS FROM THE PERMANENT COLLECTION
1/20 - 3/19/95	DORIT CYPIS
2/4 - 4/16/95	MEXICAN MASKS FROM LOCAL COLLECTIONS
3/31 - 5/28/95	RICHARD GREENBERG
4/28 - 6/25/95	PHOTOGRAPHS BY GARY WINOGRAND
6/9 - 8/6/95	CONTEMPORARY WORKS FROM THE PERMANENT COLLECTION

CHICAGO

The Art Institute of Chicago
111 So. Michigan Ave., **Chicago, IL 60603**
TEL: 312-443-3600
HRS: 10:30-4:30 M, & W-F; 10:30-8 Tu; 10-5 Sa; Noon-5 S & HOL! HOL: 12/25
SUGG/CONT: Y F/DAY: Tu! ADM: F ADULT: $6.50 CHILDREN: $3.25 STUDENTS: $3.25 SR CIT: $3.25
HDC/ACC: Y; Wheelchair accessible; wheelchairs available by reservation
PARKING: Y; Limited metered street parking; several paid parking lots nearby MUS/SH: Y
REST/FAC: Y; the Cafeteria & The Restaurant on the Park GR/T: Y GR/PH: call 312-443-3680
DT: Y TIME: 2:00 daily & 12:15 Tu H/B: Y
PERM/COLL: AM: all media; EU: all media; CH; JAP; IND; EU: MED; AF; OC; PHOT

Spend "Sunday in the park with George" while standing before Seurat's "Sunday Afternoon on the Island of La Grande Jatte," or any of the other magnificent examples of the school of French Impressionism, just one of the many superb collections housed in this world-class museum. **NOT TO BE MISSED:** "American Gothic" by Grant Wood; "Paris Street; Rainy Weather" by Gustave Caillebotte

ON EXHIBIT/95:

8/24/94 - 1/22/95	KNOTTED SPLENDOR - EUROPEAN AND NEAR EASTERN CARPETS FROM THE PERMANENT COLLECTION — Among the more than 30 carpets from 10 different countries that date from the 16th through the 19th centuries will be an 18th century Aubusson carpet, and an early 18th century "Dragon Carpet" from the region of the Caucasus.
10/29/94 - 1/2/95	KARL FRIEDRICH SCHINKEL, 1781-1841: THE DRAMA OF ARCHITECTURE — On view in the U.S. for the first time will be 100 drawings by architect Schinkel that focus on the theme of theatricality. WT*
11/19/94 - 1/15/95	DIETER APPELT (TENT! date) — In the first retrospective of the work of Appelt, a contemporary German photographer, 80 pieces, some of which are composed of 20 or more photographs, will be on exhibit.
12/3/94 - 3/19/95	JOEL MEYEROWITZ ON THE STREET: THE FIRST DECADE
12/3/94 - 3/19/95	ANDRE KERTESZ, 1894-1985: A CENTENNIAL CELEBRATION
12/10/94 - 3/12/95	BYSTANDER: A HISTORY OF STREET PHOTOGRAPHY

The Art Institute of Chicago - continued

2/18 - 5/28/95	GUSTAVE CAILLEBOTTE: THE URBAN IMPRESSIONIST — In commemoration of the 100th anniversary of his death, this first major international exhibition of 125 of French Impressionist Caillebotte's works will include many paintings that have never been seen in public before. CAT ATR WT*
2/18 - 5/8/95	LOUIS SULLIVAN AND THE PRAIRIE SCHOOL: SELECTIONS FROM THE COLLECTION AT THE ART INSTITUTE OF CHICAGO — In conjuction with the Caillebotte exhibition, this show will not only feature Sullivan's architectural drawings and other related matter, but will highlight student drawings from his studies in Paris in the 1870's, the same period when Caillebotte painted his famous "Paris Street; Rainy Day."
2/22 - 5/14/95	ENGRAVINGS ON CLOTH - PERTAINING TO FLORA, LITERATURE, AND MYTHOLOGY (working title)
3/11 - 5/21/95	THE AMERICAS EXHIBITION (working title) — Since 1888, The Art Institute has presented 75 surveys of U.S. based contemporary art. In this 76th exhibition works by 15 artists from Canada, Mexico, Latin America and the U.S. will continue the tradition of reflecting current cultural trends and conditions.
6/8 - 9/4/95	BRUCE GOFF — The complete architectural archive of Bruce Goff donated to the Art Institute in 1990 will survey the career of the Midwest visionary who was greatly influenced by Frank Lloyd Wright.
6/14 - 10/1/95	ROOTED IN CHICAGO - TEXTILE DESIGN TRADITIONS - ROBERT D. SAILORS, ANGELO TESTA, BEN ROSE, AND ELEANOR AND HENRY KLUCK
7/22 - 11/26/95	CLAUDE MONET: 1840-1926 — In the first comprehensive retrospective exhibition of Monet's work in an American museum in over 40 years, 140 paintings and a number of drawings from every period of his career will be gathered for viewing from collections worldwide. PLEASE NOTE: This is the only venue for this exhibition in America and advance tickets are required. CAT ATR WT*
ONGOING:	WITH EYES OPEN: A MULTIMEDIA EXPLORATION OF ART
	ART INSIDE OUT: EXPLORING ART AND CULTURE THROUGH TIME

CHICAGO

The David and Alfred Smart Museum of Art

Affiliate Institution: The University of Chicago
5550 S. Greenwood Ave., **Chicago, IL 60637**
TEL: 312-702-0200
HRS: 10-4 Tu-F; Noon-6 Sa, S   DAY CLOSED: M   HOL: LEG/HOL!
ADM: F   HDC/ACC: Y; Wheelchair accessible
PARKING: Y: Free parking on lot next to museum after 4:00 weekdays, and all day on weekends   MUS/SH: Y
GR/T: Y   GR/PH: 312-702-4540   DT: Y   TIME: 1:30 S during special exhibitions   S/G: Y
PERM/COLL: AN/AGK: Vases (Tarbell Coll); MED/SCULP; O/M: ptgs, sculp (Kress Coll); OM: gr (Epstein Coll); SCULP:20

Among the holdings of the Smart Museum of Art are Medieval sculpture from the French Romanesque church of Cluny III, outstanding Old Master prints by Durer, Rembrandt, and Delacroix from the Kress Collection, sculpture by such greats as Degas, Matisse, Moore and Rodin, and furniture by Frank Lloyd Wright from the world famous Robie House. **NOT TO BE MISSED:** Mark Rothko's "Untitled," 1962

ILLINOIS

The David and Alfred Smart Museum of Art - continued
ON EXHIBIT/95:

1/19 - 3/12/95	FROM THE OCEAN OF PAINTING: INDIA'S POPULAR PAINTING TRADITION, 1589 TO THE PRESENT — In the first major exhibition of its kind in the US, 100 folk tribal and popular paintings of India, ranging in date from 1589 to the present will be on loan from American and European private and public collections. CAT WT
3/14 - 6/4/95	POST-WAR CHICAGO WORKS ON PAPER AND SCULPTURE
4/13 - 6/11/95	MADNESS IN AMERICA
6/20 - 8/20/95	PAUL COFFEY
8/29 - 12/3/95	WOMEN IN THE EYES OF MAN: IMAGES OF WOMEN IN JAPANESE ART
10/17 - 12/10/95	THE STUDIO MUSEUM IN HARLEM: TWENTY-FIVE YEARS OF AFRICAN-AMERICAN ART WT

CHICAGO

Martin D'Arcy Gallery of Art
6525 N. Sheridan Rd., Chicago, IL **60626**
TEL: 312-508-2679
HRS: 12-4 M-F during the school year   DAY CLOSED: Sa, S   HOL: ACAD!, LEG/HOL! & SUMMER
ADM: F   HDC/ACC: Y   PARKING: Y; Free visitor parking on Loyola Campus
GR/T: Y   GR/PH: call 312-508-2679   DT: Y   TIME: often available upon request
PERM/COLL: MED & REN; ptgs, sculp, dec/art

Affiliated with Loyola University, the Martin D'Arcy Gallery is the only museum in the Chicago area that focuses on Medieval and Renaissance art. In celebration of its 25th anniversary in '95, the museum will present exhibitions that highlight special aspects of its permanent collection. **NOT TO BE MISSED:** 2 oil on marble nativity figures by Bassano; Tintaretto's "Deposition from the Cross;" Louisa Roldan's 17th century terra cotta sculpture "Madonna & Cherubs"

ON EXHIBIT/95:

ONGOING	PERMANENT COLLECTION OF MEDIEVAL, RENAISSANCE, AND BAROQUE ART

Mexican Fine Arts Center Museum
1852 W. 19th St., **Chicago, IL 60608**
TEL: 312-738-1503
HRS: 10-5 Tu-S   HOL: LEG/HOL!
ADM: F   HDC/ACC: Y   MUS/SH: Y
PERM/COLL: MEX: folk; PHOT; GR; CONT

Mexican art is the central focus of this museum, the first of its kind in the Midwest and the largest in the nation. Founded in 1982, the center seeks to promote the works of local Mexican artists and acts as a cultural focus for the entire Mexican community residing in Chicago.

ON EXHIBIT/95:   There are many special shows throughout the year. Please call for specific details on solo exhibitions and on "Dia de los Muertos," which are exhibitions held annually from the beginning of October through the end of November.

148

CHICAGO

Museum of Contemporary Art
237 E. Ontario St., **Chicago, IL 60611**
TEL: 312-280-5161
HRS: 10-5 Tu-Sa; Noon-5 S   DAY CLOSED: M   HOL: 1/1, THGV, 12/25
F/DAY: Tu   ADM: Y   ADULT: $5.00 CHILDREN: F (12 & under)   STUDENTS: $2.50   SR CIT: $2.50
HDC/ACC: Y; Wheelchair ramp at entrance, elevator available
PARKING: Y; On-street and pay lot parking available nearby MUS/SH: Y REST/FAC: Y; 11-4:30 Tu-Sa; Noon-5 S
GR/T: Y   GR/PH: 312-280-2660 education dept.   DT: Y   TIME: 12:15 Tu-F; 1 & 3 Sa, S
PERM/COLL: CONTINUALLY CHANGING EXHIBITIONS OF CONTEMPORARY ART

As indicated by its name the emphasis of this museum, founded in 1967, is on the presentation of the finest and most provocative cutting-edge art by both established and emerging talents. Plans are underway for a new ultra-modern 55 million dollar building and sculpture garden to be erected on a 2 acre site overlooking Lake Michigan. When finished in early 1996, the exhibition space will be 4 times its current size. **NOT TO BE MISSED:** "Dwellings" by Charles Simonds (an installation on a brick wall in the cafe/bookstore that resembles cliff dwellings); a 3 story sound sculpture on the stairwell by Max Neuhaus.

ON EXHIBIT/95:

11/12/94 - 1/8/95	OPTIONS 48: DAN PETERMAN — Concerned with environmental issues, Peterman, who works with discarded materials has even located his studio in a former recycling center in Chicago. For this exhibition he will create an installation that weighs the cultural value of the new MCA's building against the environmental cost of its construction.
1/14 - 3/12/95	SOME WENT MAD...SOME RAN AWAY — Exploring such themes as the theory of evolution, criminology and pornography as well as existential concerns of hope, death and fantasy will be works in a variety of media created by 15 international artists. WT
1/14 - 3/12/95	OPTIONS 49: HIROSHI SUGIMOTO — 24 black and white images of the sea photographed throughout the world by this New York based Japanese artist all contain the same format of water and sky with a central horizon line. Their variety lies in the difference that occurs in the often subtle influence of weather, time of day, reflected density of the air, texture of the water and quality of the light. WT
3/25 - 6/4/95	FRANZ KLINE — In the first exhibition to focus on Kline's black and white works that resulted from his transition from the figurative to abstraction, approximately 25 paintings will be on view accompanied by works on paper that include images on telephone book pages and the artist's Black Mountain sketch books. WT
6/17 - 8/20/95	JEFF WALL — Large (8'x 20') photographic tableaux that often resemble film stills comprised of backlit, color transparencies express the artist's complex theoretical ideas through the interaction and arrangement of settings and actors in and around the artist's native Vancouver. CAT WT

The Museum of Contemporary Photography of Columbia College
600 South Michigan Ave., **Chicago, IL 60605-1996**
TEL: 312-663-5554
HRS: 10-5 M-F, Noon-5 Sa, till 8pm T (Sep-May); 10-4 M-F, Noon-4 Sa (June-Jul)   DAY CLOSED: S
HOL: LEG/HOL! AUG   VOL/CONT: Y   ADM: F
HDC/ACC: Y   PARKING: Y; Public parking available nearly   GR/T: Y   GR/PH: call 312-663-5554
DT: Y   TIME: call for information   HB:
PERM/COLL: CONT/PHOT

ILLINOIS

The Museum of Contemporary Photography of Columbia College - continued

Contemporary photography by American artists forms the basis of the permanent collection of this college museum facility.

ON EXHIBIT/95:

11/19/94 - 1/14/95	IMAGES, OBJECTS AND IDEAS
1/28 - 3/25/95	ALFREDO JAAR: FRAME OF MIND
4/8 - 6/3/95	PHOTOGRAPHY AND BEYOND: NEW EXPRESSIONS FROM FRANCE — From established masters to emerging talents, works by French avant-garde photographers will be featured in this exhibition that is a joint venture between The Israel Museum and The Boca Raton Museum of Art. CAT WT
6/17 - 7/29/95	THE ART OF SEEING: PHOTOGRAPHS FROM THE PERMANENT COLLECTION

CHICAGO

Oriental Institute Museum
Affiliate Institution: University of Chicago
1155 E. 58th St., **Chicago, IL 60637**
TEL: 312-702-9520
HRS: 10-4 Tu-Sa; Noon-4 S; Till 8:30pm W   DAY CLOSED: M   HOL: 12/25, 1/1, 7/4, THGV
ADM: F   HDC/ACC: Y; Accessible by wheelchair from west side of building   PARKING: Y; On-street or coin operated street level parking on Woodlawn Ave. between 58th & 59th Sts. (1/2 block east of the institute)
MUS/SH: Y   GR/T: Y   GR/PH: call 312-702-9507   DT: Y   TIME: 2:30 S
PERM/COLL: AN: Mid/East

Hundreds of ancient objects are included in the impressive comprehensive collection of the Oriental Institute. Artifacts from the ancient Near East dating from earliest times to the birth of Christ provide the visitor with a detailed glimpse into the ritual ceremonies and daily lives of ancient civilized man. **NOT TO BE MISSED:** Ancient Assyrian 40 ton winged bull; 17' tall statue of King Tut; Colossal Ancient Persian winged bulls

ON EXHIBIT/95:

THROUGH 2/12/95	AYLA: ART AND INDUSTRY IN A MEDIEVAL ISLAMIC PORT — Ancient artifacts from Ayla (Aqaba, Jordon) that demonstrate the role that this Red Sea City played in international trade in the Midieval era. Included will be examples of glass, pottery, vessels, coins, weights and architectural elements.
THROUGH 2/28/95	VANISHED KINGDOMS OF THE NILE: THE REDISCOVERY OF ANCIENT NUBIA — Objects excavated by the Oriental Institute will be used to trace more than 3,500 years of ancient Nubian history and culture.

The Polish Museum of America
984 North Milwaukee Ave., **Chicago, IL 60622**
TEL: 312-384-3352
HRS: 11-6 daily   SUGG/CONT: Y   ADULT: $2.00
HDC/ACC: Y; Wheelchairs available by reservation 312-384-3352
PARKING: Y: Free parking with entrance from Augusta Blvd.   GR/T: Y   GR/PH: 312-384-3352
PERM/COLL: ETH: ptgs, sculp, drgs, gr

The Polish Museum of America - continued

The promotion of Polish heritage is the primary goal of this museum founded in 1935. One of the oldest and largest ethnic museums in the U.S., their holdings range from the fine arts to costumes, jewelry, and a broad ranging scholarly library featuring resource information on all areas of Polish life and culture. **NOT TO BE MISSED:** Polonia stained glass by Mieczyslaw Jurgielewicz

ON EXHIBIT/95:

12/2/94 - 3/6/95	TRADITIONS OF POLISH SZOPKA
3/3 - 4/23/95	MAPS OF POLAND FROM THE COLLECTION OF THE POLISH MUSEUM OF AMERICA
5/5 - 7/9/95	NEW PERSPECTIVES II — A group exhibition of Polish Artists living in the United States of America
7/21 - 9/17/95	ART OF ANNA & RAFAL OLBINSKI
9/29 - 11/26/95	LESZEK WYCZOLKOWSKI — Paintings and graphics
12/8/95 - 2/11/96	HERALDRY, BARONAGE, HERALDRY

CHICAGO

Terra Museum of American Art
664 N. Michigan Ave., **Chicago, IL 60611**
TEL: 312-664-3939
HRS: Noon-8 Tu; 10-5 W-Sa; Noon-5 S   DAY CLOSED: M   HOL: 1/1, 7/4, THGV, 12/25
SUGG/CONT: Y   F/DAY: Tu   ADM: F   ADULT: $3.00   CHILDREN: F (under 14)   SR CIT: $2.00
HDC/ACC: Y; Elevator access to all floors   MUS/SH: Y   GR/T: Y   GR/PH: 312-664-3939 education dept.
DT: Y   TIME: Noon & 2:00 daily
PERM/COLL: AM: 17-20

With over 800 plus examples of some of the finest American art ever created, the Terra, located in the heart of Chicago's "Magnificent Mile," reigns supreme as an important repository of a glorious artistic heritage. **NOT TO BE MISSED:** "Gallery at the Louvre" by Samuel Morse; Maurice Prendergast paintings and monotypes

ON EXHIBIT/95:

1/10 - 4/2/95	SHIP, SEA AND SKY: THE ART OF JAMES EDWARD BUTTERFIELD
4/15 - 6/25/95	LOUIS ARMSTRONG: A CULTURAL LEGACY
7/1 - 9/10/95	DICTATED BY LIFE: MARSDEN HARTLEY'S GERMAN PAINTINGS AND ROBERT INDIANA'S HARTLEY ELEGIES WT
9/16 - 11/26/95	DENNIS MILLER BUNKER OR SHAKER FURNITURE

ILLINOIS

EDWARDSVILLE

The University Museum
Affiliate Institution: So. Illinois Univ. at Edwardsville
Box 1150, **Edwardsville, IL 62026**
TEL: 618-692-2996
HRS: 10-4 M-F   DAY CLOSED: Sa, S   HOL: LEG/HOL!
ADM: F
HDC/ACC: Y; Elevator   PARKING: Y: Paid parking lot next to the museum building   S/G: Y
PERM/COLL: DRGS; FOLK; CER; NAT/AM

Works in many media from old masters to young contemporary artists are included in the permanent collection and available on a rotating basis for public viewing enjoyment. The museum is located in the western part of the state not far from St. Louis, Missouri. **NOT TO BE MISSED:** Louis Sullivan Architectural Ornament Collection located in the Lovejoy Library

ON EXHIBIT/95:

1/9 - 1/26/95	GONTERMAN DRAWING COMPETITION — This is the first annual drawing competition for artists working only in black and white.
2/4 - 3/1/95	ABRAHAM LINCOLN WALKER RETROSPECTIVE — Works by the late Mr. Walker, a self-taught artist from East St. Louis.
2/13 - 3/1/95	THE THIRD ANNUAL MASK COMPETITION
3/6 - 4/5/95	FIRST IMPRESSIONS — Prints in all media from the University Collection.

EVANSTON

Mary and Leigh Block Gallery
Affiliate Institution: Northwestern University
1967 South Campus Dr. on the arts circle, **Evanston, IL 60208-2410**
TEL: 708-491-4000
HRS: Noon-5 Tu-W; Noon-8pm T-S (Gallery closed summer; S/G open year round)   DAY CLOSED: M
HOL: LEG/HOL! SUMMER (Gallery only)
ADM: F   HDC/ACC: Y   PARKING: Y; Visitor parking on premises (pick up parking permits at front desk)
MUS/SH: Y   GR/T: Y   GR/PH: call 708-491-4852   S/G: Y
PERM/COLL: EU: gr, drgs 15-19; CONT: gr, phot; architectural drgs (Griffin Collection)

Best known for its collection of works on paper as well as its monumental outdoor sculptures, this fine university museum also features a continually rotating schedule of high quality exhibitions. **NOT TO BE MISSED:** The sculpture garden with works by Henry Moore, Jean Arp, Barbara Hepworth, and Jean Miro (to name but a few) is one of the major sculpture collections in the region.

ON EXHIBIT/95:

1/12 - 3/5/95	DABLOIDS AND ELEPHANTS: LEONID TISHKOV'S CREATURES
4/21 - 6/18/95	WENCESLAUS HOLLAR: 17TH CENTURY FROM THE MUSEUM BOYMANS-VAN BEUNINGEN, ROTTERDAM — Portraits, landscapes, still lifes and historical events that document his 17th century world will be seen in the more than 200 prints by Bohemian artist Hollar and his contemporaries. CAT WT
9/29 - 12/3/95	MULTIPLE VISIONS: THE COLLABORATIVE ART PRESS MOVEMENT IN AMERICA, 1960-1990

152

ILLINOIS

FREEPORT

The Freeport Art Museum and Cultural Center
121 No. Harlem, **Freeport, IL 61032**
TEL: 815-235-9755
HRS: Noon-5 Tu-S   DAY CLOSED: M   HOL: 1/1, EASTER, 7/4, THGV, 12/25
SUGG/CONT: Y   ADULT: $1.00   CHILDREN: F   STUDENTS: $0.50   SR CIT: $0.50
HDC/ACC: Y; Except for three small galleries   PARKING: Y; Lot behind museum
GR/T: Y   GR/PH: 815-235-9755
PERM/COLL: EU: 19-20; AM: 19-20; CONT: ptgs, sculp; P/COL; AN/R; NAT/AM; AN/EGT; AS; AF; OC

The Freeport Museum, located in northwestern Illinois, has six permanent galleries of paintings, sculpture, prints, and ancient artifacts as well as temporary exhibitions featuring the work of noted regional artists. It houses one of the largest Florentine mosaic collections in the world. **NOT TO BE MISSED:** Especially popular with children of all ages are the musuem's classical and Native American galleries.

ON EXHIBIT/95:

12/9/94 - 1/29/95	ILLUSTRATIONS FROM RECENT CHILDREN'S BOOKS
2/3 - 3/26/95	CHICAGO: SOLILOQUY IN FIVE VOICES (5 CHICAGO WOMEN)
	BETWEEN BLACK AND WHITE (CAROL HOUSE PHOTOGRAPHS)
5/5 - 6/25/95	CONTEMPORARY FIBER WORKS
6/30 - 8/20/95	BOTANICALS
	ARCHITECTURE
12/8/95 - 1/30/96	JOHN MARTINSON (SCREW SCULPTURE)
	RICK GEORGE AND OTHER COMPUTER ART OR HOLOGRAMS

GALESBURG

Galesburg Civic Art Center
114 E. Main St., **Galesburg, IL 61401**
TEL: 309-342-7415
HRS: 10:30-4:30 Tu-F; 10:30-3 Sa (Sep-Jul)   DAY CLOSED: S, M   HOL: LEG/HOL! MONTH OF AUG.
ADM: F   HDC/ACC: Y; Museum and museum shop
PARKING: Y; Free 2 hour parking in lot behind museum and on surrounding streets   MUS/SH: Y
GR/T: Y   GR/PH: call 309-342-7415
PERM/COLL: GR; WPA; REG; ldscp/ptgs (Not always on display)

NOT TO BE MISSED: The international exhibition competition called "Galex" presented annually during the month of March.

ON EXHIBIT/95:

1 - 2/95	PRINT COLLECTION - PARIS CONNECTION — Prints from the collection of Galesburg printmaker, Clare Smith, purchased during her studies and many visits to Paris.
3/95	GALEX 29 — Annual national juried multi-media exibition.
6 - 7/95	RAILROAD ART EXPRESS — Paintings, photography and train models by Illinois artists.

ILLINOIS

Galesburg Civic Art Center - continued

8/95	GALLERY CLOSED
9/95	TBA
10 - 11/95	ANNUAL FRIENDS AND MEMBERS SHOW — A show of works by artists living within a 50 mile radius of Galesburg.

MOUNT VERNON

Mitchell Museum

Richview Rd., **Mount Vernon, IL 62864**
TEL: 618-242-1236
HRS: 10-5 Tu-Sa; 1-5 S   DAY CLOSED: M   HOL: LEG/HOL!
VOL/CONT: Y   ADM: F
HDC/ACC: Y   PARKING: Y; On-site parking available   MUS/SH: Y   GR/T: Y   GR/PH: call 618-242-1236
S/G: Y
PERM/COLL: AM: ptgs, sculp (late 19- early 20)

Works from the "Ashcan School" with paintings by Davies, Glackens, Henri, Luks, and Maurice Prendergast are one of the highlights of the Mitchell Museum which also features significant holdings of late 19th and early 20th century American art.   The museum is located in south central Illinois.
NOT TO BE MISSED: Sculpture park

ON EXHIBIT/95:

2/11 - 4/2/95	GARO ANTREASIAN: PRINTS
4/8 - 7/16/95	DISCOVER GREATNESS: NEGRO LEAGUES BASEBALL — Black and white photographs, many taken by the players themselves, detail the triumphs and hardships of life in the Negro Baseball Leagues from 1900-1947. BOOK
7/22 - 9/3/95	LIGHT WEIGHT WORKS
9/23 - 10/29/95	SOUTHERN ILLINOIS ARTISTS OPEN COMPETITION
11/4/95 - 1/14/96	THE PAINTINGS OF ALBERT BLAKELOCK

PEORIA

Lakeview Museum of Arts and Sciences

West Lake Ave., **Peoria, IL 61614**
TEL: 309-686-7000
HRS: 10-4 Tu, T-Sa; Noon-4 S; Till 8pm W   DAY CLOSED: M   HOL: LEG/HOL!
F/DAY: W pm   ADM: Y   ADULT: $2.50   CHILDREN: $1.50   STUDENTS: $1.50   SR CIT: $1.50
HDC/ACC: Y   PARKING: Y; Free   MUS/SH: Y   GR/T: Y   GR/PH: call 309-686-7000   S/G: Y
PERM/COLL: DEC/ART; AM: 19-20; EU:19

A multi-faceted museum that combines the arts and sciences, the Lakeview offers approximately 10 touring exhibitions per year.   PLEASE NOTE: Prices of admission may change during special exhibitions!   **NOT TO BE MISSED:** Discovery Center, a particular favorite with children.

Lakeview Museum of Arts and Sciences - continued

ON EXHIBIT/95:

12/3/94 - 1/29/95	IN THE LAST HOUR: SANDY SKOGLUND PHOTOGRAPHS AND SCULPTURE — Skoglund's humorous and colorful photographs of environments which probe the values of society will be joined in this exhibition by her installation entitled "The Green House."
OPENING 3/28/95	30 YEARS OF COLLECTING AT LAKEVIEW MUSEUM — On the occasion of the 30th anniversary of the museum, objects from the permanent collection from each year of the 3 decades of its existence will be selected for viewing.
3/23 - 4/16/95	BRADLEY NATIONAL PRINT AND DRAWING EXHIBITION — Works from this 50th annual nationally recognized juried art show will be exhibited at Lakeview, Bradley University and The Peoria Art Guild.
5/6 - 7/30/95	THE LAMPS OF TIFFANY

PLEASE NOTE: Other exhibitions are planned for the rest of the year but were not confirmed at the time of publication. Please call for information.

QUINCY

Quincy Art Center

1515 Jersey St., **Quincy, IL 62301**
TEL: 217-223-5900
HRS: 1-4 Tu-S   DAY CLOSED: M   HOL: LEG/HOL!
SUGG/CONT: Y   ADULT: $1.00   CHILDREN: $.50   STUDENTS: $0.50   SR CIT: $0.50
HDC/ACC: Y   PARKING: Y; Free   MUS/SH: Y   GR/T: Y   GR/PH: call 217-223-5900
DT: Y   TIME: Often available upon request   H/B: Y; 1888 building known as the Lorenzo Bull Carriage House
PERM/COLL: PTGS; SCULP; GR

The Quincy Art Center is housed in an 1887 carriage house designed by architect Joseph Silsbee who was a mentor and great inspiration to Frank Lloyd Wright. Located in the middle of the state, the museum is not far from the Missouri border. **NOT TO BE MISSED:** The Quincy Art Center, located in an historic district that *Newsweek* magazine called one of the most architectually significant corners in the country, is composed of various buildings that run the gamut from Greek Revival to Prairie Style architecture.

ON EXHIBIT/95:

2/4 - 3/5/95	A CELEBRATION OF AFRICAN-AMERICAN LIFE
2/4 - 3/5/95	SCOTT SNYDER - WORKS BY THE WINNER OF THE 44TH ANNUAL QUAD-STATE EXHIBITION
3/26 - 4/29/95	45TH ANNUAL QUAD-STATE EXHIBITION
5/6 - 5/28/95	MIDWEST PHOTOGRAPHY EXHIBITION
5/6 - 5/28/95	COLORS OF JOY - FACETS OF MEMORY: A RETROSPECTIVE BY FRITZI MOHRENSTECHER MORRISON
6/6 - 6/25/95	QUINCY ARTISTS GUILD 40TH ANNUAL EXHIBITION
7/8 - 9/3/95	ABSTRACT V. REALISM

ILLINOIS

ROCK ISLAND

Augustana College Gallery of Art
7th Ave. & 38th St., Art & Art History Dept., **Rock Island, IL 61201-2296**
TEL: 309-794-7469
HRS: Noon-4 Tu-Sa (Sep-May)   DAY CLOSED: M, S   HOL: ACAD!
ADM: F
HDC/ACC: Y   PARKING: Y   GR/T: Y   GR/PH: by appt: 309-794-7469
PERM/COLL: SWEDISH AM: all media

Swedish American art is the primary focus of this college art gallery.

ON EXHIBIT/95:

1/29/94 - 1/21/95	CHANGING IMAGE OF WOMEN — An exploration through art history of the changing images and attitudes towards women as reflected in paintings ranging from the Baroque to the present day. BROCHURE
1/28 - 2/18/95	DECORATIVE ARTS OF WEST AFRICA — Displayed will be 65 items from 9 countries that demonstrate how the peoples of West Africa have applied their beautiful art forms to such utilitarian objects as furniture, clothing, cookware and musical instruments. WT
3/5 - 3/25/95	THE GOOD EARTH: FOLK ART AND ARTIFACTS FROM THE CHINESE COUNTRYSIDE — In this 40 item exhibition on daily life in Midwestern China, paintings, toys and clothing used to promote a spirit of progress within China in modern times will be on view. WT
4/2 - 4/30/95	NINETEENTH ANNUAL ROCK ISLAND FINE ARTS EXHIBITION — An annual juried competition in two-dimensional media open to artists living within a 150 mile radius of the Quad Cities.

CLOSED DURING THE SUMMER

9/1 - 9/30/95	A CENTURY OF ART AT AUGUSTANA COLLEGE — In celebration of 100 years of art instruction at Augustana College, this exhibition will present works acquired between 1985-1995. CAT

ROCKFORD

Rockford Art Museum
711 N. Main St., **Rockford, IL 61103**
TEL: 815-968-ARTS
HRS: 11-5 Tu-Sa; 1-5 S   DAY CLOSED: M   HOL: LEG/HOL!
SUGG/CONT: Y   ADULT: $2.00   STUDENTS: $1.00
HDC/ACC: Y   PARKING: Y; Free and ample   MUS/SH: Y   GR/T: Y   GR/PH: call 815-968-2787   S/G: Y
PERM/COLL: AM: ptgs, sculp, gr, dec/art 19-20; EU: ptgs, sculp, gr, dec/art 19-20; AM/IMPR; TAOS ART, GILBERT COLL: phot

With 10,000 square feet of exhibition space, this is the largest arts institution in the state outside of Chicago. It houses an 800 piece collection of 19th & 20th century art. **NOT TO BE MISSED:** "The Morning Sun" by Pauline Palmer, 1920; ink drawings and watercolors by Reginald Marsh (available for viewing only upon request)

Rockford Art Museum - continued

ON EXHIBIT/95:

1/27 - 5/14/95	RELATIVELY SPEAKING: MOTHERS AND DAUGHTERS IN ART — This unusual exhibition will allow the viewer a rare opportunity to compare and contrast the works between contemporary generations of mother and daughter artists. CAT WT
1/27 - 4/16/95	DAN GUSTIN: HEROIC SCALE WORKS — Large-scale multi-layered paintings by this Chicago artist will be on exhibit.
6/2 - 8/6/95	ILLINOIS ART FACULTY: A STATEWIDE SURVEY — Selected works by art faculty from academic institutions throughout the state of Illinois.
6/2 - 8/27/95	ILLINOIS ALUMNI: EMERGING ARTISTS
8/27 - 10/29/95	ALEXANDER LIBERMAN'S MONUMENTAL SCULPTURE — Maquettes, drawings and sculpture by internationally acclaimed artist, Liberman will be on exhibit.
9/9 - 11/5/95	ROCKFORD'S DIVERSE VOICES
11/19/95 - 1/21/96	A SHADOW BORN OF EARTH: NEW PHOTOGRAPHY IN MEXICO — Works by 16 young Mexican artists that explore the techniques of photomontage, photographic manipulation, large-scale Polaroid photography and photography constructed tableau will be featured in this exhibition. CAT WT
11/16/95 - 1/21/96	ROCKFORD AREA MEXICAN-AMERICAN ARTISTS — The rich heritage of their Mexican culture will be seen in selected works by Rockford area Mexican-American artists.

ROCKFORD

Rockford College Art Gallery / Clark Arts Center
5050 E. State, **Rockford, IL 61108**
TEL: 815-226-4034
HRS: 2-5 Daily Sep-May   HOL: ACAD! & SUMMER
VOL/CONT: Y   ADM: F
HDC/ACC: Y; Elevator at west side of Clark Art Center
PARKING: Y; Free; near Clark Arts Center
GR/T: Y   GR/PH: call 815-226-4034
PERM/COLL: PTGS, GR, PHOT, CER 20; ETH; REG

Located on a beautiful wooded site in a contemporary building, this museum presents a stimulating array of exhibitions ranging from American Indian baskets to contemporary mixed media and photography. **NOT TO BE MISSED:** African sculpture

ILLINOIS

SPRINGFIELD

Springfield Art Association
700 North Fourth St., **Springfield, IL 62702**
TEL: 217-523-2631
HRS: 9-4 M-F; 1-3 Sa   HOL: LEG/HOL! (including Lincoln's birthday)
ADM: F
HDC/ACC: Y   PARKING: Y; Free   MUS/SH: Y   GR/T: Y   GR/PH: call 217-523-2631
DT: Y   TIME: 1-3 W-S
PERM/COLL: AM: ptgs, gr, cer, dec/art; EU: ptgs; RUS: dec/art; CH; JAP

Fanciful is the proper word to describe the architecture of the 1833 Victorian structure that houses the Springfield Art Association, a fine arts facility that has been important to the cultural life of the city for more than a century.

ON EXHIBIT/95:

1/14 - 2/26/95	PASTEL PAINTINGS - SHERI RAMSEY & NANCY GILLESPIE
2/25 - 4/2/95	CONTEMPORARY GLASS BEADMAKERS
4/8 - 6/4/95	MICHAEL DUNBAR - MODELS & MONUMENTS

158

ANDERSON

Alford House - Anderson Fine Arts Center

226 W. Historic W. 8th St., **Anderson, IN 46016**
TEL: 317-649-1248
HRS: 10-5 Tu-Sa; 2-5 S (Sep-Jul) DAY CLOSED: M HOL: LEG/HOL! AUG
ADM: F
HDC/ACC: Y; Entryway and ramps PARKING: Y; Free MUS/SH: Y GR/T: Y GR/PH: call 317-649-1248
PERM/COLL: REG: all media; AM: all media 20

With an emphasis on education, this museum presents 2 children's exhibitions annually; one in
Dec.-Jan., and the other from May to the end of June.

ON EXHIBIT/95:

12/1/94 - 2/4/95	THE ILLUSTRATOR'S WORLD: CHILDREN'S AUTHOR ILLUSTRATORS
2/15 - 4/12/95	PATTERNS OF INFLUENCE: NINETEENTH-CENTURY AMERICAN ART
4/20 - 5/5/95	IN-FOCUS COMPETITIVE PHOTOGRAPHY EXHIBITION
5/18 - 7/30/95	THE ART OF INDIANA SPORTS II — Images of the automobile and horse racing
9/17 - 11/12/95	ROBERT MORRIS RETROSPECTIVE
11/28/95 - 1/30/96	AFROCENTRIC ART

BLOOMINGTON

Indiana University Art Museum

Affiliate Institution: Indiana University
Bloomington, IN 47405
TEL: 812-855-5445
HRS: 10-5 W & T; 10am-8pm F; Noon-5 Sa, S; (open only till 5 in the summer) DAY CLOSED: M, Tu
HOL: LEG/HOL!
VOL/CONT: Y ADM: F
HDC/ACC: Y; Use north entrance; wheelchairs available
PARKING: Y; Indiana Menorial Union pay parking lot one block west of the museum
GR/T: Y GR/PH: 812-855-IUAM DT: Y TIME: 2:00 Sa S/G: Y
PERM/COLL: AF; AN/EGT; AN/R; AN/GRK; AM: all media; EU: all media 14-20; OC; P/COL; JAP; CH; OR

Masterpieces in every category of its collection from ancient to modern, make this one of the finest
university museums to be found anywhere. Among its many treasures is the largest university
collection of African art in the United States. **NOT TO BE MISSED:** The stunning museum building
itself designed in 1982 by noted architect I. M. Pei.

ON EXHIBIT/95:

10/26/94 - 1/8/95	TURKISH TRADITIONAL ART TODAY
2/1 - 3/12/95	SYSTEMWIDE INDIANA UNIVERSITY FACULTY SHOW
9/8 - 12/17/95	A GOLDEN LEGACY: THE ART OF ANCIENT JEWELRY

INDIANA

COLUMBUS

Indianapolis Museum of Art - Columbus Gallery
390 The Commons, **Columbus, IN 47201-6764**
TEL: 812-376-2597
HRS: 10-5 Tu- T & Sa; 10-8 F; noon-4 S   DAY CLOSED: M   HOL: LEG/HOL!
VOL/CONT: Y   ADM: F
HDC/ACC: Y; Elevator to gallery; restrooms   PARKING: Y; Free   MUS/SH: Y
GR/T: Y   GR/PH: Call in advance to reserve   DT: Y   TIME: Noon W & 12:30 S
PERM/COLL: AM: ptgs; EU: ptgs; CONT; OR

In an unusual arrangement with its parent museum in Indianapolis, six exhibitions are presented annually in this satellite gallery, the oldest continuously operating satellite gallery in the country.

ON EXHIBIT/95:

12/10/94 - 2/5/95	J. M. W. TURNER PRINTS — From mountains to marine life, 71 prints and related drawings by Turner for his "Liber Studiorum" (Book of Prints) will be on view. Working from 1807 to 1819 on the theme of the universe of the landscape, this is the only series of original prints he ever produced.
2/18 - 4/30/95	WOVEN TREASURES: SELECTIONS FROM THE COLLECTION OF THE INDIANAPOLIS MUSEUM OF ART
5/13 - 7/16/95	CONTEMPORARY PAINTINGS BY INDIANA ARTISTS: SELECTIONS FROM THE INDIANAPOLIS MUSEUM OF ART
7/28 - 9/17/95	CHANGSHA CERAMICS FROM THE COLLECTION OF THE INDIANAPOLIS MUSEUM OF ART
9/30 - 11/19/95	PLACES AND POWER AND OBJECTS OF MYTH AND MYSTERY: PHOTOGRAPHS BY CORSON HIRSHFIELD
12/2/95 - 2/11/96	DIRECTOR'S CHOICE: PRINTS AND DRAWINGS FROM THE COLLECTION OF THE INDIANAPOLIS MUSEUM OF ART

ELKHART

Midwest Museum of American Art
429 S. Main St., **Elkhart, IN 46515**
TEL: 219-293-6660
HRS: 10-5 Tu-F; 1-4 Sa, S   DAY CLOSED: M   HOL: LEG/HOL!
F/DAY: S   ADM: Y   ADULT: $2.00   CHILDREN: F (under 4)   STUDENTS: $1.00   SR CIT: $1.00
HDC/ACC: Y   PARKING: Y; Free city lot just north of the museum   MUS/SH: Y
GR/T: Y   GR/PH: call 219-293-6660   DT: Y   TIME: Noon T (Noontime talks)
PERM/COLL: AM/IMPR; CONT; REG; SCULP; PHOT

Chronologically arranged, the permanent collection numbering more than 600 paintings, sculptures, photographs, and works on paper traces 150 years of American art history with outstanding examples ranging from American Primitives to contemporary works by Chicago Imagists. The museum is located in the heart of the mid-west Amish country. **NOT TO BE MISSED:** Original paintings by Grandma Moses, Norman Rockwell, and Grant Wood; The Vault Gallery (gallery in the vault of this former bank building.)

Midwest Museum of American Art - continued

ON EXHIBIT/95:

12/9/94 - 2/26/95	THE GREAT HUMAN RACE: ROLAND POSKA — On exhibit will be a suite of master lithographs created over the past 7 years.
3/31 - 4/30/95	GABOR PETERDI DRAWINGS AND SELECT DRAWINGS FROM THE PERMANENT COLLECTION
5.5 - 6/11/95	THE MARRIAGE PROJECT — Works by couples who are artists.
6 - 10/95	TBA
10/13 - 12/3/95	17TH ELKHART JURIED REGIONAL EXHIBITION — An annual 17-county all media juried competition.
12/8/95 - 2/25/96	GEORGE WINTER: THE MAN AND HIS ART — On view will be 80 works by this pioneer Indiana artist.

EVANSVILLE

Evansville Museum of Arts & Science
411 S.E Riverside Dr., **Evansville, IN 47713**
TEL: 812-425-2406
HRS: 10-5 Tu-Sa; Noon-5 S   DAY CLOSED: M   HOL: 1/1, 7/4, LAB/DAY, THGV, 12/25
ADM: F
HDC/ACC: Y; Wheelchairs available; ramps; elevators   PARKING: Y; Free and ample parking   GR/T: Y   S/G: Y
PERM/COLL: PTGS; SCULP; GR; DRGS; DEC/ART

Broad ranging in every aspect of its varied collections, the Evansville's holdings of fine art include prime examples from European medieval sculpture and American primitive paintings to ancient Peruvian and Chinese artifacts. **NOT TO BE MISSED:** "Madonna and Child" by Murillo

ON EXHIBIT/95:

12/11/94 - 1/29/95	COMING HOME — A World War I veteran comes home for the holidays in a vignette complete with period costumes, furnishings and 20th century art.
THROUGH 1/29/95	PASSAGES: MATTHEW DAUB, NOW AND THEN — A retrospective of the work of Daub, considered one of the country's most significant emerging Realist painters. WT
2/1 - 3/5/95	BLACK HISTORY MONTH EXHIBITION: "A DAY IN THE LIFE OF BLACK L.A. — Positive and hopeful views of the residents of Black L.A. as seen in the work of 10 African-American photographers will be featured in this exhibition.
2/5 - 3/19/95	MAGGIE FOSKETT PHOTOGRAPHS — Nature photographs using the 19th century "cliche verre" technique.
2/5 - 3/19/95	NO PLACE TO GO: PAINTINGS OF THE HOMELESS BY PAT BERGER — Acrylic paintings on the homeless of L.A.
3/26 - 5/7/95	GLICK GLASS COLLECTION — On loan from a private Indianapolis collection will be works of contemporary American glass including examples by Dale Chihuly and Harvey Littleton.
3/16 - 5/7/95	ROOKWOOD POTTERY — Featured will be a selection of objects produced from the 1880's to the 1930's by the internationally-acclaimed Cincinnati-based pottery works.

INDIANA

Evansville Museum of Arts & Science - continued

4/12 - 5/14/95	FINE ARTS CAMERA CLUB PHOTOGRAPHY COMPETITION — The 3rd biennial juried exhibition of work by regional photographers.
5/14 - 6/25/95	FRANCIA — Recent oil paintings and watercolors.
5/14 - 6/25/95	HOLIDAY COLLECTABLES — Rare and unusual holiday decorations from the late 19th to the early 20th centuries will be on display.
5/17 - 6/18/95	TRI-STATE ARTISTS COLLABORATIVE EXHIBITION — Works by artists from 7 counties in Southwestern Indiana will be seen in this 2nd juried annual exhibition.
7/2 - 9/10/95	BICYCLES BUILT FOR VIEW: THE HISTORY OF THE BICYCLE — Bicycles, prints, photographs, advertisements and artifacts are among the 600 objects in this exhibition that surveys the first 100 years of the bicycle in Europe and America. Social issues, including the liberating effects of the bicycle on women in the 1980's will also be addressed.
8/9 - 10/8/95	ARTIST-IN-RESIDENCE DIANE TESLER — Recent paintings
9/17 - 11/12/95	"HANDS-ON OR TACTILE GALLERY" COMMISSIONS — On exhibit will be tactile works by 8 leading regional artists specifically created in a wide variety of media to be accessible to the visually impaired visitor.
9/17 - 11/12/95	JEFFREY BURDEN — Recent drawings and photographs
10/18 - 12/3/95	OUTSIDE THE LINES: INTERNATIONAL CHILDREN'S ART
11/19 /95 - 1/14/96	35TH ANNUAL MID-STATES CRAFT EXHIBITION — A juried exhibition of contemporary craft art from 6 midwestern states
12/10/95 - 1 or 2/96	THEODORE CELMENT STEELE RETROSPECTIVE

FORT WAYNE

Fort Wayne Museum of Art
311 E. Main St., **Fort Wayne, IN 46802**
TEL: 219-422-6467
HRS: 10-5 Tu-Sa; Noon-5 S   DAY CLOSED: M   HOL: LEG/HOL!
F/DAY: 1st S   ADM: Y   ADULT: $3.00   CHILDREN: $2.00
HDC/ACC: Y; Fully accessible   PARKING: Y; Parking lot adjacent to building with entrance off Main St.
MUS/SH: Y   GR/T: Y   GR/PH: 219-422-6467 education dept.   S/G: Y
PERM/COLL: AM: ptgs, sculp, gr 19-20; EU: ptgs, sculp, gr 19-20; CONT

Since the dedication of the new state-of-the-art building in its downtown location in 1984, the Fort Wayne Museum has enhanced its reputation as a major vital community and nationwide asset for the fine arts. Its 1,300 piece collection includes important artistic masterworks from Durer to de Kooning. **NOT TO BE MISSED:** Etchings by Albrecht Durer on the theme of Adam and Eve.

ON EXHIBIT/95:

11/12/94 - 1/8/95	AN AMERICAN PICTURE GALLERY
1/14 - 3/12/95	SIGNS AND SYMBOLS: AFRICAN IMAGES IN AFRICAN-AMERICAN QUILTS FROM THE RURAL SOUTH
3/18 - 5/21/95	THE IDEAL HOME 1900-1920
5/6 - 6/18/95	SONGS OF MY PEOPLE — Photographs that document contemporary African-American life. CAT WT
6/3 - 7/30/95	CLEARLY ART: PILCHUCK'S GLASS LEGACY — 80 objects by 66 artists trained by renowned glass artist, Dale Chihuly in the famous Pacific Northwest Pilchuck Glass Factory will be on view. CAT WT

162

INDIANA

INDIANAPOLIS

Eiteljorg Museum of American Indians and Western Art

500 W. Washington, Indianapolis, IN 46204
TEL: 317-636-9378
HRS: 10-5 Tu-Sa; Noon-5 S; (Open M Jun-Aug)   DAY CLOSED: M   HOL: 1/1, THGV, 12/25
ADM: Y   ADULT: $3.00   CHILDREN: F (4 & under)   STUDENTS: $1.50   SR CIT: $2.50
HDC/ACC: Y; Fully accessible; elevator; restrooms; water fountains   PARKING: Y; On site   MUS/SH: Y
REST/FAC: Y; 11-2 M-Sa (Mem/Day - Lab/Day)   GR/T: Y   GR/PH: call 317-264-1724   DT: Y   TIME: 2:00 daily
H/B: Y; LANDMARK BUILDING; SW MOTIF DESIGN INTERIOR & EXTERIOR
PERM/COLL: NAT/AM & REG: ptgs, sculp, drgs, gr, dec/art

The Eiteljorg, one of only two museums east of the Mississippi to combine the fine arts of the American West with Native American artifacts, is housed in a Southwestern style building faced with 8,000 individually cut pieces of pink Minnesota stone. **NOT TO BE MISSED:** Works by members of the original Taos Artists Colony

ON EXHIBIT/95:

11/19/94 - 1/16/95	EITELJORG INVITATIONAL: NEW ART OF THE WEST 4 — On exhibit will be the works by 22 of the finest contemporary artists chosen from around the world who have worked with the subject matter of Western art.
3/18 - 6/20/95	SACRED ENCOUNTERS: FATHER DE SMET AND THE INDIANS OF THE ROCKY MOUNTAIN WEST — In an unusual juxtaposition of European and Native American arts, 200 objects on-loan from sources in the U.S., Canada and Western Europe will tell the story of the encounter between a band of missionaries led by Belgian-born Father De Smet and the Indian peoples of the Rocky Mountain West. Many of the pieces of art, maps and artifacts discovered by De Smet in his travels, have never been on public view before and will be enchanced in their dramatic exhibition settings by video, music, scent and photo murals.
7/15 - 9/17/95	EITELJORG MUSEUM AWARD — A lifetime achievement award and exhibition for an artist selected for significant contributions to the field of Western Art.
9/2 - 10/22/95	SANTA FE WATERCOLORS — On exhibit will be works by 7 select members of the Santa Fe Watercolor Society which is dedicated to artistic excellence in the medium.
11/18/95 - 1/7/96	SETTING THE STAGE: A CONTEMPORARY VIEW OF THE WEST — Three works of art (all of which have some 3-dimensional element) by each of 16 women artists who represent a variety of cultures will be presented in an exhibition that explores the contemporary side of popular and diverse cultures of the West.

Indianapolis Museum of Art

1200 W. 38th St., Indianapolis, IN 46208
TEL: 317-923-1331
HRS: 10-5 Tu, W, F, Sa; 10am-8:30pm T; Noon-5 S   DAY CLOSED: M   HOL: LEG/HOL!
ADM: F
HDC/ACC: Y; Wheelchairs available   PARKING: Y: Outdoor parking lots and parking garage of Krannert Pavillion
MUS/SH: Y   REST/FAC: Y; 11am-1:45pm Tu-S; (Brunch S- by reservation 926-2628); Cafe
GR/T: Y   GR/PH: 317-923-1331   DT: Y   TIME: 12 & 2:15 Tu-S; 7pm T
PERM/COLL: AM: ptgs; EU/OM; ptgs EU/REN:ptgs; CONT; OR; AF; DEC/ART; TEXTILES

Situated in a 152 acre park as part of a cultural complex, the Indianapolis Museum is home to many outstanding collections including a large group works on paper by Turner, and world class collections of Impressionist, Chinese, and African art. **NOT TO BE MISSED:** Lilly Pavilion; an 18th century style French chateau housing American & European decorative art

INDIANA

Indianapolis Museum of Art - continued

ON EXHIBIT/95:

11/20/94 - 1/15/95	GARO ANTREASIAN: WRITTEN IN STONE — 80 of the 350 prints that this master contemporary lithographer has presented to the permanent collection of the Indianapolis Museum of Art will be featured in this exhibition. **CAT**
12/4/94 - 2/5/95	DISNEY'S SNOW WHITE: AN ART IN THE MAKING — 125 handpainted "cels" used in the creation of Disney's animated version of Snow White will be on view for the first time from the largest private collection of its kind. **CAT**
2/18 - 4/16/95	NAM JUNE PAIK: ELECTRONIC SUPER HIGHWAY — In this exhibition 50 works that Korean-born artist, Paik, has created from television and related technologies will be on view. Included will be 15 new examples that explore the theme of the "Electronic Super Highway." **CAT** (both written and video) **WT**
4/29 - 7/30/95	DUTCH AND FLEMISH DRAWINGS FROM WINDSOR CASTLE — Sixty-five 15th through 18th century drawings from the Royal Collection at Windsor Castle will include works by such masters as Jacob Van Ruisdael, Sir Anthony Van Dyck, Adriaen Van Ostade and Sir Peter Paul Rubens. **CAT** **WT**
5/20 - 7/23/95	ITALIAN PAINTINGS FROM BURGHLEY HOUSE — 60 Old Master paintings will be on loan from the grandest Elizabethan house in England. **CAT** **WT**
9/3 - 12/31/95	ORIENTAL RUGS FROM THE MARKARIAN COLLECTION

LAFAYETTE

Greater Lafayette Museum of Art

101 S. Ninth St., **Lafayette, IN 47901**
TEL: 317-742-1128
HRS: 11-4 Tu-S   DAY CLOSED: M   HOL: LEG/HOL!
ADM: F
HDC/ACC: Y; Easy access sidewalk; no steps   PARKING: Y; Free parking lot at 10th St. entrance   MUS/SH: Y
GR/T: Y   GR/PH: call 317-742-1120
PERM/COLL: AM: ptgs, gr, drgs 19-20; EU: ptgs, drgs, gr 19-20; REG; CONT

Several important collections at the Greater Lafayette Museum of Art include art by regional Indiana artists, contemporary works by national artists of note, and a fine collection of art pottery. **NOT TO BE MISSED:** Arts and craft items by Hoosier artists at museum store; Baber Collection of contemporary art

ON EXHIBIT/95:

11/18/94 - 1/15/95	THE ART OF FANTASY: NANCY ECKOLM BURKERT — Beautifully detailed colored drawings by this children's book illustrator that seem to bring her fairy tale subjects to life.
1/15 - 4/7/95	HUMOR IN A JUGULAR VEIN — Featured in this exhibit will be the artists and artifacts of "MAD" Magazine from the collection of Mark Cohen.
1/20 - 4/2/95	FELLOWSHIP EXHIBIT — On display will be works by 1994 GLMA Fellows Charles Glick and Ana Lois-Bargallo created during their fellowship year.
4/7 - 6/4/95	MOTHER AND CHILD — A display of prints from the permanent collection and from an anonymous collection that depict the theme of mother and child from religion, mythology and genre.

Greater Lafayette Museum of Art - continued

5/19 - 7/31/95	ARTFORMS '95 — A biennial juried exhibition of contemporary art by artists from Indiana and Illinois
6/9 - 7/17/95	ART AMERICA: THE NARRATIVES — American visual artists interpret stories of America from literature, popular culture and history.
8/12 - 11/13/95	LURE OF THE PHYSICAL — On view will be works that address the symbolism inherent in the human figure in art.
9/2 - 10/30/95	THE HUMAN CONDITION — Contemporary artworks of the human figure that are artists' statements about art, love, life, and death in the last days of the 20th century.
9/2 - 9/25/95	ARTS INDIANA POSTCARD SERIES XIII AND COVER EXHIBIT — Miniature contemporary artworks by Indiana artists will be featured in this juried competition with 12 works selected for reproduction in previous years.

MUNCIE

Ball State University Museum of Art
2000 University Ave., **Muncie, IN 47306**
TEL: 317-285-5242
HRS: 9-4:30 Tu-F; 1:30-4:30 Sa, S   DAY CLOSED: HOL: EASTER, 1/1, 7/4, THGV, 12/25
ADM: F
HDC/ACC: Y; Barrier free   PARKING: Y; Metered street parking and metered paid garages nearby
GR/T: Y   GR/PH: call 317-285-5242   DT: Y   S/G: Y
PERM/COLL: IT/REN; EU: ptgs 17-19; AM: ptgs, gr, drgs 19-20; DEC/ART; AS; AF; OC; P/COL

5000 years of art history are represented in the 9,500 piece collection of the Ball State University Museum of Art. In addition to wonderful explanatory wall plaques, there is a fully cataloged Art Reference Terminal of the permanent collection.

ON EXHIBIT/95:

11/20/94 - 1/22/95	TWENTY-ONE ETCHINGS AND POEMS — 21 prints that combine abstract images and evocative text created by the collaborative efforts of artists and poets.
12/28/94 - 1/22/95	TOTAL VISION: PHOTOGRAPHY PORTFOLIOS FROM THE PERMANENT COLLECTION — Photographers' portfolios (collections of images that form a logical series or body of work) from 1904 to 1979 that document the changes photography has undergone during the 20th century will be featured.
5/2 - 3/19/95	MASTER SILVER BY PAUL STORR, HIS CONTEMPORARIES AND FOLLOWERS — Works by Paul Storr, a master English silversmith working in the English Regency style, will be accompanied by other examples of the craft by his contemporaries and followers. CAT WT
3/26 - 4/30/95	THE 60TH ANNUAL STUDENT ART SHOW — Annual juried exhibition

INDIANA

NOTRE DAME

The Snite Museum of Art
Affiliate Institution: University of Notre Dame
Notre Dame, IN 46556
TEL: 219-631-5466
HRS: 10-4 Tu-Sa; 1-4 S; 10-8 T (During school year)   DAY CLOSED: M   HOL: LEG/HOL!
VOL/CONT: Y   ADM: F   HDC/ACC: Y; Wheelchairs available; elevators to each level
PARKING: Y; Available southeast of the museum in the visitor lot   MUS/SH: Y
GR/T: Y   GR/PH: call 219-239-5466   S/G: Y
PERM/COLL: IT/REN; FR: ptgs 19; EU: phot 19; AM: ptgs, phot; P/COL: sculp; DU: ptgs 17-18

With 17,000 objects in its permanent collection spanning the history of art from antiquity to the present, this premier university museum is a must see for all serious art lovers. **NOT TO BE MISSED:** AF; PR/COL & NAT/AM Collections

ON EXHIBIT/95:

1/15 - 3/12/95	LEONARD BASKIN: PRINTS, DRAWINGS, AND SCULPTURE
1/29 - 3/26/95	DOUGLAS KINSEY: ONE-MAN SHOW
SPRING/SUMMER	NOTRE DAME ART DEPARTMENT PHOTOGRAPHY WORKSHOP
	RICHARD HUNT: ONE-MAN SHOW

RICHMOND

Richmond Art Museum
Affiliate Institution: The Art Association of Richmond
350 Hub Etchison Pkwy, **Richmond, IN 47374**
TEL: 317-966-0256
HRS: 9-4 M-F; 1-4 S SEP THRU DEC & FEB THRU JUL   DAY CLOSED: Sa   HOL: LEG/HOL!
ADM: F   HDC/ACC: Y; Northwest entrance wheelchair accessible
PARKING: Y: Free & handicapped accessible   MUS/SH: Y
PERM/COLL: AM: Impr/ptgs; REG

Aside from its outstanding collection of American Impressionist works, the Art Association of Richmond has the unique distinction of being one of only 2 art museums in the country to be housed in an operating high school. **NOT TO BE MISSED:** Self portrait by William Merritt Chase, considered to be his most famous work

ON EXHIBIT/95:

1/29 - 2/26/95	MARTHA SLAYMAKER AND JILL SLAYMAKER — Mother and daughter, current works
1/30 - 4/9/95	ART IS...NATIVE AMERICAN — A Hands-On exhibit for children grades K-3rd featuring Native American Arts and Culture
3/12 - 4/9/95	RICHMOND AND AREA AMATEUR ARTISTS EXHIBITION
5/20 - 8/1/95	MUSEUM CLOSED FOR RENOVATION AND CLIMATE CONTROL INSTALLATION
8/11 - 9/24/95	CHRISTO - IMAGES AND OBJECTS
10/1 - 10/29/95	LIZ QUISGARD (NEW YORK ARTIST) AND SANDRA ROWE (CALIFORNIA ARTIST)
11/12 - 12/17/95	97TH ANNUAL EXHIBITION BY RICHMOND AND AREA ARTISTS

INDIANA

SOUTH BEND

South Bend Regional Museum of Art
120 S. St. Joseph St., **South Bend, IN 46601**
TEL: 219-235-9102
HRS: 11-5 Tu-F; Noon-5 Sa, S   DAY CLOSED: M   HOL: LEG/HOL!
VOL/CONT: Y   ADM: F   HDC/ACC: Y; Fully Accessible   PARKING: Y; Free street parking. Also Century Center lot or other downtown parking garages.   MUS/SH: Y   GR/T: Y   GR/PH: 219-284-9102
PERM/COLL: AM: ptgs 19-20; EU: ptgs 19-20; CONT: reg

Since 1947 the South Bend Regional Museum of Art has been serving the artistic needs of its community by providing a wide variety of exhibitions of both a regional and national nature on a year-round schedule. **NOT TO BE MISSED:** Permanent site-specific sculptures are situated on the grounds of Century Center of which the museum is a part.

ON EXHIBIT/95:

12/10/94 - 1/29/95	JAPONISME
1/13 - 3/5/95	TODD JOHNSON
	RICHARD FAIRFIELD — ceramics and prints
3/11 - 4/23/95	DAVID ALLEN — Oil paintings
4/28 - 7/2/95	DEFINING SPACE: INSTALLATIONS BY BARBARA KENDRICK & KATHERINE ROSS
4/29 - 6/11/95	DANA GOODMAN — Ceramics
6/17 - 8/6/95	CARI BRENTAGANI — Color xerography, painting
7/30 - 8/27/95	NORTHERN INDIANA ARTISTS & ST. JOE VALLEY WATERCOLOR SOCIETY SHOW
8/12 - 9/24/95	MIKE HELBING — Wood & steel sculpture
9/9 - 11/5/95	MIDWESTERN SCULPTURE EXHIBITION
11/17/95 - 1/28/96	FOLK, NAIVES & VISIONARIES
11/18/95 - 1/7/96	LUCY SLIVINSKI — Mixed media sculpture

TERRA HAUTE

Sheldon Swope Art Museum
25 S. 7th St., **Terra Haute, IN 47807**
TEL: 812-238-1676
HRS: 10-5 Tu-F; Noon-5 Sa   DAY CLOSED: M   HOL: 1/1, MEM/DAY, 7/4, 12/25, 1/1
ADM: F
HDC/ACC: Y; Ground floor accessible ; elevator to 2nd floor   PARKING: Y; Pay lot on Ohio Blvd.   MUS/SH: Y
GR/T: Y   GR/PH: call 812-238-1676   H/B: Y
PERM/COLL: AM: ptgs, sculp, drgs 19-20; EU 14-20; DEC/ART

The Sheldon Swope, opened in 1942 as a museum devoted to contemporary American art, has expanded from the original core collection of such great regionalist artists as Thomas Hart Benton and Edward Hopper to now include works by living modern day masters. **NOT TO BE MISSED:** American Regionalist School of Art

INDIANA

Sheldon Swope Art Museum - continued
ON EXHIBIT/95:

1 - 2/95	PHILIP KOCH, EXPERIENCES AND REFLECTIONS
	DANETTE ANGERMEIER: PHOTOGRAPHY
3 - 4/95	51ST ANNUAL WABASH VALLEY EXHIBITION
4/23 - 6/4/95	PASSAGES: MATTHEW DAUB, THEN/NOW — A retrospective of the work of Daub, considered one of the country's most significant emerging realist painters. WT
6 - 7/95	CLAIRE PRUSSIAN RETROSPECTIVE
8 - 9/95	JACK FRANKFURTER - NEW YORK/PARIS
10 - 11/95	EDWARD EVANS, TROMPE L'OEIL PAINTINGS
12/95	HOLIDAY SHOW, PERMANENT COLLECTIONS

WEST LAFAYETTE

Purdue University Galleries
Affiliate Institution: Creative Arts Bldg., #1
West Lafayette, IN 47907
TEL: 317-494-3061
HRS: 10-5 & 7-9 M-F; 1-5 S   DAY CLOSED: Sa   HOL: ACAD!
ADM: F   HDC/ACC: Y   PARKING: Y; Visitor parking in designated areas (a $3.00 daily parking permit for campus garages may be purcased at the Visitors Information Services Center); some metered street parking as well; Free parking on campus after 5 and on weekends.
PERM/COLL: AM: ptgs, drgs, gr; EU: ptgs, gr, drgs; AM: cont/cer

In addition to a regular schedule of special exhibitions, this facility presents many student and faculty shows.

ON EXHIBIT/95:

11/14/94 - 1/22/95	SWISS POSTERS (Krannert Drawing Room) — Award winning posters from the annual competition sponsored by the Swiss Federal Department of the Interior and the Allgemeine Plakatgesellschaft.
11/29/94 - 1/29/95	CIMA KATZ: COMMON SIGNS/SECRET SYMBOLS (Union Gallery) — Prints and drawings by Katz, a University of Kansas art professor.
1/30 - 3/12/95	NEW GERMAN ART (Krannert Drawing Room)
2/1 - 2/10/95	JOSEF ALBERS' INTERACTION OF COLOR (Beelke Gallery) — A multi-media look at the color theories of the artist.
2/2 - 3/19/95	MAKING CHOICES: MIXED MEDIA COLLAGE (Union Gallery) — Distinctive approaches to the art form by Indianapolis artist Eleyes Reeves and Fort Dodge, Iowa artist Mada.
2/6 - 3/19/95	DIGITAL IMAGES (Stewart Center Gallery) — The use of the computer as an art making tool will be featured in this exhibition.
3/20 - 5/15/95	THE COLLECTOR'S EYE: SELECTIONS FROM THE McGILL COLLECTION (Krannert Drawing Room) — An exhibition of prints given to the permanent collection by McGill, a retiring professor of Purdue University.
3/27 - 4/30/95	JACK GATES: ART FURNITURE/FURNITURE ART
6/1 - 8/30/95	RECENT ACQUISITIONS (Krannert Drawing Room)
6/12 - 8/4/95	DOWN FROM THE ATTIC (Stewart Center Gallery) — Seldom seen selections from the permanent collection.

CEDAR FALLS

James & Meryl Hearst Center for the Arts
304 W. Seerly Blvd., **Cedar Falls, IA 50613**
TEL: 319-273-8641
HRS: 10-9 Tu, T; 10-5 W, F; 1-4 Sa, S   DAY CLOSED: M   HOL: 1/1, 7/4, 12/25, THGV
ADM: F   HDC/ACC: Y; Fully accessible with elevators & wheelchairs available
PARKING: Y; Free public parking available   GR/T: Y   GR/PH: call 319-273-8641
H/B: Y; Located in the former home of well-known farmer poet James Hearst
PERM/COLL: REG

Besides showcasing works by the region's best current artists, the Hearst Center's permanent holdings include examples of works by such well knowns as Grant Wood, Mauricio Lasansky, and Gary Kelly. **NOT TO BE MISSED:** "Man is a Shaper, a Maker," pastel by Gary Kelly; "Honorary Degree," lithograph by Grant Wood

ON EXHIBIT/95:

12/11/94 - 1/29/95	CERAMICS: MILLER, VENHUIZEN & WILSON
	PAINTINGS BY DAN HAGARTY
	RECENT GIFTS TO THE COLLECTION
2/5 - 3/26/95	WENDY EWALD: PORTRAITS & DREAMS
	EARTH, ROCK AND SKY; PRINTS BY KAPPLINGER, KENNON AND SLATTON
6/11 - 8/20/95	ART SHOW 7: ANNUAL IOWA COMPETITIVE ART EXHIBITION
8/15 - 10/8/95	IMAGES OF IOWA: PHOTOGRAPHS BY JOLENE ROSAUER
8/22 - 9/23/95	SEASONAL SONNETS: PAINTINGS BY DOUGLAS ECKHEART
9/3 - 11/19/95	KA LEI NO KANE: SET & COSTUME DESIGNS BY JOHN THOMAS
9/26 - 11/19/95	ORIGINAL ILLUSTRATIONS FOR "THE LEGEND OF SLEEPY HOLLOW"
12/3/95 - 4/28/95	PORTRAITS OF IOWA
	RECENT GIFTS TO THE COLLECTION

CEDAR RAPIDS

Cedar Rapids Museum of Art
410 Third Ave., S.E., **Cedar Rapids, IA 52401**
TEL: 319-366-7503
HRS: 10-4 Tu-W & F-Sa; 10am-7pm T; Noon-3 S   DAY CLOSED: M   HOL: LEG/HOL!
ADM: Y   ADULT: $2.50   CHILDREN: F (under 7)   STUDENTS: $1.50   SR CIT: $1.50
HDC/ACC: Y; Entrance ramp 3rd Ave.; elevator, restrooms, wheelchairs available
PARKING: Y: Lot behind museum building; some metered parking on street   MUS/SH: Y   REST/FAC: Y
GR/T: Y   GR/PH: call education office 319-366-7503   DT: Y   TIME: 5:30 3rd T; 11:30 4th F
PERM/COLL: REG: ptgs 20; PTGS, SCULP, GR, DEC/ART, PHOT 19-20

With a focus on regionalist art by two native sons, Marvin Cone and Grant Wood, and a "Hands-On Gallery" for children, the Cedar Rapids Museum, located in the heart of the city, offers something special for visitors of every age. A recently completed expansion program connects the new facility with its original 100 year old building by the use of a colorful and welcoming Winter Garden. **NOT TO BE MISSED:** Museum includes restored 1905 Beaux Art building, formerly the Carnegie Library (free to the public); collections of Grant Wood & Marvin Cone paintings, Malvina Hoffman sculptures, & Mauricio Lasansky prints and drawings

IOWA

Cedar Rapids Museum of Art - continued

DAVENPORT

Davenport Museum of Art
1737 W. Twelfth St., **Davenport, IA 52804**
TEL: 319-326-7804
HRS: 10-4:30 Tu-Sa; 1-4:30 S; Till 8pm T   DAY CLOSED: M   HOL: LEG/HOL!
VOL/CONT: Y   ADM: F
HDC/ACC: Y; Ramps, restrooms, elevator, wheelchairs available   PARKING: Y; Free   MUS/SH: Y
GR/T: Y   GR/PH: call 319-326-7804   S/G: Y
PERM/COLL: AM/REG; AM: 19-20; EU: 19-20; OM; MEXICAN COLONIAL; HAITIAN NAIVE

Works by Grant Wood and other American Regionalists are on permanent display at the Davenport Museum, the first public art museum established in the state of Iowa (1925). **NOT TO BE MISSED:** Grant Wood's "SELF PORTRAIT," & mock ups of his house

DES MOINES

Des Moines Art Center
4700 Grand Ave., **Des Moines, IA 50312**
TEL: 515-277-4405
HRS: 11-5 Tu, W, F, Sa; 11-9 T; Noon-5 S   DAY CLOSED: M   HOL: LEG/HOL!
F/DAY: 11-1 T   ADM: Y   ADULT: $2.00 CHILDREN: F (under 12)   STUDENTS: $1.00   SR CIT: $1.00
HDC/ACC: Y; North door of north addition (notify info. desk prior to visit)   PARKING: Y; Free parking
MUS/SH: Y   REST/FAC: Y; 11-2 lunch & 2-3 dessert/beverage Tu-Sa; dinner T (by reserv. only)
GR/T: Y   GR/PH: call 515-277-4405, ext. 32
PERM/COLL: AM: ptgs, sculp, gr 19-20; EU: ptgs, sculp, gr 19-20; AF

Its parklike setting is a perfect complement to the magnificent structure of this museum designed originally by Eliel Saarinen in 1948 with a south wing addition in 1968 by the noted I. M. Pei & Partners. Another spectacular wing recognized as a masterpiece of contemporary architecture was designed and built in 1985 by Richard Meier & Partners. **NOT TO BE MISSED:** "Maiastra" by Constantin Brancusi; Frank Stella's "Interlagos"

ON EXHIBIT/95:

1/21 - 4/9/95	SECRECY: AFRICAN ART THAT CONCEALS AND REVEALS — Relationships between art, knowledge and secrecy in Africa are examined in this exhibition. WT
2/19 - 5/8/95	MARY MISS: PHOTOGRAPHY— Photographic images of evocative environments created by using an interplay of forms and images.
4/22 - 7/16/95	WILL MENTOR: WORK 1984-1994 — Abstract paintings created over the last decade that incorporate the themes of landscape, product bar codes, Don Giovanni, the Civil War, and spirituality.
8/5 - 10/22/95	IOWA ARTISTS 1995
11/11/95 - 2/11/96	URBAN REVISIONS: CURRENT PROJECTS FOR THE PUBLIC REALM — The relationship between architecture and urban design is explored in this exhibit of innovative urban planning and design through the projects developed by 18 young and mid-career American architects and teams of architects. WT

Hoyt Sherman Place
1501 Woodland Ave., **Des Moines, IA 50309**
TEL: 515-243-0913
HRS: 8-4 M-Tu & T-F; closed on W from Oct.1-June 30   DAY CLOSED: Sa, S   HOL: LEG/HOL!
ADM: F
HDC/ACC: Y; Ramp, chairlift, elevator   PARKING: Y; Free   MUS/SH: Y   GR/T: Y   GR/PH: call 515-243-0913
H/B: Y; Complex of 1877 House, 1907 Art Museum, 1923 Theater
PERM/COLL: PTGS; SCULP; DEC/ART 19; EU; sculp; B.C. ARTIFACTS

A jewel from the Victorian Era, the Hoyt Sherman Art Galleries offer an outstanding permanent collection of 19th century American and European art complemented by antique decorative arts objects that fill its surroundings. Listed NRHP. **NOT TO BE MISSED:** Major works by 19th century American masters including Church, Innes, Moran, Frieseke and others

ON EXHIBIT/95:

On continuous exhibition are artworks from the permanent collection.

IOWA

DUBUQUE

Dubuque Museum of Art
8th & Central, **Dubuque, IA 52001**
TEL: 319-557-1851
HRS: 10-5 Tu-F; 1-5 Sa, S   DAY CLOSED: M   HOL: 1/1, EASTER, 7/4, THGV, 12/25
ADM: F
HDC/ACC: Y   PARKING: Y; Metered street parking   MUS/SH: Y   GR/T: Y   GR/PH: call 319-557-1851
DT: Y   TIME: daily upon request   H/B: Y; Housed in 1857 Egyptian Revivalist Jail
PERM/COLL: REG

The rare 1857 Egyptian Revivalist style building that formerly served as a jail is home to the Dubuque Museum. It has the added distinction of being the only National Landmark building in the city. Listed NRHP

ON EXHIBIT/95:

Exhibitions from the permanent collection are displayed on a rotating basis.

FORT DODGE

Blanden Memorial Art Museum
920 Third Ave., S., **Fort Dodge, IA 50501**
TEL: 515-573-2316
HRS: 10-5 Tu, W, F; 10am-8:30pm T; 1-5 Sa, S   DAY CLOSED: M
ADM: F
HDC/ACC: Y; Entrance on north side of building
PARKING: Y; Street parking and limited parking area behind the museum
MUS/SH: Y   GR/T: Y   GR/PH: 515-573-2316
PERM/COLL: AM: ptgs, sculp, gr 19-20; EU: ptgs, sculp, drgs, gr 15-20; OR: 16-20; P/COL

Established in 1930 as the first permanent art facility in the state, the Blanden's neo-classic design was based on the already existing design of the Butler Institute of American Art in Youngstown, Ohio. Listed NRHP. **NOT TO BE MISSED:** "Central Park" by Maurice Prendergast, 1901; "Self-Portrait in Cap & Scarf" by Rembrandt (etching, 1663)

ON EXHIBIT/95:

12/23/94 - 1/17/95	LEWIS HINE: AMERICANS AT WORK
12/23/94 - 2/19/95	WORKS BY KEITH ARCHIPOL
3/5 - 4/23/95	VISIONS 1995
6/11 - 7/30/95	PRINTS FROM THE HAROLD PETERSON COLLECTION
8/13 - 9/24/95	1995 THE FORT DODGE JURIED EXHIBITION
9/30 - 11/12/95	ROBERT TAPLIN
12/95 - 1/96	PRE-COLUMBIAN ART FROM THE STANLEY COLLECTION

172

GRINNELL

Grinnell College Print & Drawing Study Room
Affiliate Institution: Grinnell College
Burling Library, **Grinnell, IA 50112-0811**
TEL: 515-269-3371
HRS: 1-5 S-F   DAY CLOSED: Sa   HOL: 7/4, THGV, 12/25 THROUGH 1/1
ADM: F   HDC/ACC: Y   PARKING: Y; Available at 6th Ave. & High St.   GR/T: Y   GR/PH: call 515-269-3371
PERM/COLL: WORKS ON PAPER (available for study in the Print & Drawing Study Room)

1,400 works on paper ranging from illuminated manuscripts to 16th century European prints and drawings to 20th century American lithographs are all part of the study group of the Grinnell College Collection that started in 1908 with an original bequest of 28 etchings by J. M. W. Turner. **NOT TO BE MISSED:** Etching: "The Artist's Mother Seated at a Table" by Rembrandt

ON EXHIBIT/95:

2/10 - 4/2/95	THE PRINTS OF WAYNE THIEBAUD — 50 of Thiebaud's prints will be seen in this exhibition. BROCHURE WT
3/31 - 4/23/95	MIDWEST PHOTOGRAPHY INVITATIONAL
4/3 - 4/30/95	J. ANTHONY CROWLEY: RECENT PRINTS AND DRAWINGS
5/1 - 5/22/95	SPLENDOR OF RUINS, PRISONS OF FANTASY; ETCHINGS BY PIRANESI: THREE EXHIBITIONS IN RECOGNITION OF GRINNELL COLLEGE'S SESQUI-CENTENNIAL
6/1 - 9/23/95	ROBERT McKIBBIN: GRINNELL LANDSCAPES
9/29 - 10/27/95	RICHARD CERVENE: A RETROSPECTIVE 1951-1995
11/1 - 12/15/95	MERLE ZIRKLE: CERAMICS AND SCULPTURE

IOWA CITY

University of Iowa Museum of Art
North Riverside Dr., **Iowa City, IA 52242**
TEL: 319-335-1727
HRS: 10-5 Tu-Sa; Noon-5 S   DAY CLOSED: M   HOL: 1/1, THGV, 12/25
ADM: F   HDC/ACC: Y   PARKING: Y; Metered lots directly across Riverside Drive & north of the museum
GR/T: Y   GR/PH: call 319-335-1727 DT: S/G: Y
PERM/COLL: AM: ptgs, sculp 19-20; EU: ptgs, sculp 19-20; AF; WORKS ON PAPER

Eight thousand objects form the basis of the collection at this 25 year old university museum that features among its many strengths 19th & 20th century American and European art and the largest group of African art in any university museum collection. **NOT TO BE MISSED:** "Karneval" by Max Beckman: "Mural, 1943" by Jackson Pollock

ON EXHIBIT/95:

3/18 - 5/15/95	ODD NERDRUM: THE DRAWINGS — 25 charcoal drawings by this contemporary Norwegian-born artist will be featured in the first American exhibition of his work. CAT WT
3/18 - 4/30/95	MICHAEL MAZUR: THE INFERNO
3/18 - 5/13/95	A QUIET SONG: SUSAN BARRON AND JOHN CAGE

IOWA

MARSHALLTOWN

Central Iowa Art Association
Affiliate Institution: Fisher Community College
Marshalltown, IA 50158
TEL: 515-753-9013
HRS: 11-5 M-F; 1-5 Sa, S (Apr 15-Oct 15)   DAY CLOSED: Sa, S   HOL: LEG/HOL!
VOL/CONT: Y   ADM: F
HDC/ACC: Y; Barrier free   PARKING: Y; Free parking in front of building   MUS/SH: Y   S/G: Y
PERM/COLL: FR/IMPR: ptgs; PTGS; CER

You don't have to be a scholar to enjoy the ceramic study center of the Central Iowa Art Association, one of the highlights of this institution. The 20th century paintings and sculpture at the associated Fisher Art Gallery round out the collection. **NOT TO BE MISSED:** The Ceramic Study Collection.

MASON CITY

Charles H. MacNeider Museum
303 2nd St., S.E., **Mason City, IA 50401**
TEL: 515-421-3666
HRS: 10-9 Tu, T; 10-5 W, F, Sa; 1-5 S   DAY CLOSED: M   HOL: LEG/HOL!, PM 12/24, PM 12/31
ADM: F
HDC/ACC: Y   PARKING: Y; On street parking plus a large municipal lot nearby   MUS/SH: Y
GR/T: Y   GR/PH: call 515-421-3666
PERM/COLL: AM: ptgs, gr, drgs, cer; REG: ptgs, gr, drgs, cer;

A lovely English Tudor mansion built in 1920 is the repository of an ever growing collection that documents American art and life. Though only a short two block walk from the heart of Mason City, the MacNeider sits dramatically atop a limestone ravine surrounded by trees and other beauties of nature. **NOT TO BE MISSED:** For young and old alike, a wonderful collection of Bill Baird Marionettes

ON EXHIBIT/95:

12/29/94 - 2/12/95	BARBARA MORGAN: PHOTOGRAPHS — From the permanent collection photographs by Morgan, one of the pioneering experimental photographers of the early 20th century, this exhibition will include images of her famous series of dancer Martha Graham.
1/7 - 3/19/95	FROM THE EARTH — Pre-historic Southwest Indian pottery from the Bob & Wilma Anderson Collection will be on view.
3/23 - 5/14/95	LAND OF THE FRAGILE GIANTS: LANDSCAPES, ENVIRONMENTS, AND PEOPLES OF THE LOESS HILLS — Interpretations of the essence of Loess Hills (a unique geological site in Western Iowa) by artists selected specifically for this project. WT
4/6 - 5/21/95	THE PRINTS OF LYMAN BYXBE — Prints created by Byxbe (1886-1980) during his many summer soujourns to Estes Park, Colorado. CAT
5/21/ - 7/9/95	30th ANNUAL AREA SHOW — An all media juried exhibition of works by artists living within a 100 mile radius of Mason City.
5/25 - 7/9/95	RECENT ADDITIONS: PERMANENT COLLECTION

174

MUSCATINE

Muscatine Art Center
1314 Mulberry Ave., **Muscatine, IA 52761**
TEL: 319-263-8282
HRS: 10-5 Tu, W, F; 10-5 & 7-9 T; 1-5 Sa, S   DAY CLOSED: M   HOL: LEG/HOL!
ADM: F   HDC/ACC: Y; Fully accessible with wheelchairs available   PARKING: Y; Street and free lot nearby
GR/T: Y   GR/PH: call 319-263-8282   DT: Y   TIME: daily when possible!
H/B: Y; 1908 Edwardian Musser Mansion
PERM/COLL: AM: ptgs, sculp, gr, drgs, dec/art 19-20; NAT/AM

The original Musser Family Mansion built in Edwardian Style in 1908 has been joined since 1976 by the contemporary 3 level Stanley Gallery to form the Muscatine Art Center. In addition to its fine collection of regional and national American art, the center has recently received a bequest of 27 works by 19 important European artists including Boudin, Braque, Pissaro, Degas, Matisse and others. **NOT TO BE MISSED:** "Great River Collection"

ON EXHIBIT/95:

12/4/94 - 2/19/95	TEXTILES FROM THE ART CENTER'S PERMANENT COLLECTION AND QUILTS BY MUSCATINE MELON PATCHERS QUILT GUILD
5/28 - 7/16/95	FACES OF DESTINY — Modern plates of photographs taken by Frank Rindhart and Adolph Muhr of Native Americans from 36 tribes attending the Indian Congress of 1898 will be featured in this exhibition. WT
5/28 - 7/26/95	McKENNEY & HALL INDIAN PRINTS
7/23 - 9/17/95	MAPS FROM THE ART CENTER'S PERMANENT COLLECTION
9/24 - 11/12/95	THERE ON THE TABLE: THE AMERICAN STILL LIFE
11/19 - 12/31/95	THE ART OF ERIC CARLE

SIOUX CITY

Sioux City Art Center
513 Nebraska St., **Sioux City, IA 51101**
TEL: 712-279-6272
HRS: 10-5 Tu-Sa; 1-5 S   HOL: LEG/HOL!
ADM: F   HDC/ACC: Y; Chair lift at front door, elevator
PARKING: Y; Metered street parking & city lots within walking distance of the museum
GR/T: Y   GR/PH: call 712-279-6272   DT: Y   TIME: 2:00 1st Sa of the month
PERM/COLL: NAT/AM; 19-20; CONT/REG; PTGS, WORKS ON PAPER; PHOT

Begun as a WPA project in 1938, the Center features a permanent collection of regional art and changing exhibitions.

ON EXHIBIT/95:

12/11/94 - 2/5/95	LAND OF THE FRAGILE GIANTS: LANDSCAPES, ENVIRONMENTS, AND PEOPLES OF THE LOESS HILLS — Interpretations of the essence of Loess Hills (a unique geological site in Western Iowa) by artists selected specifically for this project. WT
12/27/94 - 2/26/95	SELECTIONS FROM THE PERMANENT COLLECTION: UNIVERSITY OF SOUTH DAKOTA PHOTOGRAPHY PORTFOLIO

IOWA

Sioux City Art Center - continued

1/3 - 2/19/95	RETHINKING THE PRINT: RECENT MONOTYPES BY THOMAS H. MAJESKI
2/19 - 4/9/95	RELATIVE MOMENTS: PHOTOGRAPHS BY DEANNA DIKEMAN
2/19 - 4/9/95	THOSE 1, 1, 2, 3, 5, 8, YEARS: THE ART OF LARRY SCHULTE
3/5 - 4/16/95	SELECTIONS FROM THE PERMANENT COLLECTION: THE ARTIST AND THE MODEL
4/23 - 6/11/95	53RD ANNUAL JURIED EXHIBITION
5/95	OLDER AMERICANS EXHIBITION — Off-site location to be determined

WATERLOO

Waterloo Museum of Art
225 Commercial St., **Waterloo, IA 50701**
TEL: 319-291-4491
HRS: 10-5 M-Sa; 2-5 S   HOL: LEG/HOL!
ADM: F
HDC/ACC: Y   PARKING: Y; Ample and free   MUS/SH: Y   GR/T: Y   GR/PH: call 319-291-4491
PERM/COLL: REG: ptgs, gr, sculp; HATIAN: ptgs, sculp; AM: dec/art

This museum notes as its strengths its collection of midwest art that includes works by Grant Wood, Haitian and other examples of Caribbean art, and American decorative art with particular emphasis on pottery. **NOT TO BE MISSED:** Small collection of Grant Wood paintings, lithographs, and drawings

ON EXHIBIT/95:

9/94 - 7/95	SELECTIONS FROM THE PERMANENT COLLECTION
10/94 - 5/95	THE BRITISH ISLES: ARTS AND ENCHANTMENT
1/8 - 3/5/95	PERSPECTIVES & PONDERINGS: WORK BY JEAN BERRY, JEAN MARIE SALEM, BRENDA JONES
3/17 - 5/14/95	CITY OF BIRDS: RECENT WORK BY MATTHEW SUGARMAN
5/23 - 7/9/95	WITHOUT CONTEXT: SCULPTURE BY REX SILVERNAIL
7/15 - 8/30/95	CURRENT WORKS IN CLAY: JOANN SCHNABEL
7 - 8/95	LAND OF THE FRAGILE GIANTS: LANDSCAPES, ENVIRONMENTS, AND PEOPLES OF THE LOESS HILLS — Interpretations of the essence of Loess Hills (a unique geological site in Western Iowa) by artists selected specifically for this project.

WT

KANSAS

GARNETT

The Walker Art Collection of the Garnett Public Library
125 W. 4th Ave., **Garnett, KS 66032**
TEL: 913-448-5496
HRS: 10-8 M, Tu, T; 10-5:30 W, F; 10-4:30 Sa   DAY CLOSED: S   HOL: 1/1, MEM/DAY, 7/4, THGV, 12/25
VOL/CONT: Y   ADM: F
HDC/ACC: Y   PARKING: Y; Free and abundant street parking   GR/T: Y   GR/PH: call 913-448-3388
DT: Y   TIME: upon request if abailable
PERM/COLL: EU & AM: ptgs: 19-20; REG

Considered one of the most outstanding collections in the state, the Walker was started with a 110 piece bequest in 1951 by its namesake, Maynard Walker, a prominent art dealer in New York during the 1930's & 40's. Brilliantly conserved works by such early 20th century American artists as John Stuart Curry, Robert Henri, and Luigi Lucioni are displayed alongside European and Midwest Regional paintings and sculpture. All works in the collection have undergone conservation in the past 5 years and are in pristine condition. **NOT TO BE MISSED:** "Lake in the Forest (Sunrise)" by Corot; "Girl in Red Tights" by Walt Kuhn; "Tobacco Plant" by John Stuart Curry

LAWRENCE

Spencer Museum of Art
Affiliate Institution: University of Kansas
1301 Mississippi St., **Lawrence, KS 66045**
TEL: 913-864-4710
HRS: 8:30-5 Tu-Sa; Noon-5 S; Till 9pm T   DAY CLOSED: M
HOL: 1/1, 7/4, THGV & FOLLOWING DAY, 12/24, 12/25
ADM: F
HDC/ACC: Y   PARKING: Y; Metered spaces in lot north of museum; free 3 hour visitor permits at traffic control booth on Mississippi, just south of museum. Park anywhere when school not in session.   MUS/SH: Y
GR/T: Y   GR/PH: Given Tu-F call 913-864-4710 ex 13
PERM/COLL: EU: ptgs, sculp, gr 17-18; AM: phot; JAP: gr; CH: ptgs; MED: sculp

The broad and diverse collection of the Spencer Museum of Art, located in the eastern part of the state not far from Kansas City, features particular strengths in the areas of European painting and sculpture of the 17th & 18th centuries, American photographs, Japanese and Chinese works of art, and Medieval sculpture. **NOT TO BE MISSED:** "La Pia de Tolommei" by Rosetti; "The Ballad of the Jealous Lover of Lone Green Valley" by Thomas Hart Benton

ON EXHIBIT/95:

11/12/94 - 1/8/95   FROM KASHMIR TO KUTCH: TEXTILES OF NORTHWEST INDIA — On exhibit from the permanent collection will be a splendid group of recently cleaned and conserved Indian textiles which have never been exhibited as an entity before.

1/14 - 3/12/95   THE LIBERATED IMAGE: CONTEMPORARY PHOTOGRAPHY SINCE 1970 — Featured will be innovative photographic images by a diverse group of contemporary artists that includes John Baldessari, Chuck Close, Lucas Samaras, Cindy Sherman, William Wegman and others.

1/21 - 3/19/95   AFRICAN-AMERICAN WORKS FROM THE SMA COLLECTION

KANSAS

Spencer Museum of Art - continued

1/21 - 3/12/95	VIRTUE, LABOR AND PROFIT: 18TH CENTURY BRITISH ART
3/25 - 5/14/95	ADRIAEN van OSTADE: ETCHINGS OF PEASANT LIFE IN HOLLAND IN THE GOLDEN AGE
4/8 - 6/18/95	THE JADE STUDIO: MASTEPIECES OF MING AND QING PAINTING FROM THE WONG NAN-PING COLLECTION
6/4 - 7/20/95	BEYOND THE DRAWING ROOM: THE ART OF MARY HUNTOON, 1896-1970
8/20 - 10/8/95	UNPAINTED TO THE LAST: MOBY-DICK AND TWENTIETH-CENTURY AMERICAN ART, 1940-1990 CAT WT
8/27 - 10/14/95	HAIGA: TATBE SOCHO AND THE HAIKU PAINTING TRADITION

LINDSBORG

Birger Sandzen Memorial Gallery
401 N. 1st St., **Lindsborg, KS 67456-0348**
TEL: 913-227-2220
HRS: 1-5 W-S   DAY CLOSED: M, Tu   HOL: LEG/HOL!
ADM: Y   ADULT: $2.00   CHILDREN: $.50 grades 1-12   SR CIT: $2.00
HDC/ACC: Y   PARKING: Y; Free parking in front of gallery and in lot behind church across from the gallery
MUS/SH: Y
PERM/COLL: REG: ptgs, gr, cer, sculp; JAP: sculp

Opened since 1957 on the campus of a small college in central Kansas about 20 miles south of Salina, the gallery has been an important cultural resource for the state. Named after the artist who taught at the College for 52 years, the gallery is the repository of many of his paintings. **NOT TO BE MISSED:** "The Little Triton" fountain by sculptor Carl Milles of Sweden located in the courtyard.

LOGAN

Dane G. Hansen Memorial Museum
110 W. Main, **Logan, KS 67646**
TEL: 913-689-4846
HRS: 9-Noon & 1-4 M-F; 9-Noon & 1-5 Sa; 1-5 S & Holidays   HOL: 1/1, THGV, 12/25
ADM: F
HDC/ACC: Y   PARKING: Y; Free and abundant on all four sides of the museum
PERM/COLL: OR; REG

Part of a cultural complex completed in 1973 in the heart of downtown Logan, the Hansen Memorial Museum is a member of the Smithsonian Associates and thus presents 5-7 traveling exhibitions annually from the Smithsonian Institution in addition to shows by regional artists. **NOT TO BE MISSED:** Artist of the month corner

ON EXHIBIT/95:

12/11/94 - 1/15/95	ENGRAVINGS BY ALBERT DECARIS	WT
	LOCAL POSTAGE STAMPS, BETTY LAPPIN	

Dane G. Hansen Memorial Museum - continued

1/22 - 3/12/95	MY AMISH FRIENDS: AN INSIDE LOOK
4/15 - 6/25/95	STRENGTHS AND DIVERSITY: JAPANESE-AMERICAN WOMEN, 1885-1990 — 71 historical photographs accompanied by artifacts, literary and artistic works and oral histories that chronicle the lives of 4 generations of Japanese women as they adjusted to their new lives in America. WT
6/28 - 8/25/95	JOHN STUART CURRY'S AMERICA — 54 drawings, prints and watercolors, many of which are being seen for the first time in this touring exhibition, will highlight the work of one of America's most revered Midwest Regionalist artists. WT
8/27 - 9/27/95	THE MENNINGER COLLECTION OF TRIBAL ARTS EXHIBIT
10/1 - 10/22/95	TELLING TALES: CHILDREN'S BOOK ILLUSTRATIONS — 40 charming illustrations from some of the best-loved children's story books will be highlighted in this exhibition. BROCHURE WT
11/5 - 12/31/95	IMPERIAL RUSSIAN PORCELAIN FROM THE RAYMOND F. PIPER COLLECTION — 86 opulent and extravagant porcelains from the Imperial Porcelain Factory in St. Petersburg, Russia, created between the reigns of Elizabeth I and Nicholas II, will be featured in this exhibition. WT

OVERLAND PARK

Johnson County Community College Gallery of Art
Affiliate Institution: Johnson County Community College
12345 College Blvd., **Overland Park, KS 66210**
HRS: 10-5 M, T, F; 10-7 Tu, W; 1-5 Sa, S; (closed Sa & S during the summer)   HOL: LEG/HOL!
ADM: F
HDC/ACC: Y; Fully accessible   PARKING: Y; Free   GR/T: Y   GR/PH: 913-469-8500
PERM/COLL: AM/ CONT: ptgs, cer, phot, works on paper

The geometric spareness of the building set among the gently rolling hills of the campus is a perfect foil for the rapidly growing permanent collection of contemporary American art and site-specific sculpture.

SALINA

Salina Art Center
242 S. Santa Fe, **Salina, KS 67401**
TEL: 913-827-1431
HRS: Noon-5 Tu-S; till 7pm T   DAY CLOSED: M   HOL: LEG/HOL!
ADM: F
HDC/ACC: Y; all entrances, galleries, restrooms, & Discovery Area   PARKING: Y; free and ample
GR/T: Y   GR/PH: 913-827-1431

Although not a collecting institution, the Salina Art Center serves its community by being the only center for the fine arts is its area. Rotating high quality traveling exhibitions and a permanent Discovery Area for children are its main features.

KANSAS

Salina Art Center - continued

ON EXHIBIT/95:

11/20/94 - 1/22/95	16TH ANNUAL JURIED EXHIBITION
2/5 - 3/12/95	CONTEMPORARY SCULPTURE: TWO ARTISTS
3/26 - 4/9/95	GERRY NEUSTROM: YOUNG ARTIST TALENT
4/23 - 6/25/95	SALINA FITES/SIGHTS — Outreach exhibitions, programs and installations
7/9 - 9/3/95	INTERACTIVE
9 - 10/95	BETYE SAAR: PERSONAL ICONS — Using an unusual variety of found and discarded objects to form her assemblages and installations, Saar's creations which reflect the magic, folklore and history of her personal African-American heritage are also influenced by her childhood experience of watching Simon Rodia build his now renowned Watts Towers. CAT WT
10/29 - 11/4/95	SALINA ART CENTER SHOW AND SALE
11/19/95 - 1/14/96	17TH ANNUAL JURIED EXHIBITION

TOPEKA

Gallery of Fine Arts-Topeka & Shawnee County
1515 W. 10th, **Topeka, KS 66604**
TEL: 913-233-2040
HRS: 9-9 M-F; 9-6 Sa; 2-6 S (LAB/DAY - MEM/DAY)   DAY CLOSED: HOL: LEG/HOL!
ADM: F
HDC/ACC: Y; Ground entry via automatic doors
PARKING: Y; Free parking in lots at the south end and to the west of the building.
PERM/COLL: REG: ptgs, gr 20; W/AF (Advance notice required to see any permanent collection pieces in storage)

Although the fine art permanent collection is usually not on view, this active institution presents rotating exhibitions that are mainly regional in nature. **NOT TO BE MISSED:** Glass paperweights; Akan gold weights from Ghana and the Ivory Coast, West Africa

ON EXHIBIT/95:

1/20 - 2/19/95	JOHN CODY: THE MOTH WATERCOLORS
2/22 - 3/20/95	THE CLAY OF PETER WILKIN
4/1 - 4/30/95	TOPEKA COMPETITION 19 (5 STATE/JURIED 3 D)
5/20 - 6/18/95	TOPEKA ART GUILD JURIED SUMMER SHOW
4/3 - 8/20/95	PERMANENT COLLECTIONS
9/1 - 9/29/95	LETITIA WETTERAUER DRAWING/ KEITH EKSTAM CLAY
10/14 - 11/11/95	WAYNE WILDCAT - PAINTINGS
11 - 12/95	CHRISTMAS EXHIBITION TBA

KANSAS

TOPEKA

Mulvane Art Museum
Affiliate Institution: Washburn University
17th & Jewell, **Topeka, KS 66621**
TEL: 913-231-1010
HRS: 10-4 W-F, 10-9 Tu, 1-4 Sa, S; (May-Aug) 10-4 Tu-F, 1-4 Sa, S   DAY CLOSED: M
HOL: 1/1, EASTER, LAB/DAY, THGV, 12/25
ADM: F   HDC/ACC: Y; Wide doorways, ramps, elevators
PARKING: Y; Free parking including handicapped accessible spaces   MUS/SH: Y   GR/T: Y   GR/PH: 913-231-1010
H/B: Y; Oldest Museum in State of Kansas (1925)
PERM/COLL: EU: dec/art 19-20; AM: dec/art 19-20; JAP: dec/art 19-20; REG: cont ptgs; GR; SCULP; CER

Built in 1925, the Mulvane is the oldest art museum in the state of Kansas.

WICHITA

Edwin A. Ulrich Museum of Art
Affiliate Institution: The Wichita State University
Box 46, The Wichita State University, **Wichita, KS 67208**
TEL: 316-689-3664
HRS: 10-5 Tu-F; 1-5 Sa, S   DAY CLOSED: M   HOL: 1/1, EASTER, 7/4, THGV, 12/25
ADM: F   HDC/ACC: Y; Outside ramp to entrance & elevator to gallery
PARKING: Y; With temporary parking permits from Police Dept. (open 24 hrs). Visitor lots also available.
GR/T: Y   GR/PH: sculpture garden 316-689-3664
H/B: Y; Museum facade is mural-size mosaic by Spanish artist Joan Miro   S/G: Y
PERM/COLL: AM: 19-20; EU: 19-20; PRIM; AM: gr; EU: gr; PHOT

Established in 1972, the superb sculpture garden with works by such greats as Rodin, Moore, Botero, Nevelson, Chadwick, and many others too numerous to mention, is a delight to visit at any time of year in its ever changing outdoor setting. Advance arrangements for tours of the Outdoor Sculpture Garden (weather permitting) may be made by calling 316-689-3664. Visitors may also use free maps provided for self-guided tours. PLEASE NOTE: Due to impending renovation of the museum building, adjustments in the scheduling of special exhibitions are possible. Please call ahead for information.
NOT TO BE MISSED: Sculpture collection on grounds of university; Collection of marine paintings by Frederick J. Waugh

ON EXHIBIT/95:

2/18 - 4/14/95	PUTT MODERNISM — A playable 18 hole miniature golf course installation where each hole is designed as an original work of art by such contemporary artists as Cindy Sherman, Jenny Holzer, Allison Saar and each hole addresses a specific theme: i.e., AIDS, homelessness, war, censorship and the like. ADM FEE
4/16 - 6/4/95	BOB BLACKBURN'S PRINTMAKING WORKSHOP: ARTISTS OF COLOR — Since its establishment in 1949, this printmaking workshop has played a chief role in encouraging artists of color to create works by using a wide variety of interesting and unusual techniques. CAT WT
8/6 - 10/1/95	ALTERNATIVE DOMESTIC OBJECTS (working title) — On exhibit will be creations by contemporary artists who will use or alter common objects found in and around the home in order to comment of ideas of gender, sexuality, identity, and class hierarchies.

181

KANSAS

Edwin A. Ulrich Museum of Art - continued

10/22/95 - 1/6/96   CHARLES GRAFLY (1862-1929) (working title) — 35 bronzes and 20 plaster studies for these bronzes by American sculptor Grafly, one of the most important and influential sculptors of his time will be featured in this exhibit.

10/22/95 - 1/6/96   THE FIGURE IN 20TH CENTURY SCULPTURE — From the permanent collections of the Ulrich and Wichita Art Museums, a survey of 20th century figurative sculpture that spans artistic styles from representational to abstract will include works by such notables as Gaston Lachaise, Auguste Rodin, Alexander Calder, Leonard Baskin and others.

WICHITA

Indian Center Museum
650 N. Seneca, **Wichita, KS 67203**
TEL: 316-262-5221
HRS: 10-5 Tu-Sa; 1-5 S   HOL: LEG/HOL!
ADM: Y   ADULT: $2.00   CHILDREN: F (6 & under)   STUDENTS: $1.00
PARKING: Y; free   MUS/SH: Y   GR/T: Y   GR/PH: call 316-262-5221
PERM/COLL: NAT/AM

The artworks and artifacts in this museum that preserve the Native American heritage also provide non-Indian people insight into the culture and traditions of the Native American. In addition to the art, Native American food is served on Tuesday from 11-2 & 4-7. **NOT TO BE MISSED:** Blackbear Bosin's 44 foot "Keeper of the Plains" located on the grounds at the confluence of the Arkansas & Little Arkansas Rivers.

Wichita Art Museum
619 Stackman St., **Wichita, KS 67203**
TEL: 316-268-4921
HRS: 10-5 Tu-Sa, Noon-5 S   DAY CLOSED: M   HOL: LEG/HOL!
VOL/CONT: Y   ADM: F   HDC/ACC: Y; Elevators; ramps   PARKING: Y; Free lot at rear of building
MUS/SH: Y   REST/FAC: Y; Restaurant 11:30-1:30 Tu-F; Noon-2:00 S
GR/T: Y   GR/PH: call 316-268-4921 (education office) S/G: Y
PERM/COLL: AM: ptgs, gr, drgs; EU: gr, drgs; P/COL; CHARLES RUSSELL: ptgs, drgs, scupl; OM: gr;

Outstanding in its collection of paintings that span nearly 3 centuries of American art, the Wichita is also known for its Old Master prints and pre-Columbian art works. Worthy of particular mention is its hands-on gallery of touchable sculpture. **NOT TO BE MISSED:** The Roland P. Murdock Collection of American Art

ON EXHIBIT/95:

12/18/94 - 11/26/95   KANSAS ROOTS: A SELECTION OF KANSAS ARTISTS FROM THE WICHITA ART MUSEUM — In celebration of the 60th anniversary of the Wichita Art Museum, works by notable Kansas artists who have fostered the development of the visual arts in Kansas and in the nation will be on view.

12/24/94 - 3/5/95   MASTER PRINTS FROM GEMINI G.E.L. AND FACES AND FIGURES: PRINTS FROM THE TAMERIND LITHOGRAPHY WORKSHOP — Featured among the 90 large-scale paperworks on loan from two superb collections at the National Gallery of Art in Washington, D.C., will be a group of prints by 22 of America's most admired artists and an assemblage of works by 10 contemporary artists showing diverse interpretations of the human figure as well as a broad range of technical effects produced in the lithographic medium.

Wichita Art Museum - continued

1/15 - 5/7/95	NEW YORK COLLECTION FOR STOCKHOLM — On exhibit will be a portfolio of contemporary graphics from the permanent collection including works by Jim Dine, Mark di Suvero, Red Grooms, Donald Judd, Roy Lichtenstein, Louise Nevelson, Kenneth Noland, James Rosenquist and others.
4/9 - 6/25/95	CELEBRATING A NEW PUBLIC TREASURE: THE LEE E. PHILLIPS, JR. AND ANNE KATHERINE PHILLIPS COLLECTION — Works of the American West as well as late 19th & early 20th century mainstream American art were donated by the Phillips' to two public arts institutions. This exhibition presents an opportunity to see both parts of the original collection reunited.
4/9 - 6/25/95	COLLECTING THE FUTURE: CONTEMPORARY ART IN THE WICHITA ART MUSEUM COLLECTION, 1960-1990 — An display of American paintings, sculpture, graphics and decorative arts created over the decades of the 1960's through the 1980's that documents the richness of the nation's ongoing artistic heritage.
5/14 - 9/3/95	THE AMERICAN SCENE — Works on paper from the WAM collection.
7/16 - 9/17/95	KANSAS WATERCOLOR SOCIETY 1995 FIVE-STATE EXHIBITION — An annual juried competition.
9/10 - 12/31/95	IDEAL FORM: THE ACADEMIC FIGURE — Figurative works on paper from the permanent collection.
10/22/95 - 1/7/96	THE HUMAN FIGURE IN AMERICAN SCULPTURE: A QUESTION OF MODERNITY — More than 100 works in stone, metal, clay and wood that document the roots of American modernist sculpture will be presented in thematic groups. This exhibition will particularly recognize the significant works of many previously ignored or poorly documented regional, women and minority artists.

WICHITA

The Wichita Center for the Arts
9112 East Central, **Wichita, KS 67206**
TEL: 316-634-2787
HRS: 10-5 Tu-F; 1-5 Sa, S   HOL: LEG/HOL!
ADM: F
HDC/ACC: Y   PARKING: Y; Over 200 on-site free parking spaces available.   GR/T: Y   GR/PH: call 316-634-2787
PERM/COLL: DEC/ART: 20; OR; PTGS; SCULP; DRGS; CER; GR

Midwest arts, both historical and contemporary, are the focus of this vital multi-disciplinary facility.
NOT TO BE MISSED: 1,000 piece Bruce Moore Collection

ON EXHIBIT/95:

1/7 - 2/19/95	ELLIOT ERWITT "TO THE DOGS" — Photographer Erwitt, who believes that dogs are people, captures in his images the character of his subjects and the special relationship that exists between humans and canines. BOOK WT
2/23 - 4/9/95	THE NICOLAS SALGO COLLECTION — 19th through 20th century Hungarian paintings collected by Mr. Salgo during the years he served as U.S. Ambassador to Hungary, 1983-86.
2/25 - 4/9/95	CONTEMPORARIES XVII: MERRIL KRABILL AND GARY KEIMIG — Charcoal and pencil drawings by Keimig and sculpture by Krabill will be featured in this exhibition.
4/15 - 5/30/95	THE WICHITA CENTER FOR THE ARTS PERMANENT COLLECTION ANNIVERSARY SHOW — A 75th anniversary retrospective that features favorite artworks in many media from the permanent collection.

KENTUCKY

LEXINGTON
University of Kentucky Art Museum
Rose & Euclid Ave., **Lexington, KY 40506**
TEL: 606-257-5716
HRS: Noon-5 Tu-S (Acad); Noon-4:30 (Summer)   DAY CLOSED: M
HOL: 1/1, Martin Luther King's Birthday, 7/4, THGV, 12/25
VOL/CONT: Y   ADM: F   HDC/ACC: Y; Fully accessible   PARKING: Y; Limited parking available in the circular drive in front of the Center. More extensive parking in the University lots on Euclid St.
GR/T: Y   GR/PH: 606-257-5716 (education dept.)
PERM/COLL: OM: ptgs, gr: AM: ptgs 19; EU: ptgs 19; CONT/GR; PTGS 20; AF; OR; WPA WORKS

Considered to be one of Kentucky's key cultural resources, this museum houses over 3,000 art objects that span the past 2,000 years of artistic creation.

ON EXHIBIT/95:

10/2/94 - 3/12/95	A SPECTACULAR VISION: THE GEORGE AND SUSAN PROSKAUER COLLEC-TION — From the Proskauer Collection, the largest gift in the museum's history, an exhibition of the finest modernist art will include examples by Picasso, Miro, Dubuffet, Avery, Rickey, Calder and many others. CAT
11/13/94 - 1/15/95	SELECTIONS FROM "THE WOODCUTS OF HARLAN HUBBARD" — On exhibit will be a selection of 28 woodcuts by this noted Ohio River artist. CAT
11/6/94 - 2/26/95	TRANSFORMING POWER: MASKS FROM SUB-SAHARAN AFRICA — Masks from the African countries of Zaire, Nigeria, Mali, the Ivory Coast and Burkina Faso will be accompanied by photographs that show the cultural context of the masks.
4/2 - SUMMER 95	THE ROBERT C. MAY COLLECTION — 70 images by Lexington photographer May will be shown with photographic works from his own collection by such artists as Ansel Adams, Minor White, Eugene Meatyard, Imogen Cunningham and others. CAT

LOUISVILLE
J. B. Speed Art Museum
2035 S. Third St., **Louisville, KY 40208**
TEL: 502-636-2893
HRS: 10-4 Tu-Sa; Noon-5 S   DAY CLOSED: M   HOL: LEG/HOL!, 1st weekend in March & 1st Sa in May
VOL/CONT: Y   ADM: F   HDC/ACC: Y; North entrance , selected restrooms & telephone
PARKING: Y; Adjacent to the museum - $2.00 fee for non-members   MUS/SH: Y
REST/FAC: Y; Cafe, 10-3:45 Tu-Sa, Noon-4:45 S (Reservations suggested 637-7774)
DT: Y   TIME: 2:00 Sa; at 1 & 3 S   S/G: Y
PERM/COLL: AM: dec/art; PTGS; SCULP: GR; PRIM; OR; DU:17; FL:17; FR: ptgs 18; CONT

Founded in 1927, and located on the main campus of the University of Louisville, the J. B. Speed Art Museum is the largest (over 3,000 works) and the most comprehensive (spanning 6,000 years of art history) public art collection in Kentucky. Free "Especially For Children" tours are offered at 11 am each Saturday. **NOT TO BE MISSED:** New acquisition: "Saint Jerome in the Wilderness" by Hendrick van Somer, 1651; "Head of a Ram,"a 2nd century marble Roman sculpture (recent acquisition); "Colossal Head of Medusa," polychromed fiberglass sculpture by Audry Flack (recent acquisition)

ON EXHIBIT/95:

11/8/94 - 1/5/95	THE IDEAL HOME — 200 items including furniture, lamps, ceramics, glass and other objects of home use will be featured in a major exhibition that surveys the American Arts & Crafts movement from 1900-1920. CAT WT

184

LOUISVILLE

Photographic Archives
Affiliate Institution: University of Louisville Libraries
Ekstrom Library, University of Louisville, **Louisville, KY 40292**
TEL: 502-852-6752
HRS: 10-4 M-F; 10-8 T   DAY CLOSED: Sa, S   HOL: LEG/HOL!
ADM: F
HDC/ACC: Y   PARKING: Y; Limited (for information call 502-588-6505)   GR/T: Y   GR/PH: call 502-588-6752
PERM/COLL: PHOT; GR

With 33 individual collections and over one million items, the Photographic Archives is one of the finest photography and research facilities in the country. **NOT TO BE MISSED:** 2,000 vintage Farm Security Administration photos; more than 1500 fine prints "from Ansel Adams to Edward Weston."

ON EXHIBIT/95:   There are approximately four exhibitions a year mounted from the permanent collection.

OWENSBORO

Owensboro Museum of Fine Art
901 Frederica St., **Owensboro, KY 42301**
TEL: 502-685-3181
HRS: 10-4 M-F, 1-4 Sa, S, Hol!   HOL: LEG/HOL!
SUGG/CONT: Y   ADULT: $2.00   CHILDREN: $1.00
HDC/ACC: Y; Totally accessible   PARKING: Y; Free street parking in front of museum   MUS/SH: Y
GR/T: Y   GR/PH: call 502-685-3181   H/B: Y; 1925 Carnegie Library Building (listed NRHP)
PERM/COLL: AM: ptgs, drgs, gr, sculp 19-20; BRIT: ptgs, drgs, gr, sculp 19-20; FR: ptgs, sculp, drgs, gr 19-20; CONT/AM; DEC/ART 14-18

The collection of the Owensboro Museum, the only fine art institution in Western Kentucky, features works by important 18-20th century American, English, and French masters. Paintings by regional artists stress the strong tradition of Kentucky landscape painting. Just opened in 9/94 was a new wing of the museum which houses several new exhibition galleries, an atrium sculpture court, a restored Civil War era mansion and the John Hampdem Smith House. **NOT TO BE MISSED:** 16 turn-of-the-century stained glass windows by Emil Frei (1867-1941) permanently installed in the new wing of the museum

ON EXHIBIT/95:

1/15 - 2/12/95	FRANCIA SMITH — A retrospective of the works of this New York based painter.
2/19 - 4/2/95	MATTHEW DAUB: AMERICAN REALIST — A retrospective of the work of Daub, considered one of the country's most significant emerging Realist painters. WT
3/5 - 4/14/95	THE SPIRIT OF EASTER — From the Kentucky Spirit Collection of the museum, an exhibition of Kentucky folk art inspired by the holiday of Easter.
10/15 - 12/24/95	BIRDS, BEASTS, BLOSSOMS AND BUGS IN EAST ASIAN ART — On loan from the extensive holdings of the Lowe Museum in Florida will be a varied selection of 186 Chinese, Japanese, Korean and East Asian objects decorated with design motifs ranging from mythical creatures to naturalistic forms. One of the highlights will be "Cranes," a six-fold panel screen from the Japanese Edo Period (1615-1868). CAT WT

KENTUCKY

PADUCAH

Yeiser Art Center
200 Broadway, **Paducah, KY 42001**
TEL: 502-442-2453
HRS: 10-4 Tu-Sa; 1-4 S   DAY CLOSED: M   HOL: LEG/HOL!
ADM: Y   ADULT: $1.00   CHILDREN: F (under 12)
HDC/ACC: Y; Completely accessible   PARKING: Y; Free parking across the street from the museum
MUS/SH: Y   GR/T: Y   GR/PH: call 502-442-2453   H/B: Y; Located in the historic Market House (1905)
PERM/COLL: ARTWORKS 19-20

The restored 1905 Market House (listed NRHP), home to the Art Center and many other community related activities, features changing exhibitions that are regional, national, and international in content. **NOT TO BE MISSED:** Annual national fiber exhibition mid Mar thru Apr (call for exact dates)

ON EXHIBIT/95:

2/1 - 3/12/95	THE PERMANENT COLLECTION OF THE YEISER ART CENTER — Selected works of 19th & 20th century American, European and Asian art.
3/19 - 4/30/95	FANTASTIC FIBERS — 8th annual national fibers invitational will feature traditional and non-traditional examples of wearables, wall hangings, sculpture, weavings, quilts and masks.
5/7 - 6/18/95	PERMANENT COLLECTION
6/25 - 8/6/95	PERMANENT COLLECTION
10/1 - 11/12/95	PADUCAH '95 — A juried regional competition of contemporary artworks in many media.

186

LOUISIANA

ALEXANDRIA

Alexandria Museum of Art
933 Main St., **Alexandria, LA 71301**
TEL: 318-443-3458
HRS: 9-5 Tu-F; 10-4 Sa   DAY CLOSED: S, M   HOL: LEG/HOL!
ADM: Y   ADULT: $3.00   CHILDREN: $1.00   STUDENTS: $2.00   SR CIT: $2.00
HDC/ACC: Y   PARKING: Y; Free but very limited parking across the street from the musuem. Some handicapped and bus parking in front of the building.   GR/T: Y   DT: Y   TIME: often available upon request!
H/B: Y; 1900 Bank Building
PERM/COLL: CONT: sculp, ptgs; REG; FOLK

Housed in a former bank building that dates back to the turn of the century, this museum features a permanent collection of contemporary art along with regional fine art and folk craft works. **NOT TO BE MISSED:** Recently opened gallery of Northern Louisiana folk art.

ON EXHIBIT/95:
1/6 - 3/31/95	AMoA PERMANENT COLLECTION EXHIBITION — Contemporary art from the American South and contemporary American/British works on paper will be on view from the permanent collection.
4/14 - 5/26/95	PAT TRIVIGNO: THE SEARCH FOR INNER FORM — A retrospective of paintings by Trivigno, a New Orleans artist/professor who has influenced the works of such artists in the community as Lynda Bengalis, Ida Kohlmeyer, Steve Rucker and others.
6/9 - 8/5/95	WILL HENRY STEVENS RETROSPECTIVE — An exhibition of abstracted paintings based on scenes of nature as seen by Stevens during his continuous travels.
9/9 - 10/28/95	14TH ANNUAL SEPTEMBER COMPETITION — An international juried competition of contemporary art.
11/10/94 - 1/6/95	CLEMSON UNIVERSITY, COLLEGE OF ARCHITECTURE, AMERICAN AND EUROPEAN PHOTOGRAPHY FROM THE 1920'S THROUGH THE 1960'S — Included in this collection and exhibition will be photos by Bravo, Cortege and Lyons.

BATON ROUGE

Louisiana Arts and Science Center
100 S. River Rd., **Baton Rouge, LA 70801**
TEL: 504-344-9463
HRS: 10-3 Tu-F; 10-4 Sa; 1-4 S   DAY CLOSED: M   HOL: LEG/HOL!
F/DAY: S   ADM: Y   ADULT: $2.00   CHILDREN: $1.00 (2-12)   STUDENTS: $1.00   SR CIT: $1.00
HDC/ACC: Y; Ramp outside; elevator   PARKING: Y; Limited free parking in front of building and behind train; other parking areas available within walking distance   GR/T: Y   GR/PH: call 504-344-9463
H/B: Y; Housed in reconstructed Illinois Central Railroad Station   S/G: Y
PERM/COLL: SCULP; ETH; GR; DRGS; PHOT; EGT; AM: ptgs 18-20; EU: ptgs 18-20

This museum is housed in a reconstructed Illinois Central Railroad station built on the site of the 1862 Civil War Battle of Baton Rouge. **NOT TO BE MISSED:** Works by John Marin, Charles Burchfield, Asher B. Durand; Baroque, Neo-Classic, & Impressionist Works

ON EXHIBIT/95:
12/6/94 - 1/29/95	AMERICAN NAIVE PAINTINGS FROM THE NATIONAL GALLERY OF ART FROM THE COLLECTION OF COLONEL EDGAR WILLIAM GARBISCH AND BERNICE CHRYSLER GARBISCH

187

LOUISIANA

Louisiana Arts and Science Center - continued

12/6/94 - 1/29/95	SELECTIONS FROM THE LASC PERMANENT COLLECTION
2/1 - 2/26/95	ELIZABETH CATLETT: WORKS ON PAPER 1944-1992
2/28 - 4/2/95	PHOTOGRAPHS BY DEBBIE FLEMING CAFFERY
4/4 - 5/21/95	ADOLPH DEHN'S FUNNY PEOPLE
5/2 - 7/3/95	ROBERT BURNS WOODWARD AND THE ART OF ORGANIC SYNTHESIS
5/23 - 6/18/95	WALLACE HERNDON SMITH: REDISCOVERED
6/20 - 7/23/95	LOUISIANA COMPETITION 1995
7/25 - 9/10/95	WHITE MOUNTAIN PAINTERS — 45 oil paintings and 5 watercolors (1834-1926) by artists inspired by the beauty of the New Hampshire landscape will be seen in this exhibition. BROCHURE WT
9/12 - 10/3/95	ELLIOT ERWITT: "TO THE DOGS" — Photographer Erwitt, who believes that dogs are people, captures in his images the character of his subjects and the special relationship that exists between humans and canines. BOOK WT
11/5 - 12/31/95	WILL HENRY STEVENS: ABSOLUTE HARMONY PREVAILS

JENNINGS

The Zigler Museum
411 Clara St., **Jennings, LA 70546**
TEL: 318-824-0114
HRS: 9-5 Tu-Sa; 1-5 S   DAY CLOSED: M   HOL: LEG/HOL!
SUGG/CONT: Y   ADULT: $2.00   CHILDREN: $1.00
HDC/ACC: Y   PARKING: Y; Free street parking   MUS/SH: Y   GR/T: Y   GR/PH: call 318-824-0114
PERM/COLL: REG; AM; EU

The gracious colonial style structure that had served as the Zigler family home since 1908 was formerly opened as a museum in 1970. Two wings added to the original building feature many works by Louisiana landscape artists in addition to those of other Amercian and European artists. PLEASE NOTE: The museum is open daily from the first weekend in Dec. to Dec. 22 for the Christmas festival. **NOT TO BE MISSED:** Largest collection of works by African-American artist, William Tolliver

ON EXHIBIT/95:   Exhibitions by artists and master craftsmen are presented throughout the year.

LAFAYETTE

University Art Museum
East Lewis & Girard Park Dr., **Lafayette, LA 70504**
TEL: 318-231-5326
HRS: 9-4 M-F; 2-5 S   DAY CLOSED: Sa   HOL: 1/1, MARDI GRAS, THGV, 12/25, EASTER
ADM: Y   ADULT: $2.00   HDC/ACC: Y   PARKING: Y; Free
PERM/COLL: AM/REG: ptgs, sculp, drgs, phot 19-20; JAP: gr; PLEASE NOTE: Selections from the permanent collection are on display approximately once a year (call for specifics)

188

University Art Museum - continued

This university art museum which serves as a cultural focal point for no less than 18 southwestern Louisiana parishes maintains a permanent collection of primarily 19th & 20th century Louisiana and American southern works of art.

ON EXHIBIT/95:

1/21 - 3/31/95	UNDER A SPELL — Antoine Oleyant, Haiti & Tina Girouard, Louisiana
1/21 - 3/31/95	JANE DOMENGEAUX — Paintings
6/3 - 7/28/95	PHOTOGLYPHS — Rimma Gerlovina and Valeriy Gerlovin
6/3 - 7/28/95	SELECTIONS FROM THE PERMANENT COLLECTION
9/1 - 10/31/95	NEW DIRECTIONS IN HOLOGRAPHY
9/1 - 10/31/95	BRAD LOUDENBACK — Drawings

MONROE

Masur Museum of Art
1400 S. Grand, **Monroe, LA 71201**
TEL: 318-329-2237
HRS: 9-5 Tu-T; 2-5 F-S   DAY CLOSED: M   HOL: LEG/HOL!
ADM: F
HDC/ACC: Y; Access to first floor only   PARKING: Y; Free parking adjacent to the Museum building
GR/T: Y   GR/PH: call 318-329-2237   S/G: Y
PERM/COLL: AM: gr 20; REG/CONT

Twentieth century prints by American artists and works by contemporary regional artists form the basis of the permanent collection and are displayed year round on a continually rotating basis. The museum is located in the stately modified English Tudor home of the Masur family situated on the tree-lined banks of the Ouachita River.

ON EXHIBIT/95:

1/7 - late 2/19/95	BARTHE & HUNT — Bronze sculpture
3/4 - 4/8/95	22ND ANNUAL JURIED COMPETITION — An exhibition of works by regional artists from Louisiana, Mississippi, Texas and Arkansas
4/22 - late 5/28/95	DALE KENNINGTON — One woman show
6 - 7/95	ANNUAL AFRICAN-AMERICAN EXHIBITION

LOUISIANA

NEW ORLEANS

The Historic New Orleans Collection
533 Royal St., **New Orleans, LA 70130**
TEL: 504-523-4662
HRS: 10-4:45 Tu-Sa   DAY CLOSED: M, S   HOL: LEG/HOL!
ADM: Y   ADULT: $2.00   HDC/ACC: Y   MUS/SH: Y   GR/T: Y   GR/PH: call 504-523-4662
DT: Y   TIME: 10, 11, 2, & 3 DAILY   H/B: Y; 1792 Jean Francois Merieult House Located in French Quarter
PERM/COLL: REG: ptgs, drgs, phot,

Merieult House, one of the most historic buildings of this complex, was built in 1792 during Louisiana's Spanish Colonial period. It is one of the few buildings in the French Quarter that escaped the fire of 1794. **NOT TO BE MISSED:** Changing exhibitions on local culture & history

ON EXHIBIT/95:

12/20/94 - 4/1/95	TENNESSEE WILLIAMS IN NEW ORLEANS
4/20 - 9/3/95	MARDI GRAS DESIGN AND PROCESS
9/13 - 12/2/95	CLARENCE JOHN LAUGHLIN: HIS PHOTOGRAPHS AND MANUSCRIPTS
12/12/95 - 3/10/96	RAISING CANE: SUGAR HARVESTING IN LOUISIANA

Louisiana State Museum
751 Chartres St., **New Orleans, LA 70116**
TEL: 504-568-6968
HRS: 10-5 Tu-S   DAY CLOSED: M   HOL: LEG/HOL!
ADM: Y   ADULT: $3.00   CHILDREN: F (12 & under)   STUDENTS: $1.50   SR CIT: $1.50
HDC/ACC: Y; Presbytere and Old U.S. Mint are accessible   MUS/SH: Y   H/B: Y
PERM/COLL: DEC/ART; FOLK; PHOT

Several historic buildings located in the famous New Orleans French Quarter are included in the Louisiana State Museum complex providing the visitor a wide array of viewing experiences that run the gamut from fine art to decorative art, textiles, and even jazz music. PLEASE NOTE: Although the entry fee of $3.00 is charged per building visited, a discounted rate is offered for a visit to two of more sites. **NOT TO BE MISSED:** Considered the State Museum's crown jewel, the recently reopened Cabildo features a walk through Louisiana history from Colonial times through Reconstruction.

New Orleans Museum of Art
Lelong Ave., City Park, **New Orleans, LA 70119**
TEL: 504-488-2631
HRS: 10-5 Tu-S   DAY CLOSED: M   HOL: LEG/HOL!
ADM: Y   ADULT: $6.00   CHILDREN: $3.00 (3-17)   HDC/ACC: Y; Fully accessible
PARKING: Y; Ample free parking adjacent to the museum   MUS/SH: Y
REST/FAC: Y; Courtyard Cafe 10:30-4:30 Tu-S (children's menu available)
GR/T: Y   GR/PH: call 504-488-2631   DT: Y   TIME: 11:00 & 2:00 Tu-S
PERM/COLL: OM: ptgs; IT/REN: ptgs (Kress Collection); FR; P/COL: MEX; AF; JAP: gr; AF; OC; NAT/AM; LAT/AM; AS; DEC/ART: 1st. C A.D.-20; REG

Located in the 1,500 acre City Park, the 75 year old New Orleans Museum has recently completed a $23 million dollar expansion and renvoation program that has doubled its size. Serving the entire Gulf South as an invaluable artistic resource, the museum houses at least one dozen major collections that cover a broad range of fine and decorative arts. **NOT TO BE MISSED:** Treasures by Faberge; Chinese Jades; Portrait Miniatures; New 3rd floor showcase for Non-Western Art

190

LOUISIANA

New Orleans Museum of Art - ontinued

ON EXHIBIT/95:

1/7 - 3/12/95	MONET: LATE PAINTINGS OF GIVERNY FROM THE MUSÉE MARMOTTAN — 22 of Monet's famous garden scenes created between 1903-1926, some never seen before in the U.S., will be on view in the first of only 2 venues in America for this exclusive exhibition. Of particular note will be several very large canvases from this remarkable collection.　　WT
3/25 - 4/30/95	1995 NEW ORLEANS TRIENNIAL
5/13 - 7/2/95	BOTTICELLI TO TIEPOLO: THREE CENTURIES OF ITALIAN PAINTING FROM BOB JONES UNIVERSITY — Forty great master paintings that trace the development of Italian painting from the high Renaissance through the Baroque and Rococo periods will include works by Tintoretto, Reni, Guercino and others　　CAT　WT
7/14 - 9/17/95	THE PEACEFUL LIBERATORS: JAIN ART FROM INDIA
9/29 - 11/5/95	SAFO - AFRICAN FLAGS
11/11/95 - 1/7/96	LOUIS ARMSTRONG: A CULTURAL LEGACY — Personal memorabilia, much of which has never before been on public display, will be joined by paintings, sculpture and photographs that document the life of Louis "Satchmo" Armstrong, one of the greatest talents in the history of American jazz.　　WT
12/2/95 - 1/28/96	ELLIS RULEY
12/2/95 - 1/28/96	NEAPOLITAN CRECHE FIGURES

SHREVEPORT

Meadows Museum of Art of Centenary College

2911 Centenary Blvd., **Shreveport, LA 71104**
TEL: 318-869-5169
HRS: Noon-4 Tu-F; 1-4 Sa, S　DAY CLOSED: M　HOL: LEG/HOL!
ADM: F
HDC/ACC: Y; Ramp to museum; elevator to 2nd floor　PARKING: Y; Free parking directly behind the building
GR/T: Y　GR/PH: call 318-869-5169　DT: Y　TIME: Upon request if available
PERM/COLL: PTGS, SCULP, GR, 18-20; INDO CHINESE: ptgs, gr

Opened in 1976 as a repository for the unique collection of works in a variety of media by French artist Jean Despujols, the Meadows Museum of Centenary College includes 360 major works created around this theme. **NOT TO BE MISSED:** The permanent collection itself which offers a rare glimpse into the people & culture of French Indochina in 1938.

ON EXHIBIT/95:

1/29 - 5/21/95	SPACE: THE ART OF ROBERT McCALL
7/8 - 8/20/95	SONGS OF MY PEOPLE — A presentation of photographs that document African-American traditions and lifestyles.　　CAT　WT

191

LOUISIANA

SHREVEPORT

The R. W. Norton Art Gallery
4747 Creswell Ave., **Shreveport, LA 71106**
TEL: 318-865-4201
HRS: 10-5 Tu-F; 1-5 Sa, S   DAY CLOSED: M   HOL: LEG/HOL!
ADM: F
HDC/ACC: Y; Access ramps off street; no steps   PARKING: Y; Free parking in front of building
MUS/SH: Y   GR/T: Y   GR/PH: call 318-865-4201
PERM/COLL: AM: ptgs, sculp (late 17-20); EU: ptgs, sculp 16-19; BRIT: cer

With its incomparable collections of American and European art, the Norton, situated in a 46 acre wooded park, had become one of the major cultural attractions in the region since its opening in 1966. Among its many attractions are the Bierstadt Gallery, the Bonheur Gallery, and the Corridor which features "The Prisons," a 16-part series of fantasy etchings by Piranesi. **NOT TO BE MISSED:** Outstanding collections of works by Frederick Remington & Charles M. Russell; The Wedgewood Gallery (one of the finest collections of its kind in the southern U.S.)

ON EXHIBIT/95:

1/8 - 2/26/95	ENGLISH SILVER: MASTERPIECES BY OMAR RAMSDEN
3/19 - 5/14/95	INTIMATE NATURE: ANSEL ADAMS AND THE CLOSE VIEW
8/6 - 10/1/95	HENRIETTE WYETH: PAINTER OF BEAUTY

MAINE

BRUNSWICK

Bowdoin College Museum of Art
Walker Art Bldg., **Brunswick, ME 04011**
TEL: 207-725-3275
HRS: 10-5 Tu-Sa; 2-5 S   DAY CLOSED: M   HOL: LEG/HOL! Also Closed Between 12/25 & New Years Day
VOL/CONT: Y   ADM: F
HDC/ACC: Y; Call for assistance (207) 725-3275   PARKING: Y; All along Upper Park Row   MUS/SH: Y
GR/T: Y   GR/PH: call education office 207-725-3064
H/B: Y; 1894 Walker Art Building Designed by Charles Follen McKim
PERM/COLL: AN/GRK; AN/R; AN/EGT; AM: ptgs, sculp, drgs, gr, dec/art; EU: ptgs, sculp, gr, drgs, dec/art; AF: sculp; INTERIOR MURALS BY LAFARGE, THAYER, VEDDER, COX

From the original bequest in 1811 by James Bowdoin III, who served as Thomas Jefferson's minister to France and Spain, the collection has grown to include important works from a broad range of nations and periods. **NOT TO BE MISSED:** Winslow Homer Collection of wood engravings, watercolors, drawings, and memorabilia (available for viewing during the summer months only).

ON EXHIBIT/95:

1/30 - 4/8/95	WEST MEXICAN CERAMICS FROM THE HUDSON MUSEUM — 25 pre-conquest terra cotta funerary objects of animals, warriers, women and musicians from the Colima, Mayarit, and Jalisco regions.
4/20 - 6/4/95	COLLECTING FOR A COLLEGE: GIFTS FROM DAVID P. BECKER — A major retrospective of artworks consisting mainly of prints donated to the college over the past 25 years by Becker, a scholar and independent curator of graphic arts. CAT
4/20 - 6/4/95	LANDSCAPE DRAWINGS — Drawings and watercolors from the permanent collection will be on view. BROCHURE
9/24 - 12/10/95	CONTEMPORARY PHOTOGRAPHS AND RELATED MEDIA — Work from contemporary photography-based artists whose careers began with the study of photography at Bowdoin College. CAT
ONGOING:	BOYD GALLERY — 14th to 20th-century European art from the permanent collection.
	BOWDOIN GALLERY — American art from the permanent collection.
	SOPHIA WALKER GALLERY — In celebration of the centennial of the Walker Art Building, selected works given to the College by Harriet and Mary Walker, donors of the building, will be on display.
	JOHN H. HALFORD GALLERY — "Crosscurrents," objects from the permanent collection originating from Africa, Asia, Ancient Greece, and the Americas that highlight the diversity of the museum's collections will be on exhibit.

LEWISTON

The Bates College Museum of Art
Affiliate Institution: Bates College
Olin Arts Center, Bates College, **Lewiston, ME 04240**
TEL: 207-786-6158
HRS: 10-5 Tu-Sa; 1-5 S   DAY CLOSED: M   HOL: LEG/HOL!
ADM: F
HDC/ACC: Y   PARKING: Y; Free on-street campus parking   GR/T: Y   GR/PH: call 207-786-6123
PERM/COLL: AM: ptgs, sculp; GR 19-20; EU: ptgs, sculp, gr; drgs:

193

MAINE

The Bates College Museum of Art - continued

The newly constructed building of the Museum of Art at Bates College houses a major collection of works by American artist Marsden Hartley. It also specializes in 20th-century American and European prints, drawings, and photographs, and has a small collection of 20th century American paintings. **NOT TO BE MISSED:** Collection of Marsden Hartley drawings and memorabilia

ON EXHIBIT/95:

1/20 - 3/31/95	DONALD LENT: NEW WORKS ON PAPER
6/16 - 8/18/95	D. D. COOMBS: LEWISTON'S PAINTER LAUREATE
9 - 12/95	THE PRINT WORKSHOP
	PRE-COLUMBIAN ART AT BATES COLLEGE

OGUNQUIT

Ogunquit Museum of American Art
181 Shore Rd., **Ogunquit, ME 03907**
TEL: 207-646-4909
HRS: OPEN 7/1 through 9/30 only) 10:30-5 M-Sa, 2-5 S   HOL: LAB/DAY
ADM: Y   ADULT: $3.00   CHILDREN: F (under 12)
HDC/ACC: Y; Enter lower level at seaside end of bldg; wheelchairs available   PARKING: Y; Free on museum grounds MUS/SH: Y   GR/T: Y   GR/PH: call 207-646-4909   DT: Y   TIME: upon request if available   S/G: Y
PERM/COLL: AM: ptgs, sculp 20

Situated on a rocky promontory overlooking the sea, this museum has been described as the most beautiful small museum in the world! Built in 1952 the Ogunquit houses many American paintings and sculptures of note spanning most of the 20th century. Spread throughout its three acres of land are site-specific sculptures. **NOT TO BE MISSED:** "Mt. Katadhin, Winter" by Marsden Hartley; "The Bowery Drunks" by Reginald Marsh; "Pool With Four Markers" by Dozier Bell; "Sleeping Girl" by Walt Kuhn

ON EXHIBIT/95:

7/1 - 8/8/95	BERNARD KARFIOL AND ISABEL BISHOP RETROSPECTIVES — A joint exhibition of nearly 50 works on loan from public and private collections.
8/14 - 9/30/95	MAINSCAPES: WOMEN ARTISTS, 1900-1995 — Works by 50 well known artists of the past, and younger less well known contemporary talents all of whom have worked in Maine will be featured in this exhibition.

ORONO

University of Maine Museum of Art
109 Carnegie Hall, **Orono, ME 04469**
TEL: 207-581-3255
HRS: 9-4:30 M-F; Weekends by appointment   DAY CLOSED: S   HOL: STATE & LEG/HOL!
ADM: F   HDC/ACC: PARKING: Y; Free with visitor permits available in director's office.
GR/T: Y   GR/PH: call 207-581-3255 DT: TIME: H/B: Y; 1904 Library of Palladian design
PERM/COLL: AM: gr, ptgs 18-20; EU: gr, ptgs 18-20; CONT; REG

Housed in a beautiful 1904 structure of classic Palladian design, this university art museum, located just to the northeast of Bangor, Maine, features American and European art of the 18th-20th centuries and works by Maine-based artists of the past and present. The permanent collection is displayed throughout the whole university and in the main center-for-the-arts building,

194

PORTLAND

Portland Museum of Art
Seven Congress Square, **Portland, ME 04101**
TEL: 207-775-6148
HRS: Jun 1-Oct 31: 10-5 Tu-Sa; 10-9 T; noon-5 S; call for summer hours   DAY CLOSED: M   HOL: LEG/HOL!
F/DAY: T pm & 1st S am   ADM: Y   ADULT: $6.00   CHILDREN: $1.00 (6-12)   STUDENTS: $5.00   SR CIT: $5.00
HDC/ACC: Y; Galleries are wheelchair accessible
PARKING: Y; free on street parking on weekends; discounted parking with validated museum ticket at nearby garages.
MUS/SH: Y   GR/T: Y   GR/PH: call 207 775-6148   DT: Y   TIME: 2:00 daily & 5:30 T
PERM/COLL: AM; ptgs, sculp 19-20; REG; DEC/ART; JAP: gr

The Joan Whitney Payson collection has become become part of the oldest and finest art museum in the state of Maine. PLEASE NOTE: Admission fees change according to the season. The fees listed are in effect from June 1 - Oct 31. Winter entry fees are $5. Also, there is a toll free number (1-800-639-4067) for museum information. **NOT TO BE MISSED:** The Charles Shipman Payson collection of 17 works by Winslow Homer.

ON EXHIBIT/95:

9/17 94 - 1/8/95	THE HAMILTON EASTER FIELD ART FOUNDATION COLLECTION — Displayed in its entirety, this collection which includes works by Marsden Hartley and Stuart Davis, offers the viewer an opportunity to glimpse into the interconnected world of art in New York and Maine during the first half of the 20th century.
10/29/94 - 1/29/95	FANTASY IN FABRIC: COSTUMES BY SEVENTEEN SKOWHEGAN ARTISTS — Costumes for 2 benefit balls created by Robert Indiana, Jacob Lawrence, Red Grooms and other artists affiliated with the Skowhegan School of Painting and Sculpture will be on display.
10/29/94 - 1/29/95	AN EYE FOR MAINE: PAINTINGS FROM A PRIVATE COLLECTION — 50 paintings which feature the art of past and present Maine will include prime examples of the works of Fitz Hugh Lane, Frederick Church, Childe Hassam, George Bellows, Louise Nevleson, Winslow Homer and many other artistic luminaries.
2/4 - 4/2/95	THE PICTOGRAHS OF ADOLPH GOTTLIEB — For the first time, this rare assemblage of 60 works (1941-1952) from museum and private collections will allow the viewer to understand how Gottlieb combined and integrated a diverse range of elements (from classical, African & modern) that resulted in his own distinctive grid-like creations. CAT WT
ONGOING:	FROM COURBET TO MOTHERWELL: 19TH AND 20TH CENTURY EUROPEAN AND AMERICAN ART — Works from the permanent collection by masters of the past two centuries will be featured.
	THE SCOTT M. BLACK COLLECTION — 19th and 20th century paintings and sculpture are on loan from the private collection of Black, a Portland native.

ROCKLAND

William A. Farnsworth Library and Art Museum
19 Elm St., **Rockland, ME 04841**
TEL: 207-596-6457
HRS: 10-5 M-Sa; 1-5 S (Jun-Sep); closed M (Oct- May)   HOL: LEG/HOL!
ADM: Y   ADULT: $5.00   CHILDREN: $3.00 (8-18)   STUDENTS: $4.00   SR CIT: $4.00
HDC/ACC: Y; Wheelchair and restroom accessible   PARKING: Y; Free   MUS/SH: Y
GR/T: Y   GR/PH: call 207-596-6457   H/B: Y; 1850 Victorian homestead on grounds adjacent to Art Museum
S/G: Y
PERM/COLL: AM: 18-20; REG; PHOT; GR

MAINE

William A. Farnsworth Library and Art Museum - continued

Nationally acclaimed for its collection of American Art, the Farnsworth, located in the mid eastern coastal city of Rockland, counts among its important holdings the largest public collection of works (60 in all) by sculptress Louise Nevelson. Recent renovations to the museum allow for the installation from the permanent collection of an abbreviated survey of American art with special emphasis on artists from the state of Maine. There is also an additional new gallery housing the Nevelson collection and other works of contemporary art. **NOT TO BE MISSED:** Major works by N. C., Andrew & Jamie Wyeth, Fitz Hugh Lane, John Marin, Edward Hopper, Neil Welliver, Louise Nevelson; The Olsen House, depicted by Andrew Wyeth in many of his most famous works

ON EXHIBIT/95:

11/13/94 - 2/5/95	COMICS, CARTOONS & ANIMATION — Original artwork by cartoonists and animators with a Maine connection.
1/29 - 2/26/95	EAST/WEST — New work by 3 Maine artists influenced by their recent travels to India and China.
2/12 - 4/2/95	WILLIAM MANNING — Paintings and works on paper by this Maine artist.
4/9 - 6/11/95	MONHEGAN: AN ARTIST'S ISLAND — Featured in this survey of paintings and watercolors by artists associated with the Monhegan Art Colony will be works by Hopper, Bellows, Henri, Kent, Wyeth and others.
6/25 - 9/24/95	ANDREW WYETH: THE OLSEN HOUSE COLLECTION — Watercolors and sketches from a major private collection of works related to the Olsen House, site of "Christina's World" one of Wyeth's most beloved images.
10/1 - 11/19/95	LOIS DODD: A RETROSPECTIVE — A retrospective of 25 years of painting by New York artist Dodd, a long-time summer resident of Maine.
11/26/95 - 1/28/96	THE STORIES THEY TELL TOO — Original artwork from some of the best-loved children's books illustrated by Maine artists.
ONGOING:	MAINE IN AMERICA — From the permanent collection a display of 19th and early 20th century paintings and sculpture by American artists whose works are related to the development of art in Maine within the larger context of American art history.

WATERVILLE

Colby College Museum of Art
Mayflower Hill, **Waterville, ME 04901**
TEL: 207-872-3228
HRS: 10-4:30 M-Sa; 2-4:30 S   HOL: LEG/HOL!
ADM: F   HDC/ACC: Y   PARKING: Y; Free parking in front of the museum   MUS/SH: Y
PERM/COLL: AM: Impr/ptgs, folk, gr; Winslow Homer: watercolors; OR: cer

Located in a modernist building on a campus dominated by neo-Georgian architecture, the museum at Colby College houses a distinctive collection of several centuries of American Art. Included among its many fine holdings is a 36 piece collection of sculpture donated to the school by Maine native, Louise Nevelson. **NOT TO BE MISSED:** 25 watercolors by John Marin; "La Reina Mora" by Robert Henri (recent acquisition)

196

Colby College Museum of Art - continued

ON EXHIBIT/95:

12/94 - 2/95	MULTICULTURALISM IN THE MUSEUM'S COLLECTION
3/95	NANCY GOETZ: FACULTY SHOW
4 - 5/95	FAR EASTERN RUG AND CARPET EXHIBITION — This major exhibition will be guest curated by Michael Marlais.
8 - 10/95	WILLIAM WEGMAN PHOTOGRAPHS
10 - 11/95	FALL CRAFT EXHIBITION — Sponsored by Colby College and the Maine Craft Association
FALL 95	JERE ABBOTT: EMERGING ARTIST PRIZE WINNERS
ONGOING:	WORKS FROM THE PERMANENT COLLECTION

MARYLAND

ANNAPOLIS

Elizabeth Myers Mitchell Art Gallery
Affiliate Institution: St. John's College
60 College Ave., **Annapolis, MD 21404**
TEL: 410-626-2556
HRS: Noon-5 Tu-S, 7pm-8pm F   DAY CLOSED: M   HOL: LEG/HOL!
ADM: F
HDC/ACC: Y; Barrier free entrance & restrooms; wheelchair available by appt.
PARKING: Y; Call the gallery to arrange in advance because parking is limited
REST/FAC: Y; College Coffee Shop open 8:15-4   GR/T: Y   GR/PH: Call 410-626-2556

Established in 1989 primarily as a center of learning for the visual arts in 1989, this institution, though young in years, presents a rotating schedule of exhibitions of the highest quality containing original works by many of the greatest artists of yesterday and today.

ON EXHIBIT/95:

1/10 - 3/3/95	THE ETCHINGS AND DRYPOINTS OF JAMES ABBOT McNEILL WHISTLER — Included in this exhibition of 40 images are Whistler's printed portfolio of "Sixteen Etchings of the Thames" and his renowned "Nocturnes."
4/7 - 5/21/95	MASTERPIECES OF RENAISSANCE AND BAROQUE PRINTMAKING — 85 superb 15th through 17th century prints that illustrate the differences bewteen art practiced in the North and in Italy, will compare the technical advances and stylistic differences of artists in both regions. Examples by Cranach, Durer, Rembrandt, Van Dyck, Carracci, Lorrain and other old masters will be included. CAT WT

BALTIMORE

The Baltimore Museum of Art
Art Museum Drive, **Baltimore, MD 21218**
TEL: 301-396-7100
HRS: 10-4 W-F; 11-6 Sa, S   DAY CLOSED: M, Tu   HOL: GOOD FRIDAY, 7/4, THGV, 12/25
F/DAY: T   ADM: Y   ADULT: $5.50   CHILDREN: $1.50 (7-18)   F (under 6))   STUDENTS: $3.50   SR CIT: $3.50
HDC/ACC: Y   PARKING: Y; Metered and limited; free parking on weekends at The Johns Hopkins University adjacent to the museum.   MUS/SH: Y   REST/FAC: Y; 301-235-3930   GR/T: Y   GR/PH: call 410-396-6320
H/B: Y; 1929 building designed by John Russell Pope   S/G: Y
PERM/COLL: AM: ptgs 18-20; EU: ptgs, sculp 15-20; MATISSE: Cone Coll; FR: phot 19; AM: dec/art, cont; EU: dec/art, cont; P/COL; AF; OC; NAT/AM; AN/R: mosaics

One of the undisputed jewels of this important artistic institution is the Cone Collection of works by Matisse, the largest of its kind in the Western Hemisphere. The museum, in 10/94, opened a new 17 gallery wing for contemporary art, the first and largest not only for this institution but for the state of Maryland as well. On view in this wing will be works by Andy Warhol from the permanent collection which is the second largest collection of paintings by the artist on regular display. **NOT TO BE MISSED:** The Cone Collection; American: dec/arts; Antioch mosaics; Sculpture gardens; American: paintings 19; OM: paintings

ON EXHIBIT/95:

10/26/94 - 4/16/95	STARRY NIGHTS: STAR-PATTERNED QUILTS FROM THE COLLECTION

198

The Baltimore Museum of Art - continued

11/23/94 - 1/29/95	RICHARD SERRA: WEIGHT AND MEASURE DRAWINGS — Large-scale paintstick drawings aligned to render the concepts of weight and mass will be presented in the first traveling exhibition of Serra's drawings to be held in the U.S. WT
1/4 - 2/26/95	ALONE IN A CROWD: PRINTS OF THE 1930'S AND 1940'S BY AFRICAN-AMERICAN ARTISTS FROM THE COLLECTION OF REBA AND DAVE WILLIAMS — The works of 41 African-American printmakers working in a wide variety of styles and techniques during the Depression decades (many under the auspices of the WPA) will be on view in this 106 piece exhibition. CAT WT
2/12 - 4/23/95	SOL LeWITT: DRAWINGS 1958-1992 — This major exhibition of 450 past and present works by the artist will include examples of his well-known wall drawings that allow the viewer to trace the development of LeWitt's creative process and ideas. WT
3/22 - 6/25/95	ABSTRACT PHOTOGRAPHS AND DRAWINGS — 75 works from the permanent collection will trace the path of abstraction in photography from the turn-of-the-century Photo-Secessionists to the post-modernists of today.
5/24 - 7/30/95	THE GARDEN OF EARTHLY DELIGHTS: PHOTOGRAPHS BY EDWARD WESTON AND ROBERT MAPPLETHORP — In the only museum venue outside of California, this exhibition of 45 photographs by each artist dealing with the subjects of the figure, the portrait, and the still life will allow the viewer to compare and contrast the styles of these two men both of whom challenged the artistic conventions of their day. WT
7/7 - 8/27/95	MASTERWORKS ON PAPER FROM THE CONE COLLECTION — Included in this exhibition of more than 100 masterworks, many of which are rarely on view, will be numerous works by Matisse and Picasso as well as single images by van Gogh, Seurat and Cézanne. WT
7/19 - 10/1/95	EXCURSIONS ALONG THE NILE: THE PHOTOGRAPHIC DISCOVERY OF EGYPT — More than 90 vintage 19th century photographs that trace travel photography in Egypt over 3 decades beginning in 1850, will reveal many of the monuments and wonders of Egypt along with images of Egyptian village and street life. WT
10/4/95 - 1/7/96	CELEBRATING CALDER — 53 of Calder's bold and colorful sculptures, jewelry, paintings and tapestries from the extensive holdings of the Whitney Museum in New York will be included in this comprehensive exhibition of his work. WT

BALTIMORE

Evergreen House
Affiliate Institution: The Johns Hopkins University
4545 N. Charles St., **Baltimore, MD 21210**
TEL: 410-516-0341
HRS: 10-4 M-F, 1-4 Sa, S   HOL: LEG/HOL!
ADM: Y   ADULT: $5.00   CHILDREN: F (under 5)   STUDENTS: $2.50   SR CIT: $4.00
HDC/ACC: Y   PARKING: Y; Free and ample   GR/T: Y   GR/PH: call 401-516-0341
DT: Y   TIME: call for specifics   H/B: Y; 1850-1860 Evergreen House
PERM/COLL: FR: Impr, Post/Impr; EU: cer; OR: cer; JAP

Restored to its former beauty and reopened to the public in 1990, the 48 rooms of the magnificent Italianate Evergreen House (c. 1878), with classical revival additions, contain an outstanding collection of French Impressionist and Post-Impressionist works of art. PLEASE NOTE: All visitors to Evergreen House are obliged to tour the house with a docent. It is recommended that large groups call ahead to reserve. It should be noted that the last tour of the day begins at 3:00. **NOT TO BE\ MISSED:** Japanese netsuke and inro; the only gold bathroom in Baltimore.

MARYLAND

BALTIMORE

James E. Lewis Museum of Art
Affiliate Institution: Morgan State University
Carl Murphy Art Center, Coldspring Lane & Hillen Rd., **Baltimore, MD 21239**
TEL: 410-319-3030
HRS: 9-5 M-F; weekends by appt!   DAY CLOSED: Sa, S   HOL: LEG/HOL!
ADM: F   HDC/ACC: Y   GR/T: Y   GR/PH: call 410-319-3030
PERM/COLL: AF: sculp; AF/AM; ptgs, sculp 19-20; EU: ptgs, sculp 19-20

Both emerging and well established artists are featured in this museum along with traditional to contemporary African art. The museum is located in two sites, namely, the Carl Murphy Fine Arts Building on Cold Spring Lane which houses the permanent collection, and the changing exhibition gallery at the Morgan's Northwood Annex (south of the campus) in the rear of Northwood Shopping Plaza - upper level.

Peale Museum
225 Holliday St., **Baltimore, MD 21202**
TEL: 410-396-1149
HRS: 10-4 Tu-Sa; Noon-4 S; Till 5 pm during daylight savings time   DAY CLOSED: M   HOL: LEG/HOL!
F/DAY: Sa   ADM: Y   ADULT: $2.00   CHILDREN: $1.50 (4-18)   STUDENTS: $2.00   SR CIT: $2.00
HDC/ACC: Y; Very limited   PARKING: Y; Metered street parking and pay parking in the Harbor Park Garage on Lombard St., one block from the museum.   MUS/SH: Y
H/B: Y; First building built as a museum in U.S. by Rembrandt Peale, 1814   S/G: Y
PERM/COLL: REG/PHOT; SCULP; PTGS; 40 PTGS BY PEALE FAMILY ARTISTS

The Peale, erected in 1814, has the distinction of being the very first museum in the U.S. and is one of the 6 City Life Museums in Baltimore. Over 40 portraits by members of the Peale Family are on view in the ongoing exhibition entitled "The Peales, An American Family of Artists in Baltimore."

Walters Art Gallery
600 N. Charles St., **Baltimore, MD 21201**
TEL: 410-547-9000
HRS: 11-5 Tu-S   DAY CLOSED: M   HOL: 1/1, 7/4, THGV, 12/25
F/DAY: W   ADM: Y   ADULT: $3.00   CHILDREN: F (under 18)
HDC/ACC: Y; Wheelchair ramps at entrances, elevators to all levels
PARKING: Y; Ample parking on the street and nearby lots   MUS/SH: Y
REST/FAC: Y; Pavillion Cafe (11:30-4:30 Tu-S) call 410-727-2233   GR/T: Y   GR/PH: call 410-547-9000 ex 232
DT: Y   TIME: 12:30 W & 2:00 S   H/B: Y; 1904 building modeled after Ital. Ren. & Baroque palace designs
PERM/COLL: ANT; DEC/ART; SCULP; PTGS

The Walters, considered one of America's most distinguished art museums, features a broad-ranging collection spanning more than 5,000 years of artistic achievement from Ancient Egypt to Art Nouveau. Remarkable collections of ancient, medieval, Islamic & Byzantine art, 19th century paintings and sculpture, and Old Master paintings are housed within the walls of the magnificent and recently renovated original building and in a large modern wing as well. **NOT TO BE MISSED:** Hackerman House, a restored mansion adjacent to the main museum building, filled with oriental decorative arts treasures.

Walters Art Gallery - continued

ON EXHIBIT/95:

9/7/94 - 3/12/95   PRIVATE LIVES: 19TH-CENTURY AMERICAN GENRE PAINTING — On exhibit will be drawings that document daily life in mid-19th century America.

11/20/94 - 1/15/95   GAUGUIN AND THE SCHOOL OF PONT-AVEN — Featured will be paintings, works on paper, and polychrome wood sculptures by Gauguin and other of his famous 19th century art school comtemporaries. Two additional paintings by Gauguin, and another, "Breton Girl" by Roderic O'Connor will be on special loan to the Walters for this exhibition. ATR! PLEASE NOTE: Admission fees to this exhibit are as follows: $7.00 adults, $5.00 seniors on weekdays ($7.00 weekends), $5.00 students, children free under 12. Tickets may be purchased through TicketMaster, and at the Walters box office. Special group rates are available.   CAT   WT

12/4/94 - 3/26/95   BRIDGING EAST AND WEST: JAPANESE CERAMICS FROM THE KOZAN STUDIO — 45 ceramic works by master potter Miyagawa Kozan (1842-1916) will be on view in Hackerman House. Kozan, a Yokohama-based Meiji period artist who was born into a traditional family of potters in Kyoto, gained international acclaim for his innovative experiments with glazing techniques.   CAT

12/13/94 - 4/9/95   FROM RICKSHAWS TO LOCOMOTIVES: THE WORLD OF THE MEIJI EMPEROR — Prints that focus on the ceremonial aspects of the Emperor Meiji who reigned from 1868-1912 and saw Japan transformed from a stagnating feudal country into a modern industrial nation.

2/12 - 4/16/95   BRONZE: THE MEDIUM AND ITS MESSAGE — From the permanent collection 60 works from the ancient Greeks to 19th century European and Asian pieces will be featured in an exhibition that highlights the casting process, and compares the medium of bronze sculpture to those of wood, ivory or marble. Rounding out this exhibit will be a stylistic comparison of animal themes rendered in bronze.

5/21 - 7/16/95   UNEARTHLY ELEGANCE: BUDDHIST ART FROM THE GRISWOLD COLLECTION — Important images of Buddha of every period from Thailand will be joined in this exhibition by Thai paintings and Buddhist art from India, all culled from the gifts and bequests to the Museum by Alexander B. Griswold.

11/5/95 - 1/7/96   PANDORA'S BOX: WOMEN IN CLASSICAL GREECE — 125 objects of marble, bronze, terracotta and pottery on loan from 40 public and private collections in the U.S. and Europe will address the manner in which women were portrayed in 5th century Grecian art, myth and ritual.   CAT   WT

EASTON

Academy of the Arts

106 South Sts., **Easton, MD 21601**
TEL: 410-822-0455
HRS: 10-4 M-Sa; Till 9 W   DAY CLOSED: HOL: LEG/HOL! month of Aug
VOL/CONT: Y   ADM: F   HDC/ACC: Y; Ramp
PARKING: Y; Free with 2 hour limit during business hours; handicapped parking available in the rear of the Academy.
GR/T: Y   GR/PH: call 410-822-5997   H/B: Y; Housed in Old Schoolhouse
PERM/COLL: PTGS; SCULP; GR: 19-20; PHOT

Housed in two 18th century buildings, one of which was an old school house, the Academy's permanent collection contains an important group of original 19th & 20th century prints. This 35 year old facility serves the artistic needs of the community with a broad range of activities including concerts, exhibitions and educational workshops. **NOT TO BE MISSED:** "Slow Dancer" sculpture by Robert Cook, located in the Academy Courtyard; Works by James McNeil Whistler, Grant Wood, Bernard Buffet, Leonard Baskin, James Rosenquist, and others.

MARYLAND

Academy of the Arts - continued

ON EXHIBIT/95:

12/9/94 - 1/4/95	CHESTERTOWN ART LEAGUE
12/9/94 - 1/28/95	CONTEMPORARY FURNITURE EXHIBITION
1/6 - 1/26/95	ANNAPOLIS WATERCOLOR
2/3 - 2/27/95	TIDEWATER CAMERA CLUB
2/10 - 3/25/95	BRIDGING THE BAY
3/3 - 3/27/95	ARTIST INSTITUTE AND GALLERY COOPERATIVE
4/7 - 5/20/95	WORKING ARTISTS FORUM
6/2 - 6/26/95	MONTPELIER CULTURAL CENTER/RESIDENT ARTISTS
6/2 - 6/29/95	ACADEMY MEMBERS EXHIBITION
6/1 - 6/29/95	FRIDAY FOUR PORTRAIT GROUP

HAGERSTOWN

Washington County Museum of Fine Arts
City Park, Box 423, **Hagerstown, MD 21741**
TEL: 301-739-5727
HRS: 10-5 Tu-Sa; 1-6 S   DAY CLOSED: M   HOL: LEG/HOL!
VOL/CONT: Y   ADM: F
HDC/ACC: Y   PARKING: Y; Free and ample.   MUS/SH: Y   GR/T: Y   GR/PH: call 301-739-5727
PERM/COLL: AM: 19-20; REG; OM: 16-18; EU: ptgs 18-19; OR

In addition to the permanent collection of 19th century American art donated by the founders of the museum, Mr. & Mrs. William H. Singer, Jr., a bequest of 110 works from the collection of Dr. Albert Miller was recently presented to the museum. This gift includes wonderful examples of the works of Barbizon school artists, two rare etchings by Cezanne, a fine early painting by Whistler, and a number of works by members of the "Ashcan School." The museum is located in the northwest corner of the state just below the Pennsylvania border. **NOT TO BE MISSED:** "Sunset Hudson River" by Frederick Church; the new wing of the museum that more than doubles its size scheduled for completion 6/95

ON EXHIBIT/95:   Exhibitions from the permanent collection are thematically displayed on a rotating basis.

202

MASSACHUSETTS

AMHERST

Mead Art Museum
Affiliate Institution: Amherst College
Amherst, MA 01002
TEL: 413-542-2335
HRS: 10-4:30 M-F; 1-5 Sa, S (Sep-May); Call ahead to check inter-term hours
HOL: LEG/HOL!; ACAD!; MEM/DAY; LAB/DAY
ADM: F   HDC/ACC: Y   PARKING: Y   GR/T: Y   GR/PH: call 413-542-2335
PERM/COLL: AM: all media; EU: all media; DU: ptgs 17; PHOT; DEC/ART; AN/GRK: cer; FR: gr 19

Surrounded by the Pelham Hills in a picture perfect New England setting, the Mead Art Museum at Amherst College houses a rich collection of 12,000 art objects dating from antiquity to the present. PLEASE NOTE: Summer hours are 1-4 Tu-S. **NOT TO BE MISSED:** American paintings and watercolors including Eakins' "The Cowboy" & Homer's "Pumpkin Patch."

ON EXHIBIT/95:

1/13 - 2/28/95   RESCUERS OF THE HOLOCAUST: PORTRAITS BY GAY BLOCK — Photographs accompanied by oral histories of over 50 "Righteous Gentiles" who risked their lives in order to save European Jews during World War II.   BOOK   WT

3/11 - 5/7/95   AN AMERICAN CENTURY OF PHOTOGRAPHY: SELECTIONS FROM THE HALLMARK PHOTOGRAPHIC COLLECTION — The 200 photographic images selected from this important collection offer an original overview of the art history of modern American photography.

University Gallery, University of Massachusetts
Affiliate Institution: Fine Arts Center
University of Massachusetts, **Amherst, MA 01003**
TEL: 413-545-3670
HRS: Closed till 9/95 for renovations.
S/G: Y
PERM/COLL: AM: ptgs, drgs, phot 20

With a focus on the works of contemporary artists, this museum is best known as a showcase for the visual arts. It is but one of a five college complex of museums, making a trip to this area of New England a worthwhile venture for all art lovers. PLEASE NOTE: This facility will be closed for renovation until 9/95.

ANDOVER

Addison Gallery of American Art
Affiliate Institution: Phillips Academy
Andover, MA 01810
TEL: 508-749-4015
HRS: 10-5 Tu-Sa; 1-5 S   DAY CLOSED: M   HOL: LEG/HOL! AUG 1 through LAB/DAY
ADM: F
HDC/ACC: Y; Wheelchair access & elevator   PARKING: Y; Limited on street parking
GR/T: Y   GR/PH: 508-749-4016   DT: Y   TIME: upon request
PERM/COLL: AM: ptgs, sculp, phot, works on paper 17-20

MASSACHUSETTS

Addison Gallery of American Art - continued

Since its inception in 1930, the Addison Gallery has been devoted exclusively to American art. The original benefactor, Thomas Cochran, donated both the core collection and the neo-classic building designed by noted architect Charles Platt. With a mature collection of more than 11,000 works, featuring major holdings from nearly every period of American art history, a visit to this museum should be high on every art lover's list. **NOT TO BE MISSED:** Marble fountain in Gallery rotunda by Paul Manship; "West Wind" by Winslow Homer

ON EXHIBIT/95:

9/1/94 - 1/15/95	1/4" SCALE MODELS OF AMERICAN SAILING SHIPS
9/25/94 - 1/8/95	PHILIP GUSTON'S POEM-PICTURES — During the last decade of his life (1970-80) Guston collaborated with writers and poets integrating their literary pieces into his graphics thereby producing works that related a sense of disunity, disorder and disintegration that he felt colored life in the late 20th century. These feelings may be assessed in the 70 drawings and 5 illustrated books on view in this exhibition. CAT WT
9/25/94 - 1/8/95	WITHIN THIS GARDEN: PHOTOGRAPHS BY RUTH THORNE-THOMSEN WT
1/21 - 7/31/95	MASTERWORKS FROM THE ADDISON COLLECTION
1/21 - 3/12/95	PRESENCE OF THE PAST: DECORATIVE ARTS FROM THE ADDISON COLLECTION
1/14 - 3/26/95	INDUSTRIAL REVOLUTION: PHOTOGRAPHIC IMAGES AND IDEAS
4/1 - 7/31/95	ROBERT FRANK - THE AMERICANS WT
4/1 - 7/31/95	ALUMNI COLLECTORS: STEPHEN SHERRIL'71 AND ALLAN STONE '50

BOSTON

Boston Athenaeum

10 1/2 Beacon St., **Boston, MA 02108**
TEL: 617-227-0270
HRS: 9-5:30 M-F (June-Aug); 9-5:30 M-F, 9-4 Sa (Sep-May)   DAY CLOSED: S   HOL: LEG/HOL!
ADM: F HDC/ACC: Y   MUS/SH: Y   GR/T: Y   GR/PH: 3:00 Tu & T call 617-227-0270
H/B: Y; National Historic Landmark Building
PERM/COLL: AM: ptgs, sculp, gr 19

The Athenaeum, one of the oldest independent libraries in America, features an art gallery established in 1827. Most of the Athenaeum building is closed to the public EXCEPT for the 1st & 2nd floors of the building (including the Gallery). In order to gain access to many of the most interesting parts of the building, including those items in the "do not miss" column, free tours are available on Tu & T at 3pm. Reservations must be made at least 24 hours in advance by calling the Circulation Desk, 617-227-8112. **NOT TO BE MISSED:** George Washington's private library; 2 Gilbert Stuart portraits; Houdon's busts of Benjamin Franklin, George Washington, and Lafayette from the Montecello home of Thomas Jefferson.

ON EXHIBIT/95:

11/21/94 - 1/6/95	ARTHUR J. STONE (1847-1938) DESIGNER AND MASTER SILVERSMITH — Tableware, presentation silver and ecclesiastical commissions will be seen in the first retrospective of Stone's works. CAT WT
1 - 3/95	BOSTON LIBRARY SOCIETY — The history of the Boston Library Society and its place within the Federal period is the focus of this exhibition.

Boston Athenaeum - continued

4 - 5/95	SOCIETY OF THE CINCINNATI EXHIBITION — On view will be historical documents, manuscripts and rare books relating to the American Revolution.
6 - 7/95	JAPANESE BOOKS (TENT!) — Rare Japanese books from a private collection.
8/95	GALLERY CLOSED
9 - 11/95	BOSTON JEWISH CULTURE — Boston's Jewish community and cultural history will be highlighted in this exhibition.

BOSTON

Boston Public Library

Copley Square, **Boston, MA 02117**
TEL: 617-536-5400
HRS: 9-9 M-T; 9-5 F-Sa   DAY CLOSED: S   HOL: LEG/HOL!
ADM: F   HDC/ACC: Y; General library only (Boylston St.); Also elevators, restrooms
GR/T: Y   GR/PH: 617-536-5400 ex 212 or 213   DT: Y   TIME: 2:30 M; 6:30 Tu & W; 11:00 T & Sa
H/B: Y; Renaissance "Palace" designed in 1895 by Charles Follen McKim
PERM/COLL: AM: ptgs, sculp; FR: gr 18-19; BRIT: gr 18-19; OM: gr, drgs; AM: phot 19, gr 19-20; GER: gr; ARCH/DRGS

Architecturally a blend of the old and the new, the building that houses the Boston Public Library has a facade planned and decorated by sculptor Augustus Saint-Gaudens which is complemented by a wing designed in 1973 by Philip Johnson. **NOT TO BE MISSED:** Facade of building by Augustus Saint-Gaudens; 1,500 lb. bronze entrance doors by Daniel Chester French

ON EXHIBIT/95:	There are a multitude of changing exhibitions throughout the year in the many galleries of both buildings. Call for current information.

Boston University Art Gallery

855 Commonwealth Ave., **Boston, MA 02215**
TEL: 617-353-3329
HRS: 10-4 M-F; 1-5 Sa, S Mid-Sep-mid-Dec & mid-Jan-mid-May   HOL: 12/25
ADM: F   PARKING: Y; On-street metered parking; pay parking lot nearby

Several shows in addition to student exhibitions are mounted annually in this 35 year old university gallery which seeks to promote under-recognized sectors of the art world including works by a variety of ethnic artists, women artists, and those unschooled in the traditional academic system. Additional emphasis is placed on the promotion of 20th century figurative art.

ON EXHIBIT/95:

1/21 - 2/26/95	VISIONS OF MODERNITY: PHOTOGRAPHS FROM THE PERUVIAN ANDES, 1900-1930 — An exhibition of early 20th-century photographs of South America that includes images by Martin Chambi and the Vargas Brothers.
3/4 - 4/9/95	DRAWINGS BY VISUAL ARTS ALUMNI — A juried exhibition that celebrates the key role of drawing in contemporary studio art.
mid-4 - mid-5/95	STUDENT ART EXHIBITIONS

MASSACHUSETTS

BOSTON

The Institute of Contemporary Art
955 Boylston St., **Boston, MA 02115**
TEL: 617-266-5151
HRS: Noon-9 W & T; Noon-5 F-S   DAY CLOSED: M, Tu
F/DAY: 5-9 T   ADM: Y   ADULT: $5.00 CHILDREN: $2.00   STUDENTS: $3.00   SR CIT: $2.00
HDC/ACC: Y   PARKING: Y: Several commercial lots nearby   MUS/SH: Y
GR/T: Y   GR/PH: 617-266-5151 (education dept)
PERM/COLL: No permanent collection

Originally affiliated with the Modern Museum in New York, the ICA has the distinction of being the oldest institution in the world dedicated to the presentation of contemporary art. Through the years the ICA has been a leader in introducing such "unknown" artists as Braque, Kokoshka, Munch and others who have changed the course of art history.

ON EXHIBIT/95:

11/2/94 - 1/9/95	TWO X IMMORTAL: ELVIS AND MARILYN — Imagesof these two American icons in all media by 75 important international artists will be on view. BOOK WT
1/25 - 4/9/95	BURNT WHOLE: 25 CONTEMPORARY ARTISTS REFLECT THE HOLOCAUST — Works by 25 international artists, all of whom were born after World War II, will offer their personal creative interpretations of the Holocaust utilizing a wide variety of media. WT
5/9 - 7/9/95	RACHEL WHITEREAD: WORKS (TENT!) — Ten large sculptures that includes a room-sized white plaster box cast (and reassembled) from a living room in London will be on view in the first solo exhibition in America for Whiteread, 1993 winner of the Turner Prize in England.

Isabella Stewart Gardner Museum
280 The Fenway, **Boston, MA 02115**
TEL: 617-566-1401
HRS: 11-5 Tu-S   DAY CLOSED: M   HOL: LEG/HOL!
ADM: Y   ADULT: $6.00   CHILDREN: $3.00 (12-17)   STUDENTS: $5.00   SR CIT: $5.00
HDC/ACC: Y; Street level access & elevator to 2nd & 3rd floor art galleries
PARKING: Y; Street parking plus garage two blocks away on Museum Road   MUS/SH: Y
REST/FAC: Y; Cafe 11:30-3 Tu-F, 11:30-4 Sa, S   GR/T: Y   GR/PH: call 617-566-1401   H/B: Y   S/G: Y
PERM/COLL: PTGS; SCULP; DEC/ART; GR; OM

Located in the former home of Isabella Stewart Gardner, the collection reflects her zest for amassing this most exceptional and varied personal art treasure trove. PLEASE NOTE: The admission fee for college students with current I.D. is $3.00 on Wed. Children under 12 admitted free of charge. **NOT TO BE MISSED:** Rembrandt's "Self Portrait;" Italian Renaissance works of art

ON EXHIBIT/95:

1/13 - 6/4/95	THE IMPRESSIONISM OF DENNIS BUNKER MILLER: THE ARTIST AND HIS CIRCLE — In collaboration with a major retrospective of Bunker's works at the Museum of Fine Arts in Boston, this complementary exhibition will examine the influence of such notable artists as Sargent, Thayer and Dewing on his work as well as the role played by his patron, Mrs. Gardner.
9/15 - 12/31/95	SCULPTURE BY JUAN MUNOZ — A combination of architectural and figurative elements will be seen in the sculptures of this Spanish-born internationally recognized artist whose works will be on exhibit in Boston for the first time.

206

MASSACHUSETTS

BOSTON

Museum of Fine Arts
465 Huntington Ave., **Boston, MA 02115**
TEL: 617-267-9300
HRS: 10-4:45 Tu; 10-9:45 W; 10-4:45 T-S; (Also 5pm - 9:45 T & F West Wing only) DAY CLOSED: M
HOL: 1/1, THGV, 12/24, 12/25
F/DAY: 4-9:45 W   ADM: Y   ADULT: $8.00   CHILDREN: $3.50 (6-17)   STUDENTS: $6.00   SR CIT: $6.00
HDC/ACC: Y; Completely wheelchair accessible   PARKING: Y; $3.50 first hour, $1.50 every half hour following
in garage on Museum Rd. across from West Wing entrance.   MUS/SH: Y
REST/FAC: Y; Cafe, Restaurant & Cafeteria   GR/T: Y   GR/PH: call 617-267-9300 ex 368
DT: Y   TIME: Tu-F for 20 people or more; no summer
PERM/COLL: AN/GRK; AN/R; AN/EGT; EU: om/ptgs; FR: Impr, post/Impr; AM: ptgs 18-20; OR: cer

A world class collection of fine art with masterpieces from every continent is yours to enjoy at this great Boston museum. Divided between two buildings the collection is housed both in the original (1918) Evans Wing with its John Singer Sargent mural decorations above the Rotunda, and the dramatic West Wing (1981) designed by I. M. Pei. PLEASE NOTE: There is a "pay as you wish" policy from 4 pm-9:45 pm on Wed. Also, portable benches that can be carried into the galleries are available free of charge near the information desk. **NOT TO BE MISSED:** Egyptian Pectoral believed to have decorated a royal sarcophagus of the Second Intermediate Period (1784 - 1570 B.C.), part of the museum's renowned permanent collection of Egyptian art.

ON EXHIBIT/95:

7/27/94 - 7/25/95	THE TASTE FOR LUXURY: ENGLISH FURNITURE, SILVER, AND CERAMICS 1690-1790 — Masterpieces of English silver, soft-paste porcelain and English furniture will trace the stylistic changes in the decorative arts during the 18th century in England.
10/21/94 - 3/12/95	SWEET DREAMS: BEDCOVERS AND BED CLOTHES FROM THE COLLECTION — Asian, Western, Mediterranean and contemporary designer approaches to the ritual of the bed will be seen in an exhibition of quilts, coverlets, lingerie, sleeping caps and the like selected from the permanent collection.
10/36/94 - 2/12/95	PRINTED ALLEGORIES: DURER TO PICASSO — Prints from the 16th to the early 20th century that deal with allegorical subject matter will be selected for viewing from the MFA permanent collection. Included will be Durer's "Knight, Death and the Devil" and Picasso's "Minotauromachia."
12/10/94 - 2/19/95	WILLEM DE KOONING: THE HIRSHHORN MUSEUM COLLECTION — In honor of the artist's 90th birthday in April, 1994, 50 works spanning de Kooning's career (1939-1985) will be on loan from the comprehensive Hirshhorn collection. CAT WT
9/14/94 - 1/1/95	GRAND ILLUSIONS: FOUR CENTURIES OF STILL LIFE PAINTING — Masterpieces of European and American paintings from the 16th through the 20th centuries selected from the permanent collection and augmented by loans from friends of the MFA will document the origins, emergence and full flowering of the still life genre.
1/13 - 6/4/95	DANNIS MILLER BUNKER: AMERICAN IMPRESSIONIST — On exhibit in the first comprehensive exhibition of his work will be 50 examples of this 19th century Boston artist whose paintings were influential to an entire generation of artists also working in Boston.
2/8 - 5/7/95	EMIL NOLDE: THE PAINTER'S PRINTS — In the first major U.S. exhibition of his works, 150 etchings, woodcuts and lithographs by this renowned German artist will be on exhibit.

MASSACHUSETTS

Museum of Fine Arts - continued

2/8 - 6/7/95	NOLDE WATERCOLORS IN AMERICA — As a complement to the above exhibition, 40 of Nolde's outstanding watercolors from American private and public collections will be on display.
3/11 - 7/2/95	DEGREES OF ABSTRACTION: FROM MORRIS LOUIS TO ROBERT MAPPLE-THORPE — From the permanent collection a selection of works that "play" abstract artworks against more representational examples.
6/7 - 8/27/95	JOHN SINGLETON COPLEY'S AMERICA — Featured in this exhibition will be 50 of Copley's finest portraits accompanied by 10 pastels and miniatures from the MFA permanent collection.
ONGOING	NUBIA: ANCIENT KINDOMS OF AFRICA — 500 objects incuding stone sculptures, gold jewelry, household articles, clothing and tools that form this comprehensive permanent collection of Nubian art will be on view indefinitely. This collection is considered the finest of its kind in the world. CAT

BOSTON

Museum of the National Center of Afro-American Artists
300 Walnut Ave., **Boston, MA 02119**
TEL: 617-442-8014
HRS: 1-6 Daily (July-Aug); 1-5 Tu-Sa (Sep-June)
ADM: Y   ADULT: $1.25   CHILDREN: STUDENTS: $0.50   SR CIT: $0.50
H/B: Y; 19th C
PERM/COLL: AF/AM: ptgs; sculp; GR

Art by African-American artists is highlighted along with art from the African continent itself.

BROCKTON

Fuller Museum of Art
455 Oak St., **Brockton, MA 02401**
TEL: 508-588-6000
HRS: Noon-5 Tu-S   DAY CLOSED: M   HOL: 1/1, 7/4, LAB/DAY, THGV, 12/25
ADM: F
HDC/ACC: Y; Fully accessible   PARKING: Y: Free   MUS/SH: Y   REST/FAC: Y; Cafe 11:30 - 2 Tu-F
DT: Y   S/G: Y
PERM/COLL: AM: 19-20; CONT: reg

A park-like setting surrounded by the beauty of nature is the ideal site for this charming museum that features art by artists of New England with emphasis on contemporary arts and cultural diversity.

ON EXHIBIT/95:

Many temporary exhibitions usually culled from the more than 3,000 works in the permanent collection are presented annually!

MASSACHUSETTS

CAMBRIDGE

Arthur M. Sackler Museum
Affiliate Institution: Harvard University
485 Broadway, **Cambridge, MA 02138**
TEL: 617-495-9400
HRS: 10-5 Daily   HOL: LEG/HOL!
F/DAY: Sa am   ADM: Y   ADULT: $5.00   CHILDREN: F (under 18)   STUDENTS: $3.00   SR CIT: $4.00
HDC/ACC: Y; Ramp at front and elevators to all floors
PARKING: Y; $5.00 3-hour valet parking for the museums at Harvard Inn, 1201 Mass. Ave.   MUS/SH: Y
GR/T: Y   GR/PH: call 617-496-8576 to reserve   DT: Y   TIME: Noon M-F
PERM/COLL: AN/ISLAMIC; AN/OR; NAT/AM

Opened in 1985, the building and its superb collection of Ancient, Asian, and Islamic art were all the generous gift of the late Dr. Arthur M. Sackler, noted research physician, medical publisher, and art collector. **NOT TO BE MISSED:** World's finest collections of ancient Chinese jades; Korean ceramics; Japanese woodblock prints; Persian miniatures

ON EXHIBIT/95:

THROUGH 5/21/95   IMPRESSIONS OF MESOPOTAMIA: SEALS FROM THE ANCIENT NEAR EAST — Ancient Near Eastern seals that span over 3,000 years of Mesopotamian history.

2/4 - 4/9/95   FRENCH DRAWINGS OF THE SIXTEENTH CENTURY FROM THE ECOLE des BEAUX-ARTS, PARIS — Virtually every leading artist of the period will be represented in the first comprehensive exhibition in the U.S. devoted to drawings created during the French Renaissance.   CAT   WT

Busch-Reisinger Museum
Affiliate Institution: Harvard University
32 Quincy St., **Cambridge, MA 02138**
TEL: 617-495-9400
HRS: 10-5 Daily   DAY CLOSED: HOL: LEG/HOL!
F/DAY: Sa am   ADM: Y   ADULT: $5.00 CHILDREN: F (under 18)   STUDENTS: $3.00   SR CIT: $4.00
HDC/ACC: Y; Ramp at front and elevators to all floors
PARKING: Y; $5.00 3-hour valet parking for the museums at Harvard Inn, 1201 Mass. Ave.   MUS/SH: Y
GR/T: Y   GR/PH: 617-495-9400   DT: Y   TIME: 2:00 M-F
PERM/COLL: GER: ptgs, sculp 20; GR; PTGS; DEC/ART; CER 18; MED/SCULP; REN/SCULP

Founded in 1901 with a collection of plaster casts of Germanic sculpture and architectural monuments, the Busch-Reisinger also acquired modern "degenerate" art purged from major German museums by the Nazis. All of this has been enriched over the years with gifts from artists and designers associated with the famous Bauhaus School including the archives of artist Lyonel Feininger, and architect Walter Gropius. **NOT TO BE MISSED:** Outstanding collection of German Expressionist art

ON EXHIBIT/95:

8/13/94 - 2/5/95   NORTHERN EUROPEAN ART FROM 1450-1550 — 35 important works ranging from late medieval sculpture to mannerist paintings will be featured in a reinstallation of these works from the permanent collection.

OPENING 3/11/95   BETWEEN CINEMA AND A HARD PLACE — The fragmentation of the perception of landscapes and pastoral scenes that roll rapidly across 23 various sized and modified video monitors will be experienced when viewing this unique installation.

209

MASSACHUSETTS

CAMBRIDGE

Fogg Art Museum
Affiliate Institution: Harvard University
32 Quincy St., **Cambridge, MA 02138**
TEL: 617-495-9400
HRS: 10-5 Daily   DAY CLOSED: HOL: LEG/HOL!
F/DAY: Sa am   ADM: Y   ADULT: $5.00   CHILDREN: F (under 18)   STUDENTS: $3.00   SR CIT: $4.00
HDC/ACC: Y; Ramp at front and elevators to all floors
PARKING: Y; $5.00 3-hour valet parking for the museums at Harvard Inn, 1201 Mass. Ave.
GR/T: Y   GR/PH: 617-496-8576   DT: Y   TIME: 11 M-F
PERM/COLL: EU: ptgs, sculp, dec/art; AM: ptgs, sculp, dec/art; GR; PHOT; DRGS

The Fogg, the largest university art museum in America, with one of the world's greatest collections, contains both European and American masterpieces from the Middle Ages to the present. **NOT TO BE MISSED:** The Maurice Wertheim Collection containing many of the finest Impressionist and Post-Impressionist paintings, sculptures, and drawings in the world.

ON EXHIBIT/95:

THROUGH 7/95	SHADES OF SIGNIFICANCE: TONAL VALUES IN ABSTRACT ART — Through the monochromatic palettes of such artists as Josef Albers, Jasper Johns, Franz Kline, Louise Nevelson, Mark Rothko and other notable talents, an examination of the multifaceted nature of abstraction will be addressed.
10/29/94 - 1/8/95	RARE PRINTS — Examples of rare monotypes, working proofs, incomplete and never printed works by a wide variety of masters from Canaletto, Delacroix, and Manet, to Dine and LeWitt will be on view in this exhibition.
11/19/94 - 1/29/95	ACADEMIC DRAWINGS — 19 drawings by turn-of-the-century American painter Oscar Fehrer will be displayed along with examples by such historic masters as Durer, Pontormo, Greuze, Ingres, Eakins and others in order to compare and contrast the development of the goals and achievements of academic drawing.
2/18 - 4/30/95	EDMONIA LEWIS — Lewis' unique role as not only the first professional African-American sculptor but also as as a female African-American/Native American artist will be seen in 30-40 of her sculptures, paintings, drawings, photographs and prints selected for this exhibition.
4/22 - 7/2/95	ACQUISITIONS FROM THE DEKNATEL PURCHASE FUND — On exhibit will be 19th & 20th century artworks that will celebrate 20 years of collecting through a purchase fund established in 1974 to honor former Harvard University professor, Frederick B. Deknatel, a specialist in this area of art.
5/20 - 7/30/95	MUNCH IN COLOR — Color prints of Norwegian artist, Edvard Munch that explore his experiments with graphic techniques, 19th century color theories, color symbolism and occult theories of auric color will be featured in this exhibition.

MIT-List Visual Arts Center
20 Ames Sr., Wiesner Bldg., **Cambridge, MA 02139**
TEL: 617-253-4680
HRS: Noon-6 Tu, T, F; Noon-8 W; 1-5 Sa, S   DAY CLOSED: M   HOL: LEG/HOL!
ADM: F
HDC/ACC: Y   PARKING: Y; Corner of Main & Ames Sts.   GR/T: Y   GR/PH: call 617-253-4680
DT: Y   TIME: call for information
PERM/COLL: SCULP; PTGS; PHOT; DRGS; WORKS ON PAPER

MIT-List Visual Arts Center - continued

Approximately 12 exhibitions are mounted annually in MIT's Wiesner Building designed by the internationally known architect I. M. Pei, a graduate of the MIT School of Architecture. **NOT TO BE MISSED:** Sculpture designed and utilized as furniture for public seating in the museum by visual artist Scott Burton

ON EXHIBIT/95:

1/21 - 3/26/95   THE MASCULINE MASQUERADE — The breadth of the masculine image as both a personal narrative and social phemonenon will be addressed in this exhibition which explores the issues of the military and the nature of aggression, heterosexuality and homosexuality, male fantasy and eroticism, the father & son relationship, the American boyhood experience, athletics, capitalism or white collar authority and the cultural differences surrounding Asian and African-American male identity.   BOOK

4/15 - 6/25/95   LEON GOLUB AND NANCY SPERO: WAR AND MEMORY — The themes of power and vulnerability will be seen in expressionistic figurative works by artists Golub and Spero, who have been married to each other for over 40 years.   WT

CHESTNUT HILL

Boston College

140 Commonwealth Ave., **Chestnut Hill, MA 02167**
TEL: 617-552-2378
HRS: 11-4 M-F; Noon-5 Sa, S (Sep-May); 11-3 M-F (June-Aug)   HOL: LEG/HOL!
ADM: F
HDC/ACC: Y   PARKING: Y; 1 hour parking on Commonwealth Ave.; in lower campus garage on weekends & as available on weekdays (call 617-552-8587 for availability)   MUS/SH: Y   REST/FAC: Y; On campus   H/B: Y
PERM/COLL: IT: ptgs 16 & 17; AM: ptgs; JAP: gr; MED & BAROQUE TAPESTRIES 15-17

The Renovation and expansion of two floors of Devlin Hall, the Neo-Gothic building that houses the museum, is now complete. Permanent collection works are displayed on one floor while the other is used for special exhibitions. **NOT TO BE MISSED:** "Madonna with Christ Child & John the Baptist" by Ghirlandaio, 1503-1577)

ON EXHIBIT/95:

2/8 - 5/21/95   MEMORY IN THE MIDDLE AGES — Planned to coincide with the international meeting of the Medieval Academy of America in Boston (3/30-4/1/95) this exhibition will be the first to explore how memory played an integral part in the formulation of images and thoughts throughout the middle ages and in the new Medieval movements in New England during the 19th century.   CAT

6/9 - 9/17/95   INSPIRED BY NATURE: CONTEMPORARY VISIONS — Works by local artists

10/6 - 12/3/95   PROTECTION, POWER AND DISPLAY: SHIELDS OF INDONESIA AND THE PACIFIC BASIN

MASSACHUSETTS

CONCORD

Concord Art Association
37 Lexington Rd., **Concord, MA 01742**
TEL: 508-369-2578
HRS: 10-4:30 Tu-Sa; 2-4:30 S (during exhibitions only)   DAY CLOSED: M
HOL: LEG/HOL!; Last 2 weeks AUG.; Last week DEC.   ADM: F
HDC/ACC: Y   PARKING: Y; Free street parking   MUS/SH: Y   H/B: Y; Housed in building dated 1720   S/G: Y
PERM/COLL: AM: ptgs, sculp, gr, dec/art

Historic fine art is appropriately featured within the walls of this historic (1720) building. The beautiful gardens are perfect for a bag lunch picnic during the warm weather months. **NOT TO BE MISSED:** Ask to see the secret room within the building which was formerly part of the underground railway.

ON EXHIBIT/95:   Rotating exhibits of fine art and crafts are mounted on a monthly basis.

COTUIT

Cahoon Museum of American Art
4676 Falsmouth Rd., **Cotuit, MA 02635**
TEL: 508-428-7581
HRS: 10-4 Tu-Sa   DAY CLOSED: M, Tu   HOL: LEG/HOL!
VOL/CONT: Y   ADM: F   HDC/ACC: Y; Limited to first floor only   PARKING: Y; Free
MUS/SH: Y   H/B: Y; 1775 Former Cape Cod Colonial Tavern
PERM/COLL: AM: ptgs 19-20; CONT/PRIM

Art by the donor artists of this facility, Ralph and Martha Cahoon, is shown along with works by prominent American Luminists and Impressionists. Located in a restored 1775 Colonial tavern on Cape Cod, the museum is approximately 9 miles west of Hyannis. **NOT TO BE MISSED:** Gallery of marine paintings

ON EXHIBIT/95:

5/19 - 7/1/95	BAA'S RELIEF — Soft sculpture and applique by Salley Mavor will be shown with original illustrations from Ms. Mavor's children's book entitled "Mary Had a Little Lamb"
6/9 - 9/30/95	HOOKED ON THE SEA — Antique and vintage hooked rugs will be on display along with an international juried exhibition of contemporary hooked rugs.
11/17/94 - 1/30/95	NINTH ANNUAL HOLIDAY EXHIBITION Recent paintings by Jan Collins Selman

The Cahoon Museum's permanent collection of American paintings is on display between special exhibitions.

DENNIS

Cape Museum of Fine Arts
Rte. 6A, **Dennis, MA 02638**
TEL: 508-385-4477
HRS: 10-5 Tu-Sa; 1-5 S; call for evening hours of operation   DAY CLOSED: M   HOL: LEG/HOL!
ADM: Y   ADULT: $2.00   CHILDREN: F   SR CIT: $2.00
HDC/ACC: Y   PARKING: Y; Free and ample parking   MUS/SH: Y   GR/T: Y   GR/PH: call 508-385-4477
DT: Y   TIME: !
PERM/COLL: REG

Art by outstanding Cape Cod artists from 1900 to the present is the focus of this rapidly growing permanent collection which is housed in the restored former summer home of the family of Davenport West, one of the original benefactors of this institution.

212

DUXBURY

Art Complex Museum
189 Alden St., **Duxbury, MA 02331**
TEL: 617-934-6634
HRS: 1-4 W-S   DAY CLOSED: M, Tu   HOL: LEG/HOL!
ADM: F   HDC/ACC: Y; Except for restrooms   PARKING: Y; Free   GR/T: Y   GR/PH: call 617-934-6634   S/G: Y
PERM/COLL: OR: ptgs; EU: ptgs; AM: ptgs; gr

In a magnificent sylvan setting that complements the naturalistic wooden structure of the building, the Art Complex houses a remarkable core collection of works on paper that includes Rembrandt's "The Descent from the Cross by Torchlight." An authentic Japanese Tea House complete with tea presentations in the summer months is another unique feature of this fine institution. The museum is located on the eastern coast of Massachusetts just above Cape Cod. **NOT TO BE MISSED:** Shaker furniture; "Lake Tahoe" by William Marple; "American" by Thomas Hill.

ON EXHIBIT/95:

11/4/94 - 1/22/95	SHARED TREASURES OF NEW ENGLAND — Works on loan from Duxbury collectors will be joined by art and objects from the permanent collection of the museum.
2/3 - 4/23/95	DUXBURY ART ASSOCIATION — Annual winter juried show
2/3 - 4/23/95	PORTRAITS BY WOMEN ARTISTS — Works from the permanent collection and on-loan from local collections.
5/5 - 7/9/95	NEW ENGLAND WATERCOLOR SOCIETY — Members show
5/5 - 7/9/95	ONWARD/NORMAN LaLIBERTE — Paintings, sculpture and other recent works of note and whimsey.
6/16 - 10/15/95	ENVIRONMENTAL ARTS AT THE ART COMPLEX MUSEUM — A juried exhibition of sculpture.
7/21 - 10/22/95	ART BY CHOICE — Selected South Shore artists.
11/3/95 - 1/7/96	BOSTON PRINTMAKERS/IN MEMORY OF SYLVIA — A members show dedicated to the memory of Sylvia Rantz, 1927-1994.

FITCHBURG

Fitchburg Art Museum
185 Elm St., **Fitchburg, MA 01420**
TEL: 508-345-4207
HRS: 11-4:00 Tu-Sa; 1-4 S   DAY CLOSED: M   HOL: LEG/HOL!
ADM: Y   ADULT: $3.00   CHILDREN: F (under 18)   SR CIT: $2.00
HDC/ACC: Y; 90% handicapped accessible   PARKING: Y; Free on-site parking   MUS/SH: Y   S/G: Y
PERM/COLL: AM: ptgs, gr; EU: ptgs, gr; CER; DEC/ART; SCULP;P/COL; AN/GRK; AN/R; AS; OR; ANT

Eleanor Norcross, a Fitchburg artist who lived and painted in Paris for 40 years became impressed with the number and quality of small museums that she visited in the rural areas of northern France. This led to the bequest of her collection and personal papers in 1925 to her native city of Fitchburg and marked the beginning of what is now a 40,000 square foot block-long museum complex. The museum is located in north central Massachusetts near the New Hampshire border. **NOT TO BE MISSED:** "Sarah Clayton" by Joseph Wright of Derby, 1770.

213

MASSACHUSETTS

Fitchburg Art Museum - continued

ON EXHIBIT/95:

11/20/94 - 1/15/95	EGYPTIAN TOMB PAINTINGS BY JOSEPH LINDON SMITH — Colorful true to scale replicas of paintings found in ancient Egyptian tombs will provide the viewer with a rare glimpse into the life and beliefs of the historical past in Egypt.
11/20/94 - 3/26/95	TRAINS — On exhibit will be models, paintings, photographs and memorabilia.
11/20/94 - 1/15/95	LIKE US: PRIMATE PORTRAITS BY ROBIN SCHWARTZ — In this photographic exhibition of images of primates residing in private homes, Schwartz has captured both young and old primates in a variety of activities that mimic the charcteristics and habits of the humans with whom they live; hence, having them appear to be much "Like Us."
1/29 - 3/26/95	STONE OFFERINGS: A PHOTOGRAPHIC INSTALLATION BY BRUCE T. MARTIN — Black and white photographs combined with color are used in this multi-image installation based on Mayan basic visual symbols to indicate how Mayan stone icons which reinforced and supported their ancient views of reality are in many ways related to how we use photographs today to understand our lives.
4/9 - 6/11/95	HISTORICAL TREASURES: OBJECTS FROM REGIONAL HISTORICAL SOCIETIES (TENT! title) — Rarely seen treasures from area historical societies will be on exhibit.
4/9 - 6/11/95	STRANGE AND AWKWARD BEAUTY: PHOTOGRAPHS OF DOMESTICATED ANIMALS BY FRANK NOELKER (TENT! title)
7/9 - 9/3/95	THE 60TH REGIONAL SHOW — Annual juried exhibition to encourage and discover regional creative talent .

FRAMINGHAM

Danforth Museum of Art

123 Union Ave., **Framingham, MA 01701**
TEL: 508-620-0050
HRS: Noon-5 W-S   DAY CLOSED: M, Tu   HOL: LEG/HOL!
ADM: Y   ADULT: $3.00   CHILDREN: F (under 12)   STUDENTS: $2.00   SR CIT: $2.00
HDC/ACC: Y   PARKING: Y; Free   MUS/SH: Y   GR/T: Y   GR/PH: call 617-620-0050
DT: Y   TIME: 1:00 W (Sep-May)
PERM/COLL: PTGS; SCULP; DRGS; PHOT; GR

The Danforth, a museum that prides itself on being known as a community museum with a national reputation, offers 19th & 20th century American and European art as the main feature of its permanent collection. **NOT TO BE MISSED:** 19th & 20th century American works with a special focus on the works of New England artists

ON EXHIBIT/95:

11/2/94 - 1/29/95	THE LITHOGRAPHS OF OSKAR KOKOSCHKA AND ALFRED KUBIN — Featured will be works from the permanent collection that express the narrative power of these two artists.
11/9/94 - 2/12/95	REFLECTIONS OF SPAIN: SPANISH ART FROM 1960-1980 — The artistic diversity of artists active in Spain during the 60's to the 80's will be seen in the lithographs, etchings, silkscreen prints, paintings and drawings on view in this exhibition.
2/8 - 4/23/95	THERE ON THE TABLE: AMERICAN STILL LIFE PAINTING — From classical realism to early abstraction, the still life paintings of the late 19th to mid-20th century in this exhibition will attest to the endless and fertile arena of the use of this subject in art.

WT

214

Danforth Museum of Art - continued

3/1 - 4/30/95   DENYS WORTMAN: CARTOONIST AND ARTIST, AN AMERICAN DAUMIER — Paintings and drawings that relate the picture of his life and times will be seen in this exhibition of works by Wortman, a nationally syndicated cartoonist of the early 20th century who was the first and only cartoonist of be named a member of the National Academy of Art and Design.

6/4 - 7/30/95   JOSH SIMPSON NEW WORK, NEW WORLDS — An exhibition of paperweights and vessels by Simpson, a nationally known artist from western Massachusetts.

6/22 - 6/25/95   DANFORTH CRAFT FESTIVAL — 90 of the nation's finest craft artists will be exhibiting and selling their works.

GLOUCESTER

Cape Ann Historical Association
27 Pleasant St., **Gloucester, MA 01930**
TEL: 617-283-0455
HRS: 10-5 Tu-Sa   DAY CLOSED: S, M   HOL: LEG/HOL!; FEB
ADM: Y   ADULT: $3.50   CHILDREN: F (under 6)   STUDENTS: $2.00   SR CIT: $3.00
HDC/ACC: Y; Wheelchairs available
PARKING: Y; In the lot adjacent to the museum and in the metered public lot across Pleasant St. from the museum.
MUS/SH: Y   GR/T: Y   GR/PH: call 617-283-0455   H/B: Y; 1804 Federal period home of Captain Elias Davis is part of museum
PERM/COLL: FITZ HUGH LANE: ptgs; AM: ptgs, sculp, DEC/ART 19-20; MARITIME COLL

Within the walls of this most charming New England treasure of a museum is the largest collection of paintings (39), drawings (100), and lithographs by the great American artist, Fitz Hugh Lane. A walking tour of the town will take the visitor past many charming small art studios & galleries that have a wonderful view of the harbor as does the Fitz Hugh Lane House built here in 1849. Be sure to see the famous Fisherman's Monument overlooking Gloucester Harbor. **NOT TO BE MISSED:** The only known watercolor in existence by Fitz Hugh Lane

ON EXHIBIT/95:
6/14/94 - 1/31/95   STEPPING OUT OF THE FRAME: THE PEOPLE IN THE PORTRAITS — Portraits of Cape Ann residents from the 1780's through the 1970's accompanied by personal possessions allow for memorable glimpses into their lives and times.

PLEASE NOTE: There are several other exhibitions a year usually built around a theme that pertains in some way to the locale and its history!

LINCOLN

DeCordova Museum and Sculpture Park
Sandy Pond Rd., **Lincoln, MA 01773**
TEL: 617-259-8355
HRS: 10-5 Tu-F; Noon-5 Sa, S   DAY CLOSED: M   HOL: LEG/HOL!
ADM: Y   ADULT: $4.00   CHILDREN: $3.00 (over 6)   STUDENTS: $3.00   SR CIT: $3.00
HDC/ACC: Y   PARKING: Y; free
GR/T: Y   GR/PH: call 617-259-8355   DT: Y   TIME: 2:00 S & 1:00 W   S/G: Y
PERM/COLL: AM: ptgs, sculp, gr, phot 20; REG

MASSACHUSETTS

DeCordova Museum and Sculpture Park - continued

In addition to its significant collection of modern and contemporary art, the DeCordova features the only permanent sculpture park of its kind in New England. While there is an admission charge for the museum, the sculpture park is always free and open to the public from 8 am to 10 pm daily. The 35 acre park features nearly 40 site-specific sculptures. **NOT TO BE MISSED:** Annual open air arts festival first Sunday in June; summer jazz concert series from 7/4 - Labor Day

ON EXHIBIT/95:

12/10/94 - 1/29/95	JUDITH LIBERMAN: THE HOLOCAUST WALL HANGINGS — Liberman, a former DeCordova Museum School student, is known for her complex and emotionally charged creations. The wall hangings on display created from a vast array of fibers and fiber art techniques capture the horrific images associated with the Holocaust. CAT
12/10/94 - 1/29/95	THE ART OF THE TOUCH: AN INSTALLATION BY ROSALYN DRISCOLL - NEW WORK/NEW ENGLAND — Designed to be touched as well as enjoyed visually, Driscoll's soft sculptures appeal especially to the blind. In fact, sighted visitors are even invited to wear special blindfolds in order to heighten the awareness of their other senses.
2/4 - 3/12/95	THE ART OF ARTHUR SPEAR: OBSERVATION AND FANTASY — An exhibition of New England artist Spear's works from his early Impressionist roots to the imaginary, fantastic and mythical paintings, prints and pastels of his later years.
4/1 - 8/30/95	STROKES OF GENIUS: MINI GOLF BY ARTISTS — For this unusual exhibition the galleries of the DeCordova Museum will be turned into a miniature golf course with each hole designed by regional artists. Visitors will be able to both play golf and view the art at the same time. PLEASE NOTE: There will be an admission charge of $6.00 for this exhibition and the hours will be 10-5 Tu & W, 10-8 T & F, and 10-5 Sa & S.

LOWELL

The Whistler House & Parker Gallery
243 Worthen St., **Lowell, MA 01825**
TEL: 508-452-7641
HRS: 11-4 W-Sa; 1-4 S; Open Tu Jun thru Aug only   DAY CLOSED: M   HOL: LEG/HOL! JAN. & FEB.
ADM: Y   ADULT: $3.00   CHILDREN: F (under 5)   STUDENTS: $1.00   SR CIT: $2.00
HDC/ACC: Y; Limited to first floor of museum and Parker Gallery
PARKING: Y; On street; commercial lots nearby
MUS/SH: Y   DT: Y   TIME: upon request if available
H/B: Y; 1823 Whistler Home, Birthplace of James A. M. Whistler
PERM/COLL: AM: (Including Whistler, Sargent & Gorky)

Works by James A. M. Whistler are the highlight of this collection housed in the 1823 former home of the artist. **NOT TO BE MISSED:** Collection of prints by James A. M. Whistler

ON EXHIBIT/95:   Rotating exhibitions of contemporary regional art presented on a bi-monthly basis.

MEDFORD

Tufts University Art Gallery
Affiliate Institution: Tufts University
Aidekman Arts Center, **Medford, MA 02115**
TEL: 617-628-5000
HRS: 11-5 Tu-S; Till 9pm T (Sep-mid Dec & mid Jan-May)   DAY CLOSED: M
HOL: LEG/HOL!; ACAD! ; SUMMER
ADM: F   HDC/ACC: Y   S/G: Y
PERM/COLL: PTGS, GR, DRGS, 19-20; PHOT 20; AN/R; AN/GRK; P/COL

Located just outside of Boston, the permanent collection of the Tufts University Art Museum has been elevated in stature by the generous donation of several major private family and individual gifts given to the collection and to the related performing cultural arts center.

ON EXHIBIT/95:

1/19 - 2/5/95	CARRIE TRIPPE
2/16 - 5/21/95	TUFTS & THE MUSEUM SCHOOL: A FIFTY YEAR COLLABORATION — Multi-media work by Museum School students.
2/9 - 2/29/95	JONATHAN LUCAS
2/23 - 3/5/95	ANNEY WRIGHT
3/9 - 3/19/95	KAKO WATANABE/ROBIN PAINE
3/23/- 4/2/95	MIKE MARK
4/6 - 4/23/95	ARTWORKS — A juried exhibition of art and design works by Tufts undergraduates.
4/27 - 5/21/95	MUSEUM STUDIES EXHIBITION
10/6 - 12/3/95	NEO-DADA: REDEFINING ART, 1958-62 — In this traveling exhibition, works by Duchamp and Schwitters, grand masters of the artform will be joined by those created as a direct result of their influence. Works by 31 well-known artists in the field including Jasper Johns, Claes Oldenburg, Yoko Ono, John Cage, Arman, Andy Warhol and others will be featured. WT

NORTHAMPTON

Smith College Museum of Art
Elm St. at Bedford Terrace, **Northampton, MA 01063**
TEL: 413-585-2760
HRS: Sep - Dec & Feb - May: 9:30-4 Tu-F; Noon-4 W, Sa, S; Noon-8 T; other!   DAY CLOSED: M
HOL: 1/1, 7/4, THGV, 12/25
ADM: F
HDC/ACC: Y   PARKING: Y; Nearby street parking with campus parking available on evenings and weekends only
MUS/SH: Y
PERM/COLL: AM: ptgs, sculp, gr, drgs, dec/art 17-20; EU: ptgs, gr, sculp, drgs, dec/art 17-20; PHOT; DU:17; ANCIENT ART

With in-depth emphasis on American and French 19th & 20th century art, and literally thousands of superb artworks in its permanent collection, Smith College remains one of the most highly regarded repositories for fine art in the nation. **NOT TO BE MISSED:** "Mrs. Edith Mahon" by Thomas Eakins; "Walking Man" by Rodin

217

MASSACHUSETTS

Smith College Museum of Art - continued

ON EXHIBIT/95:

10/14/94 - 1/22/95	CREATIVE COLLECTING — Paintings and sculpture from the gift of Mr. and Mrs. William A. Small, Jr.
1/26 - 3/19/95	EARLY AMERICAN ILLUMINATED MANUSCRIPTS FROM THE EPHRATA CLOISTER
1/31 - 3/31/95	PRINT ROOM EXHIBITION TBA
2/9 - 4/16/95	BEVERLY BUCHANAN: SHACK WORKS
2/23 - 4/30/95	HISTORY AND TECHNOLOGY OF PAPERMAKING
4/11 - 5/28/95	PRINT ROOM EXHIBITION TBA
5/16 - 7/2/95	DRAWINGS FROM THE GIFT OF MR. AND MRS. WILLIAM A. SMALL, JR.

NORTHAMPTON

Words & Pictures Museum
140 Main St., **Northampton, MA 01060**
TEL: 413-586-8545
HRS: Noon-5 Tu-S   DAY CLOSED: M   HOL: 1/1, MEM/DAY, 7/4, LAB/DAY, THGV, 12/25
ADM: F
HDC/ACC: Y; Fully accessible   PARKING: Y; Metered parking lots nearby
MUS/SH: Y   GR/T: Y   GR/PH: call 413-586-8545   DT: Y   TIME: Upon request if available
PERM/COLL: Original contemporary sequential/comic book art & fantasy illustration, 1970's - present

Mere words cannot describe this Words & Pictures Museum, one of only two in the country. Opening in a new building on 1/95, this museum, which follows the evolution of comic book art, intersperses traditional fine art settings with exhibits of pure fun. There are numerous interactive displays including entry into the museum through a maze and an exit-way through an area that demonstrates the history of the American comic. **NOT TO BE MISSED:** The entryway to the building featuring a life-size artist's studio built with a false perspective so that it appears to actually be viewed from above through a skylight.

ON EXHIBIT/95:

1/95	MAIN GALLERY - PERMANENT COLLECTION
	GALLERY I - UNDERWHERE (by Kevin Eastmen & Mark Martin)
	GALLERY II - UNDERGROUND COMIX
6/10 - 7/15/95	DREAM WEAVERS: FANTASY ART & CHILDREN'S BOOK ILLUSTRATION
7 - 9/95	HARVEY KURTZMAN RETROSPECTIVE — Works by the founder of Mad Magazine

PITTSFIELD

The Berkshire Museum
39 South St., **Pittsfield, MA 01201**
TEL: 413-443-7171
HRS: 10-5 Tu-Sa; 1-5 S; (10-5 M Jul & Aug)   HOL: LEG/HOL!
F/DAY: W&Sa 10-12   ADM: Y   ADULT: $3.00   CHILDREN: $1.00 (12-18)   STUDENTS: $2.00   SR CIT: $2.00
HDC/ACC: Y; Wheelchair lift south side of building; elevator to all floors
PARKING: Y; Metered street parking; inexpensive rates at the nearby Berkshire Hilton and mucicipal parking garage.
MUS/SH: Y   GR/T: Y   GR/PH: call 413-443-7171
DT: Y   TIME: 11:00 Sa "Gallery Glimpses"
PERM/COLL: AM: 19-20; EU: 15-19; AN/GRK; AN/R; DEC/ART; PHOT

Three museums in one set the stage for a varied and exciting visit to this complex in the heart of the beautiful Berkshires. The art museum is rich in its holdings of American art of the 19th & 20th centuries and houses an extensive collection of 2,900 objects of decorative art as well. **NOT TO BE MISSED:** "Giant Redwoods" by Albert Bierstadt

ON EXHIBIT/95:

10/15/94 - SUMMER/95   CONTEMPORARY ART FROM THE MUSEUM'S PERMANENT COLLECTION

12/17/94 - 3/19/95   ALICE TRUMBULL MASON - ETCHINGS AND WOODCUTS — Large woodcuts and etchings by Mason (1904-1971), a pioneer of American abstract painting, whose works were considered "Architectural Abstract Art."

2/95 - SUMMER/95   RE-OPENING OF "DESIGN BY NATURE" — A hands-on exhibition of geometry as it applies to our natural world.

11/11 - 12/3/95   THE ELEVENTH ANNUAL FESTIVAL OF TREES CELEBRATION — Over 200 decorated trees fill the galleries and are decorated by young and old community members.

PROVINCETOWN

Provincetown Art Association and Museum
460 Commercial St., **Provincetown, MA 02657**
TEL: 508-487-1750
HRS: Jul & Aug: 12- 5 & 7-10 daily; May, Jun, Sep, Oct: 12-5 daily & 7-9 F & Sa
HOL: Open most holidays!; open weekends only Nov-Apr
SUGG/CONT: Y   ADULT: $2.00   STUDENTS: $1.00   SR CIT: $1.00
HDC/ACC: Y   MUS/SH: Y   H/B: Y; 1731 Adams family house
PERM/COLL: PTGS; SCULP; GR; DEC/ART; REG

Works by regional artists is an important focus of the collection of this museum located in the former restored vintage home (1731) of the Adams family. **NOT TO BE MISSED:** Inexpensive works of art by young artists that are for sale in the galleries

MASSACHUSETTS

SOUTH HADLEY

Mount Holyoke College Art Museum
South Hadley, MA 01075
TEL: 413-538-2245
HRS: 11-5 Tu-F; 1-5 Sa-S   HOL: LEG/HOL! & ACAD!
ADM: F
HDC/ACC: Y   PARKING: Y; Free   MUS/SH: Y   GR/T: Y   GR/PH: call 413-538-2245   S/G: Y
PERM/COLL: JAP: gr; P/COL; AN/EGT; IT: med/sculp; EU: ptgs; AN/GRK; AN/CH; AM: ptgs, dec/art, gr, phot;
EU: ptgs, dec/art, gr, phot

A stop at this leading college art museum is a must for any art lover traveling in this area. Founded in 1876, it is one of the oldest college museums in the country. **NOT TO BE MISSED:** Albert Bierstadt's "Hetch Hetchy Canyon;" A Pinnacle from Duccio's "Maesta" Altarpiece

ON EXHIBIT/95:

2/3 - 3/17/95	GEORGE INNESS: PRESENCE OF THE UNSEEN — Featured in this commorative centennial exhibition of the "Father of American Landscape" will be 18 paintings and other artworks accompanied by a display of the artist's paints, brushes and palette. WT
FALL 95	FOCUS EXHIBITION: HENDRICK ANDRIESSEN AND THE VANITAS STILL-LIFE — A newly-acquired vanitas work by 17th-century Dutch artist, Andriessen will be on view accompanied by other momento mori paintings borrowed from various art institutions in the northeast.

SPRINGFIELD

George Walter Vincent Smith Art Museum
At the Quadrangle, Corner State & Chestnut Sts., **Springfield, MA 01103**
TEL: 413-739-3871
HRS: Noon-4 T-S   DAY CLOSED: M-W   HOL: LEG/HOL!
ADM: Y   ADULT: $4.00   CHILDREN: F (under 6)   STUDENTS: $1.00
PARKING: Y; Free on-street parking or in Springfield Library & Museum lots on State St. & Edwards St.
GR/T: Y   GR/PH: call 413-739-3871 ex 266   H/B: Y; Built in 1896
PERM/COLL: ENTIRE COLLECTION OF 19th C AMERICAN ART OF GEORGE WALKER VINCENT SMITH;
OR; DEC/ART 17-19; CH: jade; JAP: bronzes, ivories, armour, tsuba 17-19; DEC/ART: cer; AM: ptgs 19

With the largest collecton of Chinese cloisonné in the western world, the G. W. Smith Art Museum, built in 1895 in the style of an Italian villa, is part of a four museum complex that also includes the Museum of the Fine Arts. The museum reflects its founder's special passion for collecting the arts of 17th to 19th century Japan. **NOT TO BE MISSED:** Early 19th century carved 9' high wooden Shinto wheel shrine

ON EXHIBIT/95:

12/1/94 - 1/8/95	DOLLHOUSES FROM AREA COLLECTIONS
9/22 - 10/22/95	ART SCENE: DAVID AND DOUG BREGA — Realist and magical illusionist paintings by these contemporary artists who are brothers.

220

SPRINGFIELD

Museum of Fine Arts
At the Quadrangle, Corner of State & Chestnut Sts., **Springfield, MA 01103**
TEL: 413-739-3871
HRS: Noon-4 T-S   DAY CLOSED: M-W   HOL: LEG/HOL!
ADM: Y   ADULT: $4.00   CHILDREN: F (under 6)   STUDENTS: $1.00
HDC/ACC: Y; In progress
PARKING: Y; Free on-street parking and in Springfield Library & Museum lots on State St. and Edwards St.
MUS/SH: Y   GR/T: Y   GR/PH: call 413-739-3871 ex 266
PERM/COLL: AM: 19-20; FR: 19-20

Part of a four museum complex located on the Quadrangle in Springfield, the Museum of Fine Arts, built in the 1930's Art Deco Style, offers an overview of European and American art. **NOT TO BE MISSED:** "The Historical Monument of the American Republic, 1867 & 1888 by Erastus S. Field, a monumental painting in the court of the museum

ON EXHIBIT/95:

11/20/94 - 1/8/95	MIRACLES OF MEXICAN FOLK ART: RETABLOS AND EX-VOTOS — Rare 18th & 19th century Mexican religious folk art that celebrates Mexico's vibrant and vital artistic & religious heritage.
2/5 - 3/5/95	ART SCENE: CHILDREN OF SORROW — An installation by Slvin Paige that interprets the tragic impact of violence and the drug culture on urban youth.
3/26 - 5/4/95	UKIYO-E FROM THE SPRINGFIELD MUSEUM OF FINE ARTS — 250 17th through 19th-century Japanese woodblock prints that depict scenes from everyday life will be on exhibit.
5/21 - 6/25/95	SPRINGFIELD ART LEAGUE'S 76TH NATIONAL EXHIBITION — A juried show with works in all media by artists nationwide and from Canada.
4/23 - 6/25/95	PAPERWEIGHTS — 510 rare, antique and contemporary paperweights from the Henry Melville Fuller and Smith College Collections.
10/15/95 - 2/25/96	INSPIRED BY DREAMS: AFRICAN ART FROM THE DERBY COLLECTION

STOCKBRIDGE

Chesterwood
Off Rte. 183, Glendale Section, **Stockbridge, MA 01262**
TEL: 413-298-3579
HRS: 10-5 Daily (May 1-Oct 31)   HOL: None during open season
ADM: Y   ADULT: $6.00   CHILDREN: $1.00 (6-12)   STUDENTS: $3.00   SR CIT: $6.00
HDC/ACC: Y; Limited   PARKING: Y; Ample   MUS/SH: Y   REST/FAC: Y; Snack stand
GR/T: Y   GR/PH: several types offered 413-298-3579   DT: Y   TIME: F
H/B: Y; Two Buildings (1898 studio & 1901 house) of Daniel Chester French   S/G: Y
PERM/COLL: SCULP; PTGS; WORKS OF DANIEL CHESTER FRENCH; PHOT

Located on 120 wooded acres is the original studio and Colonial Revival house of Daniel Chester French, leading sculptor of the American Renaissance. Working models for the Lincoln Memorial and the Minute Man, his most famous works are on view along with many other of his sculptures, models, and preliminary drawings.

MASSACHUSETTS

STOCKBRIDGE

The Norman Rockwell Museum at Stockbridge
Stockbridge, MA 01262
TEL: 413-298 4100
HRS: 10-5 Daily (May - Oct); 11-4 M-F & 10-5 Sa, S, HOL (Nov-Apr)   HOL: 1/1, Last 2 weeks JAN, THGV, 12/25
ADM: Y   ADULT: $8.00   CHILDREN: $2.00 (F under 5)
HDC/ACC: Y; Main museum building but not studio   PARKING: Y; Ample free parking
MUS/SH: Y   GR/T: Y   GR/PH: call 413-298-4100 DT: Y   TIME: daily!
H/B: Y; 1800 Georgian House
PERM/COLL: NORMAN ROCKWELL ART & ARTIFACTS

With a new building opened in the spring of 1993 that more than triples its exhibition space, the Norman Rockwell Museum now displays works from all periods of the long and distinguished career of America's most beloved artist/illustrator. In addition to Rockwell's studio, moved to the new museum site in 1986, visitors may enjoy the permanent exhibition entitled "My Adventure as an Ilustrator" which contains 60 paintings that span Rockwell's entire career (1910 thru most of the 1970's). **NOT TO BE MISSED:** The "Four Freedoms" Gallery in the new museum building.

ON EXHIBIT/95:

11/5/94 - 11/5/95	A CENTENNIAL CELEBRATION — 60 original works covering a 7 decade career and drawn from both public and private collections will be brought together for the first time for this exhibition which celebrates the anniversary of Rockwell's birth.
12/94 - 1/95	THE WOMEN OF RIVERBROOK — 20 black and white photographic portraits that capture the everyday experiences of the developmentally challenged women of Riverbrook who volunteer at the Rockewll Museum.
2 - 3/95	ILLUSTRATORS OF WESTERN MASSACHUSETTS — A juried exhibit of artists living and working in Western Massachusetts.
mid 4 - early 6/95	ROCKWELL'S PHOTOGRAPHERS — Photographic images by photographers who worked with Rockwell.
mid 6 - mid 9/95	THE ARTIST AND THE BASEBALL CARD — 150 original works of art by many of the country's foremost artists and illustrators who recreate cards of popular baseball players and characters of the game.
mid 9 - 11/95	SOCIETY OF ILLUSTRATORS - HALL OF FAME — Works of award winning illustrators.
ONGOING:	A MIRROR ON AMERICA — Rockwell's images as they both influenced and depicted the American way of life is the focus of this exhibition.
	MY BEST STUDIO YET — Business, personal and social aspects of Rockwell's daily working life are revealed in this display of archival and ephemeral material. Many of the objects on view concern his relationships with his family, friends, business colleagues and even some of the models he used for his portraits of American life.
	MY ADVENTURES AS AN ILLUSTRATOR — More than 60 paintings that cover Rockwell's 60 year career from the 1910's to the 1970's will be included in this permanent installation of familiar and lesser-known works accompanied by auto-biographical quotations.

WALTHAM

Rose Art Museum
Affiliate Institution: Brandeis University
415 South St., **Waltham, MA 02254**
TEL: 617-736-3434
HRS: 1-5 Tu-S; 1-9 T   DAY CLOSED: M   HOL: LEG/HOL!
ADM: F HDC/ACC: Y PARKING: Y; Visitor parking on campus GR/T: Y GR/PH: call 617-736-3434
PERM/COLL: AM: ptgs, sculp 19-20; EU: ptgs, sculp 19-20; CONT; OC; CER PLEASE NOTE: The permanent collection is not always on view!

The Rose Art Museum, founded in 1961, and located on the campus of Brandeis University just outside of Boston, features one of the largest collections of contemporary art in New England. Selections from the permanent collection and an exhibition of the works of Boston area artists are presented annually.

ON EXHIBIT/95:

1/26 - 3/5/95	ROBERT B. MAYER ARTIST IN RESIDENCE: JUDY PFAFF — Pfaff will be in residence at the museum for 2 weeks and will create a new installation for the museum during that time.
1/26 - 3/5/95	LAURA McPHEE AND VIRGINIA BEEHHAN: COLLABORATIVE PHOTOGRAPHY — On exhibit will be photographs that are the result of a 6 year collaborative effort to capture the landscape in the volcanic regions of Hawaii, Iceland, Costa Rica, and Sicily. The works explore the tenuous connection between these environments and their inhabitants. BROCHURE
3/23 - 7/31/95	THE HERBERT W. PLIMPTON COLLECTION OF REALIST ART — Works of contemporary realism that include a braod artistic range of interpretations will be selected from this collection, now part of the Rose Museum's permanent holdings. Janet Fish, Philip Pearlstein, and William Beckmann are but a few talents whose works will be on view.

WELLESLEY

Davis Museum and Cultural Center
Affiliate Institution: Wellesley College
106 Central St., **Wellesley, MA 02181**
TEL: 617-283-2051
HRS: 11-5 Tu & F-Sa; 11-8 W & T; 1-5 S   DAY CLOSED: HOL: 1/1, 12/25
ADM: F HDC/ACC: Y REST/FAC: Y; Cafe GR/T: Y GR/PH: call 617-283-2051
PERM/COLL: AM: ptgs, sculp, drgs, phot; EU: ptgs, sculp, drgs, phot; AN; AF; MED; REN

Newly renovated and renamed the Davis Museum and Cultural Center, the former Wellesly College Museum, established over 100 years ago, has recently completed an expansion program with the addition of a stunning new 61,000 square foot state-of-the-art museum. One of the first encyclopedic college art collections ever assembled in the United States, the museum is home to more than 5,000 works of art. **NOT TO BE MISSED:** "A Jesuit Missionary in Chinese Costume," a chalk on paper work by Peter Paul Rubens (recent acquisition)

ON EXHIBIT/95:

10/26/94 - 2/19/95	CONTEMPORARY PORCELAIN FROM JAPAN — For sheer technical mastery and pure beauty the 30 spectacular contemporary porcelains from Japan on loan from the Arthur M. Sackler Gallery in Washington, D.C. are a "must see."

MASSACHUSETTS

Davis Museum and Cultural Center - continued

1/27 - 3/19/95	MODERN HEIROGLYPHS: GESTURAL DRAWING AND THE EUROPEAN VANGUARD 1900-1918 — 60 examples of gestural drawing (direct and rapid linear transcription of a model's movement or contours) by some of the foremost pioneers of this technique will include works by Picasso, Rodin, Matisse, Derain, Leger, Kokoshka, Klimt, Schiele and others.
1/27 - 3/26/95	THE SPIRIT, THE SENSES, THE MIND: 17TH-CENTURY NETHERLANDISH WORKS FROM THE COLLECTION — 40 prints and drawings of religious scenes, portraits, landscapes, genre scenes and subjects from mythology and ancient history will be included in this exhibition featuring works by well-known masters from all areas of the 17th-century Dutch empire.
3/16 - 9/95	RITUAL SERIES 1988/RETELLINGS, 1988 BY MICHAEL SINGER — On view will be a recently acquired monumental indoor sculpture by Michael Singer, an artist concerned with landscape and the environment.
4/21 - 6/4/95	THE MIA ALBUM: JULIA MARGARET CAMERON AND HER CIRCLE — 100 vintage photographs by Victorian photographer Cameron and her contemporaries used in the construction of the Mia album documenting the life of her times.
4/21 - 6/4/95	TENDER BUTTONS: WOMEN'S DOMESTIC OBJECTS, SPACES, AND INTERIORS (working title) — Everyday objects including clothespins, aprons, button collections, sewing patterns and the like that were made by women, used for work, collected or arranged by them will show the limited range of creative authorship of the women of the domestic past.
9 - 12/95	WILLEM de KOONING'S "DOOR PAINTINGS" (working title) — Images of women painted between 1964-1966 on identically sized elongated canvases will be seen together for the first time since the 1960's.
10/95 - 1/96	MARGARETT SARGENT: A MODERN TEMPERAMENT — 40 paintings and works on paper by Boston-born artist, Sargent, an early 20th century American modernist whose psychological and creative stresses caused her to abandon her then brilliant career in 1933.

CAT   WT

WILLIAMSTOWN

Sterling and Francine Clark Art Institute
225 South St., **Williamstown, MA 01267**
TEL: 413-458-9545
HRS: 10-5 Tu-S   DAY CLOSED: M!   HOL: 1/1, THGV, 12/25
ADM: F   HDC/ACC: Y; Wheelchairs available   PARKING: Y   MUS/SH: Y
GR/T: Y   GR/PH: call 413-458-9545
PERM/COLL: IT: ptgs 14-18; FL: ptgs 14-18; DU: ptgs 14-18; OM: ptgs, gr, drgs; FR: Impr/ptgs; AM: ptgs 19

More than 30 paintings by Renoir and other French Impressionist masters as well as a collection of old master paintings and a significant group of American works account for the high reputation this outstanding institution enjoys.   **NOT TO BE MISSED:** Impr/ptgs; works by Homer, Sargent, Remington, Cassatt; silver coll.; Ugolino Da Siena Altarpiece

ON EXHIBIT/95:

1 - 2/95	PERMANENT COLLECTION
3 - 5/95	ROMANTIC LANDSCAPES — 20 paintings by Johan Christian Dahl, considered to be the greatest of all Norwegian romantic landscape painters will be featured in this exhibition of works rarely seen outside of his homeland.

224

MASSACHUSETTS

Sterling and Francine Clark Art Institute - continued

3/4 - 4/16/95   WHISTLER: PROSAIC VIEWS, POETIC VISION — Works on paper

6/3 - 7/30/95   ARTHUR J. STONE, DESIGNER AND MASTER SILVERSMITH — A presentation of 80 silver objects and 20 working and presentation drawings by Stone (1847-1938) one of the last independent American silversmiths to craft his items entirely by hand.
                                                              CAT   WT

9 - 11/95   FRANCINE CLARK AS COLLECTOR

WILLIAMSTOWN

Williams College Museum of Art

Main St., Williamstown, MA 01267
TEL: 413-597-2429
HRS: 10-5 Tu-Sa; 1-5 S (open M on MEM/DAY, LAB/DAY, COLUMBUS DAY)   DAY CLOSED: M!
HOL: 1/1, THGV, 12/25
ADM: F   HDC/ACC: Y; Parking, wheelchair accessible
PARKING: Y; Limited in front of and behind museum, behind the Chapel, other lots on campus   MUS/SH: Y
GR/T: Y   GR/PH: call 413-597-2429
H/B: Y; 1846 Brich Octagon by Thomas Tefft; 1983-86 additions by Chas. Moore
PERM/COLL: AM: cont & 18-19; ASIAN & OTHER NON-WESTERN CIVILIZATIONS; BRIT: ptgs 17-19; SP: ptgs 15-18; IT/REN: ptgs ; PHOT; GR/ARTS; AN/GRK; AN/ROM;

Considered one of the finest college art museums in the U.S., Williams houses 11,000 works that span the history of art. The original museum building of 1846 was joined in 1986 by an addition designed by noted architect Charles Moore. **NOT TO BE MISSED:** Works of Maurice and Charles Prendergast

ON EXHIBIT/95:

THROUGH 1/95   VITAL TRADITIONS: OLD MASTER WORKS FROM THE PERMANENT COLLECTION — 17 superb masterworks by Guardi, Ribera, van Ostade and the like that span 300 years of art history from the Renaissance to the Baroque period will be on exhibit.

1/28 - 4/95   ROBERT MORRIS: MIRRORS (working title) — A mirror piece installation

2/11 - 4/9/95   GLENN LIGON: TO DISEMBARK — Focusing on issues of sexual and racial identity, the mixed-media works of this NY artist challenge our understanding of what it is to be African-American and male.   BROCHURE   WT

2/25 - 6/95   THE WILDERNESS CULT — An exhibition that focuses on land use and preservation of nature in America.

4/22 - 8/95   LABELTALK (working title) — Exhibition wall text by faculty members each focusing on one of 8 varied pieces chosen for this show.

THROUGH 6/95   MODERNISM! EUROPEAN & AMERICAN ART 1900-1950 FROM THE WCMA COLLECTION — 50 European and American Modernist masters (1900-1950) that show the flowering of abstraction, surrealism, and expressionism will be selected for this exhibition from the exceptional holdings of the museum collection.

7 - 12/95   AMERICAN ORIENTALISM (working title) — The early 20th century American fascination with the Orient will be explored in this exhibition of objects chosen from the collection of the museum and from local private collections.

7/9/94 - 1/8/95   ARTWORKS: AMALIA MESA-BAINS, VENUS ENVY, CHAPTER II — Known primarily for her eclectic traditional folk altars, this installation by well-known Chicana artist, Mesa-Bains will address her desire to validate Latino culture and examine the place of a woman within that tradition.

MASSACHUSETTS

WORCESTER

Iris & B. Gerald Cantor Art Gallery
Affiliate Institution: College of Holy Cross
1 College St., **Worcester, MA 01610**
TEL: 508-793-3356
HRS: 10-4 M-F, 2-5 Sa & S; Summer hours by appointment   HOL: ACAD!
ADM: F   HDC/ACC: Y   PARKING: Y; Free
PERM/COLL: SCULP; CONT/PHOT; 10 RODIN SCULPTURES

Five to seven exhibitions are mounted annually in this Gallery with themes that focus on contemporary art, art historical and social justice topics, and student work.

Worcester Art Museum
55 Salisbury St., **Worcester, MA 01609-3196**
TEL: 508-799-4406
HRS: 11-4 Tu-F; 10-5 Sa; 1-5 S   DAY CLOSED: M   HOL: LEG/HOL!
F/DAY: 10-12 Sa   ADM: Y   ADULT: $5.00   CHILDREN: F (under 13)   STUDENTS: $3.00   SR CIT: $3.00
HDC/ACC: Y; Restrooms & galleries; wheelchairs available on request   PARKING: Y; Free parking in front of museum and along side streets; handicapped parking at the Hiatt Wing entrance off Tuckerman Street.   MUS/SH: Y
REST/FAC: Y; Cafe 11:30-2 Tu-Sa Lunch (call 508-799-4406 ex 255 to reserve)
GR/T: Y   GR/PH: call 508-799-4406 ex 269   DT: Y   TIME: 3:00 most S Sep-May; 2:00 3rd Tu & Sa   S/G: Y
PERM/COLL: AM: 17-19; JAP: gr; BRIT: 18-19; FL: 16-17; GER: 16-17; DU: 17; P/COL; AN/EGT; OR: sculp;
MED: sculp; AM: dec/art

Located in central Massachusetts, The Worcester Art Museum contains more than 30,000 works of art representing 50 centuries of creative spirit. It is the second largest art museum in New England, and was one of the first museums in the country to exhibit and collect photographs as fine art. The museum features outstanding wall text for much of its permanent collection. PLEASE NOTE: Small folding stools are available for visitors to use in the galleries. **NOT TO BE MISSED:** Antiochan Mosaics; American Portrait miniatures

ON EXHIBIT/95:

9/25/94 - 1/8/95	HERITAGE OF THE LAND: CONTRASTS IN NATIVE AMERICAN LIFE — In the first major exhibition of its kind in New England and the only venue for this important exhibition in the country, 110 objects from the 19th & 20th centuries will document the rich cultural diversity of Native Americans from the 4 distinct and contrasting regions of the coastal Northeast, the pueblo communities of the Southwest, the Plains, and the Northwest Coast. WT*
10/23/94 - 2/26/95	INSIGHTS: A DISTANT VIEW — An exhibition by 6 artists who approach the subject matter of landscape in contemporary terms.
10/23/94 - 2/26/95	ANOTHER VIEW: LANDSCAPES FROM THE PERMANENT COLLECTION — As a companion exhibition to the one listed above, 16th to 19th-century American and European landscapes from the permanent collection will be on view.
1/28 - 4/9/95	WILL BARNET: AMERICAN MASTER PRINTMAKER
2/25 - 4/23/95	MEXICO: A LANDSCAPE REVISITED
4/2 - 6/18/95	CONTEMPORARY MASTERS: PRINTS FROM THE ROSE FAMILY COLLECTIONS
5/13 - 8/13/95	GREAT GIFTS! FROM BRUEGHEL TO RENOIR
11/8 - 12/31/95	THE PHOTOGRAPHER'S VISION OF THE INDUSTRIAL AGE — 50 images from the permanent collection will trace the evolution of photography against the rise of industrial society in both America and western Europe.

MICHIGAN

ANN ARBOR

The University of Michigan Museum of Art
525 S. State St. at S. Univ., Ann **Arbor, MI 48109**
TEL: 313-764-0395
HRS: 10-5 Tu-Sa, Till 9 T, & 12-5 S; SUMMER HOURS: 11-5 Tu-Sa & 12-5 S   DAY CLOSED: M
HOL: 1/1, 7/4, THGV, 12/25
ADM: F
HDC/ACC: Y; North museum entrance & all galleries; limited access to restrooms
PARKING: Y; Limited on-street parking with commercial lots nearby   MUS/SH: Y
GR/T: Y   GR/PH: call 313-764-0395
PERM/COLL: CONT; gr, phot; OM; drgs 6-20; OR; AF; OC; IS

This museum, which houses the second largest art collection in the state of Michigan, also features a changing series of special exhibitions, family programs, and chamber music concerts. With over 12,000 works of art ranging from Italian Renaissance panel paintings to Han dynasty tomb figures, this university museum ranks among the finest in the country. **NOT TO BE MISSED:** Works on paper by J. M. Whistler

ON EXHIBIT/95:

11/5/94 - 1/15/95	JOHN STEPHENSON: AFTER THE FIRE, A RETROSPECTIVE — On exhibit will be works by Stephenson, a well-known Ann Arbor ceramics artist, on the occasion of his retirement from the School of Art.
12/3/94 - 2/26/95	STAFFS OF LIFE: AFRICAN RODS, STAFFS, AND SCEPTERS FROM THE COUDRON COLLECTION — African staffs from the largest collection of its kind in the world will be featured in this exhibition.
1/14 - 3/5/95	JOSEPH BEUYS: DRAWINGS, OBJECTS AND PRINTS — Known for using unusual substances for creating his works including hare's blood, and tea, the works on view by Beuys, on loan from public and private collections in Germany, reflect his interest in all aspects of nature. WT
2/4 - 3/26/95	DIVINE ILLUMINATIONS: DEVOTIONAL BOOKS OF THE MIDDLE AGES — A selection of superb single leaves from handmade illuminated manuscripts will be on exhibit.
3/11 - 5/14/95	LABOR AND LEISURE: FRENCH PRINTS FROM THE LATTER HALF OF THE NINETEENTH CENTURY — From the permanent collection, works by Millet, Pissaro, Forain, Renoir, Vuillard and others will reveal diverse attitudes towards work and play in France during the period of 1850-1900.
3/25 - 5/21/95	FROM ANSEL ADAMS TO ANDY WARHOL — 55 important portraits and self-portraits from the permanent collection will be featured in this exhibition
4/8 - 6/4/95	IN FOCUS: KAI CHI — Four versions of a single composition by 18th century Chinese master artist Kai Chi will be on view from the permanent collection.
6/17 - 8/20/95	THE ALLURE OF THE NUDE — A survey of artistic depictions of the human body from the Renaissance to today and how the meaning of the nude is affected by narratives, allegories, and academic studies.

MICHIGAN

BLOOMFIELD HILLS

Cranbrook Academy of Art Museum
1221 North Woodward Ave., **Bloomfield Hills, MI 48013-0801**
TEL: 810-645-3323
HRS: 1-5 W-S   DAY CLOSED: M, Tu   HOL: LEG/HOL!
ADM: Y   ADULT: $3.00   CHILDREN: F (under 7)   STUDENTS: $2.00   SR CIT: $2.00
HDC/ACC: Y   PARKING: Y; Ample free parking adjacent to museum   MUS/SH: Y
GR/T: Y   GR/PH: call 313-645-3323   DT: Y   TIME: 1:30, 2:00, 3:00 & 3:30 Tu, Sa, S (Saarinen House)
H/B: Y; Designed by noted Finnish-Amer. architect, Eliel Saarinen   S/G: Y
PERM/COLL: ARCH/DRGS; CER; PTGS; SCULP; GR 19-20 ; DEC/ART 20

The newly restored Sarinen House, a building designed by noted Finnish-American architect Eliel Saarinen, is part of Cranbrook Academy, the only institution in the country devoted to graduate education in the arts. In addition to outdoor sculpture on the grounds surrounding the museum, the permanent collection includes important works of art that are influential on the contemporary trends of today. PLEASE NOTE: Tour fees of Saarinen House include museum admission. Children under 7 are not permitted on tours of the house. Private group tours are available on Wed & Fri afternoons and Thursday evenings by special advance appointment. **NOT TO BE MISSED:** Works by Eliel Saarinen; carpets by Loja Saarinen

ON EXHIBIT/95:
11/16/94 - 4/2/95	YOUNG CURATORS SELECT CERAMICS: A MUSEUM/COMMUNITY COLLABO-RATION
WINTER/95	KATHERINE AND MICHAEL McCOY AT CRANBROOK: A RETROSPECTIVE (WORKING TITLE) EXACT DATES TBA
OPENS 5/13/95	1995 GRADUATE SUMMER EXHIBITION

DETROIT

The Detroit Institute of Arts
5200 Woodward Ave., **Detroit, MI 48202**
TEL: 313-833-7900
HRS: 11-4 W-F; 11-5 Sa, S   DAY CLOSED: M, Tu   HOL: LEG/HOL!
SUGG/CONT: Y   ADULT: $4.00   CHILDREN: $1.00   STUDENTS: $1.00
HDC/ACC: Y; Wheelchairs available at barrier free Farnsworth Entrance! 833-1454
PARKING: Y; Underground parking at the science center across the street (fee charged); metered street parking
MUS/SH: Y   REST/FAC: Y; Kresge Court Cafe open 11-3:30 W-S (313-833-1855)
GR/T: Y   GR/PH: call 313-833-7978   DT: Y   TIME: 1:00 W-Sa; 1 & 2:30 S
PERM/COLL: EU: 20; AF; CONT; P/COL; NAT/AM; EU: ptgs, sculp, dec/art; AM: ptgs, sculp, dec/art

The two hundred year old Detroit Institute of Arts, consisting of 101 galleries full of centuries of artistic treasure, is considered one of the five most important and comprehensive art museums in America. **NOT TO BE MISSED:** "Detroit Industry" by Diego Rivera, a 27 panel fresco located in the Rivera court.

ON EXHIBIT/95:
8/27/94- 7/31/95	AN EVOLUTION OF 20TH-CENTURY SCULPTURE Formal and thematic developments in American and European sculpture will be traced in works selected from the permanent collection.
10/1/94 - 1/8/95	SO YOU WANT TO BUILD A MUSEUM — Plans, drawings and renderings for the 1888 Detroit Museum of Art designed by James Balfour and the 1927 Detroit Institute of Arts designed by Paul Cret will be on exhibit.

228

The Detroit Institute of Arts - continued

10/12/94 - 1/8/96	IMPRESSIONS ON A THEME: PRINT PORTFOLIOS AND SERIES — From the permanent collection, 150 prints representing 13 complete portfolios or series will feature all 16 of the DIA's rare second state impressions of Piranesi's "Prisons," the first edition of Goya's "Los Proverbios" (pub. 1864), "Jazz" by Henri Matisse, versions of the "Rake's Progress" by both David Hockney (1961-63) and William Hogarth (1735), Manet's "The Raven," and John Sloan's "New York City Life" set from 1905-06.
12/15/94 - 2/26/95	CHARLES McGEE — Paintings, sculptures, graphics, ceramics and photographs all dealing with the theme of Noah's Ark by this 70 year old Detroit artist will be featured in this exhibit of work created by McGee over the past decade.
2/1 - 3/12/95	THE MIA ALBUM: JULIA MARGARET CAMERON AND HER CIRCLE — 120 photographs that include early experimental works created by Cameron in 1863 as an album for her sister, Mia will be shown with exmples of images by some of her contemporaries. WT
2/12 - 4/2/95	THE MANY FACES OF WENCESLAUS HOLLAR: 17TH-CENTURY EUROPEAN PRINTS FROM THE MUSEUM BOYMANS-VAN BUENINGEN, ROTTERDAM — Portraits, landscapes, still lifes and historical events that document his 17th century world will be seen in the more than 200 prints by Bohemian artist Hollar and his contemporaries. CAT WT
2/12 - 4/30/95	THE ROYAL TOMBS OF SIPAN (PERU) — In its only venue in the midwest, 200 splendid gold, silver and turquoise artifacts and jewelry from 3 1700 year old burial chambers on the north coast of Peru will be on exhibit. These treasures were found in the final resting place of Moche royalty who were worshiped and buried in a manner similar to that of the Egyptian pharaohs. CAT ADM EXTRA WT
3/3 - 4/26/95	ART & FLOWERS: A FESTIVAL OF SPRING — On view will be poster designs created to commemorate this spring event whose activities include lectures, floral demonstrations & displays, and entertainment throughout the museum.
4/26 - 7/30/95	PICTURING PARIS, 1850-1950: PHOTOGRAPHS FROM THE PERMANENT COLLECTION — 19th and 20th-century photographic images of Paris by such notables as Baldus, Atget and Kertesz.
5/95	MAY IS MUSEUM MONTH — A month-long variety of programs for all ages.
5/11 - 7/9/95	JACQUES VILLON, PRINTMAKER — The long and productive career of Villon will be seen in this survey of his oeuvre that include examples of his early "Belle Epoque" manner, cubist prints from the 1920's, and landscapes & abstract compositions from his later works.
6/1 - 8/6/95	ISLAND ANCESTORS: OCEANIC ART FROM THE MASCO COLLECTION — 76 objects from New Guinea, Polynesia, Micronesia and Melanesia that date from Oceania's pre-colonial history will be featured in this exhibition. CAT ADM EXTRA WT

EAST LANSING

Kresge Art Museum
Affiliate Institution: Michigan State University
East Lansing, MI 48824-1119
TEL: 517-355-7631
HRS: 9:30-4:30 M-W, F; Noon-8 T; 1-4 Sa, S (mid Sep-mid June); Summer!
HOL: LEG/HOL!; 12/18 - 1/9, 4/2-3, 5/28-30, 6/18-7/23
VOL/CONT: Y   ADM: F   HDC/ACC: Y; Barrier free; snow melt system in sidewalk; wheelchairs available
PARKING: Y; Small fee at designated museum visitor spaces in front of the art center.   MUS/SH: Y (small)
GR/T: Y   GR/PH: call 517-353-9834   S/G: Y
PERM/COLL: GR 19-20; AM: cont/ab (1960'S), PHOT

MICHIGAN

Kresge Art Museum - continued

Founded in 1959, the Kresge, with over 4,000 works ranging from prehistoric to contemporary, is the only fine arts museum in central Michigan. **NOT TO BE MISSED:** "St. Anthony" by Francisco Zuberon; "Remorse" by Salvador Dali; Contemporary collection

ON EXHIBIT/95:

1/9 - 3/19/95	14TH MICHIGAN BIENNIAL ART EXHIBITION
10/29 - 12/15/95	CONTEMPORARY AMERICAN INDIAN ART: THE JOE FIEDDERSON COLLECTION — Jaune Qiuck-to-See and Kay Walking Stick are but two of the well-known artists represented in the collection of paintings, works on paper and mixed media on view in this exhibition.
	PLEASE NOTE: There are several student and faculty shows during the year. Please call for information. Also, the museum will be closed 7/29 - 9/4/95 and 12/16/95 - 1/7/96.

FLINT

Flint Institute of Arts
1120 E. Kearsley St., **Flint, MI 48503**
TEL: 810-234-1695
HRS: 10-5 Tu-Sa; 1-5 S   DAY CLOSED: M   HOL: LEG/HOL!
ADM: Y   ADULT: $3.00   CHILDREN: F (under 6)   STUDENTS: $1.00   SR CIT: $2.50
HDC/ACC: Y   PARKING: Y; Free parking adjacent to the building   MUS/SH: Y
GR/T: Y   GR/PH: call 313-234-1695
PERM/COLL: AM: ptgs, sculp, gr 19-20; EU: ptgs, sculp, gr 19-20; FR/REN: IT/REN: dec/art; CH: cer, sculp

In addition to the permanent collection with artworks from ancient China to modern America, visitors to this museum can enjoy the newly renovated building itself, a stunning combination of classic interior gallery space housed within the walls of a modern exterior. **NOT TO BE MISSED:** Bray Gallery of French & Italian Renaissance decorative arts

ON EXHIBIT/95:

9/18/94 - 2/12/95	NATIVE AMERICAN ART FROM THE PERMANENT COLLECTION	
11/27/94 - 1/15/95	MICHIGAN DIRECTIONS: FLINT AREA ARTISTS	
2/5 - 4/16/95	ROMARE BEARDEN AS PRINTMAKER	WT
2/19 - 4/2/95	LESS AND MORE: TWO DIRECTIONS OF ABSTRACTION — Selections from the FIA Graphic Arts Collection	
4/16 - 7/30/95	NATIVE AMERICAN ART FROM THE CHANDLER/POHRT COLLECTION AT THE FIA	
4/30 - 6/18/95	PARTIAL RECALL: PHOTOGRAPHS OF NATIVE NORTH AMERICANS	

230

GRAND RAPIDS

Calvin College Center Art Gallery
Affiliate Institution: Calvin College
Grand Rapids, MI 49546
TEL: 616-957-6326
HRS: 9-9 M-T; 9-4 F; Noon-4 Sa   DAY CLOSED: S   HOL: ACAD!
ADM: F
HDC/ACC: Y; Barrier-free   PARKING: Y; Adjacent outdoor parking
GR/T: Y   GR/PH: available upon request
DT: Y   TIME: available upon request
PERM/COLL: DU: ptgs, drgs 17-19; GR, PTGS, SCULP, DRGS 20

17th & 19th century Dutch paintings are one of the highlights of the permanent collection.

ON EXHIBIT/95:
1/12 - 2/9/95	NCECA TRAVELLING EXHIBITION
2/18 - 3/9/95	DRAWING AWAY: ROBIN JENSEN

Grand Rapids Art Museum
155 N. Division, **Grand Rapids, MI 49503**
TEL: 616-459-4677
HRS: 10-4 W, F, Sa; 10-9 T; Noon-4 Tu & S   DAY CLOSED: M   HOL: LEG/HOL!
ADM: Y   ADULT: $2.00   CHILDREN: F (under 5)   STUDENTS: $0.50   SR CIT: $0.50
HDC/ACC: Y   PARKING: Y; Less than 1 block from the museum   MUS/SH: Y
GR/T: Y   GR/PH: call 616-459-4677   DT: Y   H/B: Y; Beaux Arts Federal Building
PERM/COLL: REN: ptgs; FR: ptgs 19; AM: ptgs 19-20; GR; EXP/PTGS; PHOT; DEC/ART

Located in a renovated Federal Style Building the Grand Rapids Art Museum has, since its inception in 1911, grown to include a notable gallery of European and Oriental decorative art in addition to its highly regarded painting and print collection. **NOT TO BE MISSED:** "Harvest" by Karl Schmidt-Rottluff; "Champion of the Spirit," a bronze by Ernst Barlach; "Ingleside" by Richard Diebenkorn

ON EXHIBIT/95:
11/17/94 - 1/22/95	STEPHEN DUREN/LANDSCAPES AND DETOURS — A retrospective of works from the last 10 years by this Grand Rapids painter.
2/12 - 4/23/95	DIANNA WEGE EXHIBITION — Delicate colored pencil drawings and bold abstract paintings by Wege, a Grand Rapids native now working in Connecticut.
2/19 - 4/30/95	THE LURE AND LORE OF EGYPT — Prints and paintings by English artist, David Roberts (1796-1864).
ONGOING TILL 7/95	GRAM FOR KIDS "AN AFRICAN ART SAFARI" — African art for children presented in an interactive learning environment.
6/2 - mid 8/95	FESTIVAL '95 VISUAL ARTS EXHIBITION — A juried show of art from the West Michigan community.

MICHIGAN

KALAMAZOO

Kalamazoo Institute of Arts
314 South Park St., **Kalamazoo, MI 49007**
TEL: 616-349-7775
HRS: SEP-MAY: 10-5 Tu-Sa, 1-5 S; JUN-JUL: 10-5 Tu-Sa   DAY CLOSED: M   HOL: LEG/HOL!
ADM: F   HDC/ACC: Y   PARKING: Y; More that 100 free parking spaces   MUS/SH: Y   S/G: Y
PERM/COLL: AM: sculp, ptgs, drgs, cer, gr, phot 20

The Kalamazoo Institute, established in 1924, is best known for its collection of 20th century American art. More than 2,500 objects are housed in a building that in 1979 was voted one of the most significant structures in the state. **NOT TO BE MISSED:** "La Clownesse Aussi (Mlle. Cha-U-Ka-O)" by Henri de Toulouse Lautrec; "Sleeping Woman" by Richard Diebenkorn; "Simone in a White Bonnet" by Mary Cassatt

ON EXHIBIT/95:

11/19/94 - 1/15/95	DEALER'S CHOICE: WORKS FROM THE KIA COLLECTION
11/19/94 - 2/10/95	70 YEARS, 70 WORKS FROM THE PERMANENT COLLECTION
1/7 - 2/10/95	CULTURAL REFLECTIONS: CONTEMPORARY INUIT ART
1/14 - 3/19/95	PHOTOGRAPHS FROM THE KIA COLLECTION AND SCHOOL
1/21 - 3/5/95	RURAL JAPAN: LINDA BUTLER PHOTOGRAPHS
2/18 - 3/26/95	1995 KALAMAZOO AREA SHOW
3/11 - 6/3/95	AN ANIMAL'S TALE OF MICHIGAN HISTORY
3/18 - 5/7/95	CERAMICS AND PRINTS FROM THE KIA COLLECTION AND SCHOOL
4/1 - 5/14/95	WESTERN ART FROM MICHIANA COLLECTIONS
4/1 - 5/14/95	TUNIS PONSON RETROSPECTIVE
5/13 - 8/5/95	SCULPTURE AND DRAWINGS FROM THE KIA COLLECTION AND SCHOOL
6/10 - 8/5/95	THE PORTRAIT/THE FIGURE FROM THE KIA COLLECTION
6/17 - 8/5/95	REVOLUTION IN CLAY: AMERICAN CERAMICS, 1940-1980
6/14 - 8/5/95	BLACK ARTS & CULTURAL CENTER COMPETITION
6/17 - 8/95	WALTER O. EVANS COLLECTION OF AFRICAN-AMERICAN ART

MUSKEGON

Muskegon Museum of Art
296 W. Webster, **Muskegon, MI 49440**
TEL: 616-722-2600
HRS: 10-5 Tu-F; Noon-5 Sa, S   DAY CLOSED: M   HOL: LEG/HOL!
VOL/CONT: Y   ADM: F   HDC/ACC: Y; Fully accessible; parking, elevators, restrooms
PARKING: Y; Limited street and adjacent mall lots; handicapped parking at rear of museum   MUS/SH: Y
GR/T: Y   GR/PH: call 616-722-2600
PERM/COLL: AM: ptgs, gr 19-early 20; EU: ptgs; PHOT; SCULP; OM: gr; CONT: gr

The award winning Muskegon Museum, which opened in 1912, and has recently undergone major renovation, is home to a permanent collection that includes many fine examples of American and French Impressionistic paintings, Old Master through contemporary prints, photography, sculpture and glass. **NOT TO BE MISSED:** Glass collection

232

MICHIGAN

Muskegon Museum of Art - continued

ON EXHIBIT/95:

12/9/94 - 1/29/95   CLEARLY ART: PILCHUCK'S GLASS LEGACY — 80 objects by 66 artists trained by noted glass artist, Dale Chihuly in the famous Pacific Northwest Pilchuck Glass School will be on view.   CAT   WT

12/9/94 - 1/22/95   IMAGES OF INSIGHT: 16TH & 17TH CENTURY NORTHERN EUROPEAN PRINTS FROM THE PERMANENT COLLECTION — 30 rare works by such artists as Durer, Cranach, and Rembrandt will be selected for viewing from the permanent collection.

2/9 - 4/19/95   EXPLORING OURSELVES: PORTRAITS IN ART — An exploration of the many aspects of portraiture as seen in examples of historic portraiture, contemporary photographs (including school photographs) and self-portraits.

2/9 - 5/14/95   SPEAK! CHILDREN'S BOOK ILLUSTRATORS BRAG ABOUT THEIR DOGS — This exhibition of 43 original portraits of their favorite dogs accompanied by each illustrator's own text promises to be fun for the whole family. In addition to the artworks on view will be a family reading center.

2/9 - 3/26/95   ANIMATION ART — Original "cell" cartoon drawings will be featured in this exhibition.

4/2 - 5/28/95   HERB BABCOCK: MICHIGAN GLASS ARTIST

6 - 8/95   68TH ANNUAL WEST MICHIGAN JURIED ART COMPETITION "THE REGIONAL"

6 - 8/95   VIVA la FRANCE: PRE-IMPRESSIONIST FRENCH PRINTS FROM THE PERMANENT COLLECTION — A selection of works from the museum's extensive graphics collection.

PETOSKEY

Crooked Tree Arts Council
461 E. Mitchell St., **Petoskey, MI 49770**
TEL: 616-347-4337
HRS: 10-5 M-Sa (Spring, Fall, Winter); 10-5 M-Sa & 11-3 S (Summer)   HOL: LEG/HOL!
ADM: F   HDC/ACC: Y   PARKING: Y; 60 parking spaces on city lot next door to museum   MUS/SH: Y
H/B: Y; 1890 Methodist Church
PERM/COLL: REGIONAL & FINE ART

This fine arts collection makes its home on the coast of Lake Michigan in a former Methodist church built in 1890.

ROCHESTER

Meadow Brook Art Gallery
Affiliate Institution: Oakland University
Rochester, MI 48309-4401
TEL: 313-370-3005
HRS: 1-5 W; 2-6:30 Sa, S (7-8:30 Tu-F theater performance days)   DAY CLOSED: M
ADM: F
HDC/ACC: Y   PARKING: Y; Free   S/G: Y
PERM/COLL: AF; OC; P/COL; CONT/AM: ptgs, sculp, gr; CONT/EU: ptgs, gr, sculp

233

MICHIGAN

Crooked Tree Arts Council - continued

Located 30 miles north of Detroit on the campus of Oakland University, the Meadow Brook Art Gallery offers four major exhibitions annually. **NOT TO BE MISSED:** African art collection, a gift from the late governor of Michigan, G. Mennen Williams

ON EXHIBIT/95:

1/15 - 2/12/95	JOAN BRACE AND HER COLLECTION — An exhibition of works from this collection that will be auctioned at a later date in order to establish art gallery endowment funds.
2/16 - 4/9/95	ART OF INDONESIAN ARCHIPELAGO FROM THE COLLECTION OF DIANE AND PAUL HAIG
FALL 95	LIVING TRADITION: SHIBORI, JAPANESE INDIGO DYED TEXTILES

SAGINAW

Saginaw Art Museum
1126 N. Michigan Ave., **Saginaw, MI 48602**
TEL: 517-754-2491
HRS: 10-5 Tu-Sa; 1-5 S   DAY CLOSED: M   HOL: LEG/HOL!
VOL/CONT: Y   ADM: F
HDC/ACC: Y; Ramp at front door; only first floor is accessible   PARKING: Y; Free
GR/T: Y   GR/PH: call 517-754-2491   H/B: Y; former 1904 Clark Lombard Ring Family Home
PERM/COLL: EU: ptgs, sculp 14-20; AM: ptgs, sculp; OR: ptgs, gr, dec/art; JAP: GR; JOHN ROGERS SCULP; CHARLES ADAM PLATT: gr

The interesting and varied permanent collections of this museum that include an important group of John Rogers sculptures, are housed in a gracious 1904 Georgian-revival building designed by Charles Adam Platt. The former Clark Lombard Ring Family home is listed on the state & federal registers for historic homes. **NOT TO BE MISSED:** Full-scale model of the 28-foot tall Christ on the Cross at Indian River, MI.

ST. JOSEPH

Krasal Art Center
707 Lake Blvd., St. **Joseph, MI 49085**
TEL: 616-983-0271
HRS: 10-4 M-T, Sa; 10-1 F; 1-4 S   DAY CLOSED: F pm   HOL: EASTER, MEM/DAY, LAB/DAY, THGV, 12/25
ADM: F   HDC/ACC: Y; Ramp, restrooms, elevator   PARKING: Y; Free and ample   MUS/SH: Y
PERM/COLL: SCULP; FOLK

Located on the shores of Lake Michigan, site-specific sculptures are placed in and around the area of the center. Maps showing locations and best positions for viewing are provided for the convenience of the visitor. The center is also noted for hosting one of the Midwest's finest art fairs each July. **NOT TO BE MISSED:** "Three Lines Diagonal Jointed-Wall" by George Rickey

ON EXHIBIT/95:

11/25/94 - 1/1/95	MAYAN PAINTERS FROM HIGHLAND AND GUATAMALA — Paintings by non-professional indigenous artists from the collection of Joseph Johnston that detail the turbulence, beauty and despair of modern Latin American life.
11/15/94 - 1/1/95	HARRY AHN — A retrospective of Ahn's realist images.
1/28 - 3/12/95	JOHN STUART CURRY'S AMERICA — Drawings and studies by this renowned Midwest regionalist artist and muralist whose images of small town rural America dominated popular taste in the 1930's. WT

Krasal Art Center - continued

5/4 - 6/18/95	SHIFTING SANDS — A major 2 part exhibition of works indoors by Margo Mensing, John McQueen, Lisa Norton, and Heather McGill accompanied by an outdoor project that addresses the use of Michigan's shoreline.
6/22 - 7/23/95	GESTURAL AND GEOMETRIC ABSTRACTION — An exhibition of geometric abstractions by Thomas & Jessica Gondek juxtaposed with large gestural works by Patricia Opel and Wade Thompson.
7/27 - 8/27/95	BETH VAN LIERE: RECENT WORK — Paintings, drawings and prints by Liere of intimate corners of French and Michigan landscapes.
7/27 - 8/27/95	BOYD QUINN PAINTINGS — Meditations on the subjects of time and death influenced by Quinn's war-time experiences will be seen in his representational and non-objective paintings.
7/27 - 8/27/95	STEPHEN HOKANSON KINETIC SCULPTURE — Copper and bronze sculptures that are small monuments to balance.

UNIVERSITY CENTER

Marshall M. Fredericks Sculpture Gallery

Affiliate Institution: Saginaw Valley State University
2250 Pierce Rd., **University Center, MI 48710**
TEL: 517-790-5667
HRS: 1-5 Tu-S   DAY CLOSED: M   HOL: LEG/HOL!& ACAD/HOL!
ADM: F
HDC/ACC: Y; Barrier free building with first floor access   PARKING: Y; Free   MUS/SH: Y
GR/T: Y   GR/PH: call to reserve (may be added fee)   S/G: Y
PERM/COLL: ART OF MARSHALL M. FREDERICKS

Over 200 works that span all phases of the distinguished career of noted sculptor Marshall M. Fredericks are displayed in this museum which features his work only. Many of the greatest of his monumental sculptures can be seen here. **NOT TO BE MISSED:** Original quarter-scale model for the "Spirit of Detroit" building, Detroit, MI.

MINNESOTA

DULUTH

Tweed Museum of Art
Affiliate Institution: Univ. of Minn.
10 University Dr., **Duluth, MN 55812**
TEL: 218-726-8503
HRS: 9-8 Tu; 9-4:30 W-F; 1-5 Sa, S   DAY CLOSED: M   HOL: ACAD!
SUGG/CONT: Y   ADULT: $2.00   CHILDREN: F (under 6)   STUDENTS: $1.00   SR CIT: $1.00
HDC/ACC: Y; Barrier free   PARKING: Y   MUS/SH: Y   GR/T: Y   GR/PH: call 218-726-8222   S/G: Y
PERM/COLL: OM: ptgs; EU: ptgs 17-19; AM 19-20; CONT

Endowed with gifts of American and European paintings by industrialist George Tweed, for whom this museum is named, this fine institution also has an important growing permanent collection of contemporary art. One-person exhibitions by living American artists are often presented to promote national recognition of their work. PLEASE NOTE: The museum offers a reduced suggested contribution of $5.00 per family. **NOT TO BE MISSED:** "The Scourging of St. Blaise," a 16th century Italian painting by a follower of Caravaggio

ON EXHIBIT/95:

10/10/94 - 1/15/95	NEW ACQUISITIONS: CONTEMPORARY AMERICAN INDIAN ARTISTS — Works by Morrison, Cordova, Savage-Blue, and Bigbear will be shown.
1/17 - 3/19/95	NANCY AZARA: NEW COLLAGES & SCULPTURES FROM NEW YORK
	CHILDREN'S ART FROM ARMENIA
3/15 - 4/20/95	MASTERS OF WATERCOLOR FROM THE TWEED COLLECTION — Artworks by Burchfield, Charlot, Dove, Davies, Marin and Marsh.
3/15 - 4/20/95	127TH INTERNATIONAL EXHIBITION OF THE AMERICAN WATERCOLOR SOCIETY
6/7 - 7/10/95	TWEED CONTEMPORARY ARTIST SERIES: THE MINNESOTA & SWEDEN EXCHANGE
7/22 - 9/19/95	CONTEMPORARY SWEDISH ARTISTS: THE MINNESOTA & SWEDEN EXCHANGE

MINNEAPOLIS

James Ford Bell Museum of Natural History
Affiliate Institution: University of Minnesota
10 Church St. S.E., **Minneapolis, MN 55455**
TEL: 612-624-0225
HRS: 9-5 Tu-F; 10-5 Sa; Noon-5 S   DAY CLOSED: M   HOL: LEG/HOL!
F/DAY: T   ADM: Y   ADULT: $3.00   CHILDREN: F (under 13)   STUDENTS: $2.00   SR CIT: $2.00
HDC/ACC: Y; South Entrance & elevator access to all public areas PARKING: Y; On campus parking with handicapped ramps within one block of the museum at Church St. & Forth St. Free street parking on Sundays.
MUS/SH: Y   GR/T: Y   GR/PH: Call 612-624-1852   H/B: Y; Located in a classic 1940 Art Deco building
PERM/COLL: WILDLIFE ART

In addition to an unparalled wildlife art collection that includes a full set of Audubon's "Birds of America," the museum has recently acquired the entire collection from The American Museum of Wildlife Art. **NOT TO BE MISSED:** The dioramas painted by Francis Lee Jaques

MINNEAPOLIS

The Frederick R. Weisman Art Museum at the University of Minnesota
Affiliate Institution: University of Minnesota
333 East River Drive, **Minneapolis, MN 55455**
TEL: 612-625-9494
HRS: 10-6 M-F; Noon-5 Sa, S   HOL: ACAD!; LEG/HOL!
ADM: F   HDC/ACC: Y; Fully accessible   PARKING: Y; Paid parking in the building   MUS/SH: Y
GR/T: Y   GR/PH: call 612-625-9494   H/B: Y; Terra-cotta brick & stainless steel bldg. (1993) by Frank O. Ghery
PERM/COLL: AM: ptgs, sculp, gr 20; KOREAN: furniture 18-19; Worlds largest coll of works by Marsden Hartley
& Alfred Maurer (plus major works by their contemporaries such as Feninger & O'Keeffe)

As of November, 1993, this university museum became the recipient of the new Frederick R. Weisman
Art Museum. Mr. Weisman gererously donated the funds for the stunning fantasy building designed
by noted architect Frank Ghery, as well as the art from his own outstanding collection. All of the
permanent holdings of the University Museum are now housed in this new facility. **NOT TO BE
MISSED:** "Oriental Poppies," by Georgia O'Keeffe

ON EXHIBIT/95:

1/13 - 3/26/95	NATIONAL COUNCIL ON EDUCATION FOR THE CERAMIC ARTS CLAY NATIONAL 1995
4/14 - 6/11/95	DICTATED BY LIFE: MARSDEN HARTLEY'S GERMAN PAINTINGS AND ROBERT INDIANA'S HARTLEY ELEGIES WT
4/28 - 10/2/95	IMAGING OF WOMEN: REPRESENTATIONS OF WOMEN IN ART & CULTURE — Works from the permanent collection.
5/5 - 6/18/95	PHOTOS OF WILLIAM ALLARD — Allard is a noted photojournalist and alumnus of the University of Minnesota.
7/8 - 8/27/95	WEISMAN ART MUSEUM SCULPTURE PLAZA INSTALLATION PROJECT — Artist Kate Hunt will be featured.

The Minneapolis Institute of Arts
2400 Third Ave.So., **Minneapolis, MN 55404**
TEL: 612-870-3000
HRS: 10-5 Tu-Sa; 10-9 T; Noon-5 S   DAY CLOSED: M   HOL: LEG/HOL!
ADM: F   HDC/ACC: Y   PARKING: Y; Free and ample   MUS/SH: Y   REST/FAC: Y; Restaurant 11:30-2:30 Tu-S
GR/T: Y   GR/PH: call 612-870-3000   DT: Y TIME: 2:00 daily
H/B: Y; 1915 Neo-Classic Building by McKim Mead & White
PERM/COLL: AM: ptgs, sculp; EU: ptgs, sculp; DEC/ART; OR; P/COL; AF; OC; ISLAMIC; PHOT; GR; DRGS;
JAP: gr

Distinguished by a broad-ranging 80,000 object collection housed within the walls of a landmark
building that combines a 1915 neo-classic structure with 1974 Japanese inspired additions. With a 50
million dollar renovation just completed, the museum will be working for several years on the
reinstallation of the permanent collection. During this time certain galleries will be temporarily closed
to accommodate this effort. **NOT TO BE MISSED:** Rembrandt's "Lucretia"

ON EXHIBIT/95:

8/25/94 - 3/5/95	THE ARTS OF ISLAM — Dating from the 10th to the 17th centuries, Persian manuscripts, miniatures, ceramics, calligraphy and other items from Mamluk Egypt, Moghul India and Ottoman Turkey will be selected for viewing from the permanent collection.

MINNESOTA

The Minneapolis Institute of Arts - continued

9/10/94 - 1/8/95	THE ANCIENT ART OF FRESCO (working title) — Focusing on the work of Mark Balma, a Minnesota artist trained in Italy, this exhibit presents information on the history of the fresco and explains the processes and materials used in its creation.
10/16/94 - 1/1/95	JEWEL RIVERS: JAPANESE ART FROM THE MARY AND JACKSON BURKE COLLECTION — 80 treasures that span the history of Japanese art from an earthenware bowl of the middle Jomon period (c. 1500 BC) to a screen painting by Shibata Zeshin (1807-1891) will be on public view for the very first time. ADM FEE
11/11/94 - 1/15/95	MINNESOTA ARTISTS EXHIBITION PROGRAM (TBA)
11/19/94 - 3/95	THE PHOTOGRAPHS OF JEROME LIEBLING (closing date TBA) — Included in this first major retrospective of internationally renowned Minnesota artist, Liebling will be his images of Native Americans, views of Northern Minnesota, and other regional subjects.
1/21 - 4/23/95	ECHIZEN: 800 YEARS OF JAPANESE STONEWARE — From a famous Japanese ceramic kiln that has been in continuous operation since the 12th century, approximately 15 historic pieces on loan from the Fukui Prefectural Museum of Ceramics in Japan will be joined by both the traditionally inspired and avant-garde contemporary works of 20 internationally recognized potters.
2/5 - 4/30/95	MADE IN AMERICA: TEN CENTURIES OF AMERICAN ART — 10 centuries of art from ancient Native American works to those of the 1970's on loan from five major American museums will include superb master paintings as well as examples of decorative arts by Paul Revere, Tiffany, Frank Lloyd Wright and others.
2/10 - 4/16/95	JAMES TANNER (working title) — Ceramic, bronze and mixed media works by African-American master ceramist, Tanner, will be featured in this exhibition.
2/18 - 6/18/95	DIRTY BUSINESS: PRINCELY BRONZES — An examination and explanation of the lost-wax process in bronze casting will be highlighted by examples of bronze sculpture from the Institute's permanent collection.
5/12 - 7/16/95	RIVERS MERGING (working title) — This exhibition is concerned with cross-cultural performances, demonstrations and installations by cross-cultural collaborative teams of artists dedicated to the building of better Asian American relations.
6 - 8/95	SPOKEN BY THE LOOM: CLOTH AND SOCIETY IN BHUTAN — In addition to 18th to 20th century watercolors, sketches and photographs, textiles borrowed from several world-wide sources will focus on the relationship of Bhutanese textiles as an integral part of the history and culture of that country.
6/29 - 9/17/95	EVIDENCE 1944-1994: RICHARD AVEDON (TENT!) — A major retrospective of photographs by Richard Avedon. BOOK WT
7/15 - 9/10/95	ITALIAN DRAWINGS FROM THE KATALAN COLLECTION — Old Master paintings from the private collection of Jack Katalan.
10/22/95 - 1/14/96	TREASURES OF VENICE: PAINTINGS FROM THE MUSEUM OF FINE ARTS, BUDAPEST (working title) — 55 paintings by 44 master artists working in Venice during the 16th to 18th centuries will be on loan from one of the largest holdings of Venetian paintings outside of Venice. Many of these works will be cleaned, conserved and restored for this exhibition so that their original splendor can be fully appreciated.
10/28/95 - 1/7/96	MINNESOTA BOOK COLLECTORS

238

MINNEAPOLIS

Walker Art Center

Vineland Place, **Minneapolis, MN 55403**
TEL: 612-375-7600
HRS: 10-8 Tu-Sa; 11-5 S   DAY CLOSED: M   HOL: LEG/HOL!
F/DAY: T& 1st Sa   ADM: Y   ADULT: $4.00   CHILDREN: F (under 12))   STUDENTS: $3.00   SR CIT: $3.00
HDC/ACC: Y   PARKING: Y; Hourly metered on-street parking & pay parking at nearby Parade Stadium lot
MUS/SH: Y   REST/FAC: Y; Sculpture Garden 11:20-3 Tu-S; Terrace Cafe 3-8 Tu-Sa, 3-5 S
GR/T: Y   GR/PH: call 612-375-7600   DT: Y   TIME: 12 & 2 weekends; 2 & 6 T; 1 Sa, S in S/G   S/G: Y
PERM/COLL: AM & EU CONT: ptgs, sculp; GR; DRGS

Housed in a beautifully designed building by noted architect Edward Larabee Barnes, the Walker Art Center, with its superb 5,000 piece permanent collection, is particularly well known for its major exhibitions of 20th century art. PLEASE NOTE: The sculpture garden is open free to all from 6 am to midnight daily. **NOT TO BE MISSED:** Minneapolis Sculpture Garden at Walker Art Center (open 6- Midnight daily; ADM F); "Standing Glass Fish" by F. Gehry at Cowles Conservatory (open 10 -8 Tu-Sa, 10-5 S; ADM F)

ON EXHIBIT/95:

12/93 - 12/95	MARK LUYTEN — In the third phase of a two year project to link the Minneapolis Sculpture Garden with the Walker Art Center's indoor spaces, Belgian artist, Luyten adds and subtracts new elements to the previous 2 phases of this project. Thus each new element takes the place of a former one, forming a continuously series of objects and ideas which incorporate words, poems and text fragments in a variety of languages.
7/24/94 - 6/96	SELECTIONS FROM THE PERMANENT COLLECTION — Thematic groupings of recent works as well as many old favorites will allow the viewer the opportunity to assess changes and similarities of the works of various generations of 20th century artists.
10/2/94 - 2/5/95	ELLSWORTH KELLY — Sketchbooks, collages, and little-known photographs will be joined by works from the permanent collection and key pieces from private collections that examines the full scope of Kelly's work from the 1950's to the 1990's.
10/23/94 - 2/26/95	THE EDMOND R. AND EVELYN HALFF RUBEN BEQUEST: 20TH CENTURY MASTERWORKS — On exhibit will be 18 masterworks recently donated to the museum from the estate of Mrs. Ruben including a watercolor by Wassily Kandinsky, an oil painting by Alexej Jawlensky, and examples of Dada, Surrealist and Futurist works.
11/6/94 - 2/26/95	DUCHAMP'S LEG — In this 2-part exhibition miniature replicas of 68 of his most important works will be on display in order to emphasize the importance of the legacy of his fascination with everyday objects and his acceptance of the commonplace for its own sake. Duchamp's philosophy was to influence many diverse artists who followed in his footsteps including John Cage, Merce Cunningham, Jasper Johns and Robert Rauchenberg. WT*
2/16 - 5/21/95	ASIA/AMERICA: IDENTITIES IN CONTEMPORARY ASIAN AMERICAN ART — Paintings, sculpture, photographs and mixed-media works by 20 immigrant Asian visual artists address the questions of identity faced by Asians living in the West. CAT WT
4/9 - 7/23/95	SIGMAR POLKE — 70 newly acquired completely editioned works of German artist Polke that span the whole range of his graphic production will be featured in this 3-part exhibition. The Walker has the only comprehensive collection of its kind in any public institution in the world,
6/18 - 8/27/95	CHANTAL AKERMAN: FROM THE EAST — A museum installation by French film director Chantal Akerman consisting of 3 viewing chambers that deconstruct the basic stages of the film production process. BOOK WT*

MINNESOTA

Walker Art Center - continued

9/23 - 10/12/95   DAWOUD BEY: PORTRAITS — 125 images that cover 20 years (1975-1995) of the work of African- American portrait photographer Bey, from traditional black and white silver prints to large-scale color Polaroid works.   **CAT**

MOOREHEAD

Plains Art Museum
521 Main St., **Moorehead, MN 56560**
TEL: 701-293-0903
HRS: 10-5 Tu-Sa; Noon-5 S; Till 9pm T   DAY CLOSED: M   HOL: 1/1, 7/4, MEM/DAY, LAB/DAY, THGV, 12/25
ADM: F
HDC/ACC: Y; Elevator   PARKING: Y; Free on-street parking in front of the museum   MUS/SH: Y
GR/T: Y   GR/PH: call 218-236-7383   H/B: Y; 1915 Old Post Office Building (ListedNRHP)
PERM/COLL: AM/REG; NAT/AM; AF; PHOT 20

Located on the western border of the state near Fargo, North Dakota, the 1915 Classical Revival style building that houses the Plains Museum was used, until 1958, as a Federal Post Office building.

ST. PAUL

Minnesota Museum of American Art
Landmark Center-Fifth & Market, **St. Paul, MN 55102-1486**
TEL: 612-292-4355
HRS: 11-4 Tu-Sa; 11-7:30 T; 1-5 S   DAY CLOSED: M   HOL: LEG/HOL!
SUGG/CONT: Y   ADULT: $2.00
HDC/ACC: Y; Elevator; restroom; special entrance   PARKING: Y; Street parking and nearby parking facilities
MUS/SH: Y   REST/FAC: Y; 11:30-1:30 Tu-F; 11-1 S   GR/T: Y   GR/PH: call 612-292-4369
DT: Y   TIME: selected Sundays at 1:30!   H/B: Y   S/G: Y
PERM/COLL: AM; OC; AS; AF

Begun in 1927 as the St. Paul School of Art, the Minnesota Museum is one of the oldest visual arts institutions in the region. Housed in two historic buildings, the museum, in 1966, became the fortunate recipient of one half of the estate of noted American sculptor, Paul Manship, a native of St. Paul.

ON EXHIBIT/95:

9/25/94 - 1/8/95   PATRICK DESJARLAIT AND OJIBWE TRADITION — In the first retrospective of his work, Desjarlait, one of only 2 Ojibwe artists to achieve national acclaim in the early Native Ameican fine art movement, portrays details of Ojibwe life and pride in his cultural heritage.

1/29 - 5/14/95   WITNESS & LEGACY: CONTEMPORARY ART ABOUT THE HOLOCAUST — Works by artists who are survivors, children of survivors, and other artists will be included in an inter-generational exhibition that acts as a response to the Holocaust on the occasion of the 50th anniversary of the end of World War II and the liberation of the concentration camps.

5/28 - 9/3/95   THE REGIONAL RESPONSE — A juried exhibition of contemporary regional work.

BILOXI

George E. Ohr Arts and Cultural Center

136 George E. Ohr St., **Biloxi, MS 39530**
TEL: 601-374-5547
HRS: 9am-8pm M-W, 9-5 T-Sa   HOL: 1/1, 7/4, THGV, 12/25
ADM: F   HDC/ACC: Y   PARKING: Y; Free parking in the lot across the street from the museum.
MUS/SH: Y   GR/T: Y   GR/PH: call ahead to reserve
PERM/COLL: George Ohr pottery

This museum, formerly one of three divisions of the Mississippi Museum of Art now operates as an independent entity. **NOT TO BE MISSED:** 100 piece collection of pottery by George Ohr, often referred to as the mad potter of Biloxi

JACKSON

Mississipi Museum of Art

201 E. Pascagoula St., **Jackson, MS 39201**
TEL: 601-960-1515
HRS: 10-5 Tu-Sa   DAY CLOSED: S, M   HOL: 1/1, 7/4, THGV, 12/25
F/DAY: Tu & T students only   ADM: Y   ADULT: $3.00   CHILDREN: $2.00 (F under 3)   STUDENTS: $2.00
SR CIT: $2.00   HDC/ACC: Y   PARKING: Y; Pay lot behind museum   MUS/SH: Y   REST/FAC: Y; Restaurant
GR/T: Y   GR/PH: call 601-960-1515   DT: Y   TIME: upon request if available   S/G: Y
PERM/COLL: AM: 19-20; REG: 19-20; BRIT: ptgs, dec/art mid 18-early 19; P/COL: cer; JAP: gr

Begun as art association in 1911, the Mississippi Museum now has more than 5,000 works of art in a collection that spans more than 30 centuries. **NOT TO BE MISSED:** "hands -on" Impressions Gallery, housed in a unique stimulating architectual environment

ON EXHIBIT/95:

11/18/94 - 1/7/95	SHADOWY EVIDENCE: THE PHOTOGRAPHY OF EDWARD S. CURTIS AND HIS CONTEMPORARIES — 90 images by numerous potographers that document the upheaval and struggles with acculturation and tradition of Native Americans from 1890-1930 will be seen in this presentation.
11/18/94 - 2/18/95	ART OF THE AMERICAS — Pre-Columbian, Mexican and folk art from 3 distinctive collections aimed at enhancing our appreciation of the multi-cultural American experience will be featured in this exhibition.
12/3/94 - 1/14/95	THE MODERNS — Late 19th and early 20th century artworks from the permanent collection will include paintings, prints and watercolors by such American and European greats as Georgia O'Keeffe, Marc Chagal, and Pablo Picasso.
1/20 - 2/18/95	THE PAPER CHASE THROUGH TWENTIETH CENTURY AMERICAN ART — Works on paper that survey major artistic developments of this century features examples by Thomas Hart Benton, Edward Hopper, Andy Warhol and others.
3/3 - 4/20/95	NEW DIRECTIONS IN HOLOGRAPHY: THE LANDSCAPE REINVENTED — Images of landscapes and nature-based subjects by 8 internationally based artists whose artworks incorporate holograms will be on exhibit.
2/18 - 4/1/95	TWENTIETH-CENTURY DRAWINGS — Drawings in diverse media from the permanent collection will illustrate this century's pluralistic approach to making images.

MISSISSIPPI

Mississipi Museum of Art - continued

4/8 - 6/24/95	NEW DEAL ART: IMAGES OF MISSISSIPPI — Mississippi art of the New Deal era will be highlighted in this exhibition.
5/19 - 5/21/95	JUBILEE JAM — Featured in conjunction with this annual event will be the exhibition of the work of four contemporary artists; namely, Sandy Skoglund, Andrew Young, Carol Hepper, and Linda Frese. The works will remain on view until 7/29.

LAUREL

Lauren Rogers Museum of Art
5th Ave. at 7th St., **Laurel, MS 39440**
TEL: 601-649-6374
HRS: 10-4:45 Tu-Sa; 1-4 S   DAY CLOSED: M   HOL: LEG/HOL!
ADM: F   HDC/ACC: Y; Wheelchair accessible, elevator, restrooms
PARKING: Y; New lot at rear of museum and along side of the museum on 7th Street   MUS/SH: Y
GR/T: T GR/PH: call 601-649-6374   DT: Y   TIME: 10-12 & 1-3 Tu-F
PERM/COLL: AM:19-20; EU: 19-20; NAT/AM; JAP: gr

Located among the trees in Laurel's Historic District, the Lauren Rogers, the first museum to be established in the state, has grown rapidly since its inception in 1922. While the original Georgian Revival building still stands, the new adjoining galleries are perfect for the display of the fine art collection of American and European masterworks. **NOT TO BE MISSED:** Largest collection of Native American Indian baskets in the U.S.; Gibbons English Georgian Silver Collection

ON EXHIBIT/95:

1 - 3/95	NEW DEAL ART: IMAGES OF MISSISSIPPI
2/95	EXPRESSIONS OF MY PEOPLE: HISTORICALLY DRESSED AFRICAN-AMERICAN DOLLS BY BERNICE DURR
2/95	WORKS BY AFRICAN-AMERICAN ARTISTS
2 - MID 3/95	JAPANESE FOLK TOYS
3 - 5/95	MIXED MEDIA 1983-1993: WORKS BY SEENA DONNESON
4 - 5/95	MISSISSIPPI ARTIST SERIES: YOUR OLD MEN SHALL DREAM DREAMS

MERIDIAN

Meridian Museum of Art
25th Ave. & 7th St., **Meridian, MS 39301**
TEL: 601-693-1501
HRS: 1-5 Tu-S   DAY CLOSED: M   HOL: LEG/HOL!
ADM: F
PARKING: Y; Free but very limited   GR/T: Y   GR/PH: 601-693-1501   DT: Y   TIME: Upon request if available
PERM/COLL: AM: phot, sculp, dec/art; REG; WORKS ON PAPER 20; EU: portraits 19-20

Housed in the landmark Old Carnegie Library Building built in 1912-13, the Meridian Museum, began in 1933 as an art association, serves the cultural needs of the people of East Mississippi and Western Alabama. **NOT TO BE MISSED:** 18th century collection of European portraits

Meridian Museum of Art - continued

ON EXHIBIT/95:

1/7 - 2/4/95	SCOTT MEYER — An exhibition of archaelogicaly-inspired sculpture by Meyer, the 1994 Bi-State Best of Show winner.
1/7 - 2/4/95	BOBBY HARRISON — Moody black and white photographic images ranging in subject from nude studies to landscapes.
1/7 - 2/4/95	KENNETH PROCTOR — Charcoal drawings and oil paintings.
2/11 - 3/18/95	1995 BI-STATE ART COMPETITION — Artists from Mississippi and Alabama are featured in the 22nd presentation of this annual juried competition.
3/25 - 4/22/95	JORE ALLEN
4/29 - 6/3/95	MISSISSIPPI ART COLONY — Works from the colony's spring workshop.
4/29 - 6/3/95	PAUL CAMPBELL — A multi-media exhibit that expresses the many facets of African-American culture.
6/10 - 7/15/95	4TH ANNUAL PEOPLE'S CHOICE COMPETITION
7/22 - 9/2/95	RHYTHMS, SPIRITS, COLORS, AND EXPRESSIONS — Abstract paintings and sculpture by Martha Hopkins and Millicent Merritt Howell.
12/2 - 12/30/95	MUSEUM MEMBERS SHOW — Artworks by members of the museum will be on exhibit.

TUPELO

Mississippi Museum of Art, Tupelo
211 W. Main St., **Tupelo, MS 38801**
TEL: 601-844-2787
HRS: 10-5 Tu-Sa; 1-5 S   HOL: 1/1, 7/4, THGV, 12/25
ADM: F
HDC/ACC: Y   PARKING: Y; Non metered street parking
GR/T: Y   GR/PH: Call ahead to reserve   DT: Y   TIME: Upon request if available

Housed in the former original People's Bank Building (1904-05) this small but effective non-collecting institution is dedicated to bringing traveling exhibitions from all areas of the country to the people of the community and its visitors.

MISSOURI

COLUMBIA

Museum of Art and Archaeology
Affiliate Institution: University Of Missouri
1 Pickard Hall, **Columbia, MO 65211**
TEL: 314-882-3591
HRS: 9-5 Tu-F; Noon-5 Sa, S; Till 9pm T   DAY CLOSED: M   HOL: LEG/HOL!; 12/25, 1/1
VOL/CONT: Y   ADM: F
HDC/ACC: Y   PARKING: Y; Parking is available at the university visitors' garage on University Avenue; metered parking spaces on Ninth St.   MUS/SH: Y
PERM/COLL: AN/EGT; AN/GRK; AN/R; AN/PER; BYZ; DRGS 15-20; GR 15-20; AF; OC; P/COL; CH; JAP; OR

Ancient art and archaeology from Egypt, Palestine, Iran, Cyprus, Greece, Etruria and Rome as well as early Christian and Byzantine art, the Kress study collection, and 15th-20th century European and American artworks are among the treasures from 6 continents and five millennia that are housed in this museum.

ON EXHIBIT/95:

1/13 - 3/26/95	AFRICA THROUGH THE EYES OF WOMEN
4/15 - 6/25/95	MISSOURI ARTS COUNCIL VISUAL ARTISTS BIENNIAL
7/8 - 8/13/95	WATERWAYS WEST: PHOTOS FROM MISSOURI RIVER PORTFOLIOS
9/1 - 10/15/95	BUILT, THROWN, AND TOUCHED: CONTEMPORARY CLAY WORKS

KANSAS CITY

Federal Reserve Bank of Kansas City
925 Grand Ave., **Kansas City, MO 64198-0001**
TEL: 816-881-2000
HRS: 8-5 M-F   DAY CLOSED: Sa, S   HOL: LEG/HOL!
ADM: F   HDC/ACC: Y   PARKING: Y; Pay lots and garages nearby   H/B: Y

In 1985 the Roger Guffey Gallery of the Federal Reserve Bank was created to offer the public an ongoing high quality series of art exhbitions. The 1921 building was renovated and restored at that time in order to preserve many of the wonderful original architectural details. In addition to the art gallery, fascinating displays that encircle the lobby on the mezzanine level explain the purpose and history of the bank and exhibit such interesting objects as counterfeit money and a 27 pound bar of gold.

ON EXHIBIT/95:

2/3 - 3/24/95	BOB BLACKBURN'S PRINTMAKING WORKSHOP: ARTISTS OF COLOR — Since its establishment in 1949, this printmaking workshop has played a chief role in encouraging artists of color to create works by using a wide variety of interesting and unusual techniques. CAT WT
4/7 - 6/2/95	JOHN STUART CURRY'S AMERICA — Drawings and studies by this renowned Midwest regionalist artist and muralist whose images of small town rural America dominated popular taste in the 1930's. WT
6/9 - 8/4/95	SMALL TOWN AMERICA — On exhibit will be 48 black and white photographic images many of which appear in a book entitled "Small Town America" that were taken along with many others of a small town in Missouri each year from 1949 to the present.

244

MISSOURI

Federal Reserve Bank of Kansas City - continued

8/11 - 10/6/95   KANSAS CITY ARTISTS COALITION — Innovative, promising Midwest artistic talents whose works have not been widely shown in Kansas City before will be highlighted in this exhibition.

10/13 - 12/1/95   JOSIAH WEDGEWOOD: EXPERIMENTAL POTTER — Examples of Jasperware, red-figure Greco-Etruscan vases, a copy of the Portland vase and others will be featured in this 56 piece display of Wedgewood ceramics which date from the mid-18th century to the present.   WT

KANSAS CITY

Kemper Museum of Contemporary Art & Design of Kansas City Art Institute

Affiliate Institution: Kansas City Art Institute
4415 Warwick Blvd., **Kansas City, MO 64111-1874**
TEL: 816-561-4852
HRS: 10-4 Tu-T, 10-9 F, 10-5 Sa, 1-5 S DAY CLOSED: M HOL: 1/1, 7/4, THGV, 12/24, 12/25
ADM: F PARKING: Y; Free MUS/SH: Y REST/FAC: Y GR/T: Y GR/PH: call 816-561-4852
DT: Y TIME: call for specifics S/G: Y
PERM/COLL: CONT: figurative ptgs; Works by Contemporary Emerging and Established Artists

Designed by architect Gunnar Birkets, the stunning new (10/94) ultra-modern tripartate building of the Kemper Museum of Contemporary Art & Design (a work of art in itself) features up-turned ribbons of glass along the high walls in the exhibition wings that permit natural light to illuminate the galleries. Works by living artists, designers and craftsmen form the nucleus of the collection. **NOT TO BE MISSED:** "Ahulani," bronze sculpture by Deborah Butterfield; "Flowers, Watches, Dark Day," acrylic on canvas by Paul Wonner

ON EXHIBIT/95:

10/2/94 - 6/30/95   DEBUT: SELECTIONS FROM THE PERMANENT COLLECTION OF THE KEMPER MUSEUM OF CONTEMPORARY ART AND DESIGN — Contemporary masters from the permanent collection will be on exhibit.

10/2/94 - 6/30/95   ORIGINAL ARCHITECTURAL DRAWINGS BY GUNNER BIRKERTS FOR THE KEMPER MUSEUM OF CONTEMPORARY ART & DESIGN — Architectural drawings from every planning phase of the new museum building will be on view.

12/18/94 - 2/26/95   INSIDE OUT: CONTEMPORARY JAPANESE PHOTOGRAPHY — Creative elements combined with Japanese sensibilities are seen in the works of the 6 noted contemporary Japaneses photographers featured in this exhibition.

2/5 - 4/2/95   BEVERLY SEMMES: YELLOW POOL — This installation, a gigantic dress of velvet and organza, appeals to the absurd at the same time it acts as a metaphor for feminism and modern identity.

3/19 - 5/21/95   KEEPERS OF THE FLAME: STUDENTS OF KEN FERGUSON — In this exhibition curated by Ken Ferguson, works by many of the now famous students that he has taught at the Kansas City Art Institute will be on view. The exhibition will coincide with a retrospective for Ferguson held concurrently at the Nelson Atkins Museum.

4/23 - 3/31/95   MINNIE EVANS: AFRICAN-AMERICAN VISIONARY ARTIST — Presented will be the first retrospective of Evans' work.   CAT WT

3 - 4/95   AUSTRIAN AVANT-GARDE CINEMA: 1954-1993

245

MISSOURI

Kemper Museum of Contemporary Art & Design - continued

6/4 - 7/30/95   CROSSING BORDERS: CONTEMPORARY AUSTRALIAN TEXTILE ART — Works in 2 and 3 dimensions by artists of European, Asian and Aboriginal Australian origin. WT

6 - 7/95   AN ECCENTRIC ORBIT: VIDEO ART IN AUSTRALIA — 25 videos that present an idiosyncratic approach to Australian culture and electronic culture.

8/1 - 9/30/95   ROBERT FRANK: THE AMERICAS — Post-war America as seen in the works of this Swiss-born photographer.

KANSAS CITY

The Nelson-Atkins Museum of Art
4525 Oak St., **Kansas City, MO 64111**
TEL: 816-561-4000
HRS: 10-4 Tu-T; 10-9 F; 10-5 Sa; 1-5 S   DAY CLOSED: M   HQL: 1/1, 7/4, THGV, 12/25
F/DAY: Sa   ADM: Y   ADULT: $4.00   CHILDREN: F (under 5)   STUDENTS: $1.00   SR CIT: $4.00
HDC/ACC: Y; Elevators & ramps   PARKING: Y; Free lot on 45th St; parking lot for visitors with disabilities at Oak St. Business Entrance on west side of the Museum   MUS/SH: Y   REST/FAC: Y; Restaurant 10-3:30 Tu-Sa, 1-4 S
GR/T: Y   GR/PH: call 816-751-1238   DT: Y   TIME: 10:30, 11, 1, & 2 Tu-Sa; 1:30, 2, 2:20, 3 S   S/G: Y
PERM/COLL: AM: all media; EU: all media; PER/RMS; NAT/AM; OC; P/COL; OR

Among the many fine art treasures in this outstanding 60 year old museum is their world famous collection of Oriental art and artifacts that includes the Chinese Temple Room with its furnishings, a gallery displaying delicate scroll paintings, and a sculpture gallery with glazed T'ang dynasty tomb figures. **NOT TO BE MISSED:** Largest collection of works by Thomas Hart Benton; Henry Moore Sculpture Garden; "Shuttlecocks," a four-part sculptural installation by Claes Oldenburg and Coosje van Bruggen located in the grounds of the museum

ON EXHIBIT/95:

11/13/94 - 1/8/95   THE ART OF BOOK ILLUSTRATION: PRINTS FROM THE PERMANENT COLLECTION

12/18/94 - 2/19/95   AN AMERICAN CENTURY OF PHOTOGRAPHY: FROM DRY-PLATE TO DIGITAL, THE HALLMARK PHOTOGRAPHIC COLLECTION

2/5 - 4/2/95   ERNST HAAS IN BLACK AND WHITE — Though best known for his creative color work, the 63 less familiar black and white photographic images in this exhibition, created between 1945 and the 1960's reveal Haas' goal of achieving art and poetry in whatever subject and locale he was addressing. WT

3/19 - 5/28/95   KEN FERGUSON RETROSPECTIVE

4/23 - 6/25/95   THE PRINTS OF WAYNE THIEBAUD — 50 prints by this acclaimed representational painter dating from 1964-1991 echo many of the familiar images and graphic motifs of the artist's paintings. BROCHURE WT

6/25 - 8/20/95   HENRY OSSAWA TANNER

7/9 - 9/3/95   THE FAMILY 1976: RICHARD AVEDON'S PORTRAITS FOR ROLLING STONE

9/10 - 10/22/95   PHOTOGRAPHS BY DOROTHEA LANGE FROM THE HALLMARK COLLECTION

11/12/95 - 1/5/96   PROSAIC VIEWS, POETIC VISION: WHISTLER WORKS ON PAPER FROM THE UNIVERISTY OF MICHIGAN MUSEUM OF ART

12/17/94 - 2/11/95   THE CHANGING FACE OF EUROPE: PORTRAITS FROM THE SIXTEENTH CENTURY

MISSOURI

POPLAR BLUFF

Margaret Harwell Art Museum
421 N. Main St., **Poplar Bluff, MO 63901**
TEL: 314-686-8002
HRS: 1-4 W-Sa   DAY CLOSED: M, T, S   HOL: LEG/HOL!
VOL/CONT: Y   ADM: F   HDC/ACC: Y   H/B: Y; Located in 1883 mansion
PERM/COLL: DEC/ART; REG; CONT

The 1880's mansion in which this museum is housed is a perfect foil for the museum's permanent collection of contemporary art. Located in the south-eastern part of the state just above the Arkansas border, the museum features monthly exhibitions showcasing the works of both regional and nationally known artists.

SAINT JOSEPH

The Albrecht-Kemper Museum of Art
2818 Frederick Blvd., **Saint Joseph, MO 64506**
TEL: 816-233-7003
HRS: 10-4 Tu-Sa; 1-4 S   DAY CLOSED: M   HOL: LEG/HOL!
F/DAY: S   ADM: Y   ADULT: $3.00   CHILDREN: F (under 12)   STUDENTS: $1.00
HDC/ACC: Y; Fully wheelchair accessible (doors, lifts, restrooms, theater)   PARKING: Y; Free on-site parking
MUS/SH: Y   REST/FAC: Y; Daily Tu-F   GR/T: Y   GR/PH: call 816-233-7003   S/G: Y
PERM/COLL: AM: ldscp ptgs, Impr ptgs, gr, drgs 18-20

Considered to have the region's finest collection of American art, the Albrecht-Kemper has recently completed an extensive and transforming expansion of the 1935 Georgian-style mansion of William Albrecht. **NOT TO BE MISSED:** North American Indian Portfolio by Catlin: illustrated books by Audubon; Thomas Hart Benton collection

ON EXHIBIT/95:
1/13 - 4/2/95	LORNA SIMPSON: NEW WORK
4/7 - 6/11/95	WATERCOLOR: TECHNIQUE, CONNOISSEURSHIP AND EXPLORATION

SPRINGFIELD

Springfield Art Museum
1111 E. Brookside Dr., **Springfield, MO 65807**
TEL: 417-866-2716
HRS: 9-5 Tu-Sa; 1-5 S; 6:30pm-9:30pm W   DAY CLOSED: M   HOL: LOCAL & LEG/HOL!
VOL/CONT: Y   ADM: F   HDC/ACC: Y   PARKING: Y; West parking lot with 55 handicapped spaces; limited on-street parking north of the museum   GR/T: Y   GR/PH: call 417-866-2716
PERM/COLL: AM: ptgs, sculp, drgs, gr, phot 18-20; EU: ptgs, sculp, gr, drgs, phot 18-20; DEC/ART; NAT/AM; OC; P/COL

Watercolor U.S.A., an annual national competition is but one of the features of the Springfield Museum, the oldest cultural institution in the city. **NOT TO BE MISSED:** John Henry's "Sun Target," 1974, a painted steel sculpture situated on the grounds directly east of the museum; paintings and prints by Thomas Hart Benton

ON EXHIBIT/95:
1/95 - 5/95	PERMANENT COLLECTION — On display will be works from the permanent collection in both the Foyer Gallery and the Kelly Gallery.

247

MISSOURI

Springfield Art Museum - continued

1/14 - 2/26/95	PHILIP PEARLSTEIN — Works by one of the foremost contemporary realist painters in America.
6/3 - 7/30/95	WATERCOLOR U.S.A. 1995 — One of the most prestigious juried art competitions.

ST. LOUIS

Forum For Contemporary Art
3540 Washington St., St. **Louis, MO 63103**
TEL: 314-421-3791
HRS: 10-5 Tu, W, Sa; Noon-8 T, F; (10-5 MEM/DAY-LAB/DAY) DAY CLOSED: S, M
HOL: LEG/HOL! & INSTALLATIONS ADM: F HDC/ACC: Y; First floor accessible; elevator to third floor gallery
PARKING: Y; Street or public parking (nominal fee) at the Third Baptist Church parking lot on Washington.
REST/FAC: Y; Cafe & Bookstore GR/T: Y GR/PH: call 314-535-4660
PERM/COLL: No permanent collection. Please call for current exhibition information not listed below.

Experimental cutting-edge art of the new is the focus of The Forum which presents exhibitions of important recent national and international art enhanced by educational programming and public discussions. **NOT TO BE MISSED:**

ON EXHIBIT/95:

1/20 - 3/11/95	KIM ABELES: ENCYCLOPEDIA PERSONA, A 15 YEAR STUDY — Diverse issues of political awareness and social commentary will be seen in an exibition of books, boxes, shrines, assemblages and large & small installations created over the past 15 years by Abeles, a Los Angeles-based artist.
3/24 - 5/6/95	FELIX GONZALEZ-TORRES — An installation will be created especially for the Forum by this Cuban-American artist whose unique conceptual works might include stacks of paper printed with aphorisms or piles of cookies and/or candy pouring out of a corner onto the floor.
5/12 - 6/24/95	SANDY WALKER: WOODBLOCK PRINTS — Black and white evocations of the sun, earth, trees and water will be seen in these woodblock prints that push the limits between landscape and abstraction.

Laumeier Sculpture Park & Gallery
12580 Rott Rd., **St. Louis, MO 63127**
TEL: 314-821-1209
HRS: 8am -1/2 Hr Past Sunset Daily (Park); 10-5 Tu-Sa & Noon-5 S (Gallery)
ADM: F HDC/ACC: Y; Paved trails; ramps to museum & restrooms
PARKING: Y; Free and ample MUS/SH: Y REST/FAC: Picnic Area GR/T: Y GR/PH: call 314-821-1209
DT: Y TIME: 2pm S (May - Oct) S/G: Y
PERM/COLL: CONT/AM; sculp: 40 WORKS BY ERNEST TROVA; SITE SPECIFIC SCULP

Internationally acclaimed site-specific sculptures that complement their natural surroundings are the focus of this institution whose goal is to promote greater public involvement and understanding of contemporary sculpture. Audio cassettes are available for self-guided tours. **NOT TO BE MISSED:** Works by Alexander Liberman, Beverly Pepper, Dan Graham, Jackie Ferrara

ON EXHIBIT/95:

THROUGH 1/15/95	CONTEMPORARY MEXICAN ART
3/18 - 4/16/95	"JUDYLAND" - SCULPTURE BY JUDY ONOFRIO
5/13 - 5/14/95	LAUMEIER 8TH ANNUAL CONTEMPORARY ART & CRAFT FAIR
6/24 - 6/25/95	SAND CASTLE FESTIVAL

ST. LOUIS

The Saint Louis Art Museum
1 Fine Arts Park, Forest Park, **St. Louis, MO 63110-1380**
TEL: 314-721-0072
HRS: 1:30-8:30 Tu; 10-5 W-S   DAY CLOSED: M   HOL: 1/1, THGV, 12/25
F/DAY: Tu PM for special exhibitions   ADM: F
HDC/ACC: Y   PARKING: Y; Free parking in small lot on south side of building; also street parking availble.
MUS/SH: Y   REST/FAC: Y; Cafe 10-8 Tu; 10-3:30 W-S (S brunch 10-3)   GR/T: Y   GR/PH: call 314-721-0072
DT: Y   TIME: 1:30 W-F (30 min.); 1:30 Sa, S (60 min.)   H/B: Y; Located in a 1903 World's Fair Exhibition Building
PERM/COLL: AN/EGT; AN/CH; JAP; IND; OC; AF; P/COL; NAT/AM; REN; PTGS:18-CONT; SCULP: 18-CONT

Just 10 minutes from the heart of downtown St. Louis, this museum is home to one of the most important permanent collections of art in the country. Featuring pre-Columbian and German Expressionist works that are ranked among the best in the best in the world, the museum is also known for its Renaissance, Impressionist, American, and Asian collections. PLEASE NOTE: Although there is an admission fee for certain exhibitions, a free tour of these exhibitions is offered at 6 pm on Tuesday evenings. **NOT TO BE MISSED:** "Portrait of Lady Guildeford" by Holbien; "Portrait of a Woman" by Frans Hals

ON EXHIBIT/95:

5/31/94 - 2/1/95	ART AT THE ALTAR — From the permanent collection an exhibition of 13th through 20th century objects used in religious ceremonies will include examples of repositories for relics, candlesticks, liturgical garments and the like.
7/26/94 - 1/22/95	POTTERY FROM THE AMERICAN SOUTHWEST — An exploration of Southwest and northern Mexico pottery, both old and contemporary that demonstrates both their stylistic differences and the basic continuity of their artistic traditions.
11/1/94 - 1/1/95	GERTRUDE KASEBIER, PHOTOGRAPHER — The 45 works on exhibit will feature Kasebier's unadorned portraits of Native Americans in Buffalo Bill's traveling show, domestic genre scenes of motherhood and the family, and complex allegorical compositions.
12/94 - 2/95	CURRENTS 60: JERALD IEANS — Abstract paintings on plywood by St. Louis artist, Ieans.
1/10 - 3/12/95	MODERN GERMAN DRAWINGS FROM THE PERMANENT COLLECTION — 35 drawings by notable German artists that include works by Otto Dix, George Groz, Paul Klee, Kathe Kollwitz, Franz Marc, Max Beckman and others.
2 - 4/95	19TH CENTURY GERMAN ART FROM STUTTGART — On exhibit will be 110 paintings, drawings and sculptures, all 19th century German masterpieces that for the most part have never been seen before in the U.S. ADM FEE
3 - 8/95	METAL ARTS OF THE SUB-SAHARAN WEST AFRICA — The origins of the history of metal in this region of West Africa, an enigma for the descendants of this basically agriculturally dependent group who used metal for trade, will be addressed in this exhibition of objects used for adornment, weaponry and agriculture.
3/21 - 6/4/95	THE GRAPHIC WORK OF BRUEGEL AND BOSCH — 75 prints from a private St. Louis collection will be featured in this exhibition.
6/16 - 9/4/95	MADE IN AMERICA: TEN CENTURIES OF AMERICAN ART — 125 works from the permanent collections of 5 midwestern museums will trace ten centuries of American art under the headings of Ancient America, Colonial & Federal America, Democratic Vistas, American Impressionism, Native American Art, Art of the Early 20th Century, and Art after the War. CAT ADM FEE

MISSOURI

The Saint Louis Art Museum - continued

11/3 - 12/31/95   NIHONGA: A CENTURY OF MODERN JAPANESE-STYLE PAINTING, 1868-1968
— Nihonga, Japanese-style art that preserves aspects of traditional brush painting while
including certain Western trends, was developed as an art form in the late 19th century.
In this exhibition, drawn primarily from public and private sources in Japan, over 150
paintings from the Meiji (1868-1912), Taisho (1912-1925) and mid-Showa (1926-1968)
periods will be arranged both chronologically and thematically. In addition, screens, cedar
doors, hanging scrolls, handscrolls, albums and fans will also be on view.

CAT   ADM FEE

ST. LOUIS

Washington University Gallery of Art, Steinberg Hall

Forsyth and Skinker Campus, **St. Louis, MO 63130**
TEL: 314-935-5490
HRS: (SEP-APR) 10-5 M-F & 1-5 Sa, S; (MEM/DAY-LAB/DAY) 10-5 Tu-F, 1-5 Sa, S
HOL: LEG/HOL! Occasionally closed for major installations; Call (314-889-4523)
ADM: F
HDC/ACC: Y; Elevator recently installed   PARKING: Y; Free visitor parking on the North side of the building
MUS/SH: Y   GR/T: Y   GR/PH: call 314-5490
PERM/COLL: EU: ptgs, sculp 16-20; OM: 16-20; CONT/GR; AM: ptgs, sculp 19-20; DEC/ART; FR: academic;
AB/EXP; CUBISTS

With a well deserved reputation for being one of the premier university art museums in the nation, the
more than 100 year old Gallery of Art at Washington University features outstanding examples of
works by Picasso (25 in all) and a myriad of history's artistic greats. **NOT TO BE MISSED:** Hudson
River School Collection

ON EXHIBIT/95:

1/27 - 3/26/95   THE MATTER OF HISTORY: SELECTED WORKS BY ANNETTE LEMIEUX —
Mixed-media works by this contemporary American artist.

1/95 - 5/96   SELECTIONS FROM THE WASHINGTON UNIVERSITY ART COLLECTION

BILLINGS

Yellowstone Art Center
410 N. 27th St., **Billings, MT 59101**
TEL: 406-256-6804
HRS: 11-5 Tu-Sa; Noon-5 S; till 8pm T ; open one hour earlier summer   DAY CLOSED: M   HOL: LEG/HOL!
ADM: F   HDC/ACC: Y; Ramp   PARKING: Y; Pay lot next to building is free on weekends   MUS/SH: Y
GR/T: Y   GR/PH: call 406-256-6804   H/B: Y; Located in 1916 Building
PERM/COLL: CONT/HISTORICAL: ptgs, sculp, cer, phot, drgs, gr

Situated in the heart of downtown Billings, the focus of the museum is on displaying the works of contemporary regional artists and on showcasing artists who have achieved significant regional or national acclaim. With 2,400 works in its permanent collection, the museum is well-known for its "Montana Collection" dedicated to the preservation of Western art as a living artistic heritage. It is also the recipient of 90 Abstract Expressionist paintings from the George Poindexter family of New York. PLEASE NOTE: The museum MAY be closed for renovation and expansion for a period of 15 months starting sometime in '95. Please call ahead for information.

ON EXHIBIT/95:
1/27 - 3/3/95   27th ANNUAL ART EXHIBITION — Works in this extensive display will all be available for purchase at the auction on 3/4 at the Billings Sheraton Hotel.

GREAT FALLS

C. M. Russell Museum
400 13th St. North, **Great Falls, MT 59401**
TEL: 406-727-8787
HRS: 9-6 M-Sa & 1-5 S (May-Sep); 10-5 Tu-Sa & 1-5 S (winter)   HOL: 1/1, EASTER, THGV, 12/25
F/DAY: M (OCT-APR)   ADM: Y   ADULT: $4.00   CHILDREN: F (under 5)   STUDENTS: $2.00   SR CIT: $3.00
HDC/ACC: Y   PARKING: Y; Free parking on grounds of museum   MUS/SH: Y
GR/T: Y   GR/PH: call 406-727-8787   DT: Y   TIME: 1:00 M-F (June through Aug)   H/B: Y
PERM/COLL: REG; CONT; CER

Constructed mainly of telephone poles, the log cabin studio of the great cowboy artist, C. M. Russell still contains the original cowboy gear and Indian artifacts that were used as the artist's models. Adjoining the cabin and in stark contrast to it is the the fine art museum with its ultra modern facade. It houses more than 7,000 works of art that capture the flavor of the old west and its bygone way of life. **NOT TO BE MISSED:** Collection of Western Art by many of the American greats

ON EXHIBIT/95:
9/16/94 - 1/2/95   BILL GOLLINGS: RANAHAN ARTIST — 71 of Gollings most notable works will be featured in this exhibit.

10/27/94 - 2/12/95   WILDLIFE OF THE WEST EXHIBIT

11/9/94 - 1/8/95   C. M. RUSSELL CHRISTMAS EXHIBIT

2/24 - 3/18/95   C. M. RUSSELL AUCTION EXHIBIT

3/15 - 3/18/95   C. M. RUSSELL AUCTION OF ORIGINAL WESTERN ART

3 -5/95   INDIAN MASTERPIECES: OLD AND NEW (TENT!)

6 - 10/95   C. M. RUSSELL: THE EARLY YEARS (TENT!)

8/17 - 9/9/95   C. M. RUSSELL MUSEUM BENEFIT EXHIBIT

MONTANA

GREAT FALLS

Paris Gibson Square Museum of Art
1400 1st Ave., North, **Great Falls, MT 59401**
TEL: 406-727-8255
HRS: 10-5 Tu-F; Noon-5 Sa, S; 7-9 T; Also open M MEM/DAY to LAB/DAY   DAY CLOSED: M
HOL: LEG/HOL!   ADM: F   HDC/ACC: Y; Wheelchair accessible; elevators
PARKING: Y; Free and ample   MUS/SH: Y   REST/FAC: Y; Lunch Tu-F   GR/T: Y   GR/PH: call 406-727-8255
H/B: Y; 19th C Romanesque structure built in 1895 as a high school   S/G: Y
PERM/COLL: REG: ptgs, sculp, drgs, gr

Contemporary arts are featured within the walls of this 19th century Romanesque building which was originally used as a high school.

ON EXHIBIT/95:

11/25/94 - 1/20/95	COLLEGE OF GREAT FALLS — Works by Mirle Freel, Jack Franjevic and Sister Trinitas
1/27 - 3/26/95	PHOTOGRAPHING THE AMERICAN WEST
4/2 - 5/12/95	GFPS ALL-CITY ART EXHIBITION
5/22 - 6/30/95	ARTISTS WHO TEACH
7/7 - 8/6/95	MONTANA/CANADA COLLABORATION
8/18 - 10/1/95	5TH ANNUAL ART EQUINOX
10/13 - 11/26/95	MONTANA WATERCOLOR SOCIETY/CONTEMPORARY GLASS

KALISPELL

Hockaday Center for the Arts
Second Ave E. & Third St, **Kalispell, MT 59901**
TEL: 406-755-5268
HRS: 10-5 Tu-F; 10-3 Sa   DAY CLOSED: S, M   HOL: LEG/HOL!
ADM: F
HDC/ACC: Y   PARKING: Y; Free 2 hour street parking   MUS/SH: Y   GR/T: Y   GR/PH: call 406-755-5268
PERM/COLL: CONT/NORTHWEST: ptgs, sculp, gr, port, cer

The Hockaday Center, which places strong emphasis on contemporary art, is housed in the renovated Carnegie Library built in 1903. A program of rotating regional, national, or international exhibitions is presented approximately every 6 weeks.

MILES CITY

Custer County Art Center
Water Plant Rd., **Miles City, MT 59301**
TEL: 406-232-0635
HRS: 1-5 Tu-S; 9-5 Tu-S Summer   DAY CLOSED: M   HOL: 1/1, EASTER, THGV, 12/25
VOL/CONT: Y   ADM: F
HDC/ACC: Y; Inquire at front desk   PARKING: Y   MUS/SH: Y   GR/T: Y
H/B: Y; Located in the old holding tanks of the water plant (Listed NRHP)
PERM/COLL: CONT/REG

Custer County Art Center - continued

The old holding tanks of the water plant (c. 1914) provide an unusual location for the Custer Art Center. Situated in the middle eastern part of the state in a park-land setting overlooking the Yellowstone River, this facility features 20th century Western and contemporary art. The gift shop is worthy of mention due to the emphasis placed on available works for sale by regional artists. **NOT TO BE MISSED:** Annual Art Roundup & Quick Draw Art Auction, Sat., May 15, 1993, at 11am

ON EXHIBIT/95:

1/22 - 3/5/95	ANNUAL JURIED SHOW
3/9 - 4/23/95	ANDREW HOFMEISTER AND ALLAN FISCHER — In this dual exhibition 22 of Hofmeister's paintings donated by him to the Custer County Art Center and an installation by Fisher will be on view.
4/27 - 7/9/95	WESTERN ART ROUND-UP — Contemporary and traditional interpretations of the West will be seen in works by 10 Western artists presented as part of the Annual Jaycees Bucking Horse Sale and festivities. The "Quick Draw" sale & auction held during that time features artists who create art at the festival in a given amount of time and then have their works auctioned off for charity.
8/31 - 9/30/95	ANNUAL ART AUCTION — Over 100 works will be on display for one month before being auctioned to raise funds for the Art Center.

MISSOULA

Missoula Museum of the Arts
335 N. Pattee, **Missoula, MT 59802**
TEL: 406-728-0447
HRS: Noon-5 M-Sa   DAY CLOSED: S   HOL: LEG/HOL!.
ADM: F   HDC/ACC: Y   PARKING: Y; Limited metered on-street parking   MUS/SH: Y
GR/T: T   GR/PH: call 406-728-0447   H/B: Y
PERM/COLL: REG: 19-20

Regional art of Montana and other Western states is featured in this museum which is housed in an early 20th century building.

ON EXHIBIT/95:

11/18/94 - 1/21/95	NARRATIVE PAINTING — Featured will be works of art in the narrative tradition that act as an expression of the inner lives of the artists in this exhibition.
11/26/94 - 1/7/95	TALKING QUILTS: POSSIBILITIES IN RESPONSE — 9 contemporary quilts by Teresa Cooper Jacobs will be accompanied in this exhibition by 30 minutes of original music composed by Joseph Weisewski for each specific quilt.
1/13 - 3/11/95	JIM TODD: PORTRAITS OF PRINTMAKERS — Etchings by Todd that portray printmakers who have contributed greatly to the field will be on view.
1/30 - 4/22/95	JACOB LAWRENCE: THIRTY YEARS OF PRINTS (1963-1993) — Prints by one of the most honored and highly recognized African-American artists of the 20th century.
3 - 5/95	DAVID REGAN: WESTAF FELLOWSHIP WINNER
4/28 - 6/24/95	MISSOULA MUSEUM OF THE ARTS PERMANENT
5/19 - 7/7/95	LUCY CAPEHART: INTERIORS— Large-scale poepleless photographs of the interiors of private homes that often focus on quirky details will be featured in this exhibition.

MONTANA

MISSOULA

Museum of Fine Arts
Affiliate Institution: School of Fine Arts, University of Montana
Missoula, MT 59812
TEL: 406-243-4970
HRS: 9-12 & 1-4 M-F   DAY CLOSED: S, M   HOL: STATE/HOL & LEG/HOL!
ADM: F
HDC/ACC: Y   PARKING: Y; Free parking with visitor pass obtained in the security office.
PERM/COLL: REG

Great American artists are well represented in this University museum with special emphasis on Western painters and prints by such contemporary artists as Motherwell and Krasner. The permanent collection rotates with exhibitions of a temporary nature.

KEARNEY

Museum of Nebraska Art
Affiliate Institution: Kearney State College.
24th & Central, **Kearney, NE 68848**
TEL: 308-234-8559
HRS: 1-5 Tu-S   DAY CLOSED: HOL: LEG/HOL!
ADM: F   HDC/ACC: Y
PARKING: Y   LIB: Y   MUS/SH: Y   GT: Y   GT/PH: reservation required 308-234-8559   H/B: Y   S/G: Y
PERM/COLL: REG: Nebraskan 19-present

The Renaissance Revival style Old Kearney Post Office features artwork by Nebraskans about Nebraska. **NOT TO BE MISSED:** "The Bride," by Robert Henri

LINCOLN

Great Plains Art Collection
Affiliate Institution: University of Nebraska
205 Love Library, **Lincoln, NE 68588-0475**
TEL: 402-472-6220
HRS: 9:30-5 M-F; 10-5 Sa; 1:30-5 S   DAY CLOSED: HOL: LEG/HOL!
ADM: F   HDC/ACC: Y   PARKING: Y; Limited metered parking   LIB: Y   GT: Y Call 402-472-6220 to reserve
PERM/COLL: WESTERN: ptgs, sculp 19, 20; NAT/AM

This collection of western art which emphasizes the Great Plains features sculptures by such outstanding artists as Charles Russell & Frederic Remington, and paintings by Albert Bierstadt, John Clymer, Olaf Wieghorst, Mel Gerhold and others . **NOT TO BE MISSED:** William de la Montagne Cary, (1840-1922), "Buffalo Throwing the Hunter," bronze

ON EXHIBIT/95:

1/16 - 1/18/95	UNTITLED — Artwork by three African-American artists of the Great Plains – Pamela J. Berry, Reece Crawford, and Don Thompson.
3/7 - 5/28/95	NEW ACQUISITIONS
5/15 - 8/95	UNTITLED — Summer exhibition from permanent collection, theme undecided
9/11 - 10/27/95	UNTITLED — Photographs from the 100th Meridian Project by Monte Hartman

Sheldon Memorial Art Gallery and Sculpture Garden
Affiliate Institution: University of Nebraska
12th and R Sts., **Lincoln, NE 68588-0300**
TEL: 402-472-2461
HRS: 10-5 Tu-Sa; 7-9 T & Sa; 2-9 S   DAY CLOSED: M   HOL: LEG/HOL!
ADM: F   HDC/ACC: Y   PARKING: Y   MUS/SH: Y   GT: Y, Call 402-427-2461 to reserve   H/B: Y   S/G: Y
PERM/COLL: AM: Impr, phot, sculp, ldscp ptgs 19, 20

This highly regarded collection is housed in a beautiful Italian travertine marble building designed by internationally acclaimed architect Philip Johnson. It is located on the University of Nebraska-Lincoln campus and surrounded by a sculpture garden. **NOT TO BE MISSED:** Outdoor sculpture garden collections

NEBRASKA

Sheldon Memorial Art Gallery and Sculpture Garden - continued

ON EXHIBIT/95:

1/94 - 1/95	WAYNE THIEBAUD: OBSERVATIONS AND MEMORIES
11/94 - 4/95	INSIDE THE DANCE: DRAWINGS BY TERRY ROSENBERG
1/95 - 4/95	MARKING THE NEBRASKA PLAINS: PHOTOGRAPHS BY STEVE SZABO
1/95 - 4/95	QUIET PRIDE: AGELESS WISDOM OF THE AMERICAN WEST
3/95 - 6/95	AMERICA SEEN: PEOPLE AND PLACE
4/95 - 6/95	THE MUSEUM EYE: PIT II BY PHILIP GUSTON
4/95 - 6/95	BRIAN WALL: LYRICAL STEEL
6/95 - 7/95	CHARLES RAIN
7/95 - 9/95	SOL LEWITT
9/95 - 11/95	WARREN ROSSER DRAWINGS
9/95 - 11/95	PRECISIONISM
11/95 - 1/96	CRITIQUES OF PURE ABSTRACTION

OMAHA

Joslyn Art Museum

2200 Dodge St., **Omaha, NE 68102**
TEL: 402-342-3300
HRS: 10-5 Tu, W, F, Sa; 10-9 T; 1-5 S   DAY CLOSED: M   HOL: LEG/HOL!
F/DAY: 10-12Sa   ADM: Y   ADULT: $3.00   CHILDREN: F (under 6)   STUDENTS: $1.50   SR CIT: $1.50
HDC/ACC: Y; At north entrance   PARKING: Y; Free   LIB: Y   MUS/SH: Y   REST/FAC: Y
GT: Y   GT/PH: Call 402-342-3300 to reserve   DT: Y   TIME: W, 1pm; Sa 11am   H/B: Y   S/G: Y
PERM/COLL: AM: ptgs 19, 20; WESTERN ART; EU: 19, 20

Housing works from antiquity to the present the Joslyn, Nebraska's only art museum with an encylopedic collection, has recently completed a major $16 million dollar expansion and renovation program. **NOT TO BE MISSED:** World-renowned collection of watercolors and prints by Swiss artist Karl Bodmer that document his journey to the American West 1832-34; Noted collection of American Western art including works by Catlin, Remington, and Leigh.

ON EXHIBIT/95:

11/12/94 - 3/26/95	RECENT ACQUISITIONS TO THE PRINT COLLECTION — 16th to 19th century etchings, engravings and lithographs by master printmakers.
11/19/94 - 1/15/95	CONTEMPORARY NAVAJO WEAVING: THE GLORIA F. ROSS COLLECTION OF THE DENVER ART MUSEUM — 38 Navajo rugs and tapestries from the 1980's and early 1990's by 32 women and one man, reflecting the major trends and traditions of the '80's. The exhibition is divided into five groups which emphasize the varied sources from which weavers draw their inspiration.
11/19/94 - 1/29/95	FOSTERING EXCELLENCE (working title) — One of the inaugural exhibitions to open the Museum's new addition, this show will explore the inception and development of the expansion.

Joslyn Art Museum - continued

1/21 - 3/19/95
THE SLEEP OF REASON: REALITY AND FANTASY IN THE PRINT SERIES OF GOYA — First edition prints of four of Goya's most famous print series; "Los Caprichios, Los Desastres de la Guerra, La Tauromaquia and Los Disparates" which provide an unprecedented opportunity for audiences to view in its entirety one of the monumental acheivements in the history of printmaking.

1/28 - 3/19/95
FACE-OFF: THE PORTRAIT IN RECENT ART — The first exhibition to examine and recognize the portrait in a contemporary, cross cultural context, it reflects both new art forms and social change. Works are in all media by European, Canadian and American artists of different generations, styles and theoretical affiliations.

2/18 - 4/16/95
BOTTICELLI TO TIEPOLO: THREE CENTURIES OF ITALIAN PAINTINGS FROM BOB JONES UNIVERSITY — Forty great master paintings that trace the development of Italian painting from the High Renaissance through the Baroque and Roccoco periods. Included are works by Tintoretto, Reni, Guercino and others.   CAT WT

4/1 - 5/28/95
GEORGE CATLIN: FIRST ARTIST OF THE WEST — 35 outstanding oil paintings and rare watercolors by Catlin, the first artist to devote his entire career to the depiction of images of the West created during his many sojourns there, will be seen in this exhibition. Considered among the most enduring images in American culture, these works reflect his romanticized and idealized notions of Indian life.   CAT WT

4/1 - 6/24/95
JENNIFER BARTLETT: A PRINT RETROSPECTIVE — A first examination of the entire print work of the last 15 years and an in-depth look at this single aspect of the work of this major figure in American art.

6/17 - 9/10/95
JAMES ROSENQUIST: TIME DUST, COMPLETE GRAPHICS 1962-1992 — Beginning with a tiny monochrome etching and ending with an 82 color extravaganza involving lithography, screenprint, etching and collage, this exhibition of 100 works sums up not only Rosenquist's work to date, but also the incredible florescence of printmaking in the late 20th century.

7/8 - 9/3/95
IMAGES OF BRITISH INDIA'S GOLDEN AGE — Drawn from a private collection, these acquatints convey the romantic image of India under the first British governors. From 1780-1880 British artists portrayed the beauty and romance of an idealized land and the rich and varied subject matter provided inspired paintings, watercolors and some of the finest prints ever produced.   WT

9/16 - 11/5/95
KAREN KUNC: WOOD TO PAPER — A first significant survey of highlights from the extensive body of woodcuts created by this American printmaker who has tried to combine the delicacy of the woodblock print with bold and expressive imagery.

9/30 - 11/26/95
DOROTHEA LANGE: AMERICAN PHOTOGRAPHS — A first retrospective exhibition providing an in-depth re-evaluation of her work from the 1940's in which she documented the enormous changes in California. Included are approximately 150 works never before exhibited or published.

9/30 - 11/26/95
ODD NERDRUM: THE DRAWINGS — 25 charcoal drawings by this contemporary Norwegian-born artist will be featured in the first American exhibition of his work.   CAT WT

Late 95 - early 96
THE ART OF GRANT WOOD: DRAWINGS, STUDIES AND PAINTINGS (working title) — An exploration of Wood's stylistic development from his formative years in Europe to his fully developed scenes of the American mid-west, with particular attention to the influence of such artists such as Seurat on Wood's early and later works.   CAT WT

NEVADA

RENO

Nevada Museum of Art
Affiliate Institution: F. L. Wiegand Gallery
160 W. Liberty Street, **Reno, NV 89501**
TEL: 702-329-3333
HRS: 10-4 Tu-Sa; 12-4 S   DAY CLOSED: M   HOL: LEG/HOL!
ADM: Y   ADULT: $3.00   CHILDREN: $0.50 (6-12)   STUDENTS: $1.50   SR CIT: $1.50
HDC/ACC: Y   PARKING: Y   LIB: Y   MUS/SH: Y   GT: Y   GT/PH: call 702-329-3333 for specifics
DT: Y   TIME: "Escape for Lunch" tours of exhibitions!
PERM/COLL: AM: ptgs 19, 20, NAT/AM; REG

As "the only collecting fine art museum in the state of Nevada," this 60 year old institution has made art and artists of the Great Basin & the American West its primary focus. PLEASE NOTE: The permanent collection is not always on view. Call for specifics. **NOT TO BE MISSED:** A "welcome" collage of neon tubes & fragmented glass placed over the entryway to the museum.

CORNISH

Saint-Gaudens National Historic Site

St. Gaudens Rd, **Cornish, NH 03745-9704**
TEL: 603-675-2175
HRS: 8:30-4:30 Daily from last weekend May-Oct
ADM: Y   ADULT: $2.00   STUDENTS: $2.00   SR CIT: $2.00
HDC/ACC:N   PARKING: Y   GT: Y   GT/PH: call 603-675-2175 for specifics   H/B: Y   S/G: Y
PERM/COLL: AUGUSTUS ST. GAUDENS: sculp

The house, the studios, and 150 acres of the gardens of Augustus Saint-Gaudens (1848-1907), one of America's greatest sculptors.

ON EXHIBIT/95:
Exhibits of contemporary art throughout the season Concert Series Sundays at 2 pm

DURHAM

The Art Gallery, University of New Hampshire

Paul Creative Arts Center, 30 College Road, **Durham, NH 03824-3538**
TEL: 603-862-3712
HRS: 10-4 M-W; 10-8 T; 1-5 Sa-S (Sep-mid Jun); closed mid June thru August   DAY CLOSED: F   HOL: ACAD!
ADM: F
HDC/ACC: Y; Limited   PARKING: Y; Metered or at Visitors Center   GT: Y   GT/PH: call 603-862-3712 to reserve
PERM/COLL: JAP: gr 19; EU & AM: drgs 17-20; PHOT; EU: works on paper 19, 20

Each academic year The Art Gallery of the University of New Hampshire presents exhibitions ranging from historical eras to the contemporary art scene and featuring works in a variety of media.

ON EXHIBIT/95:

1/31 - 4/6/95 (closed 3/10 - 3/19)	THE JOURNEY INWARD: MEDITATIVE LANDSCAPES BY AMERICAN ARTISTS (1860-1920) — Highlighting the introspective mood of landscapes done in the wake of the Civil War, these tonalist paintings are by once lauded artists including J. Francis Murphy and drawings and prints by painter-etchers such as George Smillie and Thomas and Mary Moran.
1/31 - 4/6/95	ARCHITECTURE IN CONTEMPORARY PRINTMAKING — 24 artists utilize a rich variety of printmaking techniques and styles of visual expression using architecture as the central theme.
4/22 - 5/21/95	SENIOR EXHIBITION
9/7 - 10/18	THE UNIVERSITY OF NEW HAMPSHIRE FACULTY REVIEW (TENT!) — Works by Grant Drumheller, Jennifer Moses, Carol Shore and Maryse McConnell
11/1 - 12/11/95	REALISM AND INVENTION IN THE PRINTS OF ALBRECHT DURER (TENT!)

NEW HAMPSHIRE

HANOVER

Hood Museum of Art
Affiliate Institution: Dartmouth College
Hanover, NH 03755
TEL: 603-646-2808
HRS: 10-5 Tu, T, F, Sa; 10-9 W; 12-5 S   DAY CLOSED: M   HOL: LEG/HOL!
ADM: F
HDC/ACC: Y   PARKING: Y   MUS/SH: Y   REST/FAC: Y   S/G: Outdoor, No garden
PERM/COLL: AM: ptgs 19, 20; GR; PICASSO; EU: ptgs

The Museum houses one of the oldest and finest college collections in the country. **NOT TO BE MISSED:** Panathenaic Amphora by the Berlin Painter 6th C. BC.

ON EXHIBIT/95:

12/3/94 - 3/5/95	AMERICAN REGIONALIST PRINTS FROM THE PERMANENT COLLECTION — Prints from the 1930's and 1940's produced by such artists as Thomas Hart Benton, Grant Wood, Thomas Nason, and John Stuart Curry celebrate what was perceived as distinctly American in various regions of the country.
12/31/94 - 3/5/95	AFRICAN ART FROM THE COLLECTION OF NICHOLAS F. RUBANO — Masks and costumes created by the Yoruba and Igbo peoples of Nigeria and people of the Cameroon Grassfields.
3/25 - 5/28/95	SHAPING AN AMERICAN LANDSCAPE: THE ART AND ARCHITECTURE OF CHARLES A. PLATT — A survey of the artist's prolific production in several media including etching, painting, landscape architecture and architecture which examines the interrelationship of his work to its cultural, social and economic context. WT
6/10 - 9/3/95	TWO VIEWS OF ITALY: MASTER PRINTS BY CANALETTO AND PIRANESI — A comparison of the "veduta" or view of two of the greatest artists working in Italy in the 18th century. The works will be arranged thematically – scenes of ruins, public squares, modern architecture, fantasies among others – so that viewers may compare the works directly.
9/9 - 11/19/95	CONTEMPORARY NATIVE AMERICAN PHOTOGRAPHY — An exhibition of important contemporary photographs made by Native American artists is being curated by Native American and American Dartmouth College students.
9/95 - 12/95	CONTEMPORARY NATIVE AMERICAN PAINTING AND SCULPTURE — An installation of large scale contemporary Native American art.
9/23 - 11/26/95	FIRST ARTIST OF THE WEST: PAINTINGS AND WATERCOLORS BY GEORGE CATLIN FROM THE GILCREASE MUSEUM — 35 outstanding oil paintings and 25 rare watercolors by Catlin, the first artist to devote his entire career to the depiction of images of the West created during his many sojourns there, will be seen in this exhibition. Considered among the most enduring images in American culture, these works reflect his romanticized and idealized notions of Indian life. CAT WT

The Hood Museum of Art will celebrate its ten-year anniversary by presenting a year-long series of special programs and exhibitions drawn from its extensive permanent collections (over 60,000 objects) representing nearly every area of art history and ethnography.

260

NEW HAMPSHIRE

KEENE

Thorne-Sagendorph Art Gallery
Affiliate Institution: Keene State College
229 Main St, **Keene, NH 03431**
TEL: 603-358-2720
HRS: 12-4 M-W; 1-8, T-F; 1-4 Sa, S   HOL: ACAD!
ADM: F   HDC/ACC: Y   PARKING: Y; Free parking adjacent to the museum
GT: Y   GT/PH: call 603-358-2719 for specifics
PERM/COLL: REG: 19; AM & EU: cont, gr

Changing exhibitions as well as selections from the permanent collection are featured in the contemporary space of this art gallery.

ON EXHIBIT/95:
4/1 - 5/14   THE LEAGUE OF NEW HAMPSHIRE CRAFTSMEN

MANCHESTER

The Currier Gallery of Art
192 Orange St., **Manchester, NH 03104**
TEL: 603-669-6144
HRS: 10-4 Tu, W, F, Sa; 10-9 T; 1-5 S   DAY CLOSED: M   HOL: LEG/HOL!
F/DAY: 1-9 T   ADM: Y   ADULT: $4.00   CHILDREN: F (under 18)   STUDENTS: $3.00   SR CIT: $3.00
HDC/ACC: Y   PARKING: Y; Adjacent on-street parking   LIB: Y   MUS/SH: Y   GT: Y
H/B: Y; Registered in National Landmark of historic places (Circa 1929)
PERM/COLL: AM & EU: sculp 13-20; AM: furniture, dec/art

Set on beautifully landscaped grounds, The Gallery is housed in an elegant 1929 Beaux Arts building reminiscent of an Italian Renaissance villa. **NOT TO BE MISSED:** Zimmerman House (separate admission Adults $6, Seniors and Students $4) designed in 1950 by Frank Lloyd Wright. It is one of five Wright houses in the Northeast and the only Wright designed residence open to the public in New England.

ON EXHIBIT/95:
11/29/94 - 1/15/95   THE GRAPHIC WORKS OF DAUMIER, HOGARTH AND CALLOT — Using the print medium as a forum for commentary on social, political and military issues, these three European artists held up a mirror to their world that was stark, unromantic and illustrative.

12/19/94 - 1/22/95   NEW HAMPSHIRE ART ASSOCIATION EXHIBITION

2/4 - 4/1/95   LEAGUE OF NEW HAMPSHIRE CRAFTSMEN EXHIBITION

The Museum will be closed for construction from late spring 1995 until spring 1996!

NEW JERSEY

CAMDEN

Campbell Musuem
Campbell Place, **Camden, NJ 08103**
TEL: 609-342-6440
HRS: 9-4:30 M-F   DAY CLOSED: Sa, S   HOL: LEG/HOL!
ADM: F   HDC/ACC: Y   PARKING: Y   REST/FAC: Y; 9-4:30 M-F   GT: Y!   H/B: Y
PERM/COLL: SOUP TUREENS

The only museum of its type in the world that exclusively features an extensive collection of soup tureens, including many from European royal households, in all their many unusual and bizarre forms and designs. Telephone ahead to arrange showing of "Artistry in Tureens" a film illustrating the production of a porcelain and a silver soup tureen. The museum seats 50 people.

Stedman Art Gallery
Affiliate Institution: The State Univ of NJ
Rutgers Fine Arts Center, **Camden, NJ 08102**
TEL: 609-225-6245
HRS: 10-4 M-Sa   DAY CLOSED: S   HOL: MEM/DAY, 7/4, LAB/DAY, THGV, 12/24-1/2
ADM: F   HDC/ACC: Y   PARKING: Y
PERM/COLL: AM & EU: Cont works on paper

Located in southern New Jersey, the gallery brings visual arts into focus as an integral part of the human story.

ON EXHIBIT/95:

1/17 - 2/25 — SACRED CONVERSATIONS: JOHN J. GIANNOTTI RETROSPECTIVE — A retrospective exhibition of 25 years of painting and sculpture.

3/6 - 4/29/95 — SOVIET NON-CONFORMIST ART: 1956-1986 — Paintings, sculpture, photographs and mixed media art work created by artists working in a politically repressive environment and not officially recognized until the Gorbachev era of "glasnost."

JERSEY CITY

Jersey City Museum
472 Jersey Ave., **Jersey City, NJ 07302**
TEL: 201-547-4514
HRS: 10:30-5 Tu, T-Sa; 10:30-8 W; closed Sa in summer   DAY CLOSED: S, M   HOL: LEG/HOL!, 12/24, 12/31
ADM: F   HDC/ACC:N; 5 steps into building, small elevator   PARKING: Y; Street   LIB: Y   MUS/SH: Y
GT: Y   GT/PH: call for specifics   H/B: Y
PERM/COLL: AUGUST WILL COLLECTION: views of Jersey City, 19; AM: ptgs, drgs, gr, phot; HIST: dec/art;
JERSEY CITY INDUSTRIAL DESIGN

Established in 1901, the museum is located in the historic Van Vorst Park neighborhood of Jersey City in a 100-year old building which houses the public library. In addition to showcasing the works of established and emerging regional artists, the museum presents exhibitions from the permanent collection documenting regional history through the works of Jersey City artists.

NEW JERSEY

Jersey City Museum - continued

ON EXHIBIT/95:

12/7/94 - 2/18/95   CHANGO/SHANGO: AN INSTALLATION BY BEN JONES — A multi media installation dealing with the African (Yoruba Tribe) god of war Shango and his Roman Catholic identity: St. Barbara. The exhibition explores the religious commonalities of African tribal and Christian religion.

12/7/94 - 2/18/95   THE AMERICAN SCENE: PRINTS FROM THE COLLECTION — Etchings and lithographs by artists of the 1930's who specialized in depicting aspects of American life from an urban realist or social realist perspective. Works by Isabel Bishop, Hugo Gellert, Martin Lewis, Reginald Marsh, Raphael Soyer and others.

3/8 - 5/27/95   DRAWING: AN INVITATIONAL — Contemporary New York and New Jersey artists.

6/7 - 8/18/95   DON PEDRO: A VISUAL COMMEMORATION

6/7 - 8/18/95   LILLIAN MULERO: AN INSTALLATION

6/7 - 8/18/95   JOAN FINE: SCULPTURE

9/6 - 11/11/95   EVERYTHING FOR INDUSTRY: NEW JERSEY POTTERY COMPANY

9/6 - 11/11/95   MICHAEL BRAMWELL: AN INSTALLATION

9/6 - 11/11/95   FROM THE COLLECTION: 19TH CENTURY LANDSCAPES

11/13/95 - 2/17/96   SUBVERTING ABSTRACTION: ROCHELLE FEINSTEIN AND SANDI SLONE

12/13/95 - 2/17/96   JANET TAYLOR PICKETT: AN INSTALLATION

12/13/95 - 2/17/96   JONATHAN WEINBERG: THE PAST REVISITED

MILLVILLE

Museum of American Glass at Wheaton Village
Glasstown Road, **Millville, NJ 08332**
TEL: 609-825-6800
HRS: 10-5 M-S (Apr-Dec); Call for winter hrs.   DAY CLOSED: HOL: 1/1, Easter, THGV, 12/25
ADM: Y   ADULT: $6.00, Fam $12   STUDENTS: $3.50   SR CIT: $5.50
HDC/ACC: Y   PARKING: Y; Free   LIB: Y   MUS/SH: Y
REST/FAC: Y; 7am-11pm   GT: Y !   H/B: Y   S/G: Y
PERM/COLL: GLASS

Wheaton Village is a 60-acre working craft village dedicated to the history and art of American glassmaking, traditional and contemporary craft and folk art. Devoted entirely to glass, the museum has more than 7,000 objects in its collection in addition to a replica of an 1888 Glass Factory. Ongoing demonstrations of pottery, woodcarving, flame worked glass and stained glass are presented in the artist's studios.

NEW JERSEY

MONTCLAIR

The Montclair Art Museum
3 South Mountain Ave, **Montclair, NJ 07042**
TEL: 201-746-5555
HRS: 11-5 Tu, W, F, Sa; 1-5 T, S; call for summer hours   DAY CLOSED: M   HOL: LEG/HOL!
SUGG/CONT: Y   F/DAY: Sa   ADULT: $4   CHILDREN: F (under 18)   STUDENTS: $2 w/ID   SR CIT: $2.00
HDC/ACC: Y; Main floor and restroom   PARKING: Y; Free on-site parking   LIB: Y   MUS/SH: Y
REST/FAC: Y; Sunday cafe (seasonal!)   GT: Y   GT/PH: call 201-746-5555 reserv. required
DT: Y   TIME: call 201-746-5555 for specifics
PERM/COLL: NAT/AM: art 18-20; AM: ldscp, portraits 19; AM: dec/art; Hudson River School: Am Impressionists

Located just 12 miles west of midtown Manhattan and housed in a Greek Revival style building, this museum, founded in 1914, features an impressive American art collection of a quality not usually expected in a small suburb.

ON EXHIBIT/95:

8/21/94 - 6/25/95	PATTERNS AND CULTURE: THE NATIVE AMERICAN COLLECTION	
9/11/94 - 11/6/95	GEORGE INNESS: PRESENCE OF THE UNSEEN	CAT WT
9/11/94 - 2/5/95	THE KIOWA LEDGER BOOK	
11/6/94 - 3/5/95	MODERNISM FROM THE COLLECTION	
11/20/94 - 1/22/95	PRECISIONISM IN AMERICA 1915-1941: REORDERING REALITY	
12/18/94 - 3/5/95	EMMA AMOS: RECLAIMING PRESENCE	
2/26 - 4/30/95	MAURICE SANCHEZ: MASTER PRINTER	
2/26 - 5/7/95	THE WOODCUTS OF LUIGI RIST	
2/26 - 6/4/95	JAMES MCNEIL WHISTLER/CHILDE HASSAM PRINTS	
3/26 - 6/25/95	NATIVE AMERICAN JEWELRY FROM THE PERMANENT COLLECTION	
3/26 - 6/25/95	WHAT IS A PRINT	
5/21 - 8/13/95	STILL LIFE WORKS FROM THE COLLECTION	

NEW BRUNSWICK

The Jane Voorhees Zimmerli Art Museum
Affiliate Institution: Rutgers, The State University Of New Jersey
Corner George & Hamilton Streets, **New Brunswick, NJ 08903**
TEL: 908-932-7237
HRS: 10-4:30 Tu-F; Noon-5 Sa, S   DAY CLOSED: M, Sa, July   HOL: LEG/HOL! 12/25 thru 1/1
ADM: F
HDC/ACC: Y   PARKING: Y; Nearby or metered   GT: Y   GT/PH: call for Res. 908-932-7096   H/B: Y
PERM/COLL: FR: gr 19; AM: 20; EU: 15-20; P/COL: cer; CONT/AM: gr; THE NORTON AND NANCY DODGE COLLECTION OF NON-CONFORMIST ART FROM THE SOVIET UNION; AM: Texas glass

Housing the Rutgers University Collection of more than 35,000 works, this museum also incorporates the International Center for Japonisme which features related art in the Kusakabe-Griffis Japonisme Gallery. **NOT TO BE MISSED:** The George Riabov Collection of Russian Art; the Norton Dodge Collection of non-conformist Russian art

The Jane Voorhees Zimmerli Art Museum - continued

ON EXHIBIT/95:

9/11/94 - 2/12/95   TO GRANDFATHER'S HOUSE WE GO: A CHILDREN'S BOOK OF ARCHITEC-TURE — Paintings of New Jersey buildings by distinguished artist and children's book illustrator Harry Devlin.

11/26/94 - 3/26/95   THE NATIONAL ASSOCIATION OF WOMEN ARTISTS COLLECTION AT RUTGERS — Paintings, sculpture and prints by Mary Cassatt, Isabel Bishop, Judy Chicago, Miriam Schapiro and others.

Fall 1995   THE NORTON AND NANCY DODGE COLLECTION OF NONCONFORMIST ART FROM THE SOVIET UNION

NEWARK

The Newark Museum

49 Washington Street, **Newark, NJ 07101-0540**
TEL: 201-596-6550
HRS: 12-5 W-S   DAY CLOSED: M, Tu   HOL: 1/1, 7/4, THGV, 12/25
ADM: F
HDC/ACC: Y; Ramp entrance, elevators, wheelchair accessible, restrooms
PARKING: Y; $1.00 in the musuem's adjacent parking lot   MUS/SH: Y; 2
REST/FAC: Y; Cafe noon-3:30 W-S (wheelchair accessible)   GT: Y   GT/PH: call 201-596-6615 to reserve
PERM/COLL: AM: ptgs 17-20; AM: folk; AF/AM; DEC/ARTS; GLASS; JAP; CONT; AM: Hudson River School ptgs; AF; AN/GRK; AN/R; EGT

Established in 1909 as a museum of art, the Newark features one of the finest collections of Tibetan art in the world. Several connected structures of the museum consist of the historic late Victorian Ballantine House, a contemporary and recently renovated museum building, a Mini Zoo, Planetarium, and a 1784 Schoolhouse. **NOT TO BE MISSED:** "The Voice of the City of New York Interpreted," by Joseph Stella 1920-22; One of the most highly regarded collections of 19th century American furniture

PLEASE NOTE: Ballantine House will be closed for renovation until 12/94.

ON EXHIBIT/95:

1/26 - 4/23/95   TWENTIETH CENTURY AMERICAN FOLK ART (TENT!)

2/95   WILLIAM T. WILLIAMS (TENT!)

4/5 - 3/21/96   PROTECTING THE PINELANDS (TENT!)

Mid-May-Early June   PEPON OSORIO (TENT!)

9/95-10/95   ART WITH CONSCIENCE (TENT!)

11/24/95 - 1/96   NEW JERSEY CRAFTS ANNUAL (TENT!)

11/24/95 - 1/96   CONTEMPORARY AMERICAN SILVERSMITHING (TENT!)

NEW JERSEY

NEWARK

The Newark Public Library
5 Washington Street, **Newark, NJ 07101**
TEL: 201-733-7800
HRS: 9-5:30 M, F, Sa; 9-8:30 Tu, W, T   DAY CLOSED: S   HOL: LEG/HOL!
ADM: F   HDC/ACC: Y; Ramp   PARKING: LIB: Y   H/B: Y
PERM/COLL: AM & EU: gr

Since 1903 the library can be counted on for exhibitions which are of rare quality and well documented.

OCEANVILLE

The Noyes Museum
Lily Lake Rd, **Oceanville, NJ 08231**
TEL: 609-652-8848
HRS: 11-4 W-S   DAY CLOSED: M, T   HOL: LEG/HOL!
F/DAY: F, 11-4   ADM: Y   ADULT: $3.00   CHILDREN: $0.50   STUDENTS: $0.50   SR CIT: $1.50
HDC/ACC: Y   PARKING: Y; Free   LIB: Y!   MUS/SH: Y   GT: Y   GT/PH: call ahead to reserve
PERM/COLL: AM: cont, craft, folk;   NJ: reg; WORKING BIRD DECOYS

The Noyes Museum is dedicated to fostering American arts and crafts with special emphasis on New Jersey artists and American Decoys.   The sun-filled terraced galleries against a backdrop of the surrounding wooded landscape provide for a thought provoking cultural experience.

ON EXHIBIT/95:

10/16/94 - 1/8/95	THE MINI-PRINT EXHIBITION
11/6/94 - 3/6/95	SELECTIONS FROM THE NOYES MUSEUM COLLECTION OF CONTEMPORARY AMERICAN ART
1/28 - 3/26/95	ATLANTIC CITY THROUGH THE CAMERA LENS OF WILLIAM SUTTLE
2/5 - 4/2/95	JACOB LAWRENCE: THIRTY YEARS OF PRINTS 1963-1993 (TENT!)
3/26 - 6/18/95	MESSAGE FROM THE PLANET: ARTISTS WORK TO SAVE THE EARTH
4/16 - 7/9/95	LOOKING DUE SOUTH: SOUTH JERSEY LANDSCAPES BY GLENN RUDDEROW
7/2 - 9/17/95	STAYING INSIDE THE LINES: WORKS ON PAPER BY OUTSIDER ARTISTS
7/23 - 10/1/95	CAUGHT ON FILM: WILDLIFE PHOTOGRAPHY BY LEONARD BALISH

PRINCETON

The Art Museum
Affiliate Institution: Princeton University
Nassau Street, **Princeton, NJ 08544-1018**
TEL: 609-258-3788
HRS: 10-5 T-Sa; 1-5 S   DAY CLOSED: M   HOL: LEG/HOL!
ADM: F   HDC/ACC: Y   PARKING: Y; On-street or nearby garages; special parking arrangements for the handicapped are available (call ahead for information)   MUS/SH: Y
GT: Y   GT/PH: call 609-258-3043 to reserve   DT: Y   TIME: 2:00 Sa
PERM/COLL: AN/GRK; AN/R+Mosaics; EU: sculp, ptgs 15-20; CH: sculp, ptgs; GR; P/COL; OM: ptgs, drgs; AF

266

NEW JERSEY

The Art Museum - continued

An outstanding collection of Greek and Roman antiquities including Roman mosaics from Princeton University's excavations in Antioch is but one of the features of this highly regarded eclectic collection housed in a modern building on the lovely Princeton University Campus. **NOT TO BE MISSED:** Picasso sculpture, " Head of a Woman"

ON EXHIBIT/95:

10/29/94 - 1/3/95	ARSHILE GORKY AND THE GENESIS OF ABSTRACTION: DRAWINGS FROM THE EARLY 1930's
10/29/94 - 1/3/95	EUROPEAN MASTER DRAWINGS FROM THE COLLECTION OF PETER JAY SHARP, CLASS OF 1952
11/23/94 - 1/8/95	CONTEMPORARY PHOTOGRAPHS

SUMMIT

New Jersey Center for Visual Arts

68 Elm Street, **Summit, NJ 07901**
TEL: 908-273-9121
HRS: 12-4 M-F; 2-4 Sa, S   HOL: LEG/HOL! & last 2 weeks in August
ADM: Y   ADULT: $1.00   CHILDREN: F (under 12)   STUDENTS: $1.00   SR CIT: F
HDC/ACC: Y; Elevator, ramps, etc.   PARKING: Y; Free   MUS/SH: Y
GT: Y   GT/PH: call 908-273-9121 to reserve   DT: Y   TIME: !   S/G: Y
PERM/COLL: non-collecting institution

The Center presents exhibitions of contemporary art by artists of national and international reputation as well as classes for people of all ages and levels of ability.

ON EXHIBIT/95:

1/3/95 - 2/26/95	HEROS AND HEROINES: FROM MYTH TO REALITY
3/10/95 - 4/23/95	THE ARTFULL MESSAGE: CONTEMPORARY VIDEO
5/5/95 - 6/11/95	1995 JURIED COMPETITION AND EXHIBITION
6/23/95 - 7/16/95	MEMBERS SHOW

TENAFLY

African Art Museum of the S. M. A. Fathers

23 Bliss Ave, **Tenafly, NJ 07670**
TEL: 201-567-0450
HRS: 9-5 daily   HOL: LEG/HOL!
ADM: F
HDC/ACC: Y   PARKING: Y   GT: Y   GT/PH: call 201-567-0450 for specifics
PERM/COLL: AF; artifacts, sculp, masks

Items created by people from more than 40 East and West African countries are featured at this museum.

267

NEW JERSEY

TRENTON

New Jersey State Museum
205 West State Street, **Trenton, NJ 08625-0530**
TEL: 609-292-6464
HRS: 9-4:45 Tu-Sa; 12-5 S   DAY CLOSED: M   HOL: LEG/HOL!
ADM: F
HDC/ACC: Y   PARKING: Y; Pay parking nearby   MUS/SH: Y   GT: Y   GT/PH: call for specifics
PERM/COLL: AM: cont, gr; AF/AM

The museum is located in the Capitol Complex in downtown Trenton. The collections cover broad areas of interest with a special focus on New Jersey and minority artists. **NOT TO BE MISSED:** Ben Shahn Graphics Collection

ON EXHIBIT/95:

1/21 - 12/30/95	STATE MUSEUM 100TH ANNIVERSARY CELEBRATION — The exhibition includes a photographic history of the Museum as well as examples of 100 years of collecting.
10/22/94 - 9/95	MOLAS: APPLIQUE NEEDLEWORK OF THE CUNA INDIAN WOMEN OF THE SAN BLAS ISLANDS
11/19/94 - 1/15/95	NEW JERSEY ARTISTS SERIES: ELLEN LEVY
2/4 - 4/2/95	NEW JERSEY ARTIST SERIES: GERALD WOLFE
3/8 - 5/31/95	FINE AND DECORATIVE ARTS FROM THE COLLECTIONS OF NEW JERSEY'S COLONIAL DAMES
3/19 - 4/30/95	PALMER C. HAYDEN — In the 40 paintings by this African-American artist, on loan from the Museum of African Art, vivid and vital images of many of the unheroic experiences of the black man in America will be seen. CAT WT
2/25 - extended view	BASEBALL IN NEW JERSEY — An exhibition marking the 150th anniversary of the publishing of the formal rules of baseball by Alexander Cartwright in 1845 – the beginning of the game as we know it today.
4/15 - 6/3/95	NEW JERSEY ARTIST SERIES: JOAN SEMMEL
6/10 - 9/10/95	THE GRATITUDE TRAIN — The Gratitude or "Merci" Train was sent by the French to thank Americans who had provided some $40,000 in relief suppplies during the winter of 1947. The exhibition commemorates the ending of WWII, displaying New Jersey's gifts from The Gratitude Train.
Indefinitely:	WORKS BY WOMEN PHOTOGRAPHERS — The subject matter in these works from the permanent collection is wide ranging and presented with uncommon sensitivity.

NEW MEXICO

ALBUQUERQUE

University Art Museum and Jonson Gallery
Affiliate Institution: The University of New Mexico
Fine Arts Center, **Albuquerque, NM 87131**
TEL: 505-277-7312
HRS: 9-4 Tu-F; 5-8 Tu; 1-4 S; Jonson Gallery closed on weekend   DAY CLOSED: M, Sa   HOL: LEG/HOL!
ADM: F
HDC/ACC: Y   PARKING: Y; Limited free parking   MUS/SH: Y   GT: Y   GT/PH: call 505-277-7312 to reserve
DT: Y   TIME: 2nd, 3rd and 4th Tu, 5:30 pm !   S/G: Y
PERM/COLL: MEX RETABLOS 19; CONT; GR; PHOT

Works of art in all media by artists whose work is relevant to contemporary art issues is featured in this gallery. **NOT TO BE MISSED:** An early Richard Diebenkorn painting

ON EXHIBIT/95:
   11/29/94 - 3/17/95   PAINTINGS FROM TAOS: SELECTIONS FROM THE PERMANENT COLLECTION — A look at New Mexico Modernism from the 1920's and 1930's out of the Jonson Gallery and University Art Museum collections.

LOS ALAMOS

Fuller Lodge Art Center and Gallery
2132 Central Avenue, **Los Alamos, NM 87544**
TEL: 505-662-9331
HRS: 10-4 M-Sa; 1-4 S   DAY CLOSED: HOL: LEG/HOL!
ADM: F HDC/ACC: Y   PARKING: Y   MUS/SH: Y showcase H/B: Y
PERM/COLL: under development

Located in historic Fuller Lodge, this art center, nationally recognized for its juried Biennial 6-State Exhibition, also presents monthly changing exhibitions.

ON EXHIBIT/95:
1/13 - 2/5/95	5TH ANNIVERSARY GROUP EXHIBITION
2/10 - 3/5/95	NEW MEXICO WATERCOLOR SOCIETY
3.10 - 4/12/95	COLLEGE OF SANTA FE STUDENT AND FACULTY EXHIBITION
4/7 - 5/7/95	QUE PASA: ART IN NEW MEXICO — All media juried exhibition for New Mexico artists
5/12 - 6/4/95	LOS ALAMOS PIECEMAKERS
6/9 - 7/9/95	BIENNIAL PAINTING, DRAWING, PRINT, PHOTOGRAPHY AND SCULPTURE 6 STATE JURIED EXHIBITION
7/14-8/8/95	TRADITIONS: PAST AND PRESENT — An exhibition of traditional and contemporary Native American and Hispanic art forms.
8/11 - 9/9/95	STICKS AND STONES
9/8 - 10/11/95	A FREEDOM OF EXPRESSION
10/6 - 11/5/95	THROUGH THE LOOKING GLASS — National Photography juried exhibition
12/15 - 1/7/96	A FAIRY TALE

269

NEW MEXICO

ROSWELL

Roswell Museum and Art Center
100 West 11th, **Roswell, NM 88201**
TEL: 505-624-6744
HRS: 9-5 M-Sa; 1-5 S & HOL   HOL: 1/1, THGV, 12/25
ADM: F   HDC/ACC: Y   PARKING: Y   LIB: Y   GT: Y   GT/PH: call ahead for specifics
PERM/COLL: SW/ART; HISTORY; SCIENCE; NM/ART; NAT/AM

16 galleries featuring works by Santa Fe and Taos masters and a wide range of historic and contemporary art in its impressive permanent collection make this museum one of the premier cultural attractions of the Southwest. Temporary exhibitions of Native American, Hispanic, and Anglo art are often featured. **NOT TO BE MISSED:** Rogers Aston Collection of Native American and Western Art

ON EXHIBIT/95:

1/20 - 6/25/95	PERMANENT COLLECTION
3/4 - 4/30/95	DORIS CROSS: WORKS FROM 1968-1993
3/10 - 5/14/95	BILL WIGGINS RETROSPECTIVE
4/1 - 6/4/95	CELIA MUNOZ INSTALLATION
5/13 - 8/6/95	WILLIAM LUMPKINS: PAINTINGS
6/2 - 8/13/95	ARTIST-IN-RESIDENCE EXHIBITION
7/7/95 - 1/5/96	PERMANENT COLLECTION
9/9 - 11/26/95	1995 INVITATIONAL

SANTA FE

Institute of American Indian Arts Museum
108 Cathedral Place, **Santa Fe NM 87504**
TEL: 505-988-6281
HRS: 9-5 M, Tu, T-Sa; 9-6 W   DAY CLOSED: Sa, S   HOL: LEG/HOL!
VOL/CONT: Y   ADM: F   HDC/ACC: Y   MUS/SH: Y   GT: Y   GT/PH: call 505-988-6281, ext 109
PERM/COLL: NAT/AM: artifacts; CONT NAT/AM: arts and crafts

Contemporary Native American arts and crafts and Alaskan native arts are featured in this museum which also houses an outstanding archive of Native American video tapes.

Museum of New Mexico
113 Lincoln Ave., **Santa Fe, NM 87501**
TEL: 505-827-6451
HRS: All Museums 10-5 daily! Monuments, 9-6 daily 5/1-9/15; 8-5 9/16-4/30   DAY CLOSED: Fort Sumner Tu, W
HOL: 1/1, EASTER, THGV, 12/25
ADM: Y   ADULT: $5, 3 day pass all four museums, $4 single museum. Sunday $1 NM residents
CHILDREN: F (under 17)   SR CIT: W, F
HDC/ACC: Y; In most buildings   PARKING: Y   MUS/SH: Y
GT: Y   GT/PH: call 805-827-6451 to reserve   H/B: Y
PERM/COLL: (4 Museums with varied collections): TAOS & SANTA FE MASTERS; PHOT; SW/REG; NAT/AM; FOLK; 5 State Monuments

270

Museum of New Mexico- continued

In 1917 when it opened, the Museum of Fine Arts set the Santa Fe standard in pueblo-revival architecture. The Palace of the Governors, built by Spanish Colonial and Mexican governors, has the distinction of being the oldest public building in the US. **NOT TO BE MISSED:** The entire complex.

ON EXHIBIT/95:
MUSEUM OF FINE ARTS ON THE PLAZA 505-827-4468

9/16/94 - 1/8/94	ALCOVE 16: STILL CREATING — Contemporary regional artists, ages 60-80's, who have been creating in or inspired by New Mexico: William Lumpkins, Ted Egri, Toni Mygatt Lucas, Janet Lippincott, Earl Stroh and Ruben Gonzalez.
10/14/94 - continuing	GEORGIA O'KEEFFE: PAINTINGS FROM THE COLLECTION
10/14/94	NEW IDEAS: CURATORIAL SELECTIONS
11/19/94 - 2/4/95	HENRIETTE WYETH: PAINTER OF BEAUTY — A retrospective of works by this regional painter from a distinguished family of artists who painted in rural and southern New Mexico.

PALACE OF THE GOVERNORS ON THE PLAZA

Permanent	ANOTHER MEXICO: SPANISH LIFE ON THE UPPER RIO GRANDE — An overview of life in New Mexico from the Colonial period with the Spanish presence in 1540 to the present.
Permanent	SOCIETY DEFINED: THE HISPANIC RESIDENTS OF NEW MEXICO, 1790 — Artifacts and documents related to the detailed census of New Mexico taken in 1790 by order of the Spanish crown.
Permanent	PERIOD ROOMS: THE GOVERNOR PRINCE OFFICE, THE NORTHERN NEW MEXICO CHAPEL AND PERIOD KITCHEN AND PARLOR

MUSEUM OF INTERNATIONAL FOLK ART

Permanent	MULTIPLE VISIONS: A COMMON BOND — Approximately 10,000 pieces from the Girard Collection representing folk art of more than 100 nations.
Permanent	FAMILIA Y FE/FAMILY AND FAITH — Spotlighting the importance of family and faith to the New Mexican Hispanic culture.
through 7/3/95	EL RIO ABAJO: TRADITIONAL ART OF SOUTHERN NEWMEXICO — Spanish colonial and Mexican themes in rarely shown textiles, furniture, santos and metal, interpreted by southern artists and related to the folk art of northern NewMexico.
12/1/94 - 1/96	SWEDISH FOLK ART: ALL TRADITION IS CHANGE — Sweden's vernacular architecture, furniture, textiles, costumes and wall images in context promote dialog between traditional and modern, urban and rural. Includes "Lekstugan," a 19th century farmhouse replica with scaled-down, child-sized furniture.

MUSEUM OF INDIAN ARTS AND CULTURE

continuing	FROM THIS EARTH: POTTERY OF THE SOUTHWEST — A survey of archeological, historical and contemporary Southwest Indian pottery examines techniques, styles, materials and regions.
	PEOPLE OF THE MIMBRES — A comprehensive examination of the ancient people whose civilization is being reconstructed by archeologists despite destruction of cultural sites by pothunters and fortune seekers.
	DANCING SPIRITS: JOSE REY TOLEDO, TOWA ARTIST — The paintings of this late artist whose many careers included health educator, actor and lecturer, are witness to his love of the traditions and ceremonies of his people.

NEW MEXICO

Museum of New Mexico- continued
NEW MEXICO STATE MONUMENTS

FORT SELDEN 505-526-8911 — A 19th century adobe fort.

FORT SUMNER 505-355-2573 — Site of the internment of 9,500 Apaches and Navajos in the 1860's. Billy the Kid was killed here by Sheriff Pat Garrett.

JEMEZ 505-829-3530 — The ruins of Giusewa, an ancient Indian settlement near present-day Jemez Pueblo and San Jose de los Jemez, a 17th century Spanish mission church.

LINCOLN 505-653-4372 — This well preserved old west town was the site of the Lincoln County War and of Billy the Kid's capture and escape.

CORONADO 505-867-5351 — Site of the ruins of the ancient Tiwa Pueblo of Kuaua.

SANTA FE

Wheelwright Museum of the American Indian
704 Camino Lejo, **Santa Fe, NM 87502**
TEL: 505-982-4636
HRS: 10-5 M-Sa; 1-5 S   HOL: 1/1, THGV, 12/25
ADM: F   HDC/ACC: Y, Main Gallery only; rest rooms and gift shop downstairs
PARKING: Y, in front of building   LIB: Y   MUS/SH: Y   GT: Y   GT/PH: ! 505-982-4636   DT: Y
TIME: Tu, F 2pm   S/G: Y
PERM/COLL: NAT/AM, Navajo; SW Ind (not always on view)

Inside this eight sided building, shaped like a Navajo "hooghan" or home, on a hillside with vast views, you will find breathtaking American Indian art. **NOT TO BE MISSED:** Sandpainting reproductions and Hastiin Klah's sandpainting textiles

ON EXHIBIT/95:
MAIN (KLAH) GALLERY:

11/25/94 - 1/25/95	RECENT ACQUISITIONS (working title)
2/4 - 5/10/95	JURIED EXHIBITION OF CONTEMPORARY NATIVE AMERICAN ART
5/10 - 9/27/95	THE MANOOGIAN COLLECTION (ART OF THE PLAINS, GREAT LAKES AND WOODLANDS (WORKING TITLE)
Fall 95	NATIVE AMERICAN VETERANS (TENT!)
SKYLIGHT GALLERY	CHANGING EXHIBITS OF EMERGING NATIVE AMERICAN ARTISTS

TAOS

Millicent Rogers Museum
1504 Millicent Rogers Road, 4 miles n of Taos, **Taos, NM 87571**
TEL: 505-758-2462
HRS: 9-5 Daily   DAY CLOSED: HOL: LEG/HOL!
ADM: Y   ADULT: $4.00, Fam $8   CHILDREN: 6-16 $2.00   STUDENTS: $3.00   SR CIT: $3.00
HDC/ACC: Y   PARKING: Y   LIB: Y   MUS/SH: Y
GT: Y   GT/PH: call 505-758-2462 to reserve H/B: Y   S/G: Y
PERM/COLL: NAT/AM & HISP: textiles, basketry, pottery, jewelry

272

Millicent Rogers Museum - continued

Dedicated to the display and interpretation of the art and material of Native American and Hispanic peoples of the Southwest, the Millicent Rogers Museum places particular focus on northern New Mexico.

ON EXHIBIT/95:

7/16/94 - 1/15/95   VIVA BERNIE/OSCAR E. BERNINGHAUS — Oils, watercolors, etchings and lithographs by this noted early Taos artist.

9/23/94 - 1/8/95   NATIVE AMERICAN INVITATIONAL — Works from five Northern Pueblos: Taos, Picuris, San Juan, Santa Clara and San Ildefonso.

TAOS

The Harwood Foundation Museum of the University of New Mexico
Affiliate Institution: University of New Mexico
238 Ledoux St, **Taos, NM 87571**
TEL: 505-758-9826
HRS: 10-5 M-F; 10-4 Sa   DAY CLOSED: S   HOL: LEG/HOL!
ADM: Y   ADULT: $2.00
HDC/ACC: Y; Partial!   PARKING: Y; Limited parking with parking lots nearby   LIB: Y   MUS/SH: Y
GT: Y   GT/PH: call 505-758-9826 to reserve   H/B: Y
PERM/COLL: TAOS ARTISTS: 19, 20

Many of the finest artists who have worked in Taos are represented in this collection. The building housing the museum is one of the first twentieth-century buildings that set the architectural style which became popular in northern New Mexico. **NOT TO BE MISSED:** "Winter Funeral," By Victor Higgins

ON EXHIBIT/95:   The Harwood Foundation Museum will be closed for renovation during part of 1995, probably May-August. Call!

NEW YORK

ALBANY

Albany Institute of History & Art
125 Washington Ave., **Albany, NY 12210**
TEL: 518-463-4478
HRS: 10-5 Tu-F; 12-5 Sa, S   DAY CLOSED: M   HOL: LEG/HOL!
VOL/CONT: Y   ADM: F   HDC/ACC: Y   PARKING: Y; Nearby pay garage   LIB: Y   MUS/SH: Y
REST/FAC: Y; 11:30-1:30 Tu-F (Sep-May)   GT: Y   GT/PH: call 518-463-4478 to reserve   H/B: Y
PERM/COLL: PTGS: Hudson River School & Limner; AM: portraits 19; CAST IRON STOVES; DEC/ARTS: 19

Founded in 1791, this is one of the oldest museums in the country featuring changing exhibitions throughout the year. There are over 15,000 objects in the permanent collection. **NOT TO BE MISSED:** Hudson River School Ptgs by Cole, Durand, Church, Kensett, Casilear and the Hart Brothers.

ON EXHIBIT/95:

Continuing	MADE IN ALBANY: DECORATIVE ARTS FROM THE COLLECTION
Through Feb. 26, 1995	THE MOTORCYCLE: ACTION/REACTION
1/21 - 5/7/95	OUT OF THE ORDINARY: COMMUNITY TASTES AND VALUES IN CONTEMPORARY FOLK ART
2/4 - 5/18/95	RECENT ACQUISITIONS: ERASTUS CORNING AND POLITICS IN ALBANY
3/7 - 5/28	WHAT'S A WOMAN TO DO
6/15 - 8/27/95	KINGS AND QUEENS AND SOUP TUREENS WT
7/1 - 11/10	RECENT ACQUISITIONS: THE LATHROPS
9/9 - 11/10/95	BOB BLACKBURN'S PRINTMAKING WORKSHOP: ARTISTS OF COLOR WT
10/21 continuing	200 YEARS OF COLLECTING

University Art Gallery
Affiliate Institution: University at Albany, State University of NY
1400 Washington Ave, **Albany,** NY 12222
TEL: 518-442-4035
HRS: 10-5 Tu-F; 12-4 Sa, S   DAY CLOSED: M   HOL: LEG/HOL!
ADM: F   HDC/ACC: Y   PARKING: Y; Collins Circle on Washington Ave. entrance to campus
REST/FAC: Y; In Campus Center
PERM/COLL: AM: gr, ptgs, dr 20

This gallery, the largest of its kind among the State University campuses and one of the major galleries of the Capitol District, features work from student and mid-career to established artists of national reputation. **NOT TO BE MISSED:** Richard Diebenkorn, "Seated Woman," 1966, (drawing)

ON EXHIBIT/95:

1/17 - 2/19/95	WARRINGTON COLESCOTT: A RETROSPECTIVE — Curated by the artist from his own collection, this exhibition of 60 prints includes examples of both his early etchings of the fifties and sixties and his experimental and mature work of the seventies and eighties. It charts his stylistic development as a satirist and captures his ultimate statement in technique and concept as it emerged in his work during the past 30 years.
9/12 - 11/12/95	CONTEMPORARY ART OF THE NAVAJO NATION — This is the first comprehensive exhibition of contemporary Navajo Folk Art to be organized for travel. It will survey the extraordinary work of 42 artists utilizing a regional approach to provide an historical context for the artists, their inspirations and their creations. WT

274

NEW YORK

ANNANDALE ON HUDSON

The Center for Curatorial Studies and Art in Contemporary Culture
Affiliate Institution: Bard College
Annandale on Hudson, NY 12504
TEL: 914-758-2424
HRS: 1-5 W-S   DAY CLOSED: M, Tu   HOL: ACAD!
ADM: F   HDC/ACC: Y   PARKING: Y   LIB: Y!   REST/FAC: GT: Y   GT/PH: !
PERM/COLL: CONT: all media; VIDEO: installation 1960-present

Housed in a new facility which opened in 1992, the Rivendell Collection, a systematic collection of art from the mid 1960's to the present, will continue to grow with the addition of works through the end of this century. **NOT TO BE MISSED:** Sol Lewitt "Double Assymetrical Pyramids," 1986, india ink wash on wall

ASTORIA

American Museum of the Moving Image
35th Ave at 36th St, **Astoria, NY 11106**
TEL: 718-784-0077
HRS: 12-4 Tu-F; 12-6 Sa-S   DAY CLOSED: M   HOL: 1/1, 12/25
ADM: Y   ADULT: $5.00   CHILDREN: $2.50   STUDENTS: $2.50   SR CIT: $4.00
HDC/ACC: Y; Through services entrance   PARKING: Y; Nearby pay garage   MUS/SH: Y   H/B: Y
PERM/COLL: MATERIAL CULTURE OF FILM, TELEVISION, AND VIDEO

The only Museum in the US devoted exclusively to film, television, video and interactive media and their impact on 20th century American life. **NOT TO BE MISSED:** "Tut's Fever Movie Palace," Red Grooms and Lysiane Luongs interpretation of a 1920's neo-Egyptian movie palace showing screenings of classic movie serials daily.

AUBURN

Schweinfurth Memorial Art Center
205 Genesee St, **Auburn, NY 13021**
TEL: 315-255-1553
HRS: 12-5 Tu-F; 10-5 Sa; 1-5 S   DAY CLOSED: M   HOL: THGV, 12/25
ADM: Y   ADULT: $1.00   CHILDREN: F (under 12)   STUDENTS: F   SR CIT: $1.00
HDC/ACC: Y   PARKING: Y   MUS/SH: Y
PERM/COLL: Non collecting institution

Regional fine art, folk art and crafts are featured in changing exhibitions at this cultural center located in central New York State.

ON EXHIBIT/95:
2/95 - 4/95	CALL ME COLLECTOR, WE CELEBRATE DIVERSITY: ART BY CITIZENS
5/95 - 6/95	BOTH ENDS OF THE RAINBOW

275

NEW YORK

Schweinfurth Memorial Art Center - continued

6/95 - 9/95	ART CENTER JURIED INVITATIONAL
9/95 - 10/95	MICHAEL SICKLER: PAINTINGS
	BOOK ART
11/95 - 1/96	QUILTS = ART = QUILTS

BAYSIDE

QCC Art Gallery
Affiliate Institution: Queensborough Community College
222-05 56th Ave., **Bayside, NY 11364-1497**
TEL: 718-631-6396
HRS: 9-5 M-F and by appt.   DAY CLOSED: Sa, S   HOL: ACAD!
ADM: F   HDC/ACC: Y   GT: Y   GT/PH: call 718-631-6396 for specifics
PERM/COLL: AM: after 1950; WOMEN ARTISTS

The Gallery which reflects the ethnic diversity of Queensborough Community College and its regional residents also highlights the role art plays in the cultural history of people.

BINGHAMTON

Roberson Center for the Arts and Sciences
30 Front St., **Binghamton, NY 13905**
TEL: 607-772-0660
HRS: 10-5 Tu, T, Sa; 10-9 F; 12-5 S   DAY CLOSED: M   HOL: LEG/HOL!
ADM: Y   ADULT: $3.00   CHILDREN: 5-16, $1.50   STUDENTS: $3.00   SR CIT: $2.00
HDC/ACC: Y   PARKING: Y   LIB: Y   MUS/SH: Y   GT: Y   GT/PH: call 607-772-0660
PERM/COLL: TEXTILES; PHOT; PTGS; DEC/ART: late 19, 20

This regional museum and science center features the history of Broome County spanning 10,000 years, Edward A. Link's accomplishments in aviation and oceanography, and the Lee J. Loomis Wildlife Collection. **NOT TO BE MISSED:** "Blue Box" trainer circa 1942 by Edward Link

BLUE MOUNTAIN LAKE

Adirondack Museum
Blue Mountain Lake, NY 12812
TEL: 518-352-7311
HRS: 9:30-5:30 M-S; MEM/DAY weekend to 10/15   HOL: None
ADM: Y   ADULT: $10.00   CHILDREN: 7-15 $6.00   STUDENTS: SR CIT: $8.50
HDC/ACC: Y   PARKING: Y   LIB: Y   MUS/SH: Y   REST/FAC: Y   H/B: Y
PERM/COLL: An excellent small collection of paintings entirely related to the Adirondacks

Perched on the shoulder of Blue Mountain overlooking Mountain Lake, this regional museum of art and history features a small but fine collection of paintings related entirely to the Adirondacks. A luxurious private railroad car, the Bill Gates Diner, a trolley eatery from Bolton Landing, and other buildings that tell the history of the largest wilderness area in the East are also part of this complex.

NEW YORK

BROCKPORT

Tower Fine Arts Gallery
Affiliate Institution: SUNY Brockport
Tower Fine Arts Building, **Brockport, NY 14420**
TEL: 516-395-5280
HRS: 12-5 M & T-Sa; 12-5 & 7-9 Tu, W   DAY CLOSED: S   HOL: ACAD!
ADM: F   HDC/ACC: Y   PARKING: Y
PERM/COLL: WORKS OF e.e CUMMINGS

BRONX

The Bronx Museum of the Arts
1040 Grand Concourse, **Bronx, NY 10456**
TEL: 718-681-6000
HRS: 10-5 W-F; 1-6 Sa, S   DAY CLOSED: M, Tu   HOL: THGV, 12/25
F/DAY: S   ADM: Y   ADULT: $3.00   CHILDREN: F (under 12)   STUDENTS: $2.00   SR CIT: $1.00
HDC/ACC: Y   PARKING: Y; Nearby pay garage   MUS/SH: Y
PERM/COLL: AF: LAT/AM: SE/ASIAN: works on paper 20; CONT/AM: eth

Noted for its reflection of the multi-ethnicity of this "borough of neighborhoods" this is the only fine arts museum in the Bronx. The collection and exhibitions are a fresh perspective on the urban experience.

ON EXHIBIT/95:

10/7/94 - 1/22/95	CARTOGRAPHIES: FOURTEEN ARTISTS FROM LATIN AMERICA — Paintings, sculpture, photographs and installations exploring the artistic production of Latin America in terms of language, the transitional nature of curren t art issues and the dissolution of Latin American cultural boundaries. WT
2/95 - 6/95	DIVISION OF LABOR: "WOMEN'S WORK" IN CONTEMPORARY ART — An examination of the notion of gender specific art practices from the 1970's until the present. This exhibition will trace the shifting discourse on gender roles and focus on strategies that counter conventional gender stereotypes through the work of 25 artists.
7/95 - 9/95	ARTIST IN THE MARKETPLACE — The 15th anniversary of this program highlighting the work of several alumni artists.
10/95 - 1/96	RECAPTURING THE PAST: MEMORY AND HISTORY IN CONTEMPORARY ART — Works by 12 artists of African, Asian and Latin American descent who use the recreation of memory as a tool for exploring their private and collective histories.

The Hall of Fame for Great Americans
Affiliate Institution: Bronx Community College
University Ave and W. 181 St, **Bronx, NY 10453**
TEL: 718-220-6003
HRS: 10-5 Daily   HOL: None
ADM: F   HDC/ACC: Y; Ground level entrance to Colonnade   PARKING: Y   GT: Y   GT/PH: call for specifics
DT: Y   TIME: !   H/B: Y   S/G: Y
PERM/COLL: COLONNADE OF 97 BRONZE BUSTS OF AMERICANS ELECTED TO THE HALL OF FAME
SINCE 1900, includes works by Daniel Chester French, James Earle Fraser, Frederick MacMonnies, August Saint-Gaudens

Overlooking the Bronx & Harlem Rivers, this beautiful Beaux arts style architectural complex, once a Revolutionary War fort, contains a Stanford White designed library modeled after the Pantheon in Rome. 97 recently restored bronze portrait busts of famous Americans elected to the Hall of Fame since 1900 and placed within the niches of the "Men of Renown" classical colonnade allow the visitor to come face-to-face with history through art.

NEW YORK

BROOKLYN

The Brooklyn Museum

200 Eastern Pkwy, **Brooklyn, NY 11238**
TEL: 718-638-5000
HRS: 10-5 W-S   DAY CLOSED: M, T   HOL: 1/1, THGV, 12/25
ADM: Y   ADULT: $4.00   CHILDREN: F (under 12)   STUDENTS: $2 w ID   SR CIT: $1.50
HDC/ACC: Y   PARKING: Y; Pay parking on site   LIB: Y!   MUS/SH: Y   REST/FAC: Y
GT: Y   GT/PH: call 718-638-5000, ext 221   DT: Y   TIME: !W-F, 2pm; Sa, S, 1 & 2pm   H/B: Y   S/G: Y
PERM/COLL: EGT; AM: ptgs, scupl, dec/art 18-20; AF; OC; NW/AM; W/COL

The Brookyn Museum is one of the nation's premier art institutions. Housed in a Beaux-Arts structure designed in 1893 by McKim, Mead & White, its collections represent virtually the entire history of art from Egyptian artifacts to modern American paintings. **NOT TO BE MISSED:** Newly renovated and brilliantly installed Charles A. Wilbur Egyptian Collection

ON EXHIBIT/95:

9/30/94 - 9/10/95	DALE CHIHULY INSTALLATION — Blurring the lines between "fine"and "decorative" art, between "art" and "craft," Chihuly uses fantastical shapes and vibrant colors to lend movement to his often large molten-glass sculptures.
10/14/94 - 1/8/95	REALMS OF HEROISM: INDIAN PAINTINGS AT THE BROOKLYN MUSEUM — Approximately 80 Indian miniature paintings from the collection provide an exploration into heroism in a South Asian context.
1/13 - 4/2/94	THOMAS COLE: LANDSCAPE INTO HISTORY — A significant retrospective of one of New York's most important painters. Centerpieces of the exhibition are Cole's two important allegorical series, "The Course of Empire" and "The Voyage of Life."
2/3 - 3/26/95	GRAND RESERVES: REDISCOVERED PAINTINGS — 10 rediscovered and restored or recently acquired major American paintings from The Brooklyn Museum Collection
extended through 2/95	RED GROOMS'S DAME OF THE NARROWS AND THE GREATER NEW YORK HARBOR
6/3/94 - 11/5/95	MORE ROOM FOR A VIEW: LARGE SCALE WORKS ON PAPER — 20 works from the permanent collection.
9/29/95 - 1/7/96	LEON POLK SMITH: A RETROSPECTIVE — The exhibition will chronicle Smith's steadfast devotion to geometric forms and spatial relationships conveyed through solid areas of color. CAT

Ongoing reinstallations:

12/94	ANDEAN REINSTALLATION - permanent — A fully reconstructed quadrant in the Great Hall will display the Museum's impressive Andean collection.
3/9/95	OCEANIC REINSTALLATION - permanent
3/9/95	AFRICAN REINSTALLATION - permanent
Long term Installation	TWENTIETH CENTURY DESIGN FROM THE BROOKLYN MUSEUM

BROOKLYN

The Rotunda Gallery
33 Clinton Street, **Brooklyn, NY 11201**
TEL: 718-875-4047
HRS: 12-5 Tu-F; 11-4 Sa   DAY CLOSED: S, M   HOL: LEG/HOL!
ADM: F   HDC/ACC: Y; Wheelchair lift   PARKING: Y; Metered street parking; nearby pay garage
GT: Y   GT/PH: call 718-875-4047 for specifics   DT: Y   TIME: 10-11:30 am M-F
PERM/COLL: non-collecting institution

The Gallery's facility is an architecturally distinguished space designed for exhibition of all forms of contemporary art. It is located in Brooklyn Heights which is well known for its shops, restaurants and historic brownstone district.

The Rubelle & Norman Schafler Gallery
Affiliate Institution: Pratt Institute
200 Willoughby Ave, **Brooklyn, NY 11205**
TEL: 718-636-3517
HRS: 9-5 M-F   DAY CLOSED: Sa, S   HOL: LEG/HOL!
ADM: F
HDC/ACC: Y   PARKING: Y; on street parking only
PERM/COLL: Currently building a Collection of Art and Design Works by Pratt Alumni, Faculty and Students

Varied programs of thematic, solo, and group exhibitions of contemporary art, design and architecture are presented in this gallery.

ON EXHIBIT/95:

12/9/94 - 1/20/95	A NATURAL DIALOGUE
2/10 - 3/24/95	COLLECTIVE PAN-AFRICAN, HISPANIC AND KOREAN EXHIBITION
4/7 - 5/5/95	LETTERFORMS - FROM HAND TO DIGITAL

BUFFALO

Albright-Knox Art Gallery
1285 Elmwood Ave, **Buffalo, NY 14222**
TEL: 716-882-8700
HRS: 11-5 Tu-Sa; 12-5 S   DAY CLOSED: M   HOL: 1/1, THGV, 12/25
ADM: Y   ADULT: $4.00   CHILDREN: F (under 12)   STUDENTS: $3.00   SR CIT: $3.00
HDC/ACC: Y   PARKING: Y   LIB: Y!   MUS/SH: Y   REST/FAC: Y
GT: Y   GT/PH: call 716-883-8700 to reserve
DT: Y   TIME: !   H/B: Y   S/G: Y
PERM/COLL: AB/EXP; CONT: 70's & 80's; POST/IMPR; POP; OP; CUBIST; AM & EU: 18-19

With one of the world's top international surveys of twentieth-century painting and sculpture, the Albright-Knox is especially rich in American and European art of the past fifty years. The permanent collection which also offers a panorama of art through the centuries dating from 3000 BC., is housed in a 1905 Greek Revival style building designed by Edward B. Green with a 1962 addition by Gordon Bunshaft of Skidmore, Owings and Merrill.

NEW YORK

Albright-Knox Art Gallery - continued

ON EXHIBIT/95:

1/14 - 3/5/95	AMERICAN ARTS AND CRAFTS: VIRTUE IN DESIGN	
3/18 - 5/7/95	MASTER PRINTS FROM UPPER NEW YORK STATE COLLECTIONS	
5/27 - 7/9/95	IN WESTERN NEW YORK 1995	
7/22 - 10/1/95	THE WILLIAM S. PALEY COLLECTION	CAT WT
10/14 - 12/31/95	ARSHILE GORKY: THE BREAKTHROUGH YEARS — 45 paintings and drawings from Gorky's mature years (1940-1948) will document the artist's crucial role as a link between European surrealism and American abstract impressionism. Highlighted in this exhibition will be his painting "The Liver is the Cock's Comb," a work that is rarely allowed to travel.	CAT WT

BUFFALO

Burchfield-Penney Art Center
Affiliate Institution: Buffalo State College
1300 Elmwood Ave, **Buffalo, NY 14222**
TEL: 716-878-6012
HRS: 10-5 Tu-Sa; 1-5 S   DAY CLOSED: M   HOL: LEG/HOL!
SUGG/CONT: Y
HDC/ACC: Y; Elevator access, wheelchairs available   PARKING: Y; Some on campus and metered parking.
LIB: Y   MUS/SH: Y   GT: Y   GT/PH: call 716-878-6020 to reserve
DT: Y   TIME: usually available 10-5 Sa, 1-5 S
PERM/COLL: AM; WEST/NY: 19, 20

The Burchfield-Penney Art Center is dedicated to the art and artists of Western New York. Particular emphasis is given to the works of renowned American watercolorist Charles E. Burchfield and his contemporaries such as Reginald Marsh. **NOT TO BE MISSED:** Burchfield's "Appalachian Evening" and "Oncoming Spring." Charles Rand Penney collections of works by Burchfield, Roycroft movement artists, and other craft artists.

ON EXHIBIT/95:

11/5/94 - 4/9/95	ENDI POSKOVIC: EUROPA SERIES-ALTER CRUX II
12/3 - 1/29/95	ROYCROFT DESKTOP
date not determined	NORMAN BELLOWS COLLECTION OF C. D. ARNOLD PAN AM EXPO PHOTOS
2/11 - 3/26/95	EMERGING ARTISTS: ARTISTS INFLUENCED BY HALLWALLS
4/8 - 5/28/95	SIENA
6/17 - 9/3/95	FOREST LAWN CEMETARY
7/29 - 9/10/95	ETTORE PORRECA: WORLD WAR II PHOTOGRAPHS
9/16 - 11/26/95	THE CHARLES RAND PENNEY COLLECTION OF WORKS BY CHARLES E. BURCHFIELD
12/8 - 2/4/96	THE GREAT LAKES

CANAJOHARIE

Canajoharie Library and Art Gallery
Erie Blvd, **Canajoharie, NY 13317**
TEL: 518-673-2314
HRS: 10-4:45 M-W; 1:30-8:30 T; 1:30-4:45 F; 10:30-1:30 Sa; Summer Only 1-3:45 S   DAY CLOSED: Tu, S
HOL: LEG/HOL!
ADM: F
HDC/ACC: Y   PARKING: Y   LIB: Y   GT: Y   GT/PH: call for specifics   S/G: Y
PERM/COLL: WINSLOW HOMER; AMERICAN IMPRESSIONISTS; "The Eight"

Located in downtown Canjoharie, the gallery's collection includes 21 Winslow Homers.

CATSKILL

Thomas Cole Foundation
218 Spring St., **Catskill, NY 12414**
TEL: 518-943-6533
HRS: 11-4 W-Sa; 1-5 S (Jul-Lab/Day); by appt rest of year   DAY CLOSED: M, Tu   HOL: LEG/HOL!
ADM: F
PARKING: Y   LIB: Y
PERM/COLL: AM: ptgs 19

The Residence and Studio of Thomas Cole is an 1815 building with paintings relating to the development of the Hudson River School and the works of Cole himself, a leading American master painter and influential teacher of his day.

CLINTON

Emerson Gallery
Affiliate Institution: Hamilton College
198 College Hill Road, **Clinton, NY 13323**
TEL: 315-859-4396
HRS: 12-5 M-F; 1-5 Sa, S; closed weekends June, Jul & Aug   HOL: LEG/HOL!
ADM: F
HDC/ACC: Y   PARKING: Y
PERM/COLL: NAT/AM; AM & EU: ptgs, gr 19, 20; WEST INDIES ART

While its ultimate purpose is to increase the educational scope and opportunity for appreciation of the fine arts by Hamilton students, the gallery also seeks to enrich campus cultural life in general, as well as to contribute to the cultural enrichment of the surrounding community. **NOT TO BE MISSED:** Outstanding collection of works by Graham Sutherland

ON EXHIBIT/95:
1/16 - 2/19/95   DREAMS AND VISIONS: CONTEMPORARY WOODLANDS INDIAN ARTISTS —
                      Native American groups in central Canada and the north-central United States continue
                      to depict traditional themes using modern media and styles.

NEW YORK

Emerson Gallery - continued

1/16 - 2/19/95   GEORGE CATLIN PRINTS AND PLAINS BEADWORK FROM THE COLLECTION — A selection of hand colored lithographs by the 19th century artist who documented the customs and rituals of the Plains Indians, is supplemented by examples of their beadwork.

1/16 - 4/7/95   LANDSCAPES FROM THE HAMILTON COLLEGE COLLECTION — Changing conceptions of landscape as seen in paintings, drawings and prints from the 16th-20th century.

3/3 - 4/7/95   LISTENING TO THE EARTH: ARTISTS AND THE ENVIRONMENT — Paintings, sculptures and mixed-media installations focus on environmental problems and possible remedies.

6/3 - 9/10/95   GLORIA GARFINKEL: COLOR PRINTS — Colorful abstract images achieved through complex manipulation of various printmaking techniques.

9/21 - 10/29/95   SANDY WALKER: WOODBLOCK PRINTS — Fresh interpretations of landscape that hover between recognizable and pure abstraction using an old printmaking technique.

Nov - Dec   MONUMENTS AND MEMORIES: REFLECTIONS ON THE FORMER SOVIET UNION (TENT!) — Works by nine contemporary Russian photographers.

CORNING

The Corning Museum of Glass

1 Museum Way, **Corning, NY 14830-2253**
TEL: 607-937-5371
HRS: 9-5 M-S   DAY CLOSED: HOL: LEG/HOL!
ADM: Y ADULT: $6.00 CHILDREN: 6-17, $4 STUDENTS: SR CIT: $5.00
HDC/ACC: Y PARKING: Y LIB: Y MUS/SH: Y REST/FAC: Y GT: Y! GT/PH: call for specifics DT: Y
PERM/COLL: GLASS: worldwide 1500 BC - present

The Museum houses the world's premier glass collection – more than 26,000 objects representing 3,500 years of achievements in glass design and craftsmanship. It is part of the Corning Glass Center complex, which also includes the Hall of Science and Industry and the Steuben factory, where visitors can watch artisans make world-famous Steuben crystal. **NOT TO BE MISSED:** Visit the Steuben Factory where Steuben Glass is made.

The Rockwell Museum

111 Cedar St. at Denison Parkway, **Corning, NY 14830**
TEL: 607-937-5386
HRS: 9-5 M-Sa; 12-5 S; additional evening hours Jul & Aug DAY CLOSED: HOL: 1/1, THGV, 12/25 (EVE.), 12/25
ADM: Y ADULT: $3.00 CHILDREN: F (under 17) STUDENTS: SR CIT: $2.50
HDC/ACC: Y PARKING: Y; Municipal lot across Cedar St. LIB: Y MUS/SH: Y
GT: Y! GT/PH: call for specifics (fee charged) DT: Y! TIME: 10am & 2pm F (Jun, Jul, Aug)
H/B: Y; 1893 City Hall, Corning, NY
PERM/COLL: PTGS & SCULP: by Western Artists including Bierstadt, Remington and Russell 1830-1920; FREDERICK CARDER STEUBEN GLASS; ANT: toys

Located in the 1893 City Hall of Corning, NY, and nestled in the lovely Finger Lake Region of NY State is the finest collection of American Western Art in the Eastern U.S. The museum building, a Romanesque revival style that served as a City Hall, firehouse and jail until the 1970's is also home to the world's most comprehensive collection of Frederick Carder Steuben glass. **NOT TO BE MISSED:** Model of Cyrus E. Dallin's famous image, "Appeal to the Great Spirit."

282

CORTLAND

Dowd Fine Arts Gallery
Affiliate Institution: State University of New York at Cortland
SUNY Cortland,
Cortland, NY 13045
TEL: 607-753-4216
HRS: 11-4 Tu-Sa   DAY CLOSED: S, M   HOL: ACAD!
VOL/CONT: Y   ADM: F   HDC/ACC: Y   PARKING: Y; Adjacent to building   S/G: Y
PERM/COLL: Am & EU: gr, drgs 20; CONT: art books

Temporary exhibitions of contemporary and historic art which are treated thematically are presented in this university gallery.

DUNKIRK

Adams Art Gallery
Affiliate Institution: Access to the Arts
600 Central Avenue, **Dunkirk, NY 14048**
TEL: 716-366-7450
HRS: 11-4 W-F; 1-4 Sa, S; (Summer 12-5 W-S)   DAY CLOSED: M, Tu   HOL: 1/1, 7/4, 12/25
VOL/CONT: Y   SUGG/CONT: Y   ADM: summer $2.50
HDC/ACC:N; 12 steps to enter gallery   PARKING: Y, on street   MUS/SH: Y
GT: Y   GT/PH: call 716-366-7450 to reserve   H/B: Y
PERM/COLL: non-collecting institution

Located in a former Unitarian church, the Gallery presents changing bi-monthly exhibitions of fine contemporary art emerging from the crafts tradition.

ON EXHIBIT/95:

1/20 - 2/19/95	CAROL MINNEERLY (Chautauqua, NY) — Paintings
	ELIZABETH SAMUELS (Buffalo, NY) — Mixedmedia assemblage
2/24 - 3/25/95	ROBERT BOOTH (Dunkirk, NY) — Sculpture
3/31 - 5/7/95	IRIS DAWN PARKER (Pittsburgh, PA) — Photographs
	DIANE SOPHRIN (Perry, NY) — Oil painting and drawing
5/12 - 6/11/95	ACCESS INVITED REGIONAL EXHIBITION '95 — Creative and diverse works by artists who have exhibited individually at the Gallery between 1985 and 1991
9/1 - 10/1/95	NICOLE MARTIN (Erie, PA) — Manipulated Polaroids
	GREGORY STEWART (West Park, NY) — Mixed media sculpture
10/6 - 11/12/95	DANIELLE KROMAR (Shutesbury, MA) — Mixed media sculpture and assemblage
	BRYAN MCGRATH (Utica, NY) — Raku vessels
11/17 - 12/17/95	JOHN TRACEY (Hilton, NY) — Clay and porcelain sculpture

NEW YORK

EAST HAMPTON

Guild Hall Museum
158 Main Street, **East Hampton, NY 11937**
TEL: 516-324-0806
HRS: 11-5 daily (Summer); 11-5 W-Sa; 12-5 S (Winter)   HOL: 1/1; THGV; 12/25
ADM: F
HDC/ACC: Y   PARKING: Y   LIB: Y   MUS/SH: Y   H/B: Y   S/G: Y
PERM/COLL: AM: 19, 20

Located within America's foremost art colony this cultural center combines a fine art museum and a 400 seat professional theater.

EAST ISLIP

Islip Art Museum
50 Irish Lane, **East Islip, NY 11730**
TEL: 516-224-5402
HRS: 10-4 W-Sa; 2-4:30 S   DAY CLOSED: M, Tu   HOL: LEG/HOL!
VOL/CONT: Y   ADM: F
HDC/ACC: Y   PARKING: LIB: Y   MUS/SH: Y   H/B: Y
PERM/COLL: AM/REG: ptgs, sculp, cont

The Islip Museum, the leading exhibition space for contemporary and Avant Garde Art on Long Island, also features a satellite gallery called the Anthony Giordamo Gallery located at Dowling College in Oakdale, L. I.

ELMIRA

Arnot Art Museum
235 Lake St, **Elmira, NY 14901-3191**
TEL: 607-734-3697
HRS: 10-5 Tu-Sa; 1-5 S   DAY CLOSED: M   HOL: THGV, 12/25, 1/1
ADM: Y   ADULT: $2.00   CHILDREN: 6-12, $0.50   STUDENTS: $1.00   SR CIT: $1.00
HDC/ACC: Y   PARKING: Y; Free   LIB: Y   MUS/SH: Y   GT: Y   GT/PH: call 607-734-4121 to reserve
DT: Y   H/B: Y
PERM/COLL: AM: salon ptgs 19, 20; AM: sculp 19

Housed in a neo-classical mansion built in 1833 in downtown Elmira, the museum also features a modern addition designed by Graham Gund. **NOT TO BE MISSED:** Matthias Arnot Collection; one of the last extant private collections housed intact in its original showcase

NEW YORK

FLUSHING

Frances Godwin & Joseph Ternbach Museum
Affiliate Institution: Queens College
65-30 Kissena Blvd, **Flushing, NY 11367**
TEL: 718-520-7129
HRS: Hours unavailable at press time, Call!   HOL: ACAD!
ADM: F   HDC/ACC: Not at present   PARKING: Y; On campus
PERM/COLL: GR: 20; ANT: glass; AN/EGT; AN/GRK; PTGS; SCULP

This is the only museum in Queens with a broad and comprehensive permanent collection which includes a large collection of WPA/FAP prints.

GLENS FALLS

The Hyde Collection
161 Warren St., **Glens Falls, NY 12801**
TEL: 518-792-1761
HRS: 10-5 Tu-S; 10-9 T (5/1-8/31)   DAY CLOSED: M   HOL: LEG/HOL!
F/DAY: S   ADM: Y   ADULT: $4.50   CHILDREN: F, under 5   STUDENTS: $3.50   SR CIT: $3.50
HDC/ACC: Y   PARKING: Y   LIB: Y   MUS/SH: Y   GT: Y   GT/PH: call to reserve   H/B: Y   S/G: Y
PERM/COLL: O/M: ptgs; AM: ptgs; ANT; IT/REN; FR: 18

The central focus of this museum complex is an Italian Renaissance style villa which houses an original collection of noted European Old Master and American works of art displayed among an important collection of Renaissance and French 18th century furniture.   Since 1985 temporary collections are housed in the Edward Larabee Barnes Education Wing.

HAMILTON

The Picker Art Gallery
Affiliate Institution: Colgate University
Charles A Dana Center For the Creative Arts, **Hamilton, NY 13346-1398**
TEL: 315-824-7634
HRS: 10-5 Daily   HOL: ACAD!; (also open by request!)
ADM: F   HDC/ACC: Y   PARKING: Y; 2 large lots nearby   GT: Y   GT/PH: call 315-824-7634 to reserve
PERM/COLL: ANT; PTGS & SCULP 20; AS; AF

Located on the Colgate University campus, the Charles A. Dana Art Center is surrounded by expansive lawns.

HEMPSTEAD

Hofstra Museum
Affiliate Institution: Hofstra University,
Hempstead, NY 11550
TEL: 516-463-5672
HRS: 10-9 Tu; 10-5 W-F; 1-5 Sa, S   DAY CLOSED: M   HOL: EASTER WEEKEND
ADM: F   HDC/ACC: Y   PARKING: Y   MUS/SH: Y   REST/FAC: Y   H/B: Y   S/G: Y
PERM/COLL: SCULP: Henry Moore, H. J. Seward Johnson, Jr., Tony Rosenthal

285

NEW YORK

Hofstra Museum - continued

Hofstra University is a living museum. Eleven exhibition areas are located throughout the 238-acre campus, which is also a national arboretum. **NOT TO BE MISSED:** Sondra Rudin Mack Garden designed by Oehme, Van Sweden and Assoc.; Henry Moore's "Upright Motive No. 9," and "Hitchhiker," and Tony Rosenthal's "T"s.

ON EXHIBIT/95:

1/22 - 3/95	FIFTIETH ANNIVERSARY OF THE UNITED NATIONS
1/31 - 3/19/95	1995 FACULTY EXHIBITION FROM THE FINE ARTS, ART HISTORY AND GRADUATE HUMANITIES AND NEW COLLEGE
2/1 - 4/2/95	ROMARE BEARDEN FROM THE HOFSTRA MUSEUM COLLECTION
4/2 - 5/19/95	THE ARTIST AND THE BASEBALL CARD WT
4/95 - 5/95	BABE RUTH MEMORABILIA
6/95 - 8/95	60 YEARS OF HOFSTRA HISTORY FROM THE UNIVERSITY ARCHIVES
6/95 - 8/95	LUCIEN LECLERQUE PHOTOGRAPHS FROM THE HOFSTRA MUSEUM COLLECTION
9/7 - 10/29/95	THE BUTCHER, THE BAKER, THE CANDLESTICKMAKER: JAN LUYKEN'S DRAWINGS OF AMSTERDAM'S WORKING PEOPLE IN THE 17TH CENTURY
9/95 - 10/95	AFRICA THROUGH THE EYES OF WOMEN ARTISTS ET
11/95 - 12/95	RECENT ACQUISITIONS
11/95 - 12/95	ONE AND ANOTHER: PRINTS BY YAAKOV AGAM FROM THE HOFSTRA MUSEUM COLLECTION

HUDSON

Olana State Historic Site
State Route 9G, **Hudson, NY 12534**
TEL: 518-828-0135
HRS: 10-4 W-Sa & 12-4 S (4/15-Lab/Day); 12-4 W-S (Lab/Day-10/31)   DAY CLOSED: M, T   HOL: MEM/DAY, 7/4, LAB/DAY, COLUMBUS DAY
ADM: Y   ADULT: $3.00   CHILDREN: $1.50 (5-11)   STUDENTS: $3.00   SR CIT: $3.00
HDC/ACC: Y!   PARKING: Y; Limited   LIB: Y!   MUS/SH: Y
GT: Y   GT/PH: call to reserve 2 weeks in advance   H/B: Y
PERM/COLL: FREDERIC CHURCH: ptgs, drgs; PHOT COLL; CORRESPONDENCE

Olana, the magnificent home of Hudson River School artist Frederick Edwin Church, was designed by him in the Persian style, and furnished in the Aesthetic style. Many of Church's paintings are on view throughout the house.

NEW YORK

HUNTINGTON

Heckscher Museum
Prime Ave, **Huntington, NY 11743**
TEL: 516-351-3250
HRS: 10-5 Tu-F; 1-5 Sa, S   DAY CLOSED: M   HOL: !
SUGG/CONT: Y   ADULT: $2.00   CHILDREN: $1.00   STUDENTS: $1.00   SR CIT: $1.00
HDC/ACC: Y; Steps to restrooms
PARKING: Y   LIB: Y   MUS/SH: Y   GT: Y   GT/PH: call 516-351-3250
DT: Y   TIME: 2:30 & 3:30 S; 1 & 3 W   H/B: Y;
PERM/COLL: AM: ldscp ptg 19; AM: Modernist ptgs, drgs, works on paper

Located in a 18.5 acre park, the museum, whose collection numbers more than 750 works, was presented as a gift to the people of Huntington by philanthropist August Heckscher. **NOT TO BE MISSED:** "Eclipse of the Sun," by George Grosz.

ON EXHIBIT/95:

12/3/94 - 2/26/95	MILTON AVERY: PAINTINGS FROM THE NEUBERGER COLLECTION (working title) — selection of paintings by the noted 20th century artist. CAT
3/4 - 4/23/95	WHITE MOUNTAIN PAINTERS, 1834-1926 — The important 19th century landscape movement established by landscape painters in the White Mountains of New Hampshire has been largely eclipsed by the Hudson River School. This exhibition examines such artists as Albert Bierstadt, Benjamin Champney, Alvan Fisher and Willard Metcalf. CAT WT
5/13 - 5/11/95	40TH ANNUAL LONG ISLAND ARTISTS EXHIBITION — An annual juried group exhibition.

HYDE PARK

The Edwin A. Ulrich Museum
Wave Crest On-The-Hudson, Albany Post Rd., **Hyde Park, NY 12538**
TEL: 914-229-7107
HRS: 10-4 M-F May-Oct; rest of year by appt!   DAY CLOSED: Sa-S   HOL: LEG/HOL!
ADM: Y   ADULT: $2.50   CHILDREN: $2.50   STUDENTS: $2.50   SR CIT: $2.50
HDC/ACC:N   PARKING: Y   LIB: Y   MUS/SH: Y
GT: Y   GT/PH: call for specifics; fee charged
DT: Y $2.50pp fee charged   H/B: Y; 19th C barn   S/G: Y
PERM/COLL: S. B. WAUGH, PORTRAIT PAINTER (1814-1884); F. J. WAUGH, SEA SCAPE PAINTER (1861-1940); C. WAUGH, PALLETTE KNIFE PAINTER (1896-1973)

The Ulrich is home to 3 generations of an American family of painters that span a 160 year period (1814-1973). The vast differences in each artist increases the variety in the collection and shows an evolution in their art.

NEW YORK

ITHACA

Herbert F. Johnson Museum of Art
Affiliate Institution: Cornell University
Cornell University, **Ithaca, NY 14853**
TEL: 607-255-6464
HRS: 10-5 Tu-S; 10-8 W   DAY CLOSED: M   HOL: MEM/DAY, 7/4, THGV + F
ADM: F   HDC/ACC: Y   PARKING: Y; Metered   LIB: Y!   GT: Y   GT/PH: call 607-255-6464 for specifics
DT: Y   TIME: 12 noon every other T; 1 Sa, S!   S/G: Y
PERM/COLL: AS; AM: gr 19, 20

The Gallery, with a view of Cayuga Lake, is located on the Cornell Campus in Ithaca, NY. **NOT TO BE MISSED:** "Fields in the Month of June," by Daubigny

ON EXHIBIT/95:

8/19 - 10/22/95   AUGUSTUS VINCENT TACK: LANDSCAPE OF THE SPIRIT — The first comprehensive retrospective ever organized of the work of Tack (1870-1949) traces his evolution from Impressionism to spiritual abstractions. He depicts nature as chaotic yet ordered, thunderous and awe-inspiring.   CAT   WT

KATONAH

Caramoor Center for Music and the Arts
Girdle Ridge Road, **Katonah, NY 10536**
TEL: 914-232-5035
HRS: 11-4 Tu-Sa, 1-4 S (Jun-Sep); 11-4 Tu-F (by appt Oct-May)   DAY CLOSED: M   HOL: LEG/HOL!
ADM: Y   ADULT: $5.00   CHILDREN: $4.00   HDC/ACC: Y   PARKING: Y; Free   MUS/SH: Y
REST/FAC: Picnic facilities and snack bar   GT: Y   GT/PH: call 914-232-5035 to reserve   H/B: Y   S/G: Y
PERM/COLL: FURNITURE; PTGS; SCULP; DEC/ART; REN; OR: all media

Built in the 1930's by Walter Rosen as a country home, this 54 room Italianate mansion is a treasure trove of splendid collections spanning 2,000 years. Caramoor also presents a festival of outstanding concerts each summer and many other programs throughout the year. **NOT TO BE MISSED:** Extraordinary house-museum with entire rooms from European villas and palaces

The Katonah Museum of Art
Route 22 at Jay Street, **Katonah, NY 10536**
TEL: 914-232-9555
HRS: 1-5 Tu-F, S; 10-5 Sa   DAY CLOSED: M   HOL: 1/1, MEM/DAY; PRESIDENTS/DAY, 7/4, THGV, 12/25
VOL/CONT: Y   ADM: F   HDC/ACC: Y   PARKING: Y; Free on-site parking   MUS/SH: Y
REST/FAC: Y; Snack bar   GT: Y   GT/PH: call for specifics   DT: T, Th, S   TIME: 2pm   S/G: Y
PERM/COLL: No Permanent Collection

Moved to a building designed by Edward Larabee Barnes in 1990, the museum has a committment to outstanding special exhibitions which bring to the community art of all periods, cultures and mediums.

ON EXHIBIT/95:

9/18/94 - 1/14/95   ANIMATED INTERACTIONS — The notion of play as reflected in the modern arts, and specifically, in cartoonswill be seen in this exhibition which explores the way that complicated interactions between static and animated cartoons have evolved. Included are paintings, drawings, sculpture and photography by contemporary artists who work with cartoon imagery such as Sue Coe, Mike Kelley, Billy Copley, Peter Halley, Art Spiegelman and William Wegman.

The Katonah Museum of Art - continued

12/4/94 - 4/16/95	CREIGHTON MICHAEL LANDSCAPE — The artist has been commissioned to design five site specific sculptures to be exhibited in the Museum's Sculpture Garden. His work is fashioned from interior and exterior webs that are made from multiple materials. They are designed to engage the viewer in a complex dialogue and are a vehicle for questioning the way in which we identify the physical world. The location of the works is essential. These are set in a magnificent stand of Norway spruce. Some drawings will also be shown. <div align="right">CAT</div>
1/14 - 4/16/95	MEDIEVAL MONSTERS: BIZARRE BEASTS IN THE ART OF THE MIDDLE AGES — Why were animals so commonly depicted in the Middle Ages? What accounts for the medieval fascination with bizarre, composite creatures? By examining the rich variety of imaginary animals that were widely used as religious and utilitarian objects during the 12th-15th centuries in Western Europe, visitors gain remarkable insight into the medieval vision of the world. <div align="right">CAT</div>
4/9 - 10/29/95	MAKING SENSE: FIVE INSTALLATIONS ON FIVE SENSATIONS — Five artists have been commissioned to design installations for the garden and grounds of the Museum. Sight, hearing, smell, touch and taste will each be the subject of a project that considers the experience of a single sense and the role it plays in environmental perception and the experience of art. The installations will accentuate the meaning and characteristics of each sense and its cooperative and co-dependent nature. Included are the artists Mary and Bill Buchen, Amy Hauft, Eve Andree Laramee and Jeffrey Shiff.
6/24 - 9/17/95	CONTEMPORARY REALISTS
10/1 - 12/31/95	WITHIN THE FRAME: ART IN AMERICAN INTERIORS — The exhibition traces the history of American taste and art patronage in the context of the decorated interior. Fifty works from the late 18th century to the early 20th century address aesthetic styles in American homes of the past and the uses of art in home decor. The exhibition has three sections: 1) 19th century interiors including works by such artists as Charles Wilson Peale and Alexander Jackson Davis; 2) Lush mid century parlors including artists Edmund D. Hawthorne and Edward Lamsen Henry; 3) Interiors associated with Impressionism in America including works by Edmund Tarbell.

LONG ISLAND CITY

Isamu Noguchi Garden Museum
32-37 Vernon Blvd., **Long Island City, NY 11106**
TEL: 718-204-7088
HRS: 11-6 W, Sa & S (Apr-Nov only)   DAY CLOSED: M. Tu, T, F
SUGG/CONT: Y   ADULT: $4.00   CHILDREN: $2.00   STUDENTS: $2.00   SR CIT: $2.00
HDC/ACC: Y; 1/3 of the collection is accessible   PARKING: Y; Street parking   MUS/SH: Y
GT: Y   GT/PH: call 718-204-7088   H/B: Y   S/G: Y
PERM/COLL: WORKS OF ISAMU NOGUCI

Designed by Isamu Noguchi (1904-1988), this museum offers visitors the opportunity to explore the work of the artist on the site of his Long Island City studio. The centerpiece of the collection is a tranquil outdoor sculpture garden. **PLEASE NOTE**: A shuttle bus runs to the museum on Sat. & Sun. every hour on the half hour starting at 11:30am from the corner of Park Ave. & 70th St, NYC, and returns on the hour till 5pm. The round trip fare is $5.00 and DOES NOT include the price of museum admission. **NOT TO BE MISSED:** Permanent exhibition of over 250 sculptures as well as models, drawings, and photo-documentation of his works; stage sets designed for Martha Graham; paper light sculptures called Akari.

NEW YORK

MOUNTAINVILLE

Storm King Art Center
Old Pleasant Hill Rd, **Mountainville, NY 10953**
TEL: 914-534-3115
HRS: 11-5:30 Daily (Apr-Nov.15); Special eve hours Sa, June, July, Aug   HOL: closed 11/16-3/31
ADM: Y   ADULT: $8   CHILDREN: F (under 6)   STUDENTS: $6.00   SR CIT: $6.00
HDC/ACC: Y; Partial, 1st floor of building and portions of 400 acres   PARKING: Y   MUS/SH: Y
GT: Y   GT/PH: call 914-534-3190   DT: Y   TIME: 2pm daily   H/B: Y   S/G: Y
PERM/COLL: SCULP: David Smith, Alexander Calder, Isamu Noguchi, Louise Nevelson, Alice Aycock, Mark di Suvero

America's leading open-air sculpture museum features over 120 masterworks on view amid 400 acres of lawns, fields and woodlands. Works are also on view in a 1935 Norman style mansion that has been converted to museum galleries. NOT TO BE M ISSED: "Momo Taro," a 40 ton, nine-part sculpture by Isamu Noguchi designed for seating and based on a Japanese Folk tale

ON EXHIBIT/95:
    5/13 - 10/31/95   MARK DI SUVERO

MUMFORD

Genesee Country Museum
Flint Hill Road, **Mumford, NY 14511**
TEL: 716-538-6822
HRS: 10-5 Tu-S; July, Aug; 10-4 Tu-F, 10-5 Sa, S Spring and Fall; season mid Oct-mid May
DAY CLOSED: M except Leg/Hols
ADM: Y   ADULT: $10.00   CHILDREN: 6-12 $5.00   STUDENTS: $5.00   SR CIT: $8.50
HDC/ACC: Y; Partial   PARKING: Y; Free   MUS/SH: Y   REST/FAC: Y   H/B: Y   S/G: Y
PERM/COLL: AM: ptgs, sculp; AM/SW: late 19; NAT/AM: sculp; WILDLIFE: art: EU & AM: sport art 17-20

The John L. Wehle collection of sporting art is the only major fine art museum in New York specializing in sport, hunting and wildlife subjects. The collection and carriage museum are housed in an assembled village of 19th century shops, homes and farm buildings.

NEW PALTZ

College Art Gallery
Affiliate Institution: State University of New York College at New Paltz
New Paltz, NY 12561
TEL: 914-257-3844
HRS: 10-4 M-T; 7-9 Tu; 1-4 Sa, S   DAY CLOSED: F   HOL: 1/1, EASTER, THGV, 12/25, ACAD!
ADM: F
HDC/ACC: Y; Wheelchair ramp   PARKING: Y   GT: Y   GT/PH: call 914-257-3844 for sepcifics
PERM/COLL: AM: gr, ptgs 19, 20; JAP: gr; CH: gr; P/COL; CONT: phot

A major cultural resource for the mid-Hudson Valley region.

NEW YORK CITY: SEE LISTINGS UNDER: Astoria, Bayside, Bronx, Brooklyn, Flushing, Long Island City, New York, Queens, Staten Island

NEW YORK

Alternative Museum

594 Broadway, New York, NY 10012
TEL: 212-966-4444
HRS: 11-6 Tu-Sa   DAY CLOSED: S, M   HOL: 12/25
SUGG/CONT: Y   ADULT: $3.00
HDC/ACC: Y; Elevator access   PARKING: Y; Nearby pay garage only
PERM/COLL: CONT

This contemporary arts institution is devoted to the exploration and dissemination of new avenues of thought on contemporary art and culture.

ON EXHIBIT/95:

12//10/94 - 2/11/95	MAUREEN CONNOR — 20 multi-media environments constructed of fabric, wire, mylar, video, audio tape, found objects and white canvas. CAT
2/25 - 4/8/95	JAIME PALACIOS - Gallery One — Born amidst China's Cultural Revolution and still a child when his family returned to Chile the year Allende was elected, Palacios went into exile in Mexico when Allende's government was toppled. His paintings are an answer to the social upheaval that characterizes our age's lack of concrete symbols or values.
2/25 - 4/8/95	GEERDA MEYER-BERNSTEIN - Gallery Two — Bernstein's work addresses brutality and injustice and stems out of her own experiences in her native Germany during the war.
2/25 - 4/8/95	MARINA GUTIERREZ - Gallery Three — Committed to examining issues of social and political injustice, Gutierrez's current series of large scale drawings are centered around Nutt, the Egyptian goddess of the sky, who gives birth to the sun each morning and swallows the sun every night.
4/23 - 6/24/95	THE NEW CLANS — A group exhibition featuring artists who are grappling with questions of self definition and cultural definition. CAT

Americas Society

680 Park Avenue, New York, NY 10021
TEL: 212-249-8960
HRS: 12-6 Tu-S (Sep-June)   HOL: LEG/HOL!
SUGG/CONT: Y
HDC/ACC: Y   PARKING: Y; Nearby pay Garage   LIB: Y
GT: Y   GT/PH: call 212-249-8950, ext 360   H/B: Y   S/G: N
PERM/COLL: No permanent collection

Located in a historic new-federal townhouse built in 1909, the goal of the Americas Society is to increase public awareness of the rich cultural heritage of our geographic neighbors.

ON EXHIBIT/95:

1/95 - 3/95	ARTE DO MARFIM (THE ART OF IVORY) — A beautiful collection of approximately 100 ivory sculptures created in India and Ceylon during the Portuguese colonial period, largely 17th and 18th centuries. CAT

NEW YORK

Americas Society - continued

4/95 - 5/95	TOMIE OHTAKE 25 — Large-scale paintings produced in the last decade by this recognized Brazilian abstractionist born in Kyoto, Japan in 1913. CAT
Summer 1995	TBA
9/95 - 12/95	CANADIAN IMPRESSIONISM, 1885-1925 — The first in-depth scholarly exhibition to be presented in the United States on the development and history of the Impressionist movement as practiced by Canadian artists working both at home and abroad will feature the works of approximately 40 important artists. CAT WT

NEW YORK

The Asia Society
725 Park Ave., **New York, NY 10021**
TEL: 212-288-6400
HRS: 11-6 Tu-T, Sa; 11-8 F; 12-5 S   DAY CLOSED: M   HOL: LEG/HOL!
F/DAY: F, 6-8pm   ADM: Y   ADULT: $2   CHILDREN: $1   STUDENTS: $1.00   SR CIT: $1.00
HDC/ACC: Y   PARKING: Y; Nearby pay garages   MUS/SH: Y   GT: Y   GT/PH: call for specifics
PERM/COLL: IND & S/E ASIAN: sculp; CH & JAP: cer

The Asia Society is dedicated to presenting the richness and diversity of Asia to the American people and to increasing American understanding of the culture, history and contemporary affairs of Asia.

ON EXHIBIT/95:

10/7/94 - 1/15/95	AN ENDURING LEGACY: THE MR. AND MRS. JOHN D. ROCKEFELLER, 3RD COLLECTION
2/15 - 5/14/95	NEW FINDS, OLD TREASURES: CHINESE CERAMICS FROM THE MEIYINTANG COLLECTION
4/25 - 7/30/95	MONKEY
10/18 - 12/31/95	ACTUAL PLACES AND IMAGINARY LOCALES: JAPANESE SCREENS FROM THE IDEMITSU MUSEUM OF ARTS

China Institute Gallery, China Institute in America
125 East 65th Street, **New York, NY 10021-7088**
TEL: 212-744-8181
HRS: 10-5 M, W-Sa; 1-5 S; 10-8 Tu   HOL: LEG/HOL!, CHINESE NEW YEAR
SUGG/CONT: Y   ADULT: $5.00
HDC/ACC:N   PARKING: Y; Pay garage   MUS/SH: Y   DT: Y   TIME: Varies!   H/B: Y
PERM/COLL: CH: artifacts, ptgs, sculp, furniture

The only museum in New York and one of five in the entire country specializing in exhibitions of Chinese art and civilization.

ON EXHIBIT/95:

1/20 - 3/4/95	ANIMALS OF THE CHINESE ZODIAC: CELEBRATING CHINESE NEW YEAR — Fine art and folk art will illustrate the influence of the zodiac on Chinese life whose magic and mystery have inspired stories and folk beliefs for over 2,000 years, influencing millions of people.

China Institute Gallery, China Institute in America - continued

4/22 - 8/5/95   CLEAR MOON, FRESH BREEZE: CHINESE PORCELAINS OF THE SEVEN-TEENTH CENTURY — The new group of "literati" who emerged from the turbulent years between the demise of the Ming and establishment of the Qing dynasties commissioned porcelains that offered escape in their serene landscapes and scholarly themes. This exhibition of 70 blue and white and polychrome works provides a new look at the beauty and meaning of these decorative motifs.

10/95 through 12/95   ON FLYING HOOVES: THE HORSE IN CHINESE ART — The horse is the most widely used animal image in Chinese art. The exhibition will examine this motif in Chinese painting and sculpture and the fascinating way they reflect the influence of Chinese interaction with non-Chinese peoples of Asia.

NEW YORK

The Cloisters
Affiliate Institution: The Metropolitan Museum of Art
Fort Tryon Park, New York, NY 10040
TEL: 212-923-3700
HRS: 9:30-5:15 Tu-S (3/1-10/30); 9:30-4:45 Tu-S (11/1-2/28)   DAY CLOSED: M   HOL: 1/1, THGV, 12/25
SUGG/CONT: Y   ADM: ADULT: $7   CHILDREN: F (under12)   STUDENTS: $3.50   SR CIT: $3.50
HDC/ACC: Y; Limited, several half-floors are not accessible to wheelchairs
PARKING: Y; Free limited street parking in Fort Tryon Park   LIB: Y!   MUS/SH: Y
GT: Y   GT/PH: call for specifics
DT: Y   TIME: !   H/B: Y, 1938 bldg resembling med monastery, incorporates actual med arch elements
PERM/COLL: ARCH: Med/Eu; TAPESTRIES; ILLUMINATED MANUSCRIPTS; STAINED GLASS; SCULP; LITURGICAL OBJECTS

This unique 1938 building set on a high bluff in a tranquil park overlooking the Hudson River recreates a medieval monastery in both architecture and atmosphere. Actual 12th - 15th century medieval architectural elements are incorporated within various elements of the structure which is filled with impressive art and artifacts of the era. **NOT TO BE MISSED:** "The Unicorn Tapestries;" "The Campin Room;" Gardens; Treasury; the "Belles Heures" illuminated manuscript of Jean, Duke of Breey

Cooper-Hewitt, National Museum of Design, Smithsonian Institution
2 East 91st Street, New York, NY 10128
TEL: 212-860-6868
HRS: 10-9 Tu; 10-5 W-Sa; Noon-5 S   DAY CLOSED: M   HOL: LEG/HOL!
F/DAY: T 5-9   ADM: Y   ADULT: $3.00   CHILDREN: Free   STUDENTS: $1.50   SR CIT: $1.50
HDC/ACC: Y   PARKING: Y: Nearby pay garages   LIB: Y   MUS/SH: Y
GT: Y   GT/PH: call(212) 860-6321 for specifics   DT: Y   TIME: times vary; call212-860-6321   H/B: Y   S/G: Y
PERM/COLL: DRGS; TEXTILES; DEC/ART; CER

Cooper Hewitt, housed in the landmark Andrew Carnegie Mansion, has more than 165,000 objects which represent 3000 years of design history from cultures around the world.

NEW YORK

Cooper-Hewitt, National Museum of Design, Smithsonian Institution - continued

ON EXHIBIT/95:

9/13/94 - 2/19/95   GOOD OFFICES AND BEYOND: THE EVOLUTION OF THE WORKPLACE — The office environment has changed dramatically in the past two decades. A brief historical survey of office functions introduces the themes of the exhibition with a major focus on office design in the 1970's and 1980's when traditional design confronted emerging technologies that would change offices forever.   WT

10/4/94 - 3/5/95   THE STRUCTURE OF STYLE: DUTCH MODERNISM AND THE APPLIED ARTS — This is the first exhibition organized in America to focus solely on turn-of-the-century Dutch and applied arts. Architects and designers in the Netherlands created a distinctive national style that bridged the Arts and Crafts movement and the emerging field of modern industrial design. They transformed traditional media such as metalwork, ceramics, textiles, wallcoverings, furniture and graphics into vehicles for the expression of modern and innovative ideas about form, pattern and the role of the ornament.

3/21 - 8/20/95   MIXING MESSAGES: GRAPHIC DESIGN IN CONTEMPORARY CULTURE — Using the idea of "mixing" to link three basic aspects of contemporary design: aesthetics, culture and technology, the exhibition will feature magazines, books, typefaces, film and television, graphics, corporate identity, multimedia projects and other artifacts.

9/26 - 3/5/96   HENRY DREYFUSS: DIRECTING DESIGN — The Honeywell round thermostat, the Hoover "150" vacuum cleaner and the Bell Telephone "Trimline" phone are among some of the enduring household objects designed by Henry Dreyfus (1904-1972). By displaying his work it is hoped that the essentials of good design he advocated can be rediscovered.

NEW YORK

Dia Center for the Arts

548 West 22nd Street, **New York, NY 10011**
TEL: 212-431-9232
HRS: 12-6 T-S Sep-Jun   DAY CLOSED: M-W   HOL: LEG/HOL!
SUGG/CONT: Y   ADM: ADULT: $3.00   HDC/ACC: Y   MUS/SH: Y
PERM/COLL: not permanently on view

With several facilities and collaborations Dia has committed itself to working with artists to determine optimum environments for their most ambitious and uncompromising works which are usually on view for extended exhibition periods. **NOT TO BE MISSED:** Two Walter De Maria extended exhibitions, THE NEW YORK EARTH ROOM at the gallery at 141 Wooster Street and THE BROKEN KILOMETER at 393 Broadway. Both are open 12-6 W-Sa, closed July and August, adm F

ON EXHIBIT/95:   The 1995 schedule includes exhibitions by Irish artist James Coleman, Andy Warhol, Alighiero Boetti and Frederick Bruly Bovabie. Call for dates.

The Drawing Center

35 Wooster Street, **New York, NY 10013**
TEL: 212-219-2166
HRS: 10-6 Tu-F; 10-8 W; 11-6 Sa, S   DAY CLOSED: M   HOL: 12/25, 1/1, all of AUG
ADM: F   HDC/ACC: Y; Lift   PARKING: Y; Nearby pay garages   MUS/SH: Y   H/B: Y
PERM/COLL: non collecting institution

Featured at The Drawing Center are contemporary and historical drawings and works on paper both by internationally known and emerging artists.

NEW YORK
El Museo Del Barrio
1230 Fifth Ave., **New York, NY 10029**
TEL: 212-831-7272
HRS: 11-5 W-S   DAY CLOSED: M-Tu   HOL: LEG/HOL!
ADM: Y   ADULT: $2.00   CHILDREN: F (under 12)   STUDENTS: $1.00   SR CIT: $1.00
HDC/ACC: Y   PARKING: Y; Discount at Pkg. Corp 1214 E 107 St.
PERM/COLL: LAT/AM: P/COL; CONT: drgs, phot, sculp

One of the foremost Latin American cultural institutions in the United States, this museum is also the only one in the country that specializes in the arts and culture of Puerto Rico. **NOT TO BE MISSED:** Juan Sanchez: "Bleeding Reality: Asi Estamos"

The Frick Collection
1 East 70th Street, **New York, NY 10021**
TEL: 212-288-0700
HRS: 10-6 Tu-Sa; 1-6 S   DAY CLOSED: M   HOL: 1/1, 7/4, THGV, 12/24, 12/25
ADM: Y   ADULT: $5   CHILDREN: under 10 not adm   STUDENTS: $3.00   SR CIT: $3.00
HDC/ACC: Y   PARKING: Y; Pay garages nearby   LIB: Y   MUS/SH: Y   H/B: Y   S/G: Y
PERM/COLL: PTGS; SCULP; FURNITURE; DEC/ART; Eur, Or, PORCELAINS

The beautiful Henry Clay Frick mansion built in 1913-14, houses this exceptional collection while preserving the ambiance of the original house. In addition to the many treasures to be found here, the interior of the house offers the visitor a tranquil respite from the busy pace of city life outside of its doors. PLEASE NOTE: Children under 10 are not permitted in the museum and those from 11-16 must be accompanied by an adult. **NOT TO BE MISSED:** Boucher Room; Fragonard Room; Paintings by Rembrandt, El Greco, Holbein and Van Dyck

ON EXHIBIT/95:
11/13/95 - 1/28/96   THE BUTTERFLY AND THE BAT: WHISTLER AND ROBERT MONTESQUIOU —
This exhibition is devoted to the Frick Collection's well known portrait by Whistler of Comte Robert de Montesquiou-Fezenec. It will include other portraits of the artist and his subject as well as members of their circle; correspondence exchanged between the two; fine and decorative works of art by other artists whom Montesquiou favored and other memorabilia.   CAT

George Gustav Heye Center of the National Museum of the American Indian
Affiliate Institution: Smithsonian Institution
One Bowling Green, **New York, NY 10004**
TEL: 212-668-6624
HRS: 10-5 daily   HOL: 12/25
ADM: F   PARKING: Y; Nearby pay   LIB: Y   MUS/SH: Y   GT: Y   GT/PH: call 212-283-2782 for specifics
DT: Y   TIME: daily   H/B: Y
PERM/COLL: NAT/AM; Iroq silver, jewelry, NW Coast masks

The Heye Foundation collection contains more than 10,000 works which span the entire Western Hemisphere and present a new look at Native American peoples and cultures. Newly opened in the historic Alexander Hamilton Customs House it presents masterworks from the collection and contemporary Indian art.

NEW YORK

George Gustav Heye Center - continued
ON EXHIBIT/95:
Inaugural Exhibitions: CREATION'S JOURNEY: MASTERWORKS OF NATIVE AMERICAN IDENTITY AND BELIEF — Objects of beauty and historical significance, representing numerous cultures throughout the Americas, ranging from 3200 B.C. to the present.

ALL ROADS ARE GOOD: NATIVE VOICES ON LIFE AND CULTURE — Artifacts chosen by 23 Indian selectors.

THIS PATH WE TRAVEL: CELEBRATIONS OF CONTEMPORARY NATIVE AMERICAN CREATIVITY — A collaborative exhibition featuring works by 15 contemporary Indian artists.

NEW YORK

The Grey Art Gallery and Study Center
Affiliate Institution: New York University Art Collection
33 Washington Place, **New York, NY 10003**
TEL: 212-998-6780
HRS: 11-6:30 Tu, T, F; 11-8:30 W; 11-5 Sa; Summer 11-6 M-F   DAY CLOSED: S, M   HOL: LEG/HOL!
SUGG/CONT: Y   ADULT: $2.00   HDC/ACC: Y   PARKING: Y; Nearby pay garages
PERM/COLL: AM: ptgs 1940-present; CONT; AS; MID/EAST

Located at Washington Square Park and adjacent to Soho, the Grey Art Gallery occupies the site of the first academic fine arts department in America established by Samuel F. B. Morse in 1835.

ON EXHIBIT/95:
1/95 through 2/95   NARELLE JUBELIN: SOFT SHOULDER — This Australian artist's conceptually intricate art works address the influence of international commerce and travel on local cultures. In this exhibition she turns her attention to the unpublished "autobiography" of Marion Burley Griffin, an architect who worked in Frank Lloyd Wrights' office and looks at the craft ideologies and gender roles of that era. Her trademark, cross-referential style will be maintained including juxtapositions of copper plates attributed to Chicago Hull House with petit points, wall painting, hardware store signage, and string art.   CAT

3/95 through 4/95   ANN MANDELBAUM — These silver prints are still-life-like photographs and photograms which have a luminous, magical, unreal quality which seems to take up the legacy of Symbolism.   CAT

5/95 through 6/95   THE CREATIVE WILL: PROJECT REMBRANDT XI — A juried, national biennial exhibition of works by professional artists who share in common a debilitating disease--multiple sclerosis. The strength of the exhibition arises from the strength of the art and demonstrates that disability is not synonymous with inability.

Guggenheim Museum Soho
575 Broadway at Prince St., **New York, NY 10012**
TEL: 212-423-3500
HRS: 11-6 S & W-F; 11-8 Sa   DAY CLOSED: M, Tu   HOL: 1/1, 12/25
ADM: Y   ADULT: $5.00   CHILDREN: F (under 12)   STUDENTS: $3.00   SR CIT: $3.00
HDC/ACC: Y; Wheelchairs and folding chairs available in coatroom   PARKING: Y; Nearby pay garages
MUS/SH: Y   GT: Y   GT/PH: call 212-423-3555   H/B: Y
PERM/COLL: INTERNATIONAL CONT ART

As a branch of the main museum uptown, this facility, located in a historic building in Soho, was designed as a museum by Arata Isozaki.

NEW YORK

The Hispanic Society of America
155th Street and Broadway, **New York, NY 10032**
TEL: 212-926-2234
HRS: 10-4:30 Tu-Sa; 1-4, S   DAY CLOSED: M   HOL: LEG/HOL!
VOL/CONT: Y   ADM: F   HDC/ACC: Y; Limited, exterior and interior stairs   PARKING: Y; Nearby pay garage
LIB: Y!   MUS/SH: Y   GT: Y   GT/PH: call 212-926-2234 to reserve   H/B: Y   S/G: Y
PERM/COLL: SP: ptgs, sculp; arch; HISPANIC

Representing the culture of Hispanic peoples from prehistory to the present, this facility is one of several diverse museums located within the same complex on Audubon Terrace in NYC. **NOT TO BE MISSED:** Paintings by El Greco, Goya, Velazquez

International Center of Photography
Midtown, 1133 Broadway, New York City
Uptown, 1130 Fifth Ave., **New York, NY 10128**
TEL: 212-860-1777
HRS: 11-8 Tu; 11-6 W-S   DAY CLOSED: M   HOL: 1/1, 7/4, THGV, 12/25
F/DAY: Tu, 6-8 midtown, Tu 5-8 uptown   ADM: Y   ADULT: $4.00   STUDENTS: $2.50   SR CIT: $2.50
HDC/ACC: Y!   PARKING: Y; Nearby pay garages   LIB: Y   MUS/SH: Y   REST/FAC: Y; Nearby
GT: Y   GT/PH: Uptn, 212-860-1485; Mdtn, 212-768-4682   H/B: Y
PERM/COLL: DOCUMENTARY PHOT: 20

The ICP was established in 1974 to present exhibitions of photography, to promote photographic education at all levels, and to study 20th century images. The uptown museum is housed in a 1915 Neo-Georgian building designed by Delano and Aldrich.

ON EXHIBIT/95:
At 1130 Fifth Avenue:
   12/2/94 - 2/26/95   WILLIAM KLEIN: IN AND OUT OF FASHION

At 1133 Avenue of the Americas
   12/10/94 - 2/12/95   A SINGULAR ELEGANCE: THE PHOTOGRAPHS OF BARON ADOLPH DE MEYER

   12/2/94 - 2/12/95   FRED STEIN: VIEWS OF NEW YORK

Japan Society Gallery
333 E. 47th Street, **New York, NY 10017**
TEL: 212-832-1155
HRS: 11-5 Tu-S   DAY CLOSED: M   HOL: LEG/HOL!
SUGG/CONT: Y   ADULT: $3.00   CHILDREN: $3.00   STUDENTS: $3.00   SR CIT: $3.00
HDC/ACC: Y   PARKING: Y; Nearby pay garages   LIB: Y   MUS/SH: Book Shop
GT: Y   GT/PH: ! 212-715-1253 to reserve   H/B: Y   S/G: Y; Reflecting Pool
PERM/COLL: JAPANESE ART

Exhibitions of the fine arts of Japan are presented along with performing and film arts at the Japan Society Gallery which attempts to promote better understanding and cultural enlightenment between the peoples of the U.S. and Japan.

NEW YORK

Japan Society Gallery - continued

ON EXHIBIT/95:

11/16/94 - 1/8/95	OTSU-E: JAPANESE FOLK PAINTINGS FROM THE HARRIET AND EDSON SPENSER COLLECTION (With selections from the Japan Society collection) — Spirited brushwork and bold palette characterize Otsu-e, the simple paintings produced with unaffected abandon in Japan during the Edo period (1600-1868) by anonymous artists with little or no formal training.
2/17 - 4/2/95	NINGYO: THE ART OF THE HUMAN FIGURINE — In addition to being fine examples of artistic ideals and craft techniques, ningyo also embody an otherworldly character. The unique Japanese concept of the doll as an art and cult object separates it from the toy role assigned in other cultures.
4/21 - 6/4/95	GEMS OF THE FLOATING WORLD: JAPANESE WOODBLOCK PRINTS FROM THE DRESDEN KUPFERSTICH-KABINET — The first exhibition outside of Dresden of more than 70 masterpieces from this outstanding, rarely displayed collection.

NEW YORK

The Jewish Museum
1109 5th Ave., New York, NY 10128
TEL: 212-423-3200
HRS: 11-5:45 S, M, W & T; 11-8 Tu;   DAY CLOSED: F, Sa   HOL: LEG/HOL!; JEWISH/HOL!
F/DAY: after 5, Tu   ADM: Y   ADULT: $6.00   CHILDREN: F (under 12)   STUDENTS: $4.00   SR CIT: $4.00
HDC/ACC: Y!   PARKING: Y; Nearby pay garages   MUS/SH: Y   REST/FAC: Y; Cafe Weissman
GT: Y   GT/PH: call 212-423-3224 to reserve   DT: Y   TIME: Noon & 2:30 M-T   H/B: Y
PERM/COLL: JUDAICA: ptgs by Jewish and Israeli artists; ARCH; ARTIFACTS

27,000 works of art and artifacts covering 4000 years of Jewish history created by Jewish artists or illuminating the Jewish experience are displayed in the original building (the 1907 Felix Warburg Mansion), and in the new addition added in 1993. The collection is the largest of its kind outside of Israel. **NOT TO BE MISSED:** "The Holocaust," by George Segal

ON EXHIBIT/95:

PERMANENT:	CULTURE AND CONTINUITY: THE JEWISH JOURNEY
10/2/94 - 1/29/95	MARIO CAVAGLIERI: THE GLITTERING YEARS, 1912-1922 — In the first one-man show in North America of works by this important Italian Jewish artist (1887-1969), the works reveal the artist's exuberant brushwork, and richly decorative application of paint, and provide rare insight into the opulent world of the aristocratic classes on the eve of WWI and before the onslaught of mass culture.
10/9/94 - 3/5/95	JEWISH LIFE IN TSARIST RUSSIA: A WORLD DISCOVERED — In this collection from the State Ethnographic Museum in St. Petersburg, American audiences will see their first glimpse of a legendary assemblage of objects and lore related to Russian Jewish life prior to WWI collected by the renowned ethnographer, revolutionary and writer Shlomo Ansky. WT*
3/26 - 7/30/95	TOO JEWISH: RECLAIMING JEWISH IDENTITY IN THE AGE OF MULTI-CULTURALISM — A group exhibition of works by contemporary artists who use provocative subject matter to assert their cultural backgrounds. Included are traditional media as well as installation, conceptual and performance and video artists.
through 7/31/95	IN THIS HOUSE: A HISTORY OF THE JEWISH MUSEUM — An introduction to the Museum and the Warburg Mansion is provided in this exhibition of objects and photographs from the collection.
4/23 - 8/6/95	WOMEN PHOTOGRAPHERS OF THE WEIMAR REPUBLIC

298

The Metropolitan Museum of Art

5th Ave at 82nd Street, **New York, NY 10028**
TEL: 212-879-5500
HRS: 9:30-5:15 Tu-T, S; 9:30-8:45pm F, Sa   DAY CLOSED: M   HOL: 1/1, 12/25
SUGG/CONT: Y   ADULT: $6.00   CHILDREN: F (under 12)   STUDENTS: $3.00   SR CIT: $3.00
HDC/ACC: Y   PARKING: Y; Pay garage   LIB: Y   MUS/SH: Y   REST/FAC: Y
GT: Y   GT/PH: call for specifics   H/B: Y   S/G: Y; Seasonal
PERM/COLL: EU: all media; GR & DRGS: Ren-20; MED; GR; PHOT; AM: all media; DEC/ART: all media; AS: all media; AF; ISLAMIC; CONT; AN/EGT; AN/R; AN/AGR; AN/ASSYRIAN

The Metropolitan is the largest world class museum of art in the Western Hemisphere. Its comprehensive collections include more than 2 million works from the earliest historical artworks thru those of modern times and from all areas of the world. Just recently, the museum opened the Florence & Herbert Irving Galleries for the Arts of South & Southeast Asia, one of the best and largest collections of its kind in the world. **NOT TO BE MISSED:** Temple of Dendur; The recently renovated 19th century European Beaux-Arts painting & sculpture galleries (21 in all), designed to present the permanent collection in chronological order and to accommodate the promised Walter Annenberg collection now on view approximately 6 months annually.

ON EXHIBIT/95:

8/2/94 - 1/8/95   FOUR SILK KASHAN RUGS — These silk rugs are among 15 known to exist and have never before been shown together.

8/9/94 - 1/27/95   PHARAOH'S GIFTS: STONE VESSELS FROM ANCIENT EGYPT — Made of alabaster, anhydride, obsidian and other, often rare materials, the vessels show Egyptian stone-working on the highest artistic level.

9/27/94 - 1/8/95   ORIGINS OF IMPRESSIONISM — 150 paintings in all genre by avant-garde artists working in Paris in the 1860's.   CAT

1/4/94 - 1/8/95   OMINOUS HUSH: THE THUNDERSTORM PAINTINGS OF MARTIN JOHNSON HEADE — 13 paintings by the American luminist examined in the light of contemporary social develpments of his time, especially the Civil War.   CAT

10/11/94 - 1/8/95   WILLEM DE KOONING: PAINTINGS — The first major exhibition devoted exclusively to the artist's finest paintings from the 1930's through the mid-1980's.   CAT WT

11/15/94 - 5/21/95   LUCIE RIE AND HANS COPER — Some 80 of the finest examples of ceramics by these artists who are better known in Europe than the United States.

11/18/94 - 2/26/95   PAINTING AND ILLUMINATION IN EARLY RENAISSANCE FLORENCE 1300-1450 — Panel paintings and manuscript illuminations by the masters of the Gothic style in Florence.   CAT

Late 11/94 - 1/8/95   THOMAS EAKINS AT THE METROPOLITAN MUSEUM OF ART — A survey of every aspect of the artists' work in recognition of the sesquicentennial of his birth.

12/8/94 - 3/19/95   ORIENTALISM — Western fashion's absorption and assimilation of Eastern dress including India, China, Japan, Southeast Asia and the Middle East.

12/2/94 - 3/24/95   GREEK GOLD: JEWELRY OF THE CLASSICAL WORLD — A thorough and comprehensive selection of some of the most revealing masterpieces of Classical gold of the 5th and 4th centuries B.C.

1/10 - 3/19/95   THE FRENCH RENAISSANCE IN PRINTS FROM THE BIBLIOTHEQUE NATIONAL, PARIS — In the first comprehensive survey of the origins of Renaissance printmaking in France, works by over 50 artists working during the 16th to early 17th enturies will document the artistic development and production of the medium.   CAT WT

NEW YORK

The Metropolitan Museum of Art - continued

2/1 - 4/30/95	I TELL MY HEART: THE ART OF HORACE PIPPIN — A selection of paintings from a larger traveling exhibition by one of the country's best known self-taught painters. CAT
2/15/ - 5/14/95	R. B. KITAJ: A RETROSPECTIVE — This American artist has lived and worked in England for more than three decades. Themes of his work refer to his years as a merchant seaman, to writers such as Pound, Kafka, Eliot and Joyce, to the history of film and to the discovery of his own Jewish heritage. CAT
3/14 - Fall 1995	AN ANCIENT EGYPTIAN BESTIARY: ANIMALS IN EGYPTIAN ART — The 150 pieces in this exhibition explore the art of animal reprsentation in ancient Egypt in sculpture, relief, painting, and the decorative and minor arts.
3/15 - 7/9/95	HERTER BROTHERS: FURNITURE AND INTERIORS FOR A GILDED AGE — Furniture by these Stuttgart-born, European-trained craftsmen who worked in New York will be on view in the first comprehensive exhibition of its kind. The Herter Brothers were adept at blending high style, elegant design, rare woods and excellent craftsmanship for America's most famous 19th century patrons including Wm. Vanderbilt, Jay Gould and Frederick Church. CAT WT
3/25 - 7/9/95	DECORATING THE AMERICAN HOME, 1850-1900 —Paintings of interiors, trade catalogs, prints and home decorating books of the period of Herter Brothers furniture.
4/3 - 7/9/95	NADAR — The first comprehensive survey of the work of this premier portraitist in photography during the Second Empire. CAT
4/95 - 9/10/95	ART AND EMPIRE: TREASURES FROM ASSYRIA IN THE BRITISH MUSEUM — Large scale reliefs from first millenium B.C. palaces of the Assyrian kings at Nimrud and Nineveh will be displayed along with a selection of metalwork, seals and tablets. CAT
4/95 - 7/95	ASSYRIAN ORIGINS: DISCOVERIES AT ASHUR ON THE TIGRES: ANTIQUITIES FROM THE VORDERASIATISCHE MUSEUM, BERLIN — Large scale sculptures, seals, tablets as well as jewelry, ivories, and metalwork from the third and second century B.C. CAT

NEW YORK

Miriam and Ira D. Wallach Art Gallery

Affiliate Institution: Avery Library, Columbia University
116th and Broadway, **New York, NY 10027**
TEL: 212-854-7288
HRS: 1-5 W-Sa   DAY CLOSED: S, M, Tu   HOL: 1/1, week of THGV, 12/25
ADM: F
HDC/ACC: Y; Enter on Amsterdam Avenue   PARKING: Y; Nearby pay garages   H/B: Y
PERM/COLL: non-collecting institution

Operated under the auspices of Columbia University and situated on its wonderful campus, the gallery functions to complement the educational goals of the University.

ON EXHIBIT/95:

Spring 1995	FACULTY EXHIBITION (working title)
10/10 - 12/16/95	THE POST RAPHAELITE PRINT: ETCHING, ILLUSTRATION, REPRODUCTIVE ENGRAVING AND PHOTOGRAPHY IN ENGLAND IN AND AROUND THE 1860'S

NEW YORK

The Museum for African Art
593 Broadway, New York, NY 10012
TEL: 212-966-1313
HRS: 10:30-5:30 Tu-F; 12-8 Sa; 12-6 S   DAY CLOSED: M   HOL: LEG/HOL!
ADM: Y   ADULT: $4.00   CHILDREN: $2.00   STUDENTS: $2.00   SR CIT: $2.00
HDC/ACC: Y   PARKING: Y; Nearby pay garages   MUS/SH: Y   GT: Y   GT/PH: call 212-966-1313
DT: Y   TIME: call for specifics   H/B: Y
PERM/COLL: AF: all media

This new facility in a historic building with a cast iron facade was designed by Maya Lin, architect of the Vietnam Memorial in Washington, D.C. Her conception of the space is "less institutional, more personal and idiosyncratic." She is using "color in ways that other museums do not, there will be no white walls here." **NOT TO BE MISSED:** Sub-Saharan art

ON EXHIBIT/95:

10/13/94 - 3/5/95	EXHIBITION-ism — What shapes our experience of art: the work itself or its setting and display? Do objects speak to us or do we impose meaning on them through their presentation? Are objects static and exhibitions mere frames, or do objects have life histories which make exhibitions organic and alive? These questions will be addressed visually through a dramatic installation of the Museum's acclaimed exhibition "Secrecy" which showed the role of African art in concealing and revealing knowledge. This radical re-staging asks audiences to reflect on the nature of museums as institutions of learning and the exhibition as a living format that shapes how we experience and understand the world. CAT WT
4/6 - 12/31/95	BORDER CROSSINGS: ANIMALS AND HUMANS IN AFRICAN ART — How African cultures define relationships between animals and humans is examined in this exhibition presenting one hundred 19th and 20th century works of art from Western and Central Africa. The works depict a variety of animals noted for curious or remarkable attributes such as aardvarks, antelopes, bats, buffaloes, pangolins, chameleons, spiders and spotted cats. All have special meanings and roles to play in African Societies. The exhibition is an integral part of a city-wide collaboration organized by the New School for Social Research. Conceived for both children and adults it will contain a "kids level" exhibition within the exhibition. It will add an African perspective to universal questions about human nature and what can be learned by examining the culture/nature divide. CAT WT
9/8/95 - 1/7/96	ART THAT HEALS: THE IMAGE AS MEDICINE IN ETHIOPIA — Creating art to facilitate spiritual as well as physical healing was exquisitely articulated in Ethiopia from the 13th century until the present. ART THAT HEALS traces the historically shifting relationship between religion as practiced by Ethiopian Christians, art and healing in the Ethiopian context, and the African use of art as an essential therapeutic tool. The exhibition includes 100 objects, the majority of which are healing scrolls custom made for individuals and cut to their height. CAT WT

Museum of American Folk Art
Two Lincoln Square, New York, NY 10023-6214
TEL: 212-595-9533
HRS: 11:30 -7:30 Tu-S   DAY CLOSED: M   HOL: LEG/HOL!
ADM: F   HDC/ACC: Y   PARKING: Y; Nearby garages   LIB: Y   MUS/SH: Y
GT: Y   GT/PH: call 212-595-9533 to reserve
PERM/COLL: FOLK: ptgs, sculp, quilts, textiles, dec/art

NEW YORK

Museum of American Folk Art - continued

The museum is known both nationally and internationally for its leading role in bringing quilts and other folk art to a broad public audience. **NOT TO BE MISSED:** "Girl in Red with Cat and Dog," by Ammi Phillips; major works in all areas of folk art

ON EXHIBIT/95:

9/17/94 - 1/15/95	EVERY PICTURE TELLS A STORY: WORD AND IMAGE IN AMERICAN FOLK ART — The first museum exhibition to emphasize the pervasive uses to which pictorial narrative and the written word are applied to the many forms of folk art and the ways in which they fulfill a variety of purposes.
1/21 - 4/2/95	THE GIFT IS SMALL, THE LOVE IS GREAT — An exploration of the unexplored aspect of "fractur" art as a gift rather than the familiar usage of documenting milestones in family life in German-American communities.
1/21 - 4/2/95	MINNIE EVANS: ARTIST — An in-depth examination of the work of this self taught North Carolina Artist (1892-1987). WT
4/8 - 9/10/95	VICTORIAN SHOW QUILTS — A new perspective on the textile arts of the Victorian period.

NEW YORK

Museum of American Illustration
128 East 63rd St., **New York, NY 10021**
TEL: 212-838-2560
HRS: 10-5 W-F; 10-8 Tu: 12-4 Sa   DAY CLOSED: M, S   HOL: LEG/HOL!
ADM: F   HDC/ACC: Y   PARKING: Y; Nearby pay garages   LIB: Y   MUS/SH: Y
PERM/COLL: NORMAN ROCKWELL

A very specialized collection of illustrations familiar to everyone.

ON EXHIBIT/95:

1/4 - 2/4/95	PAPERBACK 1995 — A juried exhibit of the best of the past five years in this active market for illustrators: Romance, Western, Sci-Fi.
2/11 - 3/11/95	BOOK AND EDITORIAL — Annual juried show of the best of the previous year.
3/18 - 4/15/95	37TH ANNUAL ADVERTISING AND INSTITUTIONAL
4/25 - 5/13/95	MIKE DOOLING — A young artist who specializes in American Historical subjects for the Young Adult book market.
4/25 - 5/13/95	STUDENT SCHOLARSHIP — Annual national juried show of college level art students.
5/24 - 6/17/95	"SPOTS" — An exhibition of "spots" which are small reproductions in a magazine. They are big on thought, craft and imagination.
5/24 - 6/24/95	EUGENE HOFFMAN — A Colorado artist who specializes in recycling roadside debris into compositions for posters and corporate clients.
6/28 - 7/29/95	MAGAZINE COVERS — 100 paintings (1900 to the present) from the collection which were created originally for magazine covers.
6/28 - 7/29/95	RAMSEY — This Hawaiian artist has mastered both line and wash using architecture as a basic theme.

Museum of American Illustration - continued

9/7 - 10/7/95	OUR OWN SHOW '95 — Annual non-juried exhibit in wide range of media, subject and markets.
10/25 - 11/22/95	ORIGINAL ART — The best in children's book illustration for the year.
11/29 - 12/23/95	25 YEARS OF SESAME STREET — A retrospective of the art which has been produced for the TV show, the magazine and the many ancillary products.

NEW YORK

The Museum of Modern Art
11 West 53rd Street, New York, NY 10019
TEL: 212-708-9400
HRS: 11-6 Sa-Tu; 12-8:30 T, F   DAY CLOSED: W   HOL: THGV, 12/25
F/DAY: T, F 5:30-8:30 vol contr   ADM: Y   ADULT: $7.50   CHILDREN: F under16 w adult
STUDENTS: $4.50 ID   SR CIT: $4.50
HDC/ACC: Y   PARKING: Y:Pay nearby   LIB: Y!   MUS/SH: Y   REST/FAC: Y
GT: Y   GT/PH: Y; call for specifics   DT: Y   TIME: ! 212-708-9795 Weekdays, Sa, S 1 & 3pm; T, F 6 & 7pm
H/B: Y; 1939 Bldg by Goodwin & Stone considered one of first examples of Int. Style   S/G: Y
PERM/COLL: WORKS BY PICASSO, MATISSE, BRANCUSI; AB/IMP; PHOT & DESIGN 20

The MOMA offers the world's most comprehensive survey of 20th century art in all media as well as an exceptional film library. **NOT TO BE MISSED:** Outstanding collection of 20th century photography, film and design.

ON EXHIBIT/95:

10/12/94 - 1/10/95	NEW PHOTOGRAPHY 10 — An annual exhibition of recent photographic work not previously widely seen in New York.
10/23/94 - 1/24/95	A CENTURY OF ARTISTS BOOKS — The printed book has intrigued and inspired generations of artists. From Henri de Toulouse-Lautrec's innovative YVETTE GUIL-BERT (1894) and Paul Gaugin's manuscript and prints for his planned book NOA-NOA (1894) to volumes by Matisse, Chagall and Picasso from the first half of this century to avant-garde experiments from World War I through the 60's, and contemporary artists such as Louise Bourgeois, Anselm Kiefer and Barbara Kruger, the exhibition reveals the scope of work artists have dedicated both to enhancing texts with their images and to the book form itself.
11/3/94 - 2/21/95	THRESHOLDS/O.M.A. AT MOMA: REM KOOLHAAS AND THE PLACE OF PUBLIC ARCHITECTURE — This exhibition features five architectural projects, as well as three urban designs by Koolhaass for the French cities of Melun-Senat and Lille and for Yokohama, Japan. It includes video documentation of the EuroLille Project which is now under construction.
1/12 - 4/13/95	JACOB LAWRENCE: THE MIGRATION SERIES — The 60 panels in this 1940-41 narrative cycle depict the causes and effects of the African-American population shift from the rural south to the industrial North during and after World War I. Derived from Synthetic Cubism, this work is marked by a distinctive style, small scale format and expressive intensity. The collection was divided between the Museum of Modern Art and the Phillips Collection in a split purchase in 1942 and is now being shown together for the first time since 1972. CAT WT
1/26 - 4/25/95	VASILY KANDINSKY: APOCALYPTIC COMPOSITIONS — The first exhibition in which the four extant canvas from the artists' suite of seven, entitled COMPOSITIONS (I-VII) are presented together and in the context of approximately seventy related works many of which have not been seen before in the United States CAT WT

NEW YORK

The Museum of Modern Art - continued

Late 1/95 - late 5/95	MAX BECKMANN PRINTS FROM THE MUSEUM OF MODERN ART — Approximately 85 prints present work from all periods of Beckmann's printmaking career including his most ambitious portfolio, HELL completed in 1919. CAT WT
3/5 - 5/23/95	BRUCE NAUMAN: INSIDE/OUT — Widely recognized as one of the most inventive and influential American figures of the generation after that of Jasper Johns and Robert Rauschenberg, this first major retrospective since 1970 will survey works in all media except drawings. CAT WT
5/4 - 8/15/95	POSTERS BY THE STEINBERG BROTHERS — These posters produced from the mid 1920's until 1933 for the Russian cinema possess an extraordinary inventiveness and originality which helped revolutionize modern poster design. CAT WT
5/25 - 8/22/95	TRANSPARENCIES — A group exhibition presenting a younger generation of international architects all of whom explore transparency, minimalism and rationalized geometry.
9/7/95 - 1/2/96	STIEGLITZ AT LAKE GEORGE — Some 50 photographs made mainly in the 1920's and 1930's record his response to the landscape at Lake George as well as to the family and friends who vacationed there with him. CAT
10/1/95 - 1/23/96	PIET MONDRIAN: 1872-1944 — The fiftieth anniversary of the death of the great Dutch painter is marked by this 160 work survey featuring his characteristic form of abstract painting which he called Neo-Plasticism. CAT WT
10/12/95 - 1/16/96	ANNETTE MESSAGER — A small retrospective of the work of this French artist who combines photographed, painted and drawn images with found and constructed objects and written language. CAT WT

NEW YORK

Museum of the City of New York
Fifth Ave. at 103rd Street, New York, NY 10029
TEL: 212-634-1672
HRS: 10-5 W-Sa; 1-5 S   DAY CLOSED: M, T   HOL: LEG/HOL!
SUGG/CONT: Y   ADULT: $5, Family $8   CHILDREN: $3.00   STUDENTS: $3.00   SR CIT: $3.00
HDC/ACC: Y; 104th St Entrance   PARKING: Y; Nearby pay garages   MUS/SH: Y
GT: Y   GT/PH: ! open Tu for pre-registered groups   DT: Y   TIME: !   H/B: Y
PERM/COLL: NEW YORK: silver 1678-1910; INTERIORS: 17-20; THE ALEXANDER HAMILTON COLLECTION; PORT OF THE NEW WORLD MARINE GALLERY

Founded in 1933, this was the first American museum dedicated to the history of a major city. The Museum's collections encompass the City's heritage, from its exploration and settlement to the NY of today. **NOT TO BE MISSED:** Period Rooms

ON EXHIBIT/95:

10/7/94 - 1/22/95	THE MAKING OF A MURAL: REGINALD MARSH AT THE CUSTOM HOUSE — In a series of large and colorful fresco panels painted on the ceiling of the historic United States Custom House and completed in 1937, Marsh traced the course of a ship from the time it entered New York Harbor until it was unloaded at the pier. In conjunction with the reopening of the Custom House as a branch of the Smithsonian Institution, the Museum is presenting its collection of Marsh's preparatory sketches, watercolors, photographs and slides used in the creation of this important mural.
10/12/94 - 5/1/95	CITY FARMERS: OPERATION GREENTHUMB — Color photographs of gardens nurtured under Operation GreenThumb and portraits of Greenthumb project gardeners who establishh vegetable and flower gardens on City-owned vacant property.

NEW YORK

Museum of the City of New York - continued

10/28/94 - 2/19/95   RECENT ACQUISITIONS: PRESENTS OF THE PAST — New acquisitions which underscore the diversity of subjects, periods and media that enable the Museum to convey the complex history of New York City will be featured. Included in the display will be a contemporary "photorealist" cityscape by Charles Ford, watercolors by both Hugh Condo Miller and Dong Kingman, an oil by Elinor Schnurr depicting the interior of Katz's Deli, and a large modernist canvas by Israeli artist Beys Afroyin.

11/1/94 - 12/23/95   A NEW YORK HOLIDAY — A selection of winter scenes and an installation of toys and ephemera from the collection.

11/23/94 - 6/11/95   LADIES MILE: EMPORIA AND ENTERTAINMENTS — Costumes and accessories for men, women and children associated with the department stores, shops, restaurants and theaters of the area bounded by Union Square and Madison Square from Broadway to Sixth Avenue.

1/18 - 9/3/95   A CENTURY APART: IMAGES OF STRUGGLE AND SPIRIT 1880-1990, JACOB RIIS AND FIVE CONTEMPORARY PHOTOGRAPHERS — A major exhibition integrating Jacob Riis contact "printing out paper," (prints made from original negatives and lantern slides) some of which have never been on public view, with contemporary photographs by Martine Barrat, Fred Conrad, Mary Ellen Mark, Margaret Morton and Jeffrey Scales.

2/1 - 9/8/95   WHAT'S IN A NAME — Paintings, prints and photographs will demystify the source of many names of New York streets. Also explored will be how lifestyles and the urban landscape have inspired such names as "gridlock," "straphanger," etc.

6/24 - 12/31/95   NEW YORK: DINING IN, DINING OUT — Table settings and menus from public and private dinners and restaurants as well as paintings and photographs to provide a light-hearted look at yesterday's New York.

3/4 - 9/8/95   CURATING NEW YORK: A TRIBUTE TO GRACE MAYER — In tribute to Ms. Mayer who was a curator at the Museum and was responsible for major acquisitions and in recognition of Women's History Month, this exhibition includes a broad sampling of prints and photographs as well as her curatorial notes and letters.

5/13 - 11/5/95   UNION SETTLEMENT ASSOCIATION: THE FIRST ONE HUNDRED YEARS IN EAST HARLEM — The centennial of this second largest settlement in New York City, will present photographs and documents from past and present and plans for the next hundred years in East Harlem.

9/5 - 12/31/95   GROWING UP IN NEW YORK — Well known photographer Arthur Leipzig has used his camera and unerring eye to document growing up in New York. This exhibition will contain a selection of gelatin silver prints from the book of the same name being released in the fall of 1995.

10/15/95 - 3/31/96   GAELIC GOTHAM: THE IRISH AND NEW YORK — An interpretive exhibition which will introduce audiences to the cultural, social, political and economic experiences of Irish New Yorkers. The entire first floor of the Museum will be dedicated to the Irish and New York and how the Irish experience has mirrored the uniqueness and universality of the immigrant experience for over 300 years.

Ongoing: BROADWAY — A survey of the magical Broadway comedies, dramas and musicals from 1866 to the present

BROADWAY CAVALCADE — The history of the street known as Broadway from its origins as a footpath in Colonial New York to its development into the City's most dynamic, diverse and renowned boulevard.

FAMILY TREASURES: TOYS AND THEIR TALES — Toys from the Museum's renowned collection present a history of New York City through their individual stories.

NEW YORK

NEW YORK

National Academy Museum
Affiliate Institution: Cooper Hewitt Museum
1083 Fifth Avenue, **New York, NY 10128**
TEL: 212--369-4880
HRS: 12-5 W-S; 12-8 F   DAY CLOSED: M, Tu   HOL: LEG/HOL!
ADM: Y   ADULT: $3.50   STUDENTS: $2.00   SR CIT: $2.00
HDC/ACC: Y   PARKING: Y; Nearby pay garage
PERM/COLL: AM: all media 19-20

With outstanding special exhibitions as well as rotating exhibits of the permanent collection, this facility is a school as well as a resource for American Art. **NOT TO BE MISSED:** The oldest juried annual art exhibition in the nation is held in March with National Academy members only exhibiting in the odd-numbered years and works by all U.S. artists considered for inclusion in even-numbered years.

ON EXHIBIT/95:

4/5 - 6/13/95   NATURE OBSERVED, NATURE INTERPRETED: NINETEENTH CENTURY AMERICAN LANDSCAPE DRAWINGS AND WATERCOLORS FROM THE NATIONAL ACADEMY MUSEUM AND COOPER HEWITT, NATIONAL MUSEUM OF DESIGN, SMITHSONIAN INSTITUTION — For the first time, a selection of 19th century American works ranging from pencil sketches to dazzling large-scale watercolors from these two imporant collections will be shown together. It will display the complex and varied techniques artists used to transform nature observed into nature interpreted. Featured are over 80 works by masters including Frederic Church, Thomas Cole, William Haseltine, Winslow Homer and Elihu Vedder.

National Arts Club
15 Gramercy Park South, **New York, NY 10024**
TEL: 212-475-3424
HRS: 1-6 daily   HOL: LEG/HOL!
ADM: F   HDC/ACC:N   PARKING: Y; Nearby pay garage, some metered street parking   LIB: Y!   MUS/SH: Y
REST/FAC: Y; For members   H/B: Y
PERM/COLL: AM: ptgs, sculp, works on paper, dec/art 19, 20; Ch: dec/art

The building which houses this private club and collection was the 1840's mansion of former Governor Samuel Tilden. The personal library of Robert Henri which is housed here is available for study on request.

The New Museum of Contemporary Art
583 Broadway, **New York, NY 10012**
TEL: 212-219-1355
HRS: 12-6 W-F, S; 12-8 Sa   DAY CLOSED: M, TU   HOL: 1/1, 12/25
F/DAY: Sa, 6-8   ADM: Y   ADULT: $3.50   CHILDREN: F (under 12)   STUDENTS: $2.50   SR CIT: $2.50
HDC/ACC: Y   PARKING: Y; Nearby pay garages   MUS/SH: Y
GT: Y   GT/PH: 212-219-1222 ed. dept. to reserve   H/B: Y; Astor Building
PERM/COLL: CONT

Featuring a unique semi-permanent collection, this museum purchases artworks on a ongoing basis and sells older works before they are retained for a maximum of 20 years.

NEW YORK

The New Museum of Contemporary Art - continued
ON EXHIBIT/95:

1/27 - 4/9/95   ANDRES SERRANO: 1983-1994 — A mid-career survey of this provocative artist's work providing a critical examination of work exploring issues of race, religion, death, and voyeurism that have often been controversial. Included are works never seen before.   **CAT**

5/14 - 8/20/95   COLLECTIONS PROJECT (working title) — An exhibition of selected works from the Museum's Semi-Permanent Collection.

9/15/95 - 1/28/96   A LABOR OF LOVE — This group exhibition addresses the relationship between labor-intensive, hand work that is seen as belonging to the craft or folk art traditions, utilitarian objects made in religious or secular communities, and works of "fine art." Component parts of the show will change on an ongoing basis.

NEW YORK

The New-York Historical Society
170 Central Park West, **New York, NY 10024**
TEL: 212-873-3400
HRS: Temporarily closed, opening 5/5/95; Library: 11-5 Tu-F; Print, photograph and architecture collections by appt 11-5 W-F   HOL: LEG/HOL
HDC/ACC: Y; Limited!   PARKING: Y; Pay garages nearby   LIB: Y   H/B: Y
PERM/COLL: NOT ON VIEW UNTIL 5/95: AM: Ptgs 17-20; HUDSON RIVER SCHOOL; AM: gr, phot 18-20; TIFFANY GLASS; CIRCUS & THEATER: post early 20; COLONIAL: portraits (includes Governor of NY dressed as a woman)

Housed in an elegant turn of the century neoclassical building is a collection of all but 2 of the 435 "Birds of America" watercolors by John James Audubon. In addition there are 150 works from Tiffany Studios. **NOT TO BE MISSED:** 435 original watercolors by John James Audubon

ON EXHIBIT/95:

5/5 - summer   THE TREASURES OF THE NEW-YORK HISTORICAL SOCIETY — After a two year renovation the public will be afforded a new look at the museum's most precious holdings including the Audubon watercolors, Hudson River paintings and Tiffany glass as well as other objects that have not usually been put on display.

May - Fall 95   THE GRAND AMERICAN AVENUE — The exhibition documents in prints, photographs and decorative objects the post-Civil War development of America's great avenues.

10/15/94 - 1/8/95   ELVIS + MARILYN: 2 x IMMORTAL — A joint exhibition with CULTURE HEROS FROM THE NEW-YORK HISTORICAL SOCIETY'S COLLECTIONS. Historical trends in hero worship will be examined through the lens of the Elvis Presley-Marilyn Monroe show which examines their impact on contemporary culture. The 100 works of art will explore, compare, and contrast the power of these quintessentially American icons. Artists represented include Andy Warhol, Robert Rauschenberg, Robert Arneson, Audrey Flack and Alexis Smith.   **WT**

307

NEW YORK

NEW YORK

The Pierpont Morgan Library
29 East 36th Street, New York, NY 10016
TEL: 212-685-0610
HRS: 10:30-5 Tu-F; 10:30-6 Sa; noon-6 S   DAY CLOSED: M   HOL: LEG/HOL!
ADM: Y   ADULT: $5.00   CHILDREN: $3.00   STUDENTS: $3.00   SR CIT: $3.00
HDC/ACC: Y; except original Library   PARKING: Y; Nearby pay garage   LIB: Y   MUS/SH: Y
REST/FAC: Y; Cafe open daily for luncheon and afternoon tea 212-685-0008   GT: Y GT/PH: call 212-685-0008, ext
347 to reserve DT: Y TIME: Exh, W & F 2:30; Hist rooms, Tu & T 2:30   H/B: Y
PERM/COLL: MED: drgs, books, ptgs, manuscripts, obj d'art

The Morgan Library is a perfect Renaissance style gem both inside and out. Set in the heart of prosaic NY, this monument comes to the city as a carefully thought out contribution to the domain for the intellect and of the spirit. NOT TO BE MISSED: Stavelot Triptych, a jeweled 12th century reliquary regarded as one of the finest medieval objects in America.

ON EXHIBIT/95:

11/23/94 - 1/8/95	CHARLES DICKENS: "A CHRISTMAS CAROL" — The original manuscript, a part of the library collection is the centerpiece of this holiday exhibition. Also featured are drawings and other material relating to the book.
9/21/94 - 1/22/95	THE THAW COLLECTION: MASTER DRAWINGS AND NEW ACQUISITIONS — This collection which extends from works by leading Italian Renaissance artists to drawings by Cezanne and Picasso is extraordinary in its scope and quality. CAT
1/10 - 4/9/95	THE ALDINE PRESS 1495-1995: AN AMERICAN HOMAGE — This exhibition celebrates the 500th anniversary of the Aldine Press founded by Aldus Manutius in Venice and presents 75 of the finest and most representative works produced by this historic printing house. CAT WT
2/12 - 4/2/95	THE COLLECTOR'S EYE: GIFTS FROM THE COLLECTION OF JULIA PARKER WIGHTMAN — A broad spectrum of outstanding rare books, illuminated manuscripts and bindings ranging from the 1440 Flemish Book of Hours to 18th century "miniature libraries" of children's books created during the late 18th century in England by John Marshall will be on exhibit.
2/15 - 5/7/95	THE PAINTED PAGE: ITALIAN RENAISSANCE BOOK ILLUMINATION, 1450-1550 — This is the sole American venue for this outstanding international loan exhibition representative of major artistic acheivements in this field. CAT
4/6 - 8/27/95	ANIMALS AS SYMBOL IN MEDIEVAL ILLUMINATED MANUSCRIPTS — Animals, real and imaginary, played a central role in medieval life. This exhibition explores different types of animal imagery and is presented in conjunction with "Animals and Humans" a collaborative city-wide project of the New School for Social Research.

Pratt Manhattan Gallery
295 Lafayette Street, 2nd floor, New York, NY 10012
TEL: 718-636-3517
HRS: 10-5 M-Sa   DAY CLOSED: S   HOL: LEG/HOL!
ADM: F   HDC/ACC: Y; Possible but difficult   PARKING: Y; Nearby pay garage   H/B: Y; Puck Building
PERM/COLL: Not continuously on view.

Pratt Manhattan and Schaffler Galleries in Brooklyn present a program of exhibitions of contemporary art, design, and architecture in thematic exhibitions as well as solo and group shows of work by faculty, students and alumni.

Pratt Manhattan Gallery - continued

ON EXHIBIT/95:
2/18 - 3/18/95 LETTERFORMS - FROM HAND TO DIGITAL
3/24 - 4/29/95 SOUL SEARCHING - BLACK ALUMNI OF PRATT

NEW YORK

Salmagundi Museum of American Art
47 Fifth Avenue, New York, NY 10003
TEL: 212-255-7740
HRS: 1-5 daily HOL: LEG/HOL!
ADM: F HDC/ACC:N PARKING: Y; Nearby pay garage LIB: Y REST/FAC: Members Only H/B: Y
PERM/COLL: AM: Realist ptgs 19, 20

An organization of artists and art lovers in a splendid landmark building on lower 5th Avenue.

Sidney Mishkin Gallery of Baruch College
135 East 22nd Street, New York, NY 10010
TEL: 212-387-1006
HRS: 12-5 M-W, F; 12-7 T ACAD DAY CLOSED: Sa, S HOL: ACAD!
ADM: F HDC/ACC: Y PARKING: Y; Nearby pay garages H/B: Y
PERM/COLL: GR; PHOT 20

The building housing this gallery was a 1939 Federal Courthouse Building erected under the auspices of the WPA. **NOT TO BE MISSED:** Marsden Hartley's "Mount Katahdin, Snowstorm," 1942

Solomon R. Guggenheim Museum
1071 Fifth Ave., New York, NY 10128
TEL: 212-423-3500
HRS: 10-6 S-W; 10-8 F & Sa DAY CLOSED: T HOL: 1/1, 12/25
F/DAY: F 6-8 ADM: Y ADULT: $7.00 CHILDREN: F (W/ADULT) STUDENTS: $4 W/ID SR CIT: $4.00
HDC/ACC: Y; wheelchairs and folding chairs available in coatroom PARKING: Y; Nearby pay garages
MUS/SH: Y REST/FAC: Y GT: Y GT/PH: call 212-423-3555 to reserve DT: Y H/B: Y S/G: Y
PERM/COLL: AM & EU: ptgs, sculp; PEGGY GUGGENHEIM COLL: cubist, surrealist, & ab/exp artworks; PANZA diBIUMO COLL: minimalist art 1960's -70's

Designed by Frank Lloyd Wright in 1950, and designated a landmark building by New York City, the museum was recently restored and expanded. Originally called the Museum of Non-Objective Painting, the Guggenheim houses one of the world's largest collections of paintings by Kandinsky as well as prime examples of works by such modern masters as Picasso, Giacometti, Mondrian and others. **NOT TO BE MISSED:** Kandinsky's "Blue Mountain"

ON EXHIBIT/95:
10/7/94 - 1/22/95 THE ITALIAN METAMORPHOSIS: 1943-1968

NEW YORK

Solomon R. Guggenheim Museum - continued

2/10 - 5/7/95	ROSS BLECKNER
2/14 - 5/7/95	FELIX GONZALEZ-TORRES
10/7 - 1/21/96	CLAES OLDENBURG: AN ANTHOLOGY — 200 drawings, collages and sculptures by Oldenburg, a key figure of pop art, will be on exhibit. CAT WT

NEW YORK

The Studio Museum in Harlem
144 West 125th Street, **New York, NY 10027**
TEL: 212-864-4500
HRS: 10-5 W-F; 1-6 Sa, S   DAY CLOSED: M, Tu   HOL: LEG/HOL!
ADM: ADULT: $5.00   CHILDREN: $1.00 (under 12)   STUDENTS: $3.00   SR CIT: $3.00
HDC/ACC: Y   PARKING: Y; Pay garages nearby   MUS/SH: Y   S/G: Y
PERM/COLL: AF/AM; CARIBEAN; LATINO

This is the premier center for the collection, interpretation and exhibition of the art of Black America and the African Diaspora. The five-story building is located on 125th Street, Harlem's busiest thoroughfare and hub of its commercial rebirth and redevelopment.

ON EXHIBIT/95:

1/15 - 3/12/95	EMMA AMOS: PAINTINGS AND PRINTS, 1982-1992 — A ten year retrospective of this outstanding African-American artist at mid career. CAT WT
1/15 - 5/24/95	SAM GILLIAM: NEW MONOPRINTS — Recent large scale works utilizing screenprints, intaglio, woodblock, offset lithography and collage, the exhibition will also reflect on the artist's aesthetic concerns dealt with in his paintings and will measure his inventive and unique way of approaching the print media.
3/26 - 6/95	AFRICAN TRADITIONS: ART AND ARTIFACTS FROM THE PERMANENT COLLECTION OF THE STUDIO MUSEUM IN HARLEM
Summer 95	JEAN-MICHEL BASQUIAT: THE BLUE RIBBON PAINTINGS — Paintings that comment on urban street culture and societal concerns. CAT WT

Whitney Museum of American Art
945 Madison Ave., **New York, NY 10021**
TEL: 212-570-3676
HRS: 11-6 W; 1-8 T; 11-6 F-S   DAY CLOSED: M, Tu   HOL: 1/1, 7/4, THGV, 12/25
F/DAY: 6-8 T   ADM: Y   ADULT: $6.00   CHILDREN: F (under 12)   STUDENTS: $4.00   SR CIT: $4.00
HDC/ACC: Y   PARKING: Y; Nearby pay parking lots   MUS/SH: Y   REST/FAC: Y
GT: Y   GT/PH: call 212-570-3652   DT: Y   TIME: W-S, & T eve 212-570-3652   H/B: Y   S/G: Y
PERM/COLL: AM: all media, 20

Founded by leading art patron Gertrude Vanderbilt Whitney in 1930, the Whitney is housed in an award winning building designed by Marcel Breuer. The museum's mandate, to devote itself solely to the art of the US, is reflected in its significant holdings of the works of Edward Hopper (2,500 in all), and more than 850 works by Reginald Marsh. New directions and developments in art are featured every 2 years in the often cutting edge and controversial "Whitney Biennial." **NOT TO BE MISSED:** Alexander Calder's "Circus"

NEW YORK

Whitney Museum of American Art - continued

ON EXHIBIT/95:

Through 2/26/95	FROM THE COLLECTION: PHOTOGRAPHY, SCULPTURE AND PAINTING
11/10/94 - 3/5/95	BLACK MALE: REPRESENTATIONS OF MASCULINITY
12/15/94 - 3/12/95	COLLECTION IN CONTEXT: GERTRUDE VANDERBILT WHITNEY, PRINTMAKERS' PATRON — An exhibition that reveals the taste, aesthetics and collecting strategies of the Museum's first years.
12/16/94 - 3/12/95	FRANZ KLINE — This exhibition demonstrates Kline's major contribution to Abstract Impressionism with his vigorously black and white palette.
3/23-5/4/95	1995 BIENNIAL EXHIBITION — The Museum's signature exhibition of the most significant developments in American art, film and video over the past two years.
6/22-10/15/95	EDWARD HOPPER AND THE AMERICAN IMAGINATION — A major exhibition of the paintings of this quintessential American Artist. CAT
11/15/95 - 2/11/96	ROBERT FRANK: MOVING OUT CAT WT

Also: The Whitney Museum of American Art at Champion

The Whitney Museum of American Art at Philip Morris

THE PERMANENT COLLECTION
Beginning in the summer of '94, the Museum will present a series of installations of selected works in the Permanent Collection designed to give the public the opportunity to enjoy some of the finest examples of American Art of this century. The works on view will complement the Museum's changing exhibitions by providing an historical context to illustrate the diversity and richness of 20th century art in the US.

NEW YORK

Yeshiva University Museum
2520 Amsterdam Avenue, **New York, NY 10033**
TEL: 212-960-5390
HRS: 11-5 Tu, W, T & 12-6 S Sep-Jul; other times by appt   DAY CLOSED: Sa, M
HOL: LEG/HOL!, RELIGIOUS/HOL!
ADM: Y   ADULT: $3.00   CHILDREN: $1.50   STUDENTS: $1.50   SR CIT: $1.50
HDC/ACC: Y; 4th floor accessible, main floor partially assessible   PARKING: Y; Of-street   LIB: Y   MUS/SH: Y
REST/FAC: Y; Cafeteria on campus   GT: Y   GT/PH: call to reserve
PERM/COLL: JEWISH: ptgs, gr, textiles, ritual objects, cer

Major historical and contemporary exhibitions of Jewish life and ceremony are featured in this museum. **NOT TO BE MISSED:** Architectural models of historic synagogues

ON EXHIBIT/95:

10/94 - 1/95	DI VELT FUN A MOLAR: A PAINTERS WORLD — On view will be poignant oil paintings which evoke the world of Eastern European Jewry prior to the Holocaust and the impact it had on the artist during his prolonged visit.
10/94 - 1/95	A JEWELERS EDITION OF JUDAICA BY HANNA BECHAR-PANETH — "Hanukkiot," spice boxes, Torah pointers and more by this Jerusalem artist.
10/94 - 1/95	GIVE LUCK A CHAIR: WOOD SCULPTURE BY AARON BEN ARIEH — The Israeli sculptor known for his large outdoor installations has created a series of whimsical wood and nickel silver small works interpreting Yiddish proverbs.

311

NEW YORK

Yeshiva University Museum - continued

10/94 - 1/95	PRAYERS, PROVERBS, AND PSALMS: PAINTINGS BY PHILIP PEARLMAN — This New York graphic designer's interpretations of Hebrew proverbs and prayers are filled with color and energy.
11/94 - 2/95	QUILTED VISIONS: MODERN QUILTS WITH JEWISH THEMES
11/94 - 1/95	MOUNTAINS ROUND ABOUT: JERUSALEM IN ISRAELI PRINTMAKING FROM THE SEVENTIES AND EIGHTIES

NIAGARA FALLS

Castellani Art Museum-Niagara University
Niagara Falls, NY 14109
TEL: 716-286-8200
HRS: 11-5 W-Sa; 1-5 S   DAY CLOSED: M, Tu   HOL: ACAD!
ADM: F
HDC/ACC: Y   PARKING: Y
PERM/COLL: AM: ldscp 19; CONT: all media; WORKS ON PAPER: 19-20; PHOT: 20

Housed in a 1990 grey marble building in the middle of the Niagara University campus, the museum is minutes away from Niagara Falls, Artpark, and the New York State Power Vista. **NOT TO BE MISSED:** "Begonia," 1982, by Joan Mitchell

ON EXHIBIT/95:

2/5 - 3/19/95	ROBERT MORRISSEY — A formally intriguing large installation employing wood, magnets and other media, focussing on issues of gravity and suspension.
2/5 - 5/19/95	ZHUQING FUCHA — Traditional Chinese brush painting by this native of Bejing whose family has been known for generations for their skill in both brush painting and calligraphy.
3/26 - 4/16/95	SUNY MFA THESIS EXHIBITION
4/2 - Indefinite	JUDY PFAFF — A mixed-media installation in the interior sculpture court which will cover the walls with the artists' characteristic vibrant colors and mixed media forms.
4/23 - 5/28/95	ALBERTO REY — This foremost Hispanic artist in Western New York finds contemporary expressions for ethnic traditions, autobiographical memories, and organic forms.
4/23 - 5/14/95	SUNY MFA THESIS EXHIBITION
6/11 - 7/23/95	WOMEN'S STUDIO WORKSHOP ARTISTS — Recent print and handmade paper series as well as a small exhibition of works from the museum's collection.
9/17 - 11/5/95	ADELE HENDERSON — A multi-media installation involving prints, audio and mixed media works.
11/12/95 - 1/14/96	KATHLEEN CAMPBELL — A large installation of this artist-photographer's "angel" works.
11/12/95 - 1/14/96	COMMUNITY CELEBRATIONS AND PUERTO RICAN FOLK CATHOLIC TRADITIONS — A folk art exhibition featuring the visual as well as music and performance traditions of Western New York Puerto Rican communities.

NIAGARA FALLS

Native American Center for the Living Arts
25 Rainbow Boulevard, **Niagara Falls, NY 14303**
TEL: 716-284-2427
HRS: 9-6 daily (May-Sep); 9-5 Tu-F; 12-5 Sa, S (Oct-Apr)   HOL: 1/1, THGV, 12/25
ADM: Y   ADULT: $3.50   CHILDREN: $2   STUDENTS: $2.00   SR CIT: $3.00
HDC/ACC: Y   PARKING: Y   LIB: Y   MUS/SH: Y   REST/FAC: GT: Y   GT/PH: call for specifics   DT: Y
PERM/COLL: NAT/AM: arch, eth, cont Mexican, US, Canada

NORTH SALEM

Hammond Museum
Deveau Rd. Off Route 124, **North Salem, NY 10560**
TEL: 914-669-5033
HRS: 10-4 W-S   DAY CLOSED: M, Tu   HOL: 1/1, 12/25
ADM: Y   ADULT: $4.00   CHILDREN: F (under 5)   STUDENTS: $3.00   SR CIT: $3.00
HDC/ACC: Y   PARKING: Y   REST/FAC: Y; Apr through Oct
PERM/COLL: Changing exhibitions

The Hammond Museum and Japanese Stroll Garden provide a place of natural beauty and tranquility to delight the senses and refresh the spirit.

OGDENSBURG

Frederic Remington Art Museum
303/311 Washington Street, **Ogdensburg, NY 13669**
TEL: 315-393-2425
HRS: 10-5 M-Sa & 1-5 S (5/1-10/31); 10-5 Tu-Sa (11/1-4/30)   HOL: LEG/HOL!
ADM: Y   ADULT: $3.00   CHILDREN: F (under 13)   STUDENTS: 13-16 $2.   SR CIT: $2.00
HDC/ACC: Y; Back entrance of museum   LIB: Y   MUS/SH: Y   GT: Y   GT/PH: call for specifics   H/B: Y
PERM/COLL: REMINGTON: ptgs, w/col, sculp, works on paper

The library, memorabilia, and finest single collection of Frederick Remington originals are housed in a 1809-10 mansion with a modern gallery addition. **NOT TO BE MISSED:** "Charge of the Rough Riders at San Juan Hill"

ONEONTA

The Museums at Hartwick
Affiliate Institution: Hartwick College
Oneonta, NY 13820
TEL: 607-431-4480
HRS: 10-4 M-Sa; 1-4 S   HOL: LEG/HOL!
ADM: F   HDC/ACC: Y   PARKING: Y   LIB: Y   MUS/SH: Y
PERM/COLL: NAT/AM: artifacts; P/COL: pottery; VAN ESS COLLECTION OF REN, BAROQUE & AM (ptgs 19); masks; shells; botanical specimens

An excellent college museum with community involvement and travelling exhibitions.

NEW YORK

S. U. N. Y. Plattsburgh Art Museum
Affiliate Institution: State University Of New York
State University of New York, **Plattsburgh, NY 12901**
TEL: 518-564-2474
HRS: 12-4 M-T, Sa, S   DAY CLOSED: F   HOL: LEG/HOL!
ADM: F
HDC/ACC:N; Elevator   PARKING: Y; Free   LIB: Y   MUS/SH: Y
GT: Y   GT/PH: call 518-564-2813   S/G: Y
PERM/COLL: ROCKWELL KENT: ptgs, gr, cer; LARGEST COLLECTION OF NINA WINKEL SCULPTURE

This University Gallery features a "museum without walls" with artworks displayed throughout its campus. **NOT TO BE MISSED:** Largest collection of Rockwell Kent works

POTSDAM

Roland Gibson Gallery
Affiliate Institution: State University College
State University College at Potsdam, **Potsdam, NY 13676-2294**
TEL: 315-267-2250
HRS: 12-5 M-F; 12-4 Sa, S; 7-9:30 M-T eve   HOL: LEG/HOL!
ADM: F
HDC/ACC: Y   PARKING: Y
GT: Y   GT/PH: !   S/G: Y
PERM/COLL: CONT: sculp; WORKS ON PAPER; JAP: ptgs

Based on the New York State University campus in Potsdam, this is the only museum in northern New York that presents a regular schedule of exhibitions. **NOT TO BE MISSED:** "Untitled," by Miro

POUGHKEEPSIE

The Frances Lehman Loeb Art Center at Vassar College
Affiliate Institution: Vassar College
Raymond Ave., **Poughkeepsie, NY 12601**
TEL: 914-437-5235
HRS: 10-5 W-Sa; 1-5 S   DAY CLOSED: M, Tu
ADM: F
HDC/ACC: Y   PARKING: Y
LIB: Y   MUS/SH: Y
PERM/COLL: AM & EU: ptgs, sculp; AN/GR & AN/R: sculp; GR: old Master to modern

The only Museum between Westchester County and Albany exhibiting art of all periods. **NOT TO BE MISSED:** Magoon Collection of Hudson River Paintings

314

PURCHASE

Neuberger Museum of Art
Affiliate Institution: State University of New York
735 Anderson Hill Rd., **Purchase, NY 10577-1400**
TEL: 914-251-6100
HRS: 10-4 Tu-F; 11-5 Sa, S   DAY CLOSED: M   HOL: LEG/HOL!
ADM: Y   ADULT: $4   CHILDREN: F   STUDENTS: $2.00   SR CIT: $2.00
HDC/ACC: Y   PARKING: Y; Free and ample   LIB: Y   MUS/SH: Y   REST/FAC: Y; College Cafeteria
GT: Y!   GT/PH: $5pp adult, $1.50pp stu 914-251-6110
PERM/COLL: PTGS, SCULP, DRGS 20; ROY R. NEUBERGER COLLECTION; EDITH AND GEORGE RICKEY
COLLECTION OF CONSTRUCTIVIST ART; AIMEE HIRSHBERG COLLECTION OF AFRICAN ART

Located on the campus of SUNY Purchase, the Neuberger is among the 10 largest museums in the state and the sixth largest university museum.

ON EXHIBIT/95:

1/22 - 3/12/95   CRITICAL DISTANCE — Four New York artists create environments that incorporate the history, shape and constructs of the Museum's architecture.

3/26 - 5/28/95   CROSSING STATE LINES: TWENTIETH CENTURY ART FROM PRIVATE COLLECTIONS IN WESTCHESTER AND FAIRFIELD COUNTIES — The exhibition features paintings, sculpture, and works on paper by key figures iin modern and contemporary post-War American art.

5/18 - 8/6/95   A SHADOW BORN OF EARTH: NEW PHOTOGRAPHY IN MEXICO — 100 works by 16 young Mexican artists will explore the techniques of photomontage, photographic manipulation, large scale Polaroid photography and photography constructed tableau.
CAT   WT

9/24-12/24/95   JOCHEN GERZ — In a comprehensive overview of two decades of Gerz's work, his emphasis on language and image as co-equal elements which destabilize notions of time and place challenge the certainties with which identities are constructed.   WT

ONGOING: ROY R. NEUBERGER COLLECTION — More than sixty works from the permanent collection which are the heart and soul of the Museum's collection are displayed on a rotating basis and include major works by Romare Bearden, Jackson Pollack, Edward Hopper, Georgia O'Keeffe and others.

OBJECT AND INTELLECT; AFRICAN ART FROM THE PERMANENT COLLECTION — Over forty objects created in the 19th and 20th century which reflect African tradition, rites and religious beliefs will be on view. The exhibition presents the African view of the universe as being composed of two inseparable realms: a visible, tangible world of the living and an invisible world of the sacred.

The Donald M. Kendall Sculpture Gardens at Pepsico
700 Anderson Hill Road, **Purchase, NY 10577**
HRS: 9-5 daily   HOL: LEG/HOL!
ADM: F   HDC/ACC: Y   PARKING: Y; Free and ample   S/G: Y
PERM/COLL: 44 SITE-SPECIFIC SCULPTURES BY 20TH CENTURY ARTISTS

42 site-specific sculptures are located throughout the 168 magnificently planted acres that house the headquarters of PepsiCo, designed in 1970 by noted architect Edward Durell Stone. A large man-made lake and wandering ribbons of pathway invite the visitor to enjoy the sculptures within the ever-changing seasonal nature of the landscape. The garden, located in Westchester County about 30 miles outside of NYC, is an art lover's delight.

NEW YORK

QUEENS

The Queens Museum of Art
New York City Building, Flushing Meadows, Corona Park, **Queens NY 11368-3393**
TEL: 718-592-9700
HRS: 10-5 W-F; 12-5 Sa, S   DAY CLOSED: M, Tu   HOL: 1/1, THGV, 12/25
ADM: Y   ADULT: $3.00   CHILDREN: F (under 5)   STUDENTS: $1.50   SR CIT: $1.50
HDC/ACC: Y   PARKING: Y; Free   MUS/SH: Y   GT: Y   GT/PH: call 718-592-9700 to reserve   H/B: Y
PERM/COLL: CHANGING EXHIBITIONS OF 20TH CENTURY ART AND CONTEMPORARY ART

The Panorama is where all of NYC fits inside one city block. You'll feel like Gulliver when you experience it for the first time. The building was built for the 1939 World's Fair and was later used for United Nations meetings.   **NOT TO BE MISSED:** "The Panorama of NYC," largest architectural scale model of an Urban Area

ON EXHIBIT/95:

Permanent Exhibition:	THE HISTORY OF THE BUILDING AND WORLD'S FAIR GALLERIES
2/2 - 4/9/95	THE HALL COLLECTION OF AMERICAN FOLK ART
5/11 - 7/15/95	JAPANESE-AMERICAN ART FROM THE INTERNMENT CAMPS
5/11 - 7/15/95	YUKINORI YANAGI-PROJECT: ARTICLE 9

ROCHESTER

George Eastman House, International Museum of Photography and Film
900 East Ave., **Rochester, NY 14607**
TEL: 716-271-3361
HRS: 10-4:30 Tu-Sa; 1-4:30 S   DAY CLOSED: M   HOL: LEG/HOL!
ADM: Y   ADULT: $6.50   CHILDREN: $2.50 (5-12)   STUDENTS: $5.00   SR CIT: $5.00
HDC/ACC: Y   PARKING: Y   LIB: Y   MUS/SH: Y, two   REST/FAC: Y
GT: Y   GT/PH: call for specifics   DT: Y   TIME: 10:30 & 2, Tu-Sa; 2, S   H/B: Y
PERM/COLL: PHOT: prints; MOTION PICTURES; MOTION PICTURE STILLS; CAMERAS; BOOKS

The historic home of George Eastman, founder of Eastman Kodak Co. includes a museum that contains an enormous and comprehensive collection of over 500,000 photographic prints, 15,000 motion pictures, 15,000 cameras, 38,000 books and 3,000,000 motion picture stills. **NOT TO BE MISSED:** Discovery room for children.

ON EXHIBIT/95:

11/22/94 - 1/15/95	PEOPLE LIVING WITH HIV: PORTRAITS BY ANNIE LEIBOVITZ WITH PERSPECTIVES BY OUR COMMUNITY — This dramatic exhibition is made up of 13 portraits of people living with HIV. Each individual's philosophy about it is written in their own handwriting and will be shown beside his or her portrait.
9/17/94 - 2/12/95	PASSPORT: INTERNATIONAL PHOTOGRAPHY FROM THE MUSEUM'S FORD MOTOR COMPANY COLLECTION — Included are works by Pedro Meyer, Christine Spengler and Michal Rovner.
1/29 - 4/23/95	SOUVENIRS OF ASIA — A selection of photographs taken in Asia during the 19th century providing an interesting introduction to the still under-appreciated role of photography in the West's increasingly complex relationship with the Far East from the 1840's through the end of the century.
2/18 - 5/4/95	Selected works of local abstract photographer Carl Chiarenza.

George Eastman House - continued

11/19/94 - 10/1/95   SEEING THE UNSEEN: DR. HAROLD E. EDGERTON AND THE WONDERS OF STROBE ALLEY — The exhibition will enable an exploration of the ingenuity behind the creativity in the career of the developer and popularizer of the stroboscope and electronic flash for photographic illumination.

ROCHESTER

Memorial Art Gallery
Affiliate Institution: University of Rochester
500 University Ave., **Rochester, NY 14607**
TEL: 716-473-7720
HRS: 12-9 Tu; 10-4 W-F; 10-5 Sa; 12-5 S   DAY CLOSED: M   HOL: LEG/HOL!
ADM: Y   ADULT: $5.00, Tu, 5-9 pm $2.00   CHILDREN: 6-18 $3.00   STUDENTS: $4.00   SR CIT: $4.00
HDC/ACC: Y   PARKING: Y   LIB: Y   MUS/SH: Y   REST/FAC: Y
GT: Y   GT/PH: call 716-473-7720 ext. 1370
DT: Y   TIME: 2pm, F, S; 7:30 pm Tu   H/B: Y   S/G: Y
PERM/COLL: MED; DU: 17; FR: 19; AM: ptgs, sculp 19, 20; FOLK

The Gallery's permanent collection of 10,000 works span 50 centuries of world art and includes masterworks by artists such as Monet, Cezanne, Matisse, Homer and Cassatt. **NOT TO BE MISSED:** "Waterloo Bridge, Veiled Sun" 1903, by Monet

ON EXHIBIT/95:

10/29/94 - 1/8/95   HEAD, HEART AND HAND: ELBERT HUBBARD AND THE ROYCROFTERS — Showcased will be the furniture, metalwork, leathercraft and bookbinding and art work produced at Roycroft, a turn-of-the-century Arts and Crafts community at East Aurora, New York.   WT

1/28 - 3/26/95   THE IMPRESSIONISTS, NEW YORK — New York City was the mecca for American Impressionist painters such as William Merritt Chase, Childe Hassam, Edward Redfield and many others whose works will be featured in this exhibition.

4/13 - 5/18/95   FROM BRANDT POINT TO THE BOCA TIGRIS: NANTUCKET AND THE CHINA TRADE — The porcelains, paintings, silk, lacquer and silver brought back with the expansion of trade from 1800 until the War of 1812 are part of a fascinating page from American maritime, commercial and decorative history.   WT

7/8 - 9/17/95   MAG WORKS BY WOMEN: A CELEBRATION OF WOMEN — Works in all media by women in the museum collection including Lilly Martin Spenser, Angelica Kaufmann, Georgia O'Keeffe and others.

10/8 - 11/17/95   ROCHESTER-FINGER LAKES EXHIBITION — Rochester's oldest and largest juried exhibition of works in all media by artists from a 23 county region.

12/9/95 - 12/9/96   DEMOCRATIC VISTAS: THE PRINTS OF CURRIER AND IVES — A selection of the best Currier and Ives lithographs from the collection of the Museum of the City of New York.

NEW YORK

ROSLYN HARBOR

Nassau County Museum of Fine Art
Northern Blvd & Museum Dr., **Roslyn Harbor, NY 11576**
TEL: 516-484-9337
HRS: 11-5 Tu-S   DAY CLOSED: M   HOL: LEG/HOL!
F/DAY: F   ADM: Y   ADULT: $3.00   CHILDREN: $2.00   STUDENTS: $2.00   SR CIT: $2.00
HDC/ACC: Y   PARKING: Y, F   MUS/SH: Y   GT: Y   GT/PH: call for reservations   H/B: Y   S/G: Y
PERM/COLL: AM: gr, sculp

Situated on 145 acres of formal gardens, rolling lawns and meadows, the museum presents four major exhibitions annually and is home to one of the east coast's largest publicly accessible outdoor sculpture gardens.

SARATOGA SPRINGS

The Schick Art Gallery
Affiliate Institution: Skidmore College
Skidmore Campus, North Broadway, **Saratoga Springs, NY 12866-1632**
TEL: 518-584-5000
HRS: 9-5 M-F; 1-3:30 Sa, S   HOL: LEG/HOL!, ACAD!
ADM: F   HDC/ACC: Y; Elevator   PARKING: Y; On campus   LIB: Y   REST/FAC: Y
GT: Y   GT/PH: call 518-584-5000, ext. 2370
PERM/COLL: non-collecting institution

Theme oriented or one person exhibitions that are often historically significant are featured in this gallery located on the beautiful Skidmore Campus.

ON EXHIBIT/95:

1/27 - 2/26/95	ANNUAL JURIED STUDENT EXHIBITION
3/2 - 4/2/95	CALIFORNIA ARTISTS:WORKS ON PAPER
4/6 - 5/10/95	D. BRACKETT/R. UPTON — Two person faculty show
5/19 - 5/27/95	SENIOR THESIS EXHIBITION

SOUTHAMPTON

The Parrish Art Museum
25 Job's Lane, **Southampton, NY 11968**
TEL: 516-283-2118
HRS: 11-5 Tu-Sa; 1-5 S (Jun 15-Sep 14); 11-5 W-M (Sep 14-Jun 14)   HOL: 1/1, EASTER, 7/4, THGV, 12/25
SUGG/CONT: Y   ADULT: $2
HDC/ACC: Y;!   PARKING: Y   MUS/SH: Y   GT: Y   GT/PH: call for specifics   H/B: Y   S/G: Y
PERM/COLL: AM: ptgs, gr 19; WILLIAM MERRITT CHASE; FAIRFIELD PORTER

Situated in a fashionable summer community, this Museum is a "don't miss" when one is near the Eastern tip of Long Island. It is located in an 1898 building designed by Grosvenor Atterbury.

The Parrish Art Museum - continued
ON EXHIBIT/95:

through 1/8/95	SUGIMOTO/INNESS
1/9 - 1/20/95	MUSEUM CLOSED FOR ANNUAL MAINTENANCE
1/21 - 2/5/95	SCHOOL ART FESTIVAL
2/12 - 4/9/95	SCHOOL COLLABORATIVE EXHIBITION
4/16 - 5/28/95	ACQUISITIONS
6/4 - 7/23/95	THINGS IN PLACE: LANDSCAPES AND STILL-LIFES BY SHERIDAN LORD
7/30 - 10/1/95	AMERICAN PORTRAITS
10/8 - 11/26/95	ROBERT FRANK: THE AMERICANS WT
12/3/95 - 1/14/96	AGNES PELTON: POET OF NATURE

STATEN ISLAND

Jacques Marchais Center of Tibetan Art
338 Lighthouse Ave., **Staten Island, NY 10306**
TEL: 718-987-3500
HRS: 1-5 W-S (Apr-Nov or by appt.)   DAY CLOSED: M, T   HOL: EASTER, 7/4, LAB/DAY, THGV & day after
ADM: Y   ADULT: $3   CHILDREN: $1.00 (under 12)   STUDENTS: $3.00   SR CIT: $2.50
MUS/SH: Y   GT: Y   GT/PH: call 718-987-3500 for specifics   S/G: Y
PERM/COLL: TIBET; OR: arch; GARDEN

This unique museum of Himalayan art within a Tibetan setting consists of two stone buildings resembling a temple. A quiet garden and a goldfish pond help to create an atmosphere of serenity and beauty. It is the only museum in this country devoted primarily to Tibetan art.

Snug Harbor Cultural Center
Affiliate Institution: Newhouse Center for Contemporary Art
1000 Richmond Terrace, **Staten Island, NY 10301**
TEL: 718-448-2500
HRS: 12-5 W-S   DAY CLOSED: M, T   HOL: LEG/HOL!
VOL/CONT: Y   ADM: F   PARKING: Y; Free   LIB: Y   MUS/SH: Y   REST/FAC: Y
GT: Y   GT/PH: call 718-448-2500, ext 30   H/B: Y   S/G: Y
PERM/COLL: Non-collecting institution

Once a 19th century home for retired sailors Snug Harbor is a landmarked 83 acre, 28 building complex being preserved and adapted for the visual and performing arts. The Newhouse Center for Contemporary art provides a forum for regional and international design and art. **NOT TO BE MISSED:** The award winning newly restored 1884 fresco ceiling.

ON EXHIBIT/95:
10/23/94 - 1/8/95   AUTO: ON THE EDGE OF TIME — Seven stripped cars altered by artist Suzanne Lacy will be featured outdoors with an indoor component, in an exhibition that uses the car as a rich metaphor with contemporary associations of domestic violence and battered women. The installation will coincide with the release of a Public Service Announcement on domestic violence made for television in association with the Public Art Fund.

NEW YORK

Snug Harbor Cultural Center - continued

10/23/94 - 1/8/95	ARTIST IN RESIDENCE — Czech artist Vladimir Kokolia will create a new project in the galleries and will be introduced to local artists and regional arts organizations.
11/6/94 - 1/8/95	RELATIVELY SPEAKING: MOTHERS AND DAUGHTERS IN ART — The exhibition honors a rarely observed connection between generations of artists and examines the common thread in familial artists. It will present in addition to 14 pairs of artists, two mothers with two artist daughters, one three generation family and one four generation family. Included among others are Harriet Shorr, Janet Fish, Betye Saar, Nancy Azara and Jane Freilicher.　　　　　　CAT　WT
10/94 - 1/95	OUTSIDE THE FRAME: PERFORMANCE AND THE OBJECT — Performance Art, a 20th century phenomenon has been an undisputed yet unexalted influence not only on visual art, but on dance, music, theatre, film, video, television and radio. This exhibition will sample the work from the late 1950's to the present. Works will include interactive and performative sculpture, new original artworks or installations, recreations of earlier work etc. by artists who have played a significant or innovative roll in the field.　　WT
3/95 - 6/95	NEIGHBORHOODS: THE STORY OF STATEN ISLAND (diverse locations around Staten Island) — In conjuction with an upcoming History Conference sponsored by the Education Department, the exhibition will include four artists who will develop new works to be presented at various locations around Staten Island. The conference is a collaborative effort of the art and history institutions of Staten Island.
4/95 - 9/95	ARTIST IN RESIDENCE — In collaboration with the Gulbenkian Foundation in Lisbon, Portugal, Snug Harbor will choose a Portuguese artist in residence to participate in the first component of an international exchange and exhibition program.
6/18 - 10/95	1995 SNUG HARBOR OUTDOOR SCULPTURE EXHIBITION — The tenth anniversary of this annual exhibition featuring outdoor site-specific works.
10/95 - 1/96	ABSTRACTION AFTER THE FALL: ASPECTS OF ABSTRACT PAINTING SINCE 1970 — The exhibition will review the substance and importance of work that came into its own in the 1970's, how work by artists of the 70's evolved over the last 25 years, and how work by a younger generation of painters has furthered explorations of 25 years ago. The show will survey approximately 50 painters from the 70's, 80's and 90's.　　CAT

STATEN ISLAND

Staten Island Institute of Arts and Sciences
75 Stuyvesant Place, **Staten Island, NY 10301**
TEL: 718-727-1135
HRS: 9-5 M-Sa; 1-5 S　HOL: LEG/HOL!
SUGG/CONT: Y
HDC/ACC: Y; Limited　LIB: Y　MUS/SH: Y　GT: Y　GT/PH: call for specifics
PERM/COLL: PTGS; DEC/ART; SCULP; STATEN ISLAND: arch

One of Staten Islands oldest and most diverse cultural institutions, this facility explores and interprets the art, natural resources and cultural history of Staten Island. **NOT TO BE MISSED:** Ferry Collection on permanent exhibition. This exhibition on the history of the world-famous ferry service is located in the Staten Island Ferry terminal.

ON EXHIBIT/95:

9/23/94 - 1/29/95	STATEN ISLAND BIENNIAL JURIED ART EXHIBITION
12/2/94 - 3/5/95	STATEN ISLAND COLLECTS: ANTIQUES FROM THE COLLECTION OF GEORGE WAY

320

Staten Island Institute of Arts and Sciences - continued

1/27 - 5/7/95	STATEN ISLAND COMMUNITY - TRAVIS
2/17 - 5/7/95	SILVER COLLECTION OF ALAN HARTMAN
5/26 - 10/1/95	STATEN ISLAND COLLECTS
6/23 - 9/1095	A CENTURY OF AFRICAN-AMERICAN EXPERIENCE
	GREENWOOD: FROM RUINS TO RENAISSANCE
8/11/95 - 11/12/95	STATEN ISLAND BIENNIAL JURIED CRAFT EXHIBITION

STATEN ISLAND

The John A. Noble Collection at Snug Harbor
Affiliate Institution: Snug Harbor Cultural Center
270 Richmond Terrace, **Staten Island, NY 10301**
TEL: 718-447-6490
HRS: 9-2 M-F and by appt.   DAY CLOSED: Sa, S   HOL: LEG/HOL!
SUGG/CONT: Y
HDC/ACC: Y PARKING: Y LIB: Y MUS/SH: Y REST/FAC: Y GT: Y GT/PH: call for specifics H/B: Y
PERM/COLL: PTGS; LITHOGRAPHS; DOCUMENTS AND ARTIFACTS; SALOON HOUSEBOAT OF JOHN A. NOBLE

John Noble wrote "My life's work is to make a rounded picture of American Maritime endeavor of modern times." He is widely regarded as America's premier marine lithographer. The collection, in a new site at historic Snug Harbor Cultural Center, is only partially on view as renovation continues.

STONY BROOK

The Museums at Stony Brook
1208 Rte. 25A, **Stony Brook, NY 11790**
TEL: 516-715-0066
HRS: 10-5 W-Sa; 12-5 S   DAY CLOSED: M, T   HOL: THGV, 1/1, 12/24, 12/25
ADM: Y   ADULT: $6.00   CHILDREN: $3 (6-12)   STUDENTS: $4(13-18   SR CIT: $4.00
HDC/ACC: Y PARKING: Y LIB: Y MUS/SH: Y GT: Y GT/PH: call for reservations & specifics
PERM/COLL: AM: ptgs; HORSE DRAWN CARRIAGES; MINIATURE ROOMS; ANT: decoys; COSTUMES; TOYS

The finest collection of American horse-drawn carriages in the world as well as the largest holdings of works by American genre artist William Sidney Mount (1807-1868) are to be found here.

ON EXHIBIT/95:

10/8/94 - 1/8/95   MRS. STICKLES' WORLD IN MINIATURE: AMAZING DOLL HOUSES — The exhibition features toys as well as this private collection.

10/15/94 - 2/5/95   ART EN ROUTE: MTA ARTS FOR TRANSIT — Featured will be works ranging from turn of the century mosaic tile assemblages, furniture and light fixtures to contemporary commissions by artists including Roy Lichtenstein, Romare Bearden, Maya Lin, Elizabeth Murray and Milton Glaser all commissioned by the New York Metropolitan Transportation Authority for its four divisions.

NEW YORK

The Museums at Stony Brook - continued

2/18 - 4/30/95	PRINTMAKERS OF THE SPRINGS (working title) — In 1972 New York printmaker Arnold Hoffman, Jr. established the Screen Print Workshop in The Springs in Long Island's Hamptons. Highlighted are a selection of his prints as those of other artists who lived or worked there including James Brooks, Bill Durham, Bill King, Estaban Vicente, Roy Nicholson and others.
1/21 - 5/21/95	STYLE FROM THE TOP: HATS AND ACCESSORIES FROM THE MUSEUM'S COLLECTION — An exploration of the social meaning and implications of hats and their relationship to fashion history.
6/3 - 11/7/95	CREATING A CONSUMER CULTURE IN AMERICA (TENT!) — An exploration of how and why Americans were enticed to purchase and desire goods and how huge department and supermarkets steadily replaced small neighborhood markets and goods from mail order catalogs.
9/23 - 11/26/95	RESCUERS OF THE HOLOCAUST: PORTRAITS BY GAY BLOCK — An important addition to the vast Holocaust record, this exhibition documents in photographs, reminiscences, family albums and letters the efforts of many people alive today who protected, hid and saved Jews in Europe during World War II. CAT WT

SYRACUSE

Everson Museum of Art
401 Harrison Street, **Syracuse, NY 13202**
TEL: 315-474-6064
HRS: 12-5 Tu-F; 10-5 Sa; 12-5 S   DAY CLOSED: M   HOL: 1/1, 7/4, THGV, 12/25
VOL/CONT: Y   ADM: F
HDC/ACC: Y   PARKING: Y; Nearby pay garages, limited metered on street
LIB: Y   MUS/SH: Y
REST/FAC: Y   GT: Y   GT/PH: call for specifics   DT: Y   TIME: !   H/B: Y   S/G: Y
PERM/COLL: AM: cer; AM: ptgs 19, 20; AM: Arts/Crafts Movement Objects

When it was built, the first museum building designed by I. M. Pei was called "a work of art for Works of Art." The Everson's Syracuse China Center for the Study of Ceramics, one of the nation's most comprehensive, features an ever increasing collection of America's ceramics housed in an open-storage gallery. The installation is arranged chronologically by culture and includes samples from the ancient classical world, the Americas, Asia and Europe. **NOT TO BE MISSED:** One of the largest, most comprehensive permanent exhibitions of American and world ceramics

ON EXHIBIT/95:

ONGOING	ONE HUNDRED FIFTY YEARS OF AMERICAN ART — An overview of American art featuring turn-of-the-century portraits and genre paintings, late 19th century landscapes and American modernism through the 1950's, including American Scene painting by some of America's best known artists.
	INTERNATIONAL CONTEMPORARY CERAMICS
	SYRACUSE CHINA CENTER FOR THE STUDY OF AMERICAN CERAMICS

322

UTICA

Munson-Williams-Proctor Institute Museum of Art

310 Genesee Street, **Utica, NY 13502**
TEL: 315-797-0000
HRS: 10-5 Tu-Sa; 1-5 S   DAY CLOSED: M   HOL: LEG/HOL!
SUGG/CONT: Y   HDC/ACC: Y   PARKING: Y   LIB: Y   MUS/SH: Y
GT: Y   GT/PH: call 315-797-0000 to reserve   H/B: Y   S/G: Y
PERM/COLL: AM: ptgs, dec/art; EU: manuscripts, gr, drgs

The Museum is a combination of the first art museum designed by renowned architect Philip Johnson (1960) and Fountain Elms, an 1850 historic house which was the home of the museum's founders.

ON EXHIBIT/95:

11/12/94 - 1/29/95	BARBIZON TO BOULEVARD: NINETEENTH-CENTURY FRENCH PRINTS — This exhibition examines the shift in subject matter from bucolic scenery to city life on the grand boulevards of Paris as well as the change in fine printmaking techniques from intaglio processes to lithography. Featured are works by Daumier, Delacroix, Cezanne, Bonnard and Vuillard.
12/17/94 - 2/12/95	EASTON PRIBBLE: PAINTINGS AND DRAWINGS — Landscapes and urban scenes from the 1950's to the present in a variety of media.
2/18 - 4/16/95	EMPIRE VISTAS — The scenic beauties of New York State are featured in paintings, drawings and prints from the Museum collection.
3/4 - 4/30/95	THE 56TH EXHIBITION OF CENTRAL NEW YORK ARTISTS
4/22 - 7/16/95	ARTISTRY IN ROSEWOOD: THE WORK OF ELIJAH GALUSHA — The craftsmanship and contribution to nineteenth century decorative arts by this creator of high style Rococo and Renaissance Revival designs will be examined in the context of other New York State cabinetmakers such as John Henry Belter.
5/10 - 7/30/95	THE STUDIO MUSEUM IN HARLEM: 25 YEARS OF AFRICAN-AMERICAN ART — In celebration of the Studio Museum's 25th Anniversary, this traveling exhibition will highlight paintings, sculpture and works on paper created between 1968-1993 by noted African-American artists. WT
9/9 - 11/19/95	SCULPTURE SPACE: CELEBRATING 20 YEARS — Sculpture Space is a not-for-profit studio housed on the grounds formerly occupied by Utica Boiler Works. This exhibition will feature diverse works by internationally recognized sculptors as well as emerging artists.

YONKERS

The Hudson River Museum of Westchester

511 Warburton Ave., **Yonkers, NY 10701**
TEL: 914-963-4550
HRS: 10-5 W, T, Sa; 10-9 F; 12-5 S   DAY CLOSED: M, Tu   HOL: LEG/HOL!
ADM: Y   ADULT: $3.00   CHILDREN: $1.50 (12-under)   STUDENTS: SR CIT: $1.50(over 62)
HDC/ACC: Y; Entire building; also, a "Touch Gallery" for visually-impaired   PARKING: Y; Free   MUS/SH: Y
REST/FAC: Y   GT: Y   GT/PH: call 914-963-4550, ext 40 to reserve   H/B: Y   S/G: Y
PERM/COLL: AM: ldscp/ptgs 19, 20; DEC/ART; GR: 19, 20; COSTUMES; PHOT: 19, 20.

NEW YORK

The Hudson River Museum of Westchester - continued

The Hudson River Museum of Westchester overlooking the Palisades provides a dramatic setting for changing exhibitions of art, architecture, design, history and science. Discover the Hudson River's special place in American life as you enjoy the art. **NOT TO BE MISSED:** Hiram Power's "Eve Disconsolate," marble statue, 1871, (gift of Berol family in memory of Mrs. Gella Berolzheimer, 1951). Also, woodwork and stencils in the decorated period rooms of the 1876 Glenview Mansion.

ON EXHIBIT/95:

9/30/94 - 1/15/95	WINSLOW HOMER THE ILLUSTRATOR: HIS WOOD ENGRAVINGS	WT
2/3 - 5/14/95	LOOKING AT OURSELVES: 200 YEARS OF AMERICAN PORTRAITURE — Portraiture is a means for establishing identity as well as identification: we know someone not only by physical recognition but by association with other attributes, e.g., class, ethnicity, profession, etc. This exhibition is a wide investigation of how Americans distinguish and acknowledge themselves, ranging from a traditionally painted portrait to postage stamps, passports and baseball cards. Included are paintings, photography, video and computerization.	
2/3 - 5/21/95	VICTORIAN MOURNING RITUALS — Included in this exploration of 19th century American attitudes, responses, depictions and customs surrounding death are memorial photography, prints, costumes and related artifacts.	
6/25 - 8/27/95	OUT OF THE ORDINARY: COMMUNITY TASTES AND VALUES IN CONTEMPORARY FOLK ART — The connection of forms and expressions to the rich interaction of the artist, community and cultural values are here explored. The audience is challenged to consider the multicultural nature of contemporary folk art while prompting an examination of the viewers own connections with folk culture.	WT
6/25 - 8/27/95	A BRIDGE TO THE PAST: WESTCHESTER FOLK ART IN CONTEXT — Complementing OUT OF THE ORDINARY (see above) are 19th and 20th century folk art from local historical societies and private collections.	
6/25 - 9/3/95	GEORGE INNESS: A CENTENNIAL COMMEMORATION — Approximately 25 paintings, drawings and artifacts from the Montclair Museum of Art follow the artist's development from an adherent of the Hudson River School to one whose vision is transformed by his encounter with Barbizon painting and the religious thought of Emanuel Swedenborg. CAT WT	
10/95 - 1/96	NETWORK OF IRON: THE RAILROAD TRANSFORMS WESTCHESTER, 1840-1916 — From its arrival in the late 1830's through the turn of the century when four major lines ran within the counties borders, the railroad ushered in a quickly paced transformation which was a turning point in Westchester's own definition and its relationship with New York City. This complex topic is examined through an interdisciplinary exhibit combining history, art and technology as well as social, economic and urban planning issues and featuring photographs, prints, paintings, posters, historical documents and artifacts.	
10/95 - 1/96	TRY THIS ON: CONNECTING HISTORY, CLOTHING AND SOCIAL IDENTITY — An examination of how rules for dress mirror and shape attitudes about men, women, children, cultural identity and class in our society. WT	
10/95 - 1/96	OUTERWEAR/INNER WARMTH: COLLECTION OF COATS, SHAWLS AND BOOTS — The forms taken by late 19th to 20th century outerwear and how they responded to changes in fashionable silhouettes as well as serving as indicators of social transformations in lifestyles will be shown in this exhibition.	
Late 10/95 - 12/95	THE AIDS MEMORIAL QUILT	

324

ASHEVILLE

Asheville Art Museum
2 S. Pack Square, **Asheville, NC 28801**
TEL: 704-253-3227
HRS: 10-5 Tu-F; 1-5 Sa, S   DAY CLOSED: M   HOL: 1/1, 7/4, LAB/DAY, THGV, 12/25
F/DAY: Sa   ADM: Y   ADULT: $3.00   CHILDREN: $0.50 under 12 F   STUDENTS: $2.00   SR CIT: $3.00
PARKING: Y; On-street/parking deck   GT: Y   GT/PH: call 704-253-3227   H/B: Y
PERM/COLL: AM/REG: ptgs, sculp, crafts 20

The museum is housed in the Old Pack Memorial Library, a splendidly restored 1920's Beaux Arts building. **NOT TO BE MISSED:** ART IS...The Museum's collection of 20th century art asks this question and the permanent collect ion includes historical and contemporary responses by noted artists.

ON EXHIBIT/95:

1/95 - 2/95	ELIZABETH AUGUSTA CHANT — Arts and Crafts painter
3/95 - 4/95	ELLIOT ERWITT: TO THE DOGS WT
3/30-5/6/95	SOUTHERN EXPRESSIONS: CERAMICS BY TRIESCH VOELKER AND GINA BOBROWSKI
	PAINTINGS BY JULIE LEONARD
	MIXED MEDIA BY LARRY CAVENEY
5/11 - 7/2/95	SOUTHEAST REGIONAL GLASS ARTISTS
5/11 - 6/25/95	HARVEY LITTLETON GLASS COLLECTION
7/6 - 9/17/95	RICHARD SHARPE SMITH
5/29 - 9/10/95	MYSTERIOUS PLACES — Paintings by Liz Quisgard and Katherine Alexamder
9/14 - 11/4/95	SALLY MIDDLETON PAINTINGS
9/21 - 11/11/95	CHEROKEE ART AND LANGUAGE
11/9 - 12/30/95	DONALD SULTAN — DRAWINGS
11/16 - 1/6/96	STEPHEN RUECKERT: INSTALLATION

CHAPEL HILL

The Ackland Art Museum
Columbia & Franklin Sts, Univ. of North Carolina, **Chapel Hill, NC 27599**
TEL: 919-966-5736
HRS: 12-3 W-F; 10-5 Sa; 2-5 S   DAY CLOSED: M, Tu   HOL: 12/25
ADM: F
HDC/ACC: Y   PARKING: Y   LIB: Y   GT: Y   GT/PH: call 919-966-5736 to reserve
PERM/COLL: EU & AM: ptgs, gr 15-20; PHOT; REG

The Ackland, with a collection of more than 12,000 works of art ranging from ancient times to the present, includes a wide variety of categories conveying the breadth of mankind's achievements.

NORTH CAROLINA

CHARLOTTE

Mint Museum of Art
2730 Randolph Road, **Charlotte, NC 28207**
TEL: 704-337-2000
HRS: 10-10 Tu; 10-5 W-Sa; 12-5 S   DAY CLOSED: M   HOL: LEG/HOL!
F/DAY: Tu 5-10; 2nd S of each month   ADM: Y   ADULT: $4.00   CHILDREN: under 12 F
STUDENTS: $2.00   SR CIT: $3.00
HDC/ACC: Y   PARKING: Y; Free & ample   LIB: Y!   MUS/SH: Y   GT: Y, call 1 mo adv 704-337-2032   H/B: Y
PERM/COLL: EU & AM: ptgs; REN; CONT; CH; DEC/ART; AM: pottery, glass; BRIT: cer

The building, erected in 1836 as the first branch of the US Mint, produced 5 million dollars in gold coins before the Civil war. In 1936 it opened as the first art museum in North Carolina. When the museum was moved to its present parkland setting the facade of the original building was integrated into the design of the new building. **NOT TO BE MISSED:** Extensive Delhom collection of English pottery beautifully displayed.

ON EXHIBIT/95:

7/30/94 - 1/15/95	SOUTHWESTERN NATIVE AMERICAN CERAMICS — A survey of both the traditional and contemporary.
11/26/94 - 1/22/95	PROJECT FACE TO FACE — Using finely detailed plaster face castings, recorded oral histories and printed excerpts from individual stories, viewers are invited to interact in a non-threatening way with a diverse group of people with aids.
1/14 - 3/12/95	PARTIAL RECALL — A look inside the images of Native North American people that have survived since photography appeared in the mid-nineteenth century.
1/27 - 3/2/95	ARTCurrents 17
4/15 - 6/30/95	ELVIS + MARILYN: 2 X IMMORTAL — The first major museum exhibition to examine the impact of Elvis Presley and Marilyn Monroe on American culture. The more than 100 works will explore, compare, and contrast the power of these quintessentially American icons. Included are works by Andy Warhol, Robert Arneson, Robert Rauschenberg, Audrey Flack and Alexis Smith. WT

Spirit Square Center for the Arts
345 N. College Street, **Charlotte, NC 28202**
TEL: 704-372-9664
HRS: 12-6 M-Sa   DAY CLOSED: S   HOL: LEG/HOL!
ADM: F
HDC/ACC: Y   PARKING: Y   MUS/SH: Y   H/B: Y
PERM/COLL: non-collecting institution

At Spirit Square, the performing arts, the visual arts, and art education are combined in a remarkable atmosphere of exploration and creativity.

DALLAS

Gaston County Museum of Art and History

131 W. Main Street, **Dallas, NC 28034**
TEL: 704-922-7681
HRS: 10-5 Tu-F; 1-5 Sa; 2-5 S   DAY CLOSED: M   HOL: LEG/HOL!
ADM: F   HDC/ACC: Y; Ramps, elevators   PARKING: Y   LIB: Y   MUS/SH: Y
GT: Y, call to reserve   H/B: Y   S/G: Y: in courtyard
PERM/COLL: CONT; ARTIFACTS RELATING TO THE U.S, N.C., & THE SOUTHEAST

Housed in the 1852 Hoffman Hotel located in historic Court Square, the museum contains period rooms and contemporary galleries which were renovated in 1984. **NOT TO BE MISSED:** Carriage exhibit, the largest in the Southeast

ON EXHIBIT/95:

11/20/94 - 1/8/95	KEEPING WARM — Winter clothing and textiles
	TOYS WERE US — Toys from the Detroit Antique Toy Museum
1/15 - 3/5/95	UNDER AFRICAN SKIES — African Art from area collection
	THE AFRICAN-AMERICAN EXPERIENCE IN GASTON COUNTY
3/19 - 4/15/95	CATCH A RISING STAR
4/23 - 5/21/95	GASTON COUNTY ART GUILD SPRING SHOW
5/28 - 9/3/95	OPEN WIDE: A MEDICAL HISTORY OF GASTON COUNTY
9/10 - 11/12/95	COSTUMES FROM THE COLLECTION — with watercolors by Kathryn Crowe
	JENNIFER CALDWELL
11/19/95-1/7/96	TOYS WERE US

DAVIDSON

William H. Van Every Gallery/Edward M. Smith Gallery

Davidson College, Visual Arts Center, **Davidson, NC 28036**
TEL: 704-892-2000
HRS: 10-4 M-F; Sa, S 2-5 (Jan-May, Sep-Dec)   HOL: LEG/HOL!
ADM: F   PARKING: Y
PERM/COLL: WORKS ON PAPER

In the fall of 1993 the Gallery moved to a new building designed by Graham Gund where selections from the 2,500 piece permanent collection are displayed at least once during the year. The Gallery also presents a varied roster of both traveling and student exhibitions. **NOT TO BE MISSED:** Auguste Rodin's "Jean d'Aire," bronze

ON EXHIBIT/95:

Van Every Gallery	
mid 1/95 - Mid 2/95	ANSEL ADAMS
mid 2/95 - mid 3/95	ARNOLD MENSCHES
mid 3/95 - Mid 4/95	STUDENT SHOW
Smith Gallery	CHANGING STUDENT EXHIBITIONS

NORTH CAROLINA

DURHAM

Duke University Museum of Art
Affiliate Institution: Duke University
Buchanan Blvd at Trinity, **Durham, NC 27701**
TEL: 919-684-5135
HRS: 9-5 Tu-F; 11-2 Sa; 2-5 S   DAY CLOSED: M   HOL: LEG/HOL!
ADM: F   HDC/ACC: Y   PARKING: Y   MUS/SH: Y   GT: Y, call 919-477-2271 to reserve
PERM/COLL: MED: sculp; DEC/ART; AF: sculp; AM & EU: all media

Duke University Art Museum, with its impressive collection ranging from ancient to modern works includes the Breumner collection of Medieval art, widely regarded as a one of a kind in the US, and a large pre-Columbian collection from Central and South America.

FAYETTEVILLE

Fayetteville Museum of Art
839 Stamper Road, **Fayetteville, NC 28303**
TEL: 919-485-5121
HRS: 10-5 Tu-F; 1-5 Sa, S   DAY CLOSED: M   HOL: 1/1, EASTER, 7/4, THGV, 12/23-12/31
ADM: F   HDC/ACC: Y   PARKING: Y   LIB: Y   MUS/SH: Y   S/G: Y
PERM/COLL: CONT: North Carolina art; PTGS, SCULP, CER

The museum, whose building was the first in the state designed and built as an art museum, also features an impressive collection of outdoor sculpture on its landscaped grounds. **NOT TO BE MISSED:** "Celestial Star Chart," by Tom Guibb

GREENSBORO

Weatherspoon Art Gallery
Affiliate Institution: University of North Carolina
Spring Garden & Tate Street, **Greensboro, NC 27412-5001**
TEL: 910-334-5770
HRS: 10-5 Tu, T, F; 1-5 Sa-S; 10-8 W   DAY CLOSED: M   HOL: ACAD! and vacations
ADM: F
HDC/ACC: Y   PARKING: Y   MUS/SH: Y   GT: Y, call 910-334-5770   H/B: Y   S/G: Y
PERM/COLL: AM: 20; MATISSE LITHOGRAPHS; OR

Designed by renowned architect, Romaldo Giurgola, the Weatherspoon Art Gallery houses a predominantly 20th century collection of American art with works by de Kooning, Alex Katz, Louise Nevelson, David Smith, and Robert Rauschenberg. **NOT TO BE MISSED:** The Cone Collection of Matisse lithographs and bronzes

ON EXHIBIT/95:
    11/6/94 - 1/8/95   LUCIEN FREUD: DRAWINGS AND PRINTS — Drawings and prints by the British artist done in the last eight years including familiar subject matter such as interiors, portraits and nudes as well as less familiar landscapes.

Weatherspoon Art Gallery - continued

11/13/94 - 1/8/95	ART ON PAPER — An annual exhibition showcasing a wide variety of nationally known artists who create works on paper.
11/22/94 - 2/12/95	THE GRID: SELECTIONS FROM THE WEATHERSPOON COLLECTION — An exploration of the use of grids as forms and symbols in contemporary art. Relationships to broader historical and cultural uses will be considered.
1/19 - 2/26/95	MFA THESIS EXHIBITION
2/22 - 3/26/95	INTO THE NINETIES: PRINTS FROM THE TAMARIND INSTITUTE — Examples of the very best examples of contemporary lithography made at Tamarind during the last decadewill be featured.
2/26 - 5/21/95	LOOKING BACK, LOOKING FORWARD: AMERICAN ART 1893-1913 SELECTIONS FROM THE WEATHERSPOON COLLECTION — A revisiting of developments in the art of the United States between 1893-1913 focusing on three major exhibitions: the 1893 Columbian Exposition in Chicago; the 1908 exhibit of "The Eight: organized by Realist painter Robert Henri; and the Armory Show of 1913.
3/12 - 4/23/95	FALK VISITING ARTIST EXHIBITION: STEPHEN TALASNIK — Talasnik creates fictional structures and spaces that fuse together a complex amalgem of visual, cultural and formal codes.
4/9 - 5/28/95	FACE OFF: THE PORTRAIT IN RECENT ART — An examination of new portraiture which manifests itself in untraditional ways that reflect both new art forms and social change, as seen in a fundamental shift from the traditional commissioned portrait. WT
5/7 - 6/11/95	MFA THESIS EXHIBITION
6/4 - 8/27/95	THE EVERYDAY WORLD: SELECTIONS FROM THE WEATHERSPOON COLLECTION — This exhibition looks at representations of daily life as part of the ongoing program of shows on the evolution of traditional categories of subject matter in the 20th century.

GREENVILLE

Greenville Museum of Art, Inc
802 Evans Street, **Greenville, NC 27834**
TEL: 919-758-1946
HRS: 10-4:30 T-F; 1-4 S   DAY CLOSED: Sa, SHOL: LEG/HOL!
ADM: F
HDC/ACC: Y   PARKING: Y   LIB: Y   GT: Y   GT/PH: !
PERM/COLL: AM: all media 20

Founded in 1939 as a WPA Gallery, the Greenville Museum of Art focuses primarily on the achievements of 20th century American art. Many North Carolina artists are represented in its collection which also includes works by George Bellows, Thomas Hart Benton, Robert Henri, Louise Nevelson, and George Segal, to name but a few. **NOT TO BE MISSED:** Major collection of Jugtown pottery.

ON EXHIBIT/95:

1/12 - 4/7/95	SELECTED WORKS FROM THE TRYON PALACE
4/13 - 5/28/95	LOUIS ORR: THE NORTH CAROLINA ETCHINGS
9/8 - 10/29/95	CLIFFORD SMITH: TEN YEARS OF LANDSCAPE PAINTING, 1986-1995
11/10 - 12/31/95	CLAUDE HOWELL: CAROLINA INTERPRETER

NORTH CAROLINA

GREENVILLE

Wellington B. Gray Gallery
Affiliate Institution: East Carolina University
Jenkins Fine Arts Center, **Greenville, NC 27858**
TEL: 919-757-6336
HRS: 10-5 M-W, F & Sa; 10-8 T   DAY CLOSED: S   HOL: LEG/HOL!
ADM: F
HDC/ACC: Y; Ramp, elevators   PARKING: Y; Limited metered   LIB: Y   S/G: Y
PERM/COLL: CONT

One of the largest contemporary art galleries in North Carolina. **NOT TO BE MISSED:** Print portfolio, Larry Rivers "The Boston Massacre"

ON EXHIBIT/95:

1/20 - 3/3/95	JANE HAMMOND — Paintings and Drawings - New York artist
	ANDERS KNUTTSON - TREE LIGHT — Luminescent paintings - New York artist
	YVES PAQUETTE - INSTALLATION — Large scale installation - Charlotte, NC artist
5/27/95	JOSEPH BUEYS: PRINTS DRAWINGS AND OBJECTS and JOSEPH BUEYS: A VIDEO PROGRAM
7/18 - 10/30/95	TRI-STATES SCULPTURE GUILD JAPANESE POSTER EXHIBITION: IMAGINATION OF LETTERS — Posters by leading Japanese designers
11/10 - 12/2/95	MEMORIES OF CHILDHOOD — Fifteen contemporary international artists respond to the theme of personal narratives in children's books.

HICKORY

The Hickory Museum of Art
243 Third Ave. NE, **Hickory, NC 28601**
TEL: 704-327-8576
HRS: 10-5 Tu-F; 1-4 Sa, S   DAY CLOSED: M   HOL: LEG/HOL!
ADM: F
HDC/ACC: Y   PARKING: Y   LIB: Y   MUS/SH: Y   GT: Y, call 704-327-8576 to reserve   H/B: Y
PERM/COLL: AM: all media 19, 20 ; ART POTTERY; AM: Impr

Located in one of Hickory's finest examples of neo-classic revival architecture, the museum is giving new life to the old Claremont Central High School, now renovated as the Arts and Science Center of Catawba Valley. **NOT TO BE MISSED:** William Merritt Chase painting (untitled)

ON EXHIBIT/95:

12/2/94 - 1/8/95	WORKS BY PAT VILES — Although other media will be displayed, this exhibition will emphasize the unique way the artist uses French dyes on silk, using different methods to create landscapes, still-lifes and abstracts.
12/2/94 - 1/8/95	NORTH CAROLINA INVITATIONAL

330

The Hickory Museum of Art - continued

3/1 - 3/31/95	JAMES MCNEIL WHISTLER: LITHOGRAPHS AND LITHOTINTS — One sees Whistler's interest in lithography as a reproductive tool and his excitement with the medium as a unique form of expression in the 20 works on view created between 1878-1896 in collaboration with the firm of Thomas Way. WT
4/2 - 4/30/95	PAUL WHITENER MEMORIAL SCHOOL ART SHOW
5/95 - 6/95	PAINTINGS BY ROBERT TYNES — A combination of abstract brushwork and trompe l'oeil illustration in which Tynes hopes to reflect a sense of the humor and mystery inherent in the nature of illusion, and in life itself.
6/28 - 8/19/95	HENLEY SOUTHEASTERN SPECTRUM — A juried show in conjunction with the Associated Artists of Winston Salem.
10/22 - 12/31/95	MINNIE REINHARDT: A RETROSPECTIVE — A self-taught artist who began to paint in 1975 at the age of 72, Reinhardt painted in the "primitive" style of Grandma Moses or Minnie Evans. Her husband made the frames for her paintings from rough lumber, carrying out the "country life" theme. WT
11/95-12/95	NORTH CAROLINA INVITATIONAL

NORTH WILKESBORO

Wilkes Art Gallery

800 Elizabeth Street, **North Wilkesboro, NC 28659**
TEL: 910-667-2841
HRS: 10-5 M-F; 12-4 Sa   DAY CLOSED: S   HOL: 1/1, EASTER, EASTER MONDAY, 7/4, 12/25
ADM: F
HDC/ACC: Y; Entrance ways & bathrooms   PARKING: Y   MUS/SH: Y, craft
PERM/COLL: REG & CONT: all media

This 80 year old neighborhood facility which was formerly the Black Cat Restaurant presents monthly changing exhibitions often featuring minority artists.

RALEIGH

North Carolina Museum of Art

2110 Blue Ridge Boulevard, **Raleigh, NC 27607**
TEL: 919-833-1935
HRS: 9-5 Tu-T, Sa; 9-9 F; 11-6 S   DAY CLOSED: M   HOL: LEG/HOL!
ADM: F   HDC/ACC: Y   PARKING: Y   LIB: Y   MUS/SH: Y
REST/FAC: Y; Cafe serves lunch daily & dinner Fri 5:30-8:45
GT: Y   GT/PH: call 919-833-1935   DT: Y   TIME: 1:30 daily
PERM/COLL: EU/OM: ptgs; AM: ptgs 19; ANCIENT ART; AF; REG; JEWISH CEREMONIAL ART

The Kress Foundation, in 1960, added to the museum's existing permanent collection of 139 prime examples of American and European artworks, a donation of 71 masterworks. This gift was second in scope and importance only to the Kress bequest to the National Gallery in Washington, D.C. **NOT TO BE MISSED:** Kress Collection

NORTH CAROLINA

North Carolina Museum of Art - continued

ON EXHIBIT/95:

10/15/94 - 2/12/95   NEW YORK, NEW YORK: RECENT CITYSCAPES — Four painters who live in New York (Martha Diamond, Jane Dickson, Yvonne Jacquette and David Kapp), work in distinctly different styles, have made Manhattan a central theme in their work, offering varying interpretations of a city famous for rewarding and abusing its inhabitants. CAT

1/28 - 4/16/95   DUTCH AND FLEMISH DRAWINGS FROM THE ROYAL LIBRARY, WINDSOR CASTLE — A splendid selection of drawings surveying the rich and varied legacy of Dutch and Flemish art from the 16th to the 19th centuries. Assembled from the incomparable collection of H. M. Queen Elizabeth II and exhibited together for the first time, the exhibition includes works by Anthony van Dyck, Peter Paul Rubens and others. CAT WT

3/4 - 7/9/95   THE FACE OF CHILDHOOD — An expressive group of children's drawings gathered by Dr. Robert Coles, renowned child psychiatrist and writer, explores the influences of personal experiences on a child's emotional and intellectual development. The children are of varied backgrounds from the US and other countries. CAT

6/17 - 8/27/95   PASSIONATE VISIONS OF THE AMERICAN SOUTH: SELF TAUGHT ARTISTS FROM 1940 TO THE PRESENT — Bright paintings on cardboard, chunky stone carvings and chain saw sculpture are among the more than 200 "folk art" works by 80 self taught artists. The show is organized into six thematic areas: autobiography, daily life, religion, pop culture, patriotism, and nature. CAT WT

RALEIGH

North Carolina State University Visual Arts Center

Cates Ave.-Room 4110-University Student Center, **Raleigh, NC 27695**
TEL: 919-515-3503
HRS: 12-8 Tu-F; 2-8 Sa, S   DAY CLOSED: M   HOL: ACAD!
ADM: F   HDC/ACC: Y   PARKING: Y   LIB: Y   REST/FAC: Y
PERM/COLL: AM: cont, dec/art, phot

The Center hosts exhibitions of contemporary arts and design of regional and national significance and houses research collections of photography, ceramics and textiles.

ON EXHIBIT/95:

2/16 - 7/8/95   A MULTITUDE OF MEMORY: THE LIFE WORK OF ANNIE HOOPER

3/9 - mid-May   METALWORK BY MARY ANN SCHEER AND SYDNEY SCHEER

TARBORO

Blount Bridgers House/Hobson Pittman Memorial Gallery

130 Bridgers Street, **Tarboro, NC 27886**
TEL: 919-823-4159
HRS: 10-4 M-F; 2-4 S (Jan-May); 10-4 M-F; 2-4 Sa, S (Apr-Dec)   HOL: LEG/HOL!
ADM: Y   ADULT: $2.00
HDC/ACC: Y   PARKING: Y; Street   LIB: Y   GT: Y   GT/PH: call 919-823-4159   H/B: Y
PERM/COLL: AM: 20; DEC/ART

In a beautiful North Carolina town, the 1808 Plantation House and former home of Thomas Blount houses decorative arts of the 19th Century and the Hobson Pittman (American, 1899-1972) Collections of paintings and memorabilia. **NOT TO BE MISSED:** "The Roses," oil, by Hobson Pittman

NORTH CAROLINA

WILMINGTON

St. John's Museum of Art
114 Orange Street, **Wilmington, NC 28401**
TEL: 910-763-0281
HRS: 10-5 Tu-Sa; 12-4 S   DAY CLOSED: M   HOL: LEG/HOL!
VOL/CONT: Y   ADM: Y   ADULT: $2.00   CHILDREN: $1.00 under 18
HDC/ACC: Y; Ramp, elevators   PARKING: Y   MUS/SH: Y   H/B: Y
PERM/COLL: AM: ptgs, sculp

Housed in three architecturally distinctive buildings dating back to 1804, the museum is the primary visual arts center in Southeastern North Carolina. **NOT TO BE MISSED:** Mary Cassatt color prints

ON EXHIBIT/95:

11/10/94 - 2/26/95	JAMES MCNEILL WHISTLER: LITHOGRAPHS AND LITHOTINTS — One sees Whistler's interest in lithography as a reproductive tool and his excitement with the medium as a unique form of expression in the 20 works on view created between 1878-1896 in collaboration with the firm of Thomas Way. WT
1/12 - 3/5/95	DALE CHIHULY: FORM FROM FIRE — Works by America's foremost studio glass artist who studied with North Carolina artist Harvey Littleton. WT
1/12 - 3/5	VITREOGRAPHS FROM THE HARVEY LITTLETON STUDIO — Examples of this medium invented by Harvey Littleton will be on view.
3/7 - 5/28	CLAUDE HOWELL: CAROLINA INTERPRETER — Paintings, drawings and prints comprehensively representing the 60 year artistic career of this important North Carolina artist. WT
6/15 - 9/3	MARTIN JOHNSON HEADE: THE FLORAL AND HUMMINGBIRD STUDIES FROM THE ST. AUGUSTINE HISTORICAL SOCIETY — Newly conserved oil "sketches" by the 19th century American artist will be shown publicly to American audiences for the first time . WT
6/15 - 9/3	MINNIE EVANS: ARTIST — An in-depth examination of the work of this self-taught North Carolina Artist (1892-1987). WT

WINSTON-SALEM

Reynolda House, Museum of American Art
Reynolda Road, **Winston-Salem, NC 27106**
TEL: 910-725-5325
HRS: 9:30-4:30 Tu-Sa; 1:30-4:30 S   DAY CLOSED: M   HOL: 1/1, THGV, 12/25
ADM: Y   ADULT: $6.00   STUDENTS: $3.00   SR CIT: $5.00
HDC/ACC: Y   PARKING: Y   LIB: Y!   MUS/SH: Y   GT: Y   GT/PH: !   H/B: Y
PERM/COLL: AM: ptgs 18-present; HUDSON RIVER SCHOOL; DOUGHTY BIRDS

Reynolda House, an historic home designed by Charles Barton Keen, was built between 1914 and 1917 by Richard Joshua Reynolds, founder of R. J. Reynolds Tobacco Company, and his wife, Katherine Smith Reynolds.

ON EXHIBIT/95:

3/94 - 3/95	GEORGE CATLIN

333

NORTH CAROLINA

WINSTON-SALEM

The Southeastern Center for Contemporary Art
750 Marguerite Drive, **Winston-Salem, NC 27106**
TEL: 919-725-1904
HRS: 10-5 Tu-Sa; 2-5 S   DAY CLOSED: M   HOL: LEG/HOL!
ADM: Y   ADULT: $3.00   CHILDREN: F (under 12)   STUDENTS: $2.00   SR CIT: $2.00
HDC/ACC: Y; Main floor in the galleries only. Not accessible to 2nd floor   PARKING: Y; Free   LIB: Y
MUS/SH: Y GT: Y   GT/PH: call 919-725-1904 to reserve   H/B: Y   S/G: Y
PERM/COLL: Non-collecting institution

Outstanding contemporary art being produced throughout the nation is showcased at the Southeastern Center for Contemporary Art, a cultural resource for the community and its visitors.

GRAND FORKS

North Dakota Museum of Art
Affiliate Institution: University of North Dakota
Centennial Drive, **Grand Forks, ND 58202**
TEL: 701-777-4195
HRS: 9-5, M-W, F; 1-5, Sa, S; 12-9, T Sept-May   HOL: THGV, 12/25
ADM: F
HDC/ACC: Y   PARKING: Y; Metered on street   MUS/SH: Y
REST/FAC: Y; Coffee bar   GT: Y   GT/PH: !
H/B: Y   S/G: Y; in progress
PERM/COLL: CONT: Nat/Am; CONT: reg ptgs, sculp; REG HIST (not always on display)

In ARTPAPER 1991 Patrice Clark Koelsch said of this museum "In the sparsely populated state that was the very last of all the US to build an art museum, ...(The North Dakota Museum of Art) is a jewel of a museum that presents serious contemporary art, produces shows that travel internationally, and succeeds in engaging the plain people of North Dakota." **NOT TO BE MISSED:** Collection of paintings on paper by Winnipeg artist: The work is autobiographical and includes script and image; the subject is child abuse.

OHIO

AKRON

Akron Art Museum
70 East Market Street, **Akron, OH 44308-2084**
TEL: 216-376-9185
HRS: 11-5 Tu-F; 10-5 Sa; 12-5 S   DAY CLOSED: M   HOL: LEG/HOL!
ADM: F   HDC/ACC: Y   PARKING: Y; Free   LIB: Y   GT: Y   GT/PH: call 216-376-9185
H/B: Y; 1899 Italian Renaissance Revival structure, listed NRHP   S/G: Y
PERM/COLL: EDWIN C. SHAW COLLECTION; AM: ptgs, sculp, phot 20

Three new regional, national, or international temporary exhibitions are presented every 10 weeks at the Akron, the only modern art museum serving the region between New York and Chicago. **NOT TO BE MISSED:** Claus Oldenberg's "Soft Inverted Q," 1976; The Mayers Sculpture Courtyard

ON EXHIBIT/95:

11/19/94 - 1/15/95	THE CAMERA I: THE AUDREY AND SIDNEY IRMAS COLLECTION OF PHOTOGRAPHIC SELF-PORTRAITS — A definitive survey of self-portraits by European and American photographers from 1850 to the present, this collection of 136 works is a "who's who" of photography's major figures.
1/28 - 3/26/95	HEAD, HEART AND HAND: ELBERT HUBBARD AND THE ROYCROFTERS — 150 examples of furniture, metalwork, leathergoods, and finely printed books and magazines examine the production and philosophies behind the turn-of-the-century community in East Aurora, New York modeled on the medieval guild system which had been revived by William Morris in England. CAT WT
4/8 - 5/4/95	DRIVEN TO CREATE: THE ANTHONY J. PETULLO COLLECTION OF SELF-TAUGHT AND OUTSIDER ART — Paintings and works on paper by the most significant self-trained and outsider artists from the 1920's to the present, in Europe, Canada and the United States. WT

ATHENS

Teisolini Gallery of Ohio University
Affiliate Institution: Ohio University
48 East Union Street, **Athens, OH 45701**
TEL: 614-593-1305
HRS: 12-4 M-Sa   DAY CLOSED: S   HOL: LEG/HOL!
ADM: F   PARKING: Y   GT: Y   GT/PH: call 614-593-1304   H/B: Y
PERM/COLL: GR: 20; NAT/AM; AF; textiles, jewelry

The mid 19th century former home of the Ohio University President is now home to this Gallery which houses the Southwest Native American collection of Edwin L. and Ruth E. Kennedy.

CANTON

The Canton Art Institute
1001 Market Ave., **Canton, OH 44702**
TEL: 216-453-7666
HRS: 10-5 & 7-9 Tu-T; 10-5 F, Sa; 1-5 S   DAY CLOSED: M   HOL: 1/1, THGV, 12/25
ADM: F   HDC/ACC: Y   PARKING: Y   LIB: Y   MUS/SH: Y   GT: Y   GT/PH: call 216-453-7666   S/G: Y
PERM/COLL: WORKS ON PAPER; AM & EU: ptgs 19-20; CER: after 1950

336

The Canton Art Institute - continued

Located in Cultural Center for the Arts, the Canton Art Institute is the only visual arts museum in Stark County. A mix of permanent and traveling exhibitions creates a showcase for a spectrum of visual art. **NOT TO BE MISSED:** Painting by Frank Duveneck "Canal Scene with Washer Women, Venice"

ON EXHIBIT/95:

11/25/94 - 1/29/95	GEORGE LUKS: EXPRESSIONIST MASTER OF COLOR
11/25/94 - 3/5/95	SCIENCE FICTION ART

CINCINNATI

The Contemporary Arts Center
115 E. 5th St., **Cincinnati OH 45202-3998**
TEL: 513-721-0390
HRS: 10-5 M, Tu, T-Sa   DAY CLOSED: W, S   HOL: LEG/HOL!
F/DAY: M   ADM: Y   ADULT: $2.00   CHILDREN: F (under 12)   STUDENTS: $1.00   SR CIT: $1.00
HDC/ACC: Y   PARKING: Y; Pay garage 1 block away under Fountain Square   LIB: Y   MUS/SH: Y
GT: Y   DT: Y
PERM/COLL: NONE

Contemporary art in all media including video is presented in this 50 year old museum.

ON EXHIBIT/95:

11/12/94 - 1/8/95	HORIZONS: THE ART OF HEALING
11/14/94 - 1/13/95	LIGHT INTO ART
11/19/94-1/15/95	PIETER LAURENS MOLE
11/19/94 - 1/8/95	ELIZABETH FERGUS-JEAM
11/29/94 - 1/13/95	LYNN HERSHMAN
1/23 - 4/9/95	DAVID HUMPHREY
1/28 - 4/2/95	CARRIE MAE WEEMS
1/14 - 3/5/95	HORIZONS: PAT RENICK
1/23 - 3/12/95	PAUL GIABICKI
3/14 - 5/15/95	HORIZONS: DIANE SAMUELS
3/15 - 4/9/95	ANDRES TAPIA-URZUS
4/22 - 6/25/95	ASHLEY BICKERTON
4/22 - 6/4/95	BILL VIOLA
5/22 - 7/24/95	HORIZONS: MARTIN BECK AND HANNELINE ROGEBERG
7/8 - 9/6/95	JIM NUTT — The first major retrospective of his work in 20 years. Nutt is known as the originator of the Chicago Imagism movement of the 60's and 70's which influenced a generation of artists.
7/8 - 9/6/95	WINIFRED LUTZ
7/21 - 9/6/95	REGIONAL VIDEO SALON

OHIO

CINCINNATI

Cincinnati Art Museum
Eden Park, Cincinnati, OH 45202-1596
TEL: 513-721-5204
HRS: 10-5 Tu-Sa; 11-5 S; 11-5 Hol!   DAY CLOSED: M   HOL: LEG/HOL!
F/DAY: Sa   ADM: Y   ADULT: $5.00   CHILDREN: F (under 18)   STUDENTS: $4.00   SR CIT: $4.00
HDC/ACC: Y   PARKING: Y; Free   LIB: Y   MUS/SH: Y   REST/FAC: Y
GT: Y   GT/PH: call 513-721-5204   S/G: Y
PERM/COLL: AS; AF; NAT/AM: costumes, textiles; AM & EU: ptgs, dec/art, gr, drgs, phot

One of the oldest museums west of the Alleghenies, The Cincinnati Art Museum's collection includes the visual arts of the past 5,000 years of almost every major civilization in the world. **NOT TO BE MISSED:** "Undergrowth with Two Figures," Vincent van Gogh, 1890

ON EXHIBIT/95:

10/22/94 - 1/16/95	NEW ART 3: CHRISTIAN BOLTANSKI — One of the large group of artists whose work is considered "photo based" yet is not viewed as a photographer, Boltanski's works border on installation art. His mixed media installations reflect on themes such as childhood innocence and the inevitability of death.
9/1/94 - 1/29/95	THE QUEST FOR QUALITY — As a salute to the retiring Director this exhibition highlights acquisitions made during his 20 year tenure.
10/1/94 - 3/5/95	EDWARD POTTHAST, 1857-1927 — Eight paintings from the collection by this Cincinnati born artist will be on exhibit.
11/20/94 - 3/5/95	MANET TO TOULOUSE-LAUTREC: FRENCH IMPRESSIONIST TO POST IMPRESSIONIST PRINTS AND DRAWINGS — Featured are 125 works from the collection and local private collections created from 1860-1900.
10/8/94 - 4/9/95	RICHARD BITTING: NINE SUMMER HAIKU — This is one of two exhibitions that are a tribute to the 100th anniversary of the Cincinnati Symphony Orchestra. The nine color lithographs contain music and text transformed in designs clearly inspired by the clean brushstrokes of Oriental characters.
11/13/94 - 5/14/95	LITHOGRAPHS OF SHINODA TOKO (b.1913) — Most of these lithographs have never been shown before and all are from the permanent collection.
2/12 - 6/4/95	SINGING THE CLAY: PUEBLO POTTERY OF THE SOUTHWEST YESTERDAY AND TODAY — Each of the Native American Pueblos of the Southwest is known for its own traditional style of pottery: the use of materials, designs, vessel forms, and methods of firing all define a specific Pueblo's traditional style. This exhibition will include approximately 110 examples from 11 different Pueblos. CAT
2/25 - 7/23/95	THE DAWN OF ENGRAVING: MASTERPIECES FROM THE 15TH CENTURY — 15th century prints were a passion with collector Herbert Greer French. Works by Martin Schongauer, Andrea Mantegna, Albrecht Durer and others are among those bequeathed to the Museum and selected for this exhibition.
3/4 - 7/30/95	ALL THE WORLD ARRAYED — An exhibition of ethnic dress and dolls attired in traditional dress celebrating the 50th anniversary of the UN.
3/11 - 9/4/95	BARNETT AND CHIDLAW: THE ART ACADEMY OF CINCINNATI AND MODERNISM — These well respected teachers at the Art Academy of Cincinnati were credited with bringing Modernism to the school when it was still steeped in traditional styles and techniques.
4/15 - 10/8/95	ROMAS VIESULAS: NOTES ON SOUND — In the second tribute to the Cincinnati Orchestra's centennial season these twelve inkless reliefs created in Rome in 1964-65 will be presented.

338

Cincinnati Art Museum - continued

4/7 - 7/16/95   NEW ART 4: RONA PONDICK — The artist is among a group, male and female, that are mining the figure, often in a fragmented state, for new meaning. All of the sculptures are composed of body parts or furniture associated with the body.

7/30 - 10/1/95   ROOTS IN HARLEM: PHOTOGRAPHS BY JAMES VAN DER ZEE — Recognized as the dean of African-American photographers, the career of James Van Der Zee (1886-1983) spanned 60 years, over fifty spent in Harlem. The exhibition includes works from the artist's little known early period in Tidewater, Virginia from 1907-1909 as well as his portraits of notable African-Americans completed in the 1980's.   WT

CINCINNATI

The Taft Museum
316 Pike Street, Cincinnati, OH 45202
TEL: 513-241-0393
HRS: 10-5 M-Sa; 1-5 S & Hol! HOL: 1/1, THGV, 12/25
ADM: Y ADULT: $3.00 CHILDREN: F (under 12) STUDENTS: $1.00 SR CIT: $1.00
HDC/ACC: Y PARKING: Y; Limited free parking LIB: Y MUS/SH: Y
GT: Y GT/PH: call 513-241-0343 H/B: Y S/G:
PERM/COLL: PTGS; CH: Kangzi-period cer; FR/REN: Limoges enamels; EU & AM: furniture 19

Collections include masterpieces by Rembrandt, Hals, Gainsborough, Turner and Corot, arranged within the intimate atmosphere of the 1820 Baum-Taft house, a restored Federal-period residence. **NOT TO BE MISSED:** French Gothic ivory Virgin and Child from the Abbey Church of St. Denis, ca. 1260.

ON EXHIBIT/95:
12/2/94 - 1/29/95   AMERICAN EXPATRIATE PAINTERS

11/25/94 - 1/8/95   TAFT HOLIDAY DISPLAY

2/10 - 2/26/95   ARTISTS REACHING CLASSROOMS: STUDENT ART

3/10 - 5/28/95   CHINESE SNUFFBOTTLES FROM THE PAMELA R. LESSING FRIEDMAN COLLECTION   WT

6/16 - 8/20/95   LIFE LINES: AMERICAN MASTER DRAWING, 1788-1962, FROM THE MUNSON, WILLIAMS PROCTOR MUSEUM

9/15 - 11/19/95   LIFTING THE VEIL: ROBERT S. DUNCANSON AND THE EMERGENCE OF THE AFRICAN-AMERICAN ARTIST

CLEVELAND

The Cleveland Museum of Art
11150 East Blvd, Cleveland, OH 44106
TEL: 216-416-7340
HRS: 10-5:45 Tu-T, F; 10-9:45 W; 9-4:45 Sa; 1-5:45 S DAY CLOSED: M HOL: 1/1, 7/4, THGV, 12/25
ADM: F HDC/ACC: Y PARKING: Y; Pay LIB: Y! MUS/SH: Y REST/FAC: Y
GT: Y GT/PH: ! DT: Y TIME: ! H/B: Y S/G: Y
PERM/COLL: ANCIENT: Med, Egt, Gr, R; EU; AM; AF; P/COL; OR

OHIO

The Cleveland Museum of Art - continued

One of the world's major art museums, The Cleveland Museum of Art is located in the University Circle area of Cleveland, the largest concentration of cultural, educational and medical institutions in the nation. A portion of the museum includes a wing designed in 1970 by Marcel Breuer. **NOT TO BE MISSED:** Guelph Treasure, especially the Portable Altar of Countess Gertrude (Germany, Lower Saxony, Brunswick, c 1040; gold, red porphyry, cloisonne, enamel, niello, gems, glass, pearls.

ON EXHIBIT/95:

10/18/94 - 2/19/95	FROM HAND TO MOUTH: A HISTORY OF FLATWARE — Chronicling the development of the knife, fork and spoon from antiquity to the 20th century, this exhibition will include a few rare examples from the late Roman/early Byzantine period.
11/23/94 - 1/8/95	ALL THAT GLITTERS; GREAT SILVER VESSELS IN CLEVELAND'S COLLECTION — On exhibit will be works dating from 1000 BC to the early 20th century. Silversmiths and firms represented by American, English and European pieces include Nathaniel Hurd, Tiffany and Co., Paul Storr, Liberty and Co., and the Firm of Carl Faberge. Results of technical examinations by the conservation department including x-rays, metal analyses, and diagrams of the construction of certain vessels will be on view nearby.
12/2/94 - 1/22/95	ANDREW BOROWIEC PHOTOGRAPHS: AFTER THE DELUGE — Poignant large scale black and white images of the Mississippi flood plain in 1993 just as the waters were beginning to recede will be on view.
12/13/94 - 3/12/95	SANDY WALKER: WOODBLOCK PRINTS — Among the boldest and most powerful of contemporary works on paper, these very large prints exploit black-white drama, and hover betweeen abstraction and representation. WT
12/13/94 - 3/12/95	FRENCH DRAWINGS FROM THE COLLECTION — Portraits, landscapes, genre scenes, sketches, watercolors and charcoals are included with works by Watteau, Bocher, Degas, Renoir, Picasso and Matisse.
1/27 - 4/2/95	ALBERT CHONG PHOTOGRAPHS — A survey of works from the late 1980's to the present, many of which are drawn from his "Ancestral Throne" series, in which the artist embellished found wooden chairs, transforming them into altars and shrines and then photographed them.
2/15 - 4/23/95	A PASSION FOR ANTIQUITIES: ANCIENT ART FROM THE COLLECTION OF BARBARA AND LAWRENCE FLEISCHMAN — For the first time ever, 200 works from this magnificent collection will be on public view. Among the many remarkable sculptures, wall paintings, terracotta vases and jewelry will be treasures that include the head of a large Cycladic idol (2500 B.C.), a 4th century Macedonian grave stele, a rare South Italian vase, and a late Helenistic bronze vessel containing relief decoration and silver inlay. CAT WT
4/7 - 6/4/95	SHELBY LEE ADAMS: APPALACHIAN PORTRAITS — Remarkable, evocative portraits of isolated people in eastern Kentucky who have been removed from the mainstream of American culture.
5/31 - 7/16/95	VISIONS OF LOVE AND LIFE: ENGLISH PRE-RAPHAELITE ART FROM THE BIRMINGHAM COLLECTION — 100 works of painting, drawings, sculpture and stained glass from the world's largest Pre-Raphaelite collection at the Birmingham (England) Museum and Art Gallery. The vision of these artists was completely romantic, replete with intense emotion, spirituality, and poetic symbolism. WT
5/9 - 8/13/95	ROSAMOND WOLFF PURCELL: COLOR PHOTOGRAPHS — This artist is known for her luminous, strangely beautiful pictures of specimens gathered by collectors over the centuries and for the disquieting, layered effects she achieves by using reflective or translucent surfaces.
5/14 - 8/13/95	FOCUS: FIBER — An annual juried exhibition of works by members of The Textile Art Alliance, Cleveland encompassing many fiber techniques.

The Cleveland Museum of Art - continued

8/2 - 9/24/95	ELVIS + MARILYN: 2 x IMMORTAL — The first major museum exhibition to examine the impact and explore, compare and contrast the power of these two quintessentially American icons. More than 100 works by such artists as Robert Rauschenberg, Robert Arneson, Andy Warhol, Audrey Flack and Alexis Smith are included. This Cleveland venue coincides with the opening of the Rock and Roll Hall of Fame. WT
8/18 - 11/12/95	RALPH BURNS PHOTOGRAPHS: GRACELAND — For 17 years this artist has traveled to Memphis for the anniversaries of Elvis Presley's birth and death to interview and photograph fans recording with equal immediacy their moments of reverence and exuberent impersonation. Six of his works are in "Elvis + Marilyn," in addition to about 20 in this complementary show.
11/15/95 - 1/7/96	AFRICAN ZION: THE SACRED ART OF ETHIOPIA — Some of the finest surviving examples of religious art from the foremost collections all over the world trace the religious history of the Christian kingdom of Ethiopia. These sacred masterpieces include icons, illuminated manuscripts, and metalwork in silver and gold from the 4th through the 18th centuries. WT
11/17/95 - 1/7/96	TOSHIO SHIBATA: LANDSCAPE PHOTOGRAPHS — These photographs are done with a large-format camera mainly of public works designed to control water and erosion. The artist records these constructed structures for their formal qualities, and their strict geometry dramatically contrasting with the water and land around them.
11/21/95 - 1/21/96	POUSSIN DRAWINGS FROM WINDSOR — The Royal collection at Windsor Castle is lending 65 works for this exhibition of the most important French artist of the 17th century. The show includes preliminary sketches as well as fully finished compositions. WT

COLUMBUS

Columbus Museum of Art

480 East Broad Street, **Columbus, OH 43215**
TEL: 614-221-4848
HRS: 11-4 Tu-F; 10-5 Sa; 11-5 S   DAY CLOSED: M   HOL: LEG/HOL!
ADM: F   HDC/ACC: Y   PARKING: Y; Free   LIB: Y   MUS/SH: Y   REST/FAC: Y
GT: Y   GT/PH: call 614-221-6801 to reserve   H/B: Y   S/G: Y
PERM/COLL: EU & AM: ptgs 20

Located in a 1931 Italian Renaissance style building, this museum houses the largest single collection of George Bellows paintings.

ON EXHIBIT/95:

10/16/94 - 1/8/95	LANDSCAPE AS METAPHOR — An exhibition of commissioned works by 13 American artists that illustrates how the persistent subject of landscape in the history of art has gained new vitality today. Adm: Adults $4.75; Children, Students and Sr Cit $2.50
2/19 - 4/16/95	WEAVING A LEGACY: 19TH CENTURY AMERICAN COVERLETS FROM THE STUCK COLLECTION — Major weavers from 1820-1880 in Ohio and the Midwest region are represented in selections from this large and comprehensive collection. This was the period of greatest popularity and production of decorative loom-woven bedcoverings. Adm: Adults $4.75; Children, Students and Seniors $2.50
4/2 - 5/24/95	IN THE SPIRIT OF THE CLOTH — A quilt exhibition by The Women of Color Quilt Network

OHIO

Columbus Museum of Art - continued

4/16 - 6/18/95   CARTE BLANCHE: COLUMBUS ART LEAGUE INVITATIONAL — Adm: Adults
                     $3.00, Children, Students and Seniors $1.00

5/6 - 6/18/95   GEORGE LUKS: EXPRESSIONIST MASTER OF COLOR - THE WATERCOLORS
                     REDISCOVERED — A member of both The Eight and The Ashcan School, Luks is less
                     well known for his works in watercolor, which present a broad and colorful overview of
                     his style and true zest for life. Adm: Adults 4.75; Children, Students and Sr Cit $2.50
                                                                                              WT

5/7 - 7/2/95   REORDERING REALITY: PRECISIONIST DIRECTIONS IN AMERICAN ART —
                     American Modernist works by artists such as Charles Sheeler, Georgia O'Keeffe, Charles
                     Demuth and Preston Dickinson depict in precise line, flat color and clearly defined pattern
                     the skyscrapers, factories and bridges of the Machine Age of the 1920's to the end of
                     World War II. Adm: Adults $4.75; Children, Students and Seniors $2.50
                                                                                     CAT   WT

COLUMBUS

The Schumacher Gallery
Affiliate Institution: Capital University
2199 East Main Street, **Columbus, OH 43209**
TEL: 614-236-6319
HRS: 1-5 M-F; 2-5 Sa, S; Closed May through August   HOL: LEG/HOL!; ACAD!
ADM: F
HDC/ACC: Y   PARKING: Y   LIB: Y   MUS/SH: Y
GT: Y   GT/PH: call 614-236-6319
PERM/COLL: ETH; AS; REG; CONT; PTGS, SCULP, GR 16-19

In addition to its diverse 4,000 object collection, the gallery, located on the 4th floor of the
University's library building, hosts exhibitions which bring to the area artworks of historical and
contemporary significance.

ON EXHIBIT/95:
1/10 - 1/29/95   L'HAYIM (TO LIFE): WORKS BY ALFRED TIBOR — Selected sculptures reflecting
                     themes of humanity and the celebration of life.

2/3 - 2/23/95   A SONG OF THE ROLLING EARTH: PAINTINGS BY MICHAEL MCEWEN —
                     Evocative color harmonies, expressive brushwork, and a command of nuances of light
                     distinguish this artist's work.

2/12 - 4/9/95   THE LITURGICAL ART GUILD OF OHIO BIENNIAL EXHIBITION — A juried
                     exhibition of liturgical, religious and spiritual works by noted regional artists.

4/20 - 5/2/95   CAPITOL UNIVERSITY STUDENT ART EXHIBIT

COLUMBUS

Wexner Center for the Arts
Affiliate Institution: The Ohio State University
North High Street at 15th Avenue, **Columbus, OH 43210-1393**
TEL: 614-292-0330
HRS: 10-6 Tu, T, F; 10-8 W & Sa; 12-5 S   DAY CLOSED: M   HOL: LEG/HOL!
ADM: F   HDC/ACC: Y   PARKING: Y   LIB: Y   MUS/SH: Y   REST/FAC: Y
GT: Y   GT/PH: call 292-0330   DT: Y   TIME: 1:00 T & Sa   H/B: Y
PERM/COLL: ART OF THE 70's

Located on the campus of The Ohio State University, in the first public building designed by theoretician Peter Eisenman, the Wexner is a multi-disciplinary contemporary arts center dedicated to the visual, performing and media arts.

ON EXHIBIT/95:

1/7 - 3/26/95	ROBERT FRANK: THE AMERICANS — In 1955 Mr. Frank set off cross-country and produced this landmark body of photographs. This is first 84-image exhibition of the entire series. Concurrent with the exhibition, the artist's work in film will also be shown. WT
1/28 - 4/9/95	CHRIS MARKER: SILENT MOVIE — Marker is a close contemporary of Robert Frank and is regarded as one of the cinema's greatest living filmmakers. This is the first installation he has produced for an American institution.
	ALBERT OEHLEN AND CHRISTOPHER WILLIAMS — This first major exhibition by either artist in this country examines the inter-relation-ships of their very different work. CAT
4/14 - 5/11/95	FRAMED ENVIRONMENTAL: TWO VIDEO INSTALLATIONS BY BRUCE AND NORMAN YONEMOTO — These widely recognized video artists study, in a highly personalized and incisive fashion, American culture in the 1950's – particularly the rolling beneath the surface of the proverbial melting pot.
5/6 - 8/13/95	REM KOOLHAAS AND THE PLACE OF PUBLIC ARCHITECTURE — Featured are five projects – a museum, university building, convention center, library and "center for the study of media" – along with urban designs for Melun-Senant and Lille and for Yokohama, Japan. CAT
	LAURA LISBON AND CLAUDIA MATZKO — These two younger artists, one a sculptor and the other a painter, are fascinated with perception and their common interests in material manipulations and language used as a visual and conceptual foil.
7/1 - 8/27	A POSTCOLONIAL KINDERHOOD: INSTALLATION BY ELAINE REICHEK — This sculptor and installation artist draws on personal memories to address the issue of marginalization within American society.

DAYTON

The Dayton Art Institute
456 Belmonte Park North, **Dayton, OH 45405**
TEL: 513-223-5277
HRS: 9-5 daily   DAY CLOSED: M   HOL: 12/25
ADM: F   HDC/ACC: Y   PARKING: Y   LIB: Y   MUS/SH: Y
GT: Y   GT/PH: call 513-223-5277   H/B: Y   S/G: Y
PERM/COLL: AM; EU; AS; OCEANIC; AF; CONT

OHIO

The Dayton Art Institute - continued

The Dayton Art Institute is located at the corner of Riverview Avenue and Belmonte Park North in a Edward B. Green designed Italian Renaissance style building built in 1930. The 1982 Propylaeum (entry) was designed by Levin Porter Smith, Inc . **NOT TO BE MISSED:** "Water Lilies," by Monet; "Two Study Heads of an Old Man" by Rubens; "St. Catherine of Alexandria in Prison," by Preti; "High Noon," by Hopper

ON EXHIBIT/95:

11/18/94 - 2/26/95	GIFTS TO HONOR THE DAYTON ART INSTITUTE'S 75TH ANNIVERSARY — Highlighting gifts to the permanent collection in honor of this anniversary, the exhibition also features furniture which originated in Ohio and Kentucky communities.
3/18 - 6/11/95	THE SOUL UNBOUND: PHOTOGRAPHS BY JANE REECE (1868-1961) — Some 250 most important and representative works by this outstanding photographer, known for her romanticized portraits and her soft-focused Pictorialist style will be on view.
9/30 - 12/3/95	FROM BOTTICELLI TO TIEPOLO: THREE CENTURIES OF ITALIAN PAINTING FROM BOB JONES UNIVERSITY (dates TENT!) — A survey of paintings from Italy from 1500 to 1750 will be shown. This collection has only been seen three times before outside of it's home in South Carolina. Works included are by Titian, Granacci, Tintoretto, Ribera and Reni. WT
12/16/95 - 2/25/96	ERNEST I. BLUMENSCHEIN RETROSPECTIVE — An exciting array of landscapes, portraits and genre scenes of the Southwest by one of the most talented artists who worked in Taos, New Mexico in the early part of the century.

DAYTON

Wright State University Galleries
Affiliate Institution: Wright State University
Colonel Glenn Highway, **Dayton, OH 45435**
TEL: 513-873-2978
HRS: 10-4 Tu-F; 12-5 Sa, S   HOL: ACAD!
ADM: F
HDC/ACC: Y   PARKING: Y
PERM/COLL: PTGS, WORKS ON PAPER, SCULP 20

A subsidiary of the Dayton Art Institute, the Museum is located on the Wright State University campus. **NOT TO BE MISSED:** Aimee Rankin Morgana's "The Dream," 1988

ON EXHIBIT/95:

1/2 - 1/29/95	PERPETRATORS — An exhibition that critically examines the men behind the Nazi war machine. Original prints by Sid Chafetz.
2/12 - 3/19/95	URBAN LANDSCAPE — Painters Rackstraw Downes, John Moore and others pursue their view of the urban landscape through observation, drawing, memory, etc. and finally through pigment.
4/2 - 5/14/95	WOMEN: RITES OF PASSAGE — The work of a number of artists who have chosen to make life events shared by other women the subject of their work.

344

GRANVILLE

Denison University Gallery
Burke Hall of Music & Art, **Granville, OH 43023**
TEL: 614-587-6255
HRS: 10:00-4 M-Sa; 1-4 S early Sep-early May   HOL: ACAD!
ADM: F   HDC/ACC: Y; Includes parking on ground level   PARKING: Y
PERM/COLL: BURMESE & SE/ASIAN; EU & AM: 19; NAT/AM

Located on the Denison University Campus.

ON EXHIBIT/95:

1/13 - 2/16/95	PROFESSORS' CHOICE — Work in all media selected by the studio art faculty
2/24 - 4/14/95	CONTEMPORARY PAINTING EXHIBITION
4/21 - 5/7/95	SENIOR STUDENT EXHIBITION

KENT

Kent State University Art Galleries
Affiliate Institution: Kent State University
Kent State University, School of Art, **Kent, OH 44242**
TEL: 216-672-7853
HRS: 10-4 M-F; 2-5 S   DAY CLOSED: Sa   HOL: ACAD!
ADM: F   HDC/ACC: Y   MUS/SH: Y   GT: Y   GT/PH: call 216-672-7853 for specifics
PERM/COLL: GR & PTGS: Michener coll; IGE COLL: Olson photographs; GROPPER PRINTS: (political prints)

Operated by the School of Art Gallery at Kent State University since its establishment in 1972, the gallery consists of two exhibition spaces both exhibiting Western and non-Western 20th century art and craft.

ON EXHIBIT/95:
MAIN GALLERY:

1/21 - 2/3/95	SCHOLASTIC ART
2/22 - 3/17/95	STUDENT ANNUAL
4/5 - 4/28/95	JURIED INSTALLATION BY OUTSTANDING OHIO ARTIST

LAKEWOOD

Beck Center for the Cultural Arts
17801 Detroit Ave, **Lakewood, OH 44107**
TEL: 216-521-2540
HRS: 2-5 M, W-S   DAY CLOSED: Tu   HOL: LEG/HOL!
ADM: F   HDC/ACC: Y   PARKING: Y; Free
PERM/COLL: KENNETH BECK WATERCOLORS

The largest cultural arts center in Ohio.

OHIO

OBERLIN

Allen Memorial Art Museum
Affiliate Institution: Oberlin College
87 North Main Street, **Oberlin, OH 44074**
TEL: 216-775-8665
HRS: 10-5 Tu-Sa; 1-5 S   DAY CLOSED: M   HOL: LEG/HOL!
ADM: F   HDC/ACC: Y; Through courtyard entrance   PARKING: Y; Free   LIB: Y   MUS/SH: Y
GT: Y   GT/PH: call 216-775-8665 for specifics   H/B: Y   S/G: Y
PERM/COLL: DU & FL: ptgs; CONT/AM: gr; JAP: gr; ISLAMIC: carpets

Long ranked as one of the finest college or university art collections in the nation, the Allen continues to grow in size and distinction. The museum's landmark building designed by Cass Gilbert was opened in 1917. The Weitzheimer/Johnson House, one of Frank Lloyd Wright's Usonian designs, was recently opened. It is open on the first Sunday and third Saturday of the month from 1-5pm with tours on the hour. Admission is $5.00 pp with tickets available at the Museum. Group tours call Fridays at 216-775-8665. **NOT TO BE MISSED:** Hendrick Terbrugghen's "St. Sebastian Attended by St. Irene," 1625

ON EXHIBIT/95:

1/31 - 4/2/95	MEDIEVAL MANUSCRIPTS FROM THE COLLECTION
3/23 - 5/29/95	WORD AND IMAGE IN THE ART OF WILLIAM HOGARTH
4/4 - 5/29/95	THE LANGUAGE OF SPACE: MINIMALISM AND CONTEMPORARY ART
4/18 - 5/18/95	PAUL STRAND PHOTOGRAPHS WT
8/25 - 11/19/95	SYMBOLISM TO MODERNISM

OXFORD

Miami University Art Museum
Affiliate Institution: Miami University
Patterson Ave, **Oxford, OH 45056**
TEL: 515-529-2232
HRS: 11-5 Tu-S; 7/22-8/22 CLOSED   DAY CLOSED: M   HOL: LEG/HOL! ACAD!
ADM: F   HDC/ACC: Y   PARKING: Y   MUS/SH: Y   GT: Y   GT/PH: call 513-529-2232
PERM/COLL: AM: ptgs, sculp; FR: 16-20; NAT/AM; Ghandharan, sculp

Designed by Walter A. Netsch, the museum building is located in an outstanding natural setting featuring outdoor sculpture.

ON EXHIBIT/95:

Through 2/19/95	LA BELLE EPOCH IN CARICATURE
5/10/94 - 6/11/95	STITCHED, WOVEN AND PLAITED: CONTEMPORARY CRAFT TRADITIONS OF AFRICA WT
Through 10/1/95	FOREVER FLOWERS
1/10 - 3/10/95	DISTINCT FROM SHELLFISH: COLLABORATIONS; DIANA DUNCAN HOLMES AND TIMOTHY RIORDAN

OHIO

Miami University Art Museum - continued

3/21 - 10/1/95	LE CORBUSIER: UNITE
3/28 - 7/30/95	CAROL SUMMER: WOODCUTS
6/27 - 12/10/95	NATIVE AMERICAN WEAVING FROM THE KELLY COLLECTION
8/29/95 - 2/11/96	BARBARA HERSHEY: A RETROSPECTIVE
10/17 - 12/3/95	THE ELOQUENT LINE: JAPANESE CALLIGRAPHY

PORTSMOUTH

Southern Ohio Museum and Cultural Center
825 Gallia Street, **Portsmouth, OH 45662**
TEL: 614-354-5629
HRS: 10-5 Tu-F; 1-5 Sa, S   DAY CLOSED: M   HOL: LEG/HOL!
F/DAY: F   ADM: Y   ADULT: $1.00   CHILDREN: $1.00   STUDENTS: $1.00   SR CIT: $1.00
HDC/ACC: Y   PARKING: Y; Pay   LIB: Y   MUS/SH: Y   H/B: Y
PERM/COLL: PORTMOUTH NATIVE ARTIST CLARENCE CARTER; ANT: doll heads

Constructed in 1918, this beaux art design building is located in the heart of Portsmouth.

SPRINGFIELD

Springfield Museum of Art
107 Cliff Park Road, **Springfield, OH 45501**
TEL: 513-325-4673
HRS: 9-5 Tu-F; 9-3 Sa; 2-4 S   DAY CLOSED: M   HOL: GOOD FRI, THGV WEEKEND, 12/24-1/1
ADM: F   HDC/ACC: Y   PARKING: Y   LIB: Y   MUS/SH: Y   GT: Y   GT/PH: call 513-325-4673 for specifics
PERM/COLL: AM & EU: 19, 20; ROOKWOOD POTTERY; REG: ptgs, works on paper

Located in Cliff Park along Buck Creek in downtown Springfield, this nearly 50 year old institution is a major and growing arts resource for the people of southwest Ohio. Its 1,000 piece permanent collection attempts to provide a comprehensive survey of American art enhanced by works that represent all of the key movements in the development of Western art during the past two centuries. **NOT TO BE MISSED:** Gilbert Stuart's "Portrait of William Miller,"1795

ON EXHIBIT/95:

1/28 - 2/26/95	MIDWEST REALITIES: REGIONAL PAINTING 1920-1950
3/4/ - 4/2/95	THE BIENNIAL S. M. A. FACULTY EXHIBITION
4/9 - 5/21/95	THE MAINTRAUM GROUP
7/15 - 8/13/95	ANNUAL MEMBERS JURIED EXHIBITION
7/15 - 9/24/95	WEST FRASER
10/7 - 11/12/95	THE WESTERN OHIO WATERCOLOR SOCIETY JURIED EXHIBITION
11/4 - 11/26/95	NEW ADDITIONS TO THE SPRINGFIELD COLLECTION
12/2/95 - 1/7/96	STEPHANIE COOPER SCULPTURES
	TAMARA JAEGER SCULPTURES

347

OHIO

TOLEDO

The Toledo Museum of Art
2445 Monroe Street, **Toledo, OH 43697**
TEL: 419-255-8000
HRS: 10-4 Tu-Sa; 1-5 S; 4-9 F, mid Sept-mid-May   DAY CLOSED: M   HOL: 1/1, 7/4, THGV, 12/25
ADM: F   HDC/ACC: Y   PARKING: Y; $1.00 in lot on Grove St.
MUS/SH: Y   REST/FAC: Y
GT: Y   GT/PH: call 419-255-8000   H/B: Y
PERM/COLL: EU: glass, ptgs, sculp, dec/art; AM: ptgs

Long known as one of America's finest mid-size art museums with internationally renowned and broad ranging collections, the Toledo Musuem is located in a building of exceptional beauty. The perfectly proportioned neo-classical building was designed in the early 1900's by Edward Green who added symmetrical wings to his own design in the '20's and '30's. The new Center for the Visual Arts designed by Frank Gehry which opened early in 1993 was described in The Washington Post as a "walk-in, walk-through work of art, as original as they come." **NOT TO BE MISSED:** "The Crowning of St. Catherine, Peter Paul Rubens, 1633.

ON EXHIBIT/95:

10/16/94 - 1/15/95	VISIONES DEL PUEBLO: THE FOLK ART OF LATIN AMERICA adm fee	
2/11 - 3/26/95	AFRICA'S LEGACY IN MEXICO: PHOTOGRAPHS BY TONY GLEATON	
3/19 - 5/28/95	EDWARD WESTON'S PHOTOGRAPHY: CALIFORNIA AND THE WEST adm fee	
4/3 - 6/25/95	VIRGIL AND THE ART OF THE BOOK	
4/11 - 7/2/95	CLASSICAL INSPIRATION: PRINTS FROM THE COLLECTION	
10/8 - 12/31/95	MADE IN AMERICA: TEN CENTURIES OF AMERICAN ART adm fee	
11/7/95 - 1/9/96	MARY ELLEN MARK'S PHOTOJOURNALISM	WT

WOOSTER

College of Wooster Art Museum
Affiliate Institution: The College of Wooster
East University Street, **Wooster, OH 44691**
TEL: 216-263-2388
HRS: 9-12 & 1-5 M-F; 2-5 S (late Aug-mid Jun)   DAY CLOSED: Sa   HOL: LEG/HOL!, ACAD!
ADM: F   PARKING: Y
PERM/COLL: JOHN TAYLOR ARMS COLLECTION OF EU & AM: prints: PERSIAN: dec/art 16-20; CH: ptgs, bronze

YOUNGSTOWN

The Butler Institute of American Art
524 Wick Ave, **Youngstown, OH 44502**
TEL: 216-743-1711
HRS: 11-4 Tu, T-Sa; 11-8 W; 12-4 S   DAY CLOSED: M   HOL: 1/1, EASTER, 7/4, THGV, 12/25
ADM: F   HDC/ACC: Y; Parking, ramps, restrooms, elevators   PARKING: Y; Adjacent   LIB: Y   MUS/SH: Y
REST/FAC: Y   GT: Y   GT/PH: call 216-743-1711   H/B: Y   S/G: Y
PERM/COLL: AM: ptgs 19, 20; EARLY/AM: marine coll; AM/IMPR; WESTERN ART; AM: sports art

Dedicated exclusively to American Art, this exceptional museum, containing numerous national artistic treasures is often referred to as "America's Museum." It is housed in a McKim, Mead and White building that was the first structure erected in the United States to house an art collection. **NOT TO BE MISSED:** Winslow Homer's "Snap the Whip," 1872, oil on canvas.

ON EXHIBIT/95:

11/4/94 - 1/7/95	FIELD OF DREAMS: ARCHITECTURE AND BASEBALL
3/5 - 4/23/95	TANDEM PRESS
3/12 - 4/30/95	TRIUMPH OF COLOR AND LIGHT: OHIO IMPRESSIONISTS AND POST-IMPRESSIONISTS
3/95 - 5/28/95	GARY ERBE RETROSPECTIVE: 25 YEARS IN RETROSPECT WT
4/2 - 5/95	MARTIN JOHNSON HEADE
4/95 - 5/95	URBAN REALISM: THE ASHCAN PAINTER'S VISION OF NEW YORK WT
9/17 - 11/12/95	DENNIS OPPENHEIM
12/10/95 - 1/28/96	WHITE MOUNTAIN PAINTERS 1834-1926 WT

ZANESVILLE

Zanesville Art Center
620 Military Road, **Zanesville, Oh 43701**
TEL: 614-452-0741
HRS: 1-5 Tu-S   DAY CLOSED: M   HOL: LEG/HOL!
ADM: F
HDC/ACC: Y   PARKING: Y   LIB: Y   MUS/SH: Y   GT: Y   GT/PH: call 614-452-0741
PERM/COLL: ZANESVILLE: cer; HAND BLOWN EARLY GLASS; CONT; EU

In addition to the largest display of Zanesville pottery (Weller, Rosedale & J. B. Owens), the Art Center also has a generally eclectic collection. **NOT TO BE MISSED:** Rare areas (unique) hand blown glass and art pottery .

OKLAHOMA

ARDMORE

Charles B. Goddard Center for Visual and Performing Arts
First Ave & D Street SW, **Ardmore, OK 73401**
TEL: 405-226-0909
HRS: 9-4 M-F; 1-4 Sa, S   HOL: LEG/HOL!
ADM: F
HDC/ACC: Y; North parking and entrance   PARKING: Y   LIB: Y
GT: Y   GT/PH: call 405-226-0909
PERM/COLL: PTGS, SCULP, GR, CONT 20; AM: West/art; NAT/AM

Works of art by Oklahoma artists as well as those from across the United States & Europe are featured in this multicultural center.

BARTLESVILLE

Woolaroc Museum
State Highway 123, **Bartlesville, OK 74003**
TEL: 918-336-0307
HRS: 10-5 Tu-S; Mem day-Lab day 10-8 daily   DAY CLOSED: M   HOL: THGV, 12/25
ADM: Y   ADULT: $4.00   CHILDREN: F (under 16)   SR CIT: $3.00
HDC/ACC: Y; Wheelchair access in public areas and restrooms
PARKING: Y   MUS/SH: Y
REST/FAC: Y; Snack bar w/sandwiches, etc.   H/B: Y
PERM/COLL: WEST: ptgs; sculp

Brilliant mosaics surround the doors of this museum situated in a wildlife preserve. Now a large Western art museum, it was the country home of oilman Frank Phillips. The upper level houses the Woolaroc airplane, winner of the 1927 race across the Pacific to Hawaii.

ENID

Grace Phillips Johnson Art Gallery
Affiliate Institution: Phillips University
University Station, **Enid, OK 73702**
TEL: 405-237-4433
HRS: 10-4 Tu-F; Weekends by appointment   DAY CLOSED: M   HOL: LEG/HOL! ACAD!
ADM: F
PARKING: Y   LIB: Y   H/B: Y
PERM/COLL: AM: ptgs 19

The museum is located in the oldest of the University buildings, built in 1913.

350

MUSKOGEE

The Five Civilized Tribes Museum
Agency Hill, Honor Heights Drive, **Muskogee, OK 74401**
TEL: 918-683-1701
HRS: 10-5 M-Sa; 1-5 S   DAY CLOSED: HOL: 1/1, THGV, 12/25
ADM: Y   ADULT: $2.00   CHILDREN: F (under 6)   STUDENTS: $1.00
HDC/ACC: Y   PARKING: Y   LIB: Y   MUS/SH: Y
GT: Y   GT/PH: call 918-683-1701   H/B: Y
PERM/COLL: NAT/AM

Built in 1875 by the US Government as the Union Indian Agency, this museum was the first structure ever erected to house the Superintendency of the Cherokee, Chickasaw, Choctaw, Creek and Seminole Tribes.

ON EXHIBIT/95:

4/8 - 4/30/95	ART UNDER THE OAKS JUDGED EXHIBITION OF CRAFTS
7/9 - 7/31/95	COMPETITIVE ART SHOW — Painting, sculpture and woodcarving by artists of Five Tribes Heritage.
9/30 - 10/31/95	MASTER ART SHOW — Two and three dimensional Fine Art by Master Artists of the Museum.

NORMAN

The Fred Jones Jr. Museum of Art
Affiliate Institution: University of Oklahoma
410 West Boyd Street, **Norman, OK 73019**
TEL: 405-325-3272
HRS: 10-4:30 Tu, W, F; 10-9 T; 1-4:30 Sa, S   DAY CLOSED: M
HOL: LEG/HOL!; ACAD!; HOME FOOTBALL GAMES
ADM: F
HDC/ACC: Y   PARKING: Y; Free passes available at admission desk   MUS/SH: Y
GT: Y   GT/PH: call 10 days adv 405-325-3272
PERM/COLL: AM: cont/ptgs; PRIM; OR; gr; PHOT; NAT/AM

Considered one of the finest university museums in the country with a diverse permanent collection of nearly 6,000 objects, it also hosts the states most challenging exhibitions of contemporary art. **NOT TO BE MISSED:** Dame Barbara Hepworth's "Two Figures" bronze, 1968

ON EXHIBIT/95:

9/17 - 11/5/95	REMBRANDT ETCHINGS: SELECTIONS FROM THE CARNEGIE MUSEUM OF ART — 50 portrait, narrative, genre, figurative, landscape and religious themes by Rembrandt will be seen in this exhibition of his etchings, which will survey of artist's unsurpassed artistry of the medium. BOOKLET WT

OKLAHOMA

OKLAHOMA CITY

Kirkpatrick Center Museum Complex
2100 NE 52nd, **Oklahoma City, OK 73111**
TEL: 405-427-5461
HRS: 9-6 M-Sa, 12-6 S (Mem/Day-Lab/Day); 9:30-5 M-F, 12-6 Sa, S (Winter months)
HOL: THGV, 12/25
ADM: Y   ADULT: $6.00 + tax   CHILDREN: 3-12, $3.50 + tax   STUDENTS: $6.00   SR CIT: $4.00+tax
HDC/ACC: Y   PARKING: Y; Free   MUS/SH: Y   REST/FAC: Y; Limited   GT: Y   GT/PH: ! 405-424-0066
PERM/COLL: VARIED; REG; AF; AS

Seven museums under one roof include Omniplex (the children's hands-on Science Museum), Oklahoma Air & Space Museum, the International Photography Hall of Fame, Red Earth Indian Center, and a planetarium as well as its galleries, gardens and greenhouse. **NOT TO BE MISSED:** Sections of the Berlin Wall

ON EXHIBIT/95:

3/95 - 4/95	FIBERWORKS, '95
4/7 - 4/30/95	SUSAN GOETZ
5/95	ORIENTAL BRUSHWORKS

National Cowboy Hall of Fame and Western Heritage Center
1700 N.E. 63rd Street, **Oklahoma City, OK 73111**
TEL: 405-478-2250
HRS: 9-5 daily (Lab/Day-Mem/Day); 8:30-6 daily (Mem/Day-Lab/Day)   HOL: 1/1, THGV, 12/25
ADM: Y   ADULT: $6.00   CHILDREN: under 18, $3.00   SR CIT: $5.00
HDC/ACC: Y   LIB: Y   MUS/SH: Y   GT: Y   GT/PH: call 405-478-2250
PERM/COLL: WEST/ART

This unusual and unique museum houses the largest collection of contemporary Western art available for public view. Featured is work by Frederic Remington, Charles M. Russell, Charles Schreyvogel, Nicolai Fechin, and examples from the Taos School. There is also a large collection of American historical exhibits featuring the cowboy and the American Indian.

Oklahoma City Art Museum
3113 Pershing Blvd., **Oklahoma City, OK 73107**
TEL: 405-946-4477
HRS: 10-5 Tu-Sa, 10-8 T, 1-5 S; Fairgrounds 10-8 T; Artsplace 10-5   DAY CLOSED: M   HOL: LEG/HOL!
ADM: Y   ADULT: $3.50   CHILDREN: F (under 12)   STUDENTS: $2.50   SR CIT: $2.50
HDC/ACC: Y   PARKING: Y   LIB: Y   MUS/SH: Y   GT: Y   GT/PH: call 405-946-4477   H/B: Y   S/G: Y
PERM/COLL: AM: ptgs, gr 19, 20; ASHCAN SCHOOL COLLECTION

The Museum complex includes the Oklahoma City Art Museum at the Fairgrounds built in 1958 (where the design of the building is a perfect circle with the sculpture court in the middle), and the Oklahoma City Museum in the 1937 Buttram Mansion. **NOT TO BE MISSED:** Works by Washington color school painters and area figurative artists are included in the collection of modern art from the former Washington Gallery.

Oklahoma City Art Museum - continued

ON EXHIBIT/95:

10/18/94 - 4/30/95   MADE IN THE U.S.A. — This exhibition examines the depth of the museum's collection of American art, arranged chronologically, from the French inspired Impressionism of the late 19th century, through the WPA years, Abstract Expressionism, Photorealism, and Conceptual art of the last decade.

11/22/94 - 2/19/95   BOX IN A VALISE BY MARCEL DUCHAMP — Included in a reduced version of the major work of this most influential artist of the 20th century are replicas of major works which have inspired conceptual artists by his thinking about the manipulation of materials.

11/22/94 - 3/19/95   REALITY: ARTISTS AGAINST THE GRAIN — In 1953 a group of 45 artists signed a statement that advocated "respect and love for human qualities in painting." This statement and short lived publication were a slap in the face of the prevailing style, abstract expressionism. This exhibit looks at the art of 18 of these artists represented in the Museum's collections and places it in the context of their contemporaries. Included are Raphael Soyer, Isabel Bishop, Leon Kroll and Reginald Marsh.

11/29/94 - 2/19/95   RECENT WORK BY PAUL MEDINA — The surreal assemblages of Paul Medina on view are made out of strictly aesthetic concerns, although the artist agrees that much more can be read into them. He has become one of Oklahoma's primary artists.

2/28 - 4/8/95   CHRIS RAMSEY — One of two artists honored by the Volunteer Association of the Museum for professional acheivement in 1993, the artist is inspired by nature and shows his work all over the country.

SHAWNEE

Mabee-Gerrer Museum of Art
1900 West MacArthur Drive, **Shawnee, OK 74801**
TEL: 405-878-5300
HRS: 1-4 Tu-S DAY CLOSED: M HOL: 1/1, GOOD FRI, HOLY SAT, EASTER, THGV, 12/25
ADM: F HDC/ACC: Y; Ground level ramp access from parking PARKING: Y; Free LIB: Y REST/FAC: Y
GT: Y GT/PH: call 405-878-5300 S/G: Y
PERM/COLL: EU: ptgs (Med-20); AN/EGT; NAT/AM; GRECO/ROMAN; AM: ptgs

The oldest museum collection in Oklahoma is housed in the newest built facility, featuring earth derm technology and a pyramid roof. **NOT TO BE MISSED:** Mummy of the Egyptian Princess Henne, 32nd Dynasty (1332 BC)

TULSA

Gilcrease Museum
1400 Gilcrease Museum Road, **Tulsa, OK 74127-2100**
TEL: 918-596-2700
HRS: 9-5 Tu, W, F, Sa; 9-8 T: 1-5 S and Holidays; Mem Day-Lab Day open M DAY CLOSED: M Sept thru May
HOL: 12/25
ADM: Y ADULT: $3.00 (Fam $5) CHILDREN: F (under 18)
HDC/ACC: Y PARKING: Y; Free LIB: Y MUS/SH: Y REST/FAC: Y
GT: Y GT/PH: ! 2 weeks prior res. DT: Y TIME: 2pm daily
PERM/COLL: THOMAS MORAN, FREDERIC REMINGTON, C. M. RUSSELL, ALBERT BIERSTADT, ALFRED JACOB MILLER, GEORGE CATLIN, THOMAS EAKINS

OKLAHOMA

Gilcrease Museum - continued

Virtually every item in the Gilcrease Collection relates to the discovery, expansion and settlement of North America, with special emphasis on the Old West and the American Indian. The Museum's 440 acre grounds include historic theme gardens. **NOT TO BE MISSED:** "Acoma," by Thomas Moran

ON EXHIBIT/95:

1/21 - 4/16/95	CENTENNIAL CELEBRATION OF EAKINGS PORTRAIT OF CUSHING — Cushing spent nearly five years living at Zuni pueblo where, in spite of initial resistance, he became part of the community and possibly was initiated into the tribal war society as a Priest of the Bow. For this painting he was posed in the regalia of the secret society in a studio decorated to resemble a pueblo interior. Included are artworks, letter, photos and documents as well as Zuni and other Southwestern Indian artifacts.
TENTATIVE - 2/11/95	LATINO ARTS EXHIBITION — The reinstallation of the Zarrow Galleries will examine evolving traditions of Latino identity.
4/28 - 7/9/95	GILCREASE RENDEZVOUS 1995 — Works of painter David Leffel and sculptor Sherry Sandor will be included.
Mid - October	95 GILCREASE MUSEUM NATIVE AMERICAN ART INVITATIONAL — A juried show in conjunction with the Native American Art Studies Association.
11/5 - 12/5/95	AMERICAN ART IN MINIATURE 1995 — No larger than 9 x 12 inches, the paintings for sale represent a variety of styles, subjects and media.

TULSA

The Philbrook Museum of Art Inc
2727 South Rockford Road, **Tulsa, OK 74114**
TEL: 918-749-7941
HRS: 10-5 Tu-Sa; 10-8 T; 11-5 S   DAY CLOSED: M   HOL: LEG/HOL!
ADM: Y   ADULT: $4.00   CHILDREN: F (under 12)   STUDENTS: $2.00   SR CIT: $2.00
HDC/ACC: Y   PARKING: Y; Free   LIB: Y   MUS/SH: Y   REST/FAC: Y; 11-4 Tu-Sa; 1-4 S; 11:30-2:30 brunch
GT: Y   GT/PH: groups of 10 $2.00 each ! 918- 749-7941   H/B: Y   S/G: Y
PERM/COLL: NAT/AM; IT/REN: ptgs, sculp; EU & AM: ptgs 19-20;

An Italian Rennaisance style villa built in 1927 on 23 acres of gardens and grounds houses collections from around the world at the Philbrook Museum of Art. Visitors enter a 75,000 square foot addition via a striking rotunda which was completed in 1990 and houses special exhibitions, a shop, a restaurant, and a school.

ON EXHIBIT/95:

thru 1/8	ITALIAN PRINTS FROM THE 16TH - 18TH CENTURIES
	BOTTICELLI-TIEPOLO: THREE CENTURIES OF ITALIAN PAINTING FROM BOB JONES UNIVERSITY WT
thru 2/19	THE HISTORY OF THE OKLAHOMA ARTISTS: AN ANNUAL EXHIBITION AT PHILBROOK — The Oklahoma Artists Annual began in 1940 and ran through 1976. The chronology of the former exhibitions will be presented through photographs and materials in the museum's archives

The Philbrook Museum of Art Inc - continued

thru 1995   OKLAHOMA INDIANS FROM THE SOUTHEAST: PAINTINGS AND BASKETS

1/15 - 3/12/95   DURER AND REMBRANDT: THE FELIX WARBURG COLLECTION OF GERMAN
                   AND NETHERLANDISH PRINTS — A survey of the masters of printmaking of the
                   Northern Renaissance and the Baroque.

3/5 - 8/20/95   WAITE PHILLIPS: THE MAN AND HIS LEGACY — The life and times of the
                   businessman and philanthropist who was, with his wife, the founder of the museum.

4/2 - 5/28/95   AMERICAN ARTS AND CRAFTS: VIRTUE IN DESIGN — The Arts and Crafts
                   doctrine of functional design, simple materials and natural forms is showcased in
                   outstanding examples of furniture, metalwork, ceramics and other objects by Stickley,
                   Frank Lloyd Wright, Rookwood Pottery and others.

5/18 - 8/20/95   RIVER OF GOLD: TREASURES OF SITIO CONTE — Exquisite examples of pre-
                   Columbian gold work from 700-1100 A.D.   CAT   WT

9/10 - 11/5/95   20TH CENTURY AMERICAN ART FROM THE WILLIAMS COMPANIES
                   COLLECTION — Selections from one of the most extensive collections in the region
                   include work by Milton Avery, Thomas Hart Benton, Stuart Davis, John Marin and others.

11/17 - 12/3/95   FESTIVAL OF TREES

OREGON

COOS BAY

Coos Art Museum
235 Anderson, **Coos Bay, OR 97420**
TEL: 503-267-3901
HRS: 11-5 Tu-F; 1-4 Sa   DAY CLOSED: S, M   HOL: LEG/HOL!
ADM: F
HDC/ACC: Y; Complete facilities   PARKING: Y; Free   MUS/SH: Y   H/B: Y
PERM/COLL: CONT: ptgs, sculp, gr; AM; REG

This cultural center of Southwestern Oregon is the only art museum on the Oregon coast. Its collection includes work by Robert Rauschenberg, Red Grooms, Larry Rivers, Frank Boyden, Henk Pander and Manuel Izquierdo. **NOT TO BE MISSED:** "Mango, Mango" by Red Grooms

EUGENE

University of Oregon Museum of Art
Affiliate Institution: University of Oregon
1430 Johnson Lane, **Eugene, OR 97403**
TEL: 503-346-3027
HRS: 12-5 W-S   DAY CLOSED: M, Tu   HOL: ACAD!, 1/1, 7/4, THGV, 12/25
ADM: F
HDC/ACC: Y   MUS/SH: Y   GT: Y   GT/PH: call 503-346-3027   H/B: Y   S/G: Y
PERM/COLL: CONT: ptgs, phot, gr, cer; NAT/AM

Enjoy one of the premier art experiences in the Pacific Northwest at this museum whose collection features more than 12,500 objects from throughout the world as well as contemporary Northwest art and photography.

ON EXHIBIT/95:

Through 5/95	SCULPTURE BY AUGUSTE RODIN
12/11/94 - 2/5/95	ROYAL NEBEKER PAINTINGS — Work by this Oregon artist.
12/18/94 - 2/19/95	19TH CENTURY PHOTOGRAPHY FROM THE DAN BERLEY COLLECTION — In a rare opportunity to view some of the earliest image making in the history of the medium., this exhibition will highlight both invention and innovation.
3/5 - 4/30/95	SAM HERNANDEZ: ABSTRACT IMAGIST — Boisterously playful and colorful sculptures in wood and metals by this Bay Area artist.
5/95 - 6/95	MASTERS OF FINE ARTS EXHIBITION
9/95 - 11/95	INSIDE THE LARGE-SMALL HOUSE: THE RESIDENTIAL DESIGN OF WILLIAM W. WURSTER WT
12/10/95 - 2/26/96	THE PHOTOGRAPHS OF DORIS ULMANN

KLAMATH FALLS

Favell Museum of Western Art and Indian Artifacts
125 West Main Street, **Klamath Falls, OR 97601**
TEL: 503-882-9996
HRS: 9:30-5:30 M-Sa   DAY CLOSED: S   HOL: LEG/HOL!
ADM: Y   ADULT: $4.00   CHILDREN: $2.00, 6-16   SR CIT: $3.00
HDC/ACC: Y   PARKING: Y   MUS/SH: Y
PERM/COLL: CONT/WEST: art; NAT/AM; ARTIFACTS; MINI FIREARMS

The museum is built on an historic site of a campground for the Klamath Indians. Three Indian graves found on this site still exist there as do numerous artifacts – many of which have been incorporated into the stone walls of the museum building itself.

PORTLAND

Portland Art Museum
1219 S.W. Park Ave., **Portland, OR 97205**
TEL: 503-226-2811
HRS: 11-5 Tu-Sa; 1-5 S   DAY CLOSED: M   HOL: LEG/HOL!
F/DAY: 1st T of month   ADM: Y   ADULT: $4.50, Fam $10   CHILDREN: under 5, F   STUDENTS: $2.50
SR CIT: $3.50
HDC/ACC: Y; Ramp to main lobby, elevator to all floors   LIB: Y   MUS/SH: Y   REST/FAC: Y
GT: Y   GT/PH: call 503-226-2811   H/B: Y
PERM/COLL: NAT/AM; P/COL; AS; GR; EU & AM: ptgs; CONT: ptgs

Designed by Pietro Belluschi, the Portland Art Museum has a permanent collection that spans 35 centuries with major works of Asian, European, American, and Native-American art, and important works of art on paper.

The Douglas F. Cooley Memorial Art Gallery
Affiliate Institution: Reed College
3203 S.E. Woodstock Blvd., **Portland, OR 97202-8199**
TEL: 503-777-7790
HRS: 12-5 Tu-S   DAY CLOSED: M   HOL: LEG/HOL!
ADM: F
HDC/ACC: Y   PARKING: Y; Adjacent   LIB: Y
PERM/COLL: AM: 20; EU: 19

The gallery is committed to a program that fosters a spirit of inquiry and questions the status quo.

ON EXHIBIT/95:
2/4 - 3/19/95   MASTERPIECES OF RENAISSANCE AND BAROQUE PRINTMAKING — 85 superb 15th through 17th century prints that illustrate the difference in art practiced in the North and in Italy, will compare the technical advances and stylistic differences of artists in both regions. Examples by Cranach, Durer, Rembrandt, Van Dyck, Carraci, Lorrain and other old masters will be included.   CAT   WT

OREGON

WARM SPRINGS

The Museum at Warm Springs Oregon
Affiliate Institution: Confederated Tribes of the Warm Springs Reservation
PO Box C, **Warm Springs, OR**
TEL: 503-553-3331
HRS: 10-5 daily   HOL: THGV, 12/25, 1/1
ADM: Y   ADULT: $5.00   CHILDREN: $2.50; F under 4   SR CIT: $4.50
HDC/ACC: Y; Fully wheelchair accessible   MUS/SH: Y   GT: Y   GT/PH: call 503-553-3331 for specifics
PERM/COLL: NAT/AM: art, phot, artifacts

The Museum at Warm Springs draws from a rich collection of native artwork, photographs and stories that tell the long history of the three tribes that comprise the Confederate Tribes of Warm Springs. It is architecturally designed to evoke a creekside encampment among a stand of cottonwoods. **NOT TO BE MISSED:** A trio of traditional buildings built by tribal members; the tule mat wickiup, or house of the Paiutes, the Warm Springs summer teepee, and the Wasco wooden plank house .

ALLENTOWN

Allentown Art Museum
Fifth & Court Street, **Allentown, PA 18105**
TEL: 610-432-4333
HRS: 10-5 Tu-Sa; 1-5 S   DAY CLOSED: M   HOL: LEG/HOL!
ADM: Y   ADULT: $3.50   CHILDREN: F (under 12)   STUDENTS: $2.00   SR CIT: $3.00
HDC/ACC: Y   LIB: Y   MUS/SH: Y   GT: Y   GT/PH: call 215-432-4333
PERM/COLL: EU: Kress Coll; AM; FRANK LLOYD WRIGHT: library; OM: gr

Discover the intricate and visual riches of one of the finest small art museums in the country. **NOT TO BE MISSED:** "Piazetti in Venice," by Canaletto

ON EXHIBIT/95:

10/15/94 - 1/15/95	FAVORITE THINGS: THE COMMUNITY SELECTS — Thirty individuals from the tri-city area will select works from the Museum's permanent collection in a unique experimental exhibition that turns the community into the curator.
11/4/94 - 1/15/95	ETCHINGS FROM THE COLLECTION — Prints from the Museum's varied collection dating from the 16th to the 20th centuries will be exhibited. Highlighted will be technical aspects of the process as well as its expressive capacity. Included are Rembrandt, Charles Meryon, David Cameron, John Dowell and Michael Mazur.
opening 12/3/94	MAN AND MATERIALS AND THE JAMES C. FULLER GEM COLLECTION — An exploration of how man in the interest of aesthetics manipulates raw materials.
12/9/94 - 3/5/95	THE ROMANCE OF LACE — Drawn from the Museum collection, the exhibition will highlight pictorial elements in the art of lacemaking.
1/20 - 4/2/95	LESLIE FLETCHER: CONSTRUCTED PAINTINGS — Three dimensional paintings which hang on the wall but occupy space like sculpture will be on exhibit.
2/3 - 4/30/95	RESTRAINT AND SURRENDER: PHOTOGRAPHS BY KEN GRAVES AND EVA LIPMAN — Working as a team in the conception of their projects, realization of their work and in the darkroom, these artists have evolved a shared style poised between formal restraint and perceptional surrender to the subject. The two bodies of work shown here were done in amateur and professional boxing gyms and of high school seniors at their prom. CAT
2/3 - 4/9/95	PENNSYLVANIA PHOTOGRAPHERS 9 — An acclaimed biennial exhibition featuring artists who live and work in Pennsylvania.
3/10 - 6/4/95	COATS OF MANY COLORS — Elaborate ornamental embroidery adorns each of the garments in the exhibition which were designed for ceremonial occasions.
4/7 - 6/18/95	DRAWING FOR THE JACQUARD LOOM: TEXTILE DESIGNS BY WILLIAM GESKES — The original drawings of this designer of woven textiles (1877-1962) are decorative, colorful and highly patterned.
4/23 - 6/25/95	HEAD, HEART AND HAND: ELBERT HUBBARD AND THE ROYCROFTERS — A showcase of the furniture, metalwork, leathercraft and bookbinding and artwork produced at Roycroft, a turn-of-the-century Arts and Crafts community at East Aurora, New York. WT
7/7 - 9/17/95	HOWARD PYLE AND NORMAN ROCKWELL: LASTING LEGACIES — The exhibition highlights the work of two artists who sought to portray the ideals of American culture and society through the field of illustration. WT
9/29 - 12/31/95	KEITH HARING: FAMILY AND FRIENDS COLLECT — Family and friends of Keith Haring in Kutztown, Pennsylvania have loaned works which were made expressly for them including prints, drawings, paintings, Christmas cards, a crib and chest of drawers and his mother's microwave.

PENNSYLVANIA

AUDUBON

Mill Grove, the Audubon Wildlife Sanctuary
Audubon, PA 19407-7125
TEL: 215-666-5593
HRS: 10-4 Tu-Sa; 1-4 S   DAY CLOSED: M   HOL: 1/1, THGV, 12/25
VOL/CONT: Y   ADM: F
PARKING: Y   MUS/SH: Y   GT: Y   GT/PH: !   H/B: Y
PERM/COLL: JOHN JAMES AUDUBON: all major published artwork (complete 19th C editions)

Housed in the 1762 building which was the first American home of John James Audubon, this site is also a bird sanctuary complete with nature trails and feeding stations.

BETHLEHEM

Lehigh University Art Galleries
Bethlehem, PA 18015
TEL: 215-758-3615
HRS: 9-5 M-F; 9-12 Sa; 2-5 S   HOL: LEG/HOL!
ADM: F
HDC/ACC: Y   PARKING: Y; Limited   REST/FAC: Y; In Iacocca Bldg. open until 2 pm
GT: Y   GT/PH: call 215-758-3615   S/G: Y
PERM/COLL: EU & AM: ptgs; JAP: gr; PHOT

The Galleries do not permanently exhibit the important works in its collections. Call to inquire.

ON EXHIBIT/95:
> More than 20 temporary exhibitions a year in five campus galleries introduce students and the community to current topics in art, architecture, history, science and technology.

BRYN ATHYN

Glencairn Museum: Academy of the New Church
Cathedral Road, **Bryn Athyn, PA 19009**
TEL: 215-947-9919
HRS: 9-4 M-F, 2-5 Second S each month (except Jul & Aug)   DAY CLOSED: Sa   HOL: LEG/HOL!
ADM: Y   ADULT: $3.00   CHILDREN: F   STUDENTS: F
HDC/ACC: Y   PARKING: Y   GT: !
PERM/COLL: MED, GOTHIC & ROMANESQUE: sculp; STAINED GLASS; EGT, GRK & ROMAN: cer, sculp; NAT/AM

Glencairn is a unique structure built in the Romanesque style using building processes unknown since the middle ages. **NOT TO BE MISSED:** French Medieval stained glass and sculpture

PENNSYLVANIA

CARLISLE

Trout Art Gallery
Affiliate Institution: Dickinson College
High Street, **Carlisle, PA 17013**
TEL: 717-245-1344
HRS: 10-4 Tu-S   DAY CLOSED: M   HOL: LEG/HOL!; ACAD!
ADM: F
HDC/ACC: Y   PARKING: Y   LIB: Y   GT: Y   GT/PH: call 717-245-1344
PERM/COLL: GR; 19, 20; AF

The exhibitions and collections here emphasize all periods of art history. **NOT TO BE MISSED:**
Gerofsky Collection of African Art and the Carnegie Collection of prints. Rodin's "St. John the
Baptist" and other gifts from Meyer P. and Vivian Potamkin.

ON EXHIBIT/95:

11/18/94 - 1/28/95	AFRICAN ART FROM THE PERMANENT COLLECTION, PART II
2/3 - 3/4/95	ART HISTORICAL METHODS EXHIBITION: 19TH CENTURY EUROPEAN PRINTS
2/21 - 5/13/95	ANNUAL STUDIO STUDENTS' EXHIBITION (TENT!)
5/19 - 9/2/95	RON GRAFF: CONTEMPORARY PAINTER — Landscapes and still lifes

CHADDS FORD

Brandywine River Museum
Chadds Ford, PA 19317
TEL: 215-388-2700
HRS: 9:30-4:30 Daily   HOL: 12/25
ADM: Y   ADULT: $5.00   CHILDREN: F (under 6)   STUDENTS: $2.50   SR CIT: $2.50
HDC/ACC: Y   PARKING: Y   LIB: Y   MUS/SH: Y   REST/FAC: Y; 11-3 (Closed M and Tu Jan through Mar)
GT: Y   GT/PH: call for specifics   H/B: Y
PERM/COLL: AM: ptgs by three generations of the Wyeth Family

Situated in a pastoral setting in a charming converted 19th century grist mill, this museum is devoted
to displaying the works of three generations of the Wyeth family and other Brandywine River School
artists. Particular focus is also placed on 19th c American still-life & landscape paintings and on works
of American illustration.

ON EXHIBIT/95:

1/20 - 3/19/95	AMISH QUILTS FROM THE MUSEUM OF AMERICAN FOLK ART — Eighteen boldly designed works dating from the late 19th century to the 1930's and made by Amish women in both Pennsylvania and the midwest. WT
9/9 - 11/19/95	PAINTING IN THE GRAND MANNER: THE ART OF PETER FREDERICK ROTHERMEL — This comprehensive exhibition, the first in 100 years devoted solely to Rothermel's work, examines his remarkable career as a history painter in the grand style. Featured are drawings and paintings as well as engravings after his work. CAT

361

PENNSYLVANIA

CHESTER

Widener University Art Museum
Affiliate Institution: Widener University
1300 Potter Street, **Chester, PA 19013**
TEL: 610-499-1189
HRS: 10-4 Tu-Sa; Closed July 1995   DAY CLOSED: S, M   HOL: LEG/HOL! Month of July
ADM: F   MUS/SH: Y
PERM/COLL: AM & EU: ptgs 19, 20

A Georgian style building on the main campus of Widener University is the home of this museum, which includes in its holdings the Widener University Collection of American Impressionist paintings and the Alfred O. Deshong Collection of 19th and 20th century European and American painting.

ON EXHIBIT/95:

1/17 - 2/18/95	CONTEMPORARY CHINESE FOLK ART: A JOURNEY INTO RURAL CHINA
2/28 - 4/1/95	PHOTOGRAPHS BY MERLE SPANDORFER
4/11 - 5/6/95	PAINTINGS BY ELEANOR WILSON — The Widener University Art Museum building is her family home.
5/20 - 8/19/95	SELECTIONS FROM THE ALFRED O. DESHONG COLLECTION

COLLEGEVILLE

Philip and Muriel Berman Museum of Art
Affiliate Institution: Ursinius College
Main Street, **Collegeville, PA 19426**
TEL: 610-489-4111
HRS: 10-4 Tu-F; Noon-4:30 Sa, S   DAY CLOSED: M   HOL: LEG/HOL!
ADM: F   HDC/ACC: Y   PARKING: Y; On campus adjacent to Museum   LIB: Y
GT: Y   GT/PH: call 215-489-4111, ext.2354   DT: Y   TIME: !   H/B: Y   S/G: Y
PERM/COLL: AM: ptgs 19, 20; EU: ptgs 18; JAP: ptgs; PENNSYLVANIA GERMAN ART

With 145 works from 1956-1986, the Berman Museum of Art holds the largest private collection of sculpture by Lynn Chadwick in the US., all housed in the original Georgian Style stone facade college library built in 1921. **NOT TO BE MISSED:** "Seated Couple on a Bench" (1986 bronze), by Lynn Chadwick (English b. 1914)

ON EXHIBIT/95:

1/95 - 4/95	FRANCOIS GILOT: THE GRAPHIC WORK — The first retrospective of the artist's work in graphic media chronicles her artistic development from 1940-1993. CAT
4/95 - 9/95	A WAY OF LIFE: PENNSYLVANIA GERMAN CULTURE AND TRADITIONS — The focus is on objects, artifacts and art that were part of the simple practical approach of this unique and vital culture. CAT
9/95 - 11/95	THE FACULTY SELECTS — Objects from faculty and staff personal collections.
12/8/95 - 1/21/96	IMAGES OF BRITISH-INDIA'S GOLDEN AGE — These aquatints convey the romantic image of India under the first British governors. From 1780-1880 British artists portrayed the beauty and romance of an idealized land and the rich and varied subject matter inspired paintings, watercolors and some of the finest prints ever produced. WT

DOYLESTOWN

James A. Michener Art Museum
Ashland & Pine Street, **Doylestown, PA 18901**
TEL: 215-340-9800
HRS: 10-4:30 Tu-F; 10-5 Sa, S   DAY CLOSED: M   HOL: LEG/HOL!
ADM: Y   ADULT: $5.00   CHILDREN: F (under 12)   STUDENTS: $1.50   SR CIT: $4.50
HDC/ACC: Y   PARKING: Y; Free   LIB: Y!   MUS/SH: Y
GT: Y   GT/PH: call 215-340-9800, ext 126 to reserve   H/B: Y   S/G: Y
PERM/COLL: AM: Impr/ptgs 19-20; BUCKS CO: 18-20; AM: Exp 20; SCULP 20; NAKASHIMA READING ROOM

Situated in the handsomely reconstructed buildings of the antiquated Bucks County prison, the Museum, with its newly opened addition, provides an invigorating environment for viewing a wonderful collection of twentieth century American art.   **NOT TO BE MISSED:** Redfield, Garber & New Hope School

ON EXHIBIT/95:

11/12/94 - 1/15/95	THE ARTIST REVEALED: PHOTOGRAPHS FROM THE COLLECTION OF PETER PAONE AND ALMA ALABILIKIAN — Drawing on the long tradition of portraits of artists in their studios these more than one hundred images are of well known artists by master portraitists.
12/10/94 - 3/19/95	PATTERNS OF VISION: TRADITION AND INNOVATION IN CONTEMPORARY QUILTMAKING — Using quiltmakers from the Middle Atlantic region the exhibition explores this lively art form.
12/10/94 - 1/22/95	A COLLECTOR'S EYE: POST-DEPRESSION ERA PAINTINGS FROM THE COLLECTION OF JOHN HORTON — Social Realist and landscape paintings from this era including works by such noted artists as Reginald Marsh and Ben Shahn.
1/21 - 3/12/95	GEORGE RADESCHI: VESSELS IN WOOD — This Bucks County woodworker creates elegant vessels made with hundreds of pieces of wood, precisely measured and carefully cut to form complex patterns.
1/28 - 3/19/95	KENJIRO NOMURA: AN ARTIST'S VIEW OF THE JAPANESE-AMERICAN INTERNMENT — The artist, well known in the 1930's, was uprooted and placed in an internment campduring WW II. He continued to paint and to document life in the barracks at the same time that he was painting street and latrine signs.
3/18 - 4/30/95	BARRY SNYDER: DISCOVER, CONSTRUCT, TRANSFORM — This regional artist makes found-object sculpture of exceptional creativity and power influenced by sources as diverse as African masks and Zen calligraphy.
3/35 - 6/18/95	JOHN FULTON FOLINSBEE: A RETROSPECTIVE — One of the finest artists in the Pennsylvania Impressionist School, Folinsbee (1892-1972) was best known for his sensitive and distinctive landscapes of Bucks County.
3/25 - 4/30/95 and 5/6 - 6/18/95	THE CONTEMPORARY MUSE — Two group exhibitions which are the first in an ongoing series will bring to Bucks County some of the best work in the major genres of contemporary art, including painting, printmaking, sculpture, photography, ceramics and video.

PENNSYLVANIA

EASTON

Lafayette College Art Gallery, Williams Center for the Arts
Hamilton and High Streets, **Easton, PA 18042-1768**
TEL: 215-250-5361
HRS: 10-5 Tu-F; 2-5 S Sep-Jun   DAY CLOSED: M, Sa   HOL: ACAD!
ADM: F
HDC/ACC: Y   PARKING: Y; On-street
PERM/COLL: AM: ptgs, portraits, gr

Located in Easton, Pennsylvania, on the Delaware River, the collection is spread throughout the campus. **NOT TO BE MISSED:** 19th c American history paintings and portraits

ERIE

Erie Art Museum
411 State Street, **Erie, PA 16501**
TEL: 814-459-5477
HRS: 11-5 Tu-Sa; 1-5 S   DAY CLOSED: M   HOL: LEG/HOL!
F/DAY: W   ADM: Y   ADULT: $1.50   CHILDREN: $0.50 (under 12)   STUDENTS: $0.75   SR CIT: $0.75
HDC/ACC: Y   PARKING: Y; Street parking available   MUS/SH: Y
GT: Y   GT/PH: call 2 weeks ahead to reserve   DT: Y   TIME: F   H/B: Y
PERM/COLL: IND: sculp; OR; AM & EU: ptgs, drgs, sculp gr; PHOT

The museum is located in the 1839 Greek Revival Old Customs House built as the U. S. Bank of PA. Building plans are underway to provide more gallery space in order to exhibit works from the 4,000 piece permanent collection. **NOT TO BE MISSED:** Soft Sculpture installation "The Avalon Restaurant"

ON EXHIBIT/95:

11/8/94 - 1/7/95	COMIC BOOK ART (at The Frame Shop, 423 State St.)
11/19/94 - 1/22/95	WORKS BY SHELLE LICHTENWALTER BARRON — Large-scale mixed media works on canvas plus drawings by this regional artist will be presented.
12/31/94 - 2/26/95	ELASTIC VISIONS: COMPUTER ART EXHIBITION
3/4 - 4/19/95	FOUR SCULPTORS EXHIBIT
4/29 - 5/95	72ND ANNUAL JURIED SPRING SHOW
5/95 - 9/95	BIRDS EXHIBIT
	ARTSCAPE III — A public art project
9/95 - 10/95	ERIE IN 2095 EXHIBIT — Regional artists present their visions of Erie in 100 years
10/28 - 12/17/95	PA APPRENTICESHIPS IN TRADITIONAL ARTS EXHIBIT

364

PENNSYLVANIA

GREENSBURG

Westmoreland Museum of Art
221 North Main Street, **Greensburg, PA 15601-1898**
TEL: 412-837-1500
HRS: 10-5 Tu-Sa; 1-5 S   DAY CLOSED: M   HOL: LEG/HOL!
ADM: F   HDC/ACC: Y   PARKING: Y; Free   LIB: Y   MUS/SH: Y
GT: Y   GT/PH: call 412-837-1500 to reserve   DT: Y   TIME: !
PERM/COLL: AM: ptgs (18-20), sculp, drgs, gr, fruniture, dec/art

This important collection of American art is located in a beautiful Georgian style building situated on a hill overlooking the city. **NOT TO BE MISSED:** Painting by Mary Cassatt; Largest known collection of paintings by 19th century southwestern Pennsylvania artists.

ON EXHIBIT/95:

11/25/94 - 1/15/96   ANTIQUE TOY AND LARGE GAUGE TRAIN EXHIBITION — A wide variety of toys, both manufactured and handmade from the permanent collection and from private collectors will be on exhibit.

2/26 - 4/9/95   GEORGE LUKS: EXPRESSIONIST MASTER OF COLOR, THE WATERCOLORS REDISCOVERED — The brilliant watercolors of this well known American painter and member of the rebellious "Eight" are little known. Fifty works including some not previously exhibited will give a full view of his talent and stylistic changes.

4/23 - 5/11/95   KINGS AND QUEENS AND SOUP TUREENS FROM THE CAMPBELL MUSEUM — Silver, pewter and ceramic tureens from around the world will be included in this unique exhibition representing a multitude of cultures and periods.   WT

HARRISBURG

The State Museum of Pennsylvania
3rd and North Streets, **Harrisburg, PA 17120**
TEL: 717-787-4980
HRS: 9-5 Tu-Sa; 12-5 S   DAY CLOSED: M   HOL: LEG/HOLS
ADM: F   HDC/ACC: Y   LIB: Y   MUS/SH: Y   GT: Y   GT/PH: call 717-787-4979   DT: Y   TIME: !
PERM/COLL: VIOLET OAKLEY COLL; PETER ROTHERMEL MILITARY SERIES; PA: cont

Collecting, preserving, and interpreting art & artifacts relating to Pennsylvania's history, culture and natural heritage is the main focus of this museum whose collection includes 4,000 works of art from 1645 to the present produced by residents/natives of Pennsylvania. **NOT TO BE MISSED:** The 16' X 32' "Battle of Gettysburg: Pickett's Charge," by P. F. Rothermel (the largest battle scene on canvas in North America)

ON EXHIBIT/95:

2/3/95   JOHN W. MOSLEY (1907 - 1968): PHOTOGRAPHY

5/19 - 7/30/95   ART OF THE STATE: PENNSYLVANIA 1995 — Annual juried exhibition open to Pennsylvania residents in the categories of painting, works on paper, sculpture, photography, and art crafts.

TBA   OPENING OF OUTDOOR SCULPTURE COLLECTION

PENNSYLVANIA

HOLLIDAYSBURG

Blair Art Museum
Affiliate Institution: Southern Alleghenies Museum of Art
314 Allegheny Street, **Hollidaysburg, PA 16648**
TEL: 814-695-0648
HRS: 10-5 M-F; 1-5 Sa   DAY CLOSED: S   HOL: LEG/HOL!
ADM: F   HDC/ACC: Y   PARKING: Y   GT: Y   GT/PH: call 814-695-0648
PERM/COLL: Non-collecting institution

Built in the late 1800's and located on the main street in historic Hollidaysburg, the Blair is the primary museum in the Southern Alleghenies. It is affiliated with the Southern Alleghenies Museum of Art.

INDIANA

The University Museum
Affiliate Institution: Indiana University
John Sutton Hall, Indiana University of Penn, **Indiana, PA 15705**
TEL: 412-357-2302
HRS: 11-4 Tu-F; 7-9 T; 1-4 Sa, S   DAY CLOSED: M   HOL: ACAD!
ADM: F   HDC/ACC: Y   PARKING: Y   LIB: Y
PERM/COLL: AM: 19, 20; NAT/AM; MILTON BANCROFT: ptgs & drgs; INUIT: sculp

ON EXHIBIT/95:

1/17 - 2/5/95	GRADUATE ART ASSOCIATION JURIED EXHIBITION
2/7 - 3/3/95	NORTHWOOD/DUGAN/DIAMOND: FRAGILE FRAGMENTS FROM INDIANA GLASS AND SELECTIONS FROM THE BALSINGER MEMORIAL BANCROFT COLLECTION — This exhibition honors a part of Indiana County's treasured industrial history and teaches the devolopment of decorated glass there from 1892-1931.
3/14 - 4/11/95	THE COAL PEOPLE AND ANCIENT RULERS OF THE MIDWEST: THE MISSISSIPPIAN CULTURE A.D.1000-1460 — An exhibition of documentation photos which highlight current lifestyles of formerly active coal-mining towns in the immediate area. Also a showing of the Auld Collection of Native American artifacts to bolster understanding of Native American cultures and complexity.
4/18 - 5/13/95	CROSSING THE FINISH LINE — A decorative arts exhibition in which artists have been invited to decorate chairs and other small pieces of furniture, mostly functional, but some miniature and non-functional. Some are serious, some whimsical, all for fun.

LEWISBURG

Center Gallery of Bucknell University
Affiliate Institution: Bucknell University
Seventh Street and Moore Ave, **Lewisburg, PA 17837**
TEL: 717-524-3792
HRS: 11-4 M-F & 1-4 Sa, S; 11-4 M-F (Summer)   HOL: LEG/HOL!
ADM: F   HDC/ACC: Y   PARKING: Y; Free   LIB: Y   MUS/SH: Y   REST/FAC: Y; on campus
PERM/COLL: IT/REN: ptgs; AM: ptgs 19, 20; JAP

NOT TO BE MISSED: "Cupid Apollo," by Pontormo

LORETTO

Southern Alleghenies Museum of Art
Affiliate Institution: Saint Francis College
Saint Francis College Mall, **Loretto, PA 15940**
TEL: 814-472-6400
HRS: 10-4 M-F; 1:30-4:30 Sa, S   HOL: LEG/HOL!
ADM: F
HDC/ACC: Y; 1st floor only   PARKING: Y
REST/FAC: Y; Nearby on college campus   S/G: Y
PERM/COLL: AM: ptgs 19, 20; PHOT

This multi-cultural museum seeks to promote an appreciation of America's cultural legacy and especially the rich tradition of Pennsylvania art. **NOT TO BE MISSED:** John Sloan's "Bright Rocks"

MERION STATION

Barnes Foundation
300 North Latch's Lane, **Merion Station, PA 19066**
TEL: 215-667-0290
HRS: The Museum will reopen in 1995 Call!
PARKING: Y; Free on-street parking
PERM/COLL: FR: Impr, post/Impr; EARLY FR MODERN; AF; AM: ptgs, sculp 20

The Museum is closed for renovation during much of 1995. Many of the most outstanding works in the collection are on tour for the very first time.

MILL RUN

Fallingwater
Rt. 381 Mill, **Run, PA 15464**
TEL: 412-329-8501
HRS: 10-4 Tu-S (4/1 until 11/15); weekends only 11/15-4/1-open most Leg/Hol   DAY CLOSED: M
HOL: Some LEG/HOLS!
ADM: Y   ADULT: $6.00 Tu-F; $10 weekends, hols   SR CIT: $6.00 spec. rates weekdays
HDC/ACC: Y   PARKING: Y; Free   MUS/SH: Y   REST/FAC: Y; Open 5/1 - 11/1
GT: Y   GT/PH: ! in depth tour, $25pp, res req; children's tour by res
H/B: Y; National Historic Landmark   S/G: Y
PERM/COLL: ARCH; PTGS; JAP: gr; SCULP; NAT/AM

Magnificent is the word for this structure, one of Frank Lloyd Wright's most widely acclaimed works. The key to the setting of the house is the waterfall over which it is built. **NOT TO BE MISSED:** The Frank Lloyd Wright designed building.

PENNSYLVANIA

NEW BRIGHTON

The Merrick Art Gallery
Fifth Ave. & Eleventh Street, **New Brighton, PA 15066**
TEL: 412-646-1130
HRS: 10-4:30 Tu-Sa, 1-4 S; Summer: 10-4 W-Sa, 1-4 alternate Sundays   DAY CLOSED: M   HOL: LEG/HOL!
ADM: F
PARKING: Y; Street   H/B: Y   S/G:
PERM/COLL: EU & AM: ptgs 19

This fine cultural center in western Pennsylvania contains examples of romantic art by European and American artists. **NOT TO BE MISSED:** Small but excellent collection of Hudson River School paintings.

PAOLI

The Wharton Esherick Museum
Horseshoe Trail, **Paoli, PA 19301**
TEL: 610-644-5822
HRS: 10-4 Tu-F; 10-5 Sa; 1-5 S; (Mar-Dec)   DAY CLOSED: M   HOL: LEG/HOL!
ADM: Y   ADULT: $5.00   CHILDREN: $3.00 under 12   SR CIT: $5.00
HDC/ACC: Y   MUS/SH: Y   GT: Y   GT/PH: call 610-644-5822   DT: Y   TIME: Hourly, (reservations required)
H/B: Y
PERM/COLL: WOOD SCULP; FURNITURE; WOODCUTS; PTGS

Over 200 works in all media, produced between 1920-1970 which display the progession of Esherick's work are housed in his historic studio and residence. **NOT TO BE MISSED:** Oak spiral stairs

PHILADELPHIA

Afro-American Historical and Cultural Museum
702 Arch Streets, **Philadelphia, PA 19106**
TEL: 215-574-3121
HRS: 10-5 Tu-Sa; 12-6 S   DAY CLOSED: M   HOL: LEG/HOL!
ADM: Y   ADULT: $4.00   CHILDREN: $2.00   STUDENTS: $2.00   SR CIT: $2.00
HDC/ACC: Y   PARKING: Yes; Pay parking nearby   LIB: Y   MUS/SH: Y
GT: Y   GT/PH: call 215-574-0380 to reserve
PERM/COLL: JACK FRANK COLL: phot; PEARL JONES COLL: phot drgs, dec/art

A unique showplace, this is the first museum built by a major city to house and interpret collections of African-American art, history, and culture.

ON EXHIBIT/95:
10/29/93 - 1995   HEALING THE BODY AND THE MIND — This exhibition examines the role of sports in the African-American community, and its contribution towards strengthening and nurturing positive physical and spiritual values.

Afro-American Historical and Cultural Museum - continued

12/12/94 - 1/29/95	PHILADELPHIA AFRICAN-AMERICAN ARCHITECTS — A continuation on the theme of "Design Diaspora." This exhibit will highlight local architects whose works cover commercial and residential projects.
2/95 - 3/95	MOVING BACK BARRIERS: THE LEGACY OF CARTER G. WOODSON, 1875-1950 — Dr. Woodson was a world renowned scholar and proponent of the study of African-American life and history who has become known as the "Father of Black History."
4/95 - 5/95	AFRICAN-AMERICAN COMPOSERS OF CLASSICAL MUSIC — This first ever collaboration with the Philadelphia Orchestra will highlight African-American composers of classical music from the early 19th century to modern times.
5/95 - 10/95	AFRICAN-AMERICAN FEMALE SCULPTORS — The artists' works will be placed in an interpretive format to address the artistic, social, political and economic ramifications of their presence and impact on the art world of America. Included are Meta Warrick Fuller, Selma Burke, Edmonia Lewis, and Elizabeth Catlett.

PHILADELPHIA

La Salle University Art Museum
Affiliate Institution: LaSalle University
20th and Olney Ave, **Philadelphia, PA 19141**
TEL: 215-951-1221
HRS: 11-4 Tu-F; 2-4 S; Sep-Jul   DAY CLOSED: M, Sa   HOL: ACAD!
ADM: F
HDC/ACC: Y   PARKING: Y; Campus lot
PERM/COLL: EU: ptgs, sculp, gr 15-20; AM: ptgs

Many of the major themes and styles of Western art since the Middle ages are documemted in the comprehensive collection of paintings, prints, drawings and sculpture at this museum.

Museum of American Art of the Pennsylvania Academy of the Fine Arts
118 N Broad Street, **Philadelphia, PA 19102**
TEL: 215-972-7600
HRS: 10-5 Tu-Sa; 11-5 S   DAY CLOSED: M   HOL: LEG/HOL!
ADM: Y   ADULT: $5.00   CHILDREN: $3.00 F under 5   STUDENTS: $3.00   SR CIT: $3.00
HDC/ACC: Y   PARKING: Y; Public parking lots nearby ($2.00 discount at Parkway Corp. lots at Broad & Cherry and 15th & Cherry); some street parking   LIB: Y   MUS/SH: Y   GT: Y   GT/PH: F   DT: Y   TIME: Y   H/B: Y
PERM/COLL: AM: ptgs, sculp 18-20

The Pennsylvania Academy is located in the heart of downtown Philadelphia in a building recently restored to its original splendor. Its roster of past students includes some of the most renowned artists of the 19th & 20th centuries.

PENNSYLVANIA

PHILADELPHIA

Norman Rockwell Museum
601 Walnut Street, **Philadelphia, PA 19106**
TEL: 215-922-4345
HRS: 10-4 M-Sa; 11-4 S   HOL: LEG/HOL!
ADM: Y   ADULT: $2.00   CHILDREN: F (under 12)   STUDENTS: $1.50   SR CIT: $1.50
HDC/ACC: Y   PARKING: Y, pay parking in building   MUS/SH: Y   GT: Y   GT/PH: call for apecifics   H/B: Y
PERM/COLL: Complete collection of Saturday Evening Post cover illustrations

In the historic Curtis Publishing Building which published the Saturday Evening Post is housed the ·largest collection of art and Post covers by Norman Rockwell.

Philadelphia Museum of Art
26th Street & Benjamin Franklin Parkway, **Philadelphia, PA 19130**
TEL: 215-763-8100
HRS: 10-5 Tu-S; 10-8:45 W   DAY CLOSED: M   HOL: LEG/HOL!
F/DAY: S, 10-1   ADM: Y   ADULT: $6.00   CHILDREN: $3.00   STUDENTS: $3.00   SR CIT: $3.00
HDC/ACC: Y   PARKING: Y; Free   LIB: Y   MUS/SH: Y   REST/FAC: Y; 11;45-2:15
GT: Y   GT/PH: call 215-684-7863, res req.   DT: Y   TIME: Free-on the hour 11-3   H/B: Y   S/G: Y
PERM/COLL: EU: ptgs 19-20; CONT; DEC/ART; GR; AM: ptgs, sculp 17-20

With more than 400,000 works in the permanent collection, the Philadelphia Museum of Art is the 3rd largest art museum in the country. Housed within its more than 200 galleries are a myriad of artistic treasures from many continents and cultures. **NOT TO BE MISSED:** Van Gogh's "Sunflowers;" Newly re-opened Medieval & Early Renaissance Galleries (25 in all) which include a Romanesque cloister, a Gothic chapel, and a world-class collection of early Italian & Northern paintings.

ON EXHIBIT/95:

1/31 - 4/9/95	FROM CEZANNE TO MATISSE: GREAT FRENCH PAINTINGS FROM THE BARNES FOUNDATION — The Barnes Foundation is home to one of the world's finest collections of Impressionist, Post-Impressionist, and early modern paintings ever assembled by an individual. It represents the lifelong interest of Dr. Albert C. Barnes (1872-1951) a Philadelphia businessman and philanthropist who promoted the study and appreciation of the visual arts. 80 of the greatest masterpieces have been selected for this historic touring exhibition which represents the first and only time the works will be on view outside the Foundation galleries in Merion, Pennsylvania. This is the last stop for the tour. CAT WT*
Spring 1995	JOHN CAGE: ROLYHOLYOVER, A CIRCUS — One of the last compositions John Cage worked on before his death in September 1992, this appears to be an exhibition, but is in reality an orchestration of static works into a dramatic, non-static work of art. It includes methodologies and determines the points, placement and periods of display of 200 works by more than 50 artists. Other elements-musical performance, film and video screenings and readings-will be programmed and announced on a daily basis. WT
Fall 1995	TINA MODOTTI, PHOTOGRAPHS
Fall 1995	CONSTANTIN BRANCUSI

370

PENNSYLVANIA

PHILADELPHIA

Rodin Museum

Benjamin Franklin Parkway at 22nd Street, **Philadelphia, PA 19101**
TEL: 215-763-8100
HRS: 10-5 Tu-S   DAY CLOSED: M   HOL: LEG/HOL!
VOL/CONT: Y   ADM: F   HDC/ACC: Y   PARKING: Y; Free on-street parking   MUS/SH: Y
GT: Y   GT/PH: call for specifics   DT: Y   TIME: Free/twice a month- check schedule   H/B: Y   S/G: Y
PERM/COLL: RODIN: sculp, drgs

The largest collection of Rodin's sculptures and drawings outside of Paris is located in a charming and intimate building designed by architects Paul Cret and Jacques Greber. **NOT TO BE MISSED:** "The Thinker," by Rodin

The Rosenbach Museum & Library

2012 Delancey Place, **Philadelphia, PA 19103**
TEL: 215-732-1600
HRS: 11-4 Tu-S   DAY CLOSED: M   HOL: LEG/HOL!
ADM: Y   ADULT: $3.50   CHILDREN: $2.50   STUDENTS: $2.50   SR CIT: $2.50
LIB: Y   MUS/SH: Y   GT: Y   GT/PH: call 215-732-1600
PERM/COLL: BRIT & AM: ptgs; MINI SCALE DEC/ARTS; BOOK ILLUSTRATIONS

In the warm and intimate setting of a 19th-century townhouse, the Rosenbach Museum & Library retains an atmosphere of an age when great collectors lived among their treasures. It is the only collection of its kind open to the public in Philadelphia. **NOT TO BE MISSED:** Maurice Sendak drawings

ON EXHIBIT/95:

11/20/94 - 3/5/95   AMERICAN JUDAICA FROM THE COLLECTION OF DR. A. S. W. ROSENBACH — A collection of books, manuscripts and portraits that provide an eloquent history of the Jews in the New World, ranging from earliest colonization to immigration, Americanization, and religious organization.

4/1 - 9/30/95   SENDAK AT THE ROSENBACH The exhibition will examine the work of award winning children's author/illustrator Maurice Sendak alongside his private collection of rare books and manuscripts. It will permit a broad view of his work from his earliest picture books to his forthcoming new edition of Herman Melville's "Pierre."

Rosenwald-Wolf Gallery, The University of the Arts

Broad and Pine Streets, **Philadelphia, PA 19102**
TEL: 215-875-1116
HRS: 10-5 M-Tu & T-F; 10-9 W; 12-5 Sa, S; (10-5 weekdays Jun & Jul)   HOL: ACAD!
ADM: F   HDC/ACC: Y   PARKING: Y; Pay garages and metered parking nearby   GT: Y   GT/PH: !
PERM/COLL: non-collecting institution

This is the only university in the nation devoted exclusively to education and professional training in the visual and performing arts.

ON EXHIBIT/95:

1/27 - 3/3/95   CHRYSANNE STATHACOS — An installation and performance which will portray the fictitious life of Ann de Cybelle, a 19th century Parisian artist. It symbolizes the historical marginality of women artists denied equal historical representation.

PENNSYLVANIA

Rosenwald-Wolf Gallery, The University of the Arts - continued

3/17 - 4/21/95   PAINTINGS FROM THE HARLEM HORIZON ART STUDIO Paintings by twelve young artists from an inner city-arts program which advocate self-taught art as a vehicle for improving the health and quality of life of children and adults living in central Harlem.

PHILADELPHIA

The University of Pennsylvania Museum of Archaeology and Anthropology
Affiliate Institution: University of Pennsylvania
33rd and Spruce Streets, **Philadelphia, PA 19104**
TEL: 215-898-4000
HRS: 10-4:30 Tu-Sa; 1-5 S; closed S Mem day-Lab day   DAY CLOSED: M   HOL: LEG/HOL!
ADM: Y   ADULT: $5.00   CHILDREN: F (under 6)   STUDENTS: $2.50   SR CIT: $2.50
HDC/ACC: Y   PARKING: Y   LIB: Y   MUS/SH: Y   REST/FAC: Y   GT: Y   GT/PH: call 215-898-4015
DT: Y   TIME: 1:15 Sa, S (mid Sep-mid May)!   S/G: Y
PERM/COLL: GRECO/ROMAN; AF; AN/EGT; ASIA; MESOPOTAMIA; MESOAMERICAN; POLYNESIAN; AMERICAS

Dedicated to the understanding of the history and cultural heritage of humankind, the museum's galleries include objects from China, Ancient Egypt, Mesoamerica, South America, North America (Plains Indians), Polynesia, Africa, and the Greco-Roman world. **NOT TO BE MISSED:** Bull headed lyre, gold, lapis lazuli, shell on wooden construction; Ur, Iraq ca. 2650-2550 B.C.

ON EXHIBIT/95:
LONG TERM EXHIBITIONS:

       TIME AND RULERS AT TIKAL: ARCHITECTURAL SCULPTURE OF THE MAYA

       ANCIENT MESOPOTAMIA: THE ROYAL TOMBS OF UR.

       THE EGYPTIAN MUMMY: SECRETS AND SCIENCE

       RAVEN'S JOURNEY: THE WORLD OF ALASKA'S NATIVE PEOPLE

       BUDDHISM: HISTORY AND DIVERSITY OF A GREAT TRADITION

       THE ANCIENT GREEK WORLD — A complete reinstallation of the Museum's Ancient Greek gallery.

opening 5/20/95   THE SUN ALSO RISES: NATIVE AMERICANS OF THE SOUTHWEST (tent title) — About 300 artifacts of the Hopi, Zuni, Navajo and Apache people offer insights into the four tribes perspectives.

10/8/94 - 1/15/95   WAURA: DRAWINGS OF THE WAURA INDIANS OF BRAZIL — A glimpse of the culture and the lifestyle of this pottery making tribe of appproximately 100 members inhabiting the Uluri area in the Upper Xingu River region of Brazil.   WT

1/7 - 4/9/95   SEVEN YEARS IN TIBET, 1944-1951: PHOTOGRAPHS OF HEINRICH HARRER — 42 black and white photographs by the Austrian explorer and mountaineer who became an informal tutor and confidant to the then teenage Dalai Lama and was granted permission to photograph traditional ceremonies rarely witnessed by Westerners.   WT

4/15 - 8/31/995   ILLUMINATING THE PAST: ART AND ARTISTS OF THE BAN CHIANG PROJECT The exhibit highlights tthe partnership of artists and archeologists in the production of drawings from the field to the final publications.

PENNSYLVANIA

PHILADELPHIA

The Woodmere Art Museum
9201 Germantown Ave, **Philadelphia, PA 19118**
TEL: 215-247-0476
HRS: 10-5 Tu-Sa; 1-5 S   DAY CLOSED: M   HOL: LEG/HOL!
ADM: F   HDC/ACC: Y   PARKING: Y; Free parking adjacent to the building   LIB: Y   MUS/SH: Y
GT: Y   GT/PH: call 215-247-0476 to reserve
PERM/COLL: AM: ptgs 19, prints, gr, drgs; EU

The Woodmere Art Museum, located in a mid 1950's Victorian eclectic house, includes a large rotunda gallery, the largest exhibit space in the city. **NOT TO BE MISSED:** Benjamin West's "The Death of Sir Phillip Sydney"

ON EXHIBIT/95:

9/18/94 - 2/12/95   THE PERMANENT COLLECTION — Selected works from the collection by American artists, many local and regional, spanning the 19th and 20th centuries. Featured are Benjamin West, Frederic Church, Herman Herzog and recent acquisitions by Marlene Summers and Jimmy Leuders.

11/12/94 - 2/12/95   WATERCOLORS OF LOUIS KAHN — From the pyramids of Egypt to Bangladesh to Philadelphia, you will have the opportunity to look over the shoulder and through the eyes of one of the giants who shaped the physical world in which we live. These watercolor travel sketches have never before been exhibited in the U.S.

12/17/94 - 2/26/95   JACK GERBER AND JOANNA KLAIN — Demonstrating their printmaking expertise these noted practitioners of the burin and etching needle rely on the human figure as a focal point for their skillful compositions.

11/12/94 - 2/12/95   CARL PAPPE: WORKS ON PAPER — Approximately 60 works by this expatriate artist will be on view featuring his paintings and drawings from the 1980's with special emphasis on his distinctive abstract patterns of bright luminous colors organized in unifying compositions.

12/17/94 - 2/26/95   THE ELLA MAY FELL COLLECTION — On extended loan since 1986 this important collection of master works includes splendid examples of work by renowned European artists including Eugene Louis Boudin, Camille Corot, Honore Daumier, Pierre August Renoir and many other luminaries.

2/26 - 4/13/95   55TH ANNUAL JURIED EXHIBITION — One of Philadelphia's longest running exhibitions of its kind. Hundreds of area artists submit works and the jurors final choices reflect a vibrant cross section of the current trends in the Philadelphia arts community.

5/14 - 7/2/95   JANE PIPER: IN MEMORIAM (1916-1991) — A major retrospective of more than 100 works by this beloved artist acknowledged as one of Philadelphia's most important painters. Piper was noted for her abstract paintings with competing masses of bright color.

7/16 - 8/27/95   55TH ANNUAL MEMBERS EXHIBITION — The Annual, one of the Museum's most popular shows, celebrates its committment to and support of its members who cherish the pleasure and value inherent in the creative process.

9/10 - 12/3/95   THOMAS HOVENDEN — This first exhibition of its kind in the U.S., including work from all over the country, is dedicated to Hovenden, one of the finest artists to emerge from the 19th century. His works are charged with a penetrating dignity and deep understanding of the country people surrounding his home in Plymouth Meeting, PA.

373

PENNSYLVANIA

PITTSBURGH

The Andy Warhol Museum
Pittsburgh, PA
TEL: 412-237-8300
HRS: 11-6 W & S; 11-8 T-Sa   DAY CLOSED: M, Tu   HOL: 1/1, THGV, 12/25
ADM: Y   ADULT: $5.00   CHILDREN: $3.00   STUDENTS: $3.00   SR CIT: $4.00
HDC/ACC: Y; Ramp, elevators, restrooms
PARKING: Y; 2 pay lots adjacent to the museum (nominal fee charged); other pay lots nearby   MUS/SH: Y
REST/FAC: Y; Cafe   H/B: Y; Former Vokwein building renovated by Richard Gluckman Architects
PERM/COLL: ANDY WARHOL ARTWORKS

Newly opened, this long awaited 7 story museum with over 40,000 square feet of exhibition space will permanently highlight artworks spanning every aspect of Warhol's career. A unique feature of this museum will be a photo booth where visitors will be able to take cheap multiple pictures of themselves in keeping with the Warhol tradition. **NOT TO BE MISSED:** Rain Machine, a "daisy waterfall" measuring 132'by 240'; "Last Supper" paintings; 10' tall "Big Sculls" series

ON EXHIBIT/95:
Throughout 1995   The Museum's curators will be highlighting selected work in all media from the permanent collection which will be incorporated in the inaugural installation.

THROUGH SPRING 1995
                         INAUGURAL INSTALLATION — More than 500 works of art and extensive displays of related archival materials are shown together and offer the visitor an integrated presentation of the development of Warhol's work with emphasis on specific thematic concerns and his influence on popular culture.

5/95   SELECTED ANDY WARHOL DRAWINGS — The sixth floor gallery displays drawings from the 1949s-50's. This never-before-seen work includes assignments from Warhol's student years at Carnegie Tech (now Carnegie-Mellon University), his award-winning commercial illustrations, and masterful line drawings from the artist's sketchbooks. The work is rotated every six months, to insure that these drawings and other works on paper are not damaged by over-exposure to light.

The Carnegie Museum of Art
4400 Forbes Ave, **Pittsburgh, PA 15213**
TEL: 412-622-3131
HRS: 10-5 Tu-Sa; 1-5 S   DAY CLOSED: M   HOL: LEG/HOL!
ADM: Y   ADULT: $5.00   CHILDREN: $3.00   STUDENTS: $3.00   SR CIT: $4.00
HDC/ACC: Y   PARKING: Y; Pay garage   LIB: Y   MUS/SH: Y   REST/FAC: Y
GT: Y   GT/PH: call 412-622-3289 to reserve
DT: Y   TIME: call for specifics   H/B: Y   S/G: Y, COURT
PERM/COLL: FR/IMPR: ptgs; POST/IMPR: ptgs; AM: ptgs 19, 20; AB/IMPR; VIDEO ART

The original 1895 Carnegie Insititute, created in the spirit of opulence by architects Longfellow, Alden and Harlowe, was designed to house a library with art galleries, the museum itself, and a concert hall. A stunning light filled modern addition offers a spare purity that enhances the enjoyment of the art on the walls. **NOT TO BE MISSED:** Claude Monet's "Nympheas" (Water Lilies)

374

PENNSYLVANIA

The Carnegie Museum of Art - continued

ON EXHIBIT/95:

10/29/94 - 1/8/95	ARCHITECTURE IN A WELL ORDERED UNIVERSE: LORD BURLINGTON'S VILLA AT CHISWICK AND THOMAS JEFFERSON'S CAMPUS AT THE UNIVERSITY OF VIRGINIA
10/18/94 - 2/26/95	THE ART OF DECEPTION
3/11 - 5/21/95	SILVER IN AMERICA
11/4/95 - 2/18/96	CARNEGIE INTERNATIONAL

PITTSBURGH

The Frick Art Museum
7227 Reynolds Street, **Pittsburgh, PA 15221**
TEL: 412-371-0600
HRS: 10-5:30 Tu-Sa; 12-6 S   DAY CLOSED: M   HOL: LEG/HOL!
ADM: F   HDC/ACC: Y   PARKING: Y; Free   MUS/SH: Y   GT: Y   GT/PH: !   DT: !
PERM/COLL: EARLY IT/REN: ptgs; FR & FLEM: 17; BRIT: ptgs; DEC/ART

The Frick Art Museum features a permanent collection of European paintings, sculptures and decorative objects and temporary exhibitions from around the world.

ON EXHIBIT/95:

2/17 - 4/30/95	PAINTINGS FROM BURGHLEY HOUSE
6/17 - 8/27/95	MINGES: JAPANESE FOLK ART FROM THE MONTGOMERY COLLECTION
9/8 - 10/22/95	THE GOLDEN AGE OF DANISH ART: DRAWINGS FROM THE ROYAL MUSEUM OF FINE ARTS, COPENHAGEN
11/7/95 - 1/7/96	ITALIAN DRAWINGS FROM THE KATALAN COLLECTION
11/20/94 - 1/2/95	NINETEENTH-CENTURY GERMAN, AUSTRIAN AND HUNGARIAN DRAWINGS FROM BUDAPEST WT*

PITTSBURGH

Hunt Institute for Botanical Documentation
Affiliate Institution: Carnegie Mellon University
Pittsburgh, PA 15213
TEL: 412-268-2434
HRS: 9-12 & 1-5 M-F   DAY CLOSED: Sa, S   HOL: LEG/HOL!
ADM: F   HDC/ACC: Y   PARKING: Y; Pay parking nearby   LIB: Y   MUS/SH: Y
PERM/COLL: BOTANICAL W/COL 15-20; DRGS; GR

Botanical imagery from the Renaissance onward is well represented in this collection.

ON EXHIBIT/95:

11/17/94 - 2/95	NATURAL HISTORY ART WORKS FROM RAJASTHAN — This desert state in northwest India is known for its art, handicrafts, poetry, music and literature, beautiful palaces and rugged forts. The exhibition contains almost 80 watercolors and drawings by artists from the cities of Jaipur and Bikaner. CAT

375

PENNSYLVANIA

Hunt Institute for Botanical Documentation - continued

Spring 1995	WATERCOLORS BY TWO LONDON ARTISTS — Featured are watercolors of Alaskan wildflowers by Dr. Andrew P. Brown and tree paintings by John Wilkinson.
Fall 1995	8TH INTERNATIONAL EXHIBITION OF BOTANICAL ART AND ILLUSTRATION CAT

PITTSBURGH

Mattress Factory Ltd
500 Sampsonia Way, **Pittsburgh, PA 15212**
TEL: 412-231-3180
HRS: 10-5 Tu-Sa & 1-5 S (Sep-Jul or by appt)   DAY CLOSED: M   HOL: 1/1, EASTER, MEM/DAY, THGV, 12/25
ADM: F   HDC/ACC: Y   PARKING: Y   H/B: Y   S/G: Y

A restored turn of the century mattress factory is home to this unusual museum which primarily collects and commissions site-specific installations. **NOT TO BE MISSED:** "Danae," by James Turrell.

READING

Freedman Gallery
Affiliate Institution: Albright College
13th & Bern Streets, **Reading, PA 19604**
TEL: 215-921-2381
HRS: 12-4 M-W & F-Sa; 12-8 T; 1-4 S Sep-May; 12-4 M-F Jun, Jul   HOL: LEG/HOL!, ACAD!
ADM: F   HDC/ACC: Y   PARKING: Y
PERM/COLL: CONT: gr, ptgs

The only gallery in Southeastern Pennsylvania outside of Philadelphia that presents an on-going program of provocative work by todays leading artists. **NOT TO BE MISSED:** Mary Miss Sculpture creates an outdoor plaza which is part of the building

ON EXHIBIT/95:

2/14 - 3/19/95	BODY ECHO — British-born Hugh O'Donnell will create an environment of monumental wall drawings expressly for the Gallery. Composed of multiple square modular sheets of paper, the collective installation contains continuous lines which have contracted and mutated as they move through the two-dimensional space of the work.
2/14 - 3/19/95	DRAWINGS FROM THE HUGH O'DONNELL MASTER CLASS — Examples of the monumental drawings created by participants in the artists' master drawing class.
3/18 - 4/23/95	VISIONS OF MODERNITY: PHOTOGRAPHS FROM THE PERUVIAN ANDES, 1900-1930 — This historical exhibition of recently discovered photographs features 11 Peruvian photographers who worked in the southern Andes. Their images show the unmistakable influence of the modern movement in photography, while at the same time giving a marvelous overview of all levels of Peruvian society in the early 20th century.
5/4 - 5/4/95	ANNUAL JURIED STUDENT EXHIBITION
6/1 - 7/23/95	SUMMER EXHIBITION OF SOUTHEASTERN PENNSYLVANIA ARTISTS

376

PENNSYLVANIA

SCRANTON

Everhart Museum
Nay Aug Park, **Scranton, PA 18510**
TEL: 717-346-7186
HRS: 10-5 Tu-F; 12-5 Sa, S   DAY CLOSED: M   HOL: LEG/HOL!
ADM: F   HDC/ACC: Y   PARKING: Y   MUS/SH: Y
PERM/COLL: AM: early 19; WORKS ON PAPER; AM: folk, gr; AF; NAT/AM

This art, science, and natural history museum which includes a 40 seat planetarium is the only wide-ranging museum of its type in Northeastern Pennsylvaia.

ON EXHIBIT/95:

11/13/94 - 2/5/95	THE UTOPIA BODY PAINT COLLECTION: AUSTRALIAN ABORIGINAL PAINTINGS
11/10/94 - 4/9/95	PENNSYLVANIA PAINTERS
1/14/95	PERMANENT INSTALLATION OF 19TH AND 20TH CENTURY AMERICAN ART
2/95 - 3/95	INTIMATE VISIONS: PHOTOGRAPHS FROM THE CENTER FOR CREATIVE PHOTOGRAPHY
4/95 - 5/95	BARBIE AND OTHER TOYS
4/16 - 10/8/95	AMERICAN FOLK ART PAINTINGS
6/10 - 7/23/95	MAJOR LEAGUE/MINOR LEAGUE: AMERICA'S BASEBALL STADIUMS

UNIVERSITY PARK

Palmer Museum of Art
Affiliate Institution: The Pennsylvania State University
Curtin Road, **University Park, PA 16802**
TEL: 814-865-7472
HRS: 10-4:30 Tu-Sa; 12-4 S   DAY CLOSED: M   HOL: LEG/HOL!, 12/25-1/1
ADM: F
HDC/ACC: Y   PARKING: Y; Limited meter, nearby pay   MUS/SH: Y
GT: Y   GT/PH: call 814-865-7672 to reserve   DT: Y   TIME: !   S/G: Y
PERM/COLL: AM; EU; AS; S/AM: ptgs, sculp, works on paper, ceramics

A dramatic and exciting new facility for this collection of 35 centuries of artworks. **NOT TO BE MISSED:** The new building by Charles Moore, a fine example of post-modern architecture.

ON EXHIBIT/95:

1/10 - 3/5/95	THE STROKE OF GENIUS: REMBRANDT ETCHINGS FROM THE CARNEGIE MUSEUM OF ART — These etchings display Rembrandt's unsurpassed mastery of the medium, technical innovations, stylistic advancements, and the breadth of his subjects. WT
1/10 - 3/5/95	LOOKING FORWARD, LOOKING BACK: THE ETCHINGS OF LEONARD LEIBOWITZ — This contemporary artist has mastered 17th century techniques and using them, creates contemporary imagery.

PENNSYLVANIA

Palmer Museum of Art - continued

1/18 - 5/95	CONTINUITY, INNOVATION, AND CONNOISSEURSHIP: OLD MASTER PAINTINGS AND DRAWINGS FROM PENNSYLVANIA COLLECTIONS — The 30 Renaissance and Baroque paintings and works on paper will complement several of the periods on display in the museum.
7/18 - 9/17/95	DREAMTIME: AUSTRALIAN ABORIGINAL ART FROM THE COLLECTION OF JOHN W. KLUGE — Bark paintings, mortuary sculpture from the tropical forests of northern Australia, and acrylic dot paintings will be featured to represent a merging of two separate worlds: the 40,000 year history of the aborigines and the contemporary world of acrylic paint.
10/3 - 12/10/95	MEDIEVAL ART IN AMERICA: PATTERNS OF COLLECTING 1800-1940 — Works from 11 of the most important collections of medieval art in the country attempt to illuminate the artistic, intellectual and cultural contexts of specific collectors and their times.

WILKES-BARRE

Sordoni Art Gallery
Affiliate Institution: Wilkes University
150 S. River Street, **Wilkes-Barre, PA 18766-0001**
TEL: 717-831-4325
HRS: 12-5 M-S; 12-9 T   HOL: LEG/HOL!
ADM: F
HDC/ACC: Y   PARKING: Y
PERM/COLL: AM: ptgs 19, 20; WORKS ON PAPER

Located on the grounds of Wilkes University, in the historic district of downtown Wilkes-Barre, this facility is best known for mounting both historical and contemporary exhibitions.

KINGSTON

Fine Arts Center Galleries, University of Rhode Island
College of Arts and Sciences, **Kingston, RI 02881-0820**
TEL: 401-792-2131
HRS: Main Gallery 12-4 & 7:30-9:30 Tu-F; 1-4 Sa; Phot Gallery 12-4 Tu-F & 1-4Sa   DAY CLOSED: S
HOL: LEG/HOL!; ACAD!
ADM: F
HDC/ACC: Y   PARKING: Y   LIB: Y   GT: Y   GT/PH: call 401-792-2131 to reserve   DT: Y   TIME: !
PERM/COLL: non-collecting institution

A university affiliated "kunsthalle" distinguished for the activity of their programming (20-25 exhibitions annually) and in generating that programming internally. Contemporary exhibitions in all media are shown as well as film and video showings.

ON EXHIBIT/95:
Main Gallery
   1/24 - 3/4/95   SOFT ABSTRACTION: MARY HEILMANN; DAVID REED; MICHAEL VENEZIA; MERRILL WAGNER

   4/11 - 5/6/95   ANNUAL JURIED STUDENT SHOW

Photography Gallery
   1/25 - 2/25/95   DORIT CYPIS (Minnesota)

   3/7 - 4/8/95   WILL LARSEN (Maryland)

   4/18 - 5/6/95   AMY BLUHM

NEWPORT

Newport Art Museum
76 Bellevue Avenue, **Newport, RI 02840**
TEL: 401-848-8200
HRS: 10-4 Tu-Sa; 1-4 S   DAY CLOSED: M   HOL: 1/1, THGV, 12/25
ADM: Y   ADULT: $6.00   CHILDREN: F (under 12)   STUDENTS: $3.00   SR CIT: $3.00
HDC/ACC: Y   PARKING: Y   LIB: Y   MUS/SH: Y   H/B: Y
PERM/COLL: AM: w/col 19, 20

Historic J. N. A. Griswold House in which the museum is located was designed by Richard Morris Hunt in 1862-1864.

ON EXHIBIT/95:
   10/22/94 - 6/18/95   SELECTIONS FROM THE PERMANENT COLLECTION: THE 19TH CENTURY

   12/17/94 - 6/11/95   DIRECTOR'S CHOICE: OLD FRIENDS AND NEW

   1/13 - 3/12/95   FOLLY AND CHOICE: MYTHIC PAINTINGS BY DANIEL LUDWIG

RHODE ISLAND

NEWPORT

Redwood Library and Athenaeum
50 Bellevue Avenue, **Newport, RI 02840**
TEL: 401-847-0292
HRS: 9:30-5:30 M-S   HOL: LEG/HOL!
ADM: F   PARKING: Y   LIB: Y   H/B: Y
PERM/COLL: AM: gr, drgs, phot, portraits, furniture, dec/art 18, 19

Established in 1747, this facility serves as the oldest circulating library in the country. Designed by Peter Harrison, considered America's first architect, it is the most significant surviving public building from the Colonial period. **NOT TO BE MISSED:** Paintings by Gilbert Stuart and Charles Bird King

PROVIDENCE

David Winton Bell Gallery
Affiliate Institution: Brown University
List Art Center, 64 College Street, **Providence, RI 02912**
TEL: 401-863-2932
HRS: 11-4 M-F & 1-4 Sa-S (Sept-May)   HOL: 1/1, THGV, 12/25
ADM: F   HDC/ACC: Y   PARKING: Y; On-street   H/B: Y
PERM/COLL: GR & PHOT 20; WORKS ON PAPER 16-20; CONT: ptgs

Housed in a Philip Johnson designed building one block from downtown Providence, the Gallery features contemporary and historical exhibitions as well as works from its own collection.

ON EXHIBIT/95:

Through 1/22/95	A VIEW TO THE FUTURE: RECENT ACQUISITIONS
2/4 - 3/12/95	IN YOUR FACE: WEEGEE AND BEYOND
3/18 - 4/9/95	ANNUAL JURIED STUDENT COMPETITION
4/22 - 5/4/95	THE PICTORIAL MOTIVE IN CONTEMPORARY SCULPTURE
8/26 - 10/8/95	RICHARD FLEISCHNER: PROJECTS
10/21 - 11/26/95	SOPIE CALLE
12/9/95 - 1/21/96	BRITISH POP AND BEYOND: THE STEINBERG COLLECTION

Museum of Art
Affiliate Institution: Rhode Island School of Design
224 Benefit Street, **Providence, RI 02903**
TEL: 401-454-6500
HRS: 10:30-5 Tu, W, F, Sa; 12-8 T; 2-5 S, Hol; 12-5 W-Sa, 6/30-Lab day   DAY CLOSED: M   HOL: LEG/HOL!
F/DAY: Sa   ADM: Y   ADULT: $2.00   CHILDREN: $0.50 (5-18)   STUDENTS: $0.50   SR CIT: $1.00
HDC/ACC: Y   PARKING: Y; Nearby pay, 1/2 price with museum adm   MUS/SH: Y
GT: Y   GT/PH: call 401-454-6534 to reserve   S/G: Y
PERM/COLL: AM: ptgs, dec/art; JAP: gr, cer; LAT/AM

RHODE ISLAND

Museum of Art - continued

The museum's outstanding collections are housed on three levels: in a Georgian style building completed in 1926, in Pendleton House, completed in 1906, and in the newly constructed Daphne Farago Wing, a center dedicated to the display and interpretation of contemporary art in all media. **NOT TO BE MISSED:** "Le Repos," portrait of Berthe Morisot by Edward Monet, oil on canvas.

ON EXHIBIT/95:

Through Spring 1995	FROM THE RESERVE: OLD MASTER AND 19TH CENTURY EUROPEAN PAINTING AND SCULPTURE
10/21/94 - 1/22/95	PATTERNS AND POETRY: NOH ROBES FROM THE LUCY TRUMAN ALDRICH COLLECTION — 47 examples of spectacular costumes for the Japanese Noh theatre, primarily of the 18th and 19th centuries. The robes in this extensive collection have never before been in a travelling exhibition and have not been on view since the 1930's CAT
11/18/94 - 1/16/95	THE STUDIO MUSEUM OF HARLEM: TWENTY FIVE YEARS OF AFRICAN-AMERICAN ART — In celebration of the Studio Museum's 25th anniversary, this traveling exhibition will highlight paintings, sculpture and works on paper created between 1968-1993 by noted African-American artists. WT
11/94 - 1/95	ARTISTS BY ARNESON: POLLOCK AND OTHER ECCENTRICS — 35 sculptures and 30 works on paper by this San Francisco Bay artist (1930 - 1992).
2/3 - 4/2/95	JENNIFER BARTLETT: A PRINT RETROSPECTIVE
2/10 - 4/23/95	19TH CENTURY SCULPTURE FROM NEW ENGLAND COLLECTIONS — Works by Rodin, Hiram Power, Dalou, and Thomas Crawford.

PROVIDENCE

Rhode Island Black Heritage Society
One Hilton Street, **Providence, RI 02905**
TEL: 401-751-3490
HRS: 9-4:30 M-F   DAY CLOSED: Sa, S   HOL: LEG/HOL!
ADM: F
HDC/ACC: Y   PARKING: Y   LIB: Y   MUS/SH: Y
PERM/COLL: PHOT; AF: historical collection

The Society collects, documents and preserves the history of African-Americans in the state of Rhode Island with an archival collection which includes photos, rare books, and records dating back to the 18th century. **NOT TO BE MISSED:** Polychrome relief wood carvings by Elizabeth N. Prophet

SOUTH CAROLINA

CHARLESTON

City Hall Council Chamber Gallery
Broad & Meeting Streets, **Charleston, SC 29401**
TEL: 803-724-3799
HRS: 9-5 M-F; closed 12-1   DAY CLOSED: Sa, S   HOL: LEG/HOL!
ADM: F
HDC/ACC: Y   GT: Y   GT/PH: call 803-724-3799 for specifics   H/B: Y
PERM/COLL: AM: ptgs 18, 19

What is today Charleston's City Hall was erected in 1801 in Adamsesque style to be the Charleston branch of the First Bank of the United States. **NOT TO BE MISSED:** "George Washington," by John Trumbull is unlike any other and is considered the best portrait ever done of him.

Gibbes Museum of Art
135 Meeting Street, **Charleston, SC 29401**
TEL: 803-722-2706
HRS: 10-5 Tu-Sa; 1-5 S-M   HOL: LEG/HOL!
ADM: Y   ADULT: $3.00   CHILDREN: $1.00   STUDENTS: $2.00   SR CIT: $2.00
HDC/ACC: Y; Right side of museum   PARKING: Y; Municipal   LIB: Y   MUS/SH: Y
GT: Y   GT/PH: call 803-722-2706   S/G: Y
PERM/COLL: AM: reg portraits, miniature portraits; JAP: gr

Charleston's only fine arts museum offers a nationally significant collection of American art, American Renaissance (1920's-40's) period room interiors done in miniature scale, and a miniature portrait collection, the oldest and finest in the country. **NOT TO BE MISSED:** "The Green Gown," by Childe Hassam (1859-1935)

ON EXHIBIT/95:

Through Spring 95	TASTE AND STYLE: CLASSICISM IN CHARLESTON — Works focusing on Charleston 1815-1940 including historic portraits, landscapes, still-lifes, and genre paintings.
10/25/94 - 1/2/95	CORRIE MCCALLUM: A LIFE IN ART — Identifying and absorbing her environment and frequent travels, the artist's oils, prints and drawings reveal strong composition, color and emotion.
1/26 - 3/26/95	INFORMING SPIRIT — Works of art in Western Canada and the Southwest ranging from representational to abstract with emphasis on artists from New Mexico (1920's-40's) and Canadian painters.
4/2 - 5/28/95	ALONE IN A CROWD: PRINTS BY AFRICAN-AMERICAN ARTISTS OF THE 1930'S-40's FROM THE COLLECTION OF REBA AND DAVE WILLIAMS — The works of 41 African-American printmakers working in a wide variety of styles and techniques during the depression decades (many under the auspices of the WPA) will be on view in this 106 piece exhibition. WT
4/6 - 5/7/95	JONATHAN GREEN — 50 paintings representing a Gullah view of the Low country.
Late Spring 1995	PALM AND PINE: ART OF A REGION (TENT!) — A historic survey of subject matter in a variety of mediums, from northern Florida, Georgia (coastal to Augusta), and South Carolina.

Gibbes Museum of Art - continued

8/95 - 11/95   CHARLESTON THEN AND NOW — In cooperation with the Preservation Society of Charleston and its 75th anniversary, the city's architecture and the effects of its preservation movement will be the topic of this photographic essay.

11/95 - 1/96   THE ARCHITECTURE OF QUILTS — A unique presentation featuring the collaboration of state architects and quilters addressing architectural history, design and details of buildings. Computer generated patterns created by architects will be translated into quilts by craftpersons.

COLUMBIA

Columbia Museum of Arts & Gibbes Planetarium
1112 Bull Street, **Columbia, SC 29201**
TEL: 803-799-2810
HRS: 10-5 Tu-F; 12:30-5 Sa-S   DAY CLOSED: M   HOL: 1/1, 7/4, LAB/DAY, THGV, 12/24, 12/25
ADM: F
HDC/ACC: Y   PARKING: Y   LIB: Y   MUS/SH: Y   GT: Y   GT/PH: call 803-799-2810   H/B: Y
PERM/COLL: KRESS COLL OF MED, BAROQUE & REN; AS; REG

The Thomas Taylor Mansion, built in 1808, functions as the museum, while the Horry-Guignard House, one of the oldest in Columbia, is used as office space on the site. The Gibbs Planetarium, open weekends only, is inside the museum building.

ON EXHIBIT/95:
3/25 - 5/25/95   IMAGES OF BRITISH-INDIA'S GOLDEN AGE — The aquatints on view convey the romantic image of India under the first British governors. From 1780-1880 British artists portrayed the beauty and romance of an idealized land and the rich and varied subject matter inspired paintings, watercolors and some of the finest prints ever produced.

WT

FLORENCE

Florence Museum of Art, Science & History
558 Spruce Street, **Florence, SC 29501**
TEL: 803-662-3351
HRS: 10-5 Tu-Sa; 2-5 S   DAY CLOSED: M   HOL: LEG/HOL!
ADM: F
HDC/ACC: Y; Limited, not all areas accessible   PARKING: Y   H/B: Y
PERM/COLL: AM/REG: ptgs; SW NAT/AM; pottery; CER

Founded to promote the arts and sciences, this museum, located in a 1939 art deco style building originally constructed as a private home, is surrounded by the grounds of Timrod Park. **NOT TO BE MISSED:** "Francis Marion Crossing to Pee Dee," by Edward Arnold

ON EXHIBIT/95:
12/4/94 - 1/30/95   FRIENDS OF THE FLORENCE MUSEUM MINIATURE ART COMPETITION

12/4/94 - 1/30/95   PHOTOGRAPHY BY ANNE LANE

SOUTH CAROLINA

Florence Museum of Art, Science & History - continued

2/95	SOUTHERN NATIONAL — Florence Museum Statewide Art Competition
3/95	KEEPER OF THE GATE — Photographs of iron work by Philip Simmons
4/95	SOUTH CAROLINA WATERCOLOR SOCIETY TRAVELING SHOW
	RECENT WORKS BY SUZANNE JEBALLY
5/95 - 6/95	RECENT WORKS BY JACK DOWIS
7/95 - 8/95	RECENT WORKS BY ERNIE GERHARDT
9/95 - 10/95	42ND ANNUAL PEE DEE REGIONAL ART COMPETITION
10/95 - 11/95	CHEVIS CLARK AND CAROL MCDANIEL
12/95 - 1/96	FRIENDS OF THE FLORENCE MUSEUM MINIATURE ART COMPETITION

GREENVILLE

Bob Jones University Collection of Sacred Art
Affiliate Institution: Jones University
Jones University, **Greenville, SC 29614**
TEL: 803-242-5100
HRS: 2-5 Tu-S   DAY CLOSED: M   HOL: 1/1, 7/4, 12/20 thru 12/25
ADM: F
HDC/ACC: Y   PARKING: Y; Nearby   MUS/SH: Y
GT: Y   GT/PH: call 803-242-5100 for specifics
PERM/COLL: EU: ptgs including Rembrandt, Tintoretto, Titian Veronese, Sebastiano del Piombo

One of the finest collections of relegous art in America.

Greenville County Museum of Art
420 College Street, **Greenville, SC 29601**
TEL: 803-271-7570
HRS: 10-5 Tu-Sa; 1-5 S   DAY CLOSED: M   HOL: LEG/HOL!
ADM: F
HDC/ACC: Y   PARKING: REST/FAC:
GT: Y   GT/PH: call 803-271-7570 to reserve
PERM/COLL: AM: ptgs, sculp, gr; REG

The Southern Collection is nationally recognized as one of the country's best regional collections and provides a survey of American history as well as American art history from 1726-World War II.

ON EXHIBIT/95:

11/2/94 - 1/4/95	NOSTALGIC JOURNEY: AMERICAN ILLUSTRATION FROM THE COLLECTION OF THE DELAWARE ART MUSEUM — Almost 75 illustrations from classics such as "The Story of King Arthur," and "Grimms Fairy Tales" as well as covers and illustrations for "Saturday Evening Post," "Scribners" and many others will be on exhibit. WT

MURRELLS INLET

Brookgreen Gardens
1931 Brookgreen Gardens Drive, **Murrells Inlet, SC 29576**
TEL: 803-237-4218
HRS: 9:30-5:30   HOL: 12/25
ADM: Y   ADULT: $6.50   CHILDREN: $3.00 6-12
HDC/ACC: Y   PARKING: Y   MUS/SH: Y   REST/FAC: Y; New Terrace Cafe open year round
GT: Y   GT/PH: call 803-237-4218 to reserve   H/B: Y   S/G: Y
PERM/COLL: AM: sculp 19, 20

The first public sculpture garden created in America is located on the grounds of a 200-year old rice plantation. It is the largest permanent outdoor collection of American Figurative Sculpture in the world with 542 works by 239 sculptors on permanent display. **NOT TO BE MISSED:** "Fountain of the Muses," by Carl Milles.

SPARTANBURG

The Arts Council of Spartanburg County, Inc
385 South Spring Street, **Spartanburg, SC 29306**
TEL: 803-583-2776
HRS: 9-5 M-F; 10-2 Sa; 2-5 S   HOL: LEG/HOL!, EASTER, 12/24
ADM: F
HDC/ACC: Y   PARKING: Y; Adjacent to the building   MUS/SH: Y
PERM/COLL: AM/REG: ptgs, gr, dec/art

A multi-cultural Arts Center that presents 20 exhibits of regional art each year. **NOT TO BE MISSED:** "Girl With the Red Hair," by Robert Henri

SOUTH DAKOTA

BROOKINGS

South Dakota Art Museum
Medary Ave at Harvey Dunn Street, **Brookings, SD 57007**
TEL: 605-688-5423
HRS: 8-5 M-F; 10-5 Sa; 1-5 S, holidays   HOL: 1/1, THGV, 12/25
ADM: F
HDC/ACC: Y; Elevator service to all 3 levels from west entrance   PARKING: Y
LIB: Y! MUS/SH: Y
GT: Y   GT/PH: call 605-688-5423 for specifics   S/G: Y
PERM/COLL: HARVEY DUNN: ptgs; OSCAR HOWE: ptgs; NAT/AM; REG 19, 20

Many of the state's art treasures including the paintings by Harvey Dunn of pioneer life on the prairie, a complete set of Marghab embroidery from Madeira, outstanding paintings by regional artist Oscar Howe, and masterpieces from all the Sioux tribes are displayed in the 6 galleries of this museum established in 1970.

ON EXHIBIT/95:

12/10/94 - 1/8/95	THE GREAT OUTDOORS: FROM THE COLLECTION — Landscapes, wildlife paintings and other works with an outdoor theme.
12/10/94 - 1/8/95	THE GREAT OUTDOORS: CONTEMPORARY SOUTH DAKOTA ARTISTS
1/14 - 2/19/95	EUGENE BUECHEL, S. J.: THE ROSEBUD AND ITS PEOPLE 1922-1942 — Black and white photographs taken by Buechel when he served the Lakota (Western Sioux) on the Rosebud.
2/25 - 4/16/95	SIGNE STUART: RETROSPECTIVE — An overview of the last 30 years of Stuart's work. CAT
4/22 - 8/95	FROM THE COLLECTION: FACES AND FIGURES — The human form as depicted in a variety of styles and media.

MITCHELL

Friends of the Middle Border Museum
1311 S. Duff St., **Mitchell SD 57301**
TEL: 605-996-2122
HRS: 8-6 M-Sa & 10-6 S (Jun-Aug); 9-5 M-F & 1-5 Sa, S (May-Sep); by appt(Oct-Apr)   HOL: 1/1, THGV, 12/25
ADM: Y   ADULT: $3.00   CHILDREN: F (under 12)   STUDENTS: $1.25 (13-18)   SR CIT: $2.00
HDC/ACC: Y; Partially, half of the complex is wheelchair accessible. The area gallery is not wheelchair accessible.
PARKING: Y LIB: Y MUS/SH: Y   GT: Y   GT/PH: $1.50 call 605-996-2122   H/B: Y
PERM/COLL: AM: ptgs 19, 20; NAT/AM

This Museum of American Indian and Pioneer life also has an eclectic art collection in the Case Art Gallery, the oldest regional art gallery which includes works by Harvey Dunn, James Earle Frazer, Gutzon Borglum, Oscar Howe, Childe Hassam, Elihu Vedder, Anna Hyatt Huntington and many others.

MITCHELL

Oscar Howe Art Center
119 W. Third, **Mitchell, SD 57301**
TEL: 605-996-4111
HRS: 10-5 Tu-Sa, or by appointment   DAY CLOSED: S, M   HOL: LEG/HOL!
ADM: F
HDC/ACC: Y   PARKING: Y; On-street   MUS/SH: Y   GT: Y   GT/PH: call 605-996-4111   H/B: Y
PERM/COLL: OSCAR HOWE: ptgs, gr

Oscar Howe paintings and lithographs that document his career from his Santa Fe Indian School years through his mature work on a 1902 Carnegie Library are featured in the permanent collection of this art center that bears his name. **NOT TO BE MISSED:** "Sun and Rain Clouds Over Hills," dome painted by Oscar Howe in 1940 as a WPA project (Works Progress Administration)

PINE RIDGE

The Heritage Center, Inc
Affiliate Institution: Red Cloud Indian School
Pine Ridge, SD 57770
TEL: 605-867-5491
HRS: 9-5 M-F   DAY CLOSED: Sa, S   HOL: EASTER, THGV, 12/25
ADM: F
HDC/ACC: Y   PARKING: Y   LIB: Y   MUS/SH: Y   GT: Y   GT/PH: call 605-867-5491   H/B: Y
PERM/COLL: CONT NAT/AM; GR; NW COAST; ESKIMO: 19, 20

The Center is located on the Red Cloud Indian school campus in an historic 1888 building built by the Sioux and operated by them with the Franciscan sisters. The Holy Rosary Mission church features a Gothic interior with designs by the Sioux.

RAPID CITY

Dahl Fine Arts Center
713 Seventh Street, **Rapid City, SD 57701**
TEL: 605-394-4101
HRS: 9-5 M-Sa & 1-5 S (winter); 9-8 M-T; 9-5 F, Sa; 1-5 S (summer)   HOL: LEG/HOL!
ADM: F
HDC/ACC: Y   PARKING: Y; Metered   LIB: Y   MUS/SH: Y   GT: Y   GT/PH: call 605-394-4101
PERM/COLL: CONT; REG: ptgs; gr 20

The Dahl presents a forum for all types of fine arts: visual, theatre, and music, that serve the Black Hills region, eastern Wyoming, Montana, and Western Nebraska. **NOT TO BE MISSED:** 200 foot cyclorama depicting the history of the US.

SOUTH DAKOTA

RAPID CITY

Sioux Indian Museum and Crafts Center
515 West Boulevard, **Rapid City, SD 57701**
TEL: 605-348-0557
HRS: 9-5 M-Sa & 1-5 S Jun-Sep; 10-5 Tu-Sa & 1-5 S Oct-May   HOL: 1/1, THGV, 12/25
ADM: F
HDC/ACC: Y   PARKING: Y   MUS/SH: Y   GT: Y   GT/PH: call 605-348-0557 for specifics
PERM/COLL: SIOUX ARTS

Displays of the rich diversity of historic and contemporary Sioux art may be enjoyed at this museum and native crafts center.

SIOUX FALLS

Civic Fine Arts Center
235 West Tenth Street, **Sioux Falls, SD 57102**
TEL: 605-336-1167
HRS: 9-5 M-F; 10-5 Sa; 1-5 S & Hol   HOL: 1/1, THGV, 12/25
ADM: F
HDC/ACC: Y   PARKING: Y   H/B: Y
PERM/COLL: REG/ART: all media

The building was originally the 1902 Carnegie Library.

ON EXHIBIT/95:

12/16/94 - 1/29/95	UNITING MINORITIES: NEW ART FORMS BY A NEW COMMUNITY — Recent immigrant artists from such diverse societies as Viet Nam, Romania, Mexico and Armenia bring their rich cultural heritage to Sioux Falls.
2/3 - 3/5/95	LISA BELL REINAUER: RECENT WORKS — Emotionally charged paintings and drawings of the spiritual landscape by this Louisiana artist.
4/8 - 6/4/95	A SHUTTERING EXPERIENCE: PHOTOGRAPHS OF WORLD WAR II — Black and white photographs by noted photo-journalists.
Lower East Gallery	THE COUNTY LINE EXHIBITION SERIES

SISSETON

Tekakwitha Fine Arts Center
401 South 8th Street W., **Sisseton, SD 57262**
TEL: 605-698-7058
HRS: 9-5 daily (Mem day-Lab day); 9-5 Tu-F & 12:30-4 Sa-S (mid Sep-mid May)   HOL: LEG/HOL!
ADM: F
HDC/ACC: Y   PARKING: Y   MUS/SH: Y   GT: Y   GT/PH: call 605-698-7058 for specifics
PERM/COLL: TWO DIMENSIONAL ART OF LAKE TRAVERSE DAKOTA SIOUX RESERVATION

VERMILLION

University Art Galleries
Warren M. Lee Center, University of South Dakota, **Vermillion, SD 57069**
TEL: 605-677-5481
HRS: 10-4 M-F; 1-5 Sa, S   HOL: ACAD!
ADM: F
HDC/ACC: Y   PARKING: Y
PERM/COLL: Sioux artist OSCAR HOWE; HIST REG/ART

ON EXHIBIT/95:

12/19/94 - 1/9/95	CARTOONING AIDS AROUND THE WORLD — 50 original editorial cartoons focusing attention on the AIDS epidemic.
1/11 - 1/31/95	AFRICA: BETWEEN MYTH AND REALITY — Paintings and etchings inspired by Betty LaDuke's travels to Egypt, Kenya, Mali, Morocco, Nigeria, Senegal, the Ivory Coast and Cameroon between 1972 and 1992.
2/3 - 2/26/95	WILBER STILWELL STUDENT AWARDS EXHIBITION
3/1 - 3/21/95	INTIMATE OBJECTS: SMALL SCULPTURE INVITATIONAL — Mixed media sculptures exploring the whimsy and fantasy of artists who work in small scale assemblages and constructions.
3/23 - 4/8/95	AFRICAN ART FROM THE UNIVERSITY OF SOUTH DAKOTA COLLECTION
4/17 - 5/13/95	MFA AND BFA EXHIBITION
	AFRICA AND THE AMERICAS FESTIVAL — A University-wide festival from Martin Luther King Day until May 13th focusing on the rich cultural interaction between Africa and the Americas including lectures, performances and films as well as the exhibitions listed.
6/1 - 6/30/95	COME DANCE WITH US — 50 paintings by noted artists on the theme of dance by Native-American artists will be seen in this exhibit that presents a broad perspective on Indian dance from social dances of the Northern Plains to stomp dance of Oklahoma, to Pueblo religious dances.
7/5 - 7/30/95	SUMMER ARTS XVIII: REGIONAL EXHIBITION — A biennial, seven state exhibition sponsored by the University Art Galleries.

TENNESSEE

CHATTANOOGA

Hunter Museum of Art
10 Bluff View, **Chattanooga, TN 37403**
TEL: 615-267-0968
HRS: 10-4:30 Tu-Sa; 1-4:30 S   DAY CLOSED: M   HOL: LEG/HOL!
ADM: Y
HDC/ACC: Y   PARKING: Y   LIB: Y   MUS/SH: Y
GT: Y   GT/PH: call 615-267-0968 to reserve   H/B: Y
PERM/COLL: AM: ptgs, gr, sculp, 18-20

Blending the old and the new, the Hunter Museum consists of a 1904 mansion with a 1975 contemporary addition.

KNOXVILLE

Knoxville Museum of Art
410 Tenth Street, World's Fair Park, **Knoxville, TN 37916**
TEL: 615-525-6101
HRS: 10-5 Tu-T, Sa; 11:30-5 S; 10-9 F   DAY CLOSED: M   HOL: LEG/HOL!
ADM: F
HDC/ACC: Y   PARKING: Y; Free parking across the street   MUS/SH: Y
REST/FAC: Y; Cafe open for lunch daily 11:30-2
GT: Y   GT/PH: call 615-525-6101 for specifics
PERM/COLL: CONT; GR ; AM: 19; THORNE MINIATURE ROOMS

Though young, the Knoxville Museum, established in 1990, features a small but rapidly growing collection of contemporary American art. **NOT TO BE MISSED:** Historic Candy Factory next door; the nearby Sunsphere, trademark building of the Knoxville worlds fair

ON EXHIBIT/95:

12/16/94 - 5/28/95	EAST TENNESSEE ART CURRENTS — The first in a series of major exhibitions focusing on the most significant current work being produced by artists living in the area.
6/9 - 8/13/95	SCULPTURAL CONCERNS: CONTEMPORARY AMERICAN METALWORKING — Representing the dynamic range if artistic approaches to metal are 180 objects including working drawings sketches and maquettes to lend an element of understanding to the creative process.
6/16 - 8/18/95	REMBRANDT ETCHINGS: SELECTIONS FROM THE CARNEGIE MUSEUM OF ART — A selection of works providing a comprehensive view of Rembrandt's printmaking techniques. The exhibition presents four major themes — portraiture, landscape, biblical and genre — and examines the evolution of the artist's imagery as well as the evolution of his etched line. WT
9/8 - 11/19/95	AMERICAN ART FROM THE CURRIER GALLERY OF ART — The exhibition will provide a rich, cohesive and informative record of aesthetic developments in the United States from the Colonial period through the early 20th century. Included are paintings, decorative arts and an extensive survey of glassmaking. CAT WT

MEMPHIS

Memphis Brooks Museum of Art
Overton Park, 1934 Poplar Ave., **Memphis, TN 38104**
TEL: 901-722-3500
HRS: 10-5 Tu-Sa; 11:30-5 S   DAY CLOSED: M   HOL: 1/1, THGV, 12/25
F/DAY: F   ADM: Y   ADULT: $4.00   STUDENTS: $2.00   SR CIT: $2.00
HDC/ACC: Y   PARKING: Y; Free   MUS/SH: Y   REST/FAC: Y; To reserve call 901-722-3555
GT: Y   GT/PH: call for reservations
PERM/COLL: IT/REN, NORTHERN/REN, & BAROQUE: ptgs; BRIT & AM: portraits 18, 19; FR/IMPR; AM: modernist

Founded in 1916, this is the mid-south's largest and most encyclopedic fine arts museum. Works in the collection range from those of antiquity to present day creations. **NOT TO BE MISSED:** Global Survey Galleries

ON EXHIBIT/95:

2/19 - 4/9/95	JOHN JAMES AUDUBON: THE WATERCOLORS FOR "THE BIRDS OF AMERICA" — For the first time a major traveling exhibition of selected works by Audubon will present a rare view of many original paintings that served as models for his well known prints.	CAT WT
4/23 - 5/25/95	THE WILLIAM S. PALEY COLLECTION	CAT WT
7/16 - 9/3/95	AFRICAN-AMERICAN WORKS ON PAPER: THE COCHRAN COLLECTION	
10/7 - 12/3/95	MEXICO: A LANDSCAPE REVISITED	WT

The Dixon Gallery & Gardens
4339 Park Ave, **Memphis, TN 38117**
TEL: 901-761-5250
HRS: 10-5 Tu-Sa; 1-5 S   DAY CLOSED: M   HOL: LEG/HOL!
ADM: Y   ADULT: $5.00   CHILDREN: $1.00 under 12   STUDENTS: $3.00   SR CIT: $4.00
HDC/ACC: Y   PARKING: Y; Free   MUS/SH: Y   GT: Y   GT/PH: call 901-761-5250 to reserve
DT: Y   TIME: !   H/B: Y   S/G: Y
PERM/COLL: FR: Impr, 19; GER: cer

Located on 17 acres of woodlands and formal gardens, the Dixon was formerly the home of Hugo and Margaret Dixon, collectors and philanthropists.

ON EXHIBIT/95:

1/22 - 4/17/95	THEATRE DE LA MODE: FRENCH FASHION MINIATURES — Immediately following World War II, to bolster the faltering economy, French couture houses launched this project to raise money for war relief. On 27 inch mannequins in miniature stage sets created by top designers they presented the latest fashions of spring/summer 1945. Thought to be lost, they were rediscovered in the collection of the Maryhill Museum.	
4/30 - 9/17/95	BIRDS, BEASTS, BLOSSOMS AND BUGS IN EAST ASIAN ART — The theme of the exhibition is suggested by the important place that nature held in Chinese art and subsequently in other East Asian countries	WT
5/6 - 7/2/95	GAUGUIN AND THE PONT-AVEN SCHOOL — Although centering on Gauguin the exhibition includes works by Bernard and Serusier as well as 17 other avant-garde artists who worked in this small Brittany town and its surroundings from 1888-1900.	CAT WT
9/24 - 12/10/95	REDEFINING GENRE: FRANCO-AMERICAN PAINTING 1855-1900	

TENNESSEE

MURFREESBORO

Middle Tennessee State University Photographic Gallery
Affiliate Institution: Middle Tennessee State University
Learning Resources Center, **Murfreesboro, TN 37132**
TEL: 615-898-5628
HRS: 8-4:30 M-F; 8-noon Sa; 6-10pm S   HOL: EASTER, THGV, 12/25
ADM: F
HDC/ACC: Y; 1st floor complete with special electric door   PARKING: Y; Free parking 50 yards from gallery
PERM/COLL: CONT: phot

A college museum with major rotating photographic exhibitions.

NASHVILLE

Cheekwood - Tennessee Botanical Gardens & Museum of Art
1200 Forrest Park Drive, **Nashville, TN 37205-4242**
TEL: 615-356-8000
HRS: 9-5 M-Sa; 12-5 S (Grounds open 11-5 S)   HOL: 1/1, THGV, 12/24, 12/25, 12/31
ADM: Y   ADULT: $5.00   CHILDREN: $2.00 (7-17)   STUDENTS: $4.00   SR CIT: $4.00
HDC/ACC: Y   PARKING: Y   MUS/SH: Y
GT: Y   GT/PH: call 615-386-8000 for specifics   H/B: Y   S/G: Y
PERM/COLL: AM: ptgs, sculp, dec/art 19-20

One of the leading cultural centers in the South, the Museum of Art is a former mansion built in the 1920's. Located in a luxuriant botanical garden, it retains a charming homelike quality.

ON EXHIBIT/95:

1/15 - 2/12/95	YOUNG SCHOLASTIC ART COMPETITION
1/28 - 7/24/95	THE BILTMORE ESTATE: A CENTENNIAL CELEBRATOPM 1895-1995
2/19 - 3/19/95	FRANCESCA ANDERSON, PAINTINGS
3/26 - 4/30/95	DEANNA SIRLIN
4/9 - 5/29/95	NEW WORKS FELLOWSHIP
5/7 - 6/4/95	SHARON SHAVER, PAINTINGS
5/21 - 7/16/95	IMPERIAL RUSSIAN PORCELAIN FROM THE RAYMOND F. PIPER COLLECTION WT
6/10 - 8/13/95	RED GROOMS: WATERCOLORS
6/11 - 7/16/95	NASHVILLE ARTISTS GUILD "IN A GARDEN"
8/27 - 10/15/95	ULTRA REALISTIC SCULPTURE BY MARC SIJAN WT
9/9 - 10/8/95	JUNE MCCOY BALL, WATERCOLORS
11/4 - 12/29/95	NATIONAL CONTEMPORARY PAINTING COMPETITION

NASHVILLE

The Parthenon
Centennial Park, **Nashville, TN 37201**
TEL: 615-862-8431
HRS: 9-4:30 Tu-Sa; 12:30-4:30 S; ! for summer hours   DAY CLOSED: M   HOL: LEG/HOL!
ADM: Y   ADULT: $2.50   CHILDREN: $1.25, 4-17   SR CIT: $1.25
HDC/ACC: Y   PARKING: Y; Free   MUS/SH: Y   GT: Y   GT/PH: call 615-862-8431 to reserve   H/B: Y
PERM/COLL: AM: 19, 20; The Cowan Collection

First constructed as the Art Pavillion for the Tennessee Centennial Exposition, in 1897, The Parthenon is the world's only full size reproduction of the 4th century B.C. Greek original complete with the statue of Athena Parthenos. **NOT TO BE MISSED:** "Mt. Tamalpais," by Albert Bierstadt

ON EXHIBIT/95:

11/5/94 - 1/7/95	TENNESSEE JURIED ALL STATE REGIONAL EXHIBITION
1/14 - 2/25/95	NASHVILLE ARTIST GUILD MEMBERSHIP SHOW
3/4 - 4/15/95	KYU YAMAMOTO AND CHUCK MCCAN, SCULPTURE AND PAINTINGS
4/22 - 6/3/95	TENNESSEE WATERCOLOR SOCIETY 1995 WATERCOLOR SHOW
6/10 - 7/22/95	CENTRAL SOUTH JURIED ARTIST EXHIBITION
7/29 - 9/9/95	JIM COGSWELL, PAINTINGS
8/5 - 9/16/95	FRANCIA, PAINTING, MIXED MEDIA CONSTRUCTION
9/16 - 10/28/95	WADE THOMPSON, PAINTINGS
9/17 - 10/29/95	MILDRED JARRET: ABSTRACT PAINTING
11/14/95 - 1/6/96	TENNESSEE ALL STATE JURIED EXHIBITION

The University Galleries
Affiliate Institution: Fisk University
D. B. Todd Blvd. and Jackson Street, N., **Nashville, TN 37203**
TEL: 625-329-8543
HRS: 10-5 Tu-F; 1-5 Sa-S; summer 10-4 Tu-F   DAY CLOSED: M   HOL: ACAD!
ADM: Y   ADULT: $2.50   CHILDREN: Free   STUDENTS: Free   SR CIT: $2.50
HDC/ACC: Y   PARKING: Y   LIB: Y   MUS/SH: Y   GT: Y   GT/PH: call 615-329-8543 for specifics   H/B: Y
PERM/COLL: EU; AM; AF/AM: ptgs; AF: sculp

The 1888 neo-Romanesque revival building is located on the site of a former Civil War fort. **NOT TO BE MISSED:** The Carl Van Vechten Collection of photographs

Vanderbilt Fine Arts Gallery
23rd at West End Ave, **Nashville, TN 37203**
TEL: 615-322-0605
HRS: 1-4 M-F; 1-5 Sa, S; Summer 1-4 M-F   HOL: ACAD!
ADM: F   PARKING: Y   H/B: Y
PERM/COLL: OR: Harold P. Stern Coll; OM & MODERN: gr (Anna C. Hoyt Coll); CONTINI-VOLTERRA PHOT ARCHIVE; EU: om/ptgs (Kress Study Coll)

TENNESSEE

Vanderbilt Fine Arts Gallery - continued

The history of world art may be seen in the more than 7,000 works from over 40 countries housed in this museum. Rich in old masterworks and Oriental art, this historical collection is the only one of its kind in the immediate region. **NOT TO BE MISSED:** "St. Sebastian," 15th century Central Italian tempera on wood

ON EXHIBIT/95:

1/15 - 2/12/95	LITMUS FACE: PAINTINGS, PRINTS AND VIDEOS BY JOSEPH WHITT, THE 1993 MARGARET STONEWALL WOOLDRIDGE HAMBLET AWARD WINNER
2/19 - 4/2/95	DIVERSE VISIONS: WORK BY FACULTY OF THE DEPARTMENT OF FINE ARTS, VANDERBILT UNIVERSITY (TENT! title)
6/4 - 8/27/95	UNCLE SAM WANTS YOU! SELECTIONS FROM THE WORLD WAR I POSTER COLLECTION, PEABODY COLLEGE, VANDERBILT UNIVERSITY

OAK RIDGE

Oak Ridge Community Arts Center/Museum of Fine Arts
201 Badger Avenue, **Oak Ridge, TN 37830**
TEL: 615-482-1441
HRS: 9-5 Tu-F; 1-4 Sa-M   HOL: LEG/HOL!
ADM: F
HDC/ACC: Y   PARKING: Y   LIB: Y
PERM/COLL: AB/EXP: Post WW II; REG

NOT TO BE MISSED: Gomez Collection of Post WW II art

TEXAS

ABILENE

Museums of Abilene, Inc.
102 Cypress, **Abilene, TX 79601**
TEL: 915-673-4587
HRS: 10-5 Tu, W, F, Sa; 5-8:30 T; 1-5 S   DAY CLOSED: M   HOL: LEG/HOL!
F/DAY: T-Eve   ADM: Y   ADULT: $2.00   CHILDREN: $1.00 (3-12)   STUDENTS: $1.00   SR CIT:
HDC/ACC: Y   PARKING: Y   LIB: Y   MUS/SH: Y   GT: Y   GT/PH: call 915-673-4587 for specifics   H/B: Y
PERM/COLL: TEXAS/REG; AM: gr, CONT: gr; ABELINE, TX, & PACIFIC RAILWAY: 18-20

The museums are housed in the 1909 "Mission Revival Style" Railroad Hotel.

ON EXHIBIT/95:
Spring 95   THE 51ST ANNUAL COMPETITION — This perennial exhibition includes the work of
established and emerging Texas artists, giving Abilenians a taste of recent trends in
regional contemporary art.

ALBANY

The Old Jail Art Center
Hwy 6 South, **Albany, TX 76430**
TEL: 915-762-2269
HRS: 10-5 Tu-Sa; 2-5 S   DAY CLOSED: M   HOL: LEG/HOL!
ADM: F   HDC/ACC: Y; Except 2 story original jail building   PARKING: Y   LIB: Y   H/B: Y   S/G: Y
PERM/COLL: AM: cont; P/COL

The Old Jail Art Center is housed partly in a restored 1878 historic jail building with a small annex
which opened in 1980 and in a new wing added in 1984, featuring a courtyard and sculpture garden.
NOT TO BE MISSED: "Young Girl With Braids," by Modigliani

ON EXHIBIT/95:
1/14 - 2/26/95	DRAWING INTO THE 90'S — Texas Fine Arts Association juried exhibition
3/4 - 4/2/95	SELECTIONS FROM THE PERMANENT COLLECTION
4/8 - 5/28/95	KEN DIXON: ORDER AND DISORDER
5/3 - 8/6/95	BOB WADE (TENT! dates and title)
8/12 - 10/7/95	SELECTIONS FROM THE PERMANENT COLLECTION
10/14 - 12/31/95	THE ART OF THE SANTERA (TENT!)

AMARILLO

Amarillo Art Center
2200 S. Van Buren, **Amarillo, TX 79109**
TEL: 806-371-5050
HRS: 10-5 Tu-F; 10-9;30 T; 1-5 Sa, S   DAY CLOSED: M   HOL: LEG/HOL!
ADM: F   HDC/ACC: Y   PARKING: Y   LIB: Y   S/G: Y
PERM/COLL: CONT; ANCIENT; REG

TEXAS

Amarillo Art Center - continued

Opened in 1972, the Amarillo Art Center is a community based art museum located in the northeast corner of the Amarilllo College Campus.

ON EXHIBIT/95:
11/5/94 - 1/8/95	BAGLEY/ORR
	THE MAY COLLECTION
	DEBRA DANIELSON: PHOTOGRAPHS

ARLINGTON

Arlington Museum of Art
201 West Main St., **Arlington, TX 76010**
TEL: 817-275-4600
HRS: 10-5 W-Sa   DAY CLOSED: S, M, Tu   HOL: Daily although may be closed from 12/25-1/2!
ADM: F   HDC/ACC: Y; Partial, ramp on side of building, & restrooms
PARKING: Y; Free parking directly in front of the building with handicapped spaces; parking also on side of building
MUS/SH: Y   GT: Y   GT/PH: Call to reserve 8 17-275-4600   DT: Y   TIME: Occasional
PERM/COLL: Non-collecting institution

Texas contemporary art by both established and emerging talents is featured in this museum housed in a former J.C. Penney department store. Though relatively young, this North Texas museum located between the art-rich cities of Fort Worth and Dallas has gained a solid reputation for showcasing contemporary art in the eight exhibitions it presents annually.

The Center for Research in Contemporary Arts
Fine Arts Bldg, Cooper Street, **Arlington, TX 76019**
TEL: 817-273-2790
HRS: 10-3 M-T; 1-4 Sa-S   HOL: ACAD!
ADM: F   PARKING: Y
PERM/COLL: Non-collecting institution

A University gallery with varied special exhibitions.

AUSTIN

Archer M. Huntington Art Gallery
Affiliate Institution: University of Texas
Art Bldg, 23rd & San Jacinto Streets, **Austin, TX 78712-1205**
TEL: 512-471-7324
HRS: 9-5 M-Sa; 1-5 S   HOL: MEM/DAY, LAB/DAY, THGV, XMAS WEEK
ADM: F
HDC/ACC: Y   PARKING: Y   MUS/SH: Y   GT: Y   GT/PH: call 210-471-7324 for specifics   S/G: Y, small
PERM/COLL: LAT/AM; CONT; GR; DRGS

396

Archer M. Huntington Art Gallery - continued

The encyclopedic collection of this university gallery, one of the finest and most balanced in the southern United States, features a superb collection of medieval art. The permanent collection is located in the Harry Ransom Humanities Research Center at 21st and Guadelupe Streets.

ON EXHIBIT/95:

1/20 - 3/5/95	AUGUSTUS VINCENT TACK: LANDSCAPE OF THE SPIRIT — The first comprehensive retrospective ever assembled of the work of Tack (1870-1949) who evolved from Impressionism to spiritual abstractions depicting nature as chaotic yet ordered, thunderous and awe-inspiring.　　　　CAT　WT
1/20 - 3/5/95	NEW ACQUISITIONS
3/24 - 5/14/95	PRINT STUDY EXHIBITION
	The exhibition space in the Art Building will be closed during the summer until mid-October for renovation. The Huntington Gallery Space in the Harry Ransom Research Center will remain open.
10/13 - 12/15/95	THE EARLY PRINTS OF EDVARD MUNCH (TENT!)

AUSTIN

Laguna Gloria Art Museum

3809 W. 35th Street, **Austin, TX 78731**
TEL: 512-458-8191
HRS: 10-5 Tu-Sa; 1-5 S　DAY CLOSED: M　HOL: LEG/HOL!
F/DAY: TH　ADM: Y　ADULT: $2.00　CHILDREN: F (under 16)　STUDENTS: $1.00　SR CIT: $1.00
HDC/ACC: Y　PARKING: Y; Free　LIB: Y　MUS/SH: Y　GT: Y　GT/PH: call 512-458-8191 to reserve
H/B: Y　S/G: Y
PERM/COLL: AM: ptgs 19, 20; WORKS ON PAPER

The Museum is located on the 1916 Driscoll Estate which is listed in the National Register of Historic Places.

ON EXHIBIT/95:

10/16/94 - 1/15/95	THE HOLOCAUST PROJECT: FROM DARKNESS INTO LIGHT (presented off site at 823 Congress Avenue) — Created by artist Judy Chicago and based on eight years of extensive research, travel and intellectual inquiry, the exhibition is a visual exploration in tapestry, stained glass and large scale tableaus combining painting and photography, of the meaning of the Holocaust for all people today.　　　　CAT　WT
11/13/94 - 1/15/95	IN RESPONSE TO NATURE II
12/10/94 - 1/8/95	TFAA CURATED EXHIBITION (theme to be announced)
12/10/94 - 1/15/95	COMPELLING SPACES
1/28 - 3/26/95	MAGIC AND MYSTERY: THE EYE OF THE CHILD
4/1 - 4/30/95	TFAA NEW AMERICAN TALENT: THE 11TH EXHIBITION
5/6 - 7/2/95	MEXICO: A LANDSCAPE REVISITED
7/8 - 8/3/95	WOOD IT WERE
8/19 - 9/17/95	TFAA NATIONAL JURIED EXHIBITION

TEXAS

BEAUMONT

The Art Museum of Southeast Texas
500 Main Street, **Beaumont, TX 77704**
TEL: 409-832-3432
HRS: 9-5 M-Sa; 12-5 S; open until 8pm T   HOL: LEG/HOL!
ADM: F
HDC/ACC: Y   PARKING: Y   LIB: Y   MUS/SH: Y
REST/FAC: Y; Lunch 11:30-1:30 M-F; also available for special events
GT: Y   GT/PH: call 409-832-3432 to reserve   DT: Y   TIME: W, noon   S/G: Y
PERM/COLL: AM: ptgs, sculp, dec/art, FOLK: 19, 20

This new spacious art museum with 4 major galleries and 2 sculpture courtyards is located in
downtown Beaumont. **NOT TO BE MISSED:** Complete works of "FOX" Harris, visionary folk artist
is permanently installed in the Boyt Sculpture Garden.

ON EXHIBIT/95:

11/11/94 - 2/19/95	200 YEARS OF SILVER
11/4/94 - 3/6/95	DECORATIVE ARTS IN THE PERMANENT COLLECTION
2/24 - 4/30/95	ITALO SCANGA: TRANSFORMATIONS
3/4 - 8/27/95	PERSIAN RUGS
3/12 - 6/20/95	LONE STAR REVISITED: TEXAS ARTISTS FROM THE PERMANENT COLLECTION
5/5 - 8/27/95	HOLLY LANE
9/9 - 11/5/95	FLORA: CONTEMPORARY ARTISTS AND THE WORLD OF FLOWERS

COLLEGE STATION

MSC Forsyth Center Galleries
Affiliate Institution: Texas A and M University
Memorial Student Center, Joe Routt Blvd., **College Station, TX 77844**
TEL: 409-845-9251
HRS: 9-5 M-F; 12-5 Sa-S   HOL: 7/4, THGV, 12/25-1/1
ADM: F
HDC/ACC: Y   PARKING: Y; Underground   GT: Y   GT/PH: call 409-845-9251 for specifics
PERM/COLL: EU, BRIT, & AM; glass; AM: western ptgs

Particularly rich in its collection of American Art glass, this museum is located in the Memorial
Student Center on the Texas A & M campus. **NOT TO BE MISSED:** Works by Grandma Moses

ON EXHIBIT/95:

Spring 1995	FREDERICK REMINGTON AND THE ART OF ILLUSTRATION FROM THE STERLING C. EVANS LIBRARY AND THE BILL AND IRMA RUNYON COLLECTIONS	
7/30 - 9/24/95	JOSIAH WEDGEWOOD: EXPERIMENTAL POTTER	WT
Fall 1995	A CLEAR VIEW OF OUR ORIGINS: BRITISH GLASS AND GLASSMAKERS	

398

COLLEGE STATION

Texas A&M University/J. Wayne Stark University Center Galleries
Mem Student Ctr. Joe Routt Blvd., **College Station, TX 77844-9083**
TEL: 409-845-8501
HRS: 9-8 Tu-F; 12-6 Sa-S   DAY CLOSED: M   HOL: ACAD!
ADM: F
HDC/ACC: Y   PARKING: Y   LIB: Y
PERM/COLL: REG; GER 19

A University gallery featuring works by 20th century Texas artists

CORPUS CHRISTI

Art Museum of South Texas
1902 N. Shoreline Corpus, **Christi, TX 78401**
TEL: 210-884-3844
HRS: 10-5 Tu-Sa; 1-5 S   DAY CLOSED: M   HOL: 1/1, 7/4, THGV, 12/25
ADM: F
HDC/ACC: Y   PARKING: Y; Free   LIB: Y   MUS/SH: Y   REST/FAC: Y   S/G: Y
PERM/COLL: AM; REG

The award winning building designed by Philip Johnson, has vast expanses of glass which provide natural light for objects of art and breathtaking views of Corpus Christi Bay.

ON EXHIBIT/95:

1/95 - 3/95	MAPPING — 31 2 and 3 dimensional contemporary works which use maps as a point of departure.
Dates TBA	TEXAS FINE ARTS ASSOCIATION: THE TENTH EXHIBITION — A survey of American drawing by the Whitney Museum of American Art presenting a wide breadth of possible expression despite what some denounce as a "loss of standards" and relentless attempts at censorship.
3/95 - 4/95	IN THE LAST HOUR: SANDY SKOGLUND — A survey of the work created by this photographer during the last 13 years as well as an installation which will accompany the exhibit. WT
3/10 - 5/12/95	ARRESTED RIVERS: PAINTINGS BY CHUCK FORSMAN — Wall text and poetry accompany the art which examines the topic of water in the West.
5/19 - 7/20/95	MATRIX 5: MICHAEL COLLINS — An ongoing series which features mid-career regional artists.
5/19 - 7/20/95	PEDRO MEYER: TRUTHS AND FICTIONS — This native of Mexico offers an outsider's view of the United States and an insider's view of the Mextex culture in Oaxaca. Interactive CD-ROM computer work stations offer viewers the opportunity to "walk through" the exhibit with English or Spanish narrations of every image in the exhibit.
7/27 - 10/1/95	THE 70'S AND 80'S: A CALIFORNIA COLLECTION — A survey private collection of examplar works by mid to mature career west coast artists.

TEXAS

CORPUS CHRISTI

Museum of Oriental Cultures
418 Peoples Street, Suite 200, **Corpus Christi, TX 78401**
TEL: 210-883-1303
HRS: 10-4 Tu-Sa   DAY CLOSED: M, S   HOL: LEG/HOL!, EASTER
ADM: Y   ADULT: $1.00   CHILDREN: F (under 4)   STUDENTS: $0.50   SR CIT: $1.00
HDC/ACC: Y   PARKING: Y; Street   LIB: Y   MUS/SH: Y
GT: Y   GT/PH: call 210-883-1303 for specifics   H/B: Y
PERM/COLL: JAP

An oasis of peace and tranquility comprised predominately of one nostalgic private collection. **NOT TO BE MISSED:** Cast bronze 1500 lb BUDA-MOO'S

DALLAS

Biblical Arts Center
7500 Park Lane, **Dallas, TX 75225**
TEL: 214-691-4661
HRS: 10-5 Tu-Sa; 1-5 S   DAY CLOSED: M   HOL: 1/1, THGV, 12/24, 12/25
ADM: Y   ADULT: $3.75   CHILDREN: $2.00 (6-12)   SR CIT: $3.00
HDC/ACC: Y   PARKING: Y   MUS/SH: Y   H/B: Y
PERM/COLL: BIBLICAL ART

The sole purpose of this museum is to utilize the arts as a means of helping people of all faiths to more clearly envision the places, events, and people of the Bible. The building in the style of Romanesque architecture features early Christian era architectural details. **NOT TO BE MISSED:** "Miracle at Pentecost," painting with light and sound presentation

Dallas Museum of Art
1717 N. Harwood, **Dallas, TX 75201**
TEL: 214-922-1200
HRS: 11-4 Tu, W; 11-9 T, F; 11-5 Sa, S & Hols   DAY CLOSED: M   HOL: 1/1, THGV, 12/25
ADM: F
HDC/ACC: Y   PARKING: Y; Large underground parking facility   LIB: Y   MUS/SH: Y   REST/FAC: Y
GT: Y   GT/PH: call for infronation   S/G: Y
PERM/COLL: P/COL; AF; AM: furniture; EUR: ptgs, sculp, Post War AM; AF; AS; CONT

Designed by Edward Larabee Barnes, the new Nancy and Jake Hamon Building is a $30 million dollar addition to the museum. Housing a 14,000 square foot exhibition gallery it is billed as the first museum to focus on the art of the Americas from the pre-contact period (which includes a spectacular pre-Columbian gold Treasury of more than 1,000 works) through the mid-20th century. This fast growing museum added both a Museum of Africa & a Museum of Asia to its artistic complex in the Fall of 1994. **NOT TO BE MISSED:** "The Icebergs" by Frederick Church; 750 piece Bybee Collection of early American furniture; Education Resource Center with computer information on items in the core collection; contemporary art collection in Museum of Contemporary Art opened on 11/21/93.

Dallas Museum of Art - continued

ON EXHIBIT/95:

11/6/94 - 1/29/95	SILVER IN AMERICA, 1840-1940: A CENTURY OF SPLENDOR — This exhibition examines the critical areas of production, marketing, consumption and design of products during the height of the success of the American silverware industry and chronicles the work of both firms such as Tiffany, Gorham, Reed and Barton and others as well as lesser known makers. Adm. Chg. Adults $6.00; Stud/Seniors $4.00; Children under 12 $2.00.
2/95 - 3/95	ENCOUNTERS 6: RACHEL HECKER AND PETER HALLEY — The latest opportunity to compare and contrast two contemporary artists presents painters who deal with social issues in their work, both through image and through form.
3/12 - 5/28/95	BEYOND THE TANABATA BRIDGE: A TEXTILE JOURNEY IN JAPAN — An exploration of the role of textiles and techniques of textile weaving in daily Japanese society from the late 18th through the early 20th century. Adm. Chg. Adults $6.00; Stud/Seniors $4.00; Children under 12 $2.00 WT

DALLAS

The Meadows Museum

Affiliate Institution: SMU School of the Arts
Bishop and Binkley, **Dallas, TX 75275**
TEL: 214-768-2516
HRS: 10-5 M, Tu, F, Sa; 10-8 T; 1-5 S   DAY CLOSED: W   HOL: 1/1, EASTER, 7/4, THGV, 12/25
ADM: F   HDC/ACC: Y   PARKING: Y   LIB: Y   MUS/SH: Y   GT: Y   GT/PH: call 214-768-1675, res.req.
DT: Y   TIME: 3pm, S   S/G: Y
PERM/COLL: SP; ptgs, sculp, gr, drgs; AM: sculp 20

The collection of Spanish Art is the most comprehensive in the US with works from the last years of the 15th century through the 20th century.

ON EXHIBIT/95:

11/18/94 - 1/15/95	FATA MORGANA USA: THE AMERICAN WAY OF LIFE, PHOTOMONTAGES BY JOSEP RENAU — The artist explores the dichotomy in post-war American culture between real-world problems and the image of affluence produced by the media.
1/27 - 3/12/95	BIENNIAL FACULTY EXHIBITION
3/31 - 5/28/95	IMAGES OF PENANCE, IMAGES OF MERCY: SOUTHWESTERN SANTOS IN THE LATE NINETEENTH CENTURY — These painted wood sculptures of Christ, saints and figures of death, represent an artistic tradition brought to the "New World" from Spain by Christian priests. They were meant to convey Christian ideals of poverty, charity and obedience to the Hispanic and Indian populations of New Mexico.

Museum of African American Life and Culture

1111 First Avenue, **Dallas, TX 75215**
TEL: 214-565-9026
HRS: 10-5 M-T; 12-9 F; 10-9 Sa; 12-6 S   HOL: LEG/HOL!
ADM: F   HDC/ACC: Y   PARKING: Y   LIB: Y   MUS/SH: Y   REST/FAC: Y   GT: Y   GT/PH: ! to reserve   S/G: Y
PERM/COLL: AF/AM: folk

With the largest collection of African-American art in the country, this museum concentrates on identifying and researching Black American art and history.

TEXAS

EL PASO

El Paso Museum of Art
1211 Montana Ave., **El Paso, TX 79902-5588**
TEL: 915-541-4040
HRS: 9-5 Tu, W, F, Sa; 9-9 T, 1-5 S   DAY CLOSED: M   HOL: LEG/HOL!
ADM: F
HDC/ACC: Y   PARKING: Y; Free   LIB: Y   MUS/SH: Y   GT: Y   GT/PH: call 915-541-4040 for specifics
PERM/COLL: EU: Kress Coll 13-18; AM; MEX: 18, 19; MEX SANTOS: 20; REG

ON EXHIBIT/95:

1/15 - 3/26/95	ACROSS GENERATIONS: NEW MEXICAN FOLK TRADITION
	GENERATIONS IN BLACK AND WHITE: PHOTOGRAPHS BY CARL VAN VECHTEN WT
1/5 - 3/5/95	BRUCE BERMAN: THE URBAN BORDER
4/2 - 5/28/95	THE EGYPTIAN PROJECT PORTFOLIO: PHOTOGRAPHS BY WILLIAM EGGLESTON
6/8 - 7/30/95	GASPAR ENRIQUEZ: DOS MUNDOS
6/10 - 9/3/95	!GRONK! A LIVING SURVEY 1973-1993 WT

FORT WORTH

Amon Carter Museum
3501 Camp Bowie Blvd., **Fort Worth, TX 76107-2631**
TEL: 817-738-1933
HRS: 10-5 Tu-Sa; 1-5:30 S   DAY CLOSED: M   HOL: 1/1, 7/4, THGV, 12/25
ADM: F
HDC/ACC: Y; Side entrance   PARKING: Y; Free   LIB: Y   MUS/SH: Y
GT: Y   GT/PH: call 817-738-1933 to reserve
PERM/COLL: AM: ptgs, sculp, gr, phot 19, 20; WESTERN ART

One of the foremost museums of American Art, the Amon Carter is located in Fort Worth's cultural district. It represents the Western experience and embraces the history of 19th and 20th century American Art. **NOT TO BE MISSED:** "The Swimming Hole," by Thomas Eakins

ON EXHIBIT/95:

10/22/94 - 2/26/95	FACE VALUE
11/12/94 - 3/5/95	CHARLES M. RUSSELL, SCULPTOR
2/18 - 5/28/95	THOMAS COLE'S PAINTINGS OF PARADISE WT
3/18 - 5/28/95	FROM NEW YORK TO HOLLYWOOD: PHOTOGRAPHS BY KARL STRUSS — Known for his pictorial photographs during the 1910's Struss became better known as a cinematographer, winning the first Academy Award for cinematography for the 1927 film SUNRISE. CAT

402

FORT WORTH

Kimbell Art Museum

Camp Bowie Blvd., **Fort Worth, TX 76107**
TEL: 817-332-8451
HRS: 10-5 Tu-F; 12-8 Sa; 12-5 S   DAY CLOSED: M   HOL: 1/1, 7/4, THGV, 12/25
ADM: F   HDC/ACC: Y   PARKING: Y   LIB: Y   MUS/SH: Y   REST/FAC: Y
GT: Y   GT/PH: call 817-332-8687 for specifics   DT: Y   TIME: !2pm Tu-F; 2pm, 3pm S; 6:30 Sa   S/G: Y
PERM/COLL: EU: ptgs, sculp 17-20; AS

Designed by Louis I. Kahn, this classic museum building is perhaps his finest creation and a work of art in its own right. It was the last building completed under his personal supervision. **NOT TO BE MISSED:** Newly acquired "L'Asie" (Asia), by Henri Matisse, 1946

ON EXHIBIT/95:

11/20/94 - 2/12/95	TOMB TREASURES FROM CHINA: THE BURIED ART OF ANCIENT XI'AN — 62 objects spanning 1000 years of Chinese history from the Qin Dynasty (221-206 B.C.) through the Tang Dynasty (A.D. 618-906) marking the 20th anniversary of the discovery of the most significant archeological discovery in China's recent history. CAT WT
2/12 - 4/9/95	NINETEENTH CENTURY ITALIAN PAINTING FROM THE GAETANO MARZOTTO COLLECTION — An exceptionally complete survey of progresssive painting made in Italy in the second half of the 19th century, the exhibition provides the first showing of this neglected period of the history of Italian painting in the Southwest. WT
3/5 - 5/28/95	THE PEACEFUL LIBERATORS: JAIN ART FROM INDIA — A chronological presentation of the history and essential characteristics of Jain art which spans a period of more than 200 years. WT
11/5/95 - 1/29/96	LOUIS-LEOPOLD BOILLY (1761-1845) — The first monographic exhibition devoted to this artist outside of France. The core group of paintings will trace his achievement as a genre painter, political artist, portraitist and the first painter of modern life. WT

Modern Art Museum of Fort Worth

1309 Montgomery Street, **Fort Worth, TX 76107**
TEL: 817-738-9215
HRS: 10-5 Tu-F; 11-5 Sa, 12-5 S   DAY CLOSED: M   HOL: LEG/HOL!
ADM: F   HDC/ACC: Y   PARKING: Y   LIB: Y   MUS/SH: Y   REST/FAC: Y; Cafe open 11:30-2:30 Sa, 12-3 S
GT: Y   GT/PH: call 817-738-9215 to reserve
PERM/COLL: CONT; ptgs, sculp, works on paper

Chartered in 1892 (making it one of the oldest museums in the western U.S.), this museum has evolved into a celebrated and vital showcase for works of modern and contemporary art. Great emphasis at the Modern is placed on the presentation of exceptional traveling exhibitions making a trip to this facility and others in this "museum rich" city a rewarding experience for art lovers. **NOT TO BE MISSED:** Important collections of works by Robert Motherwell, Jackson Pollock, Morris Louis and Milton Avery

ON EXHIBIT/95:

1/15 - 4/16/95	HISTORY AND MEMORY: PAINTINGS BY CHRISTOPHER BROWN A survey of the work of this artist whose images are much indebted to photography. The canvases are contemporary in technique while they are simultaneously nostalgic in mood. CAT WT

TEXAS

Modern Art Museum of Fort Worth - continued

Fall 1995	ROBERT RAUSCHENBERG: SCULPTURE — The first museum exhibition of the artist's work devoted exclusively to sculpture. CAT
Fall 1995	HOWARD HODGKIN — Classified by some as representational and others as abstract, this important British artist fuses form and feeling in powerful, sensual paintings. CAT
8/13 - 10/1/95	THE STUDIO MUSEUM IN HARLEM: 25 YEARS OF AFRICAN-AMERICAN ART — In celebration of the Studio Museum's 25th anniversary, this traveling exhibition will highlight paintings, sculpture, and works on paper created between 1968-1993 by noted African-American artists. CAT WT

FORT WORTH

Sid Richardson Collection of Western Art

309 Main Street, **Fort Worth, TX 76102**
TEL: 817-332-6554
HRS: 10-5 Tu, W; 10-8 T, F; 11-8 Sa; 1-5 S   DAY CLOSED: M   HOL: LEG/HOL!
ADM: F   HDC/ACC: Y   PARKING: Y; 3 hours free at Chisholm Trail Lot-4th and Main with ticket validation.
MUS/SH: Y   GT: Y   GT/PH: call 817-332-6554 to reserve   H/B: Y
PERM/COLL: AM/WEST: ptgs

Dedicated to Western art the museum is located in historic Sundance Square in a reconstructed 1890's building. The area, in downtown Fort Worth, features restored turn-of-the-century buildings. **NOT TO BE MISSED:** 52 Remington and Russell paintings on permanent display.

HOUSTON

Contemporary Arts Museum

5216 Montrose Boulevard, **Houston, TX 77006-6598**
TEL: 713-526-3129
HRS: 10-5 Tu-F; 12-5 Sa, S   DAY CLOSED: M   HOL: 1/1, 7/4, THGV, 12/25
F/DAY: T   ADM: Y   ADULT: $3.00   CHILDREN: F (under 12)   STUDENTS: $1.00   SR CIT: $1.00
HDC/ACC: Y   PARKING: Y; On-street parking   MUS/SH: Y
GT: Y   GT/PH: call 713-526-0773 for specifics   S/G: Y
PERM/COLL: Non-Collecting Institution

Located in a metal building in the shape of a parallelogram this museum is dedicated to presenting the art of our time to the public. Admission to Gallery two and the Museum Shop is free.

ON EXHIBIT/95:

11/19/94 - 1/22/95	DENNIS ADAMS — Photography, architecture and text are used in the artist's public projects and installations each of which is developed specifically around the context in which it is situated. The works are meant to compel the viewer to ponder social and political injustices such as homelessness and the Holocaust.
12/3/94 - 1/15/95	LUCAS JOHNSON: THE IDAHO DRAWINGS — Although Houston based, Johnson has had his artistic roots in Mexican surrealist imagery for more than 30 years.
4/15 - 6/18/95	ART GUYS: SCHMART GUYS — A survey of 13 years of collaborative work by these artists, Michael Galbreth and Jack Massing, whose range of work includes performance, sculpture, actions, installations, photography, drawing and video.

HOUSTON

The Menil Collection
1515 Sul Ross, **Houston, TX 77006**
TEL: 713-525-9400
HRS: 11-7 W-S   DAY CLOSED: M, Tu   HOL: LEG/HOL!
ADM: F   HDC/ACC: Y   PARKING: Y   GT: Y   GT/PH: call 713-525-9404 for specifics   S/G: Y
PERM/COLL: PTGS, DRGS, & SCULP 20; ANT; TRIBAL CULTURES; MED; BYZ

The annex, scheduled to open in February 1995 is to be a minimuseum devoted to the paintings of Cy Twombley and designed by Renzo Piano, architect of the Beaubourg in Paris. It and the Museum building itself are exceptional. The 100,000 square feet of exhibition and work space look like a simple two story structure, but are, in fact, five stories with the most advanced technology possible. The "Treasure House" storage facility is available for viewing by appointment. **NOT TO BE MISSED:** No trip to the outstanding Menil Collection would be complete without a visit to the Menil Chapel, famous for its specially commissioned Mark Rothko paintings.

ON EXHIBIT/95:

3/2/94 - 2/95	SURREALISM
12/9/94 - 1/15/95	SHERRIE LEVINE: NEWBORN
2/10 - 3/19/95	CY TWOMBLY: A RETROSPECTIVE — Twombly, one of the most important American artists of the last half of this century, has pursued an imageless form of painting that combines elements of gestural abstraction, drawing and writing in a personal manner. This exhibition of his paintings, works on paper, and selected sculptures surveys his entire career and includes crucial, rarely seen works from private European collections. CAT WT
2/24 - 5/21/95	THE CABAL COLLECTION OF ICONS

The Museum of Fine Arts, Houston
1001 Bissonnet, **Houston, TX 77005**
TEL: 713-639-7300
HRS: 10-5 Tu-Sa; 5-9pm T; 12:15-6 S   DAY CLOSED: M   HOL: 1/1, 7/4, LAB/DAY, THGV, 12/25
F/DAY: Th   ADM: Y   ADULT: $3.00   CHILDREN: F (under 5), 6-18 $1.50   STUDENTS: $1.50   SR CIT: $1.50
HDC/ACC: Y   PARKING: Y; Free   LIB: Y   MUS/SH: Y   REST/FAC: Y
GT: Y   GT/PH: call 713-639-7324 for specifics   S/G: Y
PERM/COLL: STRAUS COLL OF REN & 18TH C WORKS; BECK COLL: Impr; GLASSELL COLL: Af gold

Over 27,000 works are housed in the largest and most outstanding museum in the southwest. **NOT TO BE MISSED:** Bayou Bend, a 28 room former residence with 14 acres of gardens, built in 1927 and redesigned and reopened as a museum in 1966. More than 4,800 works of fine and decorative arts from the colonial period to the early 19th century. Separate admission and hours. ! 713-520-2600 Adults, $7.50; Seniors and students, $5.00; Children 10-18, $3.75

ON EXHIBIT/95:

11/6/94 - 2/12/95	TEXAS MODERN — Focusing on the period from 1925-1965 the exhibition explores the visionary impulse of a group of Texas painters and sculptors who, in response to the advent of modernism began to produce more independent interpretations in the 1920's. CAT WT
11/20/94 - 1/29/95	JOHN JAMES AUDUBON: THE WATERCOLORS FOR "BIRDS OF AMERICA" — More than 85 original watercolors and a dozen engravings will be shown in this rare traveling exhibition of Audubon's work. CAT WT

TEXAS

The Museum of Fine Arts, Houston - continued

12/4/94 - 4/2/95
AMERICAN PAINTERS IN THE AGE OF IMPRESSIONISM — Outstanding examples of mid to late 19th century American painting from public and private collections in Texas. CAT

3/19 - 5/28/95
WILLEM DE KOONING: THE HIRSHHORN MUSEUM COLLECTION — de Kooning is unique among abstract expressionist painters in making the figure a primary subject. This retrospective features works that span his career and media. CAT WT

4/2 - 9/3/95
THE ART OF JOHN BIGGERS: VIEW FROM THE UPPER ROOM — This exhibition highlights themes that have remained constant in Biggers' work for over fifty years; family, the black man and woman, and the search for spiritual renewal. CAT

9/10 - 11/12/95
POUSSIN: DRAWINGS FROM THE COLLECTION OF HER MAJESTY QUEEN ELIZABETH II — In his drawings, Poussin builds images with both line and color. The impressive drawings all come from the Royal Collection. CAT

11/4/95 - 1/2/96
VISIONS OF LOVE AND LIFE: ENGLISH PRE-RAPHAELITE ART FROM THE BIRMINGHAM COLLECTION — The exhibition is drawn from one of the richest collections of Pre-Raphaelite paintings and sculpture in the world and will survey the full range of the movement. WT

12/17/95 - 2/25/96
TINA MODOTTI RETROSPECTIVE — The first major retrospective of the work of this photographer includes her exquisite still lifes, photographs of peasants, portraits, and of folk art and indigenous architecture. CAT

HOUSTON

Sewall Art Gallery Rice University
Sewall Hall 6100 S. Main Street, **Houston, TX 77005**
TEL: 713-527-6069
HRS: 10-5 Tu-Sa; 10-9 T (Sep-May)   DAY CLOSED: S, M   HOL: ACAD! & SUMMER
ADM: F   HDC/ACC: Y   PARKING: Y   LIB: Y
PERM/COLL: Rotating Exhibitions, collection not on permanent display

Since its founding in 1968 the gallery has provided a rich and diverse cultural experience for both Rice University and the Houston community.

KERRVILLE

Cowboy Artists of America Museum
1550 Bandera Hwy, **Kerrville, TX 78028**
TEL: 210-896-2553
HRS: 9-5 Tu-Sa; 1-5 S; (9-5 M MEM/DAY-LAB/DAY)   DAY CLOSED: M   HOL: 1/1, EASTER, THGV, 12/25
ADM: Y   ADULT: $2.50   CHILDREN: $1.00 (6-18)   SR CIT: $2.00
HDC/ACC: Y   PARKING: Y; Free   LIB: Y   MUS/SH: Y   GT: Y   GT/PH: call 210-896-2553 to reserve
H/B: Y   S/G: Y
PERM/COLL: AM/WESTERN: ptgs, sculp

Located on a hilltop site just west of the Guadalupe River, the museum is dedicated to perpetuating America's western heritage

406

TEXAS

LONGVIEW

Longview Art Museum
102 W. College, **Longview, TX 75601**
TEL: 903-753-8103
HRS: 10-5 Tu-Sa; 1-4 S   DAY CLOSED: M   HOL: 1/1, 12/25
ADM: F   HDC/ACC: Y   PARKING: Y; Adjacent to the building   LIB: Y   MUS/SH: Y   H/B: Y
PERM/COLL: CONT TEXAS ART (1958-1992)

Located in a residential neighborhood, this renovated home was used to house many of the city's "oil boomers" who came to East Texas to invest in the great East Texas Oil Boom.

ON EXHIBIT/95:

1/7 - 2/95	SILVER ANNIVERSARY EXHIBITION OF THE PERMANENT COLLECTION
2/25 - 3/31/95	2ND AND 3RD PLACE INVITATIONAL WINNERS — Texas Fine Arts Association Young Artists 1994
4/8 - 4/29/95	MARTHA DILLARD
5/6 - 7/1/95	ARTISTIC TASTE OF TAOS
	DOROTHY KENNEDY BASKET COLLECTION
7/15 - 8/26/95	CITATION SHOW
	PINE MILLS POTTERY
9/9 - 10/28/95	36TH ANNUAL INVITATIONAL
	35TH INVITATIONAL WINNERS
11/4 - 12/22/95	AIDS QUILT
	ETHNIC TREES

LUFKIN

The Museum of East Texas
503 N. Second Street, **Lufkin, TX 75901**
TEL: 409-639-4434
HRS: 10-5 Tu-F; 1-5 Sa-S   DAY CLOSED: M   HOL: LEG/HOL!
ADM: F   HDC/ACC: Y   PARKING: Y   LIB: Y   MUS/SH: Y   GT: Y   GT/PH: call 409-639-4434   H/B: Y
PERM/COLL: AM, EU, & REG: ptgs

The Museum is housed in St. Cyprians Church, whose original Chapel was built in 1906. **NOT TO BE MISSED:** Historic photographic collection covering a period of over 90 years of Lufkin's history.

MARSHALL

Michelson Museum of Art
216 N. Bolivar, **Marshall, TX 75670**
TEL: 903-935-9480
HRS: 12-5 Tu-F; 1-4 Sa-S   DAY CLOSED: M   HOL: EASTER, 7/4, THGV, 12/25
ADM: Y   ADULT: $2.00   CHILDREN: $1.00
HDC/ACC: Y   PARKING: Y   GT: Y   GT/PH: call 903-935-9480 for specifics   H/B: Y
PERM/COLL: WORKS OF RUSSIAN AMERICAN ARTIST LEO MICHELSON, 1887-1978

407

TEXAS

Michelson Museum of Art - continued

The historic Southwestern Bell Telephone Corporation building in downtown Marshall is home to this extensive collection.

ON EXHIBIT/95:

1/8 - 4/2/95	LONDON BRASS RUBBINGS — Discover the medieval knights and ladies preserved in portraits in brass. Try the age-old craft of brass rubbing!
2/25 - 5/13/95	CROSS CULTURAL LEGACIES:AN EXHIBITION OF TEN WOMEN ARTISTS — Ten artists from the Austin area who are culturally and ethnically diverse.
10/8/95 - 1/7/96	WINSLOW HOMER, THE ILLUSTRATOR: HIS WOOD ENGRAVINGS — 132 prints will be on view in this extensive exhibition.
10/14/95 - 1/13/97	THE CROSS: THE BILL BOMAR COLLECTION OF CROSSES — Included are 280 crosses from around the world with special emphasis on Northern New Mexico pieces.

MCALLEN

McAllen International Museum
1900 Nolana, **McAllen, TX 78504**
TEL: 210-682-1564
HRS: 9-5 Tu-Sa; 1-5 S   DAY CLOSED: M   HOL: THGV, 12/25
ADM: Y   ADULT: $1:00   CHILDREN: $0.25   STUDENTS: $0.25   SR CIT: $1.00
HDC/ACC: Y   PARKING: Y   LIB: Y   MUS/SH: Y   GT: Y   GT/PH: call 210-682-1564 for specifics
PERM/COLL: LAT/AM: folk; AM; EU: gr 20

The museum caters to art & science on an equal level.

ON EXHIBIT/95:

PERMANENT	METEOROLOGY — Includes a working weather station and related exhibits

MIDLAND

Museum of the Southwest
1705 W. Missouri Ave, **Midland, TX 79701-6516**
TEL: 915-683-2882
HRS: 10-5 Tu-Sa; 2-5 S   DAY CLOSED: M   HOL: LEG/HOL!
ADM: F
HDC/ACC: Y   PARKING: Y   S/G: Y
PERM/COLL: REG; GR; SW: archeological artifacts

The Museum of the Southwest is an educational resource in art and archeology focusing on the Southwest. Housed in a 1934 mansion and stables, the collection also features the Hogan Collection of works by founder members of the Taos Society of artists. **NOT TO BE MISSED:** "The Sacred Pipe," by Alan Houser, bronze

408

ORANGE

Stark Museum of Art
712 Green Ave, **Orange, TX 77630**
TEL: 409-883-6661
HRS: 10-5 W-Sa; 1-5 S   DAY CLOSED: M, Tu   HOL: 1/1, EASTER, 7/4, THGV, 12/25
ADM: F   HDC/ACC: Y   PARKING: Y   LIB: Y   MUS/SH: Y   GT: Y   GT/PH: by appt only ! 409-883-6661
PERM/COLL: AM: 1830-1950; STEUBEN GLASS; NAT/AM

In addition to Great Plains and SW Indian crafts the Stark houses one of the finest collections of Western American art in the country. The museum also features the only complete Steuben Glass collection of "The US in Crystal." **NOT TO BE MISSED:** Paul Kane Collection of Western American Art

ON EXHIBIT/95:
Through 5/95   ANDY ANDERSON: WACKY WOODCARVINGS

11/94 - 10/95   JOSEPH HENRY SHARP — Over 70 paintings by this important founding member of the Taos Society of Artists will be featured in this exhibition.

SAN ANGELO

San Angelo Museum of Fine Arts
704 Burgess, **San Angelo, TX 76903**
TEL: 915-658-4084
HRS: 10-4 Tu-Sa; 1-4 S   DAY CLOSED: M   HOL: LEG/HOL!
ADM: Y   ADULT: $0.75   CHILDREN: Free (under 6)   STUDENTS: $0.25   SR CIT: $0.25
HDC/ACC: Y   PARKING: Y; On-site   LIB: Y   MUS/SH: Y   GT: Y   GT/PH: call 915-658-4084 for specifics
H/B: Y   S/G: Y
PERM/COLL: AM: cont cer; REG; MEX: 1945-present

The completely renovated museum building was originally the 1868 quartermaster's storehouse on the grounds of Fort Concho, a National Historic Landmark. **NOT TO BE MISSED:** "Figuora Accoccolata," by Emilio Greco

SAN ANTONIO

McNay Art Museum
6000 N. New Braunfels Ave., **San Antonio, TX 78209**
TEL: 210-824-5368
HRS: 10-5 Tu-Sa; 12-5 S   DAY CLOSED: M   HOL: 1/1, 7/4, THGV, 12/25
ADM: F   HDC/ACC: Y   PARKING: Y   LIB: Y   MUS/SH: Y   GT: Y   GT/PH: call for information
DT: Y   TIME: Noon S Sep-Jun; Summer!   H/B: Y   S/G: Y
PERM/COLL: FR & AM: sculp 19, 20; SW: folk ; GR & DRGS: 19, 20; THEATER ARTS

Devoted to the French Post-Impressionist and early School of Paris artists, the McNay Art Museum also has an outstanding theatre arts collection containing over 20,000 books and drawings as well as models of stage sets. It is located on beautifully landscaped grounds in a classic mediterranean style mansion. **NOT TO BE MISSED:** The McNay Museum will begin the celebration of its 40th Anniversary in November 1994 and it will continue throughout 1995.

TEXAS

McNay Art Museum - continued

ON EXHIBIT/95:

10/4/94 - 2/5/95   MASTERWORKS FROM THE TOBIN COLLECTION OF THEATRE ARTS — A survey of the most important costume and stage designs celebrating the 10th anniversary of the collection at the Museum.

1/17 - 3/12/95   MASTER GRAPHICS FROM THE COLLECTION — Some of the best examples of graphics in the collection illustrating why it is considered the outstanding department of prints and graphics in the Southwest.

3/26 - 6/25/95   THE STAGE IS ALL THE WORLD: THE THEATRICAL DESIGNS OF TANYA MOISEIWITSCH — Sketches, photographs, models, costumes, and masks from the 50 year career of this celebrated theatrical designer will be featured in this exhibition.
CAT

4/25 - 6/18/95   FELIX VALLOTON: PRINTS AND PREPARATORY DRAWINGS — By 1892 when he was only 26 years old, Vallotton was hailed as one of the important leaders in the Paris artistic avant-garde for his revival of the original woodcut. He became a member of a group of artists called the "Nabis" whose origins were in the Symbolist movement.
CAT   WT

7/11 - 8/27/95   MELVIN EDWARDS SCULPTURE: A RETROSPECTIVE 1963-1993 — Welded steel sculptures spanning the career of this African-American artist including his signature "Lynch Fragments," "Rockers," pedestal pieces and large scale sculptures.

SAN ANTONIO

San Antonio Museum of Art
200 West Jones Street, **San Antonio, TX 78215**
TEL: 210-978-8100
HRS: 10-5 M, W, F, Sa; 10-9 Tu; 12-5 S   HOL: THGV, 12/25
F/DAY: Tu, 3-9 ADM: Y ADULT: $4.00 CHILDREN: $1.75 (4-11) STUDENTS: $2.00 SR CIT: $2.00
HDC/ACC: Y PARKING: Y; Free LIB: Y MUS/SH: Y GT: Y GT/PH: call 210-978-8129 to reserve
H/B: Y S/G: Y
PERM/COLL: AN/GRK; AN/R; EGT; CONT: ptgs, sculp

The San Antonio Museum of Art is located in the restored turn-of-the-century former Lone Star Brewery. In addition to its other varied and rich holdings it features the most comprehensive collection of ancient art in the southwest. **NOT TO BE MISSED:** The spectacular Ewing Halsell Wing for Ancient Art.

ON EXHIBIT/95:

Through 1/22/95   TEXAS QUILTS, FURNITURE, POTTERY AND PAINTINGS

Through 5/31/95   MUMMIES: THE EGYPTIAN ART OF DEATH — Featuring a 4000 year old mummy and the exquisite art objects related to the ancient tomb.

Through 6/95   PAINTINGS FROM THE BLAFFER FOUNDATION — European paintings from the 16th to 19th centuries.

410

TYLER

Tyler Museum of Art
1300 S. Mahon Ave, **Tyler, TX 75701**
TEL: 903-595-1001
HRS: 10-5 Tu-Sa; 1-5 S   DAY CLOSED: M   HOL: LEG/HOL!
ADM: F
HDC/ACC: Y   PARKING: Y   LIB: Y   MUS/SH: Y   REST/FAC: Y; Cafe open Tu-F 11-2
GT: Y   GT/PH: call 903 595-1001   H/B:
PERM/COLL: PHOT; REG 20

The Museum is located in an architecturally award winning building.

WACO

The Art Center
1300 College Drive, **Waco, TX 76708**
TEL: 817-752-4371
HRS: 10-5 Tu-Sa ; 1-5 S   DAY CLOSED: M   HOL: LEG/HOL!
ADM: F
HDC/ACC: Y; 1st floor   PARKING: Y   LIB: Y   MUS/SH: Y   GT: Y   GT/PH: call 817-752-4371 for specifics
S/G: Y
PERM/COLL: CONT; REG

Housed in the Cameron Home, The Art Center is located on the McLellan Community College campus. It features an exhibit of sculpture on the grounds. **NOT TO BE MISSED:** "Square in Black," by Gio Pomodoro

WICHITA FALLS

Wichita Falls Museum and Art Center
Two Eureka Circle, **Wichita Falls, TX 76308**
TEL: 817-692-0923
HRS: 10-5 Tu-Sa; 1-5 S   DAY CLOSED: M   HOL: LEG/HOL!
ADM: Y   ADULT: $1.00   CHILDREN: F (under 3)   STUDENTS: $1.00   SR CIT: $1.00
HDC/ACC: Y   PARKING: Y   LIB: Y   MUS/SH: Y   GT: Y   GT/PH: call 817-692-0923 for specifics
PERM/COLL: AM: gr; CONT

The art collection has the singular focus of representing the history of American art through the medium of print making. **NOT TO BE MISSED:** The "Magic Touch Gallery" featuring hands-on science and the "Discovery Gallery" emphasizing family programming. Also high energy, high tech laser programs and planet shows in the planetarium.

UTAH

LOGAN

Nora Eccles Harrison Museum of Art
Affiliate Institution: Utah State University
650 N. 1100 E., **Logan, UT 84322-4020**
TEL: 801-797-0163
HRS: 10:30-4:30 Tu, T, F; 10:30-9 W; 2-5 Sa-S   DAY CLOSED: M   HOL: LEG/HOL!
ADM: F
HDC/ACC: Y   PARKING: Y; Within one block   LIB: Y   REST/FAC: Y
GT: Y   GT/PH: call 801-797-0163 for specifics   S/G: Y
PERM/COLL: NAT/AM; AM: cont art, cer 20

NOT TO BE MISSED: "Untitled" (Standing Woman), 1959, by Manuel Neri

ON EXHIBIT/95:

9/29/94 - 12/10/95	VISUAL FUTURES: PERMANENT COLLECTION
1/17 - 3/12/95	5TH BIENNIAL PHOTOGRAPHY
4/4 - 7/2/95	SPOTLIGHT ON MOROCCO
4/15 - 5/1/95	SIDNEY CHAFETZ: THE PERPETRATORS
7/18 - 9/10/95	SARA NORTHERNER: PHOTOGRAPHY
7/18 - 9/10/95	SURREALIST EXHIBITION

SALT LAKE CITY

Salt Lake Art Center
20 S.W. Temple, **Salt Lake City, UT 84101**
TEL: 801-328-4201
HRS: 10-5 M-Sa; 10-5 S   HOL: LEG/HOL!
SUGG/CONT: Y
HDC/ACC: Y   PARKING: Y; Paid on street parking   MUS/SH: Y   GT: Y   GT/PH: call 801 328-4201 for specifics
PERM/COLL: REG: all media

The 60 year old art center is located in the Bicentennial complex in the heart of downtown Salt Lake City.

Utah Museum of Fine Arts
101 AAC, University of Utah, **Salt Lake City, UT 84112**
TEL: 801-581-7332
HRS: 10-5 M-F; 2-5 Sa, S   HOL: LEG/HOL!
ADM: F
HDC/ACC: Y   PARKING: Y; Free on campus parking Sa & S; metered parking on weekdays   MUS/SH: Y
GT: Y   GT/PH: call 801-581-3580 to reserve   S/G: Y
PERM/COLL: EU & AM: ptgs 17-19; AF; AS; EGT

412

Utah Museum of Fine Arts - continued

With a permanent collection of over 10,000 works spanning a broad spectrum of the world's art history, this major Utah cultural institution is a virtual artistic treasure house containing the only comprehensive collection of art in the state or the surrounding region. **NOT TO BE MISSED:** DANCE AROUND THE MAYPOLE by Pieter Breughel, The Younger

ON EXHIBIT/95:

10/30/94 - 1/8/95	LEE GREENE RICHARDS
11/13/94 - 1/16/95	V. DOUGLAS SNOW RETROSPECTIVE
1/22 - 3/12/95	EARL JONES: PAINTINGS
2/5 - 3/19/95	CROWN POINT PRESS
3/12 - 4/2/95	IRANGELES: IRANIANS IN LOS ANGELES
3/26 - 5/7/95	MARION SICILIANO: PAINTINGS
4/9 - 5/21/95	UTAH OPERA EXHIBITION
4/30 - 6/11/95	UTAH 95: WORKS ON PAPER
6/4 - 7/23/95	THE LEONARD LEWIS COLLECTION OF AFRICAN ART
6/25 - 9/17/95	QUILTS
10/1 - 12/24/95	THE ARTS AND CRAFTS MOVEMENT
10/1 - 11/19/95	THE JAMES PEARLE COLLECTION OF PHOTOGRAPHS
12/3/95 - 1/14/96	MEDIEVAL MANUSCRIPTS FROM THE COLLECTION OF THE MARRIOTT LIBRARY

SPRINGVILLE

Springville Museum of Art
126 E. 400 S., **Springville, UT 84663**
TEL: 801-489-2727
HRS: 10-5 Tu-Sa; 2-5 S; 10-9 W   DAY CLOSED: M   HOL: 1/1, 12/25
ADM: F
HDC/ACC: Y   PARKING: Y   LIB: Y   MUS/SH: Y   GT: Y   GT/PH: call 801-489-2727 for information
PERM/COLL: UTAH: ptgs, sculp

The museum, housed in a Spanish colonial revival style building, features a collection noted for the art of Utah dating from pioneer days to the present.

VERMONT

BENNINGTON

The Bennington Museum
W. Main Street, **Bennington, VT 05201**
TEL: 802-447-1571
HRS: 9-5 daily (3/1-12/23); 1/2-2/28 (weekends only)   HOL: THGV
ADM: Y   ADULT: $4.50   CHILDREN: F (under 12)   STUDENTS: $3.50   SR CIT: $3.50
HDC/ACC: Y; Partial first floor only   PARKING: Y   LIB: Y   MUS/SH: Y
GT: Y   GT/PH: call 802-447-1571 to reserve   H/B: Y
PERM/COLL: AM: dec/art; MILITARY HIST; AM: ptgs

Visitors can imagine days gone by while gazing at a favorite Grandma Moses painting at The Bennington, one of the finest regional art and history museums in New England. The original museum building is the 1855 St. Francis de Sales church.

BROOKFIELD

Museum of the Americas
Route 14, **Brookfield, VT 05036**
TEL: 802-276-3386
HRS: 2-5 Tu-S (May-Oct); by appt Nov-Apr   DAY CLOSED: M
ADM: F
HDC/ACC: Y   PARKING: LIB: Y   MUS/SH: Y   GT: Y   GT/PH: ! By appt
PERM/COLL: BRIT & AM: ptgs, gr; HISP/AM: dec/art; LAT/AM: folk

BURLINGTON

Robert Hull Fleming Museum
Affiliate Institution: University of Vermont
Colchester Ave, **Burlington, VT 05405**
TEL: 802-656-0750
HRS: 12-4 Tu-F; 1-5 Sa-S   DAY CLOSED: M   HOL: LEG/HOL!, ACAD!
ADM: F   HDC/ACC: Y   PARKING: Y   LIB: Y   MUS/SH: Y   GT: Y   GT/PH: ! 802-656-0750   H/B: Y
PERM/COLL: NAT/AM; AN/EGT; CONT: Eu & Am

Vermont's primary art and anthropology museum is located in a McKim, Mead and White building. **NOT TO BE MISSED:** Assyrian Relief

ON EXHIBIT/95:

through 1/5/95	CANADIAN PAINTERS ELEVEN (1953-1961)
1/95 - 3/95	ARTIST AS CATALYST
through 2/95	DOLLS AND MINIATURES FROM AROUND THE WORLD
through 1995	PASSAGE TO SAMOA: THE ORMSBEE COLLECTION OF PACIFIC ART AND ARTIFACTS

414

Robert Hull Fleming Museum - continued

1/95 - 5/95	ERIC AHO PAINTINGS
3/4 - 5/4/95	PICASSO INSIDE THE IMAGE: PICASSO PRINTS FROM THE LUDWIG MUSEUM, COLOGNE
5/18 - 8/27/95	UTOPIAN BODY PAINT: PATTERNS OF CONNECTIONS
9/95 - 11/95	ROBERT RAUSCHENBERG

MANCHESTER

Southern Vermont Art Center
West Road, **Manchester, VT 05254**
TEL: 802-362-1405
HRS: 10-5 Tu-Sa; 12-5 S   DAY CLOSED: M   HOL: COLUMBUS DAY only
F/DAY: Sa, 10-1   ADM: Y   ADULT: $3.00   CHILDREN: F (under 13)   STUDENTS: $0.50   SR CIT: $3.00
HDC/ACC: Y   PARKING: Y   LIB: Y   MUS/SH: Y   REST/FAC: Y
GT: Y   GT/PH: call 802-362-1405 to reserve   H/B: Y   S/G: Y
PERM/COLL: PTGS, SCULP, PHOT, GR; CONT: 20

Built in 1917, by Mr. & Mrs. W. M. Ritter of Washington D.C., the Art Center is housed in a Georgian Colonial Mansion located on 450 acres on the eastern slope of Mt. Equinox. **NOT TO BE MISSED:** Works by Winslow Homer and Ogden Pleissner

MIDDLEBURY

Middlebury College Museum of Art
Middlebury College, **Middlebury, VT 05753**
TEL: 802-388-3711 ext 5007
HRS: 10-5 Tu-F; 12-5 Sa, S; acad year 5-8 T   DAY CLOSED: M   HOL: ACAD!, 12/25-1/1
ADM: F
HDC/ACC: Y   PARKING: Y; Free   LIB: Y!   MUS/SH: Y   REST/FAC: Y
GT: Y   GT/PH: ! adv res 802-388-3711 ext 3007
PERM/COLL: CYPRIOT: pottery; EU & AM : sculp 19; CONT: GR

Designed by the New York firm of Hardy Holzman Pfeiffer Associates, the new (1992) Center for the Arts also includes a theater, concert hall, music library and dance studios. It is located midway between Rutland and Burlington. **NOT TO BE MISSED:** "Bimbo Malado (Sick Child)," 1893 by Menardo Rosso (wax over plaster)

ON EXHIBIT/95:

Ongoing	19TH CENTURY PAINTING FROM THE PERMANENT COLLECTION
	20TH CENTURY PAINTING FROM THE PERMANENT COLLECTION
1/31 - 3/26/95	HERE AND NOW: THE MIDDLEBURY COLLEGE FACULTY ART SHOW
1/31 - 3/26/95	THE HALL PARK MCCULLOUGH COLLECTION; PORTRAITS OF GEORGE WASHINGTON

VERMONT

Middlebury College Museum of Art - continued

1/10 - 3/19	ART AND COMMERCE: 18TH CENTURY PRINTS AND DRAWINGS FROM THE PERMANENT COLLECTION
3/21 - 5/7/95	ROOTS OF MODERNISM: EARLY 19TH CENTURY PRINTS FROM THE PERMANENT COLLECTION
4/18 - 6/4/95	INK, PAPER, METAL AND WOOD: CONTEMPORARY PRINTS FROM CROWN PRESS
5/16 - 6/18/95	27TH ANNUAL STUDENT SHOW
6/27 - 8/13/95	ELOQUENT LINE: CONTEMPORARY JAPANESE CALLIGRAPHY
7/11 - ONGOING	EVERYDAY LIFE IN THE ANCIENT WORLD

MIDDLEBURY

The Sheldon Art Museum, Archeological and Historical Society
1 Park Street, **Middlebury, VT 05753**
TEL: 802-388-2117
HRS: 10-5 M-F, 10-4 Sa(Jun-Oct); 10-4 M-F (Nov-May)   DAY CLOSED: S   HOL: LEG/HOL!
ADM: Y   ADULT: $3.50, $7.00 family   CHILDREN: $1.00 (under12)   STUDENTS: $3.00   SR CIT: $3.00
HDC/ACC: Y   PARKING: LIB: Y
GT: Y   GT/PH: call 802-388-2117 to reserve   H/B: Y
PERM/COLL: DEC/ART; PER/RMS; ARTIFACTS

Vermont's exciting and interesting history is interpreted in this century old museum located in the 1829 Judd Harris house. **NOT TO BE MISSED:** Collection of locally made 18th century Windsor chairs

MONTPELIER

Wood Gallery and Arts Center
Affiliate Institution: Vermont College
College Hall, **Montpelier, VT 05602**
TEL: 802-828-8743
HRS: 12-4 Tu-S   DAY CLOSED: M   HOL: LEG/HOL!
ADM: Y   ADULT: $2.00   CHILDREN: F (under 12)   SR CIT: $2.00
HDC/ACC: Y   PARKING: LIB: Y!   MUS/SH: Y
GT: Y   GT/PH: call 802-828-8743 to reserve   H/B: Y
PERM/COLL: THOMAS WATERMAN WOOD: ptgs; PORTRAITS; WPA WORKS

Included in the more than 200 oils and watercolors in this collection are the works of Thomas W. Wood and his American contemporaries of the 1920's and 30's including A. H. Wyant and Asher B. Durand. **NOT TO BE MISSED:** "American Citizen to the Poles," by Thomas Wood

416

VERMONT

SHELBURNE

Shelburne Museum

U.S.Route 7, **Shelburne, VT 05482**
TEL: 802-985-3344
HRS: 10-5 M-S Late-May through Late-Oct   HOL: open all Hols
ADM: Y   ADULT: $15.00   CHILDREN: $6.00 (6-14)
HDC/ACC: Y; Limited (certain buildings are handicap accessible)   PARKING: Y; Free   LIB: Y   MUS/SH: Y
REST/FAC: Y   GT: Y   GT/PH: !   DT: Y   TIME: 1 pm late-Oct - late-May   H/B: Y
PERM/COLL: FOLK; DEC/ART; HAVERMEYER COLL

37 historic and exhibition buildings on 45 scenic acres combine to form this nationally celebrated collection of American folk art, artifacts, and architecture. **NOT TO BE MISSED:** Steamboat Ticonderoga

ST. JOHNSBURY

St. Johnsbury Athenaeum

30 Main Street, **St. Johnsbury VT 05819**
TEL: 802-748-8291
HRS: 10:00-8:00 M, W; 10:00-5:30 Tu, F; 9:30-4 Sa   DAY CLOSED: S   HOL: LEG/HOL!
ADM: F
PARKING: Y; Limited   H/B: Y
PERM/COLL: AM: ptgs 19; Hudson River School

The Atheneum was built as a public library and presented to the townspeople of St. Johnsbury by Horace Fairbanks in 1871. In 1873 an art gallery, which today is an authentic Victorian period piece, was added to the main building. The collection is shown as it was in 1893, **NOT TO BE MISSED:** "Domes of The Yosemite," by Albert Bierstadt

417

VIRGINIA

CHARLOTTESVILLE

Bayly Art Museum of the University of Virginia
Rugby Road, Thomas H. Bayly Memorial Bldg, **Charlottesville, VA 22903**
TEL: 804-924-3592
HRS: 1-5 Tu-S   DAY CLOSED: M   HOL: 12/25-1/1
ADM: F
HDC/ACC: Y   PARKING: Y; Limited parking behind museum   LIB: Y   GT: Y   GT/PH: call 804-924-3592
PERM/COLL: NAT/AM; MESO/AM; AF; DEC/ART 18; OM: gr; AM: ptgs, sculp, works on paper, phot 20; P/COL

This handsome Palladian-inspired building is located on the grounds of Jefferson's University of Virginia. With its wide ranging collection it serves as a museum for all ages and interests, for art lovers and scholars alike.

ON EXHIBIT/95:

11/1/94 - 1/8/95	MOVEMENT AND MEANING: IMAGES OF DANCE IN EARLY MODERNIST ART — Drawing on the works of Picasso, Moreau, Gaugin, Rodin and others, the exhibition documents the profound effect dance had on artists working at the end of the 19th and early 20th centuries.
11/4/94 - 1/22/95	INUIT ART FROM THE CANADIAN ARTIC: PRINTS AND SCULPTURE — This second in a series presenting an overview of the contemporary art and culture of the Inuit focuses on the most recent prints produced by artists of the Cape Dorset Cooperative and a selection of sculpture from the Canadian North.
1/14 - 4/2/95	THE LUMINOUS LINE: FOUR HUNDRED YEARS OF WESTERN PRINTMAKING — An exploration of the suggestion of light and space through styles, methods and traditions of print production from the 16th century to the present time.
1/20 - 3/19/95	THE MADE LANDSCAPE: CITY AND COUNTRY IN 17TH CENTURY DUTCH PRINTS — Netherlandish landscapes as depicted by Rembrandt, Hollar, vande Velde, and others reflecting the transformation of Dutch rural wetlands into what became the most highly developed urbanized country in western Europe at that time.
2/3 - 8/19/95	ANCESTORS: TIES THAT BIND — African masks, sculptures and worship shrines.
3/31 - 5/14/95	SCULPTURE AND INSTALLATIONS BY ELLEN DRISCOLL: ARTS BOARD CONTEMPORARY ART EXHIBITION
4/8 - 6/18/95	CONSTANCE STUART LARRABEE: SELECTIONS FROM THE WWII PHOTO-JOURNAL — Documentary photos taken in South Africa and Europe during the WWII period by this noted woman photographer.
9/1 - 10/29/95	MULTIPLE EXPOSURE: THE GROUP PORTRAIT IN PHOTOGRAPHY — Artists and professional photographers interpret the convention of the group portrait. Works date from 1900 to the present and include Diane Arbus, Walter Evans, William Wegman and others.
Fall 1995	LOWELL NESBITT (1933-1993): PAINTINGS, PRINTS AND DRAWINGS IN THE PERMANENT COLLECTION

Second Street Gallery
201 2nd Street, NW, **Charlottesville, VA 22902**
TEL: 804-977-7284
HRS: 10-5 T-Sa; 1-5 S   DAY CLOSED: M   HOL: LEG/HOL!
ADM: F   HDC/ACC: Y   PARKING: Y; On-street parking   H/B: Y
PERM/COLL: Non-collecting Gallery

VIRGINIA

Second Street Gallery - continued

Nationally known for its innovative programming, Second Street Gallery presents work of talented local, regional, and national artists working in a variety of media from painting and photography, to sculpture and site-specific installations. The McGuffey Art Center which houses the Gallery is located in a historic former primary school building and is now an artists' cooperative with open studios.

ON EXHIBIT/95:

1/6 - 1/29/95	PAMELA DE MARRIS; PHOTOGRAPHS
	WILLIAM EMORY; PHOTOGRAPHS
2/3 - 2/26/95	BETH EDWARDS; PAINTINGS
3/3 - 4/2/95	CONTEMPORARY VIRGINIA REALISM; PAINTINGS
4/7 - 4/30/95	WILLIAM NOLAND; SCULPTURE
5/5 - 5/28/95	JAMES MCELHINNEY; PAINTINGS
6/2 - 6/25/95	TBA

CLIFTON FORGE

Alleghany Highlands Arts and Crafts Center
439 East Ridgeway Street, **Clifton Forge, VA 24422**
TEL: 703-862-4447
HRS: 10:30-4:30 M-Sa May-Jul; 10:30-4:30 Tu-Sa Aug-Apr   HOL: THGV, 12/25
ADM: F
HDC/ACC: Y   PARKING: Y   MUS/SH: Y
PERM/COLL: Non-collecting institution

Housed in an early 1900's building the galleries' changing exhibits feature works produced by Highlands and other artists.

ON EXHIBIT/95:

1/10 - 2/4/95	LINDA ATKINSON: SCULPTURE
2/7 - 3/4/95	CHARLIE BROUWER: SCULPTURE
3/7 - 4/1/95	DIANE PATTON: WATERCOLORS
	ANNA FARIELLO: SCULPTURE
4/4 - 4/29/95	AIR RESIDENCY ARTIST JILL JENSEN: PRINTMAKER
5/1 - 5/27/95	JOHN AND GLADYS CLINGEMPEEL: ENCAUSTIC, CHARCOAL AND MONOPRINT
5/29 - 6/24/95	LYNDALL MASON: MONOPRINTS
	MIMI HODGINS: WALL HANGINGS AND KIMONAS
6/26 - 7/22/95	NEW RIVER ART SHOW
7/24 - 8/19/95	MICHAEL FARRAR: ABSTRACT WATERCOLORS
8/21 - 9/16/95	CARLETON ABBOTT: WATERCOLOR CONSTRUCTIONS

VIRGINIA

DANVILLE

Danville Museum of Fine Arts & History
975 Main Street, **Danville, VA 24541**
TEL: 804-793-5644
HRS: 10-5 Tu-F; 2-5 Sa, S   DAY CLOSED: M   HOL: LEG/HOL!
ADM: F
HDC/ACC: Y   PARKING: Y   LIB: Y   MUS/SH: Y   H/B: Y
PERM/COLL: REG: portraits, works on paper, dec/art, furniture, textiles; SOUTHERN PORTRAITS

The museum, in Sutherlin House built about 1857, is know as the last capitol of the confederacy. **NOT TO BE MISSED:** Restored Victorian Parlor

FREDERICKSBURG

Belmont, the Gari Melchers Estate and Memorial Gallery
224 Washington St., **Fredericksburg, VA 22405**
TEL: 703-899-4860
HRS: 10-4 M-Sa, 1-4 S (12/1-2/28); 10-5 M-Sa, 1-5 S (3/1-11/30)   HOL: 1/1, THGV , 12/24, 12/25, 12/31
ADM: Y   ADULT: $3.00   CHILDREN: F (under 6)   STUDENTS: 6-18 $1   SR CIT: $2.40
HDC/ACC: Y; Very limited (with prior notice assistance will be provided)   PARKING: Y
MUS/SH: in 1995   GT: Y   GT/PH: call 703-899-4860 to reserve   H/B: Y
PERM/COLL: EU & AM: ptgs (mostly by Gari Melchers)

This 18th century estate features many paintings by Gari Melchers (its former resident). Also on view are works by his American and European contemporaries as well as some old masters.

HAMPTON

Hampton University Museum
Hampton University, **Hampton, VA 23668**
TEL: 804-727-5308
HRS: 8-5 M-F; 12-4 Sa, S   HOL: LEG/HOL!, ACAD!
ADM: F
HDC/ACC: Y   PARKING: Y   MUS/SH: Y   H/B: Y
PERM/COLL: AF; NAT/AM: AM: ptgs 20

In a 1881 building on the Hampton Campus founded in 1868 for the education of newly freed African-Americans is this remarkable museum containing art & artifacts from cultures around the world. **NOT TO BE MISSED:** "The Banjo Lesson," by Henry O. Tanner

ON EXHIBIT/95:

1/16-7/31/95	JACOB LAWRENCE: THE FREDERICK DOUGLASS AND HARRIET TUBMAN SERIES OF NARRATIVE PAINTINGS, 1938-1940 — After a more than three year tour of such premiere art institutions as the Philadelphia Museum of Art, The Studio Museum in Harlem, and the Art Institute of Chicago, these 63 works by the renowned Jacob Lawrence return home to Hampton University.

LYNCHBURG

Maier Museum of Art
Affiliate Institution: Randolph-Macon Woman's College
Quinlan Street, **Lynchburg, VA 24503**
TEL: 804-947-8136
HRS: 1-5 Tu-S Sep-May   DAY CLOSED: M   HOL: ACAD!; 6/1-8/31
ADM: F
HDC/ACC: Y; Limited (no handicap bathroom)   PARKING: Y; Limited   MUS/SH: Y
GT: Y   GT/PH: call 804-924-8136 to reserve   DT: Y   TIME: call 804-924-8136 for specifics
PERM/COLL: AM: ptgs 19, 20

19th and 20th century American paintings including works by Gilbert Stuart, Winslow Homer, Thomas Eakins, Thomas Cole, George Bellows, Mary Cassatt, Georgia O'Keeffe, and Jamie Wyeth, are among the many highlights of the Maier Museum of Art . **NOT TO BE MISSED:** Mary Cassatt's "Mother and Child Looking at the Baby"

ON EXHIBIT/95:

1/15 - 2/19/95	ASTRAY IN A DARK WOOD: WORKS BY KATHY MUEHLEMANN — Professor of Art, Randolph-Macon Woman's College.
2/26 - 4/16/95	CHILDE HASSAM: CITY STREETS AND RURAL RETREATS
4/21 - 5/13/95	SENIOR ART MAJORS' EXHIBITION

NEWPORT NEWS

Penninsula Fine Arts Center
101 Museum Drive, **Newport News, VA 23606**
TEL: 804-596-8175
HRS: 10-5 Tu-Sa; 1-5 S   DAY CLOSED: M   HOL: 1/1, 7/4, 12/25
ADM: F
HDC/ACC: Y; Limited as only exhibition wing is wheelchair accessible   PARKING: Y   MUS/SH: Y
GT: Y   GT/PH: call 804-596-8175 to reserve   S/G: Y
PERM/COLL: Non-collecting institution

Programs of changing exhibitions of primarily contemporary art by emerging artists that often contrast with exhibitions of historical significance are featured at this fine arts center.

ON EXHIBIT/95:

11/19/94 - 1/8/95	INTERIORS
	PHILIP MORRISON — Photographs
	ANNE PETERSON — Photographs
	VALERIE HARDY — Paintings
11/19/94 - 1/8/95	HOME FOR THE HOLIDAYS — Works by regional artists

VIRGINIA

NORFOLK

The Chrysler Museum
Olney Road and Mowbray Arch, **Norfolk, VA 23510**
TEL: 804-622-1211
HRS: 10-4 Tu-Sa; 1-5 S   DAY CLOSED: M   HOL: 1/1, 7/4, THGV, 12/25
ADM: F HDC/ACC: Y PARKING: Y; Free LIB: Y MUS/SH: Y REST/FAC: Y
GT: Y GT/PH: call 804-622-1211 to reserve
PERM/COLL: GLASS; IT/BAROQUE: ptgs; FR: 19; AN/EGT; AM: sculp, ptgs

Named one of the top 20 museums in the nation, The Chrysler Museum offers visitors an encyclopedic view of 30,000 works of art in an Italianate-Style building built on the picturesque Hague of the Elizabeth River. **NOT TO BE MISSED:** Gianlorenzo Bernini's "Bust of the Savior"

ON EXHIBIT/95:

10/22/94 - 1/2/95	HELENE BRANDT
11/13/94 - 1/8/95	CHINESE PAINTING
1/21 - 3/19/95	DOUG TRUMP
2/19 - 4/16/95	SHAKER FURNITURE
5/11 - 8/6/95	AFRICAN ZION: THE SACRED ART OF ETHIOPIA — 85 of the finest surviving examples of Ethiopian religious art from the foremost collections in Ethiopia, Europe and America. WT
9/30 - 12/31/95	INDELIBLE IMPRESSIONS: ONE HUNDRED YEARS OF AMERICAN CHILDREN'S BOOK ILLUSTRATIONS
	PARAMETERS EXHIBITIONS: CONTEMPORARY ART
4/15 - 5/18/95	JUDITH STREETER

Hermitage Foundation Museum
7637 North Shore Road, **Norfolk, VA 23505**
TEL: 804-423-2052
HRS: 10-5 M-Sa; 1-5 S HOL: 1/1, THGV, 12/25
ADM: Y ADULT: $4.00 CHILDREN: $1.00 STUDENTS: F SR CIT: $4.00
HDC/ACC: Y PARKING: Y H/B: Y
PERM/COLL: OR; EU; AS; 16, 17

Nestled in a lush setting along the Lafayette River is the 12 acre estate of the Hermitage Foundation Museum whose turn-of-the-century English Tudor home appears to have been frozen in time. It is, however, alive with treasures from the past. **NOT TO BE MISSED:** 1,400 year old Buddha

RADFORD

Radford University Galleries
200 Powell Hall, **Radford, VA 24142**
TEL: 703-831-5745, 5141
HRS: 10-4 Tu-F; 6-9 T; 12-4 S (9/1-5/30) DAY CLOSED: Sa, M HOL: LEG/HOL!, JUL & AUG
ADM: F HDC/ACC: Y PARKING: Y S/G: Y
PERM/COLL: CONT WORKS IN ALL MEDIA

Radford University Galleries - continued

Located in the New River Valley, the gallery is noted for the diversity of its special exhibitions.

ON EXHIBIT/95:

1/20 - 2/3/95	STUDENT JURIED SHOW
2/9 - 3/8/95	DEFINING OURSELVES — A collective self-portrait of the diverse community of humankind.
4/15 - 11/1/95	SCULPTURE COMPETITION — Annually ten sculptors are selected to exhibit their works on campus.
5/19 - 6/17/95	NEW RIVER ART — A biennial survey of works by local artists which opens here and travels to other sites in the Blue Ridge.

RICHMOND

Anderson Gallery, School of the Arts

Affiliate Institution: Virginia Commonwealth University
907 1/2 W. Franklin Street, **Richmond, VA 23284-2514**
TEL: 804-828-1522
HRS: 10-5 Tu-F; 1-5 Sa, S   DAY CLOSED: M   HOL: LEG/HOL! ACAD!
ADM: F
HDC/ACC: N, no elevator; museum has 3 floors   PARKING: Y; Metered on-street parking   MUS/SH: Y
PERM/COLL: CONT: gr, phot, ptgs, sculp

The gallery is well known in the US and Europe for exhibiting work of nationally and internationally renowned artists.

ON EXHIBIT/95:

1/20 - 3/5/95	REPICTURING ABSTRACTION: POLITICS OF SPACE — The exhibition explores the movement from subconcious impulse to concious strategy in late 20th century abstraction. A cooperative exhibition with the Virginia Museum of Fine Arts. CAT WT
1/20 - 3/5/95	DWELLING: CRAIG PLEASANT — This show culminates the artist's three years of contact, study, reflection and artmaking about homelessness and low-cost housing solutions.
3/21 - 3/30/95	STUDENT DESIGN EXHBITION
4/11 - 4/20/95	JURIED STUDENT FINE ARTS EXHIBITION
4/28 - 5/21/95	ROUNDS ONE AND TWO OF THE MFA THESIS EXHIBITION

Virginia Museum of Fine Arts

2800 Grove Ave, **Richmond, VA 23221-2466**
TEL: 804-367-0844
HRS: 11-5 Tu, W, F-S; 11-8 T   DAY CLOSED: M   HOL: 1/1, 7/4, THGV, 12/25
SUGG/CONT: Y   ADM: Y   ADULT: $4.00   CHILDREN: F (under 5)   STUDENTS: $4.00   SR CIT: $4.00
HDC/ACC: Y   PARKING: Y; Free and ample   LIB: Y   MUS/SH: Y   REST/FAC: Y
GT: Y   GT/PH: res 3 weeks adv call 807-367-0859   DT: Y   TIME: 2:30 Tu-F; 6pm T; 11:30 Sa; 2 S   S/G: Y
PERM/COLL: AM: ptgs, sculp; LILLIAN THOMAS PRATT COLL OF JEWELS BY PETER CARL FABERGE; EU: all media (Ren to cont)

VIRGINIA

Virginia Museum of Fine Arts - continued

Diverse collections and outstanding special exhibits abound in the internationally prominent Virginia Museum which houses one of the lagest collections in the world of Indian, Nepalese, and Tibetan art. It also holds the Mellon Collection of sporting art and the Sydney and Francis Lewis Collection of late 19th and early 20th century decorative arts, contemporary American paintings and sculpture. **NOT TO BE MISSED:** "Caligula," Roman, AD 38-40 marble 80" high. Also the largest public collection of Faberge Imperial Easter eggs in the West.

ON EXHIBIT/95:

7/26/94 - 5/14/95	ART OF THE ANCIENT AMERICAS: BODY AND SOUL TRANSFORMED — Exquisite examples of pre-Columbian painted and modeled ceramics, textiles, gold jewelry and metallurgy from the museum collection. These were primarily burial objects from Mesoamerica and South America and provide insights into the beliefs of many pre-Columbian people.
9/24/94 - 3/30/95	SPIRIT OF THE MOTHERLAND: AFRICAN ART AT THE VIRGINIA MUSEUM OF FINE ARTS — An exhibition of virtually the entire 300 object African collection will enhance the viewers perception of the diversity of African art and culture. CAT WT
11/9/94 - 1/8/95	DESIGNED TO SELL: AMERICAN TURN-OF-THE-CENTURY POSTERS — 110 posters from the museum collection document the "golden age" of poster design in America, ca. 1894-1905 CAT WT
1/17 - 7/2/95	INDIAN PAINTING FROM THE PUNJAB HILLS — A selection of miniature paintings produced in the 17th, 18th and 19th centuries in the small Hindu kingdoms and principalities in northern India.
1/21 - 3/19/95	REPICTURING ABSTRACTION — An exploration of the work of contemporary painters who have reinvigorated abstraction over the last decade. A cooperative exhibition with the Anderson Gallery, School of Fine Arts. CAT WT
1/31 - 6/25/95	A-HUNTING WE WILL GO: BRITISH SPORTING DRAWINGS AND PRINTS FROM THE COLLECTION OF PAUL MELLON — 18th and 19th century representations of fox hunting by all the leading sporting artists of the period.
6/14 - 9/17/95	AMERICA AROUND 1900: IMPRESSIONISM, REALISM AND MODERN LIFE — 75 works by artists of two distinct but related movements thematically treating the city, country and home, including Mary Cassatt, John Singer Sargent, William Merritt Chase and "Ashcan School" members Robert Henri, John Sloan and others. CAT WT
7/7 - 9/10/95	FACE OF THE GODS: ART AND ALTARS OF AFRICA AND THE AFRICAN-AMERICANS — An exploration of the altar as a focus of ritual and art and as a document of the enduring impact of African civilization on the black New World. CAT WT
11/13/95 - 1/7/96	HEAD, HEART AND HAND: ELBERT HUBBARD AND THE ROYCROFTERS — In celebration of the 100th anniverary of the Western New York craft colony founded by Elbert Hubbard, this major exhibition (the first of its kind devoted to all aspects of Roycroft production and aesthetics) will feature more than 200 examples of such finely crafted items as furniture, metalwork, ceramics, and leather goods in addition to period photographs of the community at work and play. CAT WT

424

ROANOKE

The Art Museum of Western Virginia
One Market Square, **Roanoke, VA 24011**
TEL: 703-342-5760
HRS: 10-5 Tu-Sa; 1-5 S   DAY CLOSED: M   HOL: 12/25
ADM: F
HDC/ACC: Y   PARKING: Y; Pay   LIB: Y   MUS/SH: Y
GT: Y   GT/PH: call 703-342-5670 to reserve   S/G: Y
PERM/COLL: AM & EU: ptgs 20; AM: folk, gr, phot

Located in the Blue Ridge Mountains of Western Virginia, the collection reflects all cultures formerly and presently found there. **NOT TO BE MISSED:** Outsider Art and regional artist exhibitions

ON EXHIBIT/95:

1/1 - 3/1/95	DONNA ESSIG — Large scale watercolors featuring stylized people and animals amidst heavily patterned fantasy landscapes.
3/9 - 5/21/95	WALTER O. EVANS COLLECTION OF AFRICAN-AMERICAN ART (TENT!) — A major collection of paintings and sculpture. WT
4/5/95	REINSTALLATION OF THE SCULPTURE COURT
4/95 - 6/95	"BIG AL" CARTER — Contemporary works by an African-American artist who paints expressionistically.
5/29 - 7/95	ROANOKE CITY ART SHOW
7/1 - 10/15/95	DREAMWEAVER — Illustrations from children's literature.
7/22 - 10/15/95	AFRICAN ARTS FROM THE VIRGINIA MUSEUM
10/95 - 1/96	LEONARD KOSCLANSKI — Dark sinister paintings filled with wild animals and images of untamed nature.

SWEET BRIAR

Sweet Briar College Art Gallery
Sweet Briar College, **Sweet Briar, VA 24595**
TEL: 804-381-6248
HRS: 12-5 Tu-S & by appt (Acad Schedule)   DAY CLOSED: M   HOL: ACAD!
ADM: F
HDC/ACC: Y; Ramp & elevator   PARKING: Y   LIB: Y
MUS/SH: Y   REST/FAC: Y; On campus
GT: Y   GT/PH: call 804-381-6100 for specifics   H/B: Y, on campus   S/G: Y
PERM/COLL: JAP: woodblock prints; EU: gr, drgs 19; AM: ptgs 20

The exterior design of the 1901 building is a rare collegiate example of Ralph Adams Cram Georgian Revival Style architecture. **NOT TO BE MISSED:** "Daisies and Anemones," by William Glackens

VIRGINIA

VIRGINIA BEACH

Virginia Beach Center for the Arts
2200 Parks Avenue, **Virginia Beach VA 23451**
TEL: 804-425-0000
HRS: 10-4 Tu-Sa; 12-4 S   DAY CLOSED: M   HOL: LEG/HOL!
ADM: F   HDC/ACC: Y   PARKING: Y   LIB: Y   MUS/SH: Y   S/G: Y
PERM/COLL: Non-collecting institution

Rotating exhibits of locally, nationally and internationally acclaimed artists are featured at this center for the arts.

WILLIAMSBURG

Abby Aldrich Rockefeller Folk Art Center
307 S. England Street, **Williamsburg, VA 23185**
TEL: 804-220-7670
HRS: 10-6 M-S
ADM: Y   ADULT: $6.00
HDC/ACC: Y   PARKING: Y; Free   LIB: Y!   MUS/SH: Y   GT: Y   GT/PH: call 804-220-7670 to reserve   H/B: Y
PERM/COLL: AM: folk

Historic Williamsburg is the site of the country's premier showcase for American folk art. The museum, originally built in 1957 and reopened in its new building in 1992, demonstrates folk arts' remarkable range and inventiveness in textiles, paintings, and decorative arts.

Muscarelle Museum of Art
College of William and Mary, **Williamsburg, VA 23185**
TEL: 804-221-2700
HRS: 10-4:45 M-F; 12-4 Sa-S   HOL: LEG/HOL!
ADM: F   HDC/ACC: Y   PARKING: Y   MUS/SH: Y   GT: Y   GT/PH: call 804-221-2700 to reserve   H/B: Y
PERM/COLL: BRIT & AM: portraits 17-19; O/M: drgs; CONT: gr; AB; EU & AM: ptgs

The "world's first solar painting" by Gene Davis, transforms the south facade of the Museum into a dramatic and innovative visual statement when monumental tubes, filled with colored water are lit from behind. **NOT TO BE MISSED:** Early Renaissance fresco fragment, St. Mary Magdalene and Donor, attributed to The Master of the Cappella di San Giorgio, Italian (Assisi), 1300-1350.

ON EXHIBIT/95:

11/19/94 - 1/8/95	ARTISANS IN SILVER
	EX-VOTO PAINTINGS OF LATIN AMERICA
1/14 - 2/19/95	WORKS BY WARHOL
	KARSH PHOTOGRAPHY
2/25 - 3/26/95	DRAWINGS AND STUDIES BY HANS GROHS
	JAMES BLAIR STUDIES BY LEWIS COHEN
4/1 - 5/21/95	THE PASSIONATE OBSERVER: PHOTOGRAPHS BY CARL VAN VECHTEN
9/1 - 10/14/95	NCECA 1995 CLAY NATIONAL
10/20 - 12/5/95	AFRICAN-AMERICAN WORKS ON PAPER

BELLEVUE

Bellevue Art Museum
301 Bellevue Square, **Bellevue, WA 98004**
TEL: 206-454-3322
HRS: 10-6 M, W, T, Sa; 10-8, Tu, F; 11-5 S   HOL: LEG/HOL !
ADM: Y   ADULT: $3.00   CHILDREN: F (under 12)
STUDENTS: $2.00   SR CIT: $2.00
HDC/ACC: Y   PARKING: Y, Free and ample   MUS/SH: Y
GT: Y   GT/PH: call to reserve   DT: Y   TIME: 2:00 daily
PERM/COLL: Non-collecting institution

Located across Lake Washington about 10 minutes drive from Seattle, the Bellevue Art Museum showcases Northwest art and the national and international influences that shape it.

ON EXHIBIT/95:

12/10/94 - 2/25/95	THE ILLUSTRIOUS ART OF BOOKS	
2/11 - 4/10/95	THE QUILT NATIONAL	WT
4/22 - 6/25/95	WASHINGTON: 100 YEARS, 100 PAINTINGS — On exhibit will be a collection of modern paintings by Washington artists dating from a period prior to the North West School to the present.	
7/1 - 7/16/95	PREVIEW: NORTH WEST ARTS AND CRAFT FAIR	
7/28 - 9/10/95	4TH ANNUAL PACIFIC NORTH WEST ANNUAL — A juried competition of regional contemporary artists	
9/23 - 11/26/95	JEAN JONGEWALD: IN THE NORTH WEST DESIGN TRADITION	
12/9/95 - 1/21/96	CELEBRATION ESPECIALLY FOR CHILDREN	

BELLINGHAM

Whatcom Museum of History and Art
121 Prospect Street, **Bellingham, WA 98225**
TEL: 206-676-6981
HRS: 12-5 Tu-S   DAY CLOSED: M   HOL: LEG/HOL!
ADM: F   HDC/ACC: Y   LIB: Y   MUS/SH: Y
GT: Y   GT/PH: call 206-676-6981 to reserve
H/B: Y   S/G: Y
PERM/COLL: KINSEY: phot coll; HANSON: Naval arch drgs; NW/COAST: ethnography; VICTORIANA

An architectural and historic landmark, this museum building is situated in a 1892 former City Hall on a bluff with a commanding view of Bellingham Bay.

WASHINGTON

CLARKSTON

Valley Art Center, Inc
842-6th Street, **Clarkston, WA 99403**
TEL: 509-758-8331
HRS: 9-4 M-F; by appt other times   DAY CLOSED: Sa, S   HOL: 7/4, THGV, 12/25-1/1
ADM: F
HDC/ACC: Y; Building accessible EXCEPT for restrooms   PARKING: Y   LIB: Y   MUS/SH: Y
GT: Y   GT/PH: call 509-758-8331 to reserve   H/B: Y
PERM/COLL: REG; NAT/AM

Valley Art Center is located in Southeast Washington at the Snake and Clearwater Rivers in the heart of the city's historic district made famous by Lewis and Clarke. **NOT TO BE MISSED:** Beadwork, Piute Cradle Board Tatouche

ELLENSBURG

The Clymer Art Museum
416 North Pearl Street, **Ellensburg, WA 98926**
TEL: 509-962-6416
HRS: 10-5 M-F; 12-5 Sa, S   HOL: 1/1, EASTER, 7/4, THGV, 12/25
ADM: Y   ADULT: $2.00   CHILDREN: $1.00   STUDENTS: $1.00   SR CIT: $1.00
HDC/ACC: Y   PARKING: Y; Street   LIB: Y!   MUS/SH: Y
GT: Y   GT/PH: call 509-962-6416 to reserve   H/B: Y
PERM/COLL: WORKS OF ELLENSBURG ARTIST, JOHN FORD CLYMER FOR THE SATURDAY EVENING POST COVER; drgs, sketches; WESTERN ART

The 1901 building with lintels from the Chicago Music Hall (and an upstairs ballroom!) is an unusual setting for the diverse work of John Clymer, an artist whose work adorned more than 80 Saturday Evening Post covers. He was equally well known as an outstanding cowboy and Western artist.

ON EXHIBIT/95:

1/6 - 2/20/95	FOCUS ON FIBER: TEXTILES AND WOVEN ART — Considered by many as mere craft, this exhibtion demonstrates that fiber art has evolved into a serious fine art form.
2/24 - 4/9/95	HIGH TEA GARDEN PARTY — Celebrate the English tradition of high tea with an exhibit of original ceramic teapots and floral paintings in oils and watercolors.
4/14 - 5/14/95	WESTERN ART SHOW AND AUCTION PREVIEW
5/19 - 7/9/95	TBA
7/14 - 9/4/95	COWBOY CARTOONISTS INTERNATIONAL — From the wildly hilarious to the deadly serious, many levels of cartoon entertainment are produced by this group of artists.
9/8 - 11/5/95	FIN FLAM AND FISH TALES: SOMETHING FISHY IN ART — Sometimes a single topic can inspire a multitude of artistic interpretations.
11/10 - 12/31/95	STOCKING THE ORNAMENTAL YULE: A DIFFERENT KIND OF HOLIDAY SHOW

428

GOLDENDALE

Maryhill Museum of Art

35 Maryhill Museum Drive, **Goldendale, WA 98620**
TEL: 509-773-3733
HRS: 9-5 Daily mid Mar-mid Nov.   HOL: Open HOL
ADM: Y   ADULT: $4.00   CHILDREN: F (under 6)   STUDENTS: $1.50   SR CIT: $3.50
HDC/ACC: Y   PARKING: Y   LIB: Y   MUS/SH: Y   REST/FAC: Y; Small cafe   H/B: Y
PERM/COLL: SCULP; ORTHODOX ICONS: 18; BRIT: ptgs; NAT/AM: baskets, dec/art; FURNISHINGS OF QUEEN MARIE of ROMANIA; INTERNATIONAL CHESS SETS

Serving the Pacific Northwest, the Maryhill Museum is a major cultural resource in the Columbia River Gorge Region. **NOT TO BE MISSED:** Rodin sculpture; nearby Stonehenge Monument

ON EXHIBIT/95:

3/15 - 6/7/95	THE HOUND OF HEAVEN: THE VISION OF R. H. IVES GAMMELL
3/15 - 6/4/95	TRUNNIONS, BASCULES AND CANTILEVERS: HISTORIC WASHINGTON BRIDGES
3/15 - 11/15/95	WORKS BY CONTEMPORARY NORTHWEST ARTISTS — One month exhibitions will feature Bud Eager, Oregon photographer; Paul Fyfield, Oregon printmaker; Marilyn Bolles, Washington watercolorist; and Mark Little, Portland painter.
6/17 - 11/5/95	CHIHULY BASKETS — Glass master Dale Chihuly's basket sets and Indian basket collection.
7/15 - 8/13/95	INFINITY CITY — A mixed-media installation commemorating the 50th anniversary of the Atomic Bomb.

LONGVIEW

The Art Gallery, Lower Columbia College Fine Arts Gallery

1600 Maple Street, **Longview, WA 98632**
TEL: 206-577-2300
HRS: 10-4 M-F; 7-9 W & T   DAY CLOSED: Sa, S   HOL: Open SEP through JUN
ADM: F   HDC/ACC: Y   PARKING: Y   GT: Y   GT/PH: call 206-577-2314 to reserve
PERM/COLL: Non-collecting institution

A College Gallery that features temporary exhibitions by local, regional, and national artists

OLYMPIA

Washington State Capital Museum

211 West 21st Avenue, **Olympia, WA 98501**
TEL: 206-753-2580
HRS: 10-4 Tu-F; 12-4 Sa-S   DAY CLOSED: M   HOL: LEG/HOL!
ADM: Y   ADULT: $2.00   STUDENTS: $1.00   SR CIT: $1.00
HDC/ACC: Y; 1st floor main gallery   PARKING: Y   LIB: Y   MUS/SH: Y   H/B: Y
PERM/COLL: REG; NAT/AM: 18, 19

WASHINGTON

Washington State Capital Museum - continued

The Museum is housed in the Lord Mansion, a 1924 California Mission Revival Style building. It also features a permanent exhibit on the history of Washington State government and cultural history. **NOT TO BE MISSED:** Southern Puget Sound American Indian exhibit; welcome healing totem pole figure.

ON EXHIBIT/95:

11/94 - 2/95	NEA EXPERIMENTAL GALLERY EXHIBIT
1/95 - 7/95	WASHINGTON'S HISTORIC PUBLIC ARCHITECTURE (working title)
7/95 - 12/95	OLYMPIA AS STATE CAPITAL

PULLMAN

Museum of Art
Washington State University, **Pullman, WA 99164**
TEL: 509-335-1910
HRS: 10-4 M-F; 7-10 Tu; 1-5 Sa-S   DAY CLOSED: HOL: ACAD!
ADM: F   HDC/ACC: Y
PARKING: Y; Parking permits may be purchased at Parking Services, adjacent to the Fine Arts Center
LIB: Y   GT: Y   GT/PH: call 509-335-1910 to reserve
PERM/COLL: NW: art; CONT/AM & CONT/EU: gr 19

The WSU Museum of Art, in the university community of Pullman, presents a diverse program of changing exhibitions, including paintings, prints, photography, and crafts. The Museum is located in a beautiful agricultural area between the university communities of Pullman and Moscow.

ON EXHIBIT/95:

1/30 - 3/17/95	OUR LAND/OURSELVES: AMERICAN INDIAN CONTEMPORARY ARTISTS — Works on paper
3/27 - 4/2/95	GEORGE TRAKAS/CATHERINE HOWETT: OPEN STUDIO — Original plans and drawings by designers of WSU's Glen Terrell Friendship MaLL.
4/10 - 5/13/95	GRADUATE THESIS EXHIBITIONS
5/17 - 7/31/95	THE ELWOOD COLLECTION — Contemporary prints including Beuys, Atkinson, Komar and Melamid.
9/5 - 10/15/95	CLEARLY ART: PILCHUCK'S GLASS LEGACY — Masterpieces in glass from the artists of the internationally known Pilchuck School. WT
10/30 - 12/19/95	ROBERT HELM 1981-1993 — Paintings on wood by Helm, a renowned Pullman artist.

WASHINGTON

SEATTLE

Henry Art Gallery
Affiliate Institution: University of Washington
15th Ave. NE & NE 41st Street, **Seattle, WA 98195**
TEL: 206-543-2280
HRS: 11-5 Tu-W & F-S; 11-9 T   DAY CLOSED: M   HOL: LEG/HOL!
F/DAY: T   ADM: Y   ADULT: $3.50   CHILDREN: F (under 12)   STUDENTS: $2.00   SR CIT: $2.00
HDC/ACC: Y; Call 206-543-6450 10 days advance to notify   PARKING: Y; Pay   MUS/SH: Y
GT: Y   GT/PH: call 206-543-2281 for specifics   H/B: Y
PERM/COLL: PTGS: 19, 20; PHOT; CER; ETH: textiles & W./Coast

The Tudor Gothic building housing the Gallery was built in 1927 as the first public museum in Washington State.

ON EXHIBIT/95:

12/4/94 - 3/5/95	AFTER ART: RETHINKING 150 YEARS OF PHOTOGRAPHY — These 180 works from the extensive R. Joseph amd Elaine R. Monsen collection span the entire history of the medium and explore photography's incomparable ability to offer images of great visual beauty while bringing forth fascinating questions about context and interpretation. CAT WT
12/4/94 - 3/5/95	DRAWINGS AND MODELS OF THE HENRY ART GALLERY EXPANSION — The Gallery will close in April 1995 for renovation of the existing historic building and a major addition designed by Charles Gwathmey. Call for precise closing and reopening dates.
12/7/94 - 2/12/95	FACT AND FICTION: PHOTOGRAPHY IN THE 20TH CENTURY — The Gallery houses the extensive R. Joseph and Elaine R. Monsen Study Collection of Photography from which this exhibition was selected. The wonderfully rich history of photography from its inception to today is explored through striking examples by world famous photographers. CAT

Nordic Heritage Museum
3014 N.W. 67th Street, **Seattle, WA 98117**
TEL: 206-789-5707
HRS: 10-4 Tu-Sa; 12-4 S   DAY CLOSED: M   HOL: 1/1, 12/24, 12/25
ADM: Y   ADULT: $3.00   CHILDREN: $1.00   STUDENTS: $2.00   SR CIT: $2.00
HDC/ACC: Y   PARKING: Y; Free   LIB: Y   MUS/SH: Y   GT: Y   GT/PH: call 206-789-5707 to reserve
PERM/COLL: SCANDINAVIAN/AM: folk; PHOT

Follow the immigrants journey across the America in this museum located in Ballard north of the Ballard Locks.

ON EXHIBIT/95:

1/13 - 3/12/95	CAROL TAIPALE NURMESNIEMI, FINNISH AMERICAN ARTIST
1/13 - 3/12/95	TONE ORVIK, NORWEGIAN ARTIST, SCULPTURES
1/13 - 4/30/95	RODE ORM:WEAVINGS OF A VIKING SAGA
	THE VIKINGS: MASTER MARINERS, TRADERS, COLONISTS AND ARTISANS
3/22 - 5/21/95	IDA LORENTZEN, NORWEGIAN PAINTER

WASHINGTON

Nordic Heritage Museum - continued

5/31 - 8/27/95	DANISH FURNITURE DESIGN
8/31 - 10/8/95	GRETE BODOGAARD HEIKES, NORWEGIAN TAPESTRY ARTIST
8/31 - 10/8/95	ROGER FALLMAN, SWEDISH LANDSCAPE ARTIST
9/15 - 12/31/95	RICHARD FAIRBANKS, AMERICAN POTTER: A RETROSPECTIVE
10/20 - 12/31/95	SIGRUN JONSDOTTIR, ICELANDIC ARTIST

SEATTLE

Seattle Art Museum

100 University Street, **Seattle, WA 98101-2902**
TEL: 206-654-3100
HRS: 10-5 Tu-Sa; 10-9 T; open M on Holidays   DAY CLOSED: M   HOL: 1/1, THGV, 12/25
F/DAY: 1st Tu   ADM: Y   ADULT: $6.00   CHILDREN: F (under 12)   STUDENTS: $4.00   SR CIT: $4.00
HDC/ACC: Y   PARKING: Y; Limited pay parking   MUS/SH: Y   REST/FAC: Y
GT: Y   GT/PH: call 206-654-3123 to reserve   DT: Y   TIME: 2 Tu-S; 7 T; Sp exh 1 Tu-S; 6 T   S/G: Y
PERM/COLL: AS; AF; NW NAT/AM; CONT; PHOT; EU: dec/art; NW/CONT

Designed by Robert Venturi, architect of the new wing of the National Gallery in London, this stunning new five story building is but one of the reasons for visiting the outstanding Seattle Art Museum. The new downtown location is conveniently located within walking distance of many of Seattle's most interesting landmarks including Pike Place Market, Seattle Waterford, and Historic Pioneer Square. The Museum features 2 complete educational resource centers with interactive computer systems. **NOT TO BE MISSED:** NW Coast Native American Houseposts; 48' kinetic painted steel sculpture "Hammering Man" by Jonathan Borovsky

ON EXHIBIT/95:

8/4/94 - 1/8/95	DOCUMENTS NORTHWEST: THE PONCHO SERIES: NATURE STUDIES — This exhibition explores artistic observation and transformation of the natural world.
12/15/94 - 2/12/95	BENIN: ROYAL ART OF AFRICA — 500 years of Benin royal regalia and sculpture from the late 14th to the 19th century illustrate the artistic triumphs of the Benin kingdom. The works are drawn from the collection of the Museum Fur Volkerkunda, Vienna. WT
12/15/94 - 2/12/95	ASAFO! AFRICAN FLAGS OF THE FANTE — Flags charged with color and allegory will be displayed alongside the above Benin exhibition. An animated graphic art form, these flags are highly patterned with images derived from myths, history, nature and proverbs. WT
1/26 - 6/4/95	DOCUMENTS NORTHWEST: THE PONCHO SERIES: BELIZ BROTHER — In the last decade this Seattle based sculptor and set and lighting designer has achieved national attention for her installations. This one takes the form of a house constructed from glass photographic negatives of images of war.
3/9 - 5/7/95	VISIONS OF LOVE AND LIFE: ENGLISH PRE-RAPHAELITE ART FROM THE BIRMINGHAM COLLECTION — About 100 paintings, drawings, sculpture and stained glass from this outstanding English collection of works, both masterpieces and intimate sketches, by the young English painters who chose romantic themes from literature. CAT WT

Seattle Art Museum - continued

5/22 - 9/17/95	TREASURES OF VENICE: PAINTINGS FROM THE MUSEUM OF FINE ARTS, BUDDAPEST — Drawn from one of the world's largest collections, the 55 works are by artists who worked in Venice from the 16th through the 18th centuries including Titian, Giorgione, Tintoretto and Tiepolo. CAT WT
6/29/95 - 2/4/96	DOCUMENTS NORTHWEST: THE PONCHO SERIES: PAST/PRESENT: HISTORICISM IN RECENT NORTHWEST GLASS — Eight artists including Ann Gardner, Dante Marioni, Richard Marquis, Josiah McElheney, Willam Morris, Seth Randall, Jill Reynolds and Catherine Thompson employ shapes and motifs including funerary urns, venetian extravagances and Depression-era knick-knacks.
9/7 - 12/10/95	DOCUMENTS NORTHWEST: THE PONCHO SERIES: FROM THE FLOATING WORLD TO THE STREET — Uniting woodblock prints from the mid-1880's with contemporary Northwest street photography, the exhibition explores personal, political and aesthetic similarities between these two widely separated bodies of work.
10/12/95 - 1/7/96	JOHN JAMES AUDUBON: THE WATERCOLORS FOR "BIRDS OF AMERICA" — 90 original watercolors from the complete set belonging to the New-York Historical Society reveal the artist's genius for dramatic and highly sophisticated compositions, as well as his passion for his subjects. The exhibition also traces the conversion of a painting into a print and includes an engraved copperplate, uncolored and finished prints and a complete bound volume of the "Double Elephant" folio CAT WT

SEATTLE

Seattle Asian Art Museum
Volunteer, **Park Seattle, WA**
TEL: 206-654-3100
HRS: 10-5 T, W, F-S; 10-9 Tu   DAY CLOSED: M   HOL: 1/1, THGV, 12/25
ADM: Y; good for both museums   ADULT: $6.00   STUDENTS $4.00   SR CIT: $4.00
HDA/ACC: Y   LIB: Y   GT: Y   H/B: Y
PERM/COLL: CH; JAP; SE/AS; IND; KOR

The historical preservation of the Carl Gould designed 1932 building (the first Art-Deco style art museum in the world) involved uniting all areas of the structure including additions of 1947, 1954, and 1955. Now a "jewel box" with plush but tasteful interiors perfectly complementing the art of each nation. 900 of the 7000 objects in the collection are on view.

SPOKANE

Cheney Cowles Museum
W. 2316 First Avenue, **Spokane, WA 99204**
TEL: 509-456-3931
HRS: 10-5 Tu-Sa; 10-9 W; 1-5 S   DAY CLOSED: M   HOL: LEG/HOL!
ADM: Y   ADULT: $3.00   CHILDREN: $2.00   STUDENTS: $2.00   SR CIT: $2.00
HDC/ACC: Y   PARKING: Y   LIB: Y   MUS/SH: Y   GT: Y   GT/PH: !   H/B: Y
PERM/COLL: NW NAT/AM; REG; DEC/ART

The purpose of the Cheney Cowles Museum is to exhibit, collect and preserve visual arts of regional, national and international importance as well as the history of the American Indian of the region.

WASHINGTON

Cheney Cowles Museum - continued

ON EXHIBIT/95:

2/16 - 3/26/95	BEYOND 15 MINUTES — A group exhibition of major contemporary Los Angeles artists working in diverse media and expression.
4/5 - 5/21/95	FROM FLOATING WORLD TO THE STREET — Combining traditional Japanese Ukiko-e woodblock prints with contemporary street photography, this exhibition will point out political and formal similarities.
5/31 - 7/23/95	ARRESTED RIVERS: CHUCK FORSMAN — Thirteen monumentally scaled paintings by this Colorado artist which form the nucleus of a multi-disciplinary examination of the topic of water in the West and the disruption to rivers by dam building.
8/1 - 9/3/95	VANESSA HELDER: COULEE DAM WATERCOLORS AND LIBBY PHOTOS OF COULEE DAM — These WPA era paintings and photos will be shown simultaneously with a multi-media live footage presentation of the dam construction.
9/13 - 10/22/95	NORTHWEST JURIED ART '95: ALL MEDIA
10/27 - 12/3/65	MEMORIALS OF AUSCHWITZ AND BIRKENAU: PHOTOGRAPHS BY MARK OLSEN
12/8/95 - 1/14/96	THE SPOKANE SAMPLER — An invitational exhibition featuring the work of 50 regional artists.

TACOMA

Tacoma Art Museum
12th and Pacific Ave, **Tacoma, WA 98402**
TEL: 206-272-4258
HRS: 10-5 Tu-Sa; 12-5 S   DAY CLOSED: M   HOL: 1/1, THGV, 12/25
F/DAY: Tu   ADM: Y   ADULT: $3.00   CHILDREN: F (under 12)   STUDENTS: $2.00   SR CIT: $2.00
HDC/ACC: Y   PARKING: Y; Street parking   LIB: Y   MUS/SH: Y   GT: Y   GT/PH: !
PERM/COLL: CONT/NW; AM: ptgs

The only comprehensive collection in a public institution of the stained glass of Dale Chihuly. **NOT TO BE MISSED:** Chihuly Retrospective Glass Collection: Early American Room

Tacoma Public Library/Thomas Handforth Gallery
1102 Tacoma Avenue South, **Tacoma, WA 98402**
TEL: 206-591-5688
HRS: 9-9 M-T; 9-6 F-Sa   DAY CLOSED: S   HOL: LEG/HOL!
ADM: F
HDC/ACC: Y   PARKING: Y   H/B: Y
PERM/COLL: HISTORICAL; PHOT; ARTIFACTS

Built in 1903 as an original Andrew Carnegie Library, the Gallery has been serving the public since then with rotating exhibits by Pacific Northwest artists. **NOT TO BE MISSED:** Rare book room containing 750 prints including "North American Indian," by Edward S. Curtice

434

WALLA WALLA

Donald Sheehan Art Gallery
900 Isaacs- Olin Hall, **Walla Walla, WA 99362**
TEL: 509-527-5249
HRS: 10-5 Tu-F; 1-4 Sa-S   DAY CLOSED: M   HOL: ACAD!
ADM: F
HDC/ACC: Y; Enter from parking lot   PARKING: Y; On campus   GT: Y   GT/PH: call for information
PERM/COLL: SCROLLS; SCREENS; BUNRAKY PUPPETS; CER

The Sheehan Gallery administrates the Davis Collection of Oriental Art which is not on permanent display.

WEST VIRGINIA

CHARLESTON

Sunrise Museums
746 Myrtle Road, **Charleston, WV 25314**
TEL: 304-344-8035
HRS: 10-5; Tu-Sa; 2-5 S   DAY CLOSED: M   HOL: LEG/HOL!
F/DAY: Tu-2-5   ADM: Y   ADULT: $2.00   CHILDREN: $1.00   STUDENTS: $1.00   SR CIT: $1.00
HDC/ACC: Y   PARKING: Y   MUS/SH: Y   GT: Y   GT/PH: call 304-344-8035   H/B: Y   S/G: Y
PERM/COLL: AM: ptgs, sculp, gr; DEC/ARTS; NAT/AM: artifacts

This multi media center occupies two historic mansions, Sunrise, a 1905 neo-classical revival style house constructed of natural stone, and Torowlstone.

HUNTINGTON

Huntington Museum of Art, Inc
2033 McCoy Road, **Huntington, WV 25701-4999**
TEL: 304-529-2701
HRS: 10-5 Tu-Sa; 12-5 S   DAY CLOSED: M   HOL: 1/1, 7/4, THGV, 12/25
F/DAY: W   ADM: Y   ADULT: $2.00   CHILDREN: F (under 12)   STUDENTS: $1.00   SR CIT: $1.00
HDC/ACC: Y   PARKING: Y   LIB: Y   GT: Y   GT/PH: call 304-529-2701 for specifics   H/B: Y   S/G: Y
PERM/COLL: AM: ptgs, dec/art 18-20; GLASS

The serene beauty of the museum complex on a lovely hilltop surrounded by nature trails, herb gardens, an outdoor amphitheatre and a sculpture courtyard is enhanced by an extensive addition designed by the great architect Walter Gropius.

ON EXHIBIT/95:

9/25 - 1/15/95	MARK ROTHKO: THE SPIRIT OF MYTH — This exhibition presents a selection of works from the mid 1930's to the late 40's documenting a critical period in the evolution of the artist's mature style. In contrast to the complete abstraction of his later work, these are landscapes, still lifes, portraits and figure studies painted in an expressionistic style.
11/94 - 6/95	DAYWOOD COLLECTION — A rich collection of American landscape paintings by the most important artists of the late 19th and early 20th century as well as drawings, prints, sculpture and glass. WT

BELOIT

Wright Museum of Art
Affiliate Institution: Beloit College
Prospect at Bushnell, **Beloit, WI 53511**
TEL: 608-363-2677
HRS: 10-5 M-F; 12-5 Sa, S   HOL: ACAD!
ADM: F
HDC/ACC: Y   PARKING: Y   GT: Y   GT/PH: call 608-363-2677 for specifics
PERM/COLL: AS; KOREAN: dec/art, ptgs, gr; HIST & CONT: phot

ON EXHIBIT/95:
1/15 - 2/11/95	CHARLES SMITH AND THE AFRICAN-AMERICAN HERITAGE MUSEUM AND BLACK VETERAN'S ARCHIVE
1/16 - 2/11/95	RECENT ACQUISITIONS OF THE MUSEUMS OF BELOIT COLLEGE
2/19 - 3/31/95	38TH ANNUAL BELOIT AND VICINITY EXHIBITION
4/10 - 5/14/95	48TH ANNUAL EXHIBITION OF STUDENT ART
	SENIOR ART STUDENT EXHIBITION

MADISON

Elvehjem Museum of Art
Affiliate Institution: University of Wisconsin-Madison
800 University Ave., **Madison, WI 53706**
TEL: 608-263-2246
HRS: M-S 9-5   HOL: 1/1, THGV, 12/24, 12/25
ADM: F
HDC/ACC: Y; Use Murray St. entrance, elevator requires security assistance
PARKING: Y; University lots 46 and 83 on Lake Street and City Lake St and Madison ramps.   LIB: Y
MUS/SH: Y   GT: Y   GT/PH: call 608-263-4421 for sp ecifics   DT: Y   TIME: !
PERM/COLL: AN/GRK: vases & coins; MIN.IND PTGS: Earnest C. & Jane Werner Watson Coll; JAP: gr (Van Vleck Coll); OR: dec/arts); RUSS & SOVIET: ptgs (Joseph E. Davies Coll)

More than 15,000 objects that date from 2300 B.C. to the present are contained in this unique university museum collection.

ON EXHIBIT/95:
12/10/94 - 2/22/95	UW-MADISON DEPARTMENT OF ART FACULTY QUADRENNIAL SHOW
3/4 - 4/30/95	JAMES ROSENQUIST:TIME DUST: THE GRAPHIC WORK — A traveling exhibition of work by this important 20th century artist surveys his graphic production in more than 100 prints from his ground-breaking pop images to the mural-sized handmade paper and lithographic collage prints in 1989. WT

WISCONSIN

MADISON

Madison Art Center
211 State Street, **Madison, WI 53703**
TEL: 608-257-0158
HRS: 11-5 Tu-T; 11-9 F; 10-5 Sa; 1-5 S   DAY CLOSED: M   HOL: LEG/HOL!
ADM: F   HDC/ACC: Y   PARKING: Y; Pay   LIB: Y!   MUS/SH: Y
GT: Y   GT/PH: call 608-257-0158 for specifics   H/B: Y
PERM/COLL: AM: works on paper 20; JAP; MEX; CONT

Located in the Old Capitol theatre is this interesting and varied collection of works on paper.

MANITOWOC

Rahr-West Art Museum
Park Street at North Eighth, **Manitowoc, WI 54220**
TEL: 414-663-4501
HRS: 9-4:30 M-F; 1-4 Sa-S   HOL: LEG/HOL!
ADM: F   HDC/ACC: Y   PARKING: Y: Free   LIB: Y   MUS/SH: Y   GT: Y   GT/PH: call 414-683-4501   H/B: Y
PERM/COLL: AM: ptgs, dec/art 19; OR: ivory, glass; CONT: ptgs

Built between 1891 & 1893, this Victorian mansion with its former parlors and bed chambers, carved woodwork and beamed ceiling provides an elegant setting for its fine collection. **NOT TO BE MISSED:** "Birch and Pine Tree No 2," by Georgia O'Keefe

ON EXHIBIT/95:

2/5 - 2/19/95	THE ART OF TABLESETTING
3/5 - 4/2/95	YOUTH ART MONTH
4/9 - 4/30/95	ART FROM THE PAROCHIAL SCHOOLS
5/7 - 5/21/95	RAHR-WEST PERMANENT COLLECTIONS
5/28 - 6/25/95	WISCONSIN DESIGNER CRAFTPERSONS
7/9 - 8/6/95	MANITOWOCK COUNTY ARTISTS EXHIBITION
8/13 - 9/24/95	RELATIVELY SPEAKING: MOTHERS AND DAUGHTERS IN ART — This exhibition of 15 pairs of artists, two 3 generation families and one 4 generation traces the familial influences. Included among the artists are Betye, Alison and Lezley Saar, Janet Fish, Harriet Shorr and Jane Freilicher. CAT WT
10/1 - 11/26/95	QUILT SAN DIEGO

MILWAUKEE

Charles Allis Art Museum
1801 North Prospect Avenue, **Milwaukee, WI 53202**
TEL: 414-278-8295
HRS: 1-5 & 7-9 W; 1-5 T-S   DAY CLOSED: M, T   HOL: LEG/HOL!
ADM: Y   ADULT: $2.00   PARKING: Y   GT: Y   GT/PH: call 414-278-8295 for specifics   H/B: Y
PERM/COLL: CH: porcelains; OR; AN/GRK; AN/R; FR: ptgs 19

With its diverse collection this museum is housed in a 1909 Tudor style house.

MILWAUKEE

Milwaukee Art Museum

750 North Lincoln Memorial Drive, **Milwaukee, WI 53202**
TEL: 414-224-3200
HRS: 10-5 Tu, W, F, Sa; 12-9 T; 12-5 S   DAY CLOSED: M   HOL: 1/1, THGV, 12/25
ADM: Y   ADULT: $4.00   CHILDREN: F (under 12)   STUDENTS: $2.00   SR CIT: $2.00
HDC/ACC: Y   PARKING: Y   LIB: Y   MUS/SH: Y   REST/FAC: Y
GT: Y   GT/PH: call 414-224-3825 to reserve   H/B: Y   S/G: Y
PERM/COLL: CONT: ptgs, sculp; GER; AM: folk art

The Milwauke Museum features an exceptional collection housed in a 1957 landmark building by Eero Saarinen, which is cantilevered over the Lake Michigan shoreline. **NOT TO BE MISSED:** Zurburan's "St. Francis"

ON EXHIBIT/95:

9/30/94 - 1/8/95	DUTCH PAINTINGS OF THE GOLDEN AGE: THE WESTERDIJK COLLECTION — A small but rich exhibition of works from the Dutch Baroque period representing the "little masters" whose works were concurrent with Rembrandt and the flowering of 17th Century Dutch art.
11/18/94 - 1/15/95	CURRENTS 24: STAN DOUGLAS — This is the 24th installment of the museum's series of exhibitions dedicated to international developments in contemporary art. Mr. Douglas works primarily with video, photography and sound.
12/2/94 - 2/12/95	FROM HANNIBAL TO ST. AUGUSTINE: ANCIENT ART OF NORTH AFRICA FROM THE MUSEE DU LOUVRE — More that 100 extraordinary marble sculptures, mosaics, jewelry, vases and other artworks which trace the history of the area encompassed today by Morocco, Tunisia, Algeria and parts of Libya CAT
1/13 - 4/23/95	NATHAN LERNER PHOTOGRAPHS — Concentrating on the early phase of Lerner's career (1935-1950), the exhibition illustrates the facility and breadth of his rapidly evolving work incorporating social documentary, dadaism, surrealism, and the principles of Bauhaus.
1/20 - 4/16/95	ARSHILE GORKY: DRAWINGS OF THE 1930'S — Gorky was one of the most important figures in the development of the avant-gard in the US before World WAR II. The 39 graphite or ink drawings relate to the first government-sponsored mural project on which Gorky worked. CAT WT
3/3 - 5/28/95	LATIN AMERICAN WOMEN ARTISTS, 1915-1995 — This will be the first major exhibition in the US to emphasize the significant role of women in 20th century art. CAT WT
3/17 - 4/9/95	20TH CENTURY MASTERWORKS FROM THE PERMANENT COLLECTION — After a tour of six major museums in Japan, this will be the only opportunity to view the exhibition as a whole before the works are returned to the galleries of the museum. CAT
5/12 - 8/20/95	CURRENTS 25: KIKI SMITH PRINTS AND MULTIPLES, 1985-1993 — One of the most provocative artists of recent years is featured in this ongoing series of exhibitions. CAT
5/2 - 9/3/95	DRINKING IN ART: METTLACH STEINS AND RELATED WARES — The art pottery from the Mettlach factory of Villeroy and Boch reached its golden age in 1880-1910. Various decorative processes will be represented. CAT
5/16 - 8/13/95	A CENTURY OF SPLENDOR: SILVER IN AMERICAN LIFE, 1840-1940 — An examination of the design, production, marketing and use of silver objects during the period in which American producers and designers became world famous for the exceptional quality of their products. CAT

WISCONSIN

MILWAUKEE

The Patrick & Beatrice Haggerty Museum of Art
Affiliate Institution: Marquette University
13th & Clybourn, **Milwaukee, WI 53233**
TEL: 414-288-7290
HRS: 10-4:30 M-Sa; 12-5 S; 10-8 T   HOL: 1/1, EASTER, 12/25
ADM: F   HDC/ACC: Y   PARKING: Y   MUS/SH: Y   GT: Y   GT/PH: call 414-288-5915 for specifics   S/G: Y
PERM/COLL: PTGS 17-20; PHOT

Selections from the European and American collections are on exhibition continuously.

ON EXHIBIT/95:

12/8/94 - 2/19/95	IAN MCKEEVER: CONTEMPORARY BRITISH PAINTING
3/10 - 6/11/95	SCULPTURE FROM THE B. GERALD CANTOR COLLECTION
6/29 - 8/27/95	ODD NERDRUM: CONTEMPORARY DRAWINGS — 25 charcoal drawings by this contemporary Norwegian-born artist will be featured in the first American exhibition of his work. CAT WT
7/14 - 8/27/95	GLORIA GARFINKEL: PAINTINGS ON PAPER
9/14 - 11/19/95	VISION QUEST: COLOR PHOTOGRAPHS OF SIOUX INDIANS
12/7/95 - 2/11/96	TURNBULL AND JONES REGIONAL PAINTINGS

UWM Art Museum
3253 N. Downer Avenue, **Milwaukee, WI 53211**
TEL: 414-226-6509
HRS: 10-4 Tu-F; 12-8 W; 1-5 Sa-S   DAY CLOSED: M   HOL: LEG/HOL!
ADM: F   HDC/ACC: Y; Automatic doors in front and elevators inside   PARKING: Y; Meters in front of building.   LIB: Y
PERM/COLL: AM & EU: works on paper, gr; RUSS: icons; REG: 20

The museum works to provide its audience with an artistic cultural and historical experience unlike that offered by other art institutions in Milwaukee. Its three spaces on the campus provide the flexibility of interrelated programming.

Villa Terrace Decorative Arts Museum
2220 North Terrace Ave, **Milwaukee, WI 53202**
TEL: 414-271-3656
HRS: 12-5 W-S   DAY CLOSED: M, Tu   HOL: LEG/HOL!
ADM: Y   ADULT: $2.00   CHILDREN: F (under 12)   HDC/ACC: Y; To first floor galleries   PARKING: Y   H/B: Y
PERM/COLL: DEC/ART; PTGS, SCULP, GR 15-20

Villa Terrace Decorative Arts Museum with its excellent and varied collections is located in a historic landmark building.

ON EXHIBIT/95:

11/23/94 - 1/15/95	THE ART OF THE PAPERWEIGHT - CHALLENGING TRADITION
1/30 - 3/12/95	JIM MIDDLETON: PHOTOGRAPHY
3/26 - 5/7/95	GRANDEUR, SIMPLICITY AND CONVENIENCE: THE UNITED STATES CAPITOL, 1793-1993

OSHKOSH

The Paine Art Center and Arboretum
1410 Algoma Blvd, **Oshkosh, WI 54901**
TEL: 414-235-4530
HRS: 10-4:30 Tu-F; 1-4:30 Sa, S   DAY CLOSED: M   HOL: LEG/HOL!
ADM: Y   ADULT: $3.00   CHILDREN: F (under 12)   STUDENTS: $1.00   SR CIT: $2.00
HDC/ACC: Y   PARKING: Y; On-street parking   LIB: Y   MUS/SH: Y
GT: Y   GT/PH: call 514-235-4530 for specifics   H/B: Y   S/G: Y
PERM/COLL: FR & AM: ptgs, sculp, gr 19, 20; OR: silk rugs, dec/art

Collections of paintings, sculpture and decorative objects in period room settings are featured in this historic 1920's Tudor Revival home surrounded by botanic gardens. **NOT TO BE MISSED:** "The Bronco Buster," sculpture by Frederic Remington

ON EXHIBIT/95:

12/27/94 - 2/12/95	WHITE MOUNTAIN PAINTERS 1834-1926	WT
2/26 - 4/2/95	BIRDS, BEASTS, BLOSSOMS AND BUGS IN EAST ASIAN ART FROM THE LOWE ART MUSEUM	WT
4/9 - 5/28/95	ULTRA-REALISTIC SCULPTURES BY MARC SIJAN	WT
5/4 - 8/20/95	OSHKOSH B'GOSH 100TH ANNIVERSARY PHOTO EXHIBITION	
10/29/95 - 1/10/96	ROLAND POSKA: THE GREAT HUMAN RACE	

RACINE

Charles A. Wustum Museum of Fine Arts
2519 Northwestern Ave, **Racine, WI 53404**
TEL: 424-636-9177
HRS: 1-5 M-S; until 9 M, T   HOL: LEG/HOL!, 12/19/94-1/7/95
ADM: F   HDC/ACC: Y   PARKING: Y; Free   LIB: Y   MUS/SH: Y
GT: Y   GT/PH: call 414-636-9177 for specifics   H/B: Y   S/G: Y
PERM/COLL: SCULP; WPA: collection on paper

In an 1856 Italianate style building on acres of landscaped sculpture gardens you will find Racine's only fine arts museum. It primarily supports active, regional living artists.

SHEBOYGAN

John Michael Kohler Arts Center
608 New York Avenue, **Sheboygan, WI 53082-0489**
TEL: 414-458-6144
HRS: 10-5 M-W, F; 10-9 T; 12-5 Sa, S   HOL: 1/1, EASTER, MEM/DAY, THGV, 12/24, 12/25, 12/31
ADM: F
HDC/ACC: Y   PARKING: Y   LIB: Y   MUS/SH: Y   GT: Y   GT/PH: call 414-458-6144 for specifics   H/B: Y
PERM/COLL: CONT: cer; DEC/ART

This multicultural center is located in the 1860's villa of John Michael Kohler, founder of the plumbing manufacturing company. Special exhibitions at the Center offer unique perspectives on art forms, artists, and various artistic concepts that have received little exposure elsewhere.

WISCONSIN

John Michael Kohler Arts Center - continued

ON EXHIBIT/95:

10/2/94 - 1/6/95	ANIMALS: CULTURALLY CONSTRUCTED (working title) — The exhibition will examine the ways in which contemporary artists use animal imagery to discourse on private and public stories, cultural diversity and economic, political and ecological issues as well as the ways we weave animals into our culture through mythology and nationalism.
11/6/94 - 2/5/95	LOU CABEEN (working title) — Emotionally and politically charged narratives created through the use of traditional embroidery techniques and the alteration of found samplers.
11/6/94 - 2/5/95	MARTHA HEAVENSTON AND STEVEN BRADFORD (working title) — Individual and collaborative works by artists who both work with the allegorical figure.
2/5 - 5/7/95	PATRICK DOUGHERTY: TENSION ZONES (working title) — Large scale, site-specific installations created by weaving branches, relying on the natural tension of bent saplings to hold the works together.
2/12 - 4/17/95	SILVIA MALAGRINO (working title) — "Habitat," a series of photographic murals, addresses the way we attempt to control the land through mythical and religious allegories, discourses on territory, mapping and photography.
4/23 - 7/30/95	SARA BELLEAU (working title) — This photographer and installation artist creates contemporary fables. This will be a narrative installation about her native city of Sheboygan.
4/23 - 7/30/95	JUDY HILL (working title) — These self-portraits are cast glass and raku figures. The glass clothing reveals rather than conceals the bodies through which one can see into the figures in which there are sometimes other figures or raku bodies.
6/4 - 8/27/95	THE SUBJECTIVE SELF (working title) — The exhibition explores the idea of the self, often noting that how we image ourselves is determined by cultural divisions of gender, race, class and occupation.
8/6 - 10/29/95	RAMONA SAKIESTEWA (working title) — Weavings which are reinterpretations of traditional Native American designs.
9/22/95 - 1/6/96	CONCEPTUAL TEXTILES (working title) — Textile based work which balances conceptual ideas such as domesticity, the body, femininity, race, and ethnicity with craft.
11/5/95 - 1/28/96	LISA NORTON (working title) — Metalworks which parody utilitarian objects such as colanders, pitchers, tin pails, and measuring cans.

WAUSAU

Leigh Yawkey Woodson Art Museum
700 North Twelfth Street, **Wausau, WI 54401-5007**
TEL: 715-845-7010
HRS: 9-4 Tu-F; 12-5 Sa-S   DAY CLOSED: M   HOL: LEG/HOL!
ADM: F   HDC/ACC: Y; 2 of three floors   PARKING: Y; Free   LIB: Y
GT: Y   GT/PH: call to reserve 2 weeks in advance   DT: Y   TIME: !   S/G: Y; four gardens
PERM/COLL: GLASS 19, 20; STUDIO GLASS; PORCELAIN; WILDLIFE; ptgs, sculp

An English style mansion surrounded by gracious lawns and sculpture gardens. **NOT TO BE MISSED:** Newly completed sculpture garden and landscaping. The first two sculptures will be installed in 1995.

442

Leigh Yawkey Woodson Art Museum - continued

ON EXHIBIT/95:

1/14 - 2/26/95
THE ART OF ERIC CARLE — A colorful roundup of more than 100 enchanting illustrations by the author of "The Very Hungry Caterpillar" and more than 40 other children's books.

1/14 - 2/26/95
IMAGES OF BRITISH INDIA'S GOLDEN AGE — 100 beautifully evocative aquatints that helped to create the Western notion of this distant and mysterious land.   WT

4/8 - 6/4/95
FLORA: CONTEMPORARY ARTISTS AND THE WORLD OF FLOWERS — 60 works ranging from the beauty and traditions of 17th century still lifes to explosions of unabashed color and energy tickle the imagination and invite exploration of what lies beyond the vegetation.   WT

6/10 - 8/27/95
BEYOND THE LENS: COMPOSITIONS BY ART WOLFE — Viewers are taken beyond the lens to an exploration of nature composed as art.

9/9 - 10/29/95
BIRDS IN ART — More than 100 paintings and sculptures of an exceptional diversity and natural harmony.

11/4 - 12/31/95
JEAN DESPUJOLS: INDOCHINA ODYSSEY — 60 watercolors, oils and drawings created in the 1930's to record the diverse people, ways of life and varied landscape of this mesmerizing land.   WT

WEST BEND

West Bend Museum of Art
300 South 6th Ave West, **Bend, WI 53095**
TEL: 414-334-9638
HRS: 10-4:30 W-Sa; 1-4:30 S   DAY CLOSED: M, Tu   HOL: LEG/HOL!
ADM: F
PARKING: Y   LIB: Y   GT: Y   GT/PH: call 414-334-9638 to reserve   S/G: Y
PERM/COLL: GER: 19; ACADEMIC ART WORK; REG: 1850-1950

This community art center and museum is dedicated to the work of artist Carl Von Marr. It also features the Walter A. Zuin Doll House which was first built in 1911 and completed four generations later, and contains more than 700 miniature items.

ON EXHIBIT/95:

8/31/94 - summer 95
OUTDOOR SCULPTURE OF ALAN JUNG — These highly creative wood sculptures will be featured throughout the next four seasons in the sculpture garden. Jung works with the natural form of branches and trees, joining them together with various other shaped pieces of wood masses to create sculptures that sometimes resemble weather vanes. They appeaar to be ephemeral but are surprisingly resilient to our climate and do not impose on landscape, but exist in harmony with nature.

11/4/94 - 1/7/95
BUILT, THROWN AND TOUCHED: CONTEMPORARY CLAY WORKS — 60 pieces representing some of the finest ceramic artists working in the US today.   WT

WYOMING

BIG HORN

Bradford Brinton Memorial Museum
239 Brinton Road, **Big Horn, WY 82833**
TEL: 307-672-3173
HRS: 9:30-5 daily MAY 15-LAB/DAY; other months by appt
ADM: Y   ADULT: $3.00   CHILDREN: F (under 12)   STUDENTS: $2.00   SR CIT: $2.00
HDC/ACC: Y   PARKING: Y   LIB: Y!   MUS/SH: Y   H/B: Y
PERM/COLL: WESTERN ART; DEC/ART; NAT/AM: beadwork

Important paintings by the best known Western artists are shown in a fully furnished 20 room ranch house built in 1892 and situated at the foot of the Big Horn Mountain. **NOT TO BE MISSED:** "Custer's Fight on the Little Big Horn," by Frederic Remington

ON EXHIBIT/95:

1995   RICHARD EVANS: CURRENT PAINTINGS Selections from Idiomythic Series and Wyoming Odysseys

The Patio Room Gallery features a changing exhibition every 3 weeks during the summer season.

CASPER

Nicolaysen Art Museum
400 East Collins Drive, **Casper, WY 82601-2815**
TEL: 307-235-5247
HRS: 10-5 Tu-S; 10-8 T   DAY CLOSED: M   HOL: 1/1; THGV; 12/24; 12/25
F/DAY: 1st & 3rd T, 4-8   ADM: Y   ADULT: $2.00   CHILDREN: $1.00 under 12   SR CIT: $2.00
HDC/ACC: Y   PARKING: Y   LIB: N   MUS/SH: Y   GT: Y   GT/PH: !   DT: Y   TIME: !   H/B: Y
PERM/COLL: CARL LINK ILLUSTRATIONS; REG

The roots of this Museum reside in the commitment of Wyoming people to the importance of having art and culture as an integral part life. **NOT TO BE MISSED:** The Discovery Center, an integral part of the museum, complements the educational potential of the exhibitions

ON EXHIBIT/95:

1/1 - 8/27/95	IMAGES OF THE LAND: WORKS FROM THE NICOLAYSEN ART MUSEUM COLLECTION
1/95 - 2/95	GERRY SPENCE PHOTOGRAPHS
1/14 - 3/12/95	WYOMING ARTS COUNCIL FELLOWSHIP RECIPIENTS
3/18 - 5/21/95	LYNN BROOKS KORN
4/29 - 6/25/95	CERAMICS INVITATIONAL
6/27 - 7/30/95	MARILYN HUGHES
9/95 - 10/95	CASPER COLLEGE ALUMNI
11/95 - 12/95	NINETEENTH CENTURY MEXICAN TIN RETABLOS

444

CHEYENNE

Wyoming State Museum
Barrett Building, 2301 Central Ave., **Cheyenne, WY 82002**
TEL: 301-777-7022 (or 7024)
HRS: 8:30-5 M-F, 9-4 Sa, Noon-4 S (Summer); 8:30-5 M-F, 12-4 Sa (Sep-May)
DAY CLOSED: S   HOL: LEG/HOL!
ADM: F
HDC/ACC: Y   PARKING: Y; Metered on nearby streets   LIB: Y   MUS/SH: Y
GT: Y   GT/PH: call 307-777-7022 for specifics   S/G: Y
PERM/COLL: PLAINS INDIAN COLLECTION; REG/W & CONT

The Wyoming State Museum is part of the Capital Complex area which includes the historic State Capitol building and the Governor's Mansion. **NOT TO BE MISSED:** Wyoming in WWII

CODY

Bufaflo Bill Historical Center
720 Sheridan Ave., **Cody, WY 82414**
TEL: 307-587-4771
HRS: 8-8 daily MAY-SEP; 7-10pm daily JUN-AUG; 10-3 Tu-S MAR- NOV; 8-5 Tu-S APR
ADM: Y   ADULT: $8.00   CHILDREN: 6-12 $2.00   STUDENTS: 13 +$4.00   SR CIT: $6.50
HDC/ACC: Y   PARKING: Y   LIB: Y   MUS/SH: Y   REST/FAC: Y; "Great Entertainer Eatery"
GT: Y   GT/PH: call 307-587-4771 for specifics   S/G: Y
PERM/COLL: WESTERN/ART: 19, 20; AM: firearms; CULTURAL HISTORY OF THE PLAINS INDIANS

The complex includes the Buffalo Bill, Plains Indian, and Cody Firearms museums as well as the Whitney Gallery which contains outstanding paintings of the American West by such artists as George Catlin, Albert Bierstadt, Frederic Remington and contemporary artists James Barna, Harry Jackson and Fritz Scholder. **NOT TO BE MISSED:** The Whitney Gallery of Western Art

JACKSON

National Wildlife Art Museum
2820 Rungius Road, **Jackson, WY 83001**
TEL: 307-733-5771
HRS: 10-5 Msa, 1-5 S   DAY CLOSED: HOL: 1/1, THGV, 12/25
ADM: Y   ADULT: $4.00 fam rate available   STUDENTS: $3.00   SR CIT: $3.00
HDC/ACC: Y   PARKING: Y; Free on-street parking   MUS/SH: Y
GT: Y   GT/PH: call 307-733-5771 for specifics
PERM/COLL: WILDLIFE ART AND ARTIFACTS

One of the few museums in the country to feature wildlife, the collection is styled to sensitize visitors to Native American wildlife and the habitat necessary to sustain this priceless natural heritage, and is exhibited in a new facility. NOT TO BE MISSED: Works by Carl Rungius

WYOMING

MOOSE

Grand Teton National Park, Colter Bay Indian Arts Museum
Moose, WY 83012
TEL: 307-543-2484
HRS: 8-5 daily 5/15-LAB/DAY
ADM: F
HDC/ACC: Y   PARKING: Y   MUS/SH: Y
PERM/COLL: NAT/AM: artifacts, beadwork, basketry, pottery, musical instruments

Organized into categories and themes, the Davis I. Vernon collection of Indian art housed in this museum is a spectacular assembly of many art forms including porcupine quillwork, beadwork, basketry, pottery, and masks, and musical instruments. **NOT TO BE MISSED:** Sitting Bull's beaded blanket strip, (Sioux, South Dakota, ca. 1875)

ROCK SPRINGS

Community Fine Arts Center
Affiliate Institution: Rock Springs Library
400 "C" Street, **Rock Springs, WY 82901**
TEL: 307-362-6212
HRS: 12-5 & 6-9 M, T; 10-12 & 1-5 Tu, W, F; 12-5 Sa   DAY CLOSED: S   HOL: LEG/HOL!
ADM: F
HDC/ACC: Y   PARKING: Y   LIB: Y   GT: Y   DT: Y   TIME: !
PERM/COLL: AM: 19, 20

The art gallery houses the nationally-acclaimed Rock Springs High School Collection, and is owned by the students. **NOT TO BE MISSED:** Loren McIver's "Fireplace," (first American woman to exhibit at the Venice Biennale 1962)

446

Selected Listing of Traveling Exhibitions

A PASSION FOR ANTIQUITIES: ANCIENT ART FROM THE COLLECTION OF BARBARA
AND LAWRENCE FLEISCHMAN
10/13/94 - 1/15/95	The J. Paul Getty Museum, Malibu, CA
2/15 - 4/23/95	The Cleveland Museum of Art, Cleveland, OH

A SHADOW BORN OF EARTH: NEW PHOTOGRAPHY IN MEXICO
3/22 - 5/21/95	Museum of Photographic Arts, San Diego, CA
5/18 - 8/6/95	Neuberger Museum of Art, Purchase, NY
11/19/95 - 1/21/96	Rockford Art Museum, Rockford, IL

AFRICAN ZION: THE SACRED ART OF ETHIOPIA
5/11 - 8/6/95	The Chrysler Museum, Norfolk, VA
11/15/95 - 1/7/96	The Cleveland Museum of Art, Cleveland, OH

ALFRED STEIGLITZ'S CAMERA NOTES
5/6 - 7/9/95	The Corcoran Gallery of Art, Washington, DC
12/5/95 - 1/28/96	Telfair Academy of Arts and Sciences, Inc., Savannah, GA

ALONE IN A CROWD: PRINTS OF THE 1930'S AND 1940'S BY AFRICAN-AMERICAN
ARTISTS FROM THE COLLECTION OF REBA AND DAVE WILLIAMS
12/8/94 - 1/28/95	The Fine Arts Museum of the South at Mobile, Mobile, AL
1/4 - 2/26/95	The Baltimore Museum of Art, Baltimore, MD
4/2 - 5/28/95	Gibbes Museum of Art, Charleston, SC
6/14 - 8/13/95	Bass Museum of Art, Miami Beach, FL
9/8 - 11/5/95	The Arkansas Arts Center, Little Rock, AR

AMERICAN IMPRESSIONISM AND REALISM: THE PAINTING OF MODERN LIFE,
1885-1915
12/3/94 - 2/5/95	The Denver Art Museum, Denver, CO
6/14 - 9/17/95	Virginia Museum of Fine Arts, Richmond, VA

AMERCIAN NAIVE PAINTING FROM THE NATIONAL GALLERY OF ART
2/1 - 4/1/95	Pensacola Museum of Art, Pensacola, FL
4/29 - 6/18/95	Boise Art Museum, Boise, ID

ARSHILE GORKY: THE BREAKTHROUGH YEARS
5/14 - 9/17/95	The National Gallery of Art, Washington, DC
10/14 - 12/31/95	Albright-Knox Art Gallery, Buffalo, NY

ARTHUR G. RIDER: AMERICAN IMPRESSIONIST
2/3 - 5/17/95	Fleisher Museum, Scottsdale, AZ
10/95 - 1/96	The Irvine Museum, Irvine, CA

ARTHUR J. STONE (1847-1938) DESIGNER AND MASTER SILVERSMITH
11/21/94 - 1/6/95	Boston Athenaeum, Boston, MA
6/3 - 7/30/95	Sterling and Francine Clark Art Institute, Williamstown, MA

Selected Listing of Traveling Exhibitions

AUGUSTUS VINCENT TACK: LANDSCAPE OF THE SPIRIT
1/20 - 3/5/95	Archer M. Huntington Art Gallery, Austin, TX
3/18 - 4/16/95	The Society of the Four Arts, Palm Beach, FL
8/19 - 10/22/95	Herbert F. Johnson Museum of Art, Ithaca, NY

BIRDS, BEASTS, BLOSSOMS AND BUGS IN EAST ASIAN ART FROM THE LOWE ART MUSEUM
2/26 - 4/2/95	The Paine Art Center and Arboretum, Oshkosh, WI
4/30 - 9/17/95	The Dixon Gallery & Gardens, Memphis, TN
10/15 - 12/24/95	Owensboro Museum of Fine Art, Owensboro, KY

BOB BLACKBURN'S PRINTMAKING WORKSHOP: ARTISTS OF COLOR
2/3 - 3/24/95	Federal Reserve Bank of Kansas City, Kansas City, MO
4/16 - 6/4/95	Edwin A. Ulrich Museum of Art, Wichita, KS
9/9 - 11/10/95	Albany Institute of History & Art, Albany, NY

BOTTICELLI TO TIEPOLO: THREE CENTURIES OF ITALIAN PAINTINGS FROM BOB JONES UNIVERSITY
through 1/8/95	The Philbrook Museum of Art Inc, Tulsa, OK
2/18 - 4/16/95	Joslyn Art Museum, Omaha, NE
5/13 - 7/2/95	New Orleans Museum of Art, New Orleans, LA
7/22 - 9/17/95	Birmingham Museum of Art, Birmingham, AL
9/30 - 12/3/95	(dates TENT!) The Dayton Art Institute, Dayton, OH

CHRISTOPHER BROWN
1/15 - 4/16/95	Modern Art Museum of Fort Worth, Fort Worth, TX
5/13 - 7/30/95	San Jose Museum of Art, San Jose, CA
8/30 - 11/5/95	The Contemporary Museum, Honolulu, HI

CIEN ANOS De CREATIVIDAD: LATIN AMERICAN WOMEN ARTISTS
7/8 - 10/1/95	The Denver Art Museum, Denver, CO
7/8 - 10/1/95	Phoenix Art Museum., Phoenix, AZ
10 - 12/95	Museo De Las Americas, Denver, CO

CLAES OLDENBURG: AN ANTHOLOGY
2/12 - 5/7/95	The National Gallery of Art, Washington, DC
6/18 - 9/3/95	The Museum of Contemporary Art, Los Angeles, Los Angeles, CA
10/7 - 1/21/96	Solomon R. Guggenheim Museum, New York, NY

CLEARLY ART: PILCHUCK'S GLASS LEGACY
12/9/94 - 1/29/95	Muskegon Museum of Art, Muskegon, MI
3/4 - 4/30/95	Birmingham Museum of Art, Birmingham, AL
6/3 - 7/30/95	Fort Wayne Museum of Art, Fort Wayne, IN
9/5 - 10/15/95	Museum of Art, Pullman, WA

CY TWOMBLY: A RETROSPECTIVE
2/10 - 3/19/95	The Menil Collection, Houston, TX
2/12 - 5/21/95	The Museum of Contemporary Art, Los Angeles, Los Angeles, CA

Selected Listing of Traveling Exhibitions

DALE CHIHULY: INSTALLATIONS 1964-1995
4/11 - 9/24/95	Anchorage Museum of History and Art., Anchorage, AK
10/95 - 1/96	San Jose Museum of Art, San Jose, CA

DICTATED BY LIFE: MARSDEN HARTLEY'S GERMAN PAINTINGS AND ROBERT
INDIANA'S HARTLEY ELEGIES
4/14 - 6/11/95	James Ford Bell Museum of Natural History, Minneapolis, MN
7/1 - 9/10/95	Terra Museum of American Art, Chicago, IL
10/13 - 12/17/95	The Art Museum at Florida International University, Miami, FL

DRIVEN TO CREATE: THE ANTHONY J. PETULLO COLLECTION OF SELF-TAUGHT AND
OUTSIDER ART
4/8 - 5/4/95	Akron Art Museum, Akron, OH
6/25 - 8/27/95	Tampa Museum of Art, Tampa, FL
9 - 11/26/95	The Arkansas Arts Center, Little Rock, AR

DUTCH AND FLEMISH DRAWINGS FROM THE ROYAL LIBRARY, WINDSOR CASTLE
1/28 - 4/16/95	North Carolina Museum of Art, Raleigh, NC
4/29 - 7/30/95	Indianapolis Museum of Art, Indianapolis, IN

ELECTRONIC SUPER HIGHWAY: NAM JUNE PAIK IN THE 90'S
11/4/94 - 1/22/95	Museum of Art, Inc., Ft. Lauderdale, FL
2/18 - 4/16/95	Indianapolis Museum of Art, Indianapolis, IN

ELLIOT ERWITT: TO THE DOGS
1/7 - 2/19/95	The Wichita Center for the Arts, Wichita, KS
3/95 - 4/95	Asheville Art Museum, Asheville, NC
9/12 - 10/3/95	Louisiana Arts and Science Center, Baton Rouge, LA

ELVIS + MARILYN: 2 x IMMORTAL
10/15/94 - 1/8/95	The New-York Historical Society, New York, NY
4/15 - 6/30/95	Mint Museum of Art, Charlotte, NC
8/2 - 9/24/95	The Cleveland Museum of Art, Cleveland, OH
11/2/94 - 1/9/95	The Institute of Contemporary Art, Boston, MA

FACE OF THE GODS: ART AND ALTARS OF AFRICA AND THE AFRICAN AMERICAS
3/19 - 5/28/95	Montgomery Museum of Fine Arts, Montgomery, AL
7/7 - 9/10/95	Virginia Museum of Fine Arts, Richmond, VA
9/28/94 - 2/19/95	University Art Museum and Pacific Film Archive, Berkeley, CA

FIRST ARTIST OF THE WEST: PAINTINGS AND WATERCOLORS BY GEORGE CATLIN
FROM THE GILCREASE MUSEUM
1/7 - 3/4/95	Frederick R. Weisman Museum of Art, Malibu, CA
9/23 - 11/26/95	Hood Museum of Art, Hanover, NH

THE FRENCH RENAISSANCE IN PRINTS FROM THE BIBLIOTHEQUE NATIONAL, PARIS
11/1/94 - 1/1/95	UCLA at the Armand Hammer Museum of Art and Cultural Center, Los Angeles, CA
1/10 - 3/19/95	The Metropolitan Museum of Art, New York, NY

Selected Listing of Traveling Exhibitions

FRENCH OIL SKETCHES OF THE 17TH, 18TH AND 19TH CENTURIES
1/7 - 2/5/95	The Society of the Four Arts, Palm Beach, FL
3/10 - 6/4/95	Arkansas Art Center, Little Rock, AR
9/22 - 11/19/95	Michael C. Carlos Museum of Art and Archaeology, Atlanta, GA

FROM THE OCEAN OF PAINTING: INDIA'S POPULAR PAINTING TRADITION, 1589 TO THE PRESENT
1/19 - 3/12/95	The David and Alfred Smart Museum of Art, Chicago, IL
6/10 - 8/13/95	Santa Barbara Museum of Art, Santa Barbara, CA

GARY ERBE RETROSPECTIVE: 25 YEARS IN RETROSPECT
1/21 - 3/5/95	The New Britain Museum of American Art, New Britain, CT
3/95 - 5/28/95	The Butler Institute of American Art, Youngstown, OH

GAUGUIN AND THE SCHOOL OF PONT-AVEN
11/20/94 - 1/15/95	Walters Art Gallery, Baltimore, MD
5/6 - 7/2/95	The Dixon Gallery & Gardens, Memphis, TN
7/29 - 9/24/95	San Diego Museum of Art, San Diego, CA

GENERATIONS IN BLACK AND WHITE: PHOTOGRAPHS BY CARL VAN VECHTEN
1/15 - 3/24/95	El Paso Museum of Art, El Paso, TX
10/20 - 12/3/95	The Fine Arts Museum of the South at Mobile, Mobile, AL

GEORGE INNESS: PRESENCE OF THE UNSEEN
9/11/94 - 1/6/95	The Montclair Art Museum, Montclair, NJ
2/3 - 3/17/95	Mount Holyoke College Art Museum, MA

!GRONK! A LIVING SURVEY 1973-1993
3/24 - 5/21/95	Tucson Museum of Art, Tucson, AZ
6/10 - 9/3/95	El Paso Museum of Art, El Paso, TX

HEAD, HEART AND HAND: ELBERT HUBBARD AND THE ROYCROFTERS
10/29/94 - 1/8/95	Memorial Art Gallery, Rochester, NY
1/28 - 3/26/95	Akron Art Museum, Akron, OH
4/23 - 6/25/95	Allentown Art Museum, Allentown, PA
7/29 - 9/24/95	Frederick R. Weisman Museum of Art, Malibu, CA
11/13/95 - 1/7/96	Virginia Museum of Fine Arts, Richmond, VA

HERTER BROTHERS: FURNITURE AND INTERIORS FOR A GILDED AGE
12/13/94 - 2/12/95	High Museum of Art, Atlanta, GA
3/15 - 7/9/95	The Metropolitan Museum of Art, New York, NY

HISTORY/MYSTERY: PHOTOGRAPHS BY JERRY N. UELSMANN, 1957-1993
1/6 - 2/19/95	Pensacola Museum of Art, Pensacola, FL
4/18 - 5/21/95	Philharmonic Center for the Arts, Naples, FL

HOWARD PYLE AND NORMAN ROCKWELL: LASTING LEGACIES
11/18/94 - 2/19/95	Delaware Art Museum, Wilmington, DE
7/7 - 9/17/95	Allentown Art Museum, Allentown, PA

Selected Listing of Traveling Exhibitions

IMAGES OF BRITISH INDIA'S GOLDEN AGE
1/14 - 2/26/95	Leigh Yawkey Woodson Art Museum, Wausau, WI
3/25 - 5/25/95	Columbia Museum of Arts & Gibbes Planetarium, Columbia, SC
7/8 - 9/3/95	Joslyn Art Museum, Omaha, NE
12/8/95 - 1/21/96	Philip and Muriel Berman Museum of Art, Collegeville, PA

IMPERIAL RUSSIAN PORCELAIN FROM THE RAYMOND F. PIPER COLLECTION
2/16 - 4/2/95	Lowe Art Museum, Coral Gables, FL
5/21 - 7/16/95	Cheekwood - Tennessee Bot. Gardens & Museum of Art, Nashville, TN
8/31 - 10/15/95	Honolulu Academy of Arts, Honolulu, HI
11/5 - 12/31/95	Dane G. Hansen Memorial Museum, Logan, KS
12/3/94 - 1/29/95	Boise Art Museum, Boise, ID

INTERNATIONAL LATHE-TURNED OBJECTS: CHALLENGE V
4/16 - 6/11/95	Huntsville Museum of Art., Huntsville, AL
10/3 - 11/5/95	Philharmonic Center for the Arts, Naples, FL

ISLAND ANCESTORS: OCEANIC ART FROM THE MASCO COLLECTION
2/2 - 3/26/95	Honolulu Academy of Arts, Honolulu, HI
6/1 - 8/6/95	The Detroit Institute of Arts, Detroit, MI

ITALIAN PAINTINGS FROM BURGHELY HOUSE
5/20 - 7/23/95	Indianapolis Museum of Art, Indianapolis, IN
8/19 - 11/12/95	Fresno Metropolitan Museum, Fresno, CA
12/2/95 - 2/25/96	Phoenix Art Museum., Phoenix, AZ

JACOB LAWRENCE: THE MIGRATION SERIES
1/12 - 4/13/95	The Museum of Modern Art, New York, NY
4/25 - 6/25/95	High Museum of Art, Atlanta, GA
7/15 - 9/9/95	The Denver Art Museum, Denver, CO

JAMES MCNEIL WHISTLER: LITHOGRAPHS AND LITHOTINTS
11/10/94 - 2/26/95	St. John's Museum of Art, Wilmington, NC
3/1 - 3/31/95	The Hickory Museum of Art, Hickory, NC

JAMES ROSENQUIST: TIME DUST, THE COMPLETE GRAPHIC WORKS: 1962-1992
10/23/94 - 1/8/95	Huntsville Museum of Art., Huntsville, AL
3/4 - 4/30/95	Elvehjem Museum of Art, Madison, WI

JEAN-MICHEL BASQUIAT: THE BLUE RIBBON PAINTINGS
1/29 - 3/26/95	Wadsworth Atheneum, Hartford, CT
Summer 95	The Studio Museum in Harlem, New York, NY

JOCHEN GERZ
1/13 - 3/19/95	Newport Harbor Art Museum, Newport Beach, CA
9/24-12/24/95	Neuberger Museum of Art, Purchase, NY

Selected Listing of Traveling Exhibitions

JOHN JAMES AUDUBON: THE WATERCOLORS FOR "BIRDS OF AMERICA"
11/20/94 - 1/29/95	The Museum of Fine Arts, Houston, Houston, TX
2/19 - 4/9/95	Memphis Brooks Museum of Art, Memphis, TN
10/12/95 - 1/7/96	Seattle Art Museum, Seattle, WA

JOHN STUART CURRY'S AMERICA
1/28 - 3/12/95	Krasal Art Center, St. Joseph, MI
4/7 - 6/2/95	Federal Reserve Bank of Kansas City, Kansas City, MO
6/28 - 8/25/95	Dane G. Hansen Memorial Museum, Logan, KS

JOSIAH WEDGEWOOD: EXPERIMENTAL POTTER
12/11/94 - 1/29/95	The Bruce Museum, Greenwich, CT
7/30 - 9/24/95	MSC Forsyth Center Galleries, College Station, TX
10/13 - 12/1/95	Federal Reserve Bank of Kansas City, Kansas City, MO

KINGS AND QUEENS AND SOUP TUREENS FROM THE CAMPBELL MUSEUM
4/23 - 5/11/95	Westmoreland Museum of Art, Greensburg, PA
6/15 - 8/27/95	Albany Institute of History & Art, Albany, NY

LAND OF THE FRAGILE GIANTS: LANDSCAPES, ENVIRONMENTS, AND PEOPLES OF THE LOESS HILLS
12/11/94 - 2/5/95	Sioux City Art Center, Sioux City, IA
3/23 - 5/14/95	Charles H. MacNeider Museum, Mason City, IA
7/95 - 8/95	Waterloo Museum of Art, Waterloo, IA

LARRY SULTAN: PICTURES FROM HOME
12/3/94 - 2/6/95	The Corcoran Gallery of Art, Washington, DC
6/2 - 8/20/95	Scottsdale Center for the Arts, Scottsdale, AZ

THE MANY FACES OF WENCESLAUS HOLLAR: 17TH-CENTURY EUROPEAN PRINTS FROM THE MUSEUM BOYMANS-VAN BUENINGEN, ROTTERDAM
2/12 - 4/2/95	The Detroit Institute of Arts, Detroit, MI
4/21 - 6/18/95	Mary and Leigh Block Gallery, Evanston, IL

MARRIAGE IN FORM: KAY SEKIMACHI AND BOB STOCKSDALE
1/15 - 2/26/95	Tampa Museum of Art, Tampa, FL
3/31 - 6/18/95	Renwick Gallery of the National Museum of American Art, Washington, DC

MARTIN JOHNSON HEADE: THE FLORAL AND HUMMINGBIRD STUDIES FROM THE ST. AUGUSTINE HISTORICAL SOCIETY
12/6/94 - 1/20/95	Pensacola Museum of Art, Pensacola, FL
4/2 - 5/95	The Butler Institute of American Art, Youngstown, OH
6/15 - 9/3	St. John's Museum of Art, Wilmington, NC

MASTER SILVER BY PAUL STORR, HIS CONTEMPORARIES AND FOLLOWERS
12/4/94 - 1/15/95	Museum of Fine Arts-St. Petersburg Florida, St. Petersburg, FL
2/5 - 3/19/95	Ball State University Museum of Art, Muncie, IN
4/15 - 5/28/95	Pensacola Museum of Art, Pensacola, FL

Selected Listing of Traveling Exhibitions

MASTERPIECES OF RENAISSANCE AND BAROQUE PRINTMAKING
2/4 - 3/19/95	The Douglas F. Cooley Memorial Art Gallery, Portland, OR
4/7 - 5/21/95	Elizabeth Myers Mitchell Art Gallery, Annapolis, MD

MINNIE EVANS: AFRICAN-AMERICAN VISIONARY ARTIST
1/21 - 4/2/95	Museum of American Folk Art, New York, NY
4/23 - 3/31/95	Kemper Museum of Contemporary Art & Design of Kansas City Art Institute, Kansas City, MO
6/15 - 9/3	St. John's Museum of Art, Wilmington, NC

MONET: LATE PAINTINGS OF GIVERNY FROM THE MUSÉE MARMOTTAN
1/7 - 3/12/95	New Orleans Museum of Art, New Orleans, LA
3/25 - 5/29/95	The Fine Arts Museums of San Francisco, San Francisco, CA

MY PEOPLE: THE PORTRAITS OF ROBERT HENRI
10/22/94 - 1/8/95	Orlando Museum of Art, Orlando, FL
4/30 - 6/25/95	The Columbus Museum, Columbus, GA

NEO-DADA: REDEFINING ART, 1958-62
11/4/94 - 1/1/95	Scottsdale Center for the Arts, Scottsdale, AZ
10/6 - 12/3/95	Tufts University Art Gallery, Medford, MA

NOSTALGIC JOURNEY: AMERICAN ILLUSTRATION FROM THE COLLECTION OF THE DELAWARE ART MUSEUM
11/2/94 - 1/4/95	Greenville County Museum of Art, Greenville, SC
2/11 - 3/12/95	The Society of the Four Arts, Palm Beach, FL
7/8 - 9/10/95	Georgia Museum of Art, Athens, GA

ODD NERDRUM: THE DRAWINGS
1/13 - 2/19/95	The Arkansas Arts Center, Little Rock, AR
3/18 - 5/15/95	University of Iowa Museum of Art, Iowa City, IA
6/29 - 8/27/95	The Patrick & Beatrice Haggerty Museum of Art, Milwaukee, WI
9/30 - 11/26/95	Joslyn Art Museum, Omaha, NE

PASSAGES: MATTHEW DAUB, NOW AND THEN
THROUGH 1/29/95	Evansville Museum of Arts & Science, Evansville, IN
2/19 - 4/2/95	Owensboro Museum of Fine Art, Owensboro, KY
4/23 - 6/4/95	Sheldon Swope Art Museum, Terra Haute, IN

PASSIONATE VISIONS OF THE AMERICAN SOUTH: SELF-TAUGHT ARTISTS FROM 1940 TO THE PRESENT
3/4 - 5/7/95	The Corcoran Gallery of Art, Washington, DC
6/17 - 8/27/95	North Carolina Museum of Art, Raleigh, NC

THE PEACEFUL LIBERATORS: JAIN ART FROM INDIA
11/6/94 - 1/22/95	Los Angeles County Museum of Art, Los Angeles, CA
3/5 - 5/28/95	Kimbell Art Museum, Fort Worth, TX

Selected Listing of Traveling Exhibitions

PHOTOGRAPHY AND BEYOND: NEW EXPRESSIONS FROM FRANCE
1/13 - 3/1/95	Boca Raton Museum of Art, Boca Raton, FL
4/8 - 6/3/95	The Museum of Contemporary Photography of Columbia College, Chicago, IL
6/21 - 9/10/95	Museum of Photographic Arts, San Diego, CA

THE PICTOGRAHS OF ADOLPH GOTTLIEB
2/4 - 4/2/95	Portland Museum of Art, Portland, ME
9/24/94 - 1/2/95	The Phillips Collection, Washington, DC
11/13/95 - 1/31/96	The Arkansas Arts Center, Little Rock, AR

PIET MONDRIAN: 1872-1944
6/4 - 9/4/95	The National Gallery of Art, Washington, DC
10/1/95 - 1/23/96	The Museum of Modern Art, New York, NY

POINTS OF ENTRY: TRACING CULTURES (working subtitle)
9/12 - 11/15/95	Museum of Photographic Arts, San Diego, CA
9/13 - 11/5/95	The Friends of Photography, Ansel Adams Center, San Francisco, CA

POINTS OF ENTRY: WORLDS LOST/A NATION FOUND (working subtitle)
9/12 - 11/5/95	Museum of Photographic Arts, San Diego, CA
11/15/95 - 1/7/96	The Friends of Photography, Ansel Adams Center, San Francisco, CA

THE PRINTS OF WAYNE THIEBAUD
2/10 - 4/2/95	Grinnell College Print & Drawing Study Room, Grinnell, IA
4/23 - 6/25/95	The Nelson-Atkins Museum of Art, Kansas City, MO

RELATIVELY SPEAKING: MOTHERS AND DAUGHTERS IN ART
11/6/94 - 1/8/95	Snug Harbor Cultural Center, Staten Island, NY
1/27 - 5/14/95	Rockford Art Museum, Rockford, IL
8/13 - 9/24/95	Rahr-West Art Museum, Manitowoc, WI

REMBRANDT ETCHINGS: SELECTIONS FROM THE CARNEGIE MUSEUM OF ART
3/26 - 5/21/95	Samuel P. Harn Museum of Art, Gainsville, FL
6/16 - 8/18/95	Knoxville Museum of Art, Knoxville, TN
9/17 - 11/5/95	The Fred Jones Jr. Museum of Art, Norman, OK

REORDERING REALITY: PRECISIONIST DIRECTIONS IN AMERICAN ART (1915-1941)
2/11 - 4/2/95	Norton Gallery and School of Art, West Palm Beach, FL
5/7 - 7/2/95	Columbus Museum of Art, Columbus, OH

REPICTURING ABSTRACTION: POLITICS OF SPACE
1/20 - 3/5/95	Anderson Gallery, School of the Arts, Richmond, VA
1/21 - 3/19/95	Virginia Museum of Fine Arts, Richmond, VA

RESCUERS OF THE HOLOCAUST: PORTRAITS BY GAY BLOCK
1/13 - 2/28/95	Mead Art Museum, Amherst, MA
9/23 - 11/26/95	The Museums at Stony Brook, Stony Brook, NY

Selected Listing of Traveling Exhibitions

RIVER OF GOLD: PRE-COLUMBIAN TREASURES FROM SITIO CONTE
1/22 - 4/2/95	The Bowers Museum of Cultural Art, Santa Ana, CA
5/18 - 8/20/95	The Philbrook Museum of Art Inc, Tulsa, OK

ROBERT FRANK - THE AMERICANS
1/7 - 3/26/95	Wexner Center for the Arts, Columbus, OH
4/1 - 7/31/95	Addison Gallery of American Art, Andover, MA
10/8 - 11/26/95	The Parrish Art Museum, Southampton, NY

SACRED GIFTS: PRE-COLUMBIAN ART & CREATIVITY
11/5/94 - 3/12/95	Santa Barbara Museum of Art, Santa Barbara, CA
6/28 - 11/27/95	The Mexican Museum, San Francisco, CA

SEAN SCULLY: TWENTY YEARS, 1976-1995
6/15 - 9/10/95	Hirshhorn Museum and Sculpture Garden, Washington, DC
10/10/95 - 1/7/96	High Museum of Art, Atlanta, GA

SHAKER FURNITURE: THE ART OF CRAFTSMANSHIP
6/13 - 9/10/95	High Museum of Art, Atlanta, GA
10/7 - 12/3/95	Wadsworth Atheneum, Hartford, CT

SONGS OF MY PEOPLE
5/6 - 6/18/95	Fort Wayne Museum of Art, Fort Wayne, IN
7/8 - 8/20/95	Meadows Museum of Art of Centenary College, Shreveport, LA

THE STUDIO MUSEUM IN HARLEM: TWENTY-FIVE YEARS OF AFRICAN-AMERICAN ART
11/18/94 - 1/16/95	Museum of Art, Providence, RI
3/24 - 5/21/95	Scottsdale Center for the Arts, Scottsdale, AZ
5/10 - 7/30/95	Munson-Williams-Proctor Institute Museum of Art, Utica, NY
8/13 - 10/1/95	Modern Art Museum of Fort Worth, Fort Worth, TX
10/17 - 12/10/95	The David and Alfred Smart Museum of Art, Chicago, IL

TALES AND TRADITIONS: STORYTELLING IN TWENTIETH CENTURY AMERICAN CRAFT
5/19 - 7/9/95	The Fine Arts Museum of the South at Mobile, Mobile, AL
8/6 - 9/24/95	The Columbus Museum, Columbus, GA

TOMB TREASURES FROM CHINA: THE BURIED ART OF ANCIENT XI'AN
11/20/94 - 2/12/95	Kimbell Art Museum, Fort Worth, TX
3/16 - 6/18/95	Honolulu Academy of Arts, Honolulu, HI

TREASURES OF VENICE: PAINTINGS FROM THE MUSEUM OF FINE ARTS, BUDAPEST
2/28 - 5/21/95	High Museum of Art, Atlanta, GA
5/22 - 9/17/94	Seattle Art Museum, Seattle, WA

URBAN REVISIONS: CURRENT PROJECTS FOR THE PUBLIC REALM
3/15 - 6/18/95	University Art Museum and Pacific Film Archive, Berkeley, CA
11/11/95 - 2/11/96	Des Moines Art Center, Des Moines, IA

Selected Listing of Traveling Exhibitions

VISIONS OF LOVE AND LIFE: ENGLISH PRE-RAPHAELITE ART FROM THE
BIRMINGHAM COLLECTION

3/9 - 5/7/95	Seattle Art Museum, Seattle, WA
5/31 - 7/16/95	The Cleveland Museum of Art, Cleveland, OH
8/11 - 10/15/95	Delaware Art Museum, Wilmington, DE
11/4/95 - 1/2/96	The Museum of Fine Arts, Houston, Houston, TX

WHITE MOUNTAIN PAINTERS 1834-1926

12/27/94 - 2/12/95	The Paine Art Center and Arboretum, Oshkosh, WI
3/4 - 4/23/95	Heckscher Museum, Huntington, NY
5/14 - 7/2/95	Orlando Museum of Art, Orlando, FL
7/25 - 9/10/95	Louisiana Arts and Science Center, Baton Rouge, LA
12/10/95 - 1/28/96	The Butler Institute of American Art, Youngstown, OH

WILLEM DE KOONING: THE HIRSHHORN MUSEUM COLLECTION

12/10/94 - 2/19/95	Museum of Fine Arts, Boston, MA
3/19 - 5/28/95	The Museum of Fine Arts, Houston, Houston, TX

THE WILLIAM S. PALEY COLLECTION

1/21 - 3/26/95	The Phillips Collection, Washington, DC
4/23 - 5/25/95	Memphis Brooks Museum of Art, Memphis, TN
7/22 - 10/1/95	Albright-Knox Art Gallery, Buffalo, NY

Selected Listing of Traveling Exhibitions

CHANTAL AKERMAN: FROM THE EAST
6/18 - 8/27/95   Walker Art Center, Minneapolis, MN

CLAUDE MONET: 1840-1926
7/22 - 11/26/95   The Art Institute of Chicago, Chicago, IL

DUCHAMP'S LEG
11/6/94 - 2/26/95   Walker Art Center, Minneapolis, MN

FROM CEZANNE TO MATISSE: GREAT FRENCH PAINTINGS FROM THE BARNES FOUNDATION
1/31 - 4/9/95   Philadelphia Museum of Art, Philadelphia, PA

GUSTAVE CAILLEBOTTE: THE URBAN IMPRESSIONIST
2/18 - 5/28/95   The Art Institute of Chicago, Chicago, IL

HERITAGE OF THE LAND: CONTRASTS IN NATIVE AMERICAN LIFE
9/25/94 - 1/8/95   Worcester Art Museum, Worcester, MA

JAMES MCNEIL WHISTLER: LITHOGRAPHS AND LITHOTINTS
5/28 - 8/20/95   The National Gallery of Art, Washington, DC

JASPER FRANCIS CROPSEY'S "THE SPIRIT OF WAR" AND "THE SPIRIT OF PEACE"
THROUGH 4/16/95   The National Gallery of Art, Washington, DC

JEWISH LIFE IN TSARIST RUSSIA: A WORLD DISCOVERED
10/9/94 - 3/5/95   The Jewish Museum, New York, NY

JOHANNES VERMEER
11/12/95 - 2/11/96   The National Gallery of Art, Washington, DC

KARL FRIEDRICH SCHINKEL, 1781-1841: THE DRAMA OF ARCHITECTURE
10/29/94 - 1/2/95   The Art Institute of Chicago, Chicago, IL

NINETEENTH-CENTURY GERMAN, AUSTRIAN AND HUNGARIAN DRAWINGS FROM BUDAPEST
11/20/94 - 1/2/95   The Frick Art Museum, Pittsburgh, PA

THE TOUCH OF THE ARTIST: MASTER DRAWINGS FROM THE WOODNER FAMILY COLLECTION
10/1 - 12/31/95   The National Gallery of Art, Washington, DC

Alphabetical Listing of Museums

Alphabetical Listing of Museums

460

Alphabetical Listing of Museums

Alphabetical Listing of Museums

462

Alphabetical Listing of Museums

Alphabetical Listing of Museums

Alphabetical Listing of Museums

Alphabetical Listing of Museums

Alphabetical Listing of Museums

Alphabetical Listing of Museums

Alphabetical Listing of Museums

Alphabetical Listing of Museums

471

Alphabetical Listing of Museums

Alphabetical Listing of Museums

Alphabetical Listing of Museums

ABOUT THE AUTHORS

Patti Sowalsky is an art collector and enthusiast. She was a docent at the Corcoran Gallery for many years, and planned and led all their out-of-gallery tours. She was chosen docent of the year in 1990. She represented American art collectors at a conference held in Moscow in June 1989, co-sponsored by Grand Central Art Galleries Educational Association and the Soviet Ministry of Culture and Artists Union. Her experience and involvement in art has included lecturing and tours with a partner for the Fine Arts Forum in Washington, and research for the core collection of the National Museum of Women in the Arts. Her special interests, in addition to her art collection, include travel, gardening and courses in contemporary art.

Judith Swirsky has been associated with the arts in Brooklyn as both staff and volunteer for more than forty years. She is listed in *Who's Who in American Women* and has received many awards. She has held both curatorial and volunteer administration positions at The Brooklyn Museum. While Executive Director of the Grand Central Art Galleries Educational Association she coordinated the 1989 Moscow Conference. She is now an independent curator and artists representative and is Director of Volunteer Resources at Snug Harbor Cultural Center, Staten Island, NY. In addition to visiting museums, galleries and art collections, Judith enjoys travel, music, cooking, and entertaining.

ON EXHIBIT 1995
The Art Lover's TRAVEL GUIDE to American Museums

☐ Please send me _____ copies, at $15.95 each plus $3.00 postage and handling, of:
ON EXHIBIT 1995 — The Art Lover's TRAVEL GUIDE to American Museums.

Enclosed is my check for $_____

Please ship to:
Name _____

Address _____

City _____ State _____ Zip_____

☐ Please reserve _____ copies of ON EXHIBIT 1996 – The Art Lover's TRAVEL
GUIDE to American Museums. Bill me when it is available.

Mail this coupon with your check to: ON EXHIBIT Fine Art Publications
                                          P. O. Box 59734
                                          Potomac, MD 20859

ON EXHIBIT 1995
The Art Lover's TRAVEL GUIDE to American Museums

☐ Please send me _____ copies, at $15.95 each plus $3.00 postage and handling, of:
ON EXHIBIT 1995 — The Art Lover's TRAVEL GUIDE to American Museums.

Enclosed is my check for $_____

Please ship to:
Name _____

Address _____

City _____ State _____Zip_____

☐ Please reserve _____ copies of ON EXHIBIT 1996 – The Art Lover's TRAVEL
GUIDE to American Museums. Bill me when it is available.

Mail this coupon with your check to: ON EXHIBIT Fine Art Publications
                                          P.O. Box 59734
                                          Potomac, MD 20859